Family Names in Australia & New Zealand

Family Names in Australia & New Zealand

Kenneth Allen

Kangaroo Press

First published in 1990 by Kangaroo Press Pty Ltd
3 Whitehall Road, (P.O. Box 75) Kenthurst NSW 2156
Typeset by Midland Typesetters Pty Ltd
Printed in Singapore by Fong & Sons Printers Pte Ltd

ISBN 0 86417 290 7 (hardcover)
ISBN 0 86417 348 2 (paperback)

CONTENTS

PREFACE

Miriam the prophetisse toke a tymbrel
in hir hande, and all the women followed
out after her with timbrels in a daunse

The verse danced in my memory as I took the hand of the swarthy young man who stood before me with his trim black beard and quick dark eyes. We were attending a conference in London, and he had introduced himself as John Tabor. The association of his name with the triumphant passage from Exodus was not to be denied.

The spelling is rather quaint. It is from the Coverdale Bible, and Miles Coverdale lived in the sixteenth century, when there was still an engaging sense of freedom about spelling. In a verse of only three lines he even offers us alternative ways of spelling timbrel.

Strange that both tabor and timbrel should have found their way into the English language from Old French, borrowed from Ancient Persian. Both words describe percussion instruments, small drums. I imagine Miriam's drum as a tambourine, played with joyful hands and flying fingers, filling the air with tinkling bells above the quick dancing rhythm of the drum.

But how, I asked myself, could this John Tabor have come by such a name? Could he be from somewhere in the ancient world of the Middle East, from the lands of the Tigris and the Euphrates? In fact he had an instantly recognisable accent and his family, he told me, had always lived in Lancashire. All the mystery fell away from him, all, that is, except for his name, and that still intrigued me. But he was quite incurious about his own name, being preoccupied with the subject of our conference.

This and other experiences of a similar kind led me to make a study of the origin and history of some of the colourful surnames of the British Isles. Half a century has passed since my conversation with John Tabor and in that time I have been collecting surnames in England, Ireland, Scotland, Wales, Australia, the U.S.A., Canada, New Zealand, wherever the roving peoples of those islands have settled, tracing, researching, interpreting and recording them.

A dictionary which included all the many thousands of surnames that originated in the British Isles would reduce the two-volume Sydney telephone directory to a mere pamphlet by comparison. I have assembled some 15,000 of the most frequent Australian and

New Zealand surnames in the following pages, including some well-known and interesting names which are unaccountably absent from British works of this kind.

This is an opportunity to express my appreciation of the research facilities of the British Public Record Office; the London Guildhall Library; the British (Museum) Library; the Hampshire County Library in Winchester, where I was able to take a treasured copy of that historic document *Winton Domesday*; the New York City Library, which published George Black's work on the surnames of Scotland; the public record offices in Edinburgh, and in Dublin, where I spent two years fostering Anglo-Irish trade, and getting acquainted with the Irish language and Irish surnames; the University of Toronto, which recently had the financial courage to reprint William Camden's *Remaines Concerning Britaine*, first published in 1605; the Australian National Library and the Australian National University for giving me access to books which are now out of print and unavailable from the publishers. I would also like to record my appreciation of the work of the English place-names societies, and of those researchers into surnames who have gone before me, and those works are listed in the Bibliography.

I could not have brought this dictionary to the stage of publication without the help of my wife Lisa, a geographer from London University and a very practical lady. She has given me her constant support and encouragement, has card-indexed the entire work so that I could type the entries from my research notes in a single alphabetical stream, and cheerfully accepted the task of proof-reading. Lisa is much experienced in this field, having participated in the publication of geographical books and journals in the universities of Singapore and Kuala Lumpur and more recently at Griffith University in Brisbane and the Australian National University in Canberra. I am grateful to her for bringing her talents and skills to my work.

Australia is becoming a cosmopolitan society, with citizens entering from many parts of the world. The opportunity lies with those of other racial and linguistic traditions to enrich Australia's culture by producing their own dictionaries of family names. This may appear to overlook Aboriginal names. Not so. The Aboriginal system of naming is unique in the world and its mysteries have been preserved.

Kenneth Allen
Canberra

INTRODUCTION

When the First Fleet landed at Botany Bay in 1788, neither the government in London nor those who landed could have had an inkling that two hundred years later, Australia, with a population of seventeen million, would have become an important sovereign state, with embassies throughout the world, and strong ties not only with the United Kingdom and Ireland (now the Irish Republic), from which the original settlers came, but also ties of friendship and cooperation with the United States of America, Canada, neighbouring New Zealand, Western Europe, and the countries of the Indian subcontinent, South-East Asia and the Pacific.

The family names of all the men, women and children of the First Fleet originated in the British Isles.* Their names still survive in Australia and have been joined by many thousands more. During the first two centuries of settlement the surnames of Australia have been predominantly English, Irish, Scottish, and Welsh. Even in an increasingly multicultural Australia our family names are still about seventy per cent Anglo/Celtic.

The colonisation of New Zealand proceeded in a different pattern from that in Australia, first the New Zealand Company and later, after the signing of the Treaty of Waitangi, the government purchasing land from the Maori Chiefs for settlement by free immigrants from the United Kingdom. Thus the Canterbury plains (Christchurch) and the Otago region (Dunedin) were settled, the first by English immigrants and the second by Scots. Even before the government in London moved, somewhat reluctantly, to annex New Zealand to the British Empire, under the threat of annexation by the French, British missionaries had established themselves in both Islands, some arriving as early as 1814.

Today New Zealand, with a population of three million, with initiative and enterprise altogether disproportionate to its size, and

* The 1,300 individuals who landed from the First Fleet shared 824 surnames because (1) all members of a family bore the same surname; (2) a number of unrelated persons had the same surname, e.g. 21 named Smith, 12 named Jones, 11 named Brown.

invigorated by its distinctive blend of British and Maori culture, is a staunch member of the Commonwealth and an active and independent participant in world affairs, exerting its own significant influence in the Pacific region.

On 22 October 1839, speaking at the departure for New Zealand of the first immigrant ship from the Clyde, Dr Macleod of the Church of Scotland, a man of vision, prophesied: 'In the future history of New Zealand, antiquarians . . . will be found tracing their descent from Scotland and England.' The family names of some of the early settlers in New Zealand and of those who helped to establish the colony will be found throughout the dictionary.

Every family name has a meaning, and a history stretching back at least five hundred years. Most surnames of English origin were formed during the 12th to 15th centuries. Some are much older, having developed from personal names which were first recorded in Domesday Book 1066–1086.

The adoption of surnames in England was spontaneous, not the result of royal or baronial decree. There were no rules for the choice of names and none governing the spelling of them. Most people were illiterate and the recorders of surnames were Norman or French monks who were unfamiliar with the Old English language and unable to pronounce or spell some English names, one of the reasons for the remarkable number of variants of many surnames.

A man could adopt any surname that appealed to him, although he probably did not do so consciously. The choice for some with an established pattern of personal names was obvious. Thus the son of Will became Willson or Wilson. People following the occupations of the time such as smith, archer, bowyer or palfreyman were equipped by their trade or calling with the ready-made surname that others applied to them.

A person living on the marsh, or by a cress-stream, or beside an ash-tree, was identified by that location as Marsh, Cresswell, or Ash. Others had nicknames which later became surnames bestowed upon them by their neighbours, such names as Lang or Long for a tall man, Foot for a man with some deformity of the foot, Sharp for a keen-witted man, Wise for a sagacious one.

These examples illustrate the four categories into which surnames may conveniently be divided:

1. Patronymics, that is, surnames descending from the personal name of an ancestor.
2. Occupational surnames, including surnames of office.
3. Locality surnames, descriptive of the locality in which an ancestor lived, or identifying the town, village, or hamlet from which he

had moved away; for example, (the man from) York, Stafford, Farnham.

4. Surnames which developed from nicknames.

Included in the nickname category are names acquired in pageants or nativity plays: for example, Bishop, King, Pope, Prince. And locality surnames include sign-names; inns, shops, houses were not numbered in medieval England and were distinguished by painted sign-boards, a custom which still survives in English inns and ale-houses. Of these four categories, locality surnames are by far the most numerous surnames of English origin, whereas patronymics predominate among surnames which originated in Ireland, Scotland, and Wales.

In this dictionary a key letter following each surname indicates its category: P Patronymic, O Occupational, L Locality, N Nickname. A second letter or combination of letters indicates the language in which the surname was formed. A complete list of abbreviations is at page 19. Most entries in the dictionary also give the form in which the surname was originally recorded, the most ancient being in Domesday Book, which was completed in 1086.

Occupational surnames offer us information about the kind of work on which our ancestors were engaged when they acquired their names. From the town and country crafts come the surnames Brewer, Chandler, Cutler, Fletcher, Hooper, Horner, Miller, Skinner, Tanner, Taylor, Thatcher, Turner, and many others. Cloth-making was an important industry in the Middle Ages and its craft names became surnames. The fouler who cleaned the cloth by trampling it in a trough of water became known as Fuller, Tucker, or Walker, depending on the part of England in which he followed his trade. The man who combed the cloth with a teazel became Tozer, and the weaver established the surnames Weaver, Webb, Webber, and Webster, the last of these originating with female weavers.

Our direct interest in family names goes beyond our own surname. Everyone has four grandparents, producing three more family names. Most people (except members of the aristocracy, who in the past sometimes married cousins) have eight great-grandparents, adding three family names other than our own. And if they are lucky, and have led well-ordered lives, they end up with grandchildren, some of whom, being girls, take husbands with yet other surnames.

I can best illustrate this with my own case. My ancestors' family names plus my wife's ancestors' family names, and the surnames accruing from marriages of members of our family, give us a direct personal interest in no fewer than twenty-five surnames over six generations, of which the following is an analysis:

Patronymic		*Locality*		*Occupational*		*Nickname*	
Stevens	OE	Wood	OE	Graves	ON	Hardy	OF
Janson	OE & Du	Lynn	OE	Hall	OE	King	OE
Godwin	OE	Croucher	OE	Silver	OE	Blakelock	OE
McGee	Ir	Noakes	OE	Smith	OE		
Allen	O Bret	Yates	OE	Legrain	OF		
		Roche	OF	Taylor	OE		
		Kinkaid	SG	Curd	SG/ME		
		London	Brit (pre-Roman)	Mayers	OF		
		Moreman	OE				

The family names of my ancestors are of Old English (Anglo-Saxon), Old Breton, Norman French, and Old Norse origin. What else would one expect to find in an individual born of generations of families living in the City of London? The Celts, whose several tribes were known collectively as Britons, were the first to settle England, then known as Britain. They were subdued and civilised by the Romans, and later vanquished by the Anglo-Saxons, who in their turn were overrun by the Danes amd Norsemen, and finally conquered by the Normans aided by the Bretons. The Normans were themselves of Viking (Scandinavian) origin and spoke Norman French. The fusion of Norman power and initiative with Anglo-Saxon organisation and industry eventually produced one of the most dynamic nations of Europe.

Most Australians and New Zealanders, if they assembled all the family names with which they are associated from past and present generations, could produce an equally varied and intriguing list. It is a fascinating study which generates much family interest in analysing the names on the basis of category and language.

Our family names have been handed down from father to son and daughter for up to thirty generations, yet many of them are still recognisable in the form in which the scribes wrote them so long ago, for all the vagaries of spelling. Some of the names in Domesday Book, such as Adam, Edwin, Elward, Martin, Roger and Vernon, have come down to us unchanged after nine centuries. Remarkably in a supposedly male-dominated society, a substantial number of our surnames have developed from women's personal names, many of them of Anglo-Saxon origin, as a perusal of the following pages will show. Surnames, our family names, are an indispensable link not only with racial and family history and customs but also with the languages spoken and written in earlier centuries.

Family Names from Ireland

When surnames began to be adopted in England, Ireland already had its own system. Patronymics have always predominated among Irish surnames, 'Mac' meaning 'son of' and 'O' indicating descent from a grandfather or earlier ancestor. There is no difference whatever between 'Mac' and the abbreviation 'Mc' in either Ireland or Scotland; both mean 'son of'.

A few Irish surnames describe ancient occupations, such as Hickey, meaning 'doctor or healer', or Macward, 'son of the bard', and some have developed from nicknames: for example, Gilligan, from *geal* 'white', for a man with white hair or beard. There are very few locality surnames of Irish origin.

The Irish stock of surnames contains some which were introduced by the Normans, who invaded Ireland from England in 1172. For centuries English influence was confined to the district known as 'The Pale'. In 1465 Edward IV tried to impose English surnames on Irish families living in counties close to Dublin but with little success. Despite the residual effect of Edward IV's statute, and generations of English settlement in Ireland, ten of the twelve most frequent surnames are Gaelic, and many of these have long been established in Australia and New Zealand.

Family Names from Scotland

The Scottish Highlands has long had its established pattern of Gaelic surnames, introduced by the Irish Gaels, the *Scoti*, who sailed from Ireland in the 2nd century and joined the Picts in their resistance to Roman penetration from Britain. After the withdrawal of the Roman legions the *Scoti* were engaged in a long struggle for supremacy with the Picts. The enigmatic Picts faded from history but the names of their kings, *Alpin, Elfin*, survive in the stock of Scottish surnames.

The clan system in the Scottish Highlands has resulted in many families bearing the same surname. In the violence of unsettled times families attached themselves to a powerful clan for protection and adopted its surname. The clan of Comyn provides an example. In the 13th century the Comyns were one of the most powerful families in Scotland. Oppressed people sought the protection of the chief of the clan, Gilbert Comyn, who adopted them as clansmen by baptising them in the stone hen-trough beside his castle gate. Henceforth they were known as Comyns of the hen-trough to distinguish them from Comyns of the true blood. The true Comyns were Bretons who had entered England with William the Conqueror and had been given lands in Scotland. Comyn(s) and its variants Cumming(s), Cummin, are well represented in Australia and New Zealand.

The *Scoti* bequeathed a legacy of Gaelic names to their descendants, most Highland surnames being prefixed by 'Mac', but some Highland names are locational. It was common for a laird to take as his surname the name of his estate, and for a farmer to be known by the name of his farm.

In Lowland Scotland many surnames are English rather than Gaelic, just as the Lowland dialects are a development of Northern English. In general, Scottish surnames are late recordings, mainly because they were slow to become hereditary, but many of them are of considerable antiquity.

Family Names from Wales

Some Welsh surnames are ancient, for example. Griffith(s), from Old Welsh *Gruffyd*, meaning 'chief, lord', which is 12th century. But in general, the Welsh were late in taking surnames. They have always made their own way with little heed to outside influences, especially in matters of religion, language, and culture. When in the 5th century, Britain was subject to successive waves of invasion by the Anglo-Saxons, the Celtic Britons joined their kinsmen in the Welsh mountains, looking down with distaste upon the Germanic tribes with their grim religion and savage gods. In 597, St Augustine began the conversion of the Anglo-Saxons to Christianity, but he had no need to go into Wales. The Welsh had clung to their Christian religion since late Roman times.

When the Welsh did take surnames their native cohesion was evident in their choice of them. Many Welshmen bear the surnames Jones, Evans, Hughes, Thomas, Williams, Davies, all patronymics. The Welsh 'ap' is used for 'son', and this changed some surnames. Preece was originally 'ap Reece', and Pugh developed from 'ap Hugh'. They occasionally broke the patronymic pattern by developing a surname from a nickname, as in Lloyd, which is from Old Welsh, *llwyd*, meaning 'grey'. There are few occupational or locational Welsh surnames.

Family Names from Cornwall

Cornish surnames are distinct from those of other parts of England. The Cornish are a Celtic people with close racial and linguistic ties with the Welsh and the Bretons. In ancient times there was a thriving commerce across the English Channel between Cornwall and Brittany. As a consequence of the Anglo-Saxon invasions many Britons escaped through Cornwall to Brittany (Little Britain as distinct from Great Britain), changing its name from Armorica, by which it was known to its earlier inhabitants and to the Romans.

The Cornish language has become extinct but it survives in Cornish place-names and surnames, many beginning with Che, meaning 'house', Tre meaning 'farm' or 'village', Pen 'head, end or top', Pol 'pool'. Such surnames are to be found throughout Australia and New Zealand.

Family Names from the Isle of Man

The turbulent history of the Isle of Man is reflected in its surnames. The Irish Gaels, the *Scoti*, who gave Scotland its name, also settled in the Isle of Man, and some two-thirds of Manx surnames are still of Irish origin. Later, Norsemen conquered the island, and intermarried with the Gaels, imposing Norse influence on Gaelic names. As in Ireland and Scotland, patronymics were formed by the use of the prefix 'Mac', 'son of'. Eventually 'Mac' ceased to be used but a vestige of it remains in a -C- sound prefixing the surnames. Thus Corkhill, previously MacThorketill; Caine, previously Mac Cathain; Quail, previously MacPhail. Manx surnames have evolved in a pattern not to be found elsewhere in the British Isles, and in their distinctive form are frequent in Australia and New Zealand.

The Old Languages

Every name is a word and every word has a meaning. Our surnames are written in modern English, and as most of them are centuries old we must trace them to the languages in which they were formed to discover their meaning. These old languages developed from a parent language, Indo-European, which was used thousands of years ago by the nomadic tribes, known to us as Aryan, who roamed the region between the Caspian and the Black Sea. A vigorous, fair-haired, fair-skinned people, their tribal organisation had an aristocratic structure, and they lived by grazing cattle and breeding horses.

Some three thousand years ago, these Aryan tribes began to move from their homelands under the stimulus of hunger induced by a growing population and diminishing food supplies. Great irresistible waves of them spread across northern Europe, becoming the ancestors of most of the European peoples of today including those of the British Isles. Some of the Aryan tribes turned south-east around the Caspian Sea and gradually made their way through present-day Afghanistan and the Khyber Pass to the fertile Indus Valley, later penetrating deep into India and Iran.

The Indo-European language has descended to us through Greek and Latin, and to the peoples of the Indian sub-continent through Sanskrit. One of the most vigorous and tenacious of the languages to develop from Indo-European was that of the Germanic tribes, from which English, the language of the Anglo-Saxons, derives. English also contains many words of French and Scandinavian origin, introduced by the Normans, Danes and Norwegians. Some of the words we use today go right back to the parent Indo-European language, such as father, mother, son, daughter, brother, sister, and words associated with migratory movement, such as axle and wheel. These words are common to all the Germanic languages.

Other words have so changed as they descended through the intermediate languages that they have become unrecognisable. Moreover, many new words have been created over the centuries to describe articles, situations and events which were unknown to our distant ancestors, or have been introduced from non-Indo-European languages such as the Semitic languages of the Arabs and the Jews.

The following are the old languages which contributed to the surnames of the British Isles, and the period in which they were in use:

Old English: The West Germanic language of the Anglo-Saxons spoken in England from the 5th to the 12th century.

Old Norse: The North Germanic language of the Scandinavian peoples before the 14th century and together with Old Danish and Old Swedish the language spoken by the Vikings.

Old French: The French language from 800 to 1550.

Anglo-Norman: The Anglo-French dialect spoken by Norman settlers in England after the Norman Conquest.

Anglo-French: The language spoken in England from the Norman Conquest through the Middle Ages.

Middle English: The English language as written and spoken between 1100 and 1500.

Celtic: A family of languages with two branches: (i) the Goidelic

branch consisting of Irish Gaelic, Scots Gaelic, and Manx; and (ii) the Brythonic branch consisting of Welsh, Breton, and Cornish.
Old Irish: Irish Gaelic before the 11th century.
Middle Irish: The Irish language as written and spoken from the 11th to the 15th century.
Old Welsh: The Brythonic language spoken in Wales (Brythonic—as for Briton).
Old Breton: The language spoken by the people of Brittany and introduced into England by the Breton contingent of Duke William's army in 1066.
Cornish: A Celtic language, now extinct but surviving in place-names and surnames

Domesday

Nineteen years after the Conquest, King William I of England (William the Conqueror) decided that he needed a detailed survey of the wealth of England. The purpose of the survey was not declared but his contemporaries were in no doubt that it was to enable the king to more effectively levy *geld* (land-tax) upon them, although it also became a record of the introduction of feudal law in England.

The survey was commissioned at the king's council at Gloucester, held during the Christmas festival, in 1085. It was completed in the astonishingly short time of eight months. The difficulties were immense, not the least being poor or non-existent roads and primitive methods of recording—quill pens on parchment (stretched sheepskin). The entire population of England at that time was about one and three quarter million, spread out over the whole country and most in rural districts. Domesday (from OE *dom* 'judgement'), as it came to be known, is in fact a survey of the whole of rural England held by the king and his tenants-in-chief, but some detail about towns was also recorded. London and Winchester were excluded but probably were subject to a separate survey of royal revenues.

Domesday is a unique document, recording the names and honours (*honour* 'the whole of a landholder's estate wherever situated') of every one of William's tenants-in-chief, together with exact measurement of the lands he held and a detailed assessment of his assets in farm implements, buildings, animal livestock, and serfs (slaves) both male and female. The holdings of under-tenants were also included in the survey, which recorded the value of each manor or estate at the time of Edward the Confessor (1066) and the value as it stood in 1085.

One example at random will serve to indicate the infinite detail of the survey: 'These are the lands of Bath Abbey. The Abbot of Bath has a manor called Weston. In the time of King Edward, it was assessed at 15 hides (to the geld), which required 10 ploughs. Of those hides, the Abbot has 8½ on the demesne there, and his men have 6. There, the Abbott has 7 villagers, 10 cottars and 7 slaves; 1 riding-horse and 204 sheep; 1 mill which renders 10 shillings each year; 20 acres of meadow, and pasture measuring a league in length and as much in breadth. And when the Abbot received this manor, it was worth £7, it is now worth £8.'

(A hide consisted of land considered sufficient to maintain a free family and dependants; a demesne is land whose produce is devoted to the lord (of the manor) rather than to his tenants; geld is land-tax; a league is twelve furlongs or one and a half miles; a cottar, or 'cottager', is a peasant of inferior status to a villain or bordar.)

There are in fact two Domesday Books, still carefully preserved in the Public Record Office in London. Great Domesday contains the entries for thirty counties of England, while Lesser Domesday records the entries for East Anglia, that is, Norfolk, Suffolk and Essex. They were compiled in abbreviated Latin (Norman shorthand) by scribes in Winchester, then the capital of England, from the returns sent in by royal commissioners, each of whom had a prescribed circuit to survey.

Curiously, Winchester was omitted from the otherwise all-embracing survey. This was remedied by Henry I, William's youngest son, who succeeded to the throne on the death of his brother Rufus. Henry instituted a survey of Winchester in 1125, recording the names of all Winchester citizens and their assets as they had stood in 1066, doubtless using English (Anglo-Saxon) tax records, which had obviously survived, and also recording similar details as they existed in the year of the survey. This third book is known as Winton Domesday.

Apart from its other historical value, such as providing evidence for the settlement of land disputes in earlier centuries in England, Domesday is an invaluable record of the names of both Anglo-Saxons and Normans in the 11th century, from which many Australian and New Zealand family names are derived. These are indicated by 'DB' or 'Winton D' in the dictionary.

Glossary

Etymology: The facts relating to the formation and derivation of a word. For the purposes of this book, etymology may be defined as 'the origin, formation and development of a surname'.

Metonymic: A word used in a transferred sense, often found in occupational surnames where the word for an object is used to describe the maker of it: for example, *Bolt* for a maker of bolts.

Toponymic: A surname which indicated nationality, or the country, county or town from which an ancestor came: for example, *Welch*, a Welshman; *Fleming*, from Flanders; *Cornwall*, from the county of Cornwall; *Spalding*, from the town of Spalding.

Patronymic: A surname derived from the personal name of a father or other male ancestor: for example, *Wilson* 'son of *Will*'. In Old English either *sunu* or the suffix *-ing* is used for 'son'.

Metronymic: A surname derived from the personal name of a mother or other female ancestor.

Diminutive: A surname derived from a familiar or endearing name. Most of these are Old French. Examples include *Dicken*, a diminutive of *Dick*, which is a pet-form of *Richard*; *Dobbin*, a diminutive of *Dobb*, which is a pet-form of *Robert*; *Willet*, a diminutive of *Will*, which is a pet-form of *William*.

Metathesis: Transposition, a change of places of letters in a surname: for example, Askell changed to Axcell.

Pipe Rolls: The Exchequer accounts kept in rolled form known as 'pipes'. For Exchequer see Chequer in dictionary.

Thane: Anglo-Saxon. One who held land of the king or of a baron by military service, roughly equivalent to a medieval knight.

Dreng: Anglo-Saxon. A free tenant holding by a tenure partly military, partly servile.

ABBREVIATIONS

AF	Anglo-French
Arab	Arabic
Brit	British (Celtic)
C	Cornish
c.	circa (about, date)
cent.	century
cf.	compare
Co.	County
cogn.	cognate (akin in origin)
deriv.	derivative
dial.	dialectal (local form of speech or writing)
DB	Domesday Book
dim.	diminutive form
Du	Dutch
el.	element (part of a compound name)
esp.	especially
fem.	feminine
Fr	French
Fris	Frisian
Ger	German
Gk	Greek
Ir	Irish
It	Italian
L	Locality Surname
Lat	Latin
masc.	masculine
ME	Middle English
MW	Middle Welsh
N	Nickname
O	Occupational Name
O Bret	Old Breton
O Brit	Old British (Celtic)
O Dan	Old Danish
OE	Old English (Anglo-Saxon)
OF	Old French
O Fris	Old Frisian
OG	Old German
OHG	Old High German
O Ir	Old Irish
ON	Old Norse
ONF	Old Norman French
O Scand	Old Scandinavian
O Sw	Old Swedish
OW	Old Welsh
P	Patronymic
R.	River
Pers	Persian
pers.	personal (name)
Port	Portuguese
pron.	pronounced
SG	Scots Gaelic
Sp	Spanish
Winton D	Winton Domesday

The following English county names are shown in abbreviated form:

Beds	Bedfordshire
Berks	Berkshire
Bucks	Buckinghamshire
Cambs	Cambridgeshire
Ches	Cheshire
Cumb	Cumberland
Devon	Devonshire
Derbys	Derbyshire
Glos	Gloucestershire
Hants	Hampshire
Herefords	Herefordshire
Herts	Hertfordshire
Hunts	Huntingdonshire
Lancs	Lancashire
Leices	Leicestershire
Lincs	Linconshire
Middx	Middlesex
Northumb	Northumberland
Northants	Northamptonshire
Notts	Nottinghamshire
Oxon	Oxfordshire
Salop	Shropshire
Som	Somerset
Staffs	Staffordshire
Warwicks	Warwickshire
Wilts	Wiltshire

Worces	Worcestershire	Yorks	Yorkshire
Wight or IOW	Isle of Wight		

The remaining counties: Cornwall, Dorset, Durham, Essex, Kent, Norfolk, Rutland, Suffolk, Surrey, Sussex, Westmorland are shown unabbreviated.

In recent years, changes have been made to English county boundaries. New counties such as Avon have been created, others such as Rutland have vanished. This dictionary is concerned with the historical past; old county names are retained and the new are ignored.

A

ABADAM, BADAM, BADHAM: P OW *ap* 'son'. 'Son of *Adam*'. 12th cent.

ABBERTON: L OE (i) 'The *tūn*' (manor) of an Anglo-Saxon woman called *Ēadburg*', (Essex) (ii) 'The *tūn* (settlement) of *Ēadbeorht's* people'. (Worces)

ABBEY, ABBIE: O OF *abet* 'abbot'. 'A layman working at the abbey'. 12th cent. ABBETT, ABBOTT: O OE *abbod* 'abbot'. 'Servant of the abbot' or N from playing abbot in a medieval play. 12th cent. ABDEY, ABDIE: O ME *abbodie*. 'A worker at the abbey'. 14th cent. [Joseph Abbott, a marine, brought the name to Australia 1788]

ABEAR: L OE *bere* 'barley'. 'At the barley field'. (*bere-aern* 'barn'.)

A'BECKETT, see BECKETT (ii).

ABEL, ABELL, ABLE: P Hebrew *Abel* 'son'. 13th cent. ABLETT: P A dim. of *Abel*. 13th cent. [Robert Able, a convict, arrived 1788]

ABERCROMBIE: L SG *aber-crombie* 'mouth of the crooked stream'. (*aber* from Pictish *inbhear* 'mouth'.) From the barony of Abercromby (Fifes) Scotland. 13th cent.

ABERNETHY: L SG + Brit *aber-Nethy* 'mouth of the R. Nethy'. (Perths, Inverness) Scotland. The Abernethy chiefs were lay abbots of the monastery of Abernethy in Strathearn.

ABLETT: P A dim. of *Abel*. 13th cent.

ABRAHAM, ABRAM: P Hebrew *Abram* 'high father'. Not exclusively Jewish; in DB the name of a priest. Also L from Abram (Lancs). 12th cent. [Henry Abraham, a convict, brought the name to Australia 1788]

ABSOLOM, ASPLEN, ASPENLON: P Hebrew *Abshalom* 'father of peace'. Not confined to Jews; Chaucer uses *Absolom* for the parish clerk in 'The Miller's Tale'.

ACASTER: L OE 'Roman *ceaster* (fort) of *Aca*'.

ACFIELD L OE *āc-feld* 'oak-tree field'. ACFORD: L OE *āc-ford* 'oak-tree ford'.

ACHARD, ASHARD, HATCHARD: P OG *Agihard*, OF *Achart*. 12th cent.

ACHESON, AITCHESON: P Scottish forms of *Atkinson*. 15th cent.

ACHURCH: L OE (i) An abbreviation of *atte church* (dweller by the church). (ii) From Achurch (Northants).

ACKARY, ZACHARY: P Hebrew *Zacharia* 'Jehovah has remembered'. 12th cent.

ACKER(S), ACRES, AKERS: L OE *aecer* 'acre', 'arable land'. 13th cent.

ACKERMAN, AKERMAN: O OE *aecer-mann* 'ploughman, farmer'. 13th cent. [Thomas Acres, a convict, brought the name to Australia 1788].

ACKLAM: L OE *āc leum* 'oak wood'. (Acklam, Yorks) ACKLAND: L OE *āc land* 'land with oak trees'. (Ackland, Devon) 13th cent. [J.B.A. Ackland grazed sheep on a Canterbury pastoral lease, New Zealand, 1855]. ACKROYD: L OE *āc rōd* 'oak rood or clearing'. 17th cent. (-y- is Yorks dialect.)

ACKLING, see HACKLING.

A'COURT, COURT(S), CURT: (i) L OF *cort*, ME *courte* 'at castle or manor house'. (ii) N OF *curt* 'short'. 12th cent.

ADAIR: P *Edzear* (z as y), Scottish form of *Edgar*. 14th cent.

ADAM, ADAMS, ADAMES, ADDAMS: P Hebrew *Adam* 'red', from *adamah* 'earth'. DB. ADAMSON: P 'Son of *Adam*'. 13th cent. ADCOCK(S): P *adecoc* a pet-forms of *Adam*. 13th cent. ADDIE, ADDY, ADDIS, ADDS: P Pet-forms of *Adam*, occasionally of *Adelaide*. 13th cent. ADES: P A pet-form of *Adam*. ADEY, ADIE: P A double dim. of *Adam*. 14th cent. [John Adams and Mary Adams, unrelated convicts, brought the name to Australia 1788].

ADDINGTON: L OE '*Eada's tūn* (farm)'. (Bucks) DB.

ADDISON: P 'Son of *Addie*'. 14th cent. ADDYMAN: O 'Servant of *Addie*'.

ADEANE, A'DEANE: L ME *atte dene* 'in the dale'. 15th cent.

ADELAIDE: P OG *Adalhaid*, NF *Adelais* (*athal* 'noble' + *haidu* 'kind'). DB.

ADELINE: P OG *Adelina* a pet-form of *Adalhaid*. DB.

ADKIN(S), ATKIN(S), ATKYNS: P *Ade-kin* a pet-form of *Adam*. 12th cent.

ADLAM: P OG *Adalhelm*, OE *Athelhelm* 'noble protector'. DB.

ADLARD, ALLARD, ELLARD, HALLARD, HALLETT: P OE *Athelheard* 'noble-hard'.

ADLINGTON: L OE '*Eadwulf's tūn* (farm)'. (Ches, Lancs) DB.

ADNEY: L OE '*īeg* (island) of *Eadwynn*, an Anglo-Saxon woman'. 13th cent.

ADRAIN, DRANE: L OE *dreahnian* 'at the drain or dyke'. 14th cent.

ADRIAN: P Lat *Hadrianus* 'of the Adriatic'. (Roman Emperor's name.)

AFFLECK: P SG From Affleck (Angus, Lanarks) Scotland, SG *achadh-leac* 'field of the flat stones'.

AGAR, see ALGAR, EDGAR.

AGASS: P OF From Gk *Agace*, vernacular form of *Agatha*. 13th cent.

AGATE(S): L OE *atte geat* 'at the gate'. 13th cent. See also Yate.

AGG(S): P O Dan *Aggi*. 12th cent.

AGGETT: P A pet-form of *Agace* or a double dim. of *Agness*. 14th cent. AGNES: P OF From Gk *Agnes* 'pure, chaste'. 12th cent.

AGNEW: (i) L OF From Agneaux (Normandy). 13th cent. (ii) N *agneau* 'lamb', an affectionate nickname. 13th cent. [A First Fleet (convict) surname].

AGUILA, AGUILAR: O OF *aiguiller* 'a needle-maker'. 12th cent.

AGUTTER: L OF *goutiere* 'at the gutter or dyke'.

AHERNE: P Ir *O hEachthighheirn* 'steed lord'. (Co. Cork).

AIKEN see AITKEN. AINGER see ANGER. AINSLEE, AINSLEY see ANNESLEY.

AINSWORTH: L OW + OE '*Eugain's worth* (enclosure)'. (Lancs).

AIRD: L SG From Aird (Ayrshire) Scotland.

AIRE: L Celtic *Isara* 'strong river'. (Yorks), *Yr* in 959.

AIREY, AIRY: L ON *eyrard* 'gravelly river-bank'.

AISTHORPE, AISTROPE: L OE '*ēaste-thorp* (farm)'. (Lincs).

AITKEN, AIKEN: P Scottish form of *Atkin* (*Adkin*). 14th cent.

AKED: L OE *āc-hēafod* 'oak-covered headland'. 13th cent.

AKEHURST, AKHURST: L OE *āc-hyrst* 'oak hirst (wood)'.

AKELEY: L OE *āc-lēah* 'oak wood or glade'. (Bucks).

ALABASTER, ALBISTER, ARBLASTER: O OF *arbalestier* 'a crossbowman'. 12th cent.

ALAN, ALAIN, ALLAN, ALLEN, ALLEYNE, FITZALAN: P O Bret The name of Breton noblemen and of the Breton Bishop of Quimper. Introduced into England by Count *Alain* of Brittany, companion of the Conqueror. DB. The Scottish *Alan*, *Allan* is from SG *ailene* 'rock'. Fitzalan is 'son of *Alan*'. [Seven convicts named Allan or Allen, three men and four women, arrived at Botany Bay with the First Fleet. In addition, Robert Allen and William Allen were crewmen on the *Friendship*].

ALAWAY, HALLAWAY: P OE *AEthelwīg* 'noble war'. DB.

ALBAN, ALBON, ALBONE, ALLBON(E), ALLIBAN, ALLIBON(E): P Lat *Albanus* 'of Alba'. St *Alban*, the first British martyr. Surname 13th cent.

ALBERT, AUBERT: P OE *AEthelbriht*, *AEthelbeorht* 'noble bright'. DB.

ALBRIGHT: P OE *AEthelbriht* 'noble bright'. 12th cent. Identical names.

ALCOCK: P A dim. of *Alan* + the affectionate cock. 13th cent.

ALCOTT: L OE *ēald-cote* 'the old cottage'. 13th cent.

ALDEN, AUDEN, OLDEN: P OE *Ealdwine* 'old friend', a pers. name. DB.

ALDER, NALDER, OLDER: L OE *alor* 'alder (tree)'. 13th cent.

ALDERMAN: O OE *ealdormann* 'alderman' or 'head of a guild'. 12th cent.

ALDERTON: L OE *alor-tūn* 'the farm in the alder-trees'. (Essex, Glos, Salop, Suffolk).

ALDIS, ALLDIS, ALDOUS, ALDUS, AUDAS, AUDUS: (i) P OE A pet-form of an Anglo-Saxon woman's name in *Eald* 'honoured, eminent'. 12th cent. (ii) L From Auldhous in Eastwood (Renfrews) Scotland.

ALDRED, ALLDRITT: P OE *AEthelraed* 'noble counsel'. DB.

ALDREN: L OE *alor* 'alder'. 'Among the alders'. 14th cent.

ALDRICH, ELDRIDGE: P OE *AElfric* 'elf-ruler' or *AEthelric* 'noble ruler'. DB.

ALDRIDGE: L OE *alor-wīc* 'dairy farm in the alders'. (Bucks, Staffs) ALDRITT: L OE *alrett* 'alder-grove'. 14th cent.

ALDWY: P OE *Ealdwig* 'old war'. DB.

ALEFOUNDER: O OE *ealu* 'ale' + Lat *fundere* 'to pour forth'. 'An official appointed by the Court Leet to inspect ale.' 13th cent.

ALEWOOD: L O Dan + OE 'The *wudu* (wood) of a Dane called *Alī*'.

ALEXANDER: P Gk 'defender of men'. 12th cent.

ALFLAT, ALFLATT: P OE *AEthelflaed* 'noble beauty'. DB.

ALFORD: L OE 'Ford of *Ealdgȳþ*, an Anglo-Saxon woman'. (Lincs, Som) DB. [A negro convict brought the name to Australia 1788].

ALFRED(S), ALLURED, ALURED: P OE *AElfraed* 'elf-counsel'. DB.

ALFREY, AFFERY, AFFRAY, ELVERY: P OE *AEthelfrith* 'noble peace'. 13th cent.

ALGAR, ALGER, AUGER, ELGAR, ALGER: P OE *AEthelgār* 'noble spear'. DB.

ALGATE: L OE From Aldgate, City of London, a gate in the Roman wall. 13th cent. In 1374, Geoffrey Chaucer, as controller of customs, was granted a house on the wall at Aldgate.

ALGER, AUGER: P OE *Ealhere* 'temple-army'. DB.

ALIMAN see ALLMAN.

ALIS, ALISE, ALLISH: P OG *Adalhaidis*, OF *Aliz* 'Alice', 'noble kind'. 12th cent. ALISON: P OF *Alison* a pet-form of *Alice*. 13th cent. Chaucer used *Alison* as a woman's name in *The Canterbury Tales*.

ALISTER: L OE from Lat *Alencester* 'Roman fort on the R. Alne'. 12th cent. (Alcester, Warwicks).

ALKER, L Celtic *Alt* 'muddy river'. (Altcar, Lancs) 14th cent.

ALKIN, ALLKINS: P Pet-form of *Allan* or *Alexander*. 13th cent.

ALLAN, ALLEN, ALLEYNE see ALAN.

ALLANBY: L O Bret + ON '*Aleyn's býr* (farm)'. (Cumb) 13th cent.

ALLANSON, ALLENSON, ALLINSON: P O Bret 'Son of *Alan, Alain*'. 14th cent.

ALLARD see ADLARD.

ALLARDICE: L From Barony of Allardyce (Kincardines) Scotland.

ALLATT see AYLETT. ALLBON, ALLBONE see ALBAN.

ALLAWAY, ALLOWAY: P OE 'Son of *Aldwy*', an Anglo-Saxon pers. name.

ALLBUT, ALLBUTT, ALBUTT: P OG *Albod*. 12th cent.

ALLCORN, ALCORN, ALCHORN, ALLCHIN, ALCHIN: (i) P OE 'Son of *Alcuin*', an Anglo-Saxon pers. name early corrupted to *Oldcorn* in northern England. *Halchein* in 1273. (ii) L OE From Alchorne, a parish of Rotherfield (Sussex).

ALLDIS see ALDIS. ALLDRITT see ALDRED.

ALLERTON: L OE *alratūn* 'farm in the alders'. (Lancs) DB.

ALLET see AYLETT.

ALLETSON, ALLATSON: P OF 'Son of *Allott*'. 14th cent.

ALLEY, ALLY: P O Dan *Alli*. DB.

ALLGOOD: P O Dan *Algot*. DB.

ALLIBAN, ALLIBON, ALLIBONE see ALBAN.

ALLINGHAM: L OE 'The *hām* (village) of the people of *AElla*, an Anglo-Saxon'. (Kent).

ALLKINS see ALKIN.

ALLMAN, ALLMEN, ALMAN, ALMOND: P OF *Aleman* 'German', used as a pers. name; L OF *de Alman, de Alemayne* 'the man from Germany'. 14th cent.

ALLMARK, ALMACK, HALLMARK: N OE *healf marc* 'half a mark' (one-third of a pound). A nickname from money of account. 13th cent.

ALLNUTT, ALLNER: P OE *AEthelnōth* 'noble daring'. DB.

ALLOTT: P OF *Aalot* a pet-form of *Alis*. 13th cent.

ALLPORT: L OE *eald port* 'old harbour' or 'old town (with market rights)', esp. Allport, (Derbys).

ALLPRESS: N OE *halig-prest* 'holy priest'. 13th cent.

ALLRED: P OE *AEthelraed* 'noble counsel'. DB.

ALLRIGHT: P OE *AEthelric* 'noble ruler'. 13th cent.

ALLSEP, ALLSOP, ALLSOPP, ALSOP: L OE '*AElle's hop* (small valley)'. (Alsop-en-le-Dale, Derbys) 12th cent.

ALLSTON: (i) P *AEthelstān* 'noble stone'. DB. (ii) L OE 'The *tūn* (farm) of Anglo-Saxons called *Aldhūn* (Cumb), *AElfwine* (Devon), *AElfsige* (Lancs), *AEthelnōth* (Som)'. 13th cent.

ALLURED see ALFRED.

ALLVEY, ALVEY, ELVEY, ELVY: P OE *AElfwīg* 'elf-war'. 11th cent.

ALLWARD, ALWARD, ELWARD: P OE *AElfweard* 'elf-guard'. 12th cent.

ALLWOOD see ELLWOOD.

ALLWORK: L OE *eald-worc* 'the old fort'. (Aldwark, Derbys, Yorks) 13th cent.

ALLY see ALLEY. ALMACK see ALLMARK. ALMAN see ALLMAN.

ALMOND: P OE *AEthelmund* 'noble protector'. DB. See also Allman.

ALPE: N ME *alp* 'bullfinch', a nickname from the bird. 13th cent.

ALPHEGE, ELPHICK(E), ELVIDGE: P OE *AElfēah* 'elf high'. DB.

ALPIN(E), ELFIN: P Gallo Lat *Alpinus* or OW *Elffin*, Celtic from both sources. *Elfin* was a popular name among Pictish kings. Surname 13th cent. See also McAlpin.

ALSOP see ALLSEP. ALSTEAD see HALSTEAD.

ALT: L OW *allt* 'hill'. (Lancs).

ALTHAM: L OE *aelfetu-hamm* 'the swans' meadow'. (Lancs) 13th cent.

ALTHORP: L O Dan 'The *thorp* (farm) of a Dane called *Ali*' (Lincs), *Aletorp* DB or '*Olla's thorp*' (Northants), *Olletorp* DB.

ALURED see ALFRED.

ALVAR: P OE *AElfhere* 'elf army'. DB.

ALVEN, ELVEN, ELVIN(S): P OE *AElfwine* 'elf-friend'. 12th cent.

ALWIN, ELWIN, ELWYN: P OE *AEthelwine* 'noble friend'. DB.

AMAND, AMENT, AMMANN: P OF *Amand* 'to be loved', a woman's name. 12th cent.

AMAR see AYMER.

AMBLER: O OF *esmailleur* 'enameller'. 14th cent.

AMBROSE, AMBRUS: P Lat *Ambrosius* 'divine, immortal'. 12th cent.

AMELOT, AMLOT: P OF *Amelot* a pet-form of *Ameline*. 12th cent. See Emblem.

AMERY, AMORY, EMBREY, EMBURY, EMERY, HEMBRY, IMRAY, IMRIE: P OG *Amalric*, OF *Amauri, Emauri* 'work-rule'. DB.

AMES, AMIES, AMIS, AMISS, AMEYS, AMOS: (i) P Lat *amicus* 'friend'. 13th cent. (ii) The biblical name *Amos* was not used in England before the Reformation.

AMEY, AMY, LAMEY: P Lat *amatus*, OF *amé* 'beloved'. 12th cent.

AMIET, AMIOT: P OF A pet-form of *Amis*. 12th cent.

AMISON, AMSON: P OF 'Son of *Amis*'. 14th cent.

AMLOT see AMELOT. AMMANN see AMAND.

AMMON, AMON, AMOND: P ON *Ǫgmundr*, O Sw *Aghmund*. DB.

AMOORE, AMORE: L ME *attę mōr* 'at marsh or fen'. 15th cent.

AMOR, AMOUR: N OF *amour* 'love', from the age of chivalry. 14th cent.

AN: P OE An Anglo-Saxon name meaning 'One'.

ANABLE, ANNABEL, ANNABLE: N Lat *amabilis* 'lovable'. 12th cent.

ANCASTER: L OE *Anna-ceaster* 'Roman fort of *Anna*'. (Lincs) 12th cent.

ANCELL see ANSELL. ANCHOR see ANKER. ANDERS see ANDRE.

ANDERSON: P Originally Gk 'Son of *Andrew*'. Mainly Scottish. 15th cent. [Alexander Anderson, a marine corporal, and two convicts named John Anderson brought the name to Australia 1788]

ANDERTON: L OE 'The *tūn* (farm) of an Anglo-Saxon called *Ēanrēd*'. (Ches, Lancs).

ANDISON: P 'Son of *Andy* (a pet-form of *Andrew*)'. 14th cent.

ANDRE, ANDREA, ANDREE, ANDERS: P OF Forms of *Andrew*. 13th cent.

ANDREW, ANDREWES, ANDREWS, ANDRUS: P Lat *Andreas*, Fr *Andre*, It *Andrea*, Sp *Andres*, Ger and Du *Andreas*, Rus *Andrei*; *Andrew*, from Gk 'manly'. Patron saint of Scotland and of Russia before 1917. DB.

ANDREWARTHA: L Cornish 'upper place'.

ANGEL, ANGELL: (i) N Lat *angelus*, OF *angele* 'angel, messenger'. A miracle play name. 12th cent. (ii) N Cornish *an gell* 'light brown, tawny'. [James Angel, a marine, brought the name to Australia 1788].

ANGER, AINGER: P Norman form of ON *Asgeirr*. DB.

ANGLE(S), NANGLE: L OE The *Angles* took their name from *Angul*, Holstein, and at the Anglo-Saxon invasion gave it to Celtic Britain (Angle-, Engle-land). A locational surname from dwelling on an angle or corner land.

ANGLESS, ANGLISS, ANGLISH: L Fr *anglais* 'Englishman'. 12th cent.

ANGOOD see OSGOOD.

ANGOVE: O Cornish *an gof* 'smith, blacksmith'. 16th cent.

ANGUS: P SG and Ir *Aonghus* 'unique choice'. 13th cent.

ANGWIN: (i) L OF The '*Angevin*', from Anjou (France). 12th cent. (ii) N Cornish *an gwynn* 'fair, white'. See also Gwinn.

ANKER(S), ANCHOR: N OF *anachorete* 'anchorite, hermit'. 13th cent.

ANKETEL, ANQUETIL, ANTELL,

ANTILL: P Norman form of ON *Asketill*. 12th cent.

ANKIN see ANTIN.

ANKRETT: P OW *Angharad*, a woman's name 'much loved one'. 13th cent.

ANN: (i) P Hebrew *Hannah* 'God has favoured'. (ii) L O Brit *Ann* 'river with ash trees'. (Hants) 12th cent.

ANNABEL, ANNABLE see ANABLE. ANNAKIN see ANTIN.

ANNAND: P O Scand *Anund*. DB.

ANNAS, ANNESS, ANNIS, ANNISS: P OF *Anes* (*Agnes*). 12 cent.

ANNESLEY, AINSLEY, AYNSLEY: L OE From Annesley (Notts) or Ansley (Warwicks) both Anglo-Saxon '*lēah*' (clearing). 13th cent.

ANNETT, ANNOTT: P OF *An-not*, a dim. of *Ann*. 13th cent.

ANNING: P OE A patronymic, from the Anglo-Saxon pers. name *An*, preserved in Onesacre (Yorks), *Ansacre* DB.

ANNISON: P OF 'Son of *Annis*'. 14th cent.

ANQUETIL see ANKETEL.

ANSELL, ANCELL, HANSEL(L): P OG *Ansehelm*, OF *Ansellus* 'god-helmet'. 11th cent.

ANSFORD, HANSFORD: L OE *Ealhmund's ford*. (Som) DB.

ANSON: P 'Son of *Ann*'.

ANSTEE, ANSTEY: L OE *ānstiga* 'narrow uphill track'. DB.

ANSTICE, ANSTIS(S): P Gk *Anastasia* 'resurrection'. 12th cent.

ANSTRUTHER: L SG From Anstruther (Fifes) Scotland.

ANTCLIFF(E), ANTLIFF: L OE *earn-clif* 'eagles' cliff'. 13th cent.

ANTELL, ANTILL see ANKETEL.

ANTHONEY, ANTHONY: P Lat *Antonius*, OF *Antoine*. 12th cent.

ANTIN, ANKIN, ANNAKIN: P Norman form of ON *Askell*. 13th cent.

ANTROBUS: L From Antrobus (Ches), *Entrebus* DB.

APLIN, APPLIN: P Hebrew *Ab-el-in*, a pet-form of *Abel*.

APPEL: O OE *aeppel*, ME *appel* 'apple'. Metonymic for a grower/seller of apples.

APPERLEY, APPERLY: L OE *apuldor-lēah* 'the apple-tree clearing'. 13th cent.

APPLEBY, APPLEBEE: L OE + ON *appel-by* 'apple farm'. (Leices, Lincs, Westmorland) 12th cent.

APPLEGARTH, APPLEGATE: L ON *apaldr-garthr* 'apple enclosure'. 12th cent.

APPLETON: L OE *appel-tūn* 'apple-farm'. (Ches, Kent, Yorks) 12th cent.

APPLEYARD: L OE *appel-geard* 'apple-yard'. (Yorks) 13th cent.

APPS, EPPS: L OE *aespe*, *aepse* 'aspen (tree)'. 13th cent.

APSIMON: P Welsh *ap* 'Son of *Simon*'.

APTHORPE: L O Dan + OE 'The *thorp* (farm) of a Dane called *Api*'. (Northants).

ARBER see HARBER. ARBLASTER see ALABASTER.

ARBUCKLE: L SG *ard-an-buachaille* 'the hill of the shepherd'. (Lanarks) Scotland.

ARBUTHNOT: L SG *aber-buadhnat* 'the holy river'. (Kincardines) Scotland.

ARCHBOLD, ARCHIBALD: P OG *Ercanbald*, OF *Archamboult* 'precious bold'. DB.

ARCHDEACON: O OE *aercediacon* 'the chief deacon'. 13th cent.

ARCHER, LARCHER: O OF *archier* 'archer, bowman'. 12th cent. [The surname was brought to Australia with the First Fleet by Isaac Archer, a marine private, and John Archer, a convict].

ARDEN, ARDERN: L OE *earn-denu* 'eagles' valley'. (Ches, Yorks) 13th cent.

ARDLEY: L OE 'The *lēah* (wood) of an Anglo-Saxon called *Eardwulf*'. (Oxon) DB.

ARDLIE: L OE *eard-leage* 'the homestead in a meadow'. (Essex).

ARGENT, LARGENT: O OF *argent* 'silver', 'a silversmith'. 12th cent.

ARKELL, ARKLE: P O Sw *Arkil*, O Dan *Arnketil* 'eagle-cauldron'. DB.

ARKWRIGHT, HARTRICK, HATTRICK: O OE *arc-wryhta* 'wright, carpenter, joiner', a maker of arks, chests, coffers. 13th cent.

ARLINGTON: L OE 'The *tūn* (farm) of an Anglo-Saxon called *Earl*'. (Glos, Sussex) DB.

ARLISS: N OE *eare-lēas*, 'ear-less', lopped for some crime, probably against the forest laws. 13th cent.

ARLOTT, ARLOTTE: N OF *herlot, harlot*, originally 'a lad, servant', then 13th cent. 'a vagabond, rogue', 14th cent. 'an itinerant jester, juggler, buffoon', 15th cent. 'a harlot, prostitute'. The surname is 12th cent. In Normandy in 1025 the daughter of a tanner, known as Harlotte of Falaise, presented Duke Robert with a son, William, who was destined to become Duke of Normandy, and King of England by conquest.

ARMER, ARMOR, ARMOUR, LARMER, LARMOUR: O OF *armurier* 'armourer'. 13th cent.

ARMETT see HERMITTE.

ARMIN: P OG A dim. of *Ermenald*. 13th cent.

ARMISON, ARMSON: P 'Son of *Armin*'. 17th cent.

ARMISTED, ARMISTEAD, ARMSTEAD: L OF *ermite-stede* 'hermitage'. 14th cent.

ARMITAGE, ARMYTAGE see HERMITAGE.

ARMSTRONG: N OE *earm-strang* 'strong of arm'. 13th cent.

ARNALD, ARNALL, ARNAUD, ARNELL, ARNOLD, ARNOLL, ARNOT, ARNOTT, ARNOULD, ARNULL, HARNETT, HARNOT: (i) P OG *Arnald*, OF *Arnaut* 'eagle-power'. DB. (ii) L OE *earn-halh* 'eagle's valley'. (Notts, Yorks), *Ernehale* DB.

ARNDELL see ARUNDEL.

ARNE: L OE *aern* 'dwelling'. (Dorset).

ARNISON: P 'Son of *Arnold*'. 15th cent.

ARROWSMITH, HARROWSMITH: O OE *arwe-smith* 'a maker of arrows'. 13th cent.

ARSCOTT: L OE 'The *cot* (cottage/hut) of an Anglo-Saxon called *Eadrēd*'. (Salop) 12th cent. [John Arscott, a convict, brought the surname to Australia 1788].

ARTHUR(S), ARTER: P Celtic *Arturus*, the pers. name of the legendary King *Arthur*. DB.

ARTHURSON: P 'Son of *Arthur*'.

ARTIS(S), ARTOIS: L OF From Artois, France. 14th cent.

ARUNDALE, ARUNDEL(L), ARONDEL, ARRANDALE, ARNDEL: L OE *hārhūn-dell* 'hoarhound valley'. (Sussex) DB. Roger *Arundel*, Domesday tenant-in-chief, was the earliest bearer of this name. He derived it from his coat of arms rather than from the place in Sussex. His arms, 'six swallows argent (silver) on a field of sable (black)', are from OF *arondel* 'swallow'. [Thomas Arundel, brother of the Baron Arundel of Wardour, brought the surname to Australia as assistant surgeon on the *Friendship* 1788, but changed his name to Arndell].

ASBURY see ASTBURY.

ASH, DASH, DAISH, NASH, NAISH, RASCH, RASH, TASH: L OE *aesc* 'ash (tree)'. 13th cent. The variants arise from *atten ash* (Nash), *de ash* (Dash, Daish), and from dial. changes.

ASHBOLT, ASHPOLE: P OF These are corruptions of *Archbold*. 16th cent.

ASHBRIDGE: L OE *aesc-brycg* 'the bridge by the ash-tree'.

ASHBROOK(E): L OE *ēast-brōc* 'eastern brook'. (Glos), *Estbroce* DB.

ASHBURNER: O OE *aesc-brinnan* 'ash burner, potash maker' or ON *aska-brenna* with same meaning. 13th cent.

ASHBY: L OE + ON *aesc-by* 'the farm in the ash-trees'. 12th cent. A frequent place-name, e.g., Ashby de la Zouch (OF *souche* '(tree) stump').

ASHCROFT, ASCROFT: L OE *aesc-croft* 'small holding in the ash-trees'. 13th cent. ASHDOWN: L OE *aesc-dūn* 'down (hill) with ash-trees'. ASHENDEN: L OE Identical in meaning with *Ashdown*. ASHFIELD: L OE *aesc-feld* 'open country with ash-trees'. 12th cent. ASHFOLD: L OE *aesc-falod* 'sheep fold by the ash-trees'. 14th cent. ASHFORD, ASHFORTH, AYSHFORD: L OE 'ford by the ash-trees'. (Devon, Derbys, Kent, Middx, Salop) 13th cent.

ASHKETTLE: P ON *Asketill* 'god cauldron (pagan sacrifice)'. DB.

ASHLEY: L OE *aesc-lēah* 'ash-tree wood'. 12th cent.

ASHMAN, ASMAN: O OE *aescmann* 'boat-builder, shipman, sailor'. DB.

ASHMEAD: L OE *aesc-maed* 'meadow with ash-trees'. (Glos) ASHMORE: L OE *aesc-mere* 'pool among ash-trees'. (Dorset, Wilts) ASHTON: L OE *aesc-tūn* 'farm by the ash-tree'. 14th cent. ASHURST: L OE *aesc-hyrst* 'ash-tree hillock'. (Essex, Hants, Kent) ASHWELL: *aesc-wella* 'stream in the ash-trees'. (Essex), *Asseuuella* DB. [B. Y. Ashwell established a mission near Otaki, New Zealand, which became a centre for Maori farming, 1839].

ASHWICK: L OE *aes-wīc* 'dairy farm among ash-trees'. (Som), *Escewiche* DB.

ASHWIN: P OE *AEscwine* 'spear-friend', the name of an Anglo-Saxon king of Wessex. Surname 14th cent.

ASHWORTH: L OE *aesce-worth* 'homestead in the ash-trees'. (Lancs, Yorks).

ASKAM, ASKHAM: L OE *aesc-hām* 'homestead in the ash-trees'. (Notts, Yorks, Westmorland) 12th cent.

ASKELL, ASTELL, ASTIL, ESKELL, HASKELL: P ON *Askell*, O Dan *Eskell*, O Sw *Aeskil*, forms of *Asketill* 'god cauldron'. DB.

ASKEW, HASKEW, ASCOUGH, AYSCOUGH, ASKEY: L O Scand *eikiskogr* 'oak-wood'. (Aiskew, Yorks) 14th cent. [Richard Asky alias Askew, a marine, brought his surnames to Australia with the first Fleet 1788].

ASKIN(S), ASTIN, HASKIN(S), HASKING: P Norman form of ON *Asketill*. 13th cent.

ASLET(T): P OF *Acelot*, OG *Azilin*, a double dim. of *Azo*. 12th cent.

ASLIN, ASHLIN: P OF *Acelin*, ultimately from OG *Azo*. 12th cent.

ASPINALL, ASPINWALL: L OE *aespe-wielle* 'the spring among the aspen-trees'. (Lancs) 13th cent.

ASQUITH: L ON *ask-vithr* 'ash-wood'. (Askwith, Yorks) 13th cent.

ASSER, ASHER: P OE *Asser*, an Anglo-Saxon pers. name. *Asser* (*Asserius Menevensis*) was preceptor to, and wrote the life of King Alfred. DB.

ASTBURY, ASBURY: L OE *ēaste-burg* 'eastern fort'. (Ches) 13th cent.

ASTELL, ASTILL, ASTLE: L OE *ēaste-hyll* 'east hill'. (Ches) 13th cent.

ASTERLEY: L OE *ēaste-lēah* 'the eastern glade or clearing'. (Oxon, Salop).

ASTLEY: L OE Identical in meaning with *Asterley*. (Lancs, Salop, Warwicks, Worces).

ASTON: (i) P OE An abbreviated form of *AEthelstān* (*AEstānus* DB). (ii) L OE *ēaste-tūn* 'the eastern farm', a frequent place-name. DB.

ASTROP: L OE *ēaste-thorp* 'the eastern hamlet'.

ATHELSTAN(E): P OE *AEthelstān* 'noble stone'. 12th cent.

ATHERDEN: L OE 'At-the-*denu* (valley)'. 13th cent.

ATHERFOLD: L OE 'At-the-*falod* (sheep-fold)'. 14th cent.

ATHERSYCH: L ME 'At-the-*sich* (drain)'. (Hathersage, Derbys).

ATHERTON: L OE 'The *tūn* (farm) of *AEthelhere*, an Anglo-Saxon'. (Lancs) 13th cent.

ATHEY: L OE 'At-the-*haeg* (enclosure)'.

ATHOL: L OE 'At-*holh* (hollow)'. (Perths) Scotland. 13th cent.

ATHORN: L OE *aet horn* 'at the horn (spit of land)'. 14th cent.

ATKEY: O OE *aet caeg* 'at quay', 'a waterside worker'. 14th cent.

ATKIN(S), ATKYNS see ADKIN.

ATKINSON: P 'Son of *Adkin*'. 14th cent. [A First Fleet (convict) surname].

ATLEE, ATLEY, ATTLEE: L OE *aet lēah* 'at glade or clearing'. (Berks, Suffolk) 13th cent.

ATMORE: L OE *aet mōr* 'at marsh'. 13th cent.

ATTACK, ATTOCK: L OE *aet āc* 'at the oak'. 13th cent.

ATTALE: L OE *aet healh* 'at a small hollow or nook'. 13th cent.

ATTAWAY: L OE *aet weg* 'at the way, road, path'. 13th cent.

ATTENBOROUGH, ATTENBROW: L OE (i) 'at *beauru* (grove)'. (ii) 'at *beorg* (hill or mound)'. (iii) 'at the *burg* of *Eada*'. (Attenborough, Notts) DB.

ATTER: N OE *ātor* 'gall, venom, bitterness'. 12th cent.

ATTERBURY: L OE *aet byrig, burg* 'at fort'.

ATTERIDGE: L OE *aet hrycg* 'at ridge'. 14th cent.

ATTERWELL: L OE *aet wielle* 'at spring, stream, waterfall'. 13th cent.

ATTREE: L OE *aet ēa* 'at water or low-lying land'. 13th cent.

ATTRIDE: L OE *aet rȳd* 'at the cleared land'. 15th cent.

ATTRILL: L OE *aet hyll* 'at the hill'. 14th cent. (*Rill* is 16th cent.)

ATTWATER: L OE *aet waeter* 'at the water'. 12th cent.

ATTWELL, ATTWILL, ATTWOOL, ATWELL, ATWILL: L OE Identical in meaning with *Atterwell*. 13th cent. [John Atwell, a seaman on the *Sirius*, brought the surname to Australia 1788].

ATTWICK, ATTICK: L OE *aet wīc* (dairy farm). 14th cent.

ATTWOOD: L OE *aet wudu* 'at the wood'. 13th cent.

ATYEO: L OE *aet eā*, ME *yo* 'at the water'. 14th cent.

AUBERT see ALBERT.

AUBREY, AUBRY: P OG *Albericus*, OF

Auberi 'elf-ruler' or OG *Alberada*, OF *Albree, Auberi* 'elf-counsel'. DB.

AUDLEY: L OE 'The *lēah* (clearing) of an Anglo-Saxon woman called *Aldgȳth*'. *(Staffs), Aldidelege* DB.

AUDREY: P OE *AEthelthrȳth* 'noble strength', a woman's name. DB.

AUDSLEY: L OE *ald-lēah* 'the old clearing', from a lost place in Yorks.

AUGER see ALGER.

AUGHTON: L OE *āc-tūn* 'farm in the oak-trees'. (Lancs, Wilts, Yorks).

AUGUSTIN(E): P Lat *Augustinus* 'venerable'. 12th cent. See also Austin.

AULD: N OE *eald* 'old'. 13th cent. Scottish form of *Old*.

AULT: L OW *allt* 'hill'. [Sarah Ault, a convict, arrived 1788].

AUSTEN, AUSTIN, AUSTON: P OF *Aoustin*, vernacular form of *Augustinus*. 13th cent

AUTY: P O Dan *Auti*. DB.

AVELING: P OG *Avelina*, OF *Aveline*, from *Avo*. 12th cent.

AVELL: P OG A dim. of *Avo*. 12th cent.

AVENT: N OF *auenant* 'comely, handsome'. 12th cent.

AVEREY, AVORY: P Norman French pronunciation of *Alfred*. 12th cent.

AVERILL, AVRIL: N Lat *aprilis*, OF *avrill* 'April', for one born in that month. 13th cent.

AVES: P OG 'Son of *Avo*'. 12th cent.

AVIS, AVISS, AVISON: P OF *Avice*, from Lat *Avitia* or OG *Aveza*, an ancient name used in Gaul. 12th cent. in England.

AVNER: O OF *avener* 'oat merchant'. 13th cent.

AXBEY: L OE + ON '*býr* (homestead) with ash-trees', places (Ashby) in several counties. *Axbey* is metathesised, e.g., Ashby, Northants, was *Axeby* in 13th cent.

AXCELL, AXEL: P O Scand *Askell* in which -s- and -k- have been transposed.

AXFORD: L OE *aesca-ford* 'ford in the ash-trees'. (Wilts) 12th cent.

AXTEL: P ON *Asketill*. 17th cent. AXELSON: P 'Son of *Axtel*'.

AYLETT, AYLOTT, ALLAT, ALLET, ALLITT, ALLIOT, ELIOT: (i) P OE *AEthelgēat* 'noble *Gēat*', name of Beowulf's Swedish tribe. (ii) P OE *AEthelgyth* an Anglo-Saxon woman's name. DB. See also Eliot.

AYLIFFE: P OE *AEthelgifu* 'noble gift'. 12th cent.

AYLING, AYLIN, AYLEN: P OE *aetheling* 'noble', 'prince of the royal blood', used also as a personal name. The first recording of 1006 predates the Norman Conquest by 60 years.

AYLMER, ELMAR, ELMER: P OE *Aethelmaer* 'noble famous'. DB.

AYLWARD: P OE *AEthelweard* 'noble protector'. 11th cent.

AYLWIN: P OE *AEthelwine* 'noble friend'. DB.

AYNSLEY see ANNESLEY.

AYR, AYER(S), AYRE(S), AIERS, AIR, AIRES, EYER(S), EYRE(S): (i) N OF *eir, heir* ME *eir, eyr*, 'an heir to property, land, estate'. 12th cent. (ii) L SG From the royal burgh of Ayr (Scotland). 13th cent. [William Ayres, a convict, brought his variant of the surname to Australia 1788].

AYSHFORD see ASHFORD.

B

BABB(S): P OE A pet-form of *Barbara* (see Barbary). 12th cent. BABBIT: P OE A double dim. of *Barbara*. BABCOCK: P OE A dim. of *Barbara* + the affectionate suffix *-cock*. BABLE: P OE A double dim. of *Barbara*. BABOT: P OE A dim. of *Babb*. 13th cent.

BACCUS, BACCHUS see BACKHOUSE.

BACH(E), BATCH: L OE *baece* 'beck, brook'. 13th cent.

BACHELOR, BACHELDER, BACKLER, BATCHELDER, BATCHELOR: O OF & ME *bacheler* 'a young knight'. 12th cent. [John Batchelor, a marine, arrived on the *Sirius* 1788].

BACHER: L OE with the same meaning as *Bach*. 13th cent.

BACK, BACKES, BAX: (i) L OE *baec* 'back, behind', used topographically, 'behind the ridge'. (ii) N OE A nickname for one with a conspicuous rump. (iii) N ME *bakke* 'bat' for one 'blind as a bat' or of nocturnal habits. 11th cent. OE Byname.

BACKHOUSE, BACCUS, BACCHUS: O OE *baechūs* 'bakery, bakehouse'. 14th cent.

BACKMAN: O OE *baec-mann* 'bakemeats man' (from *bacan* 'to bake'). 13th cent.

BACON, BAKON: O OF & ME *bacun* 'cured pork'. Metonymic for a pork-butcher. 13th cent. [Samuel Bacon, a marine on the *Sirius*, brought the surname to Australia 1788].

BADAM, BADHAM see ABADAM.

BADCOCK, BATCOCK: P OE from Hebrew. A dim. of *Bartholomew* + the affectionate *-cock*. 13th cent. BADCOE: A form of *Badcock*.

BADDELEY: L OE 'The *lēah* (clearing) of an Anglo-Saxon called *Badda*'. (Staffs).

BADDER see BATHA.

BADDICK, BADDOCK: P OE *Baduca*, an Anglo-Saxon personal name.

BADE: P OE *Bada*, an Anglo-Saxon pers. name. DB.

BADGER(S): (i) L OE 'The *ōfer*, (shore or river-bank) of an Anglo-Saxon called *Baegi*'. (Salop) 13th cent. (ii) O OE *badger* 'hawker, huckster'. 15th cent.

BADMAN: P OE *beadu* 'battle' + *mann*. 13th cent.

BADRICK, BATTRICK, BETTERIDGE, BETTRIDGE: P OE *Beaduric* 'battle-powerful'. 13th cent.

BAGG(S), BAGGE: (i) P OG *Bago*, OF *Bague*. 12th cent. (ii) O ME *bagge*. Metonymic for a maker of bags.

BAGGETT, BAGGOTT, BAGEHOT, BAGOT, BAGOTT: P OE *Bealdhere*, a dim. of OG *Bago*. 12th cent.

BAGGIS: P ON *Baggi* a Scandinavian pers. name preserved in the place-name Bagby (Yorks), *Bagebi* DB. [William Baggis, a convict, brought the name to Australia 1788].

BAGLEY, BAGALEY, BAGGALLY, BAGGULEY: L OE First el. obscure; second el. *lēah* 'woodland' or 'clearing'. (Bucks, Salop, Somerset) 13th cent. [James Bagley, a corporal, brought the name to Australia with the First Fleet 1788].

BAGNALL, BAGNELL, BAGNOLD: L OE 'The *halh* (corner) of an Anglo-Saxon called *Badeca*'. (Staffs) 13th cent. [Ralph Bagnall, a marine, brought the name to Australia 1788].

BAGSHAW: L OE *bacger-shaw* 'bacger's copse'. (*Bacger*, an unidentified wild animal. Until 16th cent. the badger was called 'brock', OE *brocc*.)

BAIL(S), BAILE(S), BALE(S), BAYLES: O OF, ME *baile* + OE *weard* 'bail-ward (guardian) of the (castle) bailey or courts'. 12th cent.

BAILEFF, BAILIFF(E), BAYLIFF: O OF *bailif* 'warrant officer of a shire court', 'a pursuivant', 'a catchpoll'. 13th cent.

BAILEY, BAILIE, BAILY, BAYLEY: O In England a form of OF *bailif*. In Scotland 'a chief magistrate'. 14th cent. Also L OE '*bēg-lēah* 'wild berry wood'. (Lancs) 13th cent. [James Bailey, a convict, brought the name to Australia 1788].

BAILHACHE: O OF *baille hache* 'give axe' (an executioner). 12th cent. BAILHATCHET: N A nickname for an executioner.

BAILISS, BAILESS see BAYLIS.

BAIN(E), BAINS, BAYNES, BONES: (i) O OF *bain* 'bath attendant'. 13th cent. (ii) N ME *bayn* 'ready, hospitable', nickname for keeper of a hostelry. (iii) N SG *bán* 'fair'.

BAINBRIDGE: L ON *beinn* 'direct, straight' + OE *brycg* 'straight bridge'. (Yorks) 14th cent.

BAIRD: O Celtic Scottish form of bard. 'Minstrel or singer'.

BAIRNSFATHER, BARNFATHER: N OE *bearn-faeder* 'child's father'. 13th cent.

BAIRSTOW, BAISTOW, BARSTOW: L First el. obscure. Second el. OE *stōw* 'place' (often holy place, e.g., hermitage or monastery). (Yorks) 13th cent.

BAISBROWN, BISBROWN: L ON *báss-brún* 'cowshed at brink', water's edge, perhaps. (Westmorland) 14th cent.

BAITMAN see BATEMAN. BAITSON see BATESON.

BAKER, BAIKER, BACKER: O OE *baecere* 'a baker'. 12th cent. [James Baker, a marine, brought the name to Australia 1788].

BAKEWELL: L OE 'The *wiell* (spring, stream) of *Badeca*', Anglo-Saxon. (Derbys), *Badecvella* DB.

BALAAM, BALLAAM: L OF From Baalon in Meuse (France). 12th cent.

BALCH, BAULCH see BELCH.

BALD, BAULD: N ME *ballede* 'bald, corpulent'. 12th cent.

BALDER: P OE *Bealdhere* 'bold army'. 12th cent.

BALDERSTON, BALDERSTONE, BOLDERSTON: L OE 'The *tūn* (farm) of an Anglo-Saxon called *Baldhere*'. (Lancs) 13th cent.

BALDEY, BALDIE, BALDY, BOLDY: P OE *Bealdyth*, an Anglo-Saxon woman's name. 12th cent.

BALDING, BOLDING, BOULDING: P OE *Bealding* 'bold, brave'. 13th cent. [James Balding, a convict, brought the name to Australia 1788. In 1838 he was living at Parramatta and was present at the jubilee].

BALDOCK, BALDICK: L OF from Arabic *Baldac* (for Baghdad), named by the Knights Templar. (Herts) 12th cent.

BALDREY, BALDRICK, BAUDREY, BALDERY, BOLDERO(E), BOLDERY: P OG *Baldrick*, OF *Baldri, Baudri* 'bold rule' DB.

BALDWIN: P OG *Baldwin* 'bold friend'. 11th cent. [Ruth Baldwin, a convict, brought the name to Australia 1788].

BALE(S) see BAIL [Robert Bales, a convict, arrived on the *Alexander* 1788].

BALF: N Ir *balbh* 'stammering', an uncommon Irish nickname. 13th cent.

BALFOUR: L SG + Brit 'Village with pasture'. 14th cent.

BALIOL: L OF From Baliol (Normandy). DB. Guy de Baliol, Norman baron, received lands in northern England for his part in the Norman invasion. The family produced two kings of Scotland, John and Edward. The Oxford college was founded by the widow of John de Baliol, father of the king of that name.

BALL(E), BALLS: L OF *balle* 'ball', used topographically, 'a round hill, a knoll'. There is also a N form from ME *bal* 'a bald spot'. Matilda Ball seems to have been losing her hair in 1296. 12th cent. [Henry Ball, commander of the *Supply*, Mr Ball, third mate of the *Lady Penrhyn*, and John Ball, a convict, brought the name to Australia 1788].

BALLANCE, BALLANS: O OF *balancier*. Metonymic for a balancer who weighed with scales. 12th cent.

BALLANTYNE: L A Scottish locality name, also established in Ulster.

BALLARD: N ME *bal* + OF suffix *-ard*. 'Bald head'. 12th cent.

BALLER: O A derivative of ME *bal*. 'A maker of balls'. 13th cent.

BALLON: O OF *balon* 'a ball or pack'. Metonymic for a packer. 13th cent.

BALMAIN: L SG *Baile Meadhon* 'middle town' (Kincardineshire). 16th cent. [Dr William Balmain, chief surgeon in the colony of N.S.W., founded the Sydney suburb of Balmain].

BALMAN: P OE *Bealdmann* 'bold man'. 12th cent.

BALMER: O ME *balme*. 'A spicer or seller of ointment'. 14th cent.

BALSDON: L ME *bal* + OE *dūn* 'round hill'.

BALSHAW: L ME *balgh* + OE *scaga* 'rounded wood or coppice'.

BALSTON(E): P OE *Bealdstān* 'bold stone'. 12th cent.

BAMBRICK: L OE *bēam-brice* 'tree-tops', an Anglo-Saxon hill name.

BAMFORD, BAMFORTH, BAMPFORD: L OE *bēam-ford* 'tree-trunk (footbridge) ford'. (Derbys, Lancs) 13th cent.

BANBURY: L OE 'the *burh* (fort) of an Anglo-Saxon called *Banna*'. (Oxon), *Banesberie* DB.

BANCROFT, BENCROFT: L OE *bēan-croft* 'arable holding growing beans'.

BANE, BAWN, BAUGHAN: N Ir *ban* 'white'. 'The white-haired one'.

BANEY, BONEY: N ME *bān, bōn* 'bone', nickname for a thin, bony person. 13th cent.

BANFIELD: L OE *bēan-feld* 'the bean field'. No particular place is identified.

BANHAM, BENHAM: L OE *bēan-hām* 'homestead where beans are grown'. (Banham in Norfolk was *Benham* in DB.)

BANKER: L O Dan & ME *banke* 'bank, ridge, hillside'. 13th cent.

BANKS, BANKES: L Meaning as for *Banker*. 13th cent. [Sir Joseph Banks, naturalist and botanist, accompanied Captain Cook on his expedition in 1769, collecting specimens of flora from Australia and New Zealand which excited great interest in Britain. The Banksia rose was named for Lady Banks].

BANNERMAN: O OF *banere* + OE *mann* 'banner-man', 'standard bearer', 'ensign'. 14th cent.

BANNISTER, BANNESTER: O OF *banastre* 'basket'. Metonymic for a basket-maker. 12th cent. [George Bannister, a 16-year-old convict, brought the name to Australia 1788].

BANNON: P Ir *O Banain*. A Fermanagh and Co. Mayo name enshrined in Ballyhannon.

BARAGWANATH: N Cornish. A surname meaning, curiously, 'wheaten bread'.

BARAT see BARRAT.

BARBARY: P OE from Gk. Medieval form of *Barbara*, meaning 'foreign, strange'. St *Barbara a* 3rd cent. Syrian saint, was one of the four virgin saints. French *Barbe*, Russian *Varvara*. All these forms have produced surnames.

BARBER, BARBOUR: O OF *barbier* 'barber', and surgeon and dentist, too. 13th cent. [Elizabeth Barber, a convict, brought the name to Australia 1788].

BARCLAY, BARKLY, BERKELEY, BURKLEY: L OE *beorc-lēah* 'birch-wood'. (Glos, Som, Sussex) DB. The Berkeleys of Glos are one of only two noble families whose ancestry traces back to Anglo-Saxon times.

BARDEN: L OE *bere-denu* 'barley-dale'. DB.

BARDOLPH: P OG *Bartholf* 'bright wolf'. 12th cent. Shakespeare uses Bardolph for Falstaff's 'white-livered, red-faced' companion in *Henry IV* and *Henry V*.

BARDSLEY: L OE '*Beornred's lēah* (clearing)'. (Lancs).

BARDWELL, BEARDWELL: L OE 'The *wielle* (spring) of *Bearda*, an Anglo-Saxon'. DB.

BARE: N OE *baer* 'bare, unclothed', usually in the sense of unarmed, defenceless. 13th cent.

BAREFOOT, BARFOOT: N OE *baer-fōt*, nickname for a penitent or pilgrim. 13th cent.

BAREHAM: L OE *bearu-hām* 'homestead in a grove'.

BARFORD: L OE *bereford* 'barley-ford', used at the barley harvest.

BARGATE: O OF *barre* + OE *geat*. Metonymic for 'keeper of the bargate', barring access to the castle or town. 13th cent.

BARGE: O OF *barge* 'bargeman, seaman'. 14th cent.

BARGH, BARFF, BARUGH: L OE *beorg* 'mound, barrow' (burial place). 14th cent.

BARHAM: (i) L OE *beorg-hām*. 'The *hām* (homestead) on the hill'. (Cambs, Suffolk), *Bercheham, Bercham* DB. (ii) 'The *hām* of an Anglo-Saxon called *Biora* (the bear)'. (Kent), *Berham* DB.

BARKER, BERKER: (i) O OF *berchier* 'shepherd'. 12th cent. (ii) O OF *barcher*, ME *barker* 'tanner'. 13th cent.

BARKHAM: L OE *beorc-hamm* 'river-meadow with birch trees'. (Berks) DB.

BARKHOUSE, BARKAS, BARKIS: O ME 'barkhouse, tannery', for a tanner. 14th cent.

BARKSHIRE see BERKSHIRE.

BARKWAY: L OE *beorc-weg* 'way, path through the birchwood'. (Herts).

BARLAND: L OE *bere-land* 'barley land'. [George Barland, a convict, brought the name to Australia 1788].

BARLETT: P OF *Ber-el-ot*, a double dim. of OG *Berard*. 13th cent.

BARLEY, BARLEE: O OE Metonymic for a maker of barley bread. 13th cent. Some may be locality names from Barley (Herts, Lancs, Yorks).

BARLEYCORN: O OE *baerlic-corn* 'a grower of barley'. 13th cent.

BARLOW: L OE *bere-lēah* 'barley-clearing' or *berehlāw* 'barley hill'. (Derbys, Lancs, Yorks) 13th cent.

BARMAN, BEARMAN, BERMAN: O OE *baermann* 'bearer, porter'. 12th cent.

BARN(E), BARNES, BARNS: (i) O ON *barn* 'child, young knight'. DB. (ii) O OE *beorn* 'warrior'. DB. (iii) O OE *bereaern* 'barn', for a worker at the barns. 13th cent. [Robert Barnes, bosun on the *Friendship*, Samuel Barnes, servant of Rev Johnson, and Stephen Barnes, convict, brought the name to Australia 1788].

BARNABAS: P Hebrew 'Son of Consolation'. 13th cent. BARNABY, BARNEBY, BARNABE: English forms of Barnabas. 14th cent.

BARNACLE: N ME Nickname for a horse trainer, from OF *bernac* 'strong bit for a horse's mouth', 14th cent.; or L OE 'barley slope'. (Warwicks).

BARNARD, BERNARD: P OF *Bernart* 'bear brave'. DB.

BARNET, BARNETT: L OE *baernet* 'burning', 'burnt land'. (Herts) 12th cent. [Daniel Barnett and Henry Barnett, both convicts, brought the name to Australia 1788].

BARNEY: L OE *bere-eg* 'barley island'. (Norfolk).

BARNFIELD: L OE *bereaern-feld* 'field with barn'.

BARNHAM: L OE 'The *hām* (homestead) of *Beorna*, an Anglo-Saxon'. DB.

BARNHILL: L OE '*Beorn's hyll*'. (Yorks) DB.

BARNSLEY: L OE 'The *lēah* (clearing) of various Anglo-Saxons with names related to *Beorn*'. (Dorset, Glos, Wight, Yorks) DB.

BARNSTAPLE: L OE '*Bearda's staple* (post)'. (Devon) DB.

BARNWELL: L OE *beorn-wielle* 'warriors' spring'. (Cambs).

BARON, BARRON: O/N OF & ME A title conferred for feudal service upon freemen of London and York paying homage to the king, and to freemen of the Cinque Ports for service at coronations. Also a surname from some of the smaller baronies of Scotland. Commonly, however, a nickname from playing the part of baron in a medieval play, and an ironical nickname for a proud and haughty individual. 13th cent.

BARR(S): (i) L OF From Barre-en-Ouche or Barre-de-Semilly, Normandy. DB. (ii) L OE From Barr (Ayr, Renfrews) Scotland. (iii) L OF *barre* 'town or castle gate', applied to one living by the *barre*.

BARRACK: L OF *baraque* 'hut'.

BARRACLOUGH, BARROWCLIFF, BERECLOTH: L OE *bearu-clōh* 'grove in a ravine or deep valley'. 14th cent. (Yorks, but the place has vanished).

BARRAT(T), BARRETT, BARRITT, BARROTT, BARAT: (i) N OF *barat*, ME *barrat*, a word of many meanings: commerce, dealing; trouble, distress; deception, fraud; strife. All would be fruitful in producing nicknames. (ii) O OF *barrette*. Metonymic for a maker of caps and bonnets. 12th cent. [Thomas Barrett, a convict, brought the name to Australia 1788. Richard Barrett was prominent in negotiating land purchases by the New Zealand Company, 1839].

BARRELL: O OF *baril* 'barrel, cask'. Metonymic for a cooper. 12th cent.

BARRER(E): L OF *barre*. Meaning as for Barr (iii). 13th cent.

BARRINGTON: L OE 'The *tūn* (farm) of *Bara's* people' (Cambs, Som), or the *tūn* of *Beorn's* people (Glos). DB.

BARROW(S), BERROW: L OE *bearu* 'grove' or *'beorg* 'barrow, mound'. 12th cent. [Mr Barrow, a midshipman on the *Supply*, brought the name to Australia 1788].

BARROWMAN, BARRYMAN see BORROWMAN.

BARRY, BARRIE: (i) L OF *barri* 'rampart', later, 'the town beyond the rampart'. 12th cent. (ii) L SG From Barry (Angus) Scotland. 14th cent. (iii) N Ir *O Baire* 'fair-head'. [John Barry, a convict, brought the name to Australia 1788].

BARSBY: L ON *barn-by 'býr* (farm) of a Norseman called *Child*'. (Leices) DB. (ON *barn* 'child'.) [Samuel Barsby, a convict, brought the name to Australia 1788].

BARSHAM, BASHAM: L OE '*Hām* (homestead) of an Anglo-Saxon nicknamed *Boar*'. (Norfolk) 12th cent.

BARSON: P OE from Hebrew 'Son of (a dim. of) *Bartholomew*'. 14th cent.

BARSTOW, BASTOW see BAIRSTOW.

BART: P OE Short form of *Bartholomew*. 13th cent.

BARTER: O OF *barater* 'to cheat, cousen, beguyle, deceive, lie, cog, foist' (Cotgrave 1611). Metonymic for a trader, barterer.

BARTHOLOMEW, BERTHELMY: P Hebrew *Bartholomew* 'son of *Talmai* (abounding in furrows)'. An English name from 12th cent.

BARTHORP(E), BARTRAP, and endings -TRIP, TROP, TRUP: L O Scand '*Thorp* (farm) of a Scandinavian called *Borkr*'. (Yorks) 12th cent.

BARTIN see BERTIN.

BARTINDALE: L OE 'The *dael* (valley) of *Beorht's* people'. (A lost place in Yorks.) 15th cent.

BARTLE(S), BARTELS: P OE A diminutive of *Bartholomew*. BARTLET, BARTELOT, BERTALOT: P OE Diminutives of *Bartelmew*, from *Bartholomew*. 12th cent.

BARTLEY: L OE *beorch-lēah* 'the birch-wood'. (Hants, Worces), *Berchelai* DB. The Hants place is now Bartley Regis.

BARTON, BARTEN: L OE *beretūn*. Originally 'barley farm', later, demesne farm or outlying grange (of a monastery). 11th cent.

BARTRAM, BERTRAM, BATTERHAM, BUTTRUM, BORTHRAM: P OG *Bertrant*, OF *Bertrand* 'bright raven'. DB.

BARWELL: L OE *bar-wielle* 'boar-stream'. (Leices) 12th cent.

BARWICK see BERWICK.

BASELEY, BASLEY, BAZELEY, BASIL, BAZELL: P OF from Gk via Lat *Basilius* 'kingly'. 12th cent.

BASH, BAISH: L OE *baece* 'beck, brook'. 13th cent. See also Bach.

BASHFORD: (i) L OE *beorc-ford* 'the birch ford'. (Ches, Staffs), *Berchesford* or *Berchesword* DB. (ii) L OE 'The ford of an Anglo-Saxon who was probably called *Basa*'. (Notts), *Baseford* DB.

BASK: N ON *beiskr* 'bitter, ungrateful'. 14th cent.

BASKERVILLE, BASTERFIELD, PASTERFIELD: L OF From Boschville, Eure (Normandy). 12th cent.

BASKETT: O ME *basket*. Metonymic for a basket-maker. 12th cent.

BASNET: O OF *basinet*. Metonymic for a maker of *basinets* (basin-shaped helmets).

BASON see BATESON. [Elizabeth Bason, a convict, brought the name to Australia 1788].

BASS, BASE, BAISS: N OF *bas*, ME *bass* 'short legs'. 12th cent. BASSET: N OF *basset*. A dim. of *bas* 'a dwarf'. DB.

BASSINGTHWAITE: L ON 'The *thwaite* (clearing or meadow) of a Norman called *Bastun*'.

BASTAPLE, BASTABLE: Forms of *Barnstaple*. 13th cent.

BASTARD: N OF *bastard* (ME *bast* + French suffix *-ard*) 'pack saddle', used as bed by muleteers. From this bastard, i.e., illegitimate. DB.

BASTER, BAISTER: O OF *bastier* 'saddler'. 13th cent.

BASTIAN, BASTIEN, BASTEN, BASTIN: P Lat dim. of *Sebastian*. 13th cent.

BASTICK: L OE *baest-wīc* 'dairy-farm in a lime grove'. (Norfolk) 14th cent.

BASTON: L ON *Bakstūn* 'The *tūn* (farm) of a Norseman called *Bak*'. (Lincs) 12th cent.

BATCH see BACH. BATCHELDER, BATCHELOR see BACHELOR. BATCOCK see BADCOCK.

BATE(S): P OE A pet-form of *Bartholomew*. 13th cent. [John Bates, a marine mason on the *Sirius*, brought the name to Australia 1788].

BATEMAN, BAITMAN, BATMAN: O OE 'Servant of *Bate*'. 13th cent.

BATER: O OF *bateor*. 'A coppersmith or dealer in beaten copperware'. 12th cent.

BATESON, BAITSON, BATSON: P OE 'Son of *Bate*'. 13th cent. BATEY, BATIE, BATY: P OE A pet-form of *Bate*. 13th cent.

BATH: L from Bath (Som), *Bade* DB. The Roman baths were called by the Romans *Aquae Sulis* and renamed by the Anglo-Saxons *Akemanceaster*.

BATHA, BATHE, BATHO, BADDER: P OW *ap Atha* 'son of *Atha*'. 14th cent.

BATHGATE: L OE From Bathgate (West Lothian), the lands and castle once owned by Robert the Bruce.

BATHURST: L OE 'The *hyrst* (wooded hill) of *Bada*, Anglo-Saxon'. (Sussex) 13th cent.

BATISSON, BATTISON: P OE 'Son of *Bate*'. 14th cent. BATKIN: P OE A pet-form of *Bate*. 13th cent.

BATLEY: L OE 'The *lēah* (clearing) of *Bata*, Anglo-Saxon'. DB. [A First Fleet surname].

BATSFORD: L OE 'The *ofer* (bank) of *Baecci*, Anglo-Saxon'. (Glos, Sussex) 12th cent.

BATT(E), BATTS: (i) P OE A pet-form of *Bartholomew*. 13th cent. (ii) N OE *batt* 'cudgel, club', used for a short, stocky individual. 13th cent.

BATTEN, BATTIN, BATTING, BATON: P OE Dim. of *Batt* (i). 13th cent.

BATTERSBY: L ON 'The *byr* (farm) of *Bothvarr*, Norseman'. (Yorks) DB.

BATTERSON, BATTESON: P OE 'Son of *Batten* or *Batty*'. 16th cent.

BATTISCOMBE: L OE 'The *cumb* (valley) of *Betti*, Anglo-Saxon'. (Dorset) 15th cent.

BATTLE, BATTELL: O OF *de la bataile* 'of the battle array', 'a warrior, soldier'. 12th cent.

BATTRICK see BADRICK.

BATTY(E), BATTEY, BATTIE: P OE A pet-form of *Batt* (*Bartholomew*). 14th cent.

BAUCH see BELCH.

BAUD: N OF *baud* 'gay', in its true and delightful sense of 'cheerful, sprightly'. 13th cent.

BAUDREY see BALDREY.

BAUGH: N OW *bach* 'little'. 14th cent.

BAUGHAN see BANE. BAVERIDGE see BEVERIDGE.

BAWCOCK, BOWCOCK, BOWCOTT, BOOCOCK: P OE A short form of *Baldwin* + the familiar *-cock*. 13th cent.

BAWN see BANE. BAX see BACK.

BAXTER, BAGSTER: O OE *baecestre* 'female baker'. 11th cent. [William Baxter, a private soldier, brought the name to Australia 1788].

BAYARD: (i) N OF Chaucer's proud *Bayard*, 'the haughty one'. DB. (ii) N OF *baiard* 'bay-coloured' (red hair).

BAYLEY see BAILEY. BAYLES see BAIL. BAYLIFF see BAILEFF.

BAYLIS, BAILISS, BAILESS: O OF *baillis* 'bailiff'. 16th cent. [A First Fleet surname].

BAYNARD: P OG *Beinhard* 'ready, willing', a pers. name. DB.

BAYNES see BAIN. BAYNHAM see BEYNON. BAZELY, BAZELL see BASELEY.

BEACH, BEECH, BECH: L OE *baece* 'stream'. 13th cent.

BEACHCROFT: L OE *baece-croft* 'croft (small arable plot) by a stream'. [Mary

Beachcroft, a convict, brought the name to Australia 1788].

BEACOCK: P OE from OF A pet-form of *Beatrice* + the suffix *-cock*. 13th cent.

BEADE, BEED: P OE *bēda, bede* 'proclaim'. The Venerable Bede made the name famous throughout England. First recorded as a surname 13th cent. The origin of *bēda* is OE *gebed* 'prayer' and *Beade, Beed* may have been a maker of prayer-beads.

BEADELL, BEADLE, BEDDALL, BEEDELL, BEEDLE, BIDDELL, BIDDLE, BUDDELL, BUDDLE: O OE *bydel* 'beadle'. DB. The change of vowel is dial.

BEADMAN: O ME *bedeman* 'a man of prayer, praying for the soul of a benefactor'. 14th cent.

BEAL(E)(S), BEALL: (i) N OF *bele* 'beautiful', a woman's name. (ii) L OE *bēo-hyll* 'bee-hill'. (Northumb) (iii) L OE *bēag-halh* 'corner by the bends (of the river)'. (Yorks) 13th cent.

BEAMES, BEAMISH, BEAMISS, BEAMS: (i) L OF from Beaumais-sur-Dive, Calvados (Normandy). (ii) L OF *Bellus Mansus* 'beautiful mansion'. (Durham) 12th cent.

BEAN(E), BEEN(E): (i) O OE *bēan* 'bean'. Metonymic for a grower of beans. 12th cent. (ii) N OE *bēne* 'pleasant, kindly'. 12th cent. (iii) P SG *beathan*, a dim. of *beatha* 'life'.

BEAR(E), BEER(S), BERE; L OE *bearu* 'grove'. 12th cent.

BEARD: N OE *beard* 'beard', a nickname for the wearer of one. DB.

BEARDWELL see BARDWELL. BEARMAN, BERMAN see BARMAN. BEASLEY, BEAZLEY see BEESLEY.

BEATER, BETTER: O OE *beatere* 'fighter, champion'. 12th cent.

BEATON see BETHUNE.

BEATSON: P Scottish form of *Bateson*. 15th cent.

BEATY, BEATEY, BEATIE, BEATTY: P Scottish forms of *Batey*. 15th cent.

BEAUCHAMP, BEACHAM, BEECHAM: L OF From Beauchamp, several places in France including Beauchamps, Manche (Normandy). DB.

BEAUCLERK: O OF 'Exemplary clerk'.

BEAUMONT, BEUMANT, BEAMAN(D), BEAMENT, BEAMONT, BEAUMAN, BEMAND, BELMONT: L OF From several places in Normandy meaning 'beautiful hill' including Beaumont-le-Roger. DB.

BEAUSIRE, BELLSYER, BOWSER: N OF *bel* + Lat *senior* 'fair sire'.

BEAVAN, BEAVEN BEAVON see BEVAN.

BEAVER(S), BEAVOR(S): (i) L OF *Belvoir* 'beautiful view'. (Leices) 12th cent. (ii) N OE *beofor*, a nickname from the beaver, once common in England.

BEAVES, BEAVIS, BEVES, BEVIS, BOVIS: (i) L OF from Gaulish. From *Beauvais*, Oise (Picardy), originally the home of the Gaulish tribe the *Bellovaci*. DB. (ii) N AF *beau fiz* 'fine son'.

BEBB: P OE *Bebbe*, a woman's name dating from the 7th cent. Queen *Bebbe* was wife of Aethelfrith, king of Northumbria.

BEBBINGTON: L OE 'The *tūn* (farm) of *Bebbe's* people'. (Ches) 12th cent.

BEC, BECK(E): (i) L OF From one of several places in France, e.g., Bec-Hellouin, Eure (Normandy). DB. (ii) L ON bekkr 'brook', frequent in the Danelaw. 13th cent. (iii) O OE *becca* 'pickaxe'. Metonymic for a maker of pickaxes and mattocks. 13th cent. (iv) N OF *bec* (bird's) 'beak', a nickname for one with a beaky nose. 12th cent.

BECKER: P OE *Becca*, an Anglo-Saxon pers. name.

BECKET(T), BECKIT, A'BECKETT: (i) N A dim. of OF *bec* 'little beak'. 12th cent. (ii) L OE *bēo-cot* 'bee-cottage'. (Berks, Devon) 13th cent.

BECKFORD: L OE 'The ford of *Becca*, Anglo-Saxon'. (Glos) DB. BECKHAM: L OE '*Becca's hām* (homestead)'. (Norfolk) DB. BECKLEY: L OE '*Becca's lēah* (clearing)'. (Kent, Oxon, Sussex).

BECKTON: L OE *baece-tūn* 'farm in a stream valley'. (Hants) 12th cent.

BECKWITH: L OE *bec-wudu* 'beechwood', later Scand influence changing *wudu* to *vithr*. 14th cent.

BEDALE: L OE 'The *halh* (hidden valley) of *Bēda* Anglo-Saxon'. (Yorks).

BEDDING: P OE *Bēada*, an Anglo-Saxon personal name. 12th cent.

BEDDINGFIELD: L OE '*Bēada's feld* (field)' (Suffolk) 13th cent.

BEDDOE(S), BEDDOW(S), BEDDOWES: P OW Derived from *Bedo*, a pet-form of *Meredith*. 15th cent.

BEDFORD: L OE *Bēda's ford*. DB.

BEDLOE: P OE *Bīedlufu*, a woman's name derived from *bēodan* 'to command' and *lufu* 'love'. 12th cent.

BEDSER: L OE The surname derives from a lost place in Sussex. First el. probably *Bēada* (see Bedding). Second el. obscure. 13th cent.

BEDWARD: P OW 'Son of *Edward*'. (Welsh *ap* 'son'.)

BEDWELL, BIDWELL, BIDDWELL, BIDEWELL: L OE *byde* 'tub or barrel', used topographically for a deep valley, + *wielle* 'spring or stream'. 'The stream in a valley'. (Beds, Devon, Essex, Herts, Northants, Som) 13th cent.

BEE: N OE *beo* 'bee'. 'A busybody'. 12th cent.

BEECHER, BECHER: L OE *bēce* 'beechtree'. 13th cent.

BEECHEY: L OE *bēce-haeg* 'beech enclosure'. 13th cent.

BEEMAN, BEMAN, BEAMAN: O OE *bēo* 'bee'. 'A bee-keeper', 13th cent.

BEEMER, BEAMER: O OE *bīemere* 'trumpeter'. 12th cent.

BEESTON, BEASTON, BEESON: (i) L OE *beonet* 'bent grass *tūn* (farm)'. (Notts) 12th cent. (ii) *bī* + ON *steinn* 'by (the) stone'. (Yorks) 13th cent.

BEET, BEAT: P OE from Lat. A pet-form of *Beatrice*. 13th cent.

BEETON, BEATON: (i) P A dim. of *Beet* (*Beatrice*). (ii) L OF From Béthune (Pas-de-Calais). 14th cent.

BEGBIE: L OE *bēg* + 0 Scand *by* 'homestead with berries'.

BEGG(E), BEGGS: N SG *beag* 'small'. A nickname for a small man. Also a Northern Ireland surname.

BEGLEY: N Ir *O Beaglaoich* 'descendant of small hero'. Originally a galloglas (armed retainer or mercenary soldier) name.

BEHAN: P Ir *O Beachain*, which may derive from Ir *beach* 'bee'.

BELCH, BELK, BALCH, BAULCH: (i) N OE *baelc* 'belching forth'. (ii) N from the same source, 'stomach, pride, arrogance'; also 'spirited'. 12th cent.

BELCHER, BELSHER, BEWSHIRE, BEAUSHAW, BOWSHER: N OF *bel-chiere* 'fair-look', 'fair-face'. 13th cent.

BELDAM, BELDHAM, BELDOM: N AF *beledame* 'fine lady'. 13th cent.

BELFRAGE, BERRIDGE: P Scottish form of *Beveridge*. 17th cent.

BELGIAN, BELGION(S): N AF *bele-jambe* 'fine leg'. 12th cent. (No connection with Belgium, Lat *Belgicus* 'of the Netherlands and Belgium'.)

BELGRAVE: L Originally OE *mearth-grāf* 'grove with martens', the name was changed in Norman times to OF *bel* + OE *grāf* 'lovely grove'. (Leices).

BELL(E): (i) P A dim. of Fr and Sp *Isabel*. DB. (ii) N OF *belle* 'beautiful'. 12th cent. (iii) O OE *belle*. Metonymic for a bellman or bell-ringer. 12th cent. (iv) L OE One who lived at the sign of the Bell. 13th cent. [Jonathon Bell, a soldier on the *Sirius*, and William Bell, a convict, brought the name to Australia 1788].

BELLAMY: N OF *bel ami* 'fair friend'. 12th cent. [Sarah Bellamy, a convict, brought the name to Australia 1788].

BELLCHAMBER(S): O OE *belle* + OF *chaimbre* 'keeper of the bell-chamber'. 14th cent.

BELLENGER see BERRINGER.

BELLER: O OE *belle* 'a bell-founder'. 13th cent.

BELLETT(E), BELLOTT(E): N A dim. of OF *bel* 'beautiful'. DB.

BELLEW: (i) L OF From Belleau (Normandy). (ii) L ON From Belleau (Lincs), named from ON *heilagr* 'holy', 'holy meadow'. DB.

BELLHAM, BELLAM: N OF *bel homme* 'handsome man'. 12th cent.

BELLHOUSE, BELLAS: L OE *belle-hūs* 'bell-house, bell-tower'. 12th cent.

BELLINGHAM: (i) L OE 'the *hām* (homestead) of the people of *Beora*, an Anglo-Saxon'. (Kent) 13th cent. (ii) L OE 'The *hām* of the dwellers on the bell-shaped hill'. (Northumb).

BELLIS(S): P 'Son of *Ellis*'. (Welsh *ap* 'son'.) 16th cent.

BELLMAN: (i) O OE *belle-mann* 'bellman, ringer'. In York and Scotland 'town-crier'. (ii) O ME *bely-man*, from *bely* 'bellows'. 'Bellows-blower'. 14th cent.

BELLSON, BELSON: P 'Son of *Bell* (*Isabel*)'. 14th cent.

BELLSYER see BEAUSIRE.

BELLY: N OE *bylig* 'belly', from *belgan* 'to swell, grow angry'. Nickname for a choleric individual.

BELMAINE: N OF *bel mains* 'beautiful hands'. 13th cent.

BELMONT see BEAUMONT.

BELT: O OE *belt.* Metonymic for a belt-maker. 13th cent.

BENBOW, BENBOUGH: N OE 'bend-bow', nickname for an archer. 14th cent.

BENCE: P OG *Benzo.* DB.

BENCH: L OE *benc* 'terrace or river-bank'. 13th cent.

BENCROFT see BANCROFT.

BENDALL, BENDLE: L OE *bēan-halh* 'nook or corner where beans grow'.

BENDER: N OE *bendan* 'to bend (the bow)'. As for Benbow. 14th cent.

BENDISH, BENDIX: L OE *bēan-edisc* 'enclosed field with beans'. (Herts, Essex) DB.

BENEDICT, BENEDIK: (i) P Lat *benedicere* 'blessed, benign'. 13th cent. (The name of five saints.) (ii) N Lat *benedicite*, nickname for one who was forever blessing all and sundry.

BENFIELD: L OE *beonet-feld* 'field or plain with bent grass.'

BENGER see BERRINGER. BENHAM see BANHAM.

BENJAMIN: P Hebrew 'Son of the south'. As an English surname 12th cent.

BENN, BENNIS, BENNS: P Pet-forms of names in *Ben*, e.g., *Benedict*, *Bennet.* DB.

BENNET(T), BENNETTS, BENNITT(S): P ME forms of *Beneit*, from Lat *Benedictus* 'blessed'. 12th cent. BENNISON: P ME 'Son of *Bennet*'. 14th cent. [John Bennett, convict, brought the name to Australia 1788].

BENSON: (i) P ME 'Son of *Benn*'. 14th cent. (i) L 'The *tūn* (farm) of the *Benesingas*, Anglo-Saxons'. (Oxon) 13th cent.

BENSTEAD: L OE *bēan-stede* 'settlement where beans are grown'.

BENT: L OE *beonet* 'bent grass'. 13th cent.

BENTALL, BENDALL, BENDLE: L OE *beonet-halh* 'angle or nook covered in bent grass'. (Salop) 13th cent.

BENTLEY, BINTLEY: L OE *beonet-lēah* 'clearing overgrown with bent grass'. 12th cent. [Joshua Bentley, sailor, brought the name to Australia 1788].

BENWELL: L OE *bionnan walle* 'inside the (Roman) wall' (between the R. Tyne and Hadrian's Wall). (Northumb) *Bynnewalle* in 1050.

BERARD: P OG *Berard*, OF *Berart* 'bear-strong'. 12th cent.

BERECLOTH see BARRACLOUGH.

BERESFORD: L OE *beofor-ford* 'beaver-ford'. (Staffs).

BERGH: L OE *beorg* 'hill, barrow, mound'. 13th cent.

BERIFF see BRIGHTIFF. BERKELEY see BARCLAY. BERKENSHAW see BIRKENSHAW. BERKER see BARKER.

BERKSHIRE, BARKSHIRE: L OE (County of) Berkshire. 13th cent. (OE *Baerrucscir* in 931, derived from O Brit (Celtic) *barro* 'top, summit'.)

BERNARD see BARNARD.

BERNERS: L OF From Bernières, Calvados (Normandy). DB.

BERNEY, BURNEY, BURNIE: L OF From Bernay, Eure (Normandy). DB.

BERRIDGE see BELFRAGE.

BERRIMAN, BERRYMAN: O OE *burh*, ME *buri* + *mann* 'servant at the manor'. 12th cent.

BERRINGER, BELLENGER, BELLINGER, BELLHANGER, BENNINGER, BENGER: P OG *Beringar*, OF *Berengier* 'bear-spear', the name of one of Charlemagne's paladins. DB. The variants are largely due to the inability of the Normans to pronounce the original form of the name. *Beringer* has a fem. form *Berengaria.* King Richard I's queen was *Berengaria* of Navarre.

BERRINGTON: L OE *byrigtūn* 'manor farm'. (Glos) DB.

BERROW see BARROW.

BERRY, BERREY, BERRIE, BURY: O OE *byrig*, from *burh* 'fort'. In ME this became *beri, buri*, used of a manor-house. 'Servant at the manor-house'. 13th cent.

BERSEY see BURSEY.

BERT, BERTA: P OG *Berhta*, OF *Berte.* 11th cent.

BERTALOT see BARTLET. BERTHELMY see BARTHOLOMEW.

BERTIN, BARTIN: P OG & OF *Bertin*, a pet-form of *Bertrand.* 12th cent.

BERTRAM see BARTRAM. BERTWHISTLE see BIRTWHISTLE.

BERWICK, BERRICK, BARWICK, BARRICK: L OE *berewīc* 'barley-farm', usually a grange where the barley was stored. 13th cent.

BESANT, BESSANT, BESSENT, BESZANT, BEZANT, BEZZANT: N OF *besan, beazanz* (Lat *byzantius*) a gold coin first minted at Byzantium. Nickname for a moneyer, one who coins money legally. 12th cent. The same device is used in heraldry to describe a golden roundel, a 'bezant', probably another source of the nickname. When the roundel is green (*vert*) it is described as 'pomeis'. Is this the origin of pommy, a 'green' English immigrant?

BESSEMER: O OE *besma* 'besom'. 'A maker of besoms (twig brooms)'. 12th cent.

BEST(E): N OF *beste* 'beast'. 'Savage, brutal as a beast'. 12th cent. [John Best, a convict, brought the name to Australia 1788].

BESTAR, BESTER: O OF *bestere*, from *beste* 'a herdsman'. 13th cent.

BESTMAN: O OF *beste* + OE *mann* 'a herdsman'. 14th cent.

BETHEL(L): P OE from Hebrew. A dim. of *Beth* (*Elizabeth*) but sometimes P OW a form of *Abethell*, see Bithel. 13th cent.

BETHUNE, BETTON, BEATON, BEETON: (i) L OF From Bethune (Pas-de-Calais). 12th cent. (ii) L OE *baece-tūn* 'farm by the stream'. (Salop) DB.

BETSON: P OE 'Son of *Bett*'. 14th cent.

BETT(E), BETTS: (i) P OE A pet-form of *Beatrice*. 12th cent. (ii) P A pet-form of *Bertelmew* (*Bartholomew*). (iii) N OE Langland's *Piers Plowman* has '*Bette* the bocher', from *boccen* 'to patch'. 14th cent.

BETTERIDGE, BETTRIDGE see BADRICK.

BETTERSON, BETTINSON, BETTISON: P OE 'Son of *Beton* (*Beatrice*)'. 13th cent.

BETTON see BETHUNE.

BEVAN(S), BEVEN(S), BEAVAN, BEAVEN, BEAVON, BEEVENS: P 'Son of *Evan*'. (Welsh *ap* 'son'.) 13th cent.

BEVERIDGE: N OF *bevrege*, ME *beverage* 'drink, liquor'. Reflecting the ancient custom of sealing a bargain with a drink, a nickname for one who got free drinks for bargains which he had no intention of completing. 13th cent.

BEVERLEY: L OE *beofor-lecc* 'beaver-stream'. (Yorks) 12th cent.

BEVES, BEVIS see BEAVES.

BEVILL(E), BEAVILL: L OF From Beuville, Calvados (Normandy). 13th cent.

BEVIN, BEAVINS, BIVINS: N OF *bei vin* 'drink wine' (rather than ale or cider). 13th cent.

BEW: N OF *bel* 'beautiful woman'. 13th cent.

BEWICK(E), BOWICK, BUICK: L OE *bēo-wīc* 'bee farm'. (Yorks, Northumb) 13th cent.

BEWLEY: L OF *Bellus Locus* 'beautiful place'. (Hants, Kent, Westmorland).

BEWS, BEWES: L OF From Bayeux, Calvados (Normandy). 13th cent.

BEWSHIRE, BEWSHAW see BELCHER.

BEYNON, BENIAN(S), BENNION, BENYON, BINNION: P 'Son of *Einion*'. 13th cent. (Welsh *ap* 'son'.)

BEZANT, BEZZANT see BESANT.

BIBB: P OE A pet-form of *Isabel*. 12th cent. BIBBEY, BIBBY: A double dim. of *Isabel*. 13th cent.

BIBLE: P OE *Bib-el*, a dim. of *Bibb*. 12th cent.

BICKER(S), BIKKER: O OE *bēocere, bīocere* 'beekeeper'. 12th cent.

BICKERSTAFF(E), BICKERSTETH: L OE *bēocere-stath* 'landing-place of the beekeepers'. (Lancs) 13th cent.

BICKFORD: L OE 'The ford of *Bica*, Anglo-Saxon'. (Staffs).

BICKLEY: L OE 'The *lēah* (clearing) of an Anglo-Saxon called *Bicca*'. (Devon, Ches, Kent, Worces), *Bicheleia* DB.

BICKNELL, BIGNEL, BIGNALL, BIGNOLD: L OE 'The hill of *Bica*'. (Som, Warwicks) 13th cent.

BIDDELL, BIDDLE see BEADEL.

BIDDICK: L OE *bī-dīc* 'by the ditch'. (Durham).

BIDDLECOMBE: L OE 'the *cumb* (valley) of *Bitel*, Anglo-Saxon'. (Som) 12th cent.

BIDDOLPH, BIDDULPH: L OE *bī-dulf* 'by the mine'. (Staffs) 12th cent.

BIDMEAD: L OE *byden* 'trough', used in the sense of small valley + *maed* 'valley meadow'.

BIELBY, BEILBY: L ON 'The *býr* (farm) of *Beli*, Norseman'. (Lincs, Yorks) 13th cent.

BIER(S) see BYARS. BIFIELD see BYFIELD.

BIGG(E): N ME *bigge* 'large, strong'.

BIGGAR: L OE From Biggar (Lanarks) Scotland. 12th cent.

BIGGER(S): N A derivative of OE *bycgan* 'to buy'. A nickname for a buyer. 14th cent.

BIGGIN(S): L O Scand *byggia*, ME *bigging* 'building, house'. 14th cent.

BIGGLESWORTH: L OE 'The *worth* (enclosure) of *Biccel*, Anglo-Saxon.'

BIGGS: N OE 'Son of *Bigg*'.

BIGNALL see BICKNELL. BIGRAVE see BYGRAVE.

BILES, BYLES: N OE *bile* 'bill, beak'. Nickname for one with a beaky nose. 12th cent. See also Beck.

BILL(S), BILLES: O OE *bil, bill, billes* 'a sword shaped like a sickle' (surviving in billhook). Metonymic for a Biller. 12th cent.

BILLER: O OE *bil.* 'A maker of bills, halberds'. 13th cent.

BILLING(S), BILLINS, BILLINGE: P OE An Anglo-Saxon people, the *Billingas*, whose name derives from 'sword', held land in ten counties from York to Sussex and gave their name to Billingsgate in London Wall. 12th cent.

BILLINGHAM: L OE 'The *hām* (homestead) of the *Billingas*, an Anglo-Saxon people'. (Durham), *Billingham* c.1050.

BILLINGSLEY: L OE 'The *lēah* (clearing) of an Anglo-Saxon called *Bylgī* (which means 'angry'). (Salop) 11th cent.

BILLINGTON: L OE '*Billa's dūn* (hill)' (Beds, Lancs), or 'the ridge of the *Billingas*' (Staffs).

BILLITER: O OE *belle-geotere* 'bell-founder'. 13th cent. (Billiter Street, London, owes its name to the bell-founders.)

BILTON: L OE '*Billa's tūn* (farm)' (Northumb, Warwicks, Yorks) 12th cent.

BINDER: O OE *bindere* 'bookbinder'. 13th cent.

BINDLOES, BINDLOSS: O OE *bindan* 'to bind' + OF *lou* 'wolf'. 'Wolf-trapper'. 13th cent.

BINDON: L OE *binnan-dūn* 'inside the *dūn* (hill)' (Dorset) 13th cent.

BING(E): L OE *bing* 'heap'.

BINGHAM: L OE *bing-hām* 'village with a heap'. (Notts) 12th cent.

BINGLEY: L OE 'The *lēah* (clearing) of the Anglo-Saxon people of *Bynna*'. (Yorks), *Bingheleia* DB. The surname is 12th cent.

BINKS: L ME *benk* (northern dial. *bench*) 'bank'. 13th cent.

BINNE(S), BINNS: O OE *binn* 'bin, manger, basket'. Metonymic for Binner. 13th cent.

BINNE, BINNIE, BINNY: (i) L OE *binnan ēa* 'inside the stream' (land enclosed by a stream). (ii) P OE *Bynna*, a pers. name. (iii) L From Binney (West Lothian) Scotland. 13th cent.

BINNER: O OE 'A maker of bins, etc.'. 13th cent.

BINNION see BEYNON. BINTLEY see BENTLEY. BIRAM, BIRON see BYRON.

BIRCH, BURCH, BYRCH: L OE *birce* 'birch (tree)'. 12th cent.

BIRCHALL, BURCHALL, BURCHELL: L OE *birce-halh* 'birch-tree nook'. (Ches) BIRCHETT, BURCHETT: L OE *bircett* 'birch-grove'. (Kent, Surrey, Sussex) 13th cent. BIRCHILL: L OE *birce-hyll* 'birch-tree hill'.

BIRD(S), BYRD(E), BRIDE: O & N *bridd* 'bird'. A nickname and metonymic for a bird-catcher. 12th cent. [A First Fleet (convict) surname].

BIRDSALL: L OE 'The *halh* (recess or secret place) of an Anglo-Saxon called *Bridd* (which means a young bird)'. (Yorks), *Briteshale* DB.

BIRDSEY, BIRDSEYE: L OE *bridd-īeg* 'bird-island'.

BIRK: L ON *bjork* 'birch (tree)'. BIRKBECK: L ON 'stream with birches'. (Westmorland) BIRKENHEAD, BIRKETT, BIRKHEAD, BRICKETT: L 'birch-tree covered headland'. 14th cent. BIRKENSHAW: L OE *birce-sceage* '*shaw* (copse) of birches'. 13th cent. BIRKIN: L OE 'birch-grove'. (Yorks) DB. BIRKS, BURKS: L OE *birce* or ON *bjork* 'the birches'. 13th cent.

BIRLEY: L OE *bȳr-lēah* 'enclosure with cowshed'. (Derbys).

BIRMINGHAM: L OE 'The *hām* (homestead) of *Beornmund's* people'. (Warwicks) DB.

BIRRELL: O OF *burel.* A variant of Burrell.

BIRTLE(S): L OE *birce-hylls* 'birch hills'. (Ches, Lancs).

BIRTWHISTLE, BERTWHISTLE, BURTWHISTLE: L OE First el. *birce* 'birch'; second el. obscure. From a lost place in Lancs. 13th cent.

BISACRE, BISIKER, BISSAKER, BISSEKER: L OE *bēos-acre* 'rush-grown field'. 12th cent. A Yorks surname.

BISCHOFF: O OG *bischoff* 'priest, bishop', 'servant of the bishop'.

BISH: L OE *bysc* 'thicket'. 14th cent.

BISHELL, BISSELL see BUSHELL.

BISHOP: O OE *bisceop* 'high priest, bishop'. The bishop being celibate, the surname is for the bishop's attendant or servant, but sometimes a nickname from playing boy-bishop in a St Nicholas Day pageant. DB. [Elias and Thomas Bishop, both marines, and Mary Bishop and Joseph Bishop, convicts, brought the name to Australia 1788].

BISHTON: L OE *bisceop-tūn* 'the bishop's farm'. DB.

BISLEY, BIZELY: L OE (i) *'Bise's lēah* (clearing)' (Glos), (ii) *Byssa's lēah* (Surrey), (both Anglo-Saxons). [John Bizely, convict, brought the name to Australia 1788].

BISMIRE: N OE *bismer* 'shame, disgrace', nickname for a pander, bawd, procuress. 15th cent.

BISPHAM: L OE *bisceopham* 'the bishop's manor'. (Lancs).

BISS: N OF *bis* 'dull grey or brown' (hair or complexion). 14th cent.

BISSETT: N OF *biset*, a dim. of *bis* and with the same meaning. 12th cent.

BITHEL: P 'Son of *Ithel*'. (Welsh *ap* 'son'.) 14th cent.

BIVINS see BEVIN.

BLACK, BLAKE: N Either OE *blaec* 'black, dark complexioned' or OE *blāc* 'pale, wan'. OE Byname 901. [Francis Blake, convict, landed with the First Fleet 1788].

BLACKADDER, BLAKETTER: L SG 'black stream'. 15th cent.

BLACKAH: L O Scand *blā-kiarr* 'dark marsh'. 15th cent.

BLACKALLER, BLACKLER: L OE *blaec-lēah* 'dark wood or clearing'. (Devon) 14th cent.

BLACKBIRD: N OE *blaec beard* 'black beard'. DB.

BLACKBORN(E), BLACKBOURN(E), BLACKBURN(E): L OE *blaec-burna* 'black-stream'. (Lancs) 13th cent. [David Blackburn, master of the *Supply*, brought the surname to Australia 1788].

BLACKBORO, BLACKBOROUGH, BLACKBORROW, BLACKBROUGH, BLAKEBOROUGH: L OE *blaec-burg* 'black fort'. (Devon, Norfolk) 13th cent.

BLACKDEN: L OE *blaec-denu* 'dark valley'. (Ches).

BLACKER, BLAKER: (i) P OE *Blaechere* 'black army'. 11th cent. (ii) O OE *blaecan* 'to bleach', 'a bleacher'. 13th cent. (iii) L O Scand *blā-kiarr* 'dark marsh'. (Yorks) See also Blackah.

BLACKETT: (i) N OE *blaec-hēafod* 'black head'. (ii) N OE *blāc-hēafod* 'bright, fair head'. (iii) N OE *blaec-hōd* 'black hood'.

BLACKFORD: L OE *blaec-ford* 'black ford'. (Cumb, Salop, Som) 13th cent.

BLACKHALL, BLACKALL: L OE *blaec-halh* 'dark nook'. 13th cent. [William Blackall, convict, brought the name to Australia 1788].

BLACKHAM: L OE 'The *hām* (homestead) of *Blaca*, Anglo-Saxon'. (Suffolk) 12th cent.

BLACKHURST: L OE *blaec-hyrst* 'black wooded hill'. (Sussex) 13th cent.

BLACKIE: N OE *blaec-ēage* 'black eye' (dark, rather than a shiner). 13th cent.

BLACKLEDGE: L OE *blaec-laecc* 'dark bog stream'. (Lancs, Som) 14th cent.

BLACKLEY, BLAKELEY, BLEAKLEY: L OE *blaec-lēah* 'black clearing'. (Lancs) 14th cent.

BLACKLOCK, BLAIKLOCK, BLAKELOCK: N OE *blaec locc* 'black lock (hair)'.

BLACKMAN, BLAKEMAN: N OE *blaecmann* 'dark man'. 12th cent.

BLACKMORE: L OE *blaec-mōr* 'black moor or morass'. (Essex, Dorset, Hants).

BLACKSHAW: L OE *blaec-sceaga* 'black *shaw* (copse)'.

BLACKSHIELD: N OE Either *blaec* 'black shield' or *blāc* 'white, bright shield'. The two words were already confused in OE, both from a Teutonic root striving to express the concept 'without colour'. The surname probably derives from a medieval tournament in which a knight whose shield (black or white) was without blazon entered the lists as a mysterious unknown.

BLACKSTOCK L OE *blaec-stocc* 'black stump'. 13th cent.

BLACKSTON(E), BLAKESTON, BLAXTON: (i) P *Blaecstān*, a pers. Anglo-Saxon name, *'Blackstone'*. DB. (ii) L OE *blaec-stān*, used as a boundary stone.

BLACKWELL: L OE *blaec-wielle* 'dark spring or stream'. OE Byname 1012.

BLACKWOOD: L OE *blaec-wudu* 'darkwood'. 14th cent.

BLADE(S), BLAYDES: O OE Metonymic for *Blader*. 13th cent. [Margaret Blades, convict, brought the name to Australia 1788].

BLADER: O OE *blaed* 'blade'. 'A blade-smith'. 14th cent.

BLAIKIE: A Scottish dim. of *Blake*. 17th cent.

BLAIN: (i) P SG *Bláán*, a pers. name from *blá* 'yellow', the name of a Celtic saint. (ii) N ME *blain* 'blister or boil', a nickname for a persistent sufferer from this painful condition.

BLAINEY see BLANEY.

BLAIR: L SG From numerous places of this name in Scotland, first recorded in the form *Blare*. 12th cent. Origin SG *blár* 'field, plain'.

BLAKE see BLACK.

BLAKENEY: L OE *blaec-ēg* 'black island'. (Glos, Norfolk).

BLAKESLEY, BLAXLEY: L OE *blaec wulf wudu* 'wood of the black wolf'. (Northants) 12th cent.

BLAKEWAY: L OE *blaec-wēg* 'dark way (road)'. 13th cent.

BLAMIRE(S), BLAYMORE, BLAYMIRE: L ON *blā-myrr* 'dark marsh'. 13th cent.

BLAMPEY, PLAMPIED: N OF *blanc pied* 'white foot'. 12th cent.

BLAMPHIN, PLAMPIN: N OF *blanc pain* 'white bread', nickname for a baker. 12th cent.

BLANC, BLANCK, BLANK(S): N OF *blanc* 'white or fair of hair or complexion'. 12th cent.

BLANCH(E): P OF *blanc* 'white, fair', a woman's pers. name which first entered England when *Blanch* of Artois married Edmund, Earl of Lancaster. Chaucer prefers the form *Blaunch*. 13th cent.

BLANCHARD, BLANSHARD: N OF *blanchart* 'whitish (of hair)'. 12th cent. [Susannah Blanchard, a convict, brought the name to Australia but died at Sydney Cove in March 1788].

BLANCHET(T), BLANKET(T): N OF *blankete*, ME *blankett*, nickname for a dealer in white undyed woollen material for clothing. 13th cent.

BLANCHFIELD: L OF *blanc* + OE *feld* 'white field or plain'.

BLANCHFLOWER, BRANCHFLOWER: N OF *blanche-flour* 'white, fair flower'. Complimentary nickname for a woman, derogatory for an effeminate man. 13th cent.

BLAND: L OE *gebland* 'storm, commotion', hence 'windy place'. (Yorks) 13th cent.

BLANDAMORE: N OF *pleyn d'amour* 'full of love'. 13th cent.

BLANDFORD: L OE *blaege* 'gudgeon (fresh water fish)' + *ford* where they may be caught. (Dorset) DB.

BLANEY, BLAINEY, BLAYNEY: P OW *blaenori* 'precedence'. Originally Welsh, the Blaneys settled in Co. Monaghan, Ireland.

BLANKLEY: L OE 'The īeg (island) of *Blancan*, Anglo-Saxon'. (Lincs) 12th cent.

BLATCH: N OE *blaec* or *blāc*, with same meaning as Black. 12th cent.

BLATCHER, BLEACHER, BLETCHER: O OE *blaecan* 'to bleach'. 'A bleacher'. 14th cent. See also Blacker.

BLATHERHORN: L OE *blaecthorn* + *horn* 'pinnacle or summit'. 'Hilltop where blackthorn grows'. [William Blatherhorn, a convict, brought the name to Australia 1788].

BLATHERWICK: L OE *blaecthorn-wīc* 'dairy farm among blackthorns'. DB.

BLAXALL: L OE 'The *halh* (nook) of *Blaec*, Anglo-Saxon'. (Suffolk) 14th cent.

BLAXLAND: L OE *blaec-land* 'black (fertile) land'.

BLAXTER: O ME Fem. form of *Blacker*. 'Bleacher'. 12th cent.

BLAXTON: L OE *blaec-stān* 'black stone'. (Yorks) 13th cent.

BLAYNEY see BLANEY. **BLEAKLEY** see BLACKLEY.

BLEASDALE, BLEASEL: L OE *blesi* 'a light spot, a blaze', applied topographically. 'Valley with a white (bare) place'.

BLENCH: N OE *blenc* 'trick, deceive, cheat'. 12th cent.

BLENCARN(E), BLENKHORN, BLENKIRON, BLINKHORN: L Brit or OW, *blaen-carn* 'cairn on the hilltop'. (Cumb) 15th cent.

BLENCOWE, BLENCO: L OW *blaen* + ON *haugr* 'hilltop'. (Cumb) 14th cent.

BLENKINSOP, BLENKINSHIP: L OW *blaen* + OE *hop*. A curious combination, a hilltop and a small enclosed valley. (Northumb) 12th cent.

BLENNERHASSETT: L OW *blaen* + ON *heysaetr* 'hay-shieling'. 'Hill-farm used for making hay'. (Cumb) 15th cent.

BLESSED, BLEST, BLISSETT: N OE *blētsian* 'to ordain, to bless, to give thanks', or 'to make happy'. 13th cent.

BLEVIN: P OW 'Son of *Blethin*'. (Welsh *ap* 'son'.) 11th cent.

BLEWETT, BLEWITT, BLUET: N OF *bleuet* 'bluish of complexion'. DB.

BLIGH, BLIGHT see BLY.

BLIND: N OE *blind* 'a blind person'. DB.

BLINKHORN see BLENCARN.

BLINMAN: N OE *blind mann* 'blind man'.

BLISS: N ME *blisse* 'joy, gladness'. 13th cent.

BLISSETT see BLESSED.

BLOCK: O OF *bloc* 'block'. Metonymic for

a blocker in shoe-making, bookbinding, etc. 12th cent.

BLOFIELD, BLOFELD: L OE *blāw-feld* 'blue pigment, i.e., woad field'. (Norfolk) DB.

BLOMFIELD, BLOOMFIELD: L OF From Blouville-sur-Mer, Calvados (Normandy). 13th cent.

BLONDEL(L), BLUNDELL: N OF *blondel*, a dim. of *blond* 'fair'. 12th cent.

BLOOD: (i) N OE *blōd* 'blood'. Term of address for a blood relative. 13th cent. (ii) O ME *blōden* 'to let blood'. 'A blood-letter, physician'. (iii) P 'Son of *Lloyd*' (Welsh *ap* 'son'), particularly the Irish form, settled in Co. Clare.

BLOODWORTH: L OE *blōd-worth* 'homestead of close kinsman'. [A First Fleet surname].

BLOOM, BLOOMER: O OE *blōma* 'an ingot of iron', 'a maker of blooms, an iron-worker'. 12th cent.

BLORE: L OE *blōr* 'blister, swelling', used topographically for a bare hill. (Staffs) DB.

BLOSSOM: N OE *blosma* 'lovely as a flower'. 12th cent.

BLOUNT see BLUNT.

BLOWER(S): O OE *blāwere* 'blower' (e.g., bellows, horn). 12th cent.

BLOXAM, BLOXHAM, BLOXSOM(E): L OE 'The *hām* (homestead) of *Blocc*, Anglo-Saxon'. (Oxon, Lincs) DB.

BLUET see BLEWETT. BLUNDELL see BLONDELL.

BLUNDEN: L OE 'The valley or pasture of *Blunt*, Anglo-Saxon'.

BLUNSDEN, BLUNSDON: L OE '*Blunt's dūn* (hill)'. (Wilts) 13th cent.

BLUNSOM: L OE '*Blunt's hām* (homestead)'. (Hunts) 13th cent.

BLUNT, BLOUNT: N OF *blond*, *blund* 'blond, fair, of hair or complexion'. DB. [William Blunt, a convict, brought the name to Australia 1788].

BLY, BLYDE, BLYTH, BLIGH, BLIGHT: N OE *blīth* 'joyous, gentle, gracious, friendly'. 12th cent. (Capt William Bligh, Governor of N.S.W., 1806-8, seems to have had a character somewhat at variance with the nickname.)

BLYTON: L ON + OE 'The *tūn* (farm) of *Blih*, a Norseman'. (Lincs).

BOAG see BOGUE.

BOAR, BOOR, BOR, BORE: N OE *bar* 'boar'. 'Ungracious, ferocious'. 12th cent.

BOARDER, BORDER, BORDIER: (i) O OE *bord* 'plank', 'a maker of boards or tables'. 12th cent. (ii) L OF *bordier* 'bordar, cottager'. 12th cent. (iii) N OF *bordeor* 'a jester, buffoon'. 15th cent.

BOARDMAN: O/L OE/OF A variant of *Boarder* (i) and (ii).

BOAST, BOST: N OE *bōst* 'vaunt, brag', 'a braggart'. 13th cent.

BOATER: O OE *bāt* 'boat', 'a boatman'. 13th cent. BOATMAN, BOTTMAN: O OE *bāt-mann* 'a boatman'. 13th cent.

BOATSWAIN: O OE *bātswegen* or ON *bātsveinn* 'boatman' (bosun). 11th cent.

BOATWRIGHT, BOTWRIGHT: O OE *bāt-wryhta*, 'a boatwright'. 15th cent.

BODDINGTON: L OE 'The *tūn* (farm) of *Bota's* people'. (Glos, Northants).

BODE: O OE *boda* 'herald, messenger'. DB.

BODER: O OE *bodere* 'crier'. 13th cent.

BODFISH: O OE *butte* 'a flat-fish'. Metonymic for a seller of flat-fish.

BODIN, BOYDEN: P OG *Baudin*, OF *Bodin*. DB.

BODKIN: P A dim. of *Baldwin*.

BODMAN: O OE *boda-mann*, 'servant of the herald'. 14th cent.

BODY, BODDY: N OE *bodig* 'body', presumably an outstanding one. 13th cent.

BODYCOTE: L OE 'The cottages of *Boda's* people'. (Oxon).

BOFF: N OF *boef* 'bullock', 'big, strong, lubberly'. 12th cent.

BOGG: (i) L ME (*atte*) *bogge* '(by the) bog'. 14th cent. (ii) N ME *bog* 'proud, bold, impudent'. BOGGERS, BOGGIS, BOGGS: N OE *bōgung* 'boastful, arrogant'. 13th cent.

BOGNAR, BOGNER, BOGNOR: L OE 'The *ōra* (shore) of *Bucge*, an Anglo-Saxon woman'. (Sussex) (The place was *Bucgauora* in 680.)

BOGUE, BOAG, BOHAN, BOHEN, BOUGHAN: P Ir *O Buadhaigh* 'victorious'.

BOLAM: L ON *bolr* 'tree-trunk (bridge)'. (Durham, Northants, Northumb).

BOLD, BOUD, BOULD: N OE *beald* 'brave, strong, confident'. 13th cent.

BOLDERSON see BALDERSON. BOLDERY, BOLDERO(E) see BALDREY. BOLDING, BOULDING see BALDING.

BOLDON: L OE *bōthl-dūn* 'cottage on the hill'. (Durham, Northumb).

BOLDRON, BOWRAN, BOWRON: L ON *boli-rūm* 'bull clearing'. (Yorks) 14th cent.

BOLDY see BALDEY.

BOLGER: P Ir *O Bolguidhir.* See also BOULGER.

BOLINGBROKE: L OE 'The *broc* (brook) of the people of *Bula*, Anglo-Saxon'. (Lincs) DB. (Henry IV bore the surname *Bolingbroke* from having been born at Bolingbroke Castle.)

BOLLAND, BOLAND: L OE *boga-land* 'land by the bow (river-bend)' (Devon, Lancs, Yorks) 13th cent.

BOLLEN, BOULLIN see BULLEN. BOLLETT see BULLETT.

BOLT(E), BOULT: (i) N OE *bolt*, ON *boltr* 'bolt, bar', 'a short, thick-set, heavy individual'. DB. (ii) O OE *bolt.* Metonymic for a maker of bolts and bars. 12th cent.

BOLTER, BOULTER: O OF *buleteor* 'a sifter of meal'. 13th cent.

BOLTON, BOULTON: L OE *bothl* 'cottage, hut, homestead'. (Derbys, Lancs, Yorks) 12th cent. [Two female convicts brought the name Boulton to Australia 1788].

BOMAN see BOWMAN.

BOMPAS, BOMPUS, BUMPUS: N OF *bon pas* 'good pace', 'a fast mover'. 12th cent.

BONALLO, BONELLA, BONELLO: (i) N OF *bon aller* 'good journey'. (ii) L SG From Bonaly (Midlothian) Scotland. 16th cent.

BOND, BONDI, BONDS, BONDY, BOUND(S), BOUNDY, BUNDEY, BUNDY: O OE *bōnda, būnda,* ON *bonde, bondi* 'to dwell, to till'. Originally 'a small freeholder, husbandman, farmer', the meaning was degraded to 'unfree tenant, bondsman, serf'. DB. [Mr Bond, a midshipman on the *Sirius*, Peter Bond and William Bond, convicts, brought the name to Australia 1788].

BONE, BONN(E), BUNN: N OF *bon* 'good', 'a good man'. 13th cent.

BONES see BAIN. BONEY see BANEY.

BONFIELD, BONDFIELD, BOMFIELD: L OF From Bonneville (Normandy). 12th cent.

BONGER(S), BONJOUR: N OF *bon jour* 'good day', for one who was constantly repeating this salutation. 12th cent.

BONHAM, BONHOMME, BONOME: N OF *bon homme* 'good man'. 12th cent.

BONIFACE, BONIFAS: P Lat *bonifatius* 'good fate'. 12th cent.

BONIFANT, BULLIVANT: N OF *bon enfant*, identical in meaning with *Goodchild.* 13th cent.

BONKER see BUNKER.

BONNAIRE, BONNAR, BONNER, BONNOR, BONAR, BONER: N OF *bonnaire*, a short form of *debonnaire* 'gentle, courteous, gracious'. 13th cent.

BONNAMY, BONAMY: N OF *bon ami* 'good friend'. 13th cent.

BONNET(T): O OF & ME *bonet.* Metonymic for a maker of bonnets. 12th cent.

BONSER, BONSIER, BONSOR: N OF *bon sire* 'good sir'. 13th cent.

BOODLE, BUDDLE: L OE *bothl* 'cottage, homestead'. (Devon, Hants, Wight, Som) 14th cent.

BOOKER: (i) O OE *bōcere* 'scribe, writer'. (ii) O ME *bouken* 'to steep in lye', 'a bleacher'. 13th cent.

BOOL(E) see BULL.

BOON(E), BONE, BOWN(E): L OF From Bohun (Manche) Normandy. DB.

BOOSEY: O OE *bōsig* 'a cowman'. 14th cent.

BOOT(E): O OF & ME *bote* 'boot'. Metonymic for a maker of boots. 12th cent.

BOOTH(E): O O Dan *bōth* 'cow-house', for a herdsman. 13th cent.

BOOTHBY, BOBY: L O Scand *bothabýr* 'farm-huts'. (Lincs) 12th cent.

BOOTHMAN: O ME *bōthe-mann* 'a cowman'. 13th cent.

BOOTLE: L OE *bothl* 'homestead'. (Cumb, Lancs).

BORDER see BOARDER.

BOREHAM: L OE *bor* 'elevation' + *hām* 'the homestead on the hill'. (Essex, Herts, Sussex), *Borham* DB.

BOREL, BORELL see BURREL.

BORER: O OE *borian* 'a borer, piercer'. 14th cent.

BORGES see BURGES.

BORGONON, BURGIN: L OF From Burgundy. 12th cent.

BORLAND: L OE *bordland* 'timber producing land'.

BORLEY: L OE *bār-lēah* 'boar's wood'. (Essex, Worces).

BORN(E): N OE *borgne* 'one-eyed'. 12th cent.

BORODALE, BORRODELL, BORROWDALE: L ON *Borgardalr* 'valley with a fort'. (Cumb, Westmorland) 15th cent.

BOROUGHES, BURROWS, BURRUS, BURRISS, BORROWS: O OE *būr-hūs* 'servant at the bower-house'. 15th cent.

BORRETT, BORRITT, BORET see BURRETT. BORROW see BURROUGH.

BORROWMAN, BORROMAN, BURKMAN, BURMAN, BARROWMAN, BARRYMAN: O OE *burhmann* 'borough-man, townsman, citizen'. 13th cent.

BORSHELL: L OE *bār-sell* 'boars' shelter'. (Sussex) 13th cent.

BORTHRAM see BARTRAM.

BORTHWICK: L OE *bord-wīc* 'home farm', i.e., the farm supplying the lord's table. (Roxburgh, Midlothian) Scotland. 14th cent.

BOSANQUET: N Languedoc *bouzanquet* 'dwarf'. A Huguenot surname. 17th cent. (Languedoc: a Romance language of Southern France.)

BOSCAWEN: L Cornish *bos* 'dwelling' + a Cornish equivalent of Welsh *ysgawen* 'elder-tree'.

BOSHELL, BOSSEL see BUSHEL.

BOSHER(E), BOSHIER, BUSHER: O OF *buschier* 'wood-seller'. 13th cent.

BOSKIN see BUSKENS.

BOSS: (i) P OG *Boso* 'wicked'. 12th cent. (ii) N ME *boce* 'a protuberance', nickname for a hunchback.

BOSSEY, BOSSY: N OF *bocu* 'hunchbacked'. 12th cent.

BOSSON(S), BOSENCE: O ON *bātsveinn*, OE *bātswgen* 'boatswain, bosun'.

BOSTEL, BOSTLE: L OE *borgsteall* 'place of refuge'. (Kent, Sussex) 12th cent.

BOSTOCK: L OE 'The *stoc* (place) of *Bōta*, Anglo-Saxon'. (Ches) DB.

BOSTON: L OE from OG (Saint) *Botulf's stān* '*St Botolph's* stone'. (Lincs) 12th cent.

BOSWALL, BOSWELL: L OF From Beuzeville (Normandy). 12th cent.

BOSWORTH: L OE *Bār's worth* 'the homestead of an Anglo-Saxon nicknamed Boar'. (Leices) 13th cent.

BOTHWELL: L OE *bōthl-wielle* 'house by the stream'.

BOTLER: O OF *bouteille* 'maker of (leather) bottles'. 14th cent.

BOTT: (i) P OE *Botta*, an Anglo-Saxon pers. name. (ii) N OF *bot* 'toad'. DB.

BOTTEN see BUTTON.

BOTTERELL, BOTTERILL, BOTTRELL, BOTTRILL, BUTTERIS(S), BUTTRESS, BUTTRISS: (i) L OF From Les Bottereaux (Normandy). 12 cent. (ii) O OF *buteri* 'buttery' (storehouse for provisions). Metonymic for keeper of the buttery. 12th cent.

BOTTOM(E), BOTTOMS, BOTTAMS, BOTHAM(S): L OE *botm* 'innermost part of a valley'. 13th cent.

BOTTOMLEY, BOTHAMLEY: L OE *botm-lēah* 'clearing in a deep valley'. (Yorks) 13th cent.

BOUCH, BUCHE, BUDGE: (i) N OF *bouche*, ME *bouge, budge* 'mouth'. Nickname for a supplier of victuals for travelling attendants. 12th cent. (ii) O OF *bouge* 'a maker of small leather goods'.

BOUCHER, BOUTCHER, BOWCHER, BOWKER see BUTCHER.

BOUFFLER: N OF *beau flour* 'fair flower'. 14th cent.

BOUGHAN see BOGUE.

BOUGHTON: L OE *bōc-tūn* 'beech (tree) farm'. (Kent, Ches).

BOULGER, BOULSHER, BOLGER: O OF *boulgier* 'maker of leather pouches'. 13th cent.

BOULTON see BOLTON.

BOUMPHREY, BOMPHREY, BUMPHRIES: P Welsh 'Son of *Humphrey*'. (Welsh *ap* 'son'.) 17th cent.

BOUNDY see BOND. BOURDEN see BURDEN. BOURGEIN, BOURGOIN see BURGOIN. BOURKE see BURK.

BOURNE, BORN(E), BURN(E): L OE *burna* 'stream'. OE Byname 1044.

BOURTON see BURTON.

BOUTALL, BOUTELL, BOUTLE, BOWTELL, BULTEEL, BOUTFLOWER: N ME *bulte-flour* 'sift flour'. Nickname for a miller. 13th cent.

BOUVERIE: L OF *bouverie* 'ox-stall'. A Huguenot surname.

BOVEY: L A Brit river-name. Bovey Tracey and North Bovey are on the river. (Devon).

BOVILL(E), BOVELL, BOWELL: L OF From Bouville (Normandy). DB.

BOVIS see BEAVES.

BOW(E), BOUGH: L OE *boga* 'bow', in the sense of 'arch, vault' for the occupant of an arched bridge. (London, Berks, Devon) 13th cent. (Underneath the arches.)

BOWBRICK: L OE *būfan-brōc* 'above the brook'. (Suffolk, Hunts) 13th cent.

BOWCOCK, BOWCOTT, BOOCOCK see BAWCOCK.

BOWDEN, BOWDON: L OE *boga-dūn* 'curved hill'. 12th cent.

BOWELL: L OF From Bouelles, Seine-Inférieure (France). DB. See also Bovill.

BOWEN: P OW 'Son of *Owen*', from *Euguein* 'well-born'. 13th cent. (Welsh *ap* 'son'.)

BOWER(S), BOUR: (i) L OE *būr* 'cottage or chamber'. (Som, Sussex), (Peebles) Scotland. 12th cent. (ii) O OE 'servant at the bower'.

BOWERMAN: O OE *būr-mann* 'servant at the bower'. 12th cent.

BOWES, BOWS: L OE *boga* Meaning as for *Bow*. (Yorks) 13th cent. [Surgeon Arthur Bowes of the *Lady Penrhyn* brought the surname to Australia 1788].

BOWGEN, BUDGEN, BUDGEON: N OF *bon Johan* 'good servant'. 13th cent.

BOWICK see BEWICK.

BOWIE, BUIE, BUY(E): N SG *buidhe* 'yellow, fair-haired'. 15th cent.

BOWLER: O OE *bolla* 'bowl'. 'A maker of bowls'. 14th cent.

BOWLES: (i) O Metonymic for a maker of bowls. (ii) L A variant of *Bowell*.

BOWMAKER: O OE *boga* 'a maker of bows (weapons)'. BOWMAN, BEAUMAN: O OE *boga-mann* 'bowman, archer'. 13th cent.

BOWNA(S), BOWNESS, BONAS(S): L ON *bogi* 'rounded headland'. (Cumb).

BOWRA(H), BOORER, BORER, BURRA: L OE *būr* 'cottage, chamber, bower'. 13th cent.

BOWRICK: O OE *boga-wyrhta* 'bow-maker'. 13th cent.

BOWRING, BOWERING: L or O OE *būring*, a derivative of *būr*, the meaning identical with *Bower* or *Bowra*. 14th cent.

BOWSER see BEAUSIRE. BOWSHER see BELCHER. BOWTELL, BOWTLE see BULTEEL.

BOWTON, BUFTON: L OE *būfan-tūn* 'above the village'. (Beds, Hunts) 13th cent.

BOWYER, BOYAR: O ME *bowyere* 'a maker or supplier of bows (weapons)'. 12th cent.

BOX, BOXER: L OE *box* 'box-tree'. (Glos, Herts, Wilts) 13th cent.

BOXLEY: L OE *box-lēah* 'box-tree clearing'. (Kent) BOXWELL: L OE *box-wielle* 'spring among the box-trees'. (Glos) BOXALL: L OE *box-wielle* 'the stream where box grows'. (Boxwell, Glos), *Boxewelle* DB.

BOYCOTT, BOYKETT: L OE 'The cottage of *Boia*, an Anglo-Saxon'. (Bucks, Salop) 13th cent.

BOYD(E): N SG & Ir *buidh* 'yellow'. In Manx the name is from *Mac Giolla Buide* 'the yellow-haired youth's son'. *Boyd* is also a Brit (Celtic) river-name in Glos.

BOYES, BOYS, BOYSE, BOICE, BOYCE: (i) P OG *Boio* or OE *Boia* 'young man', a pers. name. 11th cent. (ii) L OF *bois* 'wood', equivalent to OE *atte wudu*. 12th cent.

BOYLE: P Ir *O Baoighill*, from *geal* 'pledge'. [A First Fleet surname].

BOYMAN: O OE *boga-mann* 'bowman, archer'. 13th cent.

BOYTER: O OE *box*, originally the tree, later extended to a container made of boxwood. 'A box-maker'.

BOYTON: L OE 'The *tūn* (farm) of *Boia*, an Anglo-Saxon'. (Cornwall, Essex, Suffolk, Wilts) DB.

BRABAN(T), BRABEN, BRABIN, BRABON, BRABYN, BRABBAN, BRABBEN, BRABBINS, BRABHAM: L Flemish From Brabant (Flanders). 13th cent.

BRABAZON: L Flemish (AF *Brabaçon*) 'A native of Brabant'. 13th cent. (In 13th cent. the Brabazons were adventurers and devastators of French provinces.)

BRABINER, BRABNER, BREBNER: L Flemish + OE 'A man from Brabant'. 14th cent.

BRACEGIRDLE: O OF *braie*, ME *brec* 'breeches' + OE *gyrdel*. 'A maker of breech-girdles (belts)'.

BRACER see BRASSEUR.

BRACH(E), BREECH, BRECH, BRITCH: L OE *braec* 'land prepared for cultivation'. 13th cent. BRACHER: L OE with same meaning as *Brach*. 13th cent.

BRACHET, BRACKET(T): A dim. of *Brach*. 13th cent.

BRACK: O OF *brac* 'bitch-hound'. 'A breeder or keeper of hounds'. 13th cent.

BRACKEN: P Ir *O Breacain*, from *breac* 'speckled'.

BRACKENBOROUGH: L OE *braecen-burg* 'fort among the bracken'. (Lincs) DB.

BRACKENRIDGE, BRECKENRIDGE: L OE *braecen* or ON *brakni* 'ridge overgrown with bracken'. 14th cent.

BRACKNER: O OF *braconier* 'a keeper of hounds'. 14th cent.

BRADBOURNE: L OE *brād-burn* 'broad stream'. (Kent, Derbys).

BRADBROOK: L OE brād-*brōc* 'wide brook'. 14th cent.

BRADBURY, BRADBERY: L OE *bord-burg* 'fort built of boards'. (Durham) [William Bradbury, a convict, brought the name to Australia 1788].

BRADD: N OE *brād* 'broad'. 'A broad, thick-set man'. 13th cent.

BRADDEN, BRADEN: L OE *brād-denu* 'wide valley'. (Northants) DB.

BRADDOCK: L OE *brād-āc* 'broad oak'. (Kent, Essex) 13th cent.

BRADDON: L OE *brād-dūn* 'the wide hill'. (Devon).

BRADE see BROAD.

BRADFER: N OF *bras de fer* 'iron man'. 12th cent.

BRADFIELD: L OE *brād-feld* 'the wide field or open plain'.

BRADFORD, BRADFORTH, BRAIDFORD: L OE *brād-ford* 'wide ford', a frequent place-name. 12th cent. [William Bradford, a convict, brought the surname to Australia 1788, and was a landholder when he died at the age of 70].

BRADGATE, BROADGATE: L OE *brād-geat* 'broad gate'. (Leices) 13th cent.

BRADIE, BRADY, BROADY: (i) N OE *brād-ēage* 'wide-eyed'. 12th cent. (ii) L OE *brad-īeg* 'wide island'. (iii) P Ir *Brady* (*MacBrady*) *Mac Bradaigh* 'spirited'.

BRADING: L OE *Brerding*, a derivative of *brerd* 'border'. (Wight), *Berardinz* DB.

BRADLEY, BRATLEY, BROADLEY, BRODLEY: L OE *brad-lēah* 'broad clearing'. 12th cent. [Two convicts both named James Bradley, and William Bradley, an officer on the *Sirius*, brought the surname to Australia 1788].

BRADMAN, BRAIDMAN: N OE *brād-mann* 'broad (shouldered) man'. 13th cent.

BRADMORE, BREADMORE: L OE *brād-mere* 'wide lake'. (Notts) 12th cent.

BRADNAM, BRADNUM: L OE *brād-hām* or *hamm* 'wide homestead or water-meadow'. (Norfolk) 12th cent.

BRADNEY: L OE *brād-īeg* 'wide island'. (Som) 13th cent.

BRADRIDGE, BROADRIDGE: L OE *brād-hrycg* 'wide ridge'. 13th cent.

BRADSHAW, BRAYSHAW: L OE *brād-sc͡aga* 'wide grove or thicket' (*shaw* is dial.). (Derbys, Lancs, Yorks) 13th cent.

BRADSTREET: L OE *brād straet* 'wide street' (probably a Roman road). 14th cent.

BRADSTOCK, BRASTOCK: L OE *brād-stoc* 'the *stoc* (holy place) belonging to Braden (site of a monastery)'. (Wilts) DB.

BRADWELL, BRADDLE: L OE *brād-wielle* 'broad stream'. (Bucks, Essex, Suffolk) 13th cent.

BRAGG(E): N ME *bragge* 'brisk, brave' or 'arrogant'. 13th cent.

BRAHAM(E), BRAIME, BRAME, BRAMHAM, BRAMMAM, BRAYHAM, BREAM: L OE *bram*, *brōm-hām* 'homestead where broom grows'. 12th cent. (Norman pronunciation converted Bramham to Braham; see also Grantham which the Normans changed to Graham.)

BRAID(E), BREAD: (i) O OE *braegd, bregdan* 'braid, knit, knot'. Metonymic for brader 'maker of cords'. 13th cent. (ii) L From Braid Hills, Edinburgh.

BRAIDWOOD: L OE *brād-wudu* 'wide wood'.

BRAILSFORD: L OE *braegels-ford* 'ford by the tumulus (burial mound)'. (Derbys).

BRAIN: Probably a Brit, OW pers. name *Branuc, Branoc*, derived from Celtic *bran* 'raven', and given to one with black hair as a nickname. The Ulster surname *Mac Brain* is from the same source, see *Bran*. *Brain* is preserved in the place-name Braintree (Essex).

BRAITHEWAITE: L OE *brād-thwaite* 'broad clearing'. (Cumb, Yorks) 12th cent.

BRAKE: L OE *braec* 'copse, spinney'. 12th cent.

BRAKEFIELD: L ME *brake* + OE *feld* 'bracken-covered field'. 13th cent.

BRAKESPEAR, BRAKSPER see BREAKSPEAR.

BRAMAGE: L OE *brōm* 'broom or brushwood'. [Thomas Bramage, a private soldier, arrived with the First Fleet 1788].

BRAMAH, BRAMALD, BRAMHALL, BRAMMER: L OE *brōm-halh* 'nook where broom grows'. (Ches, Yorks) 13th cent.

BRAMBLE(S): L OE *braembel*, from *brōm*, ME *bremble* 'broom'.

BRAMLEY: L OE *brōm-lēah* 'clearing overgrown with broom'.

BRAMWELL: L OE *brōm-wielle* 'stream through the broom'. [Thomas Bramwell, a private soldier, arrived with the First Fleet 1788].

BRAN(N), MACBRAN, MACBRAIN: P Ir, SG, OW, Breton (all Celtic) *bran* 'raven'. 12th cent. BRANGHAN, BRANIGAN, BRANGAN, BRANEGAN: P Ir *O Branagain*, a dim. of *bran*. [Branegan, a First Fleet (convict) name].

BRANCHFLOWER see BLANCHFLOWER.

BRAND, BRANDT, BRANT, BRAUND, BRAUN: P ON *Brandr* 'fire-brand, torch, sword'. 12th cent. [Curtis Brand and Mary Brand, convicts, brought the name to Australia 1788].

BRANDON: L OE *brōm-dūn* 'broom-covered hill'. (Durham, Norfolk, Suffolk, Warwicks) 12th cent.

BRANDRETH: L OE *brand* 'fire, flame', 'burnt clearing'.

BRANGWIN, BRANGWYN, BRANGWYNNE: P OW *bran* + *gwen* 'fair raven', a woman's name (used in the Tristan and Isolde legend). 13th cent.

BRANNAN, BRANNON: P Ir *O Branain*, from *bruon* 'sorrow'. [John Brannon, a marine private, brought the name to Australia 1788].

BRANSBY: L O Scand 'The *byr* (farm) of *Brand*, a Scandinavian'.

BRANSCOMBE: L Brit (Celtic) '*Branoc's valley*'. (Devon) See also Brain.

BRANSON: P 'Son of *Brand*'.

BRANSTEAD: L OE *brōm-stede* 'the broom site'.

BRANSTON: L OE '*Brant's tūn* (farm)'. (Leices, Lincs, Staffs) 12th cent.

BRANTHWAITE: L OE *brōm-thwaite* 'broom-covered clearing'. (Cumb) 14th cent.

BRANTON: L OE *brōm-tūn* 'farm where broom grows'. (Devon, Yorks) 12th cent.

BRASH: N OE & Northern English dial. A development of OE *raesc* 'rash'. 'Brisk, nimble' or 'hasty, impetuous'.

BRASIER, BRASHER, BRAIZIER, BRAZIER: O A derivative of OE *brasian* 'a brass founder'. 14th cent.

BRASSETT: N OE *braes-hēafod* 'brass-head', 'hard-headed, insensitive'. 13th cent.

BRASSEUR, Le BRASSEUR, BRACER, BRASHER: O OF *braceor, brasseur* 'brewer'. 12th cent. (Brasher occurs both as a brewer and a brass-founder.)

BRATTON L OE *braec-tūn* 'newly cultivated farm'. (Devon, Wilts).

BRAY(E): (i) N Cornish *bregh* 'fine, brave'. (ii) P Ir *O Breagdha*. (iii) L ON *brā*, from one of several places called Brae in Scotland. (iv) L Ir From Bregia, a territory in Co. Meath. (v) L OE *brēg* 'brow' (of hill). (Berks, Devon) The surname also has a Breton influence in eastern England. 11th cent.

BRAYBROOK(E): L OE *brāda-brōc* 'wide brook'. (Northants).

BRAYER: O OF *broie* 'pounding, grinding'. 'A maker of pestles'. 12th cent.

BRAYSHAW see BRADSHAW.

BRAYTON: L O Scand *breithr* + OE *tūn* 'broad village'. (Cumb, Yorks).

BREACH: L ME *breach* 'breaking (the line)', 'spinney forming part of a boundary'. (Wilts).

BREAD see BRAID. BREADMORE see BRADMORE.

BREAKSPEAR, BRAKESPEAR, BRAKSPER: N OE Nickname for a knight who has honourably broken his lance on battlefield or in tournament. 13th cent.

BREAM see BRAHAM, BRIM.

BREAR(E): N OE *braer* 'prickly thorn bush'. Nickname for a prickly individual. 13th cent.

BREARLEY see BRIERLEY.

BREARTON, BREETON, BRERETON: L OE *braer-tūn* 'farm overrun with briars'. (Ches, Durham, Staffs, Yorks) 12th cent.

BREBNER see BRABINER. BRECKENRIDGE see BRACKENRIDGE.

BREDE, BREED(E), BREEDS: L OE *braedu* 'breadth', 'broad open space'. (Sussex) 12th cent.

BREECH, BRECH see BRACH.

BREEDEN: L OE *brād-dēnu* 'broad valley'.

BREEDON: L OE *brād-dūn* 'wide hill'.

BREEN: L OW *bre* Brit *brigā* 'up hill'. (Som).

BREESE, BREEZE: (i) P OW 'Son of *Rees*'. (Welsh *ap* 'son'.) 17th cent. (ii) N OE *brēosa* 'gadfly', 'a bloodsucker'. 13th cent.

BREMER: L OE *brēmer* 'bramble thicket'.

BREMNER, BRIMNER, BRYMNER: L Flemish From Brabant (Flanders). (Artisans and traders who settled on east coast of Scotland in 15th cent.)

BREND, BRENT, BRIND: (i) L OE *brend* 'burnt (cleared) land'. 12th cent. (ii) N OE *biernan-hand* 'burn hand', 'a branded criminal', 13th cent.

BRENHAM: L OE *brent-hām* 'burnt village' [A First Fleet (convict) surname].

BRENNAN: (i) P Ir *O Braonain* 'descendant of 'sorrow'. (ii) N OE *baernan-hand*, nickname for medieval official who carried out punishment of hand burning. 12th cent.

BRENNER: (i) O ON *brenner* 'lime or charcoal burner'. (ii) O OF *brenier* 'keeper of hounds'. 13th cent.

BRENT: L Brit (Celtic) *Brigantiā* river-name 'high and holy river' (Middx) and name of hill towns called Brent in Devon.

BRERETON see BREARTON.

BRET(T), BRITT(S): L OF *Bret* 'A Breton'. DB.

BRETHERTON: L ON *broethr-tūn* 'the brothers' farm'. (Lancs).

BRETON, Le BRETON, BRETTON, BRITON, BRITTON: (i) L OE *Bret, Bretun* 'A Breton', as distinct from OE *Briton*, applied by Anglo-Saxons to Welshmen and Strathclyde Britons. 12th cent. (ii) L OE *brec-tūn* 'newly cultivated farm'. (Derbys, Yorks).

BRETTEL(L), BRETTLE, BRETELLE, BRITTLE: P O Cornish *Brytthall* or O Bret *Brithael*. DB.

BRETTONER, BRITNOR, BRITNER, BRUTTNER: N ME *Bretoner, Brutiner* an uncomplimentary nickname used of Bretons in 14th cent. 'braggart, boaster'.

BREVETON, BREVITT, BREFFIT(T): O OF & ME *brevet, bref* 'an official written message', esp. papal indulgences. Metonymic for bearer of them. 13th cent.

BREW: O Manx *MacVriw* 'son of the judge'. 15th cent.

BREWER(S), BROUWER, BROWER: (i) L OF From Bruyere (Normandy). DB. (ii) O OE *breowan* 'to brew', 'a brewer'. 12th cent. [A First Fleet surname].

BREWIS, BREWSE, BROWSE: L OF From Briouze (Normandy). DB.

BREWITT, BROWETT: O OF *brouet*, ME *bruet* 'a meat broth'. Metonymic for a broth maker/seller. 13th cent.

BREWSTER, BROSTER, BRUSTER: O ME *brewestere* 'a female brewer'. 13th cent.

BRIAN, BRIANCE, BRIAND, BRIANT, BRIEN(T), BRYAN(D), BRYANS, BRYANT, O'BRIAN, O'BRIEN: (i) P A Breton name brought to England with the Breton contingent of Duke William's invading army. DB. (ii) P ON *Brjān*, Ir *O Briain*, an ancient Irish name and that of King Brian Boru, brought to England by Norsemen from Ireland. [Bryant, a First Fleet (convict) surname].

BRIAR(S), BRIER(S), BRYERS: L OE *brǣer* 'thorn-bush, brambles'. 13th cent.

BRICE, BRYCE: P Celtic A popular saint's name (St Britius or Brice was bishop of Tours). 12th cent. [William Brice, a convict, landed at Botany Bay 1788].

BRICKETT see BIRKENHEAD.

BRIDDOCK, BRIDEOAK: P SG *Brideoc*, a dim. of *Bride*. 12th cent.

BRIDE see BIRD.

BRIDEWELL: L OE *bridd-wielle* 'spring frequented by birds'. 13th cent.

BRIDGE, DELBRIDGE: L OE *brycg* 'bridge', 'de la bridge'. (Herefords) 13th cent.

BRIDGEFORD, BRIDGFORD: L OE *brycg-ford* 'ford at the bridge'. (Notts, Staff).

BRIDGEMAN, BRIDGMAN: O OE *brycg-mann* 'keeper of the bridge'. 13th cent.

BRIDGER, BRUGGER: O OE Identical in meaning with *Bridgeman*. 14th cent.

BRIDGES, BRYDGES: L Flemish From Bruges (Belgium). 13th cent.

BRIDGEWATER: L OE *brycg* 'the bridge'. William the Conqueror gave the place to Walter Dowai in 1194 and it was renamed *Bridgewaltier*. (Som).

BRIDLE: O OE *bridel* 'bridle'. 'A maker of bridles'. 12th cent.

BRIDSON, BRYDSON: P Manx '*St Bridget's* servant's son'. 12th cent.

BRIERLEY, BREARLEY: L OE *brǣer-lēah* 'clearing overgrown with briars'. (Staffs, Yorks) 13th cent.

BRIGG(S): L ON *bryggia*, ME *brigg* 'bridge'. (Lincs) 13th cent.

BRIGHAM: L ON *bryggia* + OE *hām* 'homestead by the bridge'. (Cumb, Yorks).

BRIGHOUSE: L ON *bryggia* + OE *hūs* 'house by the bridge'. (Yorks).

BRIGHT: N OE *beorht* 'fair, bright and beautiful'. 13th cent.

BRIGHTIFF, BERIFF: P OE *Beortgifu* 'fair gift', a woman's name. DB.

BRIGHTMAN: P OE *Beortmann* 'fair man', a pers. name. DB.

BRIGHTMORE, BRIMMER: P OE *Brihtmaer* 'fair-famous'. DB.

BRIGHTON: L OE *brycg-tūn* 'farm by the bridge'. (Breighton, Yorks) 14th cent.

(Brighton, Sussex, originally *Brightelmstone*, was named too late to contribute to the surname.)

BRIGHTWEEN, BRIGHTWEN: P OE *Beorhtwine* 'fair friend'. DB.

BRIGHTWELL: L OE *beorht-wielle* 'bright stream'. (Berks, Oxon, Suffolk).

BRIGHTY: O OE *Brihtwīg* 'bright war'. DB.

BRIGSTOCK(E), BRIDGSTOCK: L OE *brycg-stoc*, *stoc* 'holy place, perhaps a monastery, by the bridge'. (Northants) 13th cent.

BRIM(M), BRIMS, BREAM: N OE *brēme* 'vigorous, fierce' or 'famous, noble'. DB. See also Braham.

BRIMBLE: L OE *brēmel* 'bramble-bush'. (Som).

BRIMBLECOMBE: L OE *brēmel*, ME *brimble* + *cumb* 'bramble valley'. (Devon) 13th cent.

BRIMMER see BRIGHTMORE. BRIMNER see BREMNER.

BRIMSON, BRINSON: L OF From Briencun (Normandy). 13th cent.

BRINDLE: L OE *burna-hyll* 'the hill by a stream'. (Lancs), *Burnhull* 1206.

BRINDLEY: L OE *brend-lēah* 'burnt clearing'. [A First Fleet (convict) surname].

BRINKLEY: L OE 'The *lēah*' (clearing) of an Anglo-Saxon called *Brynca*'. (Cambs).

BRINKLOW, BRINKLER: L OE 'The *hlāw* (burial mound) of *Brynca*, Anglo-Saxon'. (Warwicks) 12th cent.

BRINKWORTH: L OE '*Brynca's worth* (homestead)'. (Wilts), *Brenchewrde* DB.

BRISBANE: N OF *brise* + OE *bān* 'break-bone', nickname for the official who carried out the fiendish punishment of breaking the bones of criminals. 13th cent. See also Crakebone.

BRISCO(E): (i) L ON *Bretaskogr* 'wood of the Britons'. (ii) L ON *birkiskogr* 'birch wood' (Cumb, Yorks) 14th cent.

BRISLEY: L OE *brīosa-lēah* 'clearing infested with gadflies'. (Norfolk).

BRISTOL(L): L OE *burg-steall* 'site of the old fort' or *brycg-stow* 'site of the bridge'. (Yorks, Glos) 12th cent. BRISTOW(E), BRISTO, BRISTER: L OE Identical in meaning with *Bristol*. 12th cent.

BRITCH see BRACH. BRITNOR, BRITNER see BRETTONER.

BRITTAIN, BRITTAN, BRITTEN, BRITTON: L OF *Bretagne* From Brittany or ME *Brittan* 'Breton'. 13th cent.

BRITTLE see BRETTEL.

BRIXEY, BRIXHE: P OE *Beorhtsige*, *Brihtsige* 'bright victory'. DB. [Charles Brixey, a marine shingler, brought the name to Australia 1788].

BROAD, BRADE, BRAID(E): N OE *brād* 'broad', 'broad-shouldered'. 13th cent. BROADBELT: N OE *brād-belt* 'the stout one'. 14th cent. BROADBENT: L OE *brād-beonet* 'wide plain with bent grass'. 16th cent. BROADFOOT: N OE *brād-fōt* 'broad foot' 12th cent. BROADHEAD: (i) N OE *brād-hēafod* 'broad head'. (ii) L OE 'broad headland'. 13th cent. BROADHURST: L OE *brād-hyrst* 'wide copse'. 13th cent. BROADLEY, BRODLEY see BRADLEY.

BROADMEAD: L OE *brād-maed* 'wide meadow'. 14th cent. BROADRIBB, BRODRIBB: N OE *brād-ribb* 'broad-rib', 'big chest'. 14th cent. BROADRIDGE see BRADRIDGE. BROADWOOD: L OE *brād-wudu* 'wide wood'. 13th cent.

BROADY see BRADIE. BROBYN see PROBIN.

BROCK(S): (i) L OE *brōc* 'marsh or water-meadow' (Kent, Sussex); 'brook' (Lancs). 13th cent. (ii) N OF *brocke* 'a young stag'. (iii) N OE *brocc* 'badger' 'a dirty, stinking individual'. 12th cent. BROCKET(T): N ME 'a stag with its first horns', 'a lusty young man'. 12th cent. BROCKHURST: L OE *brocc-hyrst* 'badger-wood'. (Warwicks) 13th cent.

BROCKLESBY: L ON 'The *býr* (farm) of *Brockless*'. (Lincs) BROCKLESS, BROCKLISS: N ON *broklauss* 'breechesless', the saga of a Norseman who lost his breeches. DB.

BROCKTON: L OE *brōc-tūn* 'farm by a brook'. (Salop, Staffs) BROCKWAY: L OE *brōc-weg* '*weg* (road) by a brook'. 13th cent.

BRODERICK: P Welsh 'Son of *Roderick*'. (Welsh) *ap* 'son'.)

BRODIE: P SG Scots form of Ir *O Brollaghan*; also from Brodie (Moray) Scotland. 14th cent.

BRODRIBB see BROADRIBB.

BRODY: P Ir *MacBruaideadha*. [Walter Brody, an armourer on the *Sirius*, brought the name to Australia 1788].

BROGAN: P Ir *O Brógáin*, a surname of uncertain derivation; *brón* 'sorrow' and *bróg* 'shoe' have both been suggested without much conviction. Perhaps both were present at the nurturing of earlier generations of Brogans.

BROKE see BROOK.

BROKENBOROUGH, BROKENBROUGH: L OE (*Brokeneberge* DB). 'The broken hill'. (Wilts).

BROMLEY: L OE *brōm-lēah* 'broom-covered clearing'. (Kent, Essex, Herts, Staffs) 12th cent. BROMPTON: L OE *brōm-tūn* 'farm overgrown with broom'. 13th cent. BROMWICH: L OE *brōm-wīc* 'dairy farm where broom grows'. (Staffs, Warwicks) 13th cent.

BRONSON see BROWNSON. BRONTE see PRUNTY.

BROOCH, BROATCH: O OF *broche* 'a pointed instrument'. Metonymic for a maker of lances or spears. 13th cent.

BROOK(E), BROOKES, BROOKS, BROKE, BRUCK: L OE *brōc* 'brook, stream or water-meadow'. 12th cent. [Thomas Brooks, bosun on the *Sirius*, and his wife Deborah brought the name to Australia 1788].

BROOKBANK, BROCKBANK: L OE *brōc* + ME *banke* 'bank of the brook or stream'. 14th cent.

BROOKER: L OE *brōc* 'by the brook'. 13th cent. BROOKFIELD: L OE *brōc-feld* 'brook in the open plain'. 12th cent. BROOKHOUSE, BROCKHOUSE, BROCKIS: L OE *brōc-hūs* 'house by the brook'. 13th cent.

BROOKING: L OE *brōc* + suffix *-ing* 'people of the water-meadows'.

BROOKINS: L OE Either a dim. of *brōc* 'little brook' or an affectionate term applied to the small son of *Brook*. BROOKMAN, BROCKMAN: L OE Identical with *Brooker*. 13th cent.

BROOM(E), BROME: L OE *brōm* 'broom, place where broom grows'. 12th cent.

BROOMER: L OE *brēmer* 'bramble-thicket'. (Sussex) 13th cent.

BROOMFIELD, BROMFIELD, BRUMFIELD: L OE *brōm-feld* 'broom-covered open land'. 13th cent.

BROOMHALL, BROMHALL, BRUMMEL(L): L OE *brōm-halh* 'nook where broom grows'. (Berks, Ches) 12th cent. BROOMHAM: L OE *brōm-hām* 'homestead among the broom'. (Beds) BROOMHEAD, BROMEHEAD, BROMHEAD, BRUMHEAD: L OE *brōm-hēafod* 'broom-grown hilltop'. (Yorks) 13th cent.

BROPHY: P Ir *O Broithe* 'descendant of *Broithe*'. (Leinster).

BROSTER see BREWSTER.

BROTHERS: (i) P OE *brōthor*, O Scand *brothir* 'a kinsman'. (ii) O ME 'fellow-member of a guild'. DB. (Brethren mixes OE plurals *brēther* and *brōthren*.) BROTHERSON: P OE *brōthor* + *sunu* 'son of the brother'.

BROTHERTON: L O Dan, O Sw *brodher-tūn* 'the farm of the brothers'. See also Bretherton.

BROUGH, BRUFF, BRUGH: L OE *burg* 'fort'. (Probably Roman fort.) 13th cent.

BROUGHAM: L OE *burg-hām* 'homestead by a fort'. (Westmorland) 12th cent.

BROUGHTON: L OE Either *brōc-tūn* 'farm by the brook' or *beorge-tūn* 'farm by the hill or barrow'. (Cumb, Lancs, Sussex, Wilts) 12th cent. [Ralph Broughton, a marine carpenter, and William Broughton, servant to Surgeon White, brought the name to Australia 1788].

BROWN(E), BROUN(E), BRON: N OE *brūn*, OF *brun* 'brown (hair or complexion)'. DB. [Thirteen persons surnamed Brown sailed with the First Fleet. One man was lost overboard. Of the remaining twelve, seven were marines or crew, one was the wife of a marine, and four were male convicts. In New Zealand, Alfred Brown and James Hamlin, missionaries with a taste for exploration, travelled from Waikato to the Firth of Thames, the journey taking five months, 1834. Gordon Brown was associated with David Ramsay and Thomas Raine in a flax and timber trading depot at Horeke on Hokianga Harbour, 1827].

BROWNING: N OE *Brūning*, a derivative of OE *brūn* 'brown'. DB. [William Browning, a marine, brought the name to Australia 1788].

BROWNJOHN: N OE *brūn* + pers. name *John*. 14th cent. BROWNLEE, BROWNLIE: L OE *brūn-lēah* 'brown clearing'. BROWNSMITH: O OE *brūn-smith* 'copper or brass smith'. 13th cent. BROWNSON: (i) N OE *Brunsunn*, an Anglo-Saxon pers. name. DB. (ii) N OE 'Son of *Brown*'.

BRUCE: L OF From Briouze (Normandy), (*de Bruis* DB). A descendant of the Domesday baron founded the Scottish house of *Bruce*. [Robert Bruce, a convict, brought the name to Australia 1788. George Bruce, a N.S.W. convict, was New Zealand's first European settler. He married the daughter of a powerful Maori chief and settled in the Bay of Islands, 1806].

BRUCK see BROOK.

BRUIN, BRUYN: N Dutch *bruin* 'brown'. The Dutch equivalent of *Brown*. 13th cent.

BRUMBLEY see BROMLEY. BRUMMEL(L) see BROOMHALL.

BRUMMER(S): P OE *Brūnmǣr*, a rare surname but to be found in Australia. DB.

BRUNDISH: L OE *burna-edisc* 'enclosed pasture by a stream'. (Suffolk).

BRUNEL see BURNEL.

BRUNGER, BRUNKER: P OE *Brūngār* 'brown (burnished) spear'. DB.

BRUNHAM: L OE *burna-hām* or *hamm* 'homestead or water-meadow among the streams'. Burnham, earlier Brunham, (Lincs, Norfolk).

BRUNNING: N OE Meaning identical with *Browning* and from the same source.

BRUNSDON, BRUNSDEN: P OE *Brūnstān* 'brown stone'. DB.

BRUNTON: L OE *burna-tūn* 'place or farm on a stream'. (Northumb).

BRUNWIN: P OE *Brūnwine* 'brown friend'. DB.

BRUSTER see BREWSTER.

BRUTON: L OW + OE 'The *tūn* (farm) on the R. Brue'. (Som) 13th cent.

BRUTTNER see BRETTONER. BRYAN(D), BRYANS, BRYANT see BRIAN.

BRYCESON, BRYSON: P Celtic + OE 'Son of *Brice*'. 14th cent.

BRYDGES see BRIDGES. BRYERS see BRIAR. BRYMNER see BREMNER.

BUB(B): P OE A contraction of *Bubba*, Anglo-Saxon, pers. name preserved in Bubbenhall (Warwicks) and Bubwith (Yorks).

BUCCA: (i) P OE Anglo-Saxon pers. name preserved in Buckenham (Norfolk). (ii) N OE A nickname from *bucca* 'he-goat'.

BUCHAN: L SG From Buchan (Aberdeenshire) Scotland. 13th cent.

BUCHANAN: L SG From Buchanan (Stirling) Scotland. 13th cent.

BUCHE, BUDGE see BOUCHE.

BUCK(E): (i) O OE *bucc*. Metonymic for a dealer in live deer or venison. (ii) N OE 'he-goat'. OE Byname 1055.

BUCKETT: O OF *bouc*, ME *buk* 'male deer or he-goat'. 'A dealer in buck-skin'. 12th cent.

BUCKHURST: L OE *bōc-hyrst* 'beech-grove'. (Essex, Sussex) 12th cent.

BUCKINGHAM: L OE 'The *hamm* (river-meadow) of the people of *Bucca*'.

BUCKLAND: L OE *bōcland* 'book land', land held by charter as distinct from *folcland*, held by squatter's right. 12th cent.

BUCKLE, BUCKELL, BUCKELS: O ME *bokel* 'buckle'. Metonymic for a buckler.

BUCKLER: O OF *bouchier* 'a maker of buckles.' 12th cent.

BUCKLEY, BUCKLEE, BUCKLEIGH: L OE *bucc-lēah* 'bucks' (male deers') glade'. (Som, Sussex, Warwicks) 13th cent. [A First Fleet (crew and convict) surname].

BUCKLIN see BUTLIN.

BUCKMAN: (i) O OE *bucca-mann* 'goat-keeper'. (ii) O OE *bōc-mann* 'writer, scholar, copier, book-binder'. 13th cent.

BUCKMASTER: L OE 'The minster or church of *Bucca*'. (Leices) 12th cent.

BUCKNALL: L OE '*Bucca's halh* (nook)'. (Lincs).

BUCKNELL, BUCKNILL: L OE '*Bucca's hyll* (hill)'. (Oxon, Salop).

BUCKTON: L OE '*Bucca's tūn* (farm)'. (Herefords, Northumb, Yorks).

BUDD(S): N OE *budda* 'beetle', nickname for a rotund body with short legs. OE Byname 11th cent.

BUDDELL, BUDDLE(S) see BEADELL. [Daniel Buddle, a seaman, brought the name to Australia 1788].

BUDDING: N OE 'Son of *Budd*'. 13th cent.

BUDDY: O OE 'Servant of *Budd*'. 13th cent.

BUDGE: N AF *buge* 'mouth'. A nickname for the garrulous one.

BUDGEN, BUDGEON see BOWGEN.

BUDGEY, BUGGEY, BUGGY: O ME *bugee* 'a dresser of *bugee* (lambs' skin with wool dressed outwardly)'. 13th cent.

BUFFARD: N OE *bouffard* 'puffing, blowing, swelling up', nickname for a choleric individual, 'bulging with rage'. 13th cent.

BUFTON see BOWTON.

BUGDEN: L OE *bucc* 'male deer', *bucc-denu* 'valley of the bucks'. (Hunts, Yorks) 12th cent.

BUGG(E): N ME *bugge* 'hobgoblin, bogy, bugbear' or 'scarecrow'.

BUICK see BEWICK. BUIE, BUY(E) see BOWIE.

BULGER: O Lat *bulga*, OF *bouge* 'a *bouget* (budget) of leather', 'a purse'. Metonymic for a maker of purses, money-bags, wallets. (Traditionally, the Chancellor of the Exchequer in England, and the Treasurer in Australia, in making his statement, opens his budget, his purse.)

BULKELEY, BULKLEY: L OE *bulluca-lēah* 'bullock pasture'. (Ches) 13th cent.

BULL(E), BOOL(E), BOOLS: (i) N OE *bula*, ME *bole* 'bull', 'strong as a bull'. (ii) L OE 'At the sign of the bull'. 12th cent. [William Bull, a marine private, brought the name to Australia 1788].

BULLAR, BULLER: (i) N OF *bouleur*, ME *bullere* 'a publisher of false bulls, a deceiver, cheat'. (ME *bul* 'falsehood'). (ii) N O Scand *bulla* 'to boil', nickname for 'one who seethes, rumbles, roars in anger'. 13th cent. [Rev James Buller was a Wesleyan missionary in New Zealand, 1835].

BULLARD: N OF *boul* 'fraud' + suffix *-ard*, from this, ME *bulling* 'fraudulent scheming'; but sometimes O a contraction of 'bull-ward'. 12th cent.

BULLAS(S), BULLUS: O OE *bula-hūs* 'worker at the bull-house'. 13th cent.

BULLED, BULLEID, BULLIED: N OE *bula-hēafod* 'bull-head', 'impetuous'. 12th cent.

BULLEN, BULLON, BOLEYN, BOLIN, BOLLEN: L OF From Boulogne (France). 12th cent.

BULLETT: N OF *boulet* 'round as a ball', 'corpulent'. 12th cent.

BULLEY, BULLY: L OF From Bouille or Bully-en-Brai (Normandy). DB.

BULLFINCH: N OE An unexplained nickname from the bird. 13th cent.

BULLICK: L OE *bula-wīc* 'bullock-farm'. (Northants) 12th cent.

BULLINGER, PULLINGER, PILLINGER: O OF *boulengier* 'baker'. 12th cent.

BULLIVANT see BONIFANT.

BULLMAN, BULMAN: O OE *bula-mann* 'bull-herd'. 13th cent.

BULLMORE: L OE *bula-mōr* 'fen or marsh where a bull grazes'.

BULLOCK(E): N OE *bulluc* 'bull-calf', 'a stolid and rather stupid fellow'. 12th cent. BULMER: L OE *bulena-mere* 'the bull's lake'. (Essex, Yorks).

BULPIN: O OE *bula-penn* 'a worker at the bull pen'. 13th cent.

BULSTRODE: L OE *burg-strod* 'fort or manor by the marsh'. (Bucks).

BULTEEL, BOUTTELL, BOWTELL, BOWTLE: O OF *buletel* 'cloth for sifting meal'. Metonymic for a sifter of meal. 13th cent. See also Bolter.

BUMPHRIES see BOUMPHREY.

BUMSTEAD, BUMPSTEAD: L OE *bune-stede* 'reedy place'. (Essex).

BUNBURY: L OE '*burg* (fort) of *Buna*, an Anglo-Saxon'. (Ches) [Major Thomas Bunbury carried out successful negotiations with Maori Chiefs in the North Island of New Zealand, leading up to the Treaty of Waitangi].

BUNCH: N ME *bunche* 'a protuberance', nickname for a hunchback. 12th cent.

BUNCLARK(E): N OF *bon clerc* 'good clerk'. 14th cent.

BUNCOMBE: L OE *bune-cumb* 'reedy valley'. 14th cent.

BUNDEY, BUNDY see BOND.

BUNGEY: L OE *buninga-ēg* 'the island of *Buna's* people'. (Suffolk).

BUNKER, BONKER: N OF *bon quer* 'good heart'. 13th cent.

BUNN see BONE.

BUNNEY, BUNNY: (i) N OF *bugne* 'a swelling', probably for a carbuncle. (ii) L OE *bune-ēg* 'reed island'. 13th cent.

BUNTEN, BUNTON: P Variants of *Bunting*.

BUNTING: P ME *Bountyng*, a font-name for girl babies (*baby Bunting*), derived from the name of the bird, and enshrined in *Bontyng the brewster* in the Coventry plays. 13th cent.

BUNYAN, BUNYON: N OF *buignon, bugnon* 'a round knob, bunch or lump', nickname for one with such a disfigurement. Unappetisingly, the term *bugnon* was also applied to a raised pattie or tart, and the surname may be for a maker of such confections.

BURBAGE, BURBIDGE: L OE *burg-bece* 'brook at the fort'. (Derbys, Leices, Wilts) 12th cent.

BURCH see BIRCH. BURCHALL see BIRCHALL.

BURCHARD, BURCHATT, BURGHARD, BURKART, BURKETT, BURKITT: P OE *Burghheard* 'fortress-hard' or OG *Burghard*, OF *Bouchart*, the OG/OF forms entering England at the Norman Conquest. DB. [Martha Burkitt, a convict, brought the name to Australia 1788].

BURCHETT see BIRCHETT.

BURD(S): N ME *burde* 'a young woman, a maiden'. Sometimes a slighting nickname for an effeminate youth.

BURDAS, BURDUS: L OF From Bordeaux (France). 13th cent.

BURDEKIN: N ME A dim. of ME *burde* 'little maid'. 16th cent.

BURDEN, BURDON, BOURDEN: (i) P OG *Burdo*. (ii) N OF *bourdon* 'a pilgrim's staff', nickname for a pilgrim. (iii) L OE *bȳre-den* 'valley with a byre' or L OE *burg-dūn* 'fort on the hill'. (Yorks, Durham) (iv) O OE *burthegn* 'bower-servant'. 12th cent.

BURDETT, BURDITT: N OF A dim. of *bourdon*, either a small pilgrim or a short staff. DB.

BURDO: P Lat 'mule'. Found also in OG as a pers. name and in France from a Gallic (Celtic) source. Introduced into England following the Norman Conquest. A rare surname but it entered Australia with the First Fleet. [Sarah Burdo, a convict, arrived on the *Lady Penrhyn* 1788].

BURFORD, BURFITT, BURFOOT: L OE *burg-ford* 'ford by a manor'. (Devon, Salop, Oxon, Suffolk) 12th cent.

BURGE, BURDGE: L OE *brycg* 'bridge'. 12th cent.

BURGER, BURGHER, BURKER: O ME *burger* 'a citizen'. 13th cent.

BURGES(S), BURGIS(S), BORGES: O OF *burgeis* 'a freeman', one possessing full municipal rights and privileges. 12th cent.

BURGETT, BURGOT: L OE *burg-geat* 'castle gate'. (Hants, Suffolk, Surrey) 12th cent.

BURGH: L OE *burg* 'fort, castle or manor house'. DB.

BURGHLEY: L OE *burg-lēah* 'wood or clearing of the manor'. (Northants).

BURGIN see BORGONON.

BURGLIN, BURLING: L OF A variant of *Bourguignon* 'the Burgundian'. 13th cent.

BURGOINE, BURGOYNE, BURGON, BURGIN, BOURGEIN, BURGAN: L OF From Burgundy. DB.

BURK(E), BOURKE, BURGH: (i) P Hiberno-Norman, frequent throughout Ireland, derived from Norman family of *de Burgh*. (ii) P ONF In England identical in origin with (i). DB.

BURKART, BURKETT, BURKITT, BURCHAT see BURCHARD. BURKMAN see BORROWMAN. BURKS see BIRKS.

BURLE(S), BURLS: O OE *byrle* 'cup-bearer (butler)'. 14th cent.

BURLEIGH, BURLEY: L OE Variants of *Burghley* and with same meaning. [James Burley, a boy convict, brought the name to Australia 1788].

BURLER: O ME *burle* 'flock of wool' 'dresser of woollen cloth'. 14th cent.

BURLINGTON: L OE 'The *tūn* (farm) of the people of *Beorhtel*, Anglo-Saxon'. (Yorks) 13th cent.

BURMAN see BORROWMAN. BURN(E) see BOURNE [Terence Burn, a sailor on the *Sirius*, and five convicts brought the surname Burn to Australia 1788].

BURNARD: N OF *brun* 'brown' + suffix *-ard*, 'brown hair or complexion'. 12th cent.

BURNBY: L OE *burna* + ON *byr* 'homestead by a spring'. (Yorks).

BURNEL(L), BRUNELL: N ME *burnel*, a dim. of OF *brun*, with the same meaning as *Burnard*. 12th cent.

BURNE(S), BURNS: L OE *burna* 'stream', mainly a northern English and Scottish surname. 13th cent. (The poet Robert Burns changed his name from Burness.) [A Dr Robert Burns led settlers from Scotland to the new Presbyterian settlement at Dunedin, 1843].

BURNET(T), BURNITT: (i) O OF *burnete*. Metonymic for a maker of cloth hose called *burnet*. (ii) N OF *burnete, brunette*, a dim. of *brun* 'brown of hair or complexion'. 13th cent.

BURNEY, BURNIE see BERNEY.

BURNHAM: L OE *burna hām* 'village by a stream'. (Bucks, Essex, Lincs, Norfolk, Som) 12th cent.

BURNLEY: L OE *burna-lēah* 'the clearing with a stream'. (Lancs).

BURNSIDE: L OE *burna-sīde* 'a stream on the hillside', mainly Scottish.

BURR: N O Dan & ME *burre, bur* 'a prickly seed or flower-head' and a nickname for a prickly individual, one easily annoyed. Shakespeare uses it in the sense of one hard to shake off but the surname is 12th cent. Langland uses it in *Piers Plowman* (14th cent.) in the sense of hoarseness from a *bur* in the throat.

BURRA see BOWRA.

BURRARD: P OE pers. name *Burgheard* 'fortress-hard'. 13th cent.

BURREL(L), BURRELS, BOREL(L): O OF *burel*. Metonymic for a maker of a reddish-brown woollen cloth. (ii) N One with hair or complexion '*burel*', from the colour of the cloth. 12th cent.

BURRETT, BORRETT, BORRITT, BORET: (i) P OE pers. name *Burgrǣd* 'fortress-counsel'. 12th cent. (ii) N OF *bourre* + OE *hēafod* 'rough (shaggy) haired'. 13th cent.

BURRIDGE, BURRAGE: P OE *Būrgric* 'fortress-powerful'. DB.

BURROUGH, BURROW, BORROW: L OE *beorge* 'hill' (Devon, Som), or OE *burg* 'fort' (Lancs, Leices). 14th cent.

BURROWS, BURRUS, BURRIS(S) see BOROUGHES.

BURSEY, BERSEY: (i) L OF From Burcy, Calvados (Normandy). DB. (ii) P OE *Beorhtsige* 'bright-war'. 12th cent.

BURSTALL: L OE *burg-stall* 'fort site'. (Suffolk, Yorks) BURSTOW: L OE *byrgstow* 'fort place'. (Surrey) BURTON, BOURTON: L OE *burg-tūn* 'farm by a fort'. 12th cent.

BURT: P OE *Beorht*, an Anglo-Saxon pers. name meaning 'bright, shining, noble'.

BURTWHISTLE see BIRTWHISTLE.

BURWARD: P OE *Burgweard* 'fortress-guard'. 12th cent.

BURWASH: L OE *burg-ersc* 'manor ploughland'. (Sussex) (Kipling's house 'Batemans' is here.)

BURWELL: L OE *burg-wielle* 'stream or spring by a fort'. (Cambs).

BUSBY: L O Scand *buski-by* 'the farm among the shrubs'. (Yorks), *Buschebi* DB. [James Busby was British Resident in New Zealand 1832-39].

BUSH(E), BUSK: L OE *busc* or ON *buskr* 'bush'. 12th cent.

BUSHEL(L), BUSHILL, BUSSEL, BOSHEL, BOSSEL, BISHEL, BISSELL: O ME *buyscel, busshel* 'bushel'. (i) 'A maker of bushels'. (ii) The man who measured the corn. DB.

BUSHER see BOSHER.

BUSKENS, BUSKIN, BOSKIN: (i) L OE *busc* 'bush'. (Devon) (ii) O OE *bucc* + ON *skinn* (replacing OE *hȳd* 'hide'). 'A worker or dealer in buckskin'. 13th cent.

BUSKY: L OE *busc-haeg* 'bush-enclosure'. 13th cent.

BUSS(E): O OF *busse* 'cask'. Metonymic for a maker of casks. 12th cent.

BUSSEY, BUSSY: L OF From Bouce (Orne) or Boucey (Manche) (Normandy). DB.

BUTCHER(S), BUCHER, BOUCHER, BOUTCHER, BOWCHER, BOWKER: O OF *bouchier*, AF *boucher* 'butcher'. 12th cent.

BUTLER, BUTTLER: O OF *bouteilier* 'servant in charge of the wine cellar'. (In medieval England an official of high rank, consequently a prominent surname in the peerage.) 11th cent. [A First Fleet (crew) surname. Samuel Butler, author of *Erewhon*, abandoned his intention of taking holy orders, emigrated to New Zealand and established a sheep-breeding farm at Canterbury, 1859].

BUTLIN, BUCKLIN: N OF *boute-vilain* 'hustle the churl', a nickname for the rouser who shook the churls (peasants) out of their lethargy. 12th cent. (The idea still seems to be prevalent in certain holiday camps.)

BUTNER: O OF *botonier* 'a maker of buttons'. 13th cent.

BUTT(S): (i) P OE *Butt* or *Butta*. The origin of the pers. name is obscure. It is preserved in Butsash (Hants) 'Butt's ash-tree', and in Butley (Ches) '*Butta's lēah* (clearing)'. (ii) L OF *but* 'end, aim', hence butts (targets), a frequent source of the surname since archery was a national activity. (iii) N ME *butt* 'stump', a nickname for a stumpy, thick-set individual. 12th cent.

BUTTER(S): O OE *butere* 'butter'. Metonymic for a maker or seller of butter. 12th cent.

BUTTERBY: L OF *beaute-trueve* 'beautiful trove'. (A place Butterby (Durham) was *Beautrove* in 1296, but no hint of the nature of the trove found there; perhaps a lovely view.)

BUTTERFIELD, BUTTERFILL: L OE *buter-feld* 'rich grazing for cows'. 12th cent. BUTTERWICKE: L OE *buter-wīc* 'butter farm'. (Durham, Lincs, Yorks, Westmorland) BUTTERWORTH: L OE *buter-worth* 'enclosure or homestead', extended to mean 'farm'. Identical in meaning with *Butterwicke*. (Lancs).

BUTTERIS see BOTTERELL.

BUTTERY, BUTTREY: O OF *boterie* 'room for storing provisions'. Metonymic for servant in charge of the buttery.

BUTTON, BOTTEN: O OF *boton* 'button'. Metonymic for *botonier, butner* 'a maker of buttons'. 13th cent. See also Butner.

BUTTRUM see BARTRAM.

BUXTON, BUCKSTON: P OE A pers. Anglo-Saxon name *Bucstān*, from OE *bucca* 'male deer' and *stān* 'stone'.

BUYERS see BYARS.

BUZZARD, BUSZARD: N OF *buzzard*, 'bird of prey considered by falconers as too stupid to be trained'. Nickname for a sluggard or blockhead. 12th cent.

BY(E), BUY(E): L OE *byge* 'curve, bend, corner'. 13th cent.

BYARS, BYERS, BYRE(S), BIER(S), BUYERS: O OE *bȳre* 'stall, cow-shed'. Metonymic for a cow-man. 13th cent.

BYAS, BYASS: L OE *byge-hūs* 'house at the bend'. 13th cent.

BYATT(E), BYOTT, BYGATE: L OE *geat* 'gate', 'by the gate'. 13th cent.

BYFIELD, BIFIELD: L OE *byge-feld* 'open land at the river-bend'. (Northants), *Bifelde* in DB. 12th cent.

BYFLEET: L OE *bī-flēot* 'near a fleet or stream'. (Surrey), *Biflet* DB. (*Flēot* is the origin of Fleet River which now flows underground into the R. Thames, hence Fleet Street, London.)

BYFORD: L OE *byge-ford* 'ford where traders meet'. (Second meaning of *byge* 'traffic, commerce'.) (Herefords).

BYGRAVE(S), BIGRAVE, BYGREAVES, BYGROVE: L OE *grafa* 'ditch'. A place Bygrave (Herts), which is also a source of the surname, was originally (AD 973) *bī Grafan* 'place by the ditch', *Bigrave* DB.

BYHAM, BYAM: L OE *bytme* 'head of a dale'. 12th cent.

BYLES see BILES. BYRCH see BIRCH. BYRD(E) see BIRD.

BYRNE(S): P Ir *O Broin* (*bran* 'raven'). [A First Fleet (convict) surname].

BYROM, BYRAM, BYRON, BYRAN: L OE *bӯre, bӯrum* 'cowshed'. (Lancs, Yorks) 13th cent.

BYTHEWAY, BYTHWAY: L OE *bī-weg* 'by way, path, road'. 13th cent.

BYTON: L OE *byge-tūn* 'farm by the bend'. (Herefords).

BYWATER(S): L OE *bī-waeter* 'by the water'. 13th cent.

BYWOOD: L OE *bī-wudu* 'by the wood'. 13th cent.

C

CABLE: L OE *cāēg-ball* 'a rounded hill'. (Lancs) 13th cent. [A First Fleet surname].

CABORNE, CABOURNE: L ME *cā-burna* 'jackdaw-stream'. (Lincs).

CADBURY: L OW *cad* + OE *burg* 'battle fort', an ancient camp, probably British. (Devon, Som) *Cada*, an Anglo-Saxon, is linked with this name.

CADD, CADE: O OF *cade* 'cask'. Metonymic for a cask-maker'. 13th cent.

CADDEL see CALDWELL.

CADDEN: P Ir *Mac Cadain*. A Co. Armagh erenagh family. (Erenagh indicates a lay lord and hereditary holder of once ecclesiastical lands.)

CADDICK, CADDOCK: N OF *caduc* 'frail, infirm'. 13th cent.

CADDOW: N OE *caddaw* 'jackdaw', regarded as a foolish bird. 14th cent.

CADMAN: O OF *cade* + OE *mann* 'cask-maker'. 13th cent.

CADOGAN: P OW *Cadwugann*, from *cad* 'battle'. 12th cent.

CADWALADER, CADWALLADER: P OW 'battle-leader'. (*Cadfwyall* 'battle-axe'.)

CADWELL, KADWELL: L OE (i) 'The *welle* (spring) of an Anglo-Saxon called *Cada*'. (Cadwell, Oxon), *Cadewell* DB, *Kadewell* 1203. (ii) *catte-dael* 'wild cat valley'. (Lincs), *Cattedale* 1202.

CAESAR: P Lat 'fleece, hairy'. *Caesar*, the cognomen of *Gaius Julius*, was later adopted as title by Slav and Teutonic languages: Czar, Kaiser. In England a pageant name. 12th cent.

CAFF see CHAFF. CAFFERY, CAFFREY see MAC CAFFRAY. CAFFYN see CHAFFIN.

CAGE, CADGE: O OF *cage* 'keeper of the cage (prison)'. 13th cent.

CAGER, CAUGER: O OF *cagier* 'a maker/seller of caps'. 14th cent.

CAHILL see McCAHILL. CAHN see COHEN.

CAIN(E), KAIN(E), CANE, KANE: (i) P Ir *O Cathain*, from *cath* 'warrior'. (ii) P Manx *MacCathain* 'son of *Cathan*'. 12th cent. (iii) P OW *Cain* 'beautiful', from *Keina*, a woman's name. (iv) L OF From Caen (Normandy).

CAINES, KAINES, KEYNES: L OF From Cahaignes (Normandy). 13th cent.

CAIRD: O Ir and SG *ceard* 'craftsman, smith, tinker'. 13th cent.

CAIRNS: L SG From the lands of Cairns (Midlothian). SG *carn* 'a pile of stones, either a memorial or a boundary mark'. Also an Ulster surname by Scottish settlement in 17th cent.

CAITHNESS: L SG A corruption of Kettins, an ancient barony in Angus.

CAKE: O ME *kake*, from ON *kaka* 'cake, loaf'. 'A maker of bread loaves called 'cakes''. 13th cent.

CAKEBREAD: O ON + OE 'A baker of flat loaves'. 12th cent.

CALCOTT, CALCUTT, CALDECOTT: L OE *ceald-cot* 'cold cottage'. 12th cent.

CALCRAFT: L OE *ceald-croft* 'cold croft (holding)'. 15th cent.

CALDBECK: L OE *ceald* + ON *bekkr* 'cold stream'.

CALDER: L Brit river-name, (Cumb, Caithness). 12th cent.

CALDERON, CAULDRON, CAWDRON: O OF *calderonnier* 'a maker of cauldrons'. 13th cent.

CALDWELL, CALWELL, CAUDWELL, CAUDELL, CADDEL, CADWELL, CARDWELL, COLDWELL, COULDWELL: L OE *ceald-wielle* 'cold spring or stream'. 12th cent. The surname is associated with places in 13 English counties. [Joseph Caldwell, a seaman on the *Sirius*, and James Caldwell, a convict, brought the name to Australia 1788. James Caddell was a ship's boy on the sealer *Sydney Cove*, and a member of a boat's crew sent ashore at Foveaux Strait, New Zealand, in 1810 to trade. Maoris killed and ate all the other members of the party but Caddell was protected by a chief's daughter, whom he later married. The couple visited Sydney in 1823 when Caddell, who had spoken no English for thirteen years, had difficulty in making himself understood. He returned with his wife to New Zealand, a confirmed Pakeha-Maori, i.e., White Maori].

CALE: O OF *cale*. Metonymic for a maker of women's head-dresses. 13th cent.

CALEY, CAYLEY, KALEY, KAYLEY: L OF From Cailly (Seine-Inférieure) France. DB. Also a Manx contraction of *MacCaolaidhe*, from Ir *cael* 'slender'.

CALF: N OE *cealf* 'calf'. A nickname. 12th cent.

CALL, CAULES: O OF *cale*, ME *caul* 'a close-fitting net worn by women'. Metonymic for a maker of cauls. 13th cent.

CALLAGHAN: P Ir *O Ceallachain*, from *ceallach* 'strife'. *Ceallachain* was king of Munster 10th cent. All the Callaghans are described as his descendants.

CALLAN, CALLEN: (i) P SG *Macallan*, a pers. name. (ii) P Ir *O Cathalain* 'descendant of *Cathalan* (battle-mighty)'.

CALLANDER, CALLENDER: (i) L From Callander (Perths) Scotland. 13th cent. (ii) O OF *calendrier* 'a worker in the cloth trade'. 14th cent.

CALLAWAY, CALLOWAY, KELLAWAY, KELLEWAY: L OF From Caillouet (Eure) Normandy. 12th cent.

CALLINAN: P Ir *O Callanain*. A Co. Galway erenagh family. (For erenagh see Cadden.)

CALLIS: L OF From Calais (France). 12th cent.

CALLISTER, COLLISTER: P Manx for *MacAlister* 'son of *Alexander*'. 15th cent.

CALLOW, CALOW: N OE *calu*. Nickname for a bald man. OE Byname 1070.

CALVER: L OE *cealf-ōfer* 'calves' ridge'. (Derbys) 12th cent.

CALVERLEY: L OE *cealf-lēah* 'calves' pasture' (Yorks).

CALVERT: O OE *cealf-hierde* 'calf-herd'. 13th cent.

CALWELL see CALDWELL.

CAM, CAMM: (i) L OF From Caen (Normandy). DB. (ii) L Brit & Welsh *cam* 'crooked', a Brit river-name. (Glos) 13th cent. (iii) N SG *cam* 'cross-eyed'. 13th cent.

CAMBER, COMBER, COMER: O OE *camb, comb* 'comb'. 'A maker of combs'. 12th cent.

CAMBOURN(E): L Cornish *cam-brou* 'crooked-hill'. 14th cent.

CAMBREY: L OF From Cambrai (Normandy) or Cambrai (Nord). DB.

CAMBRIDGE: L Brit + OE *Grantebrycg* 'bridge over River Granta'. DB.

CAMDEN: L OE *campa-denu* 'valley with camps'. 12th cent.

CAMELL, CAMMELL: (i) L OW *cant-moel* 'bare hill'. 14th cent. (ii) N OE *camel*, from Semitic via Greek *gāmāl*. Nickname for an ungainly person.

CAMERON: (i) Highlands: N SG *camshron* 'crooked nose'. A famous clan name. (ii) Lowlands: L SG From Cameron (Fifes). 13th cent.

CAMIDGE, CAMMIDGE see GAMAGE.

CAMKIN: L/N A pet-form of *Cam*.

CAMMIS, CAMIS, CAMMISH, CAMUS: (i) O ONF *camise* (OF *chemise*) 'shirt, tabard (herald's robe), priest's surplice'. Metonymic for maker of *camises*. 13th cent. (ii) N OF *camus* 'short-nose'. 13th cent.

CAMP(E): O OE *cempa* 'warrior, champion'. DB. See also Kemp.

CAMPAIGN, CAMPAIN: L ONF From Campagne (Oise, Pas-de-Calais). 12th cent.

CAMPBELL: N SG *caimbeul* 'wry or crooked mouth'. Colin Campbell (1282) established the clan of *Campbell*, whose hereditary chiefs are the dukes of Argyle. [James Campbell, a naval captain, his eight-year-old nephew, a seaman and two convicts brought the name to Australia 1788. In New Zealand, General Duncan Campbell took part in the Maori Wars].

CAMPION see CHAMPION.

CAMPLIN(G): O OF *camelin*. Metonymic for a maker of *camelin* (material woven from camel hair). 13th cent.

CAMPTON: L Brit + OE *camel-tūn* 'farm by the Camel stream'. (Beds).

CANAVAN: P Ir *O Ceanndubhain*, from *dubh* 'black'.

CANAWAY: P Ir An Ulster variant of Conway.

CANE, CANAS, KANE: (i) P OE *Cana*, An Anglo-Saxon pers. name. DB. (ii) L OF From Caen (Normandy). 13th cent. See also Cain.

CANHAM: L OE *Cāfa-hām* 'the homestead of an Anglo-Saxon nicknamed *Cāfa* (bold and active)'. 14th cent.

CANN: (i) O OE *canne*. Metonymic for a maker of cans and pots. 14th cent. (ii) L OE *canne* 'deep valley'. (Dorset) 13th cent.

CANNAN: P Ir *O Candin*, from *cano* 'wolf-cub'. 13th cent.

CANNARD: N OF *cannard*. Nickname for a sluggard.

CANNELL: O OF *canele* 'cinnamon'. Metonymic for a spicer. 14th cent.

CANNING: L OE 'The *ingas* (people) of *Cana*, an Anglo-Saxon'. (Wilts).

CANNINGTON: L Brit + OE *Cantuc-tūn* 'farm by the Quantock hills'. (Som).

CANNON(S), CANON, CHANNON: O OE *canon*, ME *chanun* 'canon-law'. 'A member of a communal clergy house'. 11th cent.

CANT, CHANT: O OF *chant*, ME *cant* 'singing'. Metonymic for a chanter. 14th cent.

CANTELLO, CANTELO: L OF From Canteloup (Normandy). 12th cent.

CANTER, CANTOR, CAUNTER, KANTER, KANTOR: (i) O Lat *cantor* 'precentor in cathedral or monastery'. 12th cent. (ii) O AF *caunter* 'leading singer'.

CANTRELL, CANTRILL see CHANTRELL. CANTWELL see KENTWELL.

CAPE, COPE: O OE *cāpe*, ME *cope* 'a tailor of copes, capes, cloaks'. 12th cent.

CAPEL, CAPELL, CAPELLE, CAPLE: L ONF *capele*, ME *capel* 'chapel'. 12th cent.

CAPEWELL: L OE *cape-wiele* 'look-out place by the spring'.

CAPLAN, CAPLIN see CHAPLAIN.

CAPON: O OE *capun* 'a breeder/seller of capons (neutered cocks)'. 13th cent.

CAPP(S): O OE *caeppe*. Metonymic for a maker of caps, hoods. 12th cent.

CAPPER: O OE *caeppe* 'cap/hood maker'. 13th cent.

CAPRON, CAPORN, CAPERON: O OF *chaperon* 'a maker of *chaperons* (a hood or cap worn by nobles)'. 12th cent. (*Chaperon*, 'minder of young unmarried women', came later, from the hood or cap worn by the minder.)

CARBERRY, CARBERY: P Ir *O Cairbre*. A Co. Fermanagh erenagh family. (For erenagh see Cadden.) Also a Co. Waterford surname.

CARBONELL: N OF *carbon* 'charcoal'. 'Swarthy or with coal-black hair'. DB.

CARD: O OF *carde*. Metonymic for a wool-card maker (teasel-head). 14th cent.

CARDEN: N OF *cardon* 'thistle'. Nickname for a prickly character. DB.

CARDER: O OF *carde* 'a carder or teaser of wool'. 14th cent.

CARDEW, CARDY, CARTHEW: L OW *caer-du* 'black fort'. (Cumb) 14th cent.

CARDIS see CARRUTHERS. CARDWELL see CALDWELL. CARE see KEAR.

CAREW: L An Anglo-Norman name Hibernicised as *de Carrun*. (Tipperary).

CAREY, CARY: L Brit river-name 'pleasant stream'. (Devon, Som) 13th cent.

CARFAX: L OF *carrefourc* 'four-forked', 'cross-roads'. (Oxon).

CARGILL: (i) L Brit/OW *kaer-geall* 'fort of the pledge'. (Scotland). 13th cent. (ii) P Ir An Irish surname from *Mac Feargail* (McCarrigle). (iii) L Cumbric + ON *cair-gil* 'the fort by the ravine'. (Perths) Scotland. 13th cent. in the form *Kergyl*. (Cumbric, the language of the Britons of the ancient kingdom of Strathclyde, which embraced Cumberland, annexed to England by William Rufus, eldest son of the Conqueror.) [Capt William Cargill together with Dr Burns led settlers from Scotland to the new Presbyterian settlement at Dunedin, 1843].

CARKER, CHARKER: O ONF *carche*, ME *cark* 'a load'. Metonymic for a carrier of *carks*. 12th cent.

CARL(E), KARL(E): (i) P OG *Karl*, O Scand

Karli 'Charles'. DB. (ii) P O Dan *karl*, ON *karli*, ME *carl*, originally 'a free peasant'. Later (1300) 'a bondman, servile tenant or villain, a churl'. Cotgrave, whose English-French dictionary appeared in 1611, noted the degeneration of such names: '*Vilain*: a villaine, slave, bondman, servile tenant. Hence also, a churl, carle, boore, clown; and a knave, rascall, varlet, filthie fellow; any base-humoured, ill-born, and worse-bred hinde, cullion, or clusterfist'.

CARLESS, CARLOSS, CARLOS: N OE *carlēas* 'carefree'. 12th cent.

CARLISLE, CARLILE, CARLILL, CARLYLE: L OW *caer* 'castle or city' + O Brit pers. name *Luguvalos* or Romano-British god *Lugus*. Surname 12th cent.

CARLTON, CARLETON: L OE *ceorlatūn* 'farm of the free peasants'. DB.

CARMAN: P ON *Karmann*, of which the meaning is simply 'man'. 12th cent.

CARMICHAEL: L O Brit + Hebrew. 'The fort of *Michael*'. From Carmichael (Lanarks) Scotland. A sept of the clan Stewart.

CARMODY: P Ir *O Cearmada*, from the ancient territory of Thomond (Co. Clare).

CARN(E): L Cornish *carn* 'a pile of stones'. A cogn. of Cairns, and a frequnt el. in Cornish place-names.

CARNABY: L ON *Kaerandis*, a pers. name, + *byr* (farm).

CARNEGIE: L SG *cather an eige* 'fort at the gap'. 14th cent.

CARNELL, CARNALL: O OF *crenel* 'battlement, embrasure'. 'An arbalester (crossbowman) at the battlements'. 13th cent.

CARNEY: P Ir *MacCearnaigh*, from *cearnach* 'victorious'. [John Carney, a convict, brought the name to Australia 1788].

CAROLAN: P Ir *O Cearbhallain* 'descendant of *Cearbhallan*', a dim. of an O Ir pers. name.

CARPENTER: O AF *carpenter*, a craft name unchanged in 800 years. 12th cent.

CARR, KER, KERR: L ON *Kiarr*, ME *Kerr* 'marsh with brushwood'. 12th cent.

CARRAGHER: P Ir *Mac Fearchair* 'man-dear'. Cos. Monoghan & Armagh.

CARRAN: P Manx from Ir *MacCiarain*, a saint's name.

CARRICK: L SG *creag*, with meaning identical with *Craig*. (Ayrs) Scotland.

CARRIER: O ONF *carier* 'a carrier, porter' 14th cent.

CARRINGTON: L OE 'The tūn (farm or village) of an Anglo-Saxon leader', whose name remains obscure. (Ches, Lothian) 13th cent. A place in Lincs was named for Robert Smith, first Lord Carrington, in 1796, too late to have contributed to the surname.

CARROL, CARROLL: P Ir *MacCearbhaill*, name of several Irish septs.

CARRUTHERS, CARROTHERS, CARRODUS, CARDIS, CROTHERS, CRUDDAS: L Brit *Caer* 'fort' of a leader whose name is obscure, possibly *Rhydderch*. The surname is from Dumfries, Scotland, and was settled in Ulster as *Caruth* in 17th cent. The Scottish surname is 14th cent.

CARSLEY, CASELEY, CASLEY, CASSLEY, KEARSLEY, KERSLEY: L OE *caerse-lēah* 'glade where cress grows'. 12th cent.

CARSON: An ancient Scottish name of uncertain derivation. Probably from the same source as *Curzon*. 13th cent. form *de Carsan*. Also a Northern Ireland surname.

CARSTAIRS: L ME *castel* (castle) of *Tarres*. (Lanarks) Scotland.

CARSWELL, CASEWELL, CASWELL, CRASSWELL, CRASWELL, CRESSWELL: L OE *caerse-wiella* 'cress-stream'. 12th cent. [A First Fleet (convict and crew) surname].

CARTER, CHARTER: O ONF *caretier*, surviving in French surnames *Carretier*, *Cartier*, and English *Carter* and variants. 12th cent.

CARTHEW see CARDEW.

CARTLAND: L ON *kartr* + OE *land* 'rocky land'.

CARTLEDGE, CARTLIDGE: L ON *kartr* + OE *laecc* 'stony stream'. (Derbys).

CARTMEL(L), CARTMILL: L ON *kartr-melr* 'sandbank by the rocks'. (Lancs).

CARTWRIGHT: O OE *craet-wyrhta* 'a maker of carts'. 13th cent.

CARUS, CARISS, CARRAS, CARRISS: L ON kiarr + OE *hūs* 'marsh house'. 14th cent.

CARUTH see CARRUTHERS.

CARVER: (i) O OE *ceorfan* 'to carve, engrave', 'a wood-carver'. 13th cent. (ii) O OF *caruier* 'ploughman'. 12th cent.

CARVILL(E): L OF From Carville (Normandy) or Carville (Seine Inférieure). 12th cent.

CARWARDINE: L OE *carr-worthign* 'rocky enclosure'. (Ches) 14th cent.

CASBOLT: N ME *casbalde* 'bald-head'. 14th cent.

CASBORNE, CASBURN: L OE *caerse-burna* 'cress-brook'. 13th cent.

CASE: O ONF *casse*. 'A maker of boxes, chests'. 13th cent.

CASEMENT: P Ir *Mac* + ON *Asmundr* 'god protector'. Early form *MacCasmonde*. An Antrim name of Manx origin. 15th cent.

CASEY: P Ir *O Cathasaigh*, from *cathasath* 'watchful'.

CASH: P Ir An early (medieval) Dublin name. In England a variant of *Case*.

CASHIN, CASHION see MAC CASHIN. CASKEY see MACASKIE. CASLAKE see CARSLAKE.

CASHMAN: P Ir A Co. Cork variant of *Kissane*.

CASS: P A dim. of Gk *Cassandra*. 12th cent.

CASSIDY: P Ir *O Caiside*. A Fermanagh name.

CASSINGHAM: L OE *caersen-hām* 'homestead where cress grows'. 13th cent.

CASSON: P OE 'Son of *Cass*'. 14th cent.

CASTELLAN, CASTLING: (i) L OF From Castellion (Normandy). DB. (ii) O OF *castelain* 'governor or constable of a castle'. 13th cent.

CASTERTON: L OE 'Site of a Roman fort developed as a *tūn* (village)'. (Rutland, Westmorland).

CASTLE(S), CASTELL, CASSEL(S), CASSELL(S): L or O ME *castel* 'worker at the castle or tenant of castle land'. 12th cent. [A First Fleet, convict, surname].

CASTLEMAN, CASTLEMAIN: O ME *castel-mann* 'worker at the castle'. 14th cent.

CASTLETON: L ME *castel* + OE *tūn* 'castle-farm'. (Derbys, Lancs).

CASWELL see CARSWELL.

CATANACH, CATTANACH: P SG 'Descendant of *Gillacatain* (servant of St *Catan*)'. 14th cent.

CATCHLOVE: O ONF *cacheleu* 'chase wolf', 'a wolf hunter'. 12th cent.

CATCHPOLE, CATCHPOOL(E): O OF *chacepol* 'chase fowl', 'a tax-gatherer who confiscated poultry in lieu of money'. Later a minor law officer. DB.

CATER, CHATER: O OF *achatour* 'purveyor for a noble household' 13th cent.

CATES, KATES: N ON *Kati* 'the merry man'. 12th cent.

CATFORD: L OE *catt-ford* 'wild cats' ford'.

CATHCART: L A Brit river-name from the Cart. (Renfrews) 13th cent.

CATHERALL see CATTERALL.

CATLETT: L 'The sign of the small wild cat'. CATLEY: L OE *catt-lēah* 'wild cats' clearing'.

CATLIN(G), CATTLIN: P OF A woman's name, *Cateline*. 13th cent. CATON: P A pet-form of *Cateline*. 13th cent.

CATT, KATTE: N OF *chat* 'cat'. A nickname for a prowler or stalker. DB.

CATTELL, CATELL, CATTLE: P Identical in meaning with Caton. 13th cent.

CATTERALL: L ON *kattar-hali* 'cat's tail', a long strip of land. 13th cent.

CATTON: (i) L OE *catt-denu* 'wild cats' valley'. (Northumb) (ii) L ON *'Kati's tūn* (farm)'. (Derbys, Norfolk, Yorks).

CAUDELL, CAUDLE, CADWELL: N ONF *caudel* 'a spiced gruel, laced with ale or wine'. A nickname for one addicted to this mess. 13th cent.

CAUDWELL, CAUDELL see (also) CALDWELL. CAULDER see CALDER. CAULDRON see CALDERON. CAULES see CALL. CAUGER see CAGER.

CAULFIELD: L OE *ceald-feld* 'cold field or open plain'.

CAUSER see CHAUCER.

CAUSEY, CAWSEY: (i) L OF From Pays-de-Caux (Seine Inférieure) France. 12th cent. (ii) L ME *cauce* 'causeway'. 12th cent.

CAUSELEY: L OE *cauce-lēah* 'road through the woodland'.

CAVALIER: (i) O Lat *caballarius*, Fr *chevalier* 'knight'. (ii) N 'A gallant attending ladies' or 'an overbearing swashbuckler'.

CAVAN: P Ir A dim. of *O'Keefe*.

CAVANAGH see KAVANAGH.

CAVE: L OE *caf* 'quick, nimble' applied to 'running stream'. (Yorks).

CAVENDISH: L OE *Cāfna-edisc* *'Cāfna's* pasture'. (Suffolk) DB.

CAVILL: L ME *cā* + OE *feld* 'jackdaw field'. (Yorks) 12th cent.

CAW, CAWSE: L OF From Pays-de-Caux (Seine Inferieure) France. 12th cent.

CAWDELL see CAUDEL. CAWDRON see CALDERON.

CAWOOD: L ME *cā* + OE *wudu* 'jackdaw wood'. (Lancs).

CAWTHORN(E), CAWTHRON: L OE *calu-thorn* 'bare thorn bush'. (Yorks) 12th cent.

CAWTON: L OE *calfa-tūn* 'calf farm'. (Yorks), *Calvetun* DB.

CAXTON: L O Scand *Kakkr* + OE *tūn* '*Kakkr's* farm'. (Cambs) 12th cent. (William Caxton, a rich mercer, and a prolific writer and translator, introduced the printing press to England in 15th cent.)

CAYLEY see CALEY.

CAYZER, KASER, KAYSER, KESOR, KEYZER: N ME *Caisere*, ultimately from Lat *Caesar* 'emperor'. A 12th cent. pageant name.

CECIL: P OW *Seisill*, from Lat *Caecilius*. William the Conqueror's daughter *Cecilia*, Abbess of Caen, introduced the name into England. DB.

CEELY, CEILEY see SEELEY. CELLIER see SELLAR.

CENTER, SENTER: O OF *ceinturier* 'a maker of girdles'. 13th cent.

CHACE see CHASE.

CHAD: P OE *Ceadda*, a pers. Anglo-Saxon name, borne by a monk of Lindisfarne who became Bishop of the Mercians in 7th cent. Surname 12th cent.

CHADDERTON: L Brit *cader* + OE *tūn* 'farm by the hill-fort'. (Lancs).

CHADWICK, CHADDOCK, SHADDICK, SHADDOCK, SHADWICK: L OE 'The *wīc* (dairy farm) of *Ceadda*'. (Lancs, Warwicks, Worces) 13th cent. [William Chadwick, a marine, and Thomas Chadwick, a convict, brought the name to Australia 1788].

CHAFER: O OE *chauffour* 'lime kiln'. 'A lime burner'. 13th cent.

CHAFF(E), CHAVE, CAFF: N OF *chauf* 'bald'. 13th cent. [A First Fleet, convict, surname].

CHAFFEN, CHAUVIN, CAFFYN: N OF A dim. of *chauf* 'bald'. 13th cent.

CHAFFER: O OE *cēapfaru* 'trade, wares'. Metonymic for a merchant. 14th cent.

CHALCRAFT: L OE *cealf-croft* 'grazing for calves'. 13th cent.

CHALK: L OE *cealce* 'chalk', 'chalk downs'. 12th cent.

CHALKER: O OE *cealcian* 'to whiten'. 'A chalker (wattle and daub)'. 12th cent.

CHALKLEY: L OE *cealce-lēah* 'clearing by the chalk quarry'.

CHALLENER, CHALONER, CHANNER: O OF *chalon*. Metonymic for a dealer in *chalons* (coverlets imported from Chalon-sur-Marne, France). 13th cent.

CHALLENGER: O OF *chalonger* 'to challenge'. 'A plaintiff, claimant'. 12th cent.

CHALLIS, CHALLICE, CHALICE: L OF From Eschalls (Pas-de-Calais). DB.

CHALMERS: O Scottish form of *Chambers*. 13th cent.

CHAM: L OF From Caen (Normandy). 12th cent.

CHAMBERLAIN, CHAMBERLAYNE, CHAMBERLIN: O OF *chamberlain* 'court official responsible for private chambers of king or nobleman'. 12th cent.

CHAMBERS: O OF *chambre*. Originally *chamberlain* but later 'servant of the chamber', e.g., chamber-maid. 13th cent.

CHAMPAIN: L OF From Champagne (France). 12th cent.

CHAMPION, CAMPION: O OF *champion*, ONF *campion* 'a professional champion, defending the interests of his employer by force of arms'. 12th cent. [Edward Champion, a sergeant on the *Sirius*, brought the name to Australia 1788].

CHAMPNESS, CHAMPNEY: L AF *le champeneis* 'the man from Champagne' (France). 13th cent. See also Champain.

CHANCE: N OF *cheance* 'luck, fortune'. Nickname for a gambler. 13th cent.

CHANCELLOR, CANCELLOR: O ME *chanceler* 'clerk in the chancery'. DB.

CHANDLER, CHANTLER, CANDLER: O AF *chandeler* 'candle maker'. 13th cent.

CHANEY see CHESNEY. CHANNER see CHALLENER. CHANNON see CANNON. CHANT see CANT.

CHANTER: O OF *chanteor* 'singer, chorister'. 13th cent. See also Canter.

CHANTRILL, CANTRELL, CANTRILL: O OF *chanterelle* 'a small bell', used of the treble in a choir. 12th cent.

CHAPLAIN, CHAPLIN, CHAPERLIN, CAPLAN, CAPLIN, CAPELIN, KAPLAN, KAPLIN: O OF *chapelain*, ONF *capelain* 'chantry priest'. 12th cent.

CHAPMAN, CHIPMAN: O OE *cēapmann* 'merchant, trader'. 12th cent. [Thomas Chapman, a marine private, and his wife and two daughters brought the name to Australia 1788].

CHAPPEL(L), CHAPEL, CHAPILL, CHAPPLE, CHAPELL: O OF *chapele*. 'A lay worker at the chapel'. 12th cent.

CHARITY: N OF *charité* 'Christian love', 'hospice, refuge', 'one giving succour to the needy'. 12th cent.

CHARKER see CARKER.

CHARLES: (i) P OF *Charles*, from Lat *Carolus*, OG *Karl* 'man'. 12th cent. See also Carl. (ii) O OE *ceorl* 'a freeman of the lowest rank'. 12th cent.

CHARLESON: P OF 'Son of *Charles*'.

CHARLESWORTH: L OE 'The *worth* (homestead) of an Anglo-Saxon with the unlikely name of *Ceafl* (jaw)'. (Derbys), *Chenneswurde* DB.

CHARLEY: L OE *cearn-lēah* 'clearing marked by a rock'. (Leices).

CHARLTON: L OE *ceorl-tūn* 'farm of the churls'. 12th cent.

CHARLWOOD: L OE *ceorl-wudu* 'churls' wood'. (Surrey).

CHARMAN: O OF *char* + OE *mann* 'a carter, carrier'. 13th cent.

CHARNELL: O OF *charnel* 'custodian of burial ground'. 12th cent.

CHARNOCK: L Brit/OW *carn* 'stone-pile', probably a memorial stone. (Lancs) See also Cairns, Carn.

CHART, CHARD: L OE *ceart* 'wild common land'. (Kent, Surrey) 13th cent.

CHARTER see CARTER.

CHARTERIS, CHARTERS, CHARTRES, CHATTERS: L OF From Chartres (Eure-et-Loire) France. 12th cent.

CHASE, CHACE: O OF *chaceur* 'hunter'. 14th cent.

CHASTON: L OF *chastaigne* 'chestnut-tree'. 13th cent.

CHATER(S), CHAYTOR see CATER.

CHATFIELD: L OE 'The *feld* (field or open plain) of an Anglo-Saxon called *Catta*'.

CHAUCER, CHAUSER, CAUSER: O OF *chaucier* 'a maker of hose, pantaloons, breeches'. Geoffrey Chaucer's grandfather lived in Cordwainer Street (the street of the shoemakers and leather workers), London, and was known by five names: Robert le Saddler, Robert Chaucer, Robert Malyn, Robert of Dennington, and Robert of Ipswich. He relinquished four of these names, and his son was known as John Chaucer. Geoffrey's great-grandfather kept a tavern and was called Andrew le Taverner; Robert was a boot-maker and sadler; John was a well-to-do vintner; and Geoffrey, having been trained as a page at court, was a Customs Officer and a diplomat, as well as England's great medieval poet. The surname is 13th cent.

CHAUMONT: L OF From Chaumont (Orne) Normandy. 12th cent.

CHAUVIN see CHAFFIN. **CHAVE** see CHAFF.

CHEADLE: L Brit *cēto* + OE *lēah* 'forest glade'. (Ches, Staffs).

CHEAL: L OE *cegel* 'pole or peg', probably a plank bridge over a dyke. (Lincs).

CHEATER: O ME *chetour* 'officer responsible for the king's escheats'. 13th cent. (Escheats were heirless lands which lapsed to the crown. Cheat is from the same source; indeed an escheat was regarded as confiscation. Shakespeare (*The Merry Wives of Windsor*): 'I will be cheater to them both, and they shall be exchequers to me'.

CHECKLEY: L OE 'The *lēah* (clearing) of *Ceacca*'. (Ches, Herefords, Staffs).

CHEEK: N OE *ceace* 'jaw', presumably a prominent one.

CHEER(S): N OF *chere*. Nickname for a happy face.

CHEESE, CHIESE: O OE *cēse* 'cheese'. Metonymic for a cheese-maker. 12th cent. CHEESEMAN, CHESEMAN, CHISMAN, CHISMON: O OE *cēse-mann* 'maker/seller of cheese'. 13th cent. CHEESEWRIGHT: O OE *cēse-wyrhta* 'cheese-maker'.

CHEETHAM: L OE *cēt-hām* 'village by the forest'. (Lancs) 13th cent.

CHEEVER(S), CHIVERS: N OF *chievre* 'she-goat', perhaps for agility. DB.

CHEGWIDDEN, CHEGWIN, CHEGWYN: L Cornish. 'White house'.

CHENHALL: L Cornish. 'House by the stone'.

CHENOWETH: L Cornish. 'New house'.

CHEQUER: O OF *eschequier* 'chess-board'. 13th cent. (The Exchequer, originally the table divided into squares on which the English revenue accounts were worked out with counters. The clerks of the Exchequer were known as *chequers*. Chequers Court, Bucks, official residence of British prime ministers, was owned by the clerk to the exchequer under Henry II, and the manor took its name from his office.)

CHERITON: L OE *cirice-tūn* 'church farm'. (Devon).

CHERRETT: O OE A Suffolk variation of *Cheesewright*.

CHERRY: O ME *cherye* 'a grower/seller of cherries'. 13th cent.

CHESHIRE, CHESSER: L OE From the county, *Cestrecire* DB. Surname 13th cent.

CHESNEY, CHEYNE, CHANEY, CHENEY: L OF *chesnai* 'oak grove'. From Quesnay, Chenay, or Chesnoy (France). DB.

CHESSELL: L OE (i) *ciest-hyll* 'chest (coffin) hill'. (Wilts), *Chesthull* 1317. (Chessel is the site of a pagan Anglo-Saxon burial ground.) (ii) From Chesthill, a lost place in Salop, with identical derivation and meaning.

CHESTER: L Lat *Castra-legionum*, OE *Legacaestir* 'Roman station'. *Cestre* DB.

CHESTERFIELD: L OE *ceaster-feld* 'field by the Roman station'. (Derbys).

CHESTERTON: L OE *ceaster-tūn* 'farm at the Roman station'. DB.

CHESTNUT(T): L OF *chastaigne* 'chestnut-tree'.

CHETTLE: L OE *cietel* 'deep valley among hills'. (Dorset).

CHETWODE, CHETWOOD: L Brit *cēt* + OE *wudu*, both meaning 'wood'. (Bucks).

CHETWYND: L OE *Ceatta-gewind* 'Ceatta's winding hill-path'. (Salop).

CHEVERALL(S): (i) O OF *chevrelle* 'kid', 'kid-leather'. Metonymic for a maker/seller of kid-leather goods. 12th cent. (ii) L Fr *chevreuil* 'roe-buck'. (Wilts), *Chevrel* DB.

CHEVIS: N OF *chevesne* 'a small fat river-fish'. 13th cent.

CHEW, CHUE: (i) L Brit river-name. (Som) 12th cent. (ii) N OE *cēo*, a chattering bird of the crow family. [John Chew, a marine, brought the name to Australia 1788].

CHEYNEY, CHEYNE see CHESNEY.

CHICK: N ME *chike* 'chicken', term of endearment. 14th cent.

CHIDGEY, CHIDZEY: L OE 'The *īeg* (island) of an Anglo-Saxon called *Cedd*'. (Som).

CHIDIAC: L Brit cogn. of OW *coediog* 'wooded', from Brit *cēto* 'wood'. (Dorset), *Cidihoc* DB.

CHIESE see CHEESE. CHISMON see CHEESEMAN.

CHIFLEY: L OE 'The *lēah* (clearing) of an Anglo-Saxon called *Cifa*'. (Berks) (The Australian prime minister of this name came of a family settled in Ireland.)

CHILCOTE: L OE *cilda-cot* 'cottages of the noble youths (training in the knightly arts)'. (Leices, Northants).

CHILCOTT: L OE 'Cottage of *Cēola*, an Anglo-Saxon'. (Som).

CHILD(S), CHILES, CHILL: O OE *cild* 'child', 'a noble youth', 'a page at court', or 'an aspirant to knighthood'. DB.

CHILDERHOUSE, CHILDERS: O OE *cildra-hūs* 'master of an orphanage'. 13th cent.

CHILMAN: O OE *cildra-mann* 'servant of a young noble'. 13th cent.

CHILTON: L OE *cildra-tūn* 'children's manor' (either training centre for knighthood or orphanage). 12th cent.

CHILVER: P OE *cēol-frith* 'ship-peace', a pers. name. CHILVERS: 'Son of *Chilver*.'

CHIN(N): N OE *cin* 'chin', nickname for a prominent chin. 13th cent.

CHINNERY: N OE Probably for a bearded chin. [Samuel Chinnery, a negro convict, brought the name to Australia 1788. On arrival he took up residence in a hollow tree].

CHIPCHASE: L OE *cipp-ceas* 'beam trap for animals'. (Northumb).

CHIPP: P OE *Cippa* 'a personal name associated with ploughshare', preserved in Chipnall (*Cippa's* knoll) Salop. [Thomas Chipp, a marine, brought the name to Australia 1788].

CHIPPENDALE: L OE *cīeping-dael* 'market in the valley'. 13th cent.

CHIPPING: O OE *cēping* 'market trader'. 12th cent.

CHISHOLM: L OE *cēse-holm* 'water-meadow cheese factory'. (Roxburghs).

CHISLETT: L OE *cysel-stede* 'gravelly place'. (Kent) CHISNALL: L OE *cysel-halh* 'gravelly corner'. (Lancs).

CHISWICK, CHISSICK; L OE *cēse-wīc* 'cheese-farm'. (Cambs, Essex, Middx, Northumb) 12th cent.

CHITTY: N ME *chitte* 'young cub, pup, kitten'. 13th cent.

CHIVERS see CHEEVER.

CHOPIN, CHOPPING; N OF *chopiner* 'a tipler'. 13th cent. (*Chopine* 'a large measure (of wine)').

CHORLEY: L OE *ceorla-lēah* 'ceorls' (peasants') clearing'. (Ches, Lancs).

CHRICHTON see CRICHTON. CHRISP see CRISP.

CHRISTIAN: P Lat *Christianus* 'a Christian'. 12th cent.

CHRISTIE, CHRISTEY, CHRISTY: P Northern England and Scottish pet-form of *Christian* or *Christine*. 13th cent.

CHRISTIN(E): P OE *Crīsten* 'Christian' 13th cent.

CHRISTMAS: N OE *Cristmaesse* Nickname for one born at Christmas. 12th cent.

CHRISTOPHER(S): P Lat from Gk *Christopherus* 'Christ-bearing'. 13th cent.

CHRYSTAL, CRYSTAL: P Lowland Scots dim. of *Christopher*. 16th cent.

CHUBB: N ME *chubbe*, regarded as a doltish fish, simple to catch. 12th cent.

CHUCK see SUCH. CHUE see CHEW.

CHURCH: O OE *cirice* 'church', usually sexton, verger. 13th cent.

CHURCHARD, CHURCHYARD: O OE *cirice-geard* 'keeper of the churchyard'. 13th cent.

CHURCHER, CHURCHES: O OE *cirice-hūs* 'caretaker of the church house'. 14th cent.

CHURCHILL: L OE *cirice-hyll* 'church hill'. (Devon, Som, Warwicks, Worces) 13th cent.

CHURCHWARD: O OE *cirice-weard* 'custodian of a church building'. 11th cent.

CHURTON: L OE *cirice-tūn* 'church farm'. (Ches).

CHUTE: L Brit *cēto* (Welsh *coed*) 'forest'. (Wilts), *Chut* 13th cent. [General Trevor Chute, an outstanding commander in the Maori wars].

CHYNOWETH see CHENOWETH.

CINNAMON: N OF *cinnamome* 'fragrant spice', a term of endearment.

CLACHER: O SG *clachan* 'a stonemason'.

CLACK: N OE *clacc* 'a compulsive chatterer'. DB

CLAGUE: P Ir and Manx *MacLiaigh* 'son of the leech'. 12th cent.

CLANCY: P Ir *MacFhlannchaidh* 'son of the ruddy warrior'.

CLAPHAM: L OE *clop-hām* 'homestead on a hillock'. (Beds, London, Surrey, Sussex, Yorks) 12th cent.

CLAPP: N OE *clop* applied as a nickname to a 'lumpy, clumsy chap'. 12th cent.

CLARE, CLAIR: (i) L OW *claear* 'bright'. (Suffolk) DB. (ii) P OF *Claire* 'bright, fair', a woman's name. 13th cent.

CLARIDGE: P Lat *clarita* 'bright, shining', *Clarice*, a woman's name. 12th cent.

CLARINGBOLD: P OG *Clarembald*, OF *Clarebald*, from Lat *clarus* 'famous' + OG *bald* 'bold'. 12th cent.

CLARK(E), CLERK(E): O Lat *clericus*, OF *clerc* 'clerk, cleric, clergyman'. DB. (The writing, recording etc., was performed by the clergy in the Middle Ages, so the occupational name included 'scholar, penman, recorder, secretary'.) [Lieutenant Ralph Clark, Zachariah Clark (agent for the contractors) and five convicts brought the name to Australia 1788].

CLATWORTHY: L OE *clotworthy* 'homestead where burdock grows'. (Som).

CLAXTON: L OE 'The *tūn* (farm) of an Anglo-Saxon called *Clac*'. (Durham, Norfolk, Yorks).

CLAY: O OE *clǣg* 'clay'. 'Worker at the claypit'. 12th cent.

CLAYDON: L OE *clǣgen-dūn* 'clayey hill'. (Bucks, Oxon, Suffolk).

CLAYFIELD: L OE *clǣg-feld* 'clayey field or plain'. CLAYMAN: O OE *clǣgmann* 'a worker in clay'. 14th cent. CLAYTON: L OE *clǣg-tūn* 'farm on the clay'. 12th cent. [Clayfield and Clayton are First Fleet surnames].

CLEAN: N OE *clǣne* 'pure, chaste', 'true, honourable'.

CLEAR: (i) P OF *Clere*, French form of *Clare*. 13th cent. (ii) L OE *clēare* 'bright', a river-name. (Hants) 14th cent. [A First Fleet, convict, surname].

CLEARY see McCLEARY. CLEAVE see CLIFF.

CLEAVER: O OE *clēofan* 'to cleave'. 'A cleaver of logs, etc'. 14th cent. [Mary Cleaver, a convict, brought the name to Australia 1788].

CLEE: L OE *clǣg* 'clayey soil'. (Lincs, Salop) 14th cent.

CLEGG: L ON *kleggi* 'haystack'. (Lancs).

CLELAND: L OE *clǣg-land* 'clayey land'.

CLEMM, CLEMENCE, CLEMENS, CLEMENT(S), CLEMONS, CLIMAS: P Lat *Clementia* 'mildness', the name of several popes. 12th cent. [Henry Clements, a private, John Clements, a seaman, and Thomas Clements, a convict, brought the name to Australia 1788]. CLEMENTSON, CLEMINSON, CLEMSON, CLIMPSON: 'Son of *Clement*'.

CLEMO, CLEMOW, CLYMO: P Cornish forms of *Clement*. 16th cent.

CLENCH, CLINCH: L OE *clenc* 'mass, bulk', used of a hill or high ground in a fen. 13th cent. [Richard Clinch, a marine sergeant, brought the name to Australia 1788].

CLENDON: L OE *clǣnan-dūn* 'the clean hill' (free from obstructive growth such as thorn-bushes). (Surrey), *Clanedun* DB. [Capt James Clendon set up a trading post at Okiato in the Bay of Plenty, 1832].

CLENNELL: L OE *clǣnan* 'clean (weed-free) hill'. (Worces).

CLERK(E) see CLARK. **CLEUGH** see CLOUGH.

CLEVELAND: L OE *clif-land* 'hilly country'. (Yorks).

CLEVELEY, CLEVERLEY, CLEVERLY: L OE *clif-lēah* 'steep clearing'. (Lancs).

CLEWER: L OE *clif-ware* 'slope of the hill'. (Berks, Som).

CLEWS see CLOUGH.

CLIFF(E), CLIVE, CLEAVE, CLEEF, CLIFT: L OE *clif* 'cliff, steep descent, promontory, steep river-bank'. 11th cent. CLIFFORD: L OE *clif-ford* 'ford by a steep bank'. (Devon, Glos, Herefords, Yorks) CLIFTON: L OE *clif-tūn* 'farm by the cliff'.

CLIMAS see CLEMM. **CLINCH** see CLENCH. **CLINE** see CLYNE.

CLIMPSON: L Cornish From a place-name of obscure etymology, *Climestone* DB. See also Clementson.

CLINK, CLINKER, CLINCH: O OE *clencean* 'to clinch, rivet'. Metonymic for a rivetter. 14th cent. See also Clench.

CLINTON: (i) L OE 'The *tūn* (settlement) with a *glind* (fence)'. (Glinton, Northants), *Clinton* 1060, *Glintone* DB. (ii) P Ir *Mac Clinton, Mac Giolla Fhionntain* 'devotee of St *Finton*'. An Ulster surname.

CLIPSHAM: L OE with O Scand influence. 'The hām (homestead) of *Cylp*, an Anglo-Saxon whose name is from O Scand *Kylp* 'sturdy''.

CLITHEROE, CLUDERAY: L O Scand *kilthra* + ON *haugra* 'hill with song thrushes'. (Lancs) 12th cent.

CLODE: O ME *clodde* 'clod of earth'. Metonymic for a clodder (harrower). 12th cent.

CLOGG: O ME *clogge*. Metonymic for a maker of clogs. 14th cent.

CLOSE, CLOSS: (i) L OF *clos* 'enclosure'. 13th cent. (ii) N ME *clos* 'reticent, discreet, secret'. 13th cent.

CLOTHIER: O OE *clāth* 'cloth, covering'. 'A maker/seller of cloth'. 13th cent.

CLOUD(S): L OE *clūd* 'rock', here meaning 'hill'. (Som) 12th cent.

CLOUGH, CLEUGH, CLUFF, CLOW, CLEWES, CLEWS, CLUE: L OE *clōh* 'ravine with a river'. 13th cent. [A First Fleet, convict, surname].

CLOUSTON: L ON *Klostathr*. An Orkney surname. 15th cent.

CLOUT, CLOUTER: O OE *clūt* 'patch, clout'. 'A clouter, patcher'. 13th cent.

CLOWSE, CLUSE: O OE *clūse* 'dam, sluice' 'keeper of the flood-gate'. 13th cent.

CLUBB: O ME *clubbe*. Metonymic for a maker of clubs. 12th cent.

CLUCAS: P SG *MacLucais* 'son of *Lucas*'. 16th cent.

CLUNES, CLUNIES: L SG From Clunes (Inverness, Perths) Scotland.

CLUNIE, CLUNEY, CLUNY: L OF From Cluny (Saône-et-Loire) France. DB.

CLUTTERBUCK: Origin uncertain. Probably one of the Flemish weavers who responded to the invitation of Edward III to establish the English weaving industry.

CLUTTON: L OE *clūd-tūn* 'farm by the hill'. (Ches).

CLYMO see CLEMO.

CLYNE(S), CLINE(S): L SG From Clyne (Sutherland). 14th cent.

COAD(E) see CODE. **COALES** see COLE. **COAT(S)**, COATE(S) see COTE.

COBB(E): (i) N Dial. *cobba* 'important, notable'. (ii) L OE *cobb* 'a rounded mass' (e.g., the Cobb, Lyme Regis, a massive breakwater sheltering the port). 13th cent. (iii) P A short form of *Jacob*. 13th cent.

COBBALD, CUTBILL: P OE *Cūthbeald* 'famous bold'. DB.

COBBY: N Dial. A nickname from the horse 'brisk, lively'.

COBDEN: L OE *cobb-dūn* 'knob' (top of hill).

COBHAM: L OE 'The *hamm* (water-meadow) of *Cobba*'. (Kent, Surrey) 12th cent.

COBLEY: L OE 'The *lēah* of an Anglo-Saxon called *Cobba*'. (Devon).

COCHRAN(E), COCKRAN(E), COLQUERAN: L Brit From Cochrane (Renfrews). 13th cent. [Mary Cockran, a convict, arrived with the First Fleet 1788].

COCK(S), COX: (i) N OE *cocc* 'wild bird', applied to scullions, pert lads, and apprentices. (ii) L a sign name. (iii) An affectionate term attached to a first name. [Joseph Cox, a marine drummer, and two male convicts, brought the variant Cox to Australia 1788].

COCKBAIN(E): N OE *cocc-bān* 'cock-bone' (strutting like a cock due to a deformity). COCKBILL: N OE *cocc-bile* 'cock-bill', 'beaky nose'. 14th cent.

COCKBURN, COBURN: L OE 'The *burna* (stream) of *Cocca*'.

COCKELL, COCKLE: (i) O OF *cokille* 'cockle' 'a gatherer/hawker of cockles'. (ii) N OF *coquille* 'shell'. Nickname for a pilgrim bedecked with shells, proclaiming his piety. 12th cent. (iii) O OF *coquillier* 'a maker of women's head coverings from *fabricant de coquilles*'. 13th cent.

COCKER: (i) L Brit river-name. (ii) O ME *coke* '(hay) cock', 'a haymaker'.

COCKERELL, COCKERILL: O OF *cocherell* 'a poultry dealer'. 12th cent.

COCKIN, COCKETT: O ME Metonymic for a baker of *cockin, cocket-bread*, an inferior loaf. 13th cent.

COCKING: L OE 'People of *Cocca*, an Anglo-Saxon'. (Sussex) 14th cent.

COCKMAN, COOKMAN: O OE *cōcmann* 'the cook's servant'. 13th cent.

COCKCROFT: L OE *cocc-croft* 'small holding frequented by birds'. 13th cent.

COCKSEDGE, COXSEDGE: L OE *cocc-secg* 'sedge (rushes, reeds) frequented by birds'.

COCKSHED, COXHEAD: N OE *cocc-hēafod* 'cock's head' (cock's comb or bird-brain). 13th cent.

COCKSHOTT, COCKSHOOT, COCKSHUTT: O OE *coccsȳte* 'nets to trap woodcock'. 'A catcher of woodcocks'. 13th cent. Shakespeare used *cockshut* for twilight.

CODD: N OE *codd* 'bag', used also of belly and scrotum. Cod-piece, a baggy piece worn in front of tight hose; perhaps for the wearer.

CODE, COAD: N ME *code* 'cobbler's wax', nickname for a cobbler. 12th cent.

CODLIN(G), QUADLING, QUODLING, GURLING: (i) O OE Metonymic for a seller of codlings (young cod). (ii) O OF *coeur-de-lion*. Metonymic for a grower or seller of 'lion-heart' apples. 13th cent.

CODRINGTON: L OE 'The *tūn* (farm) of *Cūphere*'. (Glos).

CODY, CODEY, COADY: P Ir *MacOda* 'son of *Oda*'. 13th cent.

COE: N ON *ka*, ME *co* 'jackdaw'. 12th cent.

COFFEY: P Ir *O Cobhthaigh*, name of three septs.

COFFIN, COFFEN: O OF *coffin*. Metonymic for a maker of small containers, baskets, coffins. [The name was brought to Australia by John Coffin, a negro servant and a convict in 1788].

COGAN, COGGAN, COGGIN(S), GOGAN, GOGGIN: P OW From Cogan (Glamorgan). 12th cent. The surname is Irish as well as Welsh; Richard *de Clare*, Earl of Pembroke, nicknamed 'Strongbow', mounted an expedition to assist *Dermot*, king of Leinster, and was accompanied by a *Cogan*, who settled the name there. *Gogan* and *Goggin* are Irish forms.

COGGER: O ME *cogge* 'shipman, master of a cock-boat'. 12th cent.

COGHLAN see COUGHLAN.

COHEN, CAHN: O Hebrew *kohen* 'priest'. Normally a Jewish surname but in Ireland also a variant of Coen.

COKER: L Brit *kukro* 'crooked river'. (Som).

COLBAN: P O Scand *Kolbeinn*. DB.

COLBERT: P OG *Colbert*. DB.

COLBORN(E), COLBOURNE(E), COLBURN(E): L OE *cōl-burne* 'cool stream'. 12th cent.

COLBRAN, COLBRON: P ON *Kolbrandr*. DB.

COLBY, COLBEY, COLEBY: L ON 'The *bŷr* (farm) of *Koli*, a Norseman'. (Norfolk, Lincs) 12th cent.

COLCLOUGH: L OE *ceald-clōh* 'cold clough (ravine)'.

COLDBECK, COLBECK, COULBECK: L OE *ceald* + ON *bekkr* 'cold brook'. 14th cent.

COLDHAM: L OE *ceald-hām* 'cold homestead'. (Cambs) COLDWELL: L OE *ceald-wielle* 'cold spring'. (Northumb).

COLE(S), COALES: P OE *Cola*, a pers. name from OE *col* 'swarthy'. DB.

COLEBROOK: L OE *cōl-burne* 'cool-stream'. (Devon) 12th cent.

COLEMAN, COLMAN, COULMAN: (i) P OG *Colman*. DB. (ii) P Ir *Colman, O Colmain*, from *colm* 'dove', taken to England by the Vikings. [A First Fleet (convict) surname].

COLEPITTS: O OE *col-pytt* 'a charcoal burner'. [Ann Colepitts, a convict, arrived in Australia with the First Fleet 1788].

COLERIDGE: L OE *col-hrycg* 'ridge of the charcoal burners'.

COLESON, COLSON, COULSON, COULSEN: 'Son of: (i) O Dan *Kol* or ON *Koli*, (ii) OE *Cola* (see Cole), (iii) *Coll* (*Nicholas*). 11th, 12th, 14th cent.

COLHOUN see COLQUHOUN.

COLIN: P SG *Gaileau* 'a youth'. 14th cent.

COLL(S), COULL(S), COWL, COWLES: (i) P O Scand *Koll*. DB. (ii) P Ir *MacColla*, abbreviated to Coll. (iii) P A dim. of *Nicholas*. 13th cent.

COLLAR, COLLER, COLLA: O OE A variant of *Collier*. 14th cent.

COLLARD: P A pet-form of *Nicholas*. 13th cent.

COLLEDGE, COLLIDGE: L OE *col-wīc* 'the charcoal burners' dairy farm'. (Notts, Staffs) 13th cent.

COLLET(T), COLLETE: P A dim. of *Col* (*Nicholas*). 12th cent.

COLLEY, COLLIE: N OE *colig* 'coaly', 'swarthy or dark-haired'. 13th cent. [Elizabeth and Richard Colley, convicts, brought the name to Australia 1788].

COLLICK: L OE *col-wīc*. Identical in meaning with Colledge. 12th cent.

COLLIER, COLLYER, COLYER: O OE *col* 'coal'. 'A charcoal burner/seller'. 12th cent.

COLLIN(S), COLLEN(S), COLLYNS: P A dim. of *Col* (*Nicholas*). 12th cent. [David Collins, judge-advocate and lieutenant-governor of the first settlement at N.S.W., his brother William, second-lieutenant on the *Sirius*, and Joseph Collins, a convict, brought the name to Australia 1788].

COLLING(E), COLLINGS, COWLING: P ON *Kollungr*. DB.

COLLINGRIDGE: L OE 'The *hrycg* (ridge) of *Cola*'.

COLLINGWOOD: L ONF *calenge* + OE *wudu* 'the wood of disputed ownership'. (Staffs) 14th cent.

COLLIS, COLLESS: P 'Son of *Col* (*Nicholas*)'.

COLLISHAW see COWLISHAW. COLLISTER see CALLISTER.

COLLOP: N ME *colhope* 'a tasty dish of fried eggs and bacon', especially popular on Collop Monday, before Shrove Tuesday. Nickname for the *colhope* fryer. 13th cent.

COLMAN see COLEMAN.

COLQUERAN: A variant of *Cochran*.

COLQUHOUN, COLHOUN: L SG From the lands of Colquhoun (Dumbartonshire). 13th cent. Founder of the clan was Sir Robert *Colquhoun* (14th cent.) who married the heiress of Humphrey de Luss and became lord of both Colquhoun and Luss. Colhoun is the Ulster form.

COLSTON, COULSTON: L ON 'The *tūn* (farm) of a Norseman called *Kol*'. (Notts, Wilts) 12th cent.

COLTARD, COULTARD: O OE *colt-hierde* 'a colt herd'. 13th cent.

COLTER: O OE *colt* 'a colt-keeper'. 13th cent. COLTMAN: Identical in meaning with Colter. 14th cent.

COLVILL(E): L OF From Colleville (Seine Inférieure) France. DB.

COLVIN: P OW *Coluin*. DB.

COLWELL, COLWILL: L OE *cōl-wielle* 'cool stream'. (Northumb).

COLYER see COLLIER.

COMB(S): L OE *camb* 'crest (of hill)'. (Derbys).

COMBE, COOM, COOMBES, COOMBS: L OE *cumb* 'narrow valley'. 12th cent.

COMBER, COOMER: L OE *cumb* 'valley dweller'. 13th cent.

COMER see CAMBER.

COMERFORD: L OE 'The ford of an Anglo-Saxon called *Cumbra*'. (Staffs), *Cumbreford* 12th cent.

COMFORT, COMPORT: N OF *cunfort*, ME *cumfort* 'succour, support'. 13th cent.

COMLEY: L OE *cumb-lēah* 'clearing or glade in a valley'.

COMIN, COMMIN(S) see CUMMING.

COMMANDER: O OF *comandeor* 'officer in charge of a commandery', esp. in religious military orders such as Knights Templars. 12th cent.

COMPTON: L OE *cumb-tūn* 'farm in a narrow valley'. 13th cent.

COMYN(S) see CUMMINGS.

CONAN, CONEN: P O Bret *Conan*, name of a Breton saint and of several kings of Brittany, introduced into England at the Norman Conquest.

CONDER, CONDOR: L OW *cam-dwfr* 'crooked stream'. 13th cent.

CONDIE, CONDY, CUNDEY, CUNDY: L OF From Condé (Nord, Oise, Orne) France. 12th cent.

CONDON: P Ir *Condún*, from OF. A Norman name, originally *de Caunteton* 'from Caunteton (Normandy)'. The barony of Condon (Co. Cork) is named from the Norman family.

CONDUIT, CONDY, CUNDICT, CUNDY: L OF & ME *conduit* 'water-pipe'. 14th cent.

CONEY, CONY: O ME *cony* 'dealer in rabbit skins'. 13th cent.

CONGREAVE: L OE *graefe* + *cumb* 'grove in a valley'. (Staffs) 12th cent.

CONINGSBY: L O Scand *kunungsbȳr* 'king's farm'. (Lincs).

CONNELL see O'CONNELL.

CONNELLAN, CONLAN, CONLON: P Ir *O Conalláin*. Conlan has partly absorbed *Quinlan*.

CONNER: O OE *cunnian* 'investigate'. 'An ale-conner, inspector'. 13th cent.

CONNING: N AF *coning* 'rabbit'. 13th cent.

CONNOLLY, O'CONNOLLY, CONNELLY: P Ir *O Conghaile*, from *Conall*. [William Connolly, a convict, arrived with the First Fleet 1788].

CONNOR, MACCONNER, O'CONNOR: P Ir *Mac* or *O' Conchobhair* 'son/descendant of *Connor*'. The last king of Ireland was of the Connacht *O Conor Don*. [The name was brought to Australia in 1788 by Martin Connor, a private, and Cornelius Connor, a convict].

CONQUEROR: N Lat *conquestor*, OF *conquerant* 'conqueror'. The most illustrious of nicknames and one of those given to William of Normandy. The other was 'The Tanner's Bastard'. DB.

CONQUEST: N OF *conquete* 'conquest'. Nickname for a triumphant warrior or a squire of dames.

CONROY: P Ir (i) *Mac Conraoi* (Cos. Galway and Clare). (ii) *O'Conraoi* (Galway).

CONSIDINE: P Ir *MacConsaidin*, a branch of the *O'Briens*. Also 'son of *Constantine*'. [Dennis Considen (probably an unrecorded variant of the name) arrived on the *Sirius* in 1788 and was an assistant surgeon to the colony].

CONSTABLE: O OF *conestable* 'count of the stable'. 12th cent.

CONSTANCE, CUSTANCE: (i) P OF *Constance* 'constancy'. DB. (ii) L OF From Coutances (Normandy). 12th cent.

CONSTANT: N OF *constant* 'steadfast, resolute'. 12th cent.

CONSTANTINE: P Lat *Constantinus*, with the same qualities as *Constant*. DB. (Name of the first Christian Emperor of the Roman Empire, 4th cent.)

CONSTERDINE: P Ultimately from *Constantine*. Used in Ireland as a variant of *Considine*.

CONTE: O or N OF *conte* 'count'. Usually a medieval pageant name. 13th cent.

CONVILLE, MACCONVILLE, CONWELL: P Ir *MacConmhaoil*, an Oriel sept.

CONWAY: (i) L OW From Conway (Caernarvon). 13th cent. (ii) P Ir Anglicised form of *MacConnhaig*. [A First Fleet (crew) surname].

CONYNGHAM see CUNNINGHAM.

CONYBEARE: L ME *cony* + OE *beorgan* 'rabbit burrow'.

CONYER: O OF *coignier* 'minter, authorised coiner of money'. 14th cent.

CONYERS: L OF From Coignieres (Seine-et-Oise) or Cogners (Sarthe) France. 12th cent.

COOGAN: P Ir *O Cuagain*, a sept of the Ui Maine (Galway, Roscommon).

COOK(E): O OE *cōc* 'cook', 'a cook/seller of cooked meats'. DB. See also Kew. [James Cook, Yorkshire sea captain, explorer, navigator and surveyor of genius, in 1769 charted the entire coastline of New Zealand, and discovered and charted the eastern coast of Australia. Cook is also a First Fleet surname]. COOKMAN see COCKMAN.

COOKSEY: L OE 'The *īeg* (island) of an Anglo-Saxon called *Cucu*'. (Worces).

COOKSLEY: L OE '*Cucu's lēah* (glade)'.

COOLEY: P Ir An Ulster variant of *Cowley* or *Colley*.

COOMBS, COOMBES see COMBE. COOMBER, COOMER see COMBER.

COONEY: P Ir *O Cuana*, from *cuan* 'elegant'.

COOPER, COPPER, COUPER, COWPER: O ME *couper* 'a maker of wooden casks'. 12th cent. [A First Fleet (crew and convict) surname].

COOTE(S), COOTS: N ME *coote* 'coot, diving bird', 'bald as a coot'. 12th cent.

COPE see CAPE.

COPELAND, COUPLAND, COPLAND: L ON *kaupland* 'bought land'. 12th cent.

[Benjamin Copeland, a marine, brought the name to Australia 1788].

COPEMAN, COOPMAN: O ON *kaupmathr* 'chapman, merchant'. 12th cent.

COPLEY: L OE *cop-lēah* 'hilltop clearing'.

COPP: L OE *cop* 'top, summit', 'hilltop'. (Lancs) 13th cent.

COPPARD: N OE *cop* + OF suffix *-ard* 'big-head'. 14th cent.

COPPELL see CUPPLES.

COPPER: O OE *coper* 'copper', 'a worker in copper'. 13th cent. See also Cooper.

COPPERTHWAITE, COPPERWHEAT: L ME *couper* + ON *thwaite* 'the coopers' clearing'.

COPPIN(S), COPPEN: P A pet-form of *Jacob*. 12th cent.

COPPING: (i) L OE A derivative of *copp* 'hilltop'. 12th cent. (ii) N From the same source, either 'big-head' or 'topknot'.

COPPLESTONE: L OE *cople-stān* 'logan stone'. (Devon, Suffolk).

COPSEY: P ON *Kupsi*, a Norse pers. name. DB.

CORB: N OF *corb* 'raven', 'black-haired' or 'raucous'. 13th cent.

CORBELL: O OF *corbeillier* 'a basket-maker'. 12th cent.

CORBET(T), CORBITT: N OF *corbet* 'raven'. See Corb for meaning. DB.

CORBIN, CORBEN, CORBYN: (i) L OF From Corbon (Normandy). DB. (ii) N OF *corbin*, from *corb* 'raven', 'black-haired'.

CORBY: L Ir + ON 'The *býr* (farm) of an Irishman called *Corc*'. (Lincs).

CORCORAN, CORKAN: N Ir *Mac* or *O'Corcrain*, from *corcair* 'purple (of complexion)'. 11th cent.

CORDELL: O OF *cordele* 'a maker of cords'. 13th cent.

CORDEN, CORDON: O OF *cordoan* 'Sp leather from Cordoba'. Metonymic for a *cordner* or *cordwainer*, 'worker in *Cordova* leather'. 13th cent.

CORDEROY, CORDUROY, CORDERY, CORDREY: (i) N OF *coeur-de-roi* '(having the) heart of a king'. (ii) O OF *corderie* 'rope-walk', 'worker at the ropery'. 13th cent.

CORDNER, CODNER: O OF *cordoanier* 'cordwainer', 'leather-worker'. 11th cent.

CORDWELL see CALDWELL.

CORFE: L OF *corf* 'the pass'. (Dorset, Som) 12th cent.

CORK(E), CORCK: O Sp *alcorque*, ME *cork*. Metonymic for a corker. 13th cent.

CORKER: O (i) 'a seller of dye made from cork'. (ii) 'a cork-dyer of cloth'.

CORKERY, CORCKERY: P Ir *O Corcra*, from *corcair* 'purple'.

CORKHILL, CORKILL: P Manx contraction of Gaelic *MacCorkell* or *MacCorquodale* 'son of *Thorketill*'. 15th cent.

CORLETT: P Manx contraction of Gaelic *MacThorliotr*, from ON *Thorliotr* 'Thor-people'. 15th cent.

CORMACK, CORMICK, MACCORMACK, MACCORMICK: P Ir *MacCormaic*, 'son of the chariot'. Cormick, MacCormick are Ulster forms, some of Scottish origin, a branch of the clan Buchanan-MacCormick of MacLaine.

CORMELL: L OF From Cormeilles (Normandy). DB.

CORNELIUS: Lat *cōrnu* 'horn': (i) 'a horn (trumpet)', (ii) 'crest of a helmet', (iii) 'end of a core for rolled books'. Probably the Roman *gens* (people) who bore this name derived it from *cōrnu*. The name entered England from the low countries and is 15th cent.

CORNELL: (i) L A variant of *Cornhill* or *Cornwall* (see those entries). (ii) N OF *corneille* 'crow', a nickname for a chatterer. 12th cent.

CORNELLY: L Cornish '(church of) St *Cornelius*'.

CORNER: O OF *corneor* 'hornblower', 'player on the corn'. 13th cent.

CORNET(T): O OF *cornet* 'player on the cornet (wind instrument made of horn)'. 12th cent.

CORNEY: L OE *corn-īeg* 'corn-island'. (Herts, Cumb) 13th cent.

CORNFORD, CORNFORTH: L OE *cran*, *cron* 'cranes' ford'. (Durham) 13th cent.

CORNHILL: L OE *corn-hyll* 'hill where corn is sold'. (London, Northumb) 12th cent.

CORNISH, CORNES: L ME 'from Cornwall'. 13th cent. CORNWALL: L Brit tribal name *Cornōvii* giving *Cornāvia*. Surname 13th cent.

CORNWALLIS: L Norman form 'From Cornwall'. 13th cent.

CORNWELL: L OE *cran-wielle* 'cranes' stream'. (Oxon) 12th cent.

CORP(E): N ON *korpr* (North and North-east England), OF *corp* (Southern England) 'raven' for black hair or dark complexion. 12th cent.

CORR: P Ir *O Corra*, from *corr* 'spear'. An Ulster surname.

CORRAN, CORRIN: P Manx contraction of Ir *MacOdhrain*. 15th cent.

CORRICK: N Cornish, O Bret, OW *corrach* 'elf, pygmy'.

CORRIGAN: P Ir *O Corragáin*. Kin to the *Maguires*.

CORRY, CORRIE: P Ir *Mac Gothraidh* 'son of *Godfrey*'. A branch of the *Maguires*.

CORSER: O ME *corser* 'horse-dealer'. 13th cent.

CORSON see CURZON. CORTES, CORTIS see CURTIS.

CORY: P ON pers. name *Kori*. 13th cent.

COSGRAVE, COSGROVE: (i) P Ir *Mac* & *O Coscraigh* 'victorious'. (ii) L OE '*Cof's graefe* (grove)'. (Northants).

COSH, COYSH: L ME *cosshe* 'hovel, hut, small cottage'. 13th cent.

COSIN, COSYN see COUSEN.

COSSAR, COSSER: O ME *cosser* 'horse-corser, broker'. 13th cent.

COSSINS, COSSONS see COUSEN.

COSTAIN, COSTEN: (i) P A variant of *Constantine*. 12th cent. (ii) P Ir *MacOistin* (*Augustin*). (iii) P Manx *MacAugustin* abbr. to *MacCosten*.

COSTE, COSTA: P A short form of *Constantine*. 12th cent.

COSTELLO(E): P Ir *MacOisdealbhaig*. Irish form of Norman name originally *de Angulos*, becoming *Nangle* in Connacht and Leinster.

COSTERMAN: O OF *coste*, from Lat *costa* 'rib'. *Costard* 'a ribbed apple'. 'A fruit hawker', originally *costard-monger*, whence 'coster-monger'. 16th cent.

COSTIGAN: P Ir *MacOistigin*, a branch of the Fitzpatricks of Ossory.

COSTIN(S), COSTON(S): P Short form of *Constantine*. 13th cent.

COTE(S), COAT(S), COATE(S), COATTES, COTTIS: L OE *cot, cote* 'cottage', OE *cotsetla* 'a cottager', OE *cotlif* also 'a manor'. 12th cent.

COTGREAVE: L OE *cota-graefe* 'grove with cots (cottages)'. (Derbys) 12th cent. COTMAN: L OE *cot-mann* 'a cottager'. 12th cent. COTON, COTTAM, COTTOM, COTTEN, COTTON(E): L OE *aet-cotum* 'at cottages'. 12th cent. See also Cotton.

COTTEL(L), COTTLE, CUTTELL, CUTTLE: (i) O OF *cotel* 'coat of mail'. Metonymic for a maker of mail. 11th cent. (ii) O OF *coutel* 'dagger, small knife'. Metonymic for a cutler. (iii) P Ir *O Coitil*, from a Norse pers. name, preserved in Cottlestown, Co. Sligo.

COTTER, COTTIER: O OF *cotarius* 'villein holding a cot by labour service'. DB.

COTTERAL(L), COTTERELL, COTTER-ILL, COTTRILL, COTRELL: L OF *coterel*, a dim. of *cotier* 'cottager'. 12th cent. [Thomas Cotrell, a marine, brought the name to Australia 1788].

COTTON: L OE 'The *tūn* (farm) of *Coda*, an Anglo-Saxon'. (Derbys).

COUCH(E): O OF *couch*. Metonymic for coucher. 13th cent. COUCHER, COWCHER: O AF *coucheour* 'a maker of couches, beds, pallets'. 13th cent.

COUCHMAN: Identical in meaning with Coucher. 14th cent.

COUGHLAN, COUGHLIN, COGHLAN: P Ir *Mac/O' Cochláin*, from *cochal* 'hood'.

COUL see COLL. COULBECK see COLDBECK. COULDWELL see CALDWELL. COULING see COWLING. COULMAN see COLEMAN. COULSON, COULSEN see COLESON. COULSTON see COLSTON.

COULTAS, COULTON, COULTIS, COWTAS: O OE *colt-hūs* 'colt-house'. 'A colt-keeper'. 16th cent.

COULTHARD, COULTART see COLTARD. COULTON see COLTON.

COUNSEL, COUNCIL, COUNSEL(L): O OF *conseil*, AF *counseil* 'consultation'. 'A counsellor, adviser'. 13th cent.

COUNTER: O OF *conteor*, AF *countour* 'accountant, treasurer'. 13th cent.

COUPER see COOPER. COUPLAND see COPELAND.

COURAGE: N OF *curage* 'heart, spirit, courage'. 13th cent.

COURT(E), CORTE, CURT: N OF *curt* 'short, small of stature'. 13th cent.

COURTALD, COURTAULD: N OF A dim. of *curt*. A Huguenot surname.

COURTENAY, COURTENEY, COURT-NEY: L OF From Courtenay (Loiret) France. 12th cent.

COURTICE, COURTIS see CURTIS.

COURTIER: O ME A derivative of ME *curt*, rather than ME *courteour*, a worker at the court, rather than one who courts and flatters. 13th cent.

COURTMAN: O ME *curt-mann* 'a worker at the court', which may be castle or manor-house. 13th cent.

COUSE: N ON *Kausi* (tom-cat), a Norse nickname established in Yorkshire. 12th cent. *Kausi* gave his name to Cowesby (Yorks).

COUSEN(S), COUSIN(S), COUZENS, COSSIN(S), COSSONS, COZENS, COZINS, CUSSEN(S): N OF *cusin*, ME *cousin* 'kinsman, kinswoman, a blood relative'. 12th cent.

COVE: L OE *cofa* 'cave, den, recess, valley'. (Devon, Hants).

COVENTRY: L OE 'The tree of *Cofa*, an Anglo-Saxon'. (Warwicks) 12th cent. [James Coventry, a seaman, brought the name to Australia 1788].

COVER: (i) O OF *cuvier* 'a cooper'. 13th cent. (ii) O OF *couvreor* 'a roofer, tiler'. 11th cent.

COVERDALE: L Brit river-name + OE *dael* 'valley'. (Yorks) 13th cent. (In 1537, Miles Coverdale published the first translation of the Bible in English, overcoming stiff opposition from those who wished to preserve it only in Latin.)

COWAN see MACOWEN.

COWARD: O OE *cuhyrde* 'cow-herd'. 12th cent. [A First Fleet surname].

COWCHER see COUCHER.

COWDREY, COWDRY, COWDROY, COWDEROY, COWDERY: L OF *coudraie* 'hazel-copse'. From Coudrai (Seine Inférieure) or Coudray (Eure) France. 12th cent.

COWELL: L OE *cū-hyll* 'cow-hill'. (Glos).

COWGILL: L ON 'The *gil* (deep glen) of a Norseman called *Kalli*'. (Yorks).

COWIE: L SG *colldha* 'hazel'. (Stirling) Scotland. 14th cent.

COWL, COWLES see COLL.

COWLER: O OE *cūle* 'a monk's cowl'. 'A maker of cowls'. 14th cent.

COWLEY: L OE *cū-leah* 'cow-pasture'. 12th cent.

COWLING, COULING: L OE *coll*, an Anglo-Saxon hill name. (Yorks) 13th cent.

COWLISHAW, COLLISHAW: L OE *col-scaga* 'The shaw (copse) used for charcoal-burning'. (Derbys, Lancs) 17th cent.

COWPE: L OE *cū-hop* 'cow valley'. (Lancs).

COWPER see COOPER.

COWSLADE: L OE *cū* + Dial. *slade* 'dell with cows'.

COX see COCK.

COXON, COXEN: N OE 'Son of *Cock*'. 14th cent.

COY, COEY: N OF *quei, coi* 'quiet, coy, shy'. 12th cent.

COYLE: P Ir *Mac Giolla Chomgaill* 'devotee of St *Comgal*'.

COYNE: (i) O AF *coigne*, ME *coyn* 'a die for stamping coins'. Metonymic for a coiner or minter. 13th cent. (ii) P Ir *O Cadhain* 'wild goose'. (Wild goose, a term applied to Irish exiles in 17th cent, who accepted service with European armies.)

COYSH see COSH. COZENS, COZINS see COUSEN.

CRABB(E), KRABBE: N OE *crabba* 'crab': (i) for the man with a crab-like gait, (ii) for the crabbed, ill-tempered one. 12th cent.

CRABTREE: L ME *crab-apple*, perhaps from O Sw *skrabba* 'wild-apple'. 'Wild apple tree'. 13th cent. A Yorkshire surname.

CRACKNELL: L OE 'The *halh* (nook) frequented by water-crakes'. (Yorks) 12th cent.

CRADDOCK, CRADDUCK, CRADOCK, CRADICK: P Brit & OW. A famous Welsh name and a rare survival of a Brit pers. name: *Caradoc*, chief of the Brit tribe *Catuvellauni*, known to the Romans as *Caratacus*. Surname 12th cent.

CRAFT(S): (i) N OE *craeft*, a word of several meanings: 'skill, art', 'guile, cunning'. (ii) L OE *craeft* 'machine, engine, probably water-mill'. (Herefords, Leices, Lincs, Yorks) 12th cent.

CRAGG(S): L SG & OW *creag* 'steep rough rock'. 12th cent. CRAIG: Scots and Northumb form of Cragg. 12th cent. CRAIGIE: L SG Same derivation. (Ayrs, Angus, Lothian, Perths) 14th cent.

CRAIN(E): P Manx contraction of Ir *MacCiarain*. 15th cent.

CRAKEBONE: N OE *cracian-bān* 'crack-bone'. Nickname for the merciless official who executed this fiendish punishment of medieval law. *Piers Plowman*: 'Quikliche came a cachepol and craked a-two here legges'. 13th cent.

CRAMER see CREAMER.

CRAMP: N OHG *chramph* 'curved, a hook', 'hook-nose'. 12th cent.

CRAMPTON see CROMPTON.

CRANAGE: L OE *crāwena-laecc* 'crows' stream'. (Ches) CRANDON: L OE *cran-dūn* 'cranes' hill'. (Som) CRANFIELD: L OE *cranuc-feld* 'open country with cranes'. (Beds) CRANFORD: L OE *cranuc-ford* 'cranes' ford'.

CRANE, CRAN: N OE *cran* 'crane', 'long-legs'. 12th cent.

CRANK, CRONK: N ME *cranke* 'lusty, vigorous, merry'. 12th cent.

CRANKSHAW, CRANSHAW, CRONKSHAW, CRONSHAW: L OE *cranuc-wudu* 'cranes' wood'. (Lancs) 15th cent. CRANLEY: L OE *cran-lēah* 'cranes' clearing'.

CRANMER: L OE *cran-mere* 'cranes' pool or spring'. (Salop, Som).

CRANSTON(E), CRANSTOUN: L OE *cran-tūn* 'the *tūn* (farm) frequented by cranes'. Mainly a Scottish surname.

CRAPPER see CROPPER.

CRASKE: N OF *cras* 'gross, fat'. 12th cent. CRASS, CRAZE: N OF *cras* 'gross'. DB.

CRASSWELL, CRASWELL see CARSWELL.

CRAUFORD, CRAWFORD: L OE *crāwena-ford* 'crows' ford'. (Lanarks, Dorset, Lancs) 12th cent.

CRAVEN: L OW *craf* '(wild) garlic'. 12th cent. Place-name Craven (Yorks) was *Crave* in DB. No connection with faint-hearted. [James Craven, a sailor on the *Friendship*, brought the name to Australia 1788].

CRAWCOUR, CRAKER, CROAKER, CROKER, CROCKER: (i) L OF From Crevecoeur (Normandy). 12th cent. (ii) N OF *creve-coer* 'a philanderer'.

CRAWLEY, CROWLEY: L OE *crāwe-lēah* 'crows' clearing'. 12th cent.

CRAWSHAW, CRAWSHAY, CROSHAW, CROWSHER: L OE *crāwe-scaga* 'crows' wood'.

CREAGH: N Ir *Creaobhach*, from *craobg* 'branch'. The valiant Creaghs carried branches of trees into battle with the Norsemen.

CREAMER, CRAMER: O OF *cresme* 'cream', ME *creme*. 'A pedlar of cream and oil'. In Ireland, a corruption of MacCreanor. [A First Fleet (convict) surname].

CREAN, CREHAN: P Ir *O Croidheain*, from *croidhe* 'heart'.

CREASE, CREES(E): N OE *crēas* 'fine, elegant'. 11th cent.

CRECY, CRESSY: L OF from Cressy (Seine Inférieure) France. 12th cent.

CREECH: L Brit *crūc*, OW *crug* 'hill'. (Dorset, Som) 14th cent.

CREED: P OE *Creoda*, an Anglo-Saxon pers. name. 12th cent.

CREEK, CREAK: L Du *kreek*, ON *kriki*, ME *crike* 'creek, stream', a word familiar to Chaucer: 'He knew every creek in Britaigne and in Spayne'. Surname 14th cent. [A First Fleet (convict) surname].

CREIGHTON: L OW *creigiog* 'rocky place'. (Staffs) 14th cent.

CRELLIN: P Manx form of *MacRaghnaill*, from ON *Rognvaldr* 'ruler of the gods', name of several kings of Isle of Man and of king of Dublin 1075.

CREMIN, CREMEN: P Ir *O Cruimin*, from *crom* 'bent'. A branch of the *MacCarthys*.

CRERAR: O SG *criathrar* 'a sifter or sievewright'. 16th cent.

CRESSWELL see CARSWELL.

CRESWICK: L OE *caerse-wīc* 'dairy farm where water-cress grows'.

CREWE: L OW *cryw* 'weir, or stepping-stones'. (Ches).

CREWES, CREWS, CRUISE, CRUSE, CRUWYS: N ME *crus* 'bold, fierce'. 13th cent.

CREWTHER see CROWTHER.

CRIBB, CRIBBES: O OE *crib* 'manger'. Metonymic for a cowman. 12th cent.

CRIBBEN, CREBBIN, GRIBBIN, GRIBBON: P Ir *MacRoibin*, 'son of *Robin*'.

CRICH, CRICK: L Brit *crūc* 'hill'. (Derbys, Northants), *Crice* and *Crec* DB.

CRICHTON, CRIGHTON, CHRICHTON, CREIGHTON: L SG + OE 'border-place'. From Crichton (Midlothian). 12th cent.

CRICKETT: L Brit *crūc* 'hill' + OF *et* 'little hill'. (Som).

CRIER, CRYER: O OF, ME *criere* 'a town crier'. 13th cent.

CRISP(E), CHRISP, CRIPS: N OE *crisp* 'curly-haired'. 11th cent.

CRISPIN, CRIPPEN, CRIPPIN: N Lat *crispus* 'curly'. DB.

CRITCHLEY: L Brit *cruc* + OE *lēah* 'wooded hill'.

CRITTENDEN see CRUTTENDEN.

CROCKER, CROKER: O OE *crocca* 'an earthen pot', 'a potter'. 13th cent.

CROCKET(T): N ME *croket* 'a large curl'. A nickname for one who affected this extravagant hairstyle.

CROCKFORD: L OE *crocca-ford* 'potters' ford'.

CROFT(S), CRUFT: L OE 'croft' (piece of arable land). 12th cent.

CROFTON: L OE *cropp-tūn* 'farm by the hill', or *croh-tūn* 'crocus (saffron) farm'.

CROLL see CURL.

CROMB, CROME, CRUMB: O OE *cromb* 'a hook', 'a maker of hooks'. 12th cent.

CROMBIE, CROMIE, CRUMBIE, CRUMMY: L SG *crom* 'crooked'. (Aberdeens) 15th cent.

CROMER: L OE *crāwe-mere* 'crows' lake'. (Norfolk).

CROMPTON, CRAMPTON, CRUMPTON: L OE *crōk-tūn* 'farm at the river-bend'. (Lancs) 13th cent.

CROMWELL: L OE *crumb-wielle* 'winding stream'. (Notts) 12th cent.

CRONAN, CRONE, CRONIN: P Ir *O Cronáin* 'descendant of swarthy'.

CRONK see CRANK. CRONKSHAW see CRANKSHAW.

CROOK(E), CROKE: (i) N ON *krók* 'crook-backed' or 'sly, cunning'. DB. (ii) L ON *krōkr* 'bend or nook'. (Devon, Dorset, Durham, Yorks) 14th cent.

CROOKES, CROOKS: L ME *crōc* 'crook, bend', 'road or river-bend'. (Yorks) 13th cent.

CROOKSHANK see CRUICKSHANK.

CROOM(E), CROOMBES, CROOMBS: L OE *crōh* 'narrow valley' (Yorks), or Brit *Crōmba*, a stream-name (Worces). 12th cent.

CROPPER, CRAPPER: O ME *croppen* 'a cropper, reaper'. 13th cent. [John Crapper, a convict, brought the name to Australia 1788].

CROSBY, CROSBIE, CROSSBEE: L O Scand *krossa-býr* 'village with crosses'. There are eight places called Crosby from Lincs to Kircudbright. 12th cent.

CROSHAW see CRAWSHAW.

CROSIER, CROZIER, CROSER: O OF *crosier* 'bearer of the cross or of the bishop's staff'. 13th cent.

CROSS(E), Du CROSS: L ON *kross*, ME *cruche, crouche, crois* 'cross', 'by the cross'. 13th cent. [A First Fleet (convict) surname].

CROSSLAND, CROSLAND: L ME *crois* 'land by a cross'. (Yorks) 14th cent.

CROSSLEY: L OE *crūc-lēah* 'clearing with a cross'. (Yorks) CROSSMAN: L OE 'by the cross'. 14th cent. CROSTHWAITE: L ON *kross-thwaite* 'meadow or clearing with a cross'. (Cumb, Westmorland, Yorks) 13th cent.

CROSTON: L OE *crūc-tūn* 'town or market cross'. (Lancs).

CROTHER see CROWTHER. CROTHERS see CARRUTHERS.

CROUCH, CRUTCH: L OE *crūc* 'by the cross'. 13th cent. CROUCHER, CRUTCHER: L OE *crūc* 'by the cross'. 13th cent. CROUCHMAN: L OE *crūc-mann* 'by the cross'. 13th cent. (All these surnames were acquired by dwelling by or near a cross.)

CROW(E), CRAW: N OE *crāwe* 'crow', a nickname. 12th cent.

CROWHURST: L OE *crāwe-hyrst* 'crows' wood'. (Surrey, Sussex) 12th cent.

CROWL(E): L OE *crull* 'curly', used in sense of 'winding river'. (Lincs) 12th cent.

CROWLEY see CRAWLEY.

CROWTHER, CROWDER, CROTHER, CREWTHER: O ME *crouth* 'fiddle', 'a fiddler'.

CROXALL: L ON '*Crōc's hall*'. (Staffs) (In 11th cent. *Crōc* was a moneyer to King Canute.)

CROYDEN, CROYDON: L OE *crogen-denu* 'crocus valley'. (Surrey).

CROYLE see KERRELL. CRUDDAS see CARRUTHERS. CRUFT see CROFT.

CRUIKSHANK(S), CROOKSHANK(S): N ON *krōkr* 'hook, bent + OE *sceanca* 'shank' 'crooked leg'. 13th cent.

CRUISE: L OF From Cruys-Straet (Nord) France. 13th cent. See also Crewes.

CRUMBIE see CROMBIE.

CRUMP: N OE *crump* 'bent, crooked, stooping'. 12th cent.

CRUMPTON see CROMPTON.

CRUNDALL: L OE *crundel* 'quarry or chalk-pit'. (Kent, Hants) 13th cent.

CRUSE: N ON *krūs* 'crock', for 'one too fond of the crock (bottle)'. See also Crewes.

CRUST: N OF *crouste* 'crust', 'obstinate, stubborn, hard as a crust'. 12th cent.

CRUTCH: see CROUCH. CRUTCHER see CROUCHER.

CRUTTENDEN, CRITTENDEN: L OE *crūc-denu* 'valley with a cross'. (Kent) 15th cent.

CRUWYS see CREWES. CRYER see CRIER. CRYSTAL see CHRYSTAL.

CUBBIN, CUBBON: P Manx form of SG *Mac Cubbin.*

CUCKOW: N OF *coucou* 'cuckoo'. 12th cent. (The OE name for cuckoo was gēac, which came to mean *gowk* 'fool'.) [A First Fleet (convict) surname].

CUDBIRD see CUTHBERT.

CUDD: P A pet-form of *Cuthbert.* 14th cent.

CUDLIP: N OE *clēofan-lippa* 'cleft lip'.

CUDMORE: L OE *'Cuda's mere* (lake)'.

CUDWORTH: L OE *'Cutha's worth* (homestead)'. (Yorks).

CUE, MACCUE: P Ir A variant of *MacHugh.*

CUERDEN: L OW *cerddin* 'ash-tree'. (Lancs).

CUFF(E): N OF *coif*, ME *cuffe* 'lining of helmet', later, 'head-dress'. Nickname for a wearer of a startling head-dress. 14th cent.

CULF: P OE *Cuthwulf* 'famous wolf'. DB.

CULHAM: L OE 'The *hām* (homestead) with a *cyln* (kiln)'. (Berks).

CULLEN, CULLIN: (i) L OF From Cologne. 13th cent. (ii) L SG From Cullen (Banffs) Scotland. (iii) P Ir *MacCullen*, from *cuileann* 'holly'.

CULLETON: L Brit river-name *Coly* + *tūn* (farm). (Devon).

CULPEPPER: O OF *cueillir* 'to gather, cull', + OE *pipor* 'pepper culler, a spicer'. 14th cent.

CULTER see COULTAR.

CULVER: N OE *culfre* 'dove, pigeon'. A term of endearment or an emblem of innocence. See also Pigeon. CULVERHOUSE: O OE *culfre-hūs.* Metonymic for the keeper of the dovecote. 13th cent. CULVERSTON: L OE *tūn* 'farm frequented by doves or pigeons'. CULVERWELL: L OE *wielle* 'doves' spring'.

CUMBERLAND: L Brit + OE The British kingdom of Strathclyde included present-day Cumberland 'the land of the *Cumbrians* (Britons)', annexed by William II (Rufus). Surname 12th cent.

CUMBERWORTH: L OE 'The *worth* (homestead) of *Cumbra*, an Anglo-Saxon'. (Lincs).

CUMMING(S), COMMONS, COMYN(S), COMMIN(S): (i) L OF From Bosc-Benard-Commin (Normandy) or Commines (Nord). The name, from O Bret *Cunmin*, became *Comyn* in Scotland (see Introduction). (ii) P Ir *O Comain* (Munster), *O Cuimin* (Wexford), becoming Commons in Co. Wexford and Cummings in Co. Cork.

CUNDALL: L OE *cumb* + O Scand *dalr*, both meaning 'valley'. (Yorks).

CUNDEY see CONDUIT, CONDIE. CUNDICT see CONDUIT.

CUNNEEN: P Ir *Mac/O' Coinin*, apparently from *cano* 'wolf-cub'. There are two *O'Cunneen* septs, of Thomond and Offaly. The *Mac Cunneens* are a literary family of Erris.

CUNNINGHAM: L SG from Brit Anglicised form of *Cunegan* 12th cent. From Cunningham (Ayrs) Scotland. Also P Ir *O Cuinneagain.* [A First Fleet (convict and crew) surname. Allan Cunningham, explorer and botanist, came to N.S.W. in 1816].

CUNNINGTON: L O Scand form of OE *Cyningestūn* 'king's manor'. (Cambs).

CUPPLES, COPPELL: L OE *copp-hyll* 'hill with a peak'. 12th cent.

CURD(S): O SG *gruth*, Ir *cruth* 'curd'; ME *curde* 'cheese'. Metonymic for a maker/seller of cheese.

CURL(E), CROLL: N ME *crulle* 'curly (haired)'. CURLING: N ME *crulling* 'the one with curly hair'. 13th cent.

CURLEY: P Ir *Mac Thoridealbhaig*, a variant of the Ulster surname *Turley.*

CURNOW, CURNOE: N Cornish 'the one from Cornwall'.

CURPHEY, CURPHY: P Manx contraction of Ir *MacMurchadha* 'sea-warrior'.

CURR: N ME *curre* 'cur-dog', from O Scand dial. *kurre* 'to grumble'. Nickname for a grumbler. 12th cent.

CURRAN: P Ir *O Corrain*, from *corradh* 'spear'.

CURRANT: O OF *chien courant* 'a hunter'. 12th cent.

CURRIE: L SG From Currie (Lothian), a branch of the clan *MacDonald.* 12th cent.

CURRIER, CURRYER: O OF *coureeur* 'currier, leather-dresser'. 13th cent.

CURRY, CURREY, CURRIE: (i) L Brit river-name (Som). 11th cent. (ii) O OF *curie* 'kitchen'. 'a kitchen-worker'. (Curry, spiced dish, is from Tamil *kari* 'sauce'.) See also Currie.

CURTIN: (i) N OF A dim. of *curt* 'short'. 13th cent. (ii) P Ir *MacCurtin*, a variant of *MacCruitin* 'the hunch-backed'.

CURTIS(S), CURTEIS, CURTICE, CURTIES, CURTHOYS, CURTOIS, CORTES, COURTICE, COURTIS: N OF *corteis, curteis, cortois* 'courteous', a name from the age of chivalry, 'educated', 'of good breeding'. 12th cent. [William Curtis, quartermaster of the *Lady Penhryn*, brought the name to Australia 1788].

CURWEN: L SG From Colvend (Kirkudbrightshire) Scotland. 13th cent.

CURZON, CURSON, CORSON: (i) L OF From Notre Dame-de-Courson (Normandy). DB. (ii) N OF A dim. of *curt* 'short'. 12th cent.

CUSACK: L Ir from OF Originally *de Cussac*, introduced into Ireland by Anglo-Norman settlers in 13th cent.

CUSH, CUSS(E) see KISS.

CUSHING, CUSHION: Variants of *Cousen*. 16th cent.

CUSLEY, CUSLY: L OE 'The *lēah* (clearing) of *Cūthsa*, an Anglo-Saxon'. [Benjamin Cusly, a marine, brought the name to Australia 1788].

CUSS: O OF *cuisse* Metonymic for a maker of thigh armour. 13th cent. See also Kiss. [John Cuss, a convict, brought the name to Australia 1788].

CUSSEN, CUSSON: P 'Son of *Cust*' (*Constance*)'. 14th cent. See also COUSEN.

CUSTANCE see CONSTANCE.

CUSTER: O OF *coustier* 'a maker of feather cushions, pillows'. 13th cent.

CUSWORTH: L OE 'The *worth* (homestead) of *Cūpsa*'. (Yorks) 14th cent.

CUTHBERT, CUDBIRD: P OE *Cūthbeort* 'famous-bright'. 12th cent.

CUTLACK see GOODLAKE.

CUTLER: O OF *coutelier* 'A maker/vendor of cutlery, a cutler'. 13th cent.

CUTT(S): P A pet-form of *Cuthbert*. 12th cent.

CUTTELL, CUTTLE see COTTEL.

CUTTERIDGE, CUTTRISS, GUTTERIDGE, GUTRIDGE: P OE *Cūthric* 'famous ruler'. 12th cent.

D

DABB(S): P OE A form of *Dobb*, dim. of *Robert*. 16th cent. DABINETT: P A double dim. of *Dobb*. 13th cent.

DACK: P OE *Daecca*, an Anglo-Saxon pers. name preserved in Dagenham (*Daecca's* farm) (Essex). 13th cent.

DADE see DEED.

DAFT: N OE *daeft* Originally 'meek, gentle'. In ME *dafft* 'stupid'. 13th cent.

DAFTER see DAUGHTERS.

DAGG: N OF *dague* 'dagger', a dangerous nickname. 13th cent. DAGGAR(D), DAGGER, DAGGETT: N OF Meaning identical with that of Dagg. 13th cent.

DAGLISH see DALGLEISH. DAILLEY see DOYLEY.

DAINES, DAYNE(S), DYNE(S): N OF *deigne* 'haughty' or OF & ME *digne, deyne* 'worthy, honourable'. 12th cent.

DAINTETH, DENTITH: N ME *dainteth* 'dainty'. 14th cent.

DAINTREE, DAINTREY, DAINTRY, DAVENTRY: L OE *Dafa-trēow* 'the tree of an Anglo-Saxon called *Dafa*'. (Northants) 12th cent.

DAINTY, DENTY: N OF *dainte* 'pleasant, attractive'. 12th cent.

DAISH see ASH. DAKIN see DAYKIN.

DALBY: L OE *dael* + ON *býr* 'farm in the dale'. (Leices, Lincs, Yorks).

DALE(S): L OE *dael* 'dale'. 13th cent.

DALEY see DALY.

DALGARNO: L From the lands of Dalgarnoc (Dumfries) Scotland. 15th cent.

DALGETY: L From Dalgety (Fifes, Aberdeens) Scotland. 16th cent.

DALGLEISH, DALGLIESH, DALGLISH, DAGLISH: L From Dalgleish (Selkirks) Scotland. 15th cent.

DALLAS: (i) L SG From the barony of Dallas (Moray) Scotland. 13th cent. (ii) L OE *dael-hūs* 'house in the dale'. (Yorks) 13th cent.

DALLIMORE see DELMAR.

DALLING: L OE *Dallingas* 'the people of an Anglo-Saxon called *Dalla*'. (Norfolk) 12th cent.

DALLY see DALY.

DALRYMPLE: L A Scottish surname from

lands first granted to John Kenedy of Dunure in 1371.

DALTON: L OE *dael-tūn* 'farm in the dale'. 12th cent. [Elizabeth Dalton, a convict, brought the name to Australia 1788].

DALWOOD: L OE *dael-wudu* 'wood in the dale'. (Devon).

DALY, DALEY, DALLY, DALLEY: P Ir *O Dalaigh*, from *dail* 'member of the Assembly'.

DALYELL, DALZELL, DALZIEL: L SG From the barony of Dalziel (Lanarks) Scotland. 13th cent.

DAMANT see DAMMANT.

DAMARY, D'AMERY: L OF From Daumeray (Maine-et-Loire) France. DB.

DAME: N OE *dame* 'lady', an uncomplimentary nickname for a male. 13th cent.

DAMERELL: L OF From Aumale (Normandy). DB. (The name is associated with the title of the dukes of Albermarle.)

DAMMANT, DAMANT: P OE *Daegmund* 'day-protector' or, according to Dauzat, authority on French surnames, L OF 'up-stream in the village'.

DAMPIER: L OF From one of several places in France. 13th cent. [C.E. Dampier arrived in New Zealand on the *Barbara Gordon*, one of the early immigrant ships].

DAMSON: N OF *dame* + OE *sunu* 'The Dame's son'. 12th cent.

DAMYON: P Lat *Damianus* (St *Damianus*, martyred at Cilicia 303). Surname 13th cent.

DANBY: L ON *Danebýr* 'the farm or village of the Danes'. (Yorks) 12th cent.

DANCE: O OF & ME *danser* 'dancer'. 13th cent. DANCER: O A derivative of ME *dancen* 'to dance'. 'A dancer'. 12th cent.

DANCEY, DAUNCEY: L OF *de Anisy*. From Anisy (Calvados) Normandy. DB.

DAND, DANDIE, DANDY: P A pet-form of *Andrew*. 13th cent.

DANDO, DADDOW, DAUNEY, DELANEY, DELANY: L OF From Aunou or Aunay, several places in Normandy. DB. The name is preserved at Compton Dando (Som). The Irish Delaney is *O Dubhshlaine*, from *dubh* 'black'.

DANE(S), DANN: L OE *denu* 'dene or valley'. 13th cent.

DANFORD, DANFORTH: L OE *dierne-ford* 'hidden ford'. (Suffolk) 13th cent.

DANGAR, DANGER: N OF *dangier*, *danger* (i) 'power'. (ii) 'coyness, hesitation'. 13th cent.

DANGERFIELD: L OF From Angerville, several places in France. 12th cent.

DANIEL(S), DANIELL(S): P Hebrew *Daniel* 'God has judged'. DB. [A convict named Daniel Daniels was judged at the Old Bailey and arrived on the *Scarborough* in 1788].

DANSON: P 'Son of *Dand*'. 14th cent.

DANVERS: L OF version of Flemish. From Anvers (Antwerp). 13th cent.

DARBY see DERBY.

DARCEY, DARCY, D'ARCY: (i) L OF From Arcy (Manche) Normandy. DB. (ii) P Ir *O Dorchaidhe*, from *dorcha* 'dark'. There are also descendants of the Norman Darceys in Ireland.

DARE: (i) N OE *dearr* 'dare, venture'. (ii) L Ir *dair* 'oak'.

DARELL see DAYRAL.

DARGAN, O'DARGAN: P Ir *O Deargain*, from *dearg* 'red'. [Peter Dargin (an unrecorded variant), a marine, brought his version of the name to Australia 1788].

DARK(E): N OE *deorc* 'dark', of hair or complexion. 13th cent.

DARLEY: L OE *deor-lēah* 'deer-wood'. (Derbys) 12th cent.

DARLING, DEARLING, DORLING, DURLING: N OE *dēorling* 'darling, dearly beloved' or 'minion' in sense of eldest son on whom rests the future of the family. 11th cent.

DARLINGTON: L OE 'The *tūn* (settlement) of the *ingas* (people) of an Anglo-Saxon called *Dēornōth*'. (Durham), *Dearthingtun* c. 1050.

DARMODY, DERMODY: P Ir *O Diarmada*, anglicised *Dermot*, but distinct from *McDermot*.

DARNELL: (i) N OF *darnel* 'plant once thought to be intoxicating'. Nickname for an addict. 11th cent. (ii) L 'Hidden *halh* (nook)'. (Yorks) 12th cent.

DARRAGH: P Ir *Mac Dubhdara*, a Co. Antrim surname.

DARRELL see DAYRAL.

DARROCH: L SG *darach* 'oak-wood'. (Stirling) Scotland. A branch of the clan *MacDonald*.

DART: L Brit river-name identical with Darwen, Derwent. (Devon) DARWEN, DARWENT, DERWENT: L Brit & OW 'river flowing through oak woods'. 13th cent.

DARTNALL see DURTNALL.

DARWIN: P OE *Dēorwine* 'dear friend'. 12th cent.

DASH see ASH.

DASHWOOD: L OF + OE Originally 'de Ashwood (OE *aesc-wudu*)'.

DAUBENEY: D'AUBNEY: L OF From Aubigny (Normandy). DB.

DAUBER, DAWBER: O OF *daubier* 'dauber, whitewasher' (wattle and daub). 13th cent.

DAUD: P A pet-form of *David*.

DAUGHTERS, DAFTERS, DOCTOR: P OE *dohtor*, ME *doughter* 'daughter'. 14th cent. (Daughter, a kinship surname, has descended from the mother Indo-European language with cogns. Dutch *dochter*, Ger *tochter*,ON *dōtter*, Gothic *dauhtar*, Sanskrit *duhitar*.)

DAUGHTERY, DAUGHTRY see DAWTREY. DAUNAY see DANDO. DAUNCEY see DANCEY.

DAVALL, DEAVILLE, DE VILE, DEVILL(E), DE VILLE, DIVALL, EVILL: (i) L OF From Deville (Normandy). 12th cent. (ii) N OE *deofol* 'devil', a pageant or miracle play name. DB.

DAVENPORT: L Brit river-name (R. Dane) + OE *port* 'harbour, town'. (Ches).

DAVENTRY see DAINTREE.

DAVEY, DAVIE, DAVY: P Pet-form of *David*. 12th cent.

DAVID, DAVITT: P Hebrew *David* originally 'darling', later 'friend'. Patron saint of Wales and name of two kings of Scotland. 12th cent. [A First Fleet surname].

DAVIDGE, DAVAGE: P '*David's* son'. 16th cent.

DAVIDSON, DAVISON, DAVSON: P 'Son of *David*'. 14th cent. [A First Fleet surname].

DAVIES, DAVIS, DAVES, DAVYS: P 'Son of *Davy*'. 14th cent. [Fourteen persons named Davis brought the name to Australia 1788: seven male and four female convicts, a crew member, and a marine and his wife].

DAW(E), DAWES, DAWS: (i) P A pet-form of *David*. 13th cent. (ii) N OE *dawe* 'jackdaw', regarded as a foolish bird. 13th cent. [A naval officer, William Dawes, brought the name to Australia 1788].

DAWKES: P A contracted form of *Dawkins*. 15th cent. DAWKINS: P Daw(e) + suffix -*kin*. 'Little David'. 14th cent.

DAWN: P A form of *Daw*. 14th cent.

DAWSON: P or N 'Son of *Daw*' (*David* or the jackdaw). 14th cent. [The name was brought to Australia 1788 by Richard Dawson, ship's boy, and Margaret Dawson, a convict who later lived with Chief Surgeon Balmain].

DAWTREY, DAUGHTERY, DAUGHTRY, HAWTREY, HATRY: L OF From Hauterive (Orne) Normandy. 12th cent.

DAY(E), DAY, DEYE(S): O OE *daege* 'female bread-maker'; ME *day, daye, dey* included 'dairy-maid', later extended to male servants. 11th cent. [A First Fleet (convict) surname].

DAYKIN, DAKIN: P *Day* + suffix -*kin* 'little *David*'. 13th cent.

DAYMAN: O ME *day* + OE *mann* 'dairyman', 'herdsman'. 13th cent.

DAYNE(S) see DAIN.

DAYRELL, DARRELL: L OF From Airelle (Calvados) Normandy. 12th cent.

DEACON, DEAKIN(S): O OE *dēacon* or OF *diacne* 'deacon'. 13th cent.

DEADMAN see DEBENHAM. DEAKES see DECKES.

DEAL: L OE *dael* 'dale, valley'. (Kent) 13th cent.

DEAN(E), DEANER, DEANS, DEEN, DENE: (i) L OE *denu* 'valley'. DB. (ii) O OF *deien*, ME *deen* 'dean'. 12th cent. Probably the dean's servant. [A First Fleet (crew) surname. William and John Deans were the first settlers on the Canterbury plains of New Zealand, 1843].

DEAR(E), DEARES, DEER(E), DEERR: (i) N OE *dēor* 'wild animal, esp. deer'. (ii) N OE *dēor* (same word) 'bold, brave'. (iii) N OE *deore* 'beloved'. 11th cent.

DEARING, DEERING, DORING: P OE *Dēoring*, from *dēor* 'brave, bold'. DB.

DEARLING see DARLING.

DEARMAN, DORMAN, DURMAN: P OE *Dēormann* 'brave man'. DB.

DEARSON, DAIRSON: P OE 'Son of *Dēor*, ancestor of *Dēoring*'.

DEASE: L Ir *Deise*. From Deece (Co. Meath). 13th cent. [Edward Dease, a sailor on the *Lady Penhryn*, brought the name to Australia 1788].

DEASON see DAYSON.

DEATH(E), DEETH, DEARTH, DE ATH(E): N OE *dēath*, ME *deeth* 'death'. A sinister sounding nickname but from the harmless appearance of an actor in a medieval pageant or play. 12th cent. Some may be L from immigration from Ath in the low countries (now Belgium).

DEATHRIDGE, DETHERIDGE: O OE Originally *Dethewright*, from *dyth* 'tinder'. 'A maker of tinder'. 13th cent.

DEAVE(S), DEEVES: N OE *dēaf* 'deaf'. 12th cent.

DEAVILLE see DAVALL. DEAVIN see DEVIN.

DEBBAGE: L OE *dēope-baece* 'deep back-parts' used topographically 'deep valley'.

DEBENHAM, DEBHAM, DEADMAN, DEDMAN: L OE river-name *Dēope* + hām 'settlement by the deep river'. (Suffolk) 13th cent.

DEBNEY: N OF *Dieu bénir* 'God bless', a phrase-name for one who was constantly uttering it. 12th cent.

DECOURCEY, de COURCY, de COURCEY, COURSEY: L OF From Courcy (Normandy). DB.

DECKER see DICKER.

DEED, DEEDES, DEDE(S), DADE: N OE *daed* 'deed, exploit'. 12th cent.

DEEGAN, DUFFIN: P Ir Individual surnames from the same stem, *O Duibhginn*, from *dubh-ceann* 'black-head'.

DEEKS, DEAKES: L OE *dīc*, ME *deke* 'ditch/dyke'. 14th cent.

DEEM, DEAM: O OE *dēma* 'judge'. 13th cent. DEEMER, DEAMER, DEMER: O OE *dēmere* 'deemer, judge, pronouncer of *dōm* "doom" (verdict)'. 11th cent. DEEMING, DEMINGS: O OE *dēmung* 'judgement'. 'A judge'. 13th cent.

DEEN see DEAN.

DEEPING: L OE *dēoping* 'deep place (fen)'. (Lincs).

DEER(E), DEERR see DEAR. DEERING see DEARING. DEEVES see DEAVE.

DEIGHTON, DIGHTON: L OE 'The *tūn* (farm) within a dīc (dyke)'. (Yorks) 12th cent.

DELAFIELD: L OF + OE *de la feld* 'of the field or open plain'. 12th cent.

DE la HAYE, DELAHAYE, DELAHAY: (i) L OF From Haye-du-Puits (Normandy). 12th cent. (ii) L OF + OE *de la hege* 'of the hedge or enclosure'.

DELAHUNTY, DOLAHENTY: P Ir *O Dulchaointigh* 'satirist'.

DELAMARE, DE la MARE, DELAMERE: L OF From La Mare (pool), many places in France. 12th cent. (ii) L OF + OE *mere* 'lake, pool' or *mōr* 'moor, fen, marsh'.

DELANEY see DANDO. DELAWARE see WARR.

DE la RUE: L OF + OE *raew* 'of the row (of cottages)'.

DELBRIDGE see BRIDGE.

DELF, DELPH, DELVE: O OE *delf* 'diggings', *delfan* 'to delve, burrow'. 'A quarrier, excavator'. 13th cent.

DE LISLE: L OF *del isle*. From one of the many places of this name in France, notably Lille (Nord). DB.

DELL, DELLAR, DELLER: L OE *dell* 'dell, hollow'. 13th cent.

DELLAND: L OE *denu* + *land* 'property in the valley'. 13th cent.

DELLOW: L OE *hōh* 'point of land' (hill or ridge). 13th cent.

DEMER see DEEMER.

DEMPSEY, DEMPSY: P Ir *O Diomasaigh*, from *diomasach* 'proud'. 16th cent. [William Dempsey, a marine, brought the name to Australia 1788].

DEMPSTER: O OE fem. of *Deemer* 'judge'. 13th cent.

DENBY: L OE *Denisc* 'Danish' + ON *býr* 'the Danes' farm'. (Derbys, Yorks).

DENCE, DENCH: L OE *Denisc*, ME *Denshe* 'Danish'. 14th cent.

DENCHFIELD: L ME *Denshe* + OE *feld* 'the Danes' field'.

DENFORD: L OE *denu-ford* 'valley with a ford'. (Berks, Northants).

DENGATE: L OE *denu-geat* 'valley-gate'.

DENHAM: L OE *denu-hām* 'homestead in the valley'. (Bucks, Suffolk) 12th cent.

DENHOLM(E): L OE *denu* + O Scand *holmi* 'valley with dry land in a fen'. (Yorks) 14th cent.

DENIS(E), DENNIS, DENNISS, DENNYS, DENNES, DINNIS: (i) P Gk *Dionysos*, Lat *Dionysius* masc. *Denis*, fem. *Dionysia, Denise* (OF). Both contributed to the surname. St *Denys* became patron saint of France. 12th cent. (ii) L 'Danish', a combination of OF *Daneis* and OE *Denisc*.

DENISON, DENNISON: (i) P 'Son of *Denis*'. 13th cent. (ii) O AF *deinzein* 'a burgess entitled to the privileges *deinz la cite* (within the city)'. 13th cent. [A First Fleet (convict) surname].

DENLOW: L OE *denu-hlāw* 'mound in the valley'.

DENLEIGH, DENLEY: L OE *denu-lēah* 'valley-clearing'. 13th cent.

DENMAN: L OE *denu-mann* 'valley man', 'dweller in the valley'.

DENMEAD: L OE *denu-maedw* 'meadow in the valley'. (Hants) 13th cent.

DENN(E): O OE *denn* 'swine-pasture'. 'A swineherd'. 12th cent.

DENNETT: P A dim. of *Dennis*.

DENNING see DINNEEN.

DENNY, DENNEY: L OE From Denny (Stirling) Scotland. 15th cent.

DENOVAN: L From the lands of Dunipace (Stirling). 14th cent.

DENSON: O ME *deen* 'son of the dean'. 13th cent.

DENT: L OE from Celtic *dind* 'hill'. (Yorks) 12th cent.

DENTISH see DAINTETH.

DENTON: L OE *denu-tūn* 'valley farm'. (Cumb, Northants) 11th cent.

DENVER: L OE *dena-faer* 'The passage (ferry) of the Danes'. (Norfolk).

DERBY, DARBY, DARBEY: L OE *dēor* + ON *býr* 'The farm where deer roam'. (Derbys, Lancs) 12th cent.

DERRICK: P OG *Theodoric*, Du *Dirck* 'people-rule'. 15th cent.

DERRY: P Ir *O Doirighe*, a Co. Donegal name.

DERWENT: L Brit *dervā* 'oak'. 'River lined by oak-woods'. Also a Brit river-name *Derventiō*. There are four Rivers Derwent in England and one noble one in Tasmania. See also Darwen.

DESBOROUGH: L OE *dweorge* 'penny royal' (the herb puliol royal). 'The hill where penny royal grows'. (Bucks).

DESMOND: L Ir *O Deasmhumhnaig*, from *deas* 'south' (South Munster).

DETHERIDGE see DEATHRIDGE. DEVANE see DWANE.

DEVENISH: L OE *defensic* 'from Devon'. 12th cent.

DEVERAUX, DEVEREAUX, DEVEREUX, EVEREST, EVERIST: L OF from Gaulish. From Evreux (Eure) Normandy. DB. The surname descends from the Celtic tribal name *Eburovices*.

DEVERE see VERE.

DEVERELL, DEVERILL: L Brit *Dubroialon* 'stream near the *iâl* (fertile upland)'. (Cornwall, Wilts).

DE VILE, DEVILL, DE VILLE see DAVALL.

DEVIN(E), DEAVIN, DIVINE: N OF *devin* 'divine'. A nickname given to one thought to be so immaculate that he qualified for this holy description.

DEVITT: P Ir A variant form of *MacDaid*.

DEVLIN: P Ir 'Descendant of *Dobhailen*', an Ulster sept.

DEWAR (i) L SG From Dewar (Lothian) Scotland. 13th cent. (ii) N SG *Deoireach* 'pilgrim, sojourner'.

DEWHURST, DEWHIRST: L OE *dēaw-hyrst* 'bedewed copse, wood'. 13th cent.

DEWSBURY: L OE *dēaw-burg* 'dewey-fort' (perhaps a dew-pond in the ancient earthworks, as at Cissbury, Sussex). (Yorks) 12th cent.

DEXTER: O OE *deazestre* 'dyer (of cloth)' 13th cent. See also Dyster.

DEY(E) see DAY.

DIAMANT, DIAMOND, DIMENT, DIMOND, DIMONT, DYMOND: (i) Usually forms of O *Dayman* (herdsman, dairyman), (ii) Occasionally P from *Diamanda*, a medieval woman's name. 13th cent.

DIBB(S): L Dial. *dib* 'little hollow'. 15th cent.

DIBBLE: P OG or OF Dim. of *Theobald*. 13th cent.

DIBDEN: L OE *dēop-denu* 'deep valley'. (Hants) DIBLEY: L OE *dēop-lēah* 'clearing in a hollow'.

DICE, DYCE: N ME *dyce* 'dice', nickname for a gambler. 14th cent. See also Chance, Hazard.

DICK(S), DIX: P Pet-form of *Richard*. 13th cent. [A First Fleet surname].

DICKENS, DICKIN(S), DICKINGS, DICKONS: P Dim. of *Dick*. 13th cent.

DICKENSON, DICKINSON, DICKERSON, DICKESON, DICKASON: P 'Son of *Dicun*', a form of *Dick*. 14th cent. [Mary Dickerson, a convict, brought her variant of the name to Australia 1788].

DICKER(S), DIKKERS: (i) O OE *dīcere* 'ditcher'. 13th cent. (ii) L ME *dyker* 'dicker, a number of ten'. 'Occupier of land by payment of a dicker of iron rods rent'. 13th cent. (A name of Sussex iron-working district; the original owner of Batemans, Kipling's house at Burwash, was an iron-master.)

DICKIE, DICKEY: P Scottish dim. of *Dick*. 15th cent.

DICKMAN, DIGMAN: O OE *dīc-mann* 'worker on the ditch/dyke'. 13th cent.

DICKSON, DIXON: P 'Son of *Dick*'. 14th cent. [A First Fleet (convict) surname].

DIGBY: L OE *dīc* + ON *býr* 'farm with a ditch or dyke'. 12th cent.

DIGGLE(S), DICKELS: P Dim. of *Dick*. 13th cent.

DIGNAN, DIGNUM see DUIGENAN.

DIL(L), DILLER, DILLING: (i) P OE *Dylla*, an Anglo-Saxon pers. name. 12th cent. (ii) O OE *dile* 'dill'. Metonymic for a grower of dill, a medicinal herb. 14th cent.

DILGER: L OE *dile* 'dill-field'. 13th cent.

DILLON, DYLLON: P OG *Dillo* + suffix *-on*, adopted by the Normans and taken to Ireland. Hibernicised as *Diolún*. 12th cent.

DILWORTH: L OE *dile-worth* 'homestead where dill is grown'. (Lancs).

DIMENT see DIAMANT.

DIMMACK, DIMMICK, DIMMOCK, DIMOCK, DYMOCK: L Brit/OW *ty-moch* 'pigsty'. 12th cent.

DIMMER see DISMORE.

DINAN: L OF From Dinan (Brittany). 12th cent.

DINGLE: L ME *dingle* 'deep dell (hollow)'. (Lancs) 13th cent.

DINGWALL: L O Scand 'parliament field'. (Ross and Cromarty, a northern county of Scotland.)

DINNEEN, DENNING: P Ir *O Duinnin*, from the pers. name *Donn*.

DINSDALE: L OE *Dīctūne-halh* 'The nook of Deighton'. (Durham).

DIPLOCK, DUPLOCK: L OE *dēop-lacu* 'deep stream or pond'.

DIPPER, DIAPER: L OF From *de Ipra* (Ypres) Belgium. 12th cent.

DISHER: O OE *disc* 'bowl, platter'. 'A maker of dishes (wooden measures for wine or ale)'. 13th cent.

DISNEY: L OF From Isigny (Normandy). 12th cent.

DISPER: P OF *duze pers* 'twelve equals, twelve peers', the twelve paladins of Charlemagne, later applied to other illustrious knights. 12th cent.

DISS: L OE *dīc* 'ditch (fen drain)'. (Norfolk) DITCH, DEETCH, DYKE(S): 'ditch or dyke'. 13th cent. DITCHETT: L OE *dīc-geat* 'gate in the dyke', (on the ancient road Fosse Way). (Som).

DITER, DYTER: O OF & ME *ditour* 'author, composer, summoner'. 14th cent.

DITTON: L OE *dīc-tūn* 'farm within a dyke'. (Bucks, Cambs, Surrey).

DIVALL see DAVALL. DIVAN see DWANE.

DIVER(S): O OE *dūfan* 'to dive, immerse'. 'A diver'. 13th cent.

DIVES: L OF From Dives (Normandy). DB.

DIVINE see DEVIN. DIX see DICK.

DIXEY, DIXIE: N Lat *dixi*, OF *dixie* 'I have spoken', derived from a psalm. Nickname for a chorister. 13th cent.

DIXON see DICKSON.

DOBB(E), DOBBS: P Dim. of *Robert*. 12th cent.

DOBBIE, DOBBY, DOBE, DOBY, DOBBIN(S): P Pet-forms of *Dobb*. 12th cent.

DOBEL, DOBLE: N OF *doubel* 'a twin'. 12th cent.

DOBSON: P 'Son of *Dobb*'. 14th cent. [Arthur Dudley Dobson discovered a pass through the mountains to the West Coast of New Zealand, providing a shorter route to the South Island goldfields, 1865].

DOCHERTY see DOUGHARTY.

DOCKER: L ON *dokk* 'a hollow or small valley'. (Lancs).

DOCKERAY, DOCKEREY: L OE *docce* + ON *vra* 'remote valley where dock (sorrel) grows abundantly'. 14th cent.

DOCKEREY: P Ir *O Dochraigh*. Entirely distinct from the English name.

DOCKETT see DOGGETT. DOCKSEY see DOXEY. DOCTOR see DAUGHTERS.

DOD, DODD(S), DODS: P OE Anglo-Saxon pers. name *Dodda* or *Dudda*. DB. [Henry Dodd, personal servant to Governor Phillip, brought the name to Australia 1788]. DODDING: P OE 'Son of *Dodda*'. 12th cent. [James Dodding, a convict, arrived on the *Friendship* 1788].

DODGE: P A dim. of *Roger*. 12th cent.

DODGEON, DUDGEON: P Dim. of *Dodge*. 14th cent. [Dudgeon, a female convict surname].

DODGSON: P 'Son of *Dodge*'. 14th cent.

(Dodgson was the true name of Lewis Carroll, author of *Alice in Wonderland.*)

DODWELL: L OE 'The *wielle* (stream) of *Dodda*'. (Warwicks).

DOE: (i) L OF From Eu (Normandy). 12th cent. (ii) N OE *dā* 'doe'. A nickname from the female deer.

DOGGETT, DOCKETT: (i) P OE Dim. of *Docca*, an Anglo-Saxon pers. name. 12th cent. (ii) N OE *dogca-hēafod* 'dog-head', an uncomplimentary nickname.

DOGGRELL: N OE *dogca*, applied to trivial or mean verse. cf. dog-Latin 'barbarous (uncultured) Latin'. First occurrence in English literature is in Chaucer's Tale of Sir Thopas, where the host of the Tabard describes the verse as 'dogerel and not worth a turd'. Nickname for a bad poet. See also Rimer.

DOHERTY see DOUGHARTY.

DOIDGE: P Variant of *Dodge*. 14th cent.

DOIG, DOOHIG, DOOGUE: P Ir & SG 'Devotee of *St Cadoc*, battle prince'. 15th cent.

DOLAHENTY see DELAHUNTY.

DOLAN: P Ir *O Dobhailen*. Cos. Galway and Roscommon.

DOLE: L OE *dāl*, ME *dole* 'a share of land in the common field'. 13th cent.

DOLITTLE: N OE *dōn lȳtel* 'do little', nickname for an idler. 12th cent.

DOLL: N OE *dol* 'foolish' or 'presumptuous'. Winton D.

DOLLAR: L From Dollar (Clackmannan) Scotland. 14th cent.

DOLLING, DOWLING: N OE *dolling* 'dullard'. 13th cent.

DOLLMAN, DOLMAN: L ME *dole* (see Dole). 'Boundary marking the land share'.

DOLLY, O'DOLLY: P Ir *O Dathlaoich*, from *laoch* 'champion' + *dath* 'swift'.

DOLPHIN: P ON *Dolgfinnr*. 12th cent.

DOMAN: O OE *dōm* 'a judge'. 13th cent. See also Deemer. DOMESMAN: O OE 'Man of judgement, judge'. 12th cent.

DOMM, DOMB: N OE *dumb* 'mute, speechless'. 13th cent.

DOMMET see DUMMETT. DON see DUNN.

DONALD: P SG *Domhnall*, Ir *Domnall*, from early Celtic *Dubno-valos* 'world-mighty'. 13th cent. DONALDSON: 'Son of *Donald*'. 14th cent.

DONAT, DONNET: P Lat *donatus*, OF *donat* 'given', name of several saints.

DONCASTER: L Brit + OE 'Roman fort on the River Don'. (Yorks) 12th cent.

DONKIN see DUNCAN.

DONLEVY, DUNLEVY, MACDUNLEVY: P Ir *Mac Duinnshleivhe*, from *sliabh* 'mountain'.

DONNELLAN: P Ir *O Domhuallain*, a dim. of *Domhnall* (*Donnell*). See O'DONNELL.

DONNELLY: P Ir *O Donnghaile* 'brown valour'.

DONOGHUE, DONOHOE, O'DONAGHUE: P Ir *O Donnchadha*. 'descendant of *Donagh*'.

DONOVAN: P Ir *O Donnabhain*, a Co. Cork sept. [Stephen Donovan, a midshipman on the *Sirius*, brought the name to Australia 1788].

DOOGUE see DOIG.

DOOLAN: P Ir *O Dubhlain* 'descendant of *Dubhfhlan* (black defiance)'.

DOOLEY, DOWLEY: P Ir *O Dubhlaoich* 'black hero'.

DORAN, DORRAN: P Ir *O Deoradhain* 'the exile'. One of the seven septs of Leix.

DORE: (i) L Brit river-name. (ii) L OE *dor* 'gate, pass' (on the ancient boundary between Northumbria and Mercia).

DORING see DEARING. DORLING see DARLING. DORMAN see DEARMAN.

DORMER: N OF *dormeur* 'sleeper', nickname for a sluggard. 14th cent.

DORRATT see DURWARD.

DORRINGTON: L OE 'The *tūn* (farm) of *Dēora*, an Anglo-Saxon'. (Lincs).

DORSET(T), DOSSETT: L OE *Dornsaete* 'the people of Dorset'. 13th cent. [Surgeon Dorset of the New Zealand Company arrived on the *Tory* 1839].

DORWARD, DORWOOD see DURWARD.

DOSSETTER: (i) L Brit *Dorcic* + OE *ceaster* 'fort'. (Oxon). 13th cent. (ii) L OE *Dornwaru* 'the Dorchester people' + *ceaster* 'Roman station'. (Dorset).

DOUBLEDAY: O OF + OE 'Servant of *Dobel*'. 13th cent.

DOUBLET: O OF *doublet* 'a close-fitting body garment worn with hose'. Metonymic for a maker/seller of doublets. 12th cent.

DOUCE, DOWSE, DUCE: N OF *dous*, ME *douce* 'pleasant, sweet-natured'. 13th cent.

DOUCET see DOWSETT.

DOUGAL(L), DOUGILL: P Ir & SG *Dubhghall* 'black stranger', originally an Irish name for a Viking. 12th cent. Now mainly a name of the Scottish Highlands.

DOUGAN see DUGAN.

DOUGHARTY, DOUGHERTY, DOHERTY, DOCHERTY: P Ir *O Dochartaigh* 'the stern'. 12th cent. [A First Fleet (marine) surname].

DOUGHTY, DOUTY, DOWTY, DUFTY: N OE *dohtig* 'doughty, valiant'. 13th cent.

DOUGLAS(S): L SG *dubh glas* 'black water'. (Lanarks) Scotland. 12th cent. [Two men named William Douglas, one a private soldier, the other a convict, brought the name to Australia 1788].

DOULL: P For *Domhnall*. 16th cent. See Donald.

DOUST see DUST.

DOUTHWAITE, DOWTHWAITE: L ON 'The *thwaite* (meadow or clearing) of *Duve*, a Norseman'. (Cumb). 14th cent.

DOVE: N OE *dūfe*. In his *Myrrour of the World*, William Caxton (1422–91) observed: 'The douve is a symple byrde, and of her nature nourissith well the pigeons of another dove'. Either 'a simple bird' or 'gentle as a dove', a term of endearment. 12th cent. (Caxton uses pigeon for a young dove, and to further confuse the issue, *culfre* was used both for dove and pigeon. See also Culver.)

DOVER: L Brit river-name *Dobrā*, now the Dour, *Dofras* in 7th cent. (Kent) Surname DB.

DOW(E): (i) P For *Daw*, pet-form of *David*. 13th cent. (ii) N SG *dubh* 'black'. 14th cent.

DOWD: (i) P A variant of *Daud* (*David*). 13th cent. (ii) P Ir *O Dubhda*, 'descendant of *Dubhda*'.

DOWDESWELL: L OE 'The *wielle* (stream) of *Dogod*, an Anglo-Saxon'. (Glos).

DOWELL see DOYLE.

DOWER(S): O OE *dāh* 'dough'. 'A maker of dough, a baker'. 14th cent.

DOWEY: L OF From Douai (Nord) France. DB.

DOWIE see DUFFEY.

DOWLAND: L OE *dūfe-land* 'land frequented by doves'. (Devon).

DOWLANE, DOWLAN: P A Co. Longford variant of Doolan. [A First Fleet (marine) surname].

DOWLER: O ME *dowle* 'A maker of dowels (wooden pegs)'. 13th cent.

DOWLEY see DOOLEY. DOWLING see DOLLING.

DOWN(S), DOWNE(S), DOWNS, DOWNER, DOWNMAN, DUNMAN: L OE *dūn* 'hill' (North Downs, South Downs). 12th cent.

DOWNEY: P Ir For *Muldowney* or *MacEldowney*. [A First Fleet (crew and convict) surname].

DOWNHAM: L OE 'dūn-hām 'homestead on the hill'. 12th cent.

DOWNING: P OE *Dūning* 'son of *Dūn*. 12th cent. See also Dunn.

DOWNTON see DUNTON. DOWSE see DOUCE.

DOWSETT, DOWCETT, DOUCET: N OF *doucet* 'pleasing, agreeable'. 14th cent.

DOWSING: P O Dan 'Son of *Dusi*'. 12th cent.

DOWSON: P 'Son of *Dow*'. 14th cent.

DOWTHWAITE see DOUTHWAITE. DOWTY see DOUGHTY.

DOXEY, DOCKSEY: L OE 'The *īeg* (island) of *Docc*, an Anglo-Saxon'. 13th cent.

DOYLE, DOWELL: P Ir *O Dubhghaill*, from *dubh-gall* 'black foreigner' (a Viking). (The main sept of the Doyles is of Norse origin.)

DOYLEY, DULEY, DULY, DAILEY, DAILLEY, OLLEY, OLLIE: L OF From Ouilly (Calvados) Normandy. DB. [Dailey, a First Fleet (convict) surname].

DRABBLE: (i) P A dim. of OE *Drabba*, an Anglo-Saxon pers. name. 13th cent. (ii) N A dim. of *drab* 'dirty, untidy', cf. Ir *drabog* and SG *drabag* 'slut, slattern'.

DRAGON: (i) O OF *dragonier* 'standard-bearer'. 12th cent. (ii) N OF A medieval pageant name.

DRAKE(S), DRAKER(S): O OE *draca*, Anglo-Saxon equivalent of OF *dragon*. Also O Dan *draki*. 'Standard-bearer'. DB.

DRANE: N OE *drān* 'drone', 'indolent'. 13th cent.

DRAPER, DRAPIER, DRAPPER: O OF *drapier*, AF *draper* 'a seller of woollen cloth'. 12th cent.

DRAWBRIDGE: O OE *dragan-brycg* 'keeper of the drawbridge' (at castle or fortified manor-house).

DRAY: O A development of OE *dragan*. A maker or driver of a dray (cart without wheels).

DRAYTON: L OE *draeg-tūn* 'farm by a steep hill'.

DRENG, DRING: O OE *dreng*, from O Scand *drengr* 'lad, servant'. In England, 'a free tenant holding land by tenure older than the Norman conquest, partly military, partly servile'. 12th cent. [Dring, a First Fleet (convict) surname].

DRENNEN, DRENEN: P Ir *O Draighnean*, meaning 'blackthorn'.

DRESSER: O OF *dresser* 'a dresser of textile fabrics'. 14th cent.

DREW(E), DRU: (i) P OG *Drogo* 'ghost', the name of one of Charlemagne's sons. DB. (ii) P A dim. of *Andrew*.

DREWELL: N OF A dim. of *dru* 'sweetheart, lover'. 12th cent.

DREWERY, DRUERY, DRURY: N OF *druerie* 'love, love-token'. 12th cent.

DREWES see DRUCE.

DREWETT, DREWITT, DRUETT, DRUITT: (i) P A pet-form of *Drew* (*Drogo*) 12th cent. (ii) a dim. of OF *dru*. See Drewell.

DREYER see DRYER.

DRIFFIELD, DRIFFILL: L OE *drit* 'dirt' + *feld*, 'dirty (manured) field'. (Glos, Yorks) 12th cent.

DRINKALE, DRINKALL, DRINKALD: N OE *drinc-hael* 'a drinking pledge'. 12th cent.

DRINKWATER: N OE *drinc-waeter*. Nickname for one who was too poor to drink ale at a farthing a gallon or too drunk to notice the difference. 13th cent.

DRISCOLL: P Ir *O Leiderseeoil*, from *eidirsceol* 'intermediary'. [A First Fleet (convict) surname].

DRIVER: O OE *drīfan* 'driver of an early conveyance, e.g., an ox-cart'. 13th cent.

DROOP: N ME *drup* 'gloomy, dejected'. Nickname for a pessimist. 12th cent.

DROVER: O OE A derivative of *drāf* (drove-herd) 'a drover', preceded by *docga* 'the drover's dog'. 13th cent.

DRU see DREW.

DRUCE, DREWS: L OF From Dreux (Eure-et-Loir) France. DB.

DRUERY, DRURY see DREWERY. DRUETT, DRUITT see DREWETT.

DRUMMOND: L SG From the barony of Drummond (Stirling) Scotland. 13th cent. [John Drummond, a sailor on the *Sirius*, brought the name to Australia 1788, and became beachmaster and pilot on Norfolk Island].

DRYDEN: L OE *drȳge-denu* 'dry valley'.

DRYER, DREYER: O OE *drygean* 'to dry'. 'A dryer of cloth after fulling'. 14th cent. See also Fuller, Tucker, Walker, who did the fulling (scouring).

DRYSDALE: L A river-name *Dryfe* + OE *dael* 'dale or valley'. (Dumfries) Scotland. 16th cent.

DUBBER: O ME *dubber* 'fripperer' in several trades, e.g., book-binding, garment-finishing, arms, harness-polishing. 12th cent. (The City of York had its Company of Dubbers.)

DUBOIS: L OF 'of the wood'. A Huguenot surname.

DUCAT: N OF 'a gold coin', probably a nickname for a medieval millionaire. In Chaucer's spelling it was *duket*, in Shakespeare's *ducket*. The original form survived in the surname. 14th cent.

DUCE see DOUCE.

DUCK(S), DOAK, DOKE: (i) O OE *dūce* 'diver'. 'A duck farmer/purveyor'. 13th cent. (ii) N ME *doke*, a nickname from a term of endearment. 13th cent.

DUCKER, DUKER: N ME *douker* 'a diving bird', nickname for a diver/swimmer.

DUCKERS: O OE *dūce-hūs* 'duck-house', a worker with ducks. 16th cent.

DUCKET(T), DUCKITT: (i) P OE *Ducca*, an Anglo-Saxon pers. name. (ii) P A dim. of *Marmaduke*. (iii) O or N A dim. of *Duck*. 12th cent.

DUCKHAM: L OE *dūce-hām* 'homestead with ducks'. DUCKWORTH: L OE *dūce-worth* or '*Ducca's worth* (homestead)'. (Lancs).

DUDGEON see DODGEN.

DUDLEY: L OE '*Dudda's lēah* (clearing)'. 12th cent.

DUFF: P Ir & SG A variant of SG *Dubh* 'black'. 13th cent. *MacDuff* is an Ulster surname, from Ir *MacDhuibh* 'son of *Dubh* (black)'. [J. Duff, sailing a whaleboat, was the first European to pass through the Manawatu Gorge, 1840].

DUFFET: N OE *dūfe-hēafod* 'dove-head', a nickname of uncertain meaning. (In OE *culfre* was used of both dove and pigeon, but *dūfe* for dove must have existed.) See also DOVE.

DUFFEY, DUFFIE, DUFFY, DOWIE: P Ir O *Dubhthaig* 'dark man of peace'.

DUFFIELD, DUFFELL, DUFFILL: L OE *dūfe-feld* 'field with doves'. (Derbys).

DUFFIN see DEEGAN.

DUFFUS: (i) L SG From Duffus (Moray)

Scotland. 13th cent. (ii) O ON *dūfa* + OE *hūs* 'dove-house', 'keeper of the dove-house'. 13th cent.

DUFTON: L ON *dūfa* + OE *tūn* 'farm with doves'. (Westmorland).

DUFTY see DOUGHTY.

DUGAN, DUGGAN, DOUGAN: (i) P Ir *O Dubhagáin*, from *dubh* 'black'. Also a Manx surname. (ii) N OE *dugan* 'strong, virtuous, kind'.

DUGUID: N Nickname for a 'do-gooder'. 14th cent.

DUIGNAN, DIGNAM, DIGNUM: P Ir *O Duibhgeannain* 'black head (hair)'.

DUKE: N or O OF *duc* 'duke, captain, leader'. A pageant name or from service in a ducal household. [A First Fleet (marine) surname].

DUKER see DUCKER.

DULCKEN: N ME *dul-kin*, a dim. of OE pers. name *Dylla*. 13th cent.

DULEY, DULY see DOYLEY.

DULLARD: N ME *dull* + suffix *-ard*, 'stupid' but like *Deave*, an affliction which may have lost its meaning at the next generation.

DULWICH: L OE *dile-wisce* 'meadow where dill is grown'. (Surrey).

DUMBELL, DUMBLE: N A dim. of OE *dumb* 'silent', 'slow to comprehend'. 13th cent.

DUMMER, DUMPER: L OE *dūn-mere* 'lake by a hill'. (Hants) 12th cent.

DUMMETT, DOMMETT: L OF From Dumart-en-Ponthieu (Somme) France. 12th cent.

DUNBAR: L SG *dùn-barr* 'fort at the summit'.

DUNCAN, DUNKIN, DONKIN: P Ir & SG *Donnchad* 'brown warrior'. DB. [David Duncan, ship' boy on the *Lady Penrhyn*, brought the name to Australia 1788].

DUNDAS: L SG *dun-deas* 'south hill' (Lothian) Scotland. 12th cent. [Jane Dundas, a convict, brought the name to Australia 1788, and rose to become housekeeper at Government House].

DUNGATE: L OE *dūn-geat* 'gap in the Downs'. (Sussex) 13th cent.

DUNGER: O ME A derivative of *dungen* 'a manure spreader'. 13th cent.

DUNHAM: L OE 'The *hām* (homestead) of *Dunna*, an Anglo-Saxon'. (Ches, Norfolk, Notts) 12th cent.

DUNJOHN: O OF *donjon* 'gaoler at the castle tower'. 12th cent.

DUNKERTON: L Brit *din* + OE *tūn* 'farm by the hill-fort'. (Som).

DUNLEVY see DONLEVY.

DUNLOP: L SG From the lands of Dunlop in Cunningham, Scotland. 13th cent.

DUNMALL: L OE *Dunmail*, name of the last king of Cumbria.

DUNMAN see DOWNMAN.

DUNN(E), DON(N), DONNE: (i) N OE *dunn* 'dark, swarthy'. 12th cent. (ii) L SG *dùn* 'fort', as at Dun (Angus) Scotland.

DUNNAGE: L Brit *dumnuc* + OE *wīc* 'deep port or town'. (Suffolk) 12th cent. [A First Fleet (convict) surname].

DUNNICLIFFE see TUNNICLIFFE.

DUNNING: (i) N OE *Dunning* 'son of *Dunn*'. DB. (ii) L SG *dùnan*, a dim. of *dùn* 'fort'. (Perths) Scotland.

DUNPHY, DUNFY: P Ir *O Donnchaidh*.

DUNSTAN, DUNSTON(E): L OE *dūn-stān* 'hill-stone'. (Devon, Derbys, Lincs, Norfolk, Northumb) (St *Dunstan*, archbishop of Canterbury 10th cent.)

DUNSTER: L OE '*Dunn's torr* (high rock)'. (Som) 12th cent.

DUNTON, DOWNTON: L OE *dūn-tūn* 'hill farm'. (Herefords, Kent, Wilts) 13th cent.

DUPLOCK see DIPLOCK. DUPONT see PONT.

DURACK: P Ir *O Dubhraic*, a Co. Clare surname.

DURAND, DURANT, DURRAND, DURRANT, DURRAN(S), DURRANCE: N OF *durant* 'enduring, persevering, obstinate'. Winton D.

DURDEN, DURDIN: N OF *dur-dent* 'hard-tooth', a nickname of obscure meaning. 12th cent.

DURHAM: L ON + OE *holmr* + *dūn* 'island with a hill'. Surname 12th cent.

DURKAN, MACDURKAN: P Ir *O Duarcain* 'descendant of pessimist'.

DURLEY: L OE *dēor-lēah* 'deer forest'. (Hants, Som).

DURLING see DARLING. DURMAN see DEARMAN.

DURNFORD, DORNFORD: L OE *dierne-ford* 'hidden ford'. (Wilts) 12th cent.

DURSTON: L OE 'The *tūn* (farm) of an Anglo-Saxon called *Dēor*'. (Som).

DURTNALL, DURTNELL, DARTNALL: L

OE From a lost place in Kent, *Durkinhole* 1240 and last recorded 16th cent. OE *deorc-holh* 'dark hole'.

DURWARD, DORWARD: O OE *durnweard* 'guardian of the door'. (In Scotland, the office of door-ward to the king was hereditary.)

DUST, DOUST: N OE *dūst* 'dust', nickname for a dusty wayfarer. OE Byname.

DUSTING see THURSTON.

DUTCH: O Du *duitsch* 'an immigrant Dutch weaver'. 14th cent. DUTCHMAN: O Du *duitsch* + OE *mann* 'a Flemish brick-maker'. 14th cent.

DUTTON: L OE '*Dudda's tūn* (farm)'. (Ches, Lancs) [A First Fleet (female convict) surname].

DWANE, DIVAN, DEVANE: P Ir *O Dubhain*, the name of several septs. [Edward Divan, a marine sergeant, and his wife brought his variant of the name to Australia 1788].

DWELLY: N OE *dweollic* 'misled, heretical'. 13th cent.

DWYER see O'DWYER.

DYASON: P 'Son of *Dyott*'. 14th cent.

DYBALL: P A variant of *Theobald*.

DYCE see DICE.

DYE, DYETT: P Pet-forms of *Dionysia*, see *Denis*. 13th cent.

DYER(S): O OE *dēagere*, from *dēagian* 'to dye'. 'A dyer of woollen cloth'. 13th cent. [A First Fleet (convict) surname].

DYKE(S) see DITCH. DYMOND see DIAMANT. DYMOCK see DIMMACK. DYNE see DAIN.

DYSON: P 'Son of *Dye*'. 13th cent.

DYSTER: O OE *deazestre* 'a female dyer', later also used of male dyers. 13th cent. See also Dexter.

DYTER see DITER.

E

EAD(E), EADES, EDE(S), EADIE, EADY: P OE *Ēadgȳth* a compound of 'prosperity-happiness' and 'combat'. 12th cent.

EADEN, EADON, EDEN(S): P OE *Ēadhūn* 'prosperity-happiness cub'. 12th cent.

EAGER, EAGER(S), EAGGER see EDGAR.

EAGLAND, EAGLIN see EGLIN. EAKIN see EDKINS. EALEY see ELY.

EAGLE(S): (i) L OF From Laigle (Orne) Normandy. 12th cent. (ii) N OF *aigle* 'eagle', 'eagle-power'. 12th cent.

EAMES: N OE *ēam* 'uncle'. 13th cent.

EARDLEY: L OE *eard-lēah* 'clearing with a dwelling' or 'estate with an enclosure' (it could be either). (Staffs).

EARL(E), ERLE, HEARL, HURL(E): N OE *eorl* 'earl' (comparable with ON *jarl* 'under-king'). Usually a pageant name; sometimes from service in an earl's household. 11th cent. (The Anglo-Saxon title of rank survived the Norman Conquest.) [A First Fleet (convict) surname].

EARLEY, EARLY: (i) L OE *earn-lēah* 'eagle-wood'. 12th cent. (ii) N OE *eorlic* 'chivalrous'. [A First Fleet (female convict) surname].

EARNSHAW: L OE *earn-scaga* 'eagle *shaw* (copse)'. 14th cent.

EASDALE see ESDALE.

EASON, EASOM, ESSON: P SG *Adamh* 'son of *Adam*'. 14th cent.

EAST, EASTES, ESTE: L OE *ēastan* 'east (of the settlement)'. 12th cent.

EASTABROOK: L OE *ēastan-brōc* 'east of the brook'. 13th cent.

EASTALL, ESTALL: L OE *ēast-heall* 'east hall'. 13th cent.

EASTAUGH, EASTOE, ESTAUGH: L OE *ēast-haga* 'east enclosure'. 14th cent.

EASTCOTT, ESCOT(T), ESTCOURT: L OE *ēastan-cot* 'eastern cottages'. (Beds, Middx, Wilts) 12th cent. [Jonathon Escott, a marine, arrived on the *Sirius* 1788].

EASTER: O OE *ēstre* 'sheepfold', 'worker at the sheepfold'. (Essex).

EASTGATE, ESGATE: L OE *ēast-geat* 'east gate (of castle or walled town)'. 12th cent. EASTHOPE, EASTOP: L OE *ēast-hop* 'eastern valley'. 13th cent.

EASTLEY: L OE *ēast-lēah* 'eastern clearing'. (Hants).

EASTMAN, EASTMENT, ESMOND(E): P OE *Ēastmund* 'grace or favour protection', an Anglo-Saxon pers. name. DB.

EASTMUIR: L OE *ēast* + Scots dial. *muir* 'moor', 'eastern moor'.

EASTMURE: P OE *Ēastmaer* 'grace or favour famous', an Anglo-Saxon pers. name and that of moneyers to Edward the Confessor and William I. Surname 13th cent.

EASTOE see EASTAUGH.

EASTON: L OE *ēastan-tūn* 'eastern farm'. 13th cent.

EASTWELL: L OE *ēast-wielle* 'eastern spring'. (Kent, Leices).

EASTWOOD: L OE *ēast-wudu* 'east of the wood'. 13th cent.

EATON: L OE *ēa-tūn* 'river-farm'. [Martha Eaton, a convict, brought the name to Australia 1788 but relinquished it when she married Edward Jones, a convict, soon after arrival].

EAVES, EAVIS, EVES: L OE *efes* 'forest edge, border'. 13th cent.

EBBETT, EBBITT, EBBUTT: P Dim. of *Ebb*, from *Ebbet* or *Ebbot*, women's names and pet-forms of *Isabel*. 12th cent.

EBBLEWHITE see HEPPLETHWAITE.

ECCLES: (i) L Brit *eclēs* 'a church'. (ii) L OE *āc-laes* 'oak pasture'. (There are places of this name in Berwicks, Dumfries, Kent, Lancs, Norfolk.) [A First Fleet (convict) surname].

ECCLESHALL, ECKERSHALL, EXALL, EXCELL: L Brit *eclēs* + OE *halh* 'church in the nook or corner'. (Lancs, Staffs, Yorks) 13th cent.

ECCLESTON: L OE *eclēs-tūn* 'the church farm'. (Ches), *Eclestone* DB, (Lancs).

ECKERSLEY: L Brit *eclēs* + OE *lēah* 'the church clearing'. 13th cent.

ECKHARD, ECKART, ECKERT: P OG *Eckhard* 'edge-hard'. 13th cent.

EDDINGTON, EDINGTON: L OE 'The *tūn* (farm) of an Anglo-Saxon woman called *Ēadgifu*' (Berks) or *Ēadwynn* (Som). 12th cent. [A First Fleet (convict) surname].

EDDISON see EDESON. EDDOWES see EDIS.

EDDS: P Pet-form of *Edward* or *Edwin*. 14th cent.

EDDY, EDDIE: P OE *Ēadwīg* 'prosperity-war'. 13th cent.

EDEN: (i) P Hebrew 'delight', arguably the first garden in the world. (ii) L A Brit river-name, originally *Ituna*, through *Eodune* to *Eden* (Cumb).

EDENBOROUGH: L Brit river-name *Eden* + OE *burg* 'fort'.

EDESON, EDDISON, EDISON, EDSON: P OE 'Son of *Ēad*'. 14th cent.

EDGAR(S), EDGER, EAGAR, EAGER(S), EAGGER, EGAR(R), EGER, EGGAR, EGGER(S): P OE *Ēadgār* 'prosperity-spear'. DB. A favoured name in the royal family of Wessex incl. King *Ēadgar* 944-75, grandson of King Alfred.

EDGE: L OE *ecg* 'edge, steep hillside'. (Ches) 13th cent.

EDGELEY: L OE 'The *lēah* (clearing) of *Ecgrēd*'. (Ches, Salop) 13th cent.

EDGELL: P OE *Ecgwulf* 'sword-wolf'. 13th cent.

EDGERTON, EGERTON, EGGERTON: L OE 'The *tūn* (farm) of *Echeard*'. 13th cent.

EDGEWORTH: L OE *ecg-worth* 'enclosure by a steep hill'. 13th cent.

EDHOUSE see EDIS.

EDINBOROUGH, EDINBURG: L SG *Dun-eideann* (not, as previously thought, associated with Edwin of Northumbria). Capital of Scotland, royal burgh, and county town of Midlothian. Surname 13th cent.

EDIS, EDHOUSE, EDDOWES: P OE *Edus*, short-form of *Ēadgifu*, a woman's name. 12th cent. EDISON: P 'Son of *Edis*'. See also Edeson.

EDKINS, EAKIN(S), EKINS: P OE A dim. of *Eda*, see Ead. 13th cent.

EDLESTON: L OE 'The *tūn* (farm) of *Ēadlāc*'. (Ches) 13th cent.

EDLIN: P OG *Edelina*, a woman's name, from *athal* 'noble'. 13th cent.

EDLINGTON: L OE 'The *tūn* (village) of *Ēadwulf's* people'. (Lincs, Yorks).

EDMAN: P OE *Ēadmann* 'prosperity-happiness man'. 13th cent.

EDMEAD(S), EDMED: N OE *ēadmēde* 'gentle, obedient'. 14th cent.

EDMOND(S), EDMONS, EDMUND(S): P OE *Ēadmund* 'prosperity-happiness protector'. DB. [Two men named William Edmunds, one a marine, the other a convict, brought the name to Australia 1788]. EDMONDSON, EDMUNDSON, EDMENSON, EDMINSON: P OE 'Son of *Edmund*'. 14th cent. [Also a First Fleet (marine) surname].

EDOLLS: P OE *Ēadwulf* 'riches-prosperity-happiness-good fortune wolf'.

EDRICH, EDRIDGE: P OE *Ēadric* 'prosperity-powerful'. DB.

EDWARD(S), EDWARDES: P OE 'prosperity-happiness guard'. DB. [A First Fleet surname for a convict whose guard was down]. EDWARDSON: P 'Son of *Edward*'.

EDWIN(S): P OE *Ēadwine* 'prosperity-happiness friend'. DB. Name of the first Christian king of Northumbria, 7th cent.

EELEY see ELY.

EFFEMY, EFFENEY: P Gk *Euphemia*, a woman's name meaning 'honour, good repute, worship of the gods'. The name of two martyrs. Surname 12th cent.

EGAN, MACEGAN: P Ir *Mac Aodhagain* 'son of *Egan*'. See also Kegan.

EGBERT: P OE *Ecgbeorht* 'sword-bright'. DB. Traditionally the name of the first king of all England, 9th cent.

EGER, EGAR(R), EGGER(S) see EDGAR. EGERTON see EDGERTON.

EGGINTON: L OE 'The *tūn* (farm) of *Ecga*'. (Beds, Derbys).

EGGLESTON(E), EGLESTON: L OE 'The *tūn* of *Ecgel*'. (Durham, Yorks) 12th cent. [A First Fleet (convict) surname].

EGGLETON: L OE 'The *tūn* of *Ecgwulf*'. (Herefords) [A First Fleet (convict) surname, William Eggleton, who married Mary Dickerson on arrival].

EGLEN, EGLIN, EAGLEN, EAGLAND, EAGLING, EGLON: P A Norman form of *Aquilina*, (*Egelina*), a woman's name. 12th cent.

EKINS see EDKINS.

ELCOCK(S), ELLCOCK, ELLICOCK: P OE *Eli-coc*, a dim. of *Elie*. 13th cent.

ELDER(S): N OE *eald* 'old', *ealdor* 'elder, senior'. 13th cent.

ELDRIDGE see ALDRICH.

ELESENDER: P Scottish form of *Alexander*. 14th cent.

ELFICK see ALPHEGE.

ELFORD: L OE *ellern-ford* 'ford by an elm-tree'. (Northumb).

ELGAR see ALGAR.

ELGOOD: P OG *Helgaud*, OF *Helgot*. DB.

ELIAS see ELLIS.

ELIOT, ELLIOT, ELLIOTT: (i) P A dim. of *Elias* + suffix *-ot*. 12th cent. (ii) The Scottish Eliot is from OE *AElfweald* 'elf-ruler'. 13th cent. [Joseph Elliot and Edward Elliot, both convicts, brought the name to Australia 1788].

ELKERTON: L OE 'The *tūn* (farm) of *Ēleac*'.

ELKIN(S): P A dim. of *Elie* (*Elias*). 13th cent.

ELKINGTON: L OE '*Elta's dūn* (hill)'. (Northants).

ELL, ELCE: P A dim. of *Ela* (Eleanor), a woman's name. 13th cent.

ELLARD see ADLARD.

ELLEN(S), ELLIN: (i) P *Ellen*, Anglo-Saxon form of Gk *Helen*. 12th cent. (ii) L OE *ellen* 'elder-tree'. 14th cent.

ELLENOR, ELLINOR: P *Alienor*, Provençal form of Gk *Helen*, taken to England by the wife of Henry II, *Eleanor* of Aquitaine. 12th cent.

ELLERY see HILLARY. ELLICK see ELWICK.

ELLIMAN, ELLERMAN: O OE *aele* or OF *oile* + *mann* 'oil-man, a seller of oil'. 14th cent.

ELLINGTON: L OE 'The *tūn* (settlement) of the people of *Ella* or *Ealda*'. (Hunts, Kent, Northumb, Yorks) 13th cent.

ELLIS(S), ELLICE: P ME *Elis* ((*Elias*, Gk form of Hebrew *Elijah*). 12th cent.

ELLISON: (i) P OG *Elisund*, OF *Elissent*. 12th cent. (ii) P ME 'Son of *Ellis*'. 13th cent. [Ellis, a First Fleet (crew and marine) surname].

ELLWOOD, ELWOOD, ALLWOOD: P OE *AElfweald* 'elf-ruler'. DB.

ELM, ELMES, NELMS: L OE *elm* 'elm' or 'elms'. 14th cent.

ELMER see AYLMER. ELPHIC see ALPHEGE.

ELPHINSTON(E): L From the lands of Tranent (Midlothian) Scotland. 13th cent.

ELSEY, ELSIE: P OE *Aelfsige* 'elf-victory'. DB.

ELSLEY: L OE 'The *lēah* (clearing) of *Elt*'. (Cambs) 14th cent.

ELSTON(E), ELLSTON: (i) P *Ealdstān* 'old stone' or *Ealhstān* 'temple stone'. Anglo-Saxon pers. names. (ii) L OE 'The *tūn* (farm) of *Ethelsige*' (Lancs) or of *Elias* (who held the manor in 1168) (Wilts) or ON + OE 'The *tūn* of a Norseman called *Eileifr*' (Notts). 12th cent.

ELTON: L OE '*Ella's tūn* (farm)'. 13th cent.

ELVEN, ELVIN(S) see ALVEN. ELVERY see ALFREY.

ELVEY, ELVY: P OE *AElgifu* 'elf-gift'. 14th cent. See also Allvey.

ELVIN(S) see ALVEN. ELVIDGE see ALPHEGE.

ELWELL: L OE *hael-wielle* 'omen-spring', known as 'the wishing well'. (Dorset) 13th cent.

ELWICK, ELLICK: L OE '*Ella's wīc* (dairy farm)'. (Durham).

ELWIN, ELWYN see ALWIN.

ELY, EALEY, EELEY, ELEY, HELY, HELEY: (i) P ME *Elie* (*Elijah*). 12th cent. (ii) L OE *ēl-gē* 'eel district'. According to Bede, Ely was named from the eel catch in the fens there. (Cambs) DB.

EMANUEL: P Hebrew 'God with us'. Mainly a Jewish name but popular in Cornwall in 15th and 16th cent.

EMBERSON see EMMERSON.

EMBERY, EMBURY: L OE *efn, emn* 'even', 'the smooth hill'. (Som) 13th cent.

EMBLEM, EMBLEN, EMBLIN, EMBLING: P Dim. of OF *Ameline, Emmeline*, pet-forms of names in *Adal-* (*athal*) 'noble'. DB.

EMERY see AMERY.

EMM(S): P OG *Emma*, pet-form of names compounded with *ermin* 'whole, universal'. The name of the queen of Ethelred the Unready (1002) and, the same woman, of Canute (1017). Surname 12th cent.

EMMATT, EMMETT, EMMITT, EMMOTT: P Pet-forms of *Emm*. 13th cent.

EMMERSON, EMBERSON: P 'Son of *Emery*'. 15th cent.

EMSON, EMPSON: P 'Son of *Emm*'. 14th cent.

ENDACOTT, ENDICOTT: L OE *ende-cot* 'beyond the cottages'.

ENFIELD: L OE 'The *feld* (field or open plain) of *Ēana*'. (Middx) 12th cent.

ENGELBERT see INGLEBRIGHT.

ENGLAND: L OE Development of a name given to a man from the land of the Angles as distinct from that of the Saxons and Jutes, who settled in other parts of Britain. The Angles were so named from the fact that they came from an angle-shaped area of Holstein (Schleswig-Holstein). In Britain, the name developed through Angle-land, Engleland, England.

ENGLEFIELD: L OE 'The *feld* (open, unforested country) of an Anglo-Saxon called *Ingweald*'. (Surrey).

ENGLISH, INGLISH, INGLIS: L OE *Englisc* 'English (Angle)' living among border people, e.g., in areas of Scandinavian influence or the Welsh border country. *Inglis* is the Scottish form. 12th cent. [Nicholas English, a convict, brought the name to Australia 1788].

ENION, ENNION, EYNON, ONIANS, ONION(S): P OW *Enniaun*, an ancient Welsh name associated with *einion* 'anvil' for 'stability, fortitude'. 12th cent.

ENNIS: P Ir *O hAonghuis* 'descendant of *Angus*'.

ENRIGHT, MACENRIGHT: P Ir *Mac Ionnrachtaigh*, from *indreacht* 'attack'.

ENSOR: L OE 'The *ōfer* (place over or beyond) belonging to *Ēada*'. 13th cent.

ENTICKNAP: L OE 'The *cnaepp* (hillock) belonging to *Anneca*'. 14th cent.

ENTWHISTLE: L OE 'The *twisla* (a tongue of land in a river fork) belonging to *Enna*'. (Lancs) 13th cent.

EPPS see APPS.

ERNEST, HARNESS: (i) P OG *Arnegis*, OF *Erneis*. Winton D. (ii) O OF *harneis*, ME *harnais* 'harness', 'a maker of harness or suits of mail'. 13th cent.

ERRIDGE: L OE *earu-hrycg* 'eagle ridge'. (Sussex) 13th cent.

ERRINGTON: L Brit/OW *arian-tūn* 'the farm beside the silvery river'. (Northumb), *Erienton* 1202.

ERSKINE: L SG From Erskine (Renfrews) Scotland. 13th cent.

ERVIN(E) see IRVIN.

ERWIN, IRWIN(E), URWIN: P OE *Ēorfwine* 'boar-friend'. DB.

ESCREET: L ON *eski* 'ash-tree'. (Yorks).

ESDAILE, EASDALE: L Celtic + ON *Esk-dalr* 'dale of the Esk'. (Dumfries) Scotland. 15th cent.

ESGATE see EASTGATE. ESKELL see ASKELL. ESMOND(E) see EASTMAN.

ESPLEY: L OE *aespe-lēah* 'aspen wood'. (Northumb).

ESSEX: L OE *Ēast-Seaxe* 'land of the East Saxons'. 12th cent.

ESSLEMONT: L SG from Brit. From Esslemont (hill) (Aberdeens).

ESSON see EASON. ESTALL see EASTALL. ESTAUGH see EASTAUGH. ESTE see EAST.

ESTRIDGE: L OF *estreis* 'from the east', an 'Easterling'. 12th cent.

ETCHELLS: L OE *ēcels* 'addition, increase', 'land added to estate or village'. (Ches).

ETHEREDGE, ETHERIDGE, ETTERIDGE, ETTRIDGE: P OE *AEthelrīc* 'noble rule'. DB.

ETHERINGTON see HETHERINGTON.

EUSTACE, EUSTICE: P Lat *Eustachius*, from Gk 'fruitful'. The name was introduced into England by the Normans. DB.

EVANS, EVENS, HEAVEN(S): P A Welsh form of *John*. 15th cent. [A First Fleet (convict and marine) surname].

EVASON, EVERSON, EVISON: P 'Son of *Evot*'. 14th cent. See Evatt.

EVATT, EVETT(S), EVITT(S): P From *Evot* or *Evet*, dims. of *Eve*. 14th cent.

EVE: Hebrew 'lively', a term of uncertain meaning: 'lively, brisk, spirited'? 'joy, rapture'? 'vital, lifelike'? What Hebrew *hawwah* means is equally uncertain; 'lively' and 'serpent' are both possibilities. Surname 13th cent.

EVELEIGH, EVERLEY, EVERSLEIGH: L OE *eofor-lēah* 'wild boar wood'. (Yorks, Wilts).

EVERARD, EVERETT, EVERITT: P OG *Eburhard, Everhard* 'boar-hard'. DB.

EVERDEN: L OE *eofor-dūn* 'wild boar hill'. (Northants).

EVERINGHAM: L OE 'The *hām* (homestead) of the people of *Eofor* (the boar)'. (Yorks). [A First Fleet (convict) surname].

EVEREST, EVERIST see DEVERAUX. EVERLEY, EVERSLEIGH see EVELEIGH.

EVERSHED: N or L OE *eofor-hēafod* either an uncomplimentary nickname 'boar-head' or a sign name 'at the Boar's Head'.

EVERSON: P A dim. of *Eve*.

EVERTON: L OE *eofor-tūn* 'the *tūn* (farm) where a wild boar lurks'. (Beds, Lancs, Notts) 13th cent.

EVES see EAVES. EVILL see DAVALL.

EWAN, EWEN(S), EWING(S), EWIN(S), HEWINS, YEWEN, YOUENS: P Ir *Eogan*, SG *Eoghann*, OW *Eugein, Ougein*, from Gk 'well-born'. The name was also introduced into eastern England by the Bretons. DB.

EWART, YEOWARD, YEOWART, YOUATT: (i) P *Ewart*, an OF form of *Edward*. 11th cent. (ii) O OE *eown-hierde* 'dairy-farmer'. 13th cent. (iii) L OE *ēa-worth* 'the *worth* (homestead) on a river'. (Ewart, Northumb, *Ewurthe* 13th cent.)

EWBANK: L OE *īw* + ME *banke* 'yew bank'. 13th cent.

EWER(S), LEWER(S), LOWER: O OF *euwier*, from *eau* 'water'. 'Servant offering ewers of water at table during meals'. 12th cent. (Table forks came into use in 15th cent.)

EXTON: (i) L OE *Esce*, from Brit *Escā* (river-name) + *tūn*. 'The farm on the River *Esce* (now Exe)'. (Devon) (ii) L OE *aet East Seaxatune* 'at the farm colony of the East Saxons'. (Hants).

EYER(S), EYRE(S) see AYR. EYLES see ILES. EYNON see ENNION. EZARD see ISSARD.

F

FABER: O Lat *faber* 'smith'. DB.

FABIAN: P Lat *Fabianus*, a Roman family name. English surname 12th cent.

FACEY see VAISEY.

FADDEN, MACFADDEN: P Ir *Mac Phaidin*, a dim. of *Padraig* (Patrick).

FAGAN: P Ir A surname of uncertain etymology, *O Faodhagain* in Co. Louth but apparently of Norman origin in Dublin.

FAGG, VAGG: O OE *facq, fadge* 'a baker of flat loaves'. 12th cent.

FAGGOTTER: O OF & ME *fagot* 'firewood', 'a fagot seller'. 13th cent.

FAHY, FAHEY: P Ir *O Fathartaigh*, from *fothadh* 'foundation'.

FAIL see FAYLE.

FAINER, FEINER: O OF *fenier* 'haymonger'. 13th cent.

FAIR(E), FAIRES, FAIRS, FAIERS, FAYER, FEYER, PHAIR, PHAYER, PHAYRE: N OE *faeger* 'fair, beautiful'. DB.

FAIRBAIRN: N OE *faeger-bearn* 'fair, beautiful child'. 13th cent.

FAIRBANKS: L OE *faeger* + ME *banke* 'beautiful hillside'. 16th cent.

FAIRBOURNE, FAIRBURN: L OE *fearn-burna* 'stream in the ferns'. (Kent) 12th cent.

FAIRBROTHER, FAREBROTHER: N 'Brother of *Fair*'. 16th cent.

FAIRCHILD: N OE *faeger-cild* 'beautiful child'. 11th cent.

FAIRCLOUGH, FAIRCLOTH: L OE *faeger* + ME *clough* 'fair hollow'. 14th cent.

FAIREY, FAIRY: N OE *faeger-ēage* 'fair (beautiful) eyes'. 13th cent.

FAIRFAX: N OE *faeger-feax* 'fair hair'. 12th cent.

FAIRFIELD: L OE *faeger-feld* 'beautiful field or open plain'. (Derbys) 12th cent.

FAIRFOUL, FAIRFULL: N OE *faeger-fugol* 'fair bird'. 13th cent.

FAIRHALL, FAIRALL: L OE *faeger-healh* 'beautiful secluded place'. 14th cent.

FAIRHURST: L OE *faeger-hyrst* 'beautiful wooded hill'. 13th cent.

FAIRLAMB: N OE *faeger-lamb* 'beautiful and gentle'.

FAIRLEE: L OE *faeger-lēah* 'beautiful glade'. (Wight).

FAIRLEY, FAIRLEIGH: L OE *fearn-lēah* 'ferney glade or clearing'. (Salop) DB. [Fairley, a First Fleet (convict) surname].

FAIRMAN: N OE *faeger-mann* (fair (handsome) man'. 12th cent.

FAIRWEATHER: N OE *faeger-weder* 'bright, sunny disposition'. 13th cent.

FAITH: N OF *feid* (pron. *feith*) 'faith', 'a sincerely devout person'. 14th cent. FAITHFUL: N with same meaning as Faith.

FAKE(S), FALCK see FAWKE.

FALCON: O OF *faucon* 'falcon'. Metonymic for *Falconer*. 12th cent.

FALCONER, FALKNER, FAULKINER, FAULKNER: O OF 'A keeper, trainer or hunter with falcons'. 12th cent.

FALDER, FOLDER, FAULDER, VALDER: O OE *falod* '(sheep) fold'. 'A worker at the sheep-folds'. 14th cent.

FALK, FALKUS see FAWKE.

FALL(E), FALLS, FAULL, FAWLE: L ME *falle* 'waterfall or steep slope'. 13th cent.

FALLON, FALLOON: P Ir *O Fallamhain*, from *follamhnas* 'pre-eminence'.

FALLOW(S): L OE *fealg*, ME *falwe* 'newly cultivated land'. 13th cent.

FALLOWFIELD: L OE Either *fealu* 'fallow' or *fealg* 'newly cultivated *feld* (field)'. (Northumb) 13th cent.

FALLSHAW: L OE *scaga* 'shaw, copse' + ME *falle* 'waterfall in a little wood'.

FALMER: L OE perhaps *fealu-mere* '*fallow* (in the sense of unused) *mere* (lake)'. (Sussex), *Falemere* DB. [A First Fleet (female convict) surname].

FANE, FAYNE, VAINE, VANE, VAYNE: N OE *faegen*, ME *fane, fayne* 'cheerful, glad'. 13th cent.

FANN, VAN(N), VANCE: L OE *faen, fenn* 'fen or marsh'. 12th cent.

FANNER, VANNER: (i) L OE Identical in meaning with *Fann*. (ii) O OE *fann* 'a maker of fans (winnowing baskets)'. 13th cent.

FANNING, FENNING: L OE variants of *Fenn*.

FARADAY: O OE *daege*, ME *day* 'servant', 'servant of *Farra (Farrar)*'.

FARDELL: O ME *fardel* 'bundle, burden', 'a carrier, porter'. *Hamlet* (Act III): 'who would fardels bear, to grunt and sweat under a weary life . . .?'

FAREBROTHER see FAIRBROTHER.

FARINDON, FARRINGDON: L OE *fearn-dūn* 'fern-clad down (hill)' (Berks, Devon, Dorset, Hants, Oxon) DB. (Farringdon, London, was named from an alderman, Nicholas de *Farindon*.)

FARINGTON, FARRINGTON: L OE *fearn-tūn* 'homestead among ferns'. (Lancs, Som).

FARLAM: L OE *fearn-lēam* 'fern clearings'. (Cumb) 14th cent.

FARLEY, FARLEIGH: L OE *fearn-lēah* 'fern glade or clearing'.

FARLOW: L OE *fearn-hlāw* 'fern-covered mound'. (Salop) 13th cent.

FARMAN: O ON *farmann* 'a travelling trader'. Winton D. 1066.

FARMER, FERMOR: O OF *fermier*, AF *fermer* 'tax farmer', paying an agreed sum to the Exchequer and keeping the balance. (ii) O 'Steward, bailiff'. 13th cent. (Farmer has entirely changed its meaning in general usage, replacing *churl*, husbandman.)

FARMERY: O OF *enfermerie* 'worker at the (monastic) infirmary'. 12th cent.

FARNALL, FARNELL, FARNILL, VARNAL, VERNAL(L): L OE *fearn-hyll* 'fern-covered hill'. (Ches, Kent, Hants, Wilts, Yorks) 13th cent.

FARNCOMB(E): L OE *fearn-cumb* 'ferny valley'. (Surrey) 13th cent.

FARNHAM: L OE *fearn-hām* 'homestead in the ferns'. 12th cent.

FARNSWORTH: L OE *fearn-worth* '*worth* (enclosure) overgrown with ferns'. (Lancs) 12th cent.

FARO see FARRAR. FARQUHAR see MACFARQUHAR.

FARQUARSON: P A patronymic of *Farquar*. See MacFarquar.

FARR: N OE *fearr*. A nickname from the bull. 14th cent.

FARRAND, FARRANT, FARRANCE, FARREN, FARRIN, FERRAN: (i) P OF *Ferant* (*Ferdinand*). 12th cent. (ii) N OF *ferrant* 'iron-grey' (of hair).

FARRAR, FARRER, FARRAH, FARROW, FARO, PHAROAH, PHARRO: O OF *ferreor, ferrier* 'a worker in iron, smith'. 14th cent. Pharaoh may also be a pageant name.

FARRELL, FERRALL: P Ir *O Fearghail* 'man of valour'. [Both Farrell and Ferrel are First Fleet (convict) surnames, Ferrel an unrecorded variant].

FARREN: N OE *faeger-hine* 'fair servant'. 13th cent. See also Farrand.

FARRINGTON: L OE *fearn-tūn* 'the fern-grown farm'. (Som), *Ferentone* DB.

FARSON: N OE *faeger-sunu* 'fair son'. 14th cent.

FARTHING: N OE *feorthing* 'fourth part', nickname for a holder of a farthing of land. DB. See also Halfpenny.

FATHERS: N OE *faeder* 'a protector, religious teacher or confessor'. DB.

FATT: N OE *faett* 'plump, fleshy'. OE Byname 1049.

FAUCHON: N OF *falchion* 'broadsword', nickname for the warrior who wielded it.

FAULCONER, FAULKNER see FALCONER. FAULL see FALL.

FAULDER see FALDER. FAULDS see FOLD.

FAUN, FAUNCE, FAWNS, FOWNES: (i) N OF *faon*, ME *faun*, based on Lat rural deities with horns and tail, 'fallow deer'. Nickname for a frisky youngster. 12th cent. (ii) L From the lands of Faunes (Berwicks) Scotland. 12th cent. [A rare variant, Founes, is a First Fleet (female convict) surname].

FAVELL(E): N OF *fauvel* 'tawny', usually of hair. 12th cent.

FAWCETT, FAWSETT, FAUCETT: L OE *fāg-sīde* 'multi-coloured hillside'. 13th cent.

FAWKE(S), FAUX, FALCK, FALK, FALKUS, FAULK(S), FAULKES, FAKE(S): P OG *Falco*, OF *Faugue* 'falcon', a pers. name from the bird of prey. 13th cent.

FAWLE see FALL.

FAWLEY: L OE *fealu-lēah* 'fallow-coloured clearing'. (Bucks, Hants, Herefords) [John Fawley, a seaman on the *Scarborough*, brought the name to Australia 1788].

FAY(E), FEY: (i) L OF From Fay (France). 12th cent. (ii) N OF *fae* 'fairy', 'delicate, diminutive, graceful, charming'. 14th cent.

FAYER(S), FAYRE see FAIR. FAYNE see FANE.

FAYLE, FAIL(S): P Manx for *Mac Giolla Phoil* 'son of the servant of *Paul*'. 15th cent.

FAZACKERLEY, FAZAKERLY, PHIZ-ACLEA: L OE *faes-lēah* 'strip of land at the clearing'. (Lancs) 13th cent.

FEAKES, FEAKS see FICK.

FEAR(E), PHEAR: N OF *fier* 'fierce, bold' or ME *fere* 'comrade'. 13th cent.

FEARNLEY: L OE *fearn-lēah* 'the clearing overgrown with ferns'.

FEARNSIDE: L OE *fearn-sīde* 'ferny slope'. 14th cent.

FEARON, FERON: O OF *ferron* 'iron-worker, smith'. 12th cent.

FEATHER: O OE *fether*. Metonymic for a feather-monger. 13th cent.

FEATHERBY: L ON *fegrthar-býr* 'beautiful farm'. (Yorks) 12th cent.

FEATHERSTONE, FETHERSTONE: L OE *fetherstān* 'standing stones (cromlech)'. (Northumb, Staffs) 12th cent.

FEATHERSTONEHAUGH: L OE *fetherstān-halh* 'nook by the standing stones'. 12th cent.

FEAVER, FEVER(S), LEFEVRE: O OF *fevre* 'iron-worker, smith'. 13th cent.

FEE see FOY.

FEELY, FEELEY, FEEHELY, FEHILLY: P Ir *O* & *Mac Fithcheallaigh* 'chess-player'.

FEENEY, FINNEY: P Ir *O Fiannaidhe* 'descendant of the soldier'. [Finney, a First Fleet (convict) surname].

FEILD see FIELD. FEINER see FAINER. FELD see FIELD. FELDER see FIELDER.

FELDWICK: L OE *feld-wīc* 'dairy farm in the fields'. (Sussex) 13th cent.

FELGATE see FIELDGATE.

FELICE, FILICE: P Lat *Felicia*, OF *Felise*, fem. of *Felix*. 12th cent. (*Felice* was used by Langland in *Piers Plowman*.)

FELIX: P Lat *Felix* 'happy', the name of four popes and several saints. 12th cent. (Felixtowe, Suffolk, was named for St *Felix*, the apostle of East Anglia.)

FELL(S): (i) O OE *fell-mangian*. Metonymic for *fell-monger* 'trader in hides and skins'. 13th cent. (ii) L ON *fell* 'mountain'. 14th cent.

FELLER: O OE *fellan* 'to fell', 'a timber-feller'. 13th cent.

FELLOWES, FELLOWS: N OE *fēolaga* or ON *felagi* 'companion, partner'. 13th cent.

FELSTEAD: L OE *feld-stede* 'place in a field'. *Felstede* DB. (Essex).

FELTHAM: L OE *filethe-hamm* 'hay-meadow', (Som), or OE *feld-hām* 'homestead in a field', (Middx).

FELTON: L OE *feld-tūn* 'farm or village in open country'. (Herefords, Northumb, Salop, Som) 13th cent.

FEMISTER, FIMISTER, PHEMISTER, PHIMISTER: O OE *feoh-maegester* 'fee-master', in charge of the (cattle) herds. 15th cent.

FENBY: L OE *fenn-by* 'farm or village in the fens'. (Lincs) 13th cent.

FENDER: O OF A derivative of *fend*, short-form of *defend*, 'a defender'. 13th cent.

FENDICK: L OE *fenn-dīc* 'fen-dyke'. 14th cent.

FENN, VENN: L OE *fenn* or E. Saxon *faen* 'fen or marsh'. 12th cent.

FENNEL, FENNELL: O OE *finugl 'fennel* (culinary herb). Metonymic for a grower of fennel. 14th cent.

FENNER, VENNER: L OE *fènn*. See Fenn for meaning.

FENTON: L OE *fenn-tūn* 'farm in the fens'. (Cumb, Lincs, Northumb, Notts, Staffs, E. Lothian) 12th cent.

FENWICK: L OE *fenn-wīc* 'dairy-farm or outlying farm by the fen'. (Northumb, Yorks).

FERDINAND: P OG *Ferdinand*, a compound of *fardi* 'journey' and *nanthi* 'risk, adventure', giving rise to surnames Farrand and variants.

FERGUS: P SG *Fearghus*, Ir *O Fearghuis* 'man-choice' or 'man-vigour'. 12th cent.

FERGUSON: P 'Son of *Fergus*'. 15th cent. [A First Fleet (crew and convict) surname].

FERMOR see FARMER.

FERN(E), VERN(E): L OE *fearn* 'fern', 'among the ferns'. 13th cent.

FERNEYHOUGH: L OE *fearn-holh* 'ferny hollow'. 14th cent.

FERNIE: L OE From the lands of Fernie (Fifes) Scotland. 15th cent.

FERNLEY: L OE *fearn-lēah* 'ferny glade or clearing'. (Yorks).

FERON see FEARON. FERRALL see FARRELL. FERRAN see FARRAND.

FERRAR: O OF *ferreor* 'a worker in iron, smith'. 12th cent. See also Farrar.

FERRERS: L OF From Ferrières-Saint-Hilaire (Eure) Normandy. DB.

FERRET: N OF *furet* 'ferret', nickname for a pilferer. 13th cent.

FERRIER: O OE A derivative of *fērian* 'to carry', 'fare (travel)'. 'A ferryman'. 12th cent.

FERRIS: P An Ulster variant of *Fergus*.

FERRY, FERRIE, FERRI: L OE *ferian* 'ferry', 'by the ferry'. (Yorks) 13th cent.

FERRIMAN: O ME *feri-mann*, see Ferrier for meaning. 12th cent.

FETHERSTONE see FEATHERSTONE.

FETTERPLACE: O AF *fete-place* 'make room', 'an usher'. 14th cent.

FEVER see FEAVER. FEWKES see FOLK.

FEWSTER, FOYSTER, FOISTER, FUSTER: O AF *fuster* 'a saddle-tree maker'. 12th cent.

FEWTRELL: O ME *veuterer* 'a keeper of hounds'.

FEYER see FAIR.

FICK, FEAKES, FEAKS: O OF see Fitch for meaning. 12th cent.

FIDDES: L SG From the barony of Fiddes (Kincardines) Sçotland. 12th cent.

FIDDIAN see VIVIAN.

FIDDY, FIDOE: N OF *fitz deu* 'son of God', an oath name. 14th cent.

FIDGE: O OF A variant of *Fitch*. 12th cent.

FIDLER, FIDDLER, VIDLER: O OE *fithelere*, 'a fidler', *fithelestre* 'female fidler'. 13th cent.

FIDLING, FIDDLING: L OE 'The people of an Anglo-Saxon called *Fitela*'. (Yorks) 12th cent.

FIELD(S), FEILD, FELD: L OE *feld* 'field or open country', a frequent name in previously wooded country. 12th cent. See also Delafield.

FIELDEN, FEILDEN: L OE Identical in meaning with *Field*. 13th cent.

FIELDER, FELDER: O OE 'Worker in the fields'. 14th cent.

FIELDHOUSE: L OE *feld-hūs* 'house in the fields'. 14th cent. FIELDING: L OE *felding* 'open country'. 13th cent. FIELDSEND: 'End of the field'. 13th cent.

FIENNES: L OF From Fiennes (Pas-de-Calais) France. 12th cent.

FIFE see FYFE.

FIFEHEAD, FIFEFIELD: L OE *fīf-hīde* 'five

hides of land'. 12th cent. (One hide = 120 acres, enough for one free family and dependents. Five hides was the holding of a *thegn*, thane, noble of lower rank than earl.)

FIGGISS: N OF *ficheis* 'faithful'. 13th cent.

FIGGINS: O OF Identical in meaning with *Fitch*. 16th cent.

FILBY, FILBEE, PHILBY, PHILBEY: L O Scand 'The *býr* (farm) of a Scandinavian settler called *Fili*'. (Norfolk) 12th cent.

FILDES: L OE *filde* 'field-like, open plain'. (Lancs) 13th cent.

FILER: O OE *fēol* 'file'. Metonymic for a maker of files. 13th cent.

FILKIN(S): L OE 'The people of an Anglo-Saxon called *Filica*'. (Oxon) 12th cent. Filkin is also a dim. of *Phil* (*Philip*). 14th cent.

FILLINGHAM: L OE 'The *hām* (homestead) of *Fygla*'. (Lincs).

FIMISTER see FEMISTER.

FINCH, FINK(E), VINCK, VINK: N OE *finc* 'finch', nickname for a simpleton. Chaucer: 'to pull a finch' (to swindle a simpleton). Not all were simple; Finch Lane and St Benet Fink (Clerkenwell) London, were named for a prominent freeman of the City, *AElfwin Finche*. OE Byname 1049.

FINCHAM: L OE *finc-hām* 'homestead with finches'. (Norfolk).

FINDLATER: L From Findlater (Banffs) Scotland. 14th cent.

FINDON: L OE *fīn-dūn* 'the hill heaped with wood'. (Sussex).

FINE(S): N OF *fin* 'delicate, tender'. 12th cent.

FINER: O OF *fineur* 'a refiner of gold or silver'. 12th cent.

FINLAY, FINLEY, FINDLAY, FINDLEY, FINDLOW, FINLOW: N SG *Fionnlagh* 'fair hero'. 11th cent. FINLAYSON: P 'Son of *Finlay*'. 13th cent.

FINN, FYNN, PHIN: L O Dan & O Sw *Fin*, ON *Finnr* 'The Finn, man from Finland'. DB. In Ireland, *O Finn* 'descendant of *Fionn* the fair'.

FINNEGAN, FINEGAN: P Ir *O Fionnagain* 'fair-headed'.

FINNEMORE: N OF *fin amour* 'dear love'. 12th cent.

FINNEY see FEENEY.

FIRBANK, FURBANK: L OE *fyrhth, frith* 'wooded slope or bank'. 15th cent.

FIRKIN: O OE from Du *ferdekyn, firkin* 'quarter barrel'. 'A maker of barrels'.

FIRMAGE see FURMAGE.

FIRMIN, FIRMAN, FURMAN: N OF *firmin* 'firm, strong'. 12th cent.

FIRMINGER: O OF *fromagier, formagier* 'a maker/seller of cheese'. 12th cent.

FIRTH, FRITH, FREETH, FREED, FRIFT, THRIFT, FRIGHT, FREAK, FREKE: (i) L OE *fryhth, ferhthe*, ME *firthe, ferthe* 'frith', 'woodland'. 12th cent. (ii) L ON *fjorthr firth, frith* 'woodland'. (ON *fjorthr* reached England from Scotland in 15th cent.)

FISH, FISK(E), FYSH: N OE *fisc*, a nickname from the fish. 12th cent.

FISHBORNE, FISHBOURNE, FISHBURN(E): L OE *fisc-burna* 'fish-stream'. (Durham, Sussex, Wight) 12th cent. [Andrew Fishborne, a private soldier, brought the name to Australia 1788].

FISHER: O OE *fiscere* 'fisher, fisherman'. 13th cent. [A First Fleet (crew) surname].

FISHLOCK: L OE *fisc-lacu* 'fish-lake'. (Yorks) 12th cent.

FISHMAN: O OE *fiscere-mann* 'a fisherman or seller of fish'. 15th cent.

FISHWICK, FYSHWICK: L OE *fisc-wīc* 'the dairy farm where fish also is sold'. (Lancs) 12th cent.

FITCH, FITCHETT: OF *fiche* 'an iron point' (i) O 'a worker with an iron-pointed instrument', (ii) N 'a knight famous on the battlefield or tournament for his exploits with the lance'. 13th cent.

FITTER: (i) O OE *fitt* 'struggle, contest', 'a fighter, contestant'. (ii) O OE *fit* 'song, poem'. Metonymic for a poet or song-writer. 12th cent. (To be precise, *fit* is a division of a poem: e.g., *The Hunting of the Snark: An Agony in Ten Fits* by Lewis Carroll.)

FITTON: N ME *fitten*, a common term for lying, deceit, and a nickname from this source. 12th cent.

FITZ: Lat *filius*, AF *fiz* denotes 'son of', used early in the recording of surnames to distinguish a son from his father. The prefix has assumed an aristocratic connotation, generally without justification, although some surnames in *Fitz* indicate royal bastardy. The survival of surnames preceded by Fitz has been a matter of chance. The following have survived, several being the surnames of families, originally Norman, which settled in Ireland: FitzAlan (Alan), FitzAucher (Alger), Fitzgerald (Gerald), Fitzgibbon, Fitzgibbin (Gibben), Fitzgilbert (Gilbert), Fitzhardinge (Harding), Fitzharris, Feehally, Feeharry (Harry), Fitzhenry (Henry), Fitzherbert

(Herbert), Fitzhugh (Hugh), Fitzjames (James), Fitzjohn (John), Fitzmaurice (Maurice), Fitzneal (Neal), Fitzpatrick (Patrick), Fitzpayn (Pain), Fitzroy (Fillary), Fitzsimmons (Simmons), Fitzwalter, Fitzwater (Walter), Fitzwarin (Wareing). There is no hard and fast rule about the use of capitals or small letters for the surname following the prefix. The forms given above are those generally used. [Elizabeth Fitzgerald and Jane Fitzgerald, unrelated convicts, brought the name to Australia 1788].

FLAGG, FLACK: L ON *flagg*, ME *flag* 'a sod, turf', 'the turf-cutting place', probably peat is indicated. (Derbys, Notts) 14th cent.

FLAHERTY, O'FLAHERTY: P Ir *O Flaithbheartaigh* 'descendant of bright ruler'. [Flartee, an unrecorded variant, is a First Fleet (convict) surname].

FLAMANK see FLEMING.

FLANAGAN, O'FLANAGAN: P Ir *O Flannagain* 'descendant of the ruddy one'.

FLANDERS, FLINDERS: L OF from Flemish. An immigrant from Flanders. 12th cent.

FLANNERY: P Ir *O Flannabhra*, from *flannabhar* 'ruddy eyebrow'.

FLASHMAN: L OE *flasce*, ME *flasshe* 'flask', used topographically, 'pond or marsh'. 13th cent.

FLATMAN: L ON *flatr* 'smooth, level ground'. 16th cent.

FLATT: L ON *flatr*. Identical in meaning with *Flatman*. 14th cent.

FLAXMAN, FLEXMAN: O OE *fleax* 'a dresser/seller of flax'. 13th cent.

FLEEMAN see FLEMING.

FLEET: (i) L OE *flēot* 'a stream or creek'. (Hants, Kent, Lincs, Middx) 12th cent. (ii) N ME *flete* 'swift', nickname for a fast runner. 14th cent.

FLEGG: L O Dan *flaeg* 'marsh where flags (water plants) grow'. (Norfolk).

FLEMING, FLEMMING, FLEMONS, FLAMENT: L OF *flamanc*, AF *fleming* 'a Fleming'. 12th cent. See also Flanders. [George Flemming, a marine, arrived on the *Sirius*].

FLESHER: O OE *flǣsc-hēawan*, reversing the order, 'cut flesh', 'a butcher'. 13th cent.

FLETCHER: O OF *flechier* 'an arrow maker/dealer'. 12th cent.

FLETT: L OE *flett*, Old Saxon *fletti* 'hall, mansion'.

FLEURY, FLOREY, FLORY, FLURY: (i) P Lat *Floria*, a woman's name, from *flos* 'flower'. 12th cent. (ii) L OF From Fleury (France). 12th cent.

FLEWETT, FLEWITT, FLOWITT: P OG *Hlodhard* 'fame-hardy'. 12th cent. The change of pronunciation and therefore of spelling is due to Norman influence.

FLINDERS: N ON *flindra*, dial. *flinter* 'splinters, fragments', a nickname of lost meaning. See also Flanders. [Matthew Flinders, naval officer and explorer, sailed to Australia 1795].

FLINT, FLINDT: N OE *flint* 'rock', a nickname for rock-hard character. DB.

FLOAT, FLOTE: O OE *flota* 'boat, ship, crew', 'a mariner'. 12th cent.

FLOOD, FLUDE: (i) L OE *flōd* 'tide, current', 'flood-waters' or OE *flōde* 'channel or gutter'. 12th cent. (ii) P Ir *Mac an Tuile*, hence *Tully*. *Tuile* also means 'flood'.

FLOOK, FLUKE: P ON *Flóki*, a pers. name meaning 'matted, shaggy'.

FLORENCE: P Lat *Florentius*, from *florens* 'blooming'. 12th cent.

FLORY, FLURY see FLEURY.

FLOWER(S): (i) O OE *flā* 'arrow', ME *flōer* 'an arrow-maker'. 13th cent. (ii) O OF *flur*, ME *flour*. Metonymic for a miller. 13th cent.

FLOWITT see FLEWETT.

FLOYD(E): N Welsh A variant from the pronunciation of *Lloyd*.

FLYNN, O'FLYNN, FLINN: P Ir *O Floinn*, from *flann* 'ruddy'. [Flynn and Flinn are both First Fleet (convict) surnames].

FOAD, FOAT: N OE *fōda* 'food', later the hand-fed recipient of food, 'a child'. 13th cent.

FODEN: L OE *fōding* 'feeding', 'grazing ground'. FODOR: O OE *fōdderbrytta*, from *fōdien* 'to feed', a supplier of fodder to cattle, 'a herdsman'. 14th cent.

FOGARTY: P Ir *O Fogartaigh* 'descendant of banished'.

FOGG: L *fog* (origin unknown) 'rank grass', later 'boggy, spongy', eventually, 'thick, murky' whence fog (mist). O Dan *fog* 'spray, storm' and *snefog* 'driving snow'. The surname is probably for 'bog, marsh'.

FOISTER see FEWSTER. **FOKES** see FOLK. **FOLDER** see FALDER.

FOLD(S), FOULD(S), FOWLDS, FAULDS: O OE *falod*, fāld '(sheep) fold'. 'Worker at the folds'. 13th cent.

FOLEY: P Ir *O Foghladha* 'descendant of plunderer'.

FOLK, FOLKES, FOULKES, FEWKES, FOKES, FOOKES, FOUX, FOWKE, FUKE, VOAKE, VOKE(S), VOLK(E), VOLKES: P OE, Old Saxon, Old High German *folc* 'the people'. The name was established among the Old English when the Normans recorded Domesday and has survived through the centuries. A variant is *ffoulkes*; the 'ff' form was often used in medieval manuscripts in place of the capital F. DB.

FOLKARD: P OG *Fulcard* 'people-brave'. 11th cent.

FOLL: N OF *fol* 'foolish'. 12th cent. FOLLEFANT: N OF *fol enfant* 'foolish child'. 12th cent. FOLLEY, FOLLY: N OF *folie* 'foolishness'. 12th cent. [Folly, a First Fleet (marine) surname].

FOLLETT, FOLLITT: N A dim. of *fol* 'foolish'. DB.

FONTAINE see FOUNTAIN.

FOOT(E): N OE *fot* 'foot', a nickname from some peculiarity or dexterity of the foot. DB.

FORBES: L SG From Forbes (Aberdeens) Scotland, derived from *forba* 'field'. 13th cent. [Ann Forbes, a convict, brought the name to Australia 1788].

FORD(E), FOORD, FORTH: L OE *ford* 'by the creek or river ford'. DB.

FORDER: L OE 'by the ford'. 14th cent. FORDHAM: L OE *ford-hām* 'homestead by the ford'.

FORDRED: P OE *Forthrǣd* 'forth-counsel'. 11th cent.

FORDYCE: L SG *forba-deas* 'south field'. (Banffs) Scotland. 16th cent.

FOREMAN, FORMAN: O OE *fōr-mann* 'pig-man, swineherd'. 13th cent.

FORESTER, FORESTIER, FORRESTER: O OF *forestier* 'official in charge of a forest'. 12th cent. [Forrester, a First Fleet (convict) surname].

FORGE: O OF *forge* 'smithy', 'blacksmith'. 13th cent.

FORMBY: L O Scand *forn-býr* 'old farm'. (Lancs).

FORREST: L OF *foret* 'forest'. 12th cent.

FORSDIKE see FOSDIKE. FORSE see FOSS. FORST see FROST.

FORSTER: (i) O A variant of *Forester*. (ii) O OF *forcetier* 'a cutler'. 13th cent.

FORSYTH, FORSAITH, FORSAYTH: P SG *Fearsithe* 'man of peace'. 14th cent.

FORT(E): N OF *fort* 'strong (character or physique)'. FORTESCUE: N OF *fort-escu* 'strongshield'. 12th cent.

FORTEY, FORTY: L OE *forth-ēg* 'forth island or peninsula'. 13th cent.

FORTNUM: O OF *fort anon* 'strong young ass'. 13th cent.

FORWARD, FORWOOD: O OE *fōr-weard* 'pig guard', 'a swineherd'. 13th cent.

FOSBERY, FOSBEARY: L OE *forwost-burg* 'chieftain's fort'. (Wilts).

FOSBROOK(E): L OE 'The *brōc* (brook) of an Anglo-Saxon called *Fōt*, which means 'foot'. (Staffs) 12th cent.

FOSDIKE, FOSDICK: L O Scand + OE 'The *dīc* (ditch) of a Viking settler called *Fotr*'. (Lincs).

FOSKETT: L OE *foxcot* 'foxes burrow'. (Bucks, Hants, Glos, Northants).

FOSSEY: L OE *foss-ēg* 'ditch island' (land surrounded by a dyke). 13th cent.

FOSTER: (i) O ME *foster* 'foster-parent, nurse'. 14th cent. (ii) A variant of *Forster* 'cutler'.

FOTHERGILL: L OE *fōdor* + ON *gil* 'the ravine where fodder may be found'. (Yorks).

FOTHERINGHAM: L OE From Fotheringham (Angus) Scotland. Originally from Fotheringhay (Northants) held in 12th cent. by the royal family of Scotland. (*fōd-ring-ēg* 'island used for foddering, grazing)'.

FOULCHER see FULCHER. FOULD(S) see FOLD. FOULKES see FOLK.

FOULSTONE, FOWLESTONE: L OE 'The *tūn* (farm) of *Fugol* (Bird)'. (Yorks) 12th cent.

FOUNTAIN(E), FONTAINE: L OF *fontaine* 'fountain or spring', or from Fontaine or Lafontaine (France). 12th cent.

FOURACRE(S): L OE *feower-aecer* 'a holding of four acres'. 14th cent.

FOURNEL see FURNELL. FOURNIER see FURNER. FOUX, FOWKE see FOLK.

FOWLE(S), FOWELL(S), FUGGLE, VOWELL(S), VOWLES: N OE *fugol* 'fowl, bird'. Winton D. [Fowell and Fowles are First Fleet (convict and crew) surnames].

FOWLER, FUGLER: O OE *fugelere* 'a fowler, hunter of wild birds'. 13th cent.

FOWNES see FAUN.

FOX: N OE *fox*, a nickname for cunning. 13th cent. [William Fox and Charles Heaphy discovered Lake Rotorua, 1846].

FOXLEY: L OE *fox-lēah* 'the foxes wood'. FOXTON: L OE *fox-denu* 'valley where foxes run'. FOXWELL: L OE *fox-wielle* 'the foxes spring'.

FOY, FEE: P Ir *O Fiaich*, from *fiach* 'raven'. Some may be from Foy (Herefords).

FOYLE: L OF *fouille* 'pit, excavation'. 13th cent. [A First Fleet surname].

FOYSTER see FEWSTER.

FRAIL: N OF *fresle* 'frail, weak'. DB.

FRAIN, FRAYNE, FREAN, FREEN: L OF *fresne* 'ash-tree'. 12th cent.

FRAME: L OE *fremde* 'foreigner, stranger'.

FRANCES, FRANCIS: L OF *Franceis* 'a Frenchman'. 12th cent. [A First Fleet (convict) surname].

FRANK(S), FRANCK(E): (i) L OG *Franco* 'a Frank'. 11th cent. (ii) O OF & ME *franc* 'a freeman, as distinct from a serf'. DB.

FRANKIS, FRANKISH: L OE *frencisc* 'French'. 12th cent.

FRANKLIN, FRANKLYN: O AF & ME *frankeleyn* 'a freeman and a landowner but not of noble birth'. 12th cent. Chaucer uses the *Franklin* in *The Canterbury Tales*.

FRANSHAM, FRENSHAM: L OE *fraemde-hām* 'the alien village', an Anglo-Saxon name for a village of the Danes. (Norfolk).

FRARY see FREDERICK.

FRASER, FRAZER: P The name of a Scottish clan. Numerous also in Ulster. Recorded in 11th cent. as *de Frisselle, de Freseliere, de Fresel*, suggesting a Norman origin, and in 14th cent. as *Frysel*. Family name of the barons Lovat, Saltoun, and Strathalmond. [A First Fleet (crew and convict) surname].

FRATER: O OF *fraitur* 'monk in charge of the refectory'. 13th cent.

FREAK see FIRTH. FREAN see FRAIN.

FREAR, FREER, FRERE, FRIAR, FRIER, FRYER: O OF *frere* 'friar'. 12th cent.

FREDERICK(S), FREDERIC, FRARY: P OG *Frederic* 'peace-rule'. DB. [A First Fleet (crew) surname].

FREE: O OE *frēo* 'free, not a serf'. 13th cent. FREEBAIRN: O OE *frēo-bearn* 'a child born free'. 12th cent. FREEBODY: O OE *frēo-bodig* 'free body', a free man. 13th cent. FREEBORN(E), FREEBURN: O OE *frēo-boren* 'free-born', not born to serfdom. 11th cent. [Freeborne is a First Fleet (marine) surname].

FREELAND: O OE *frēoland* 'a holder of land free of rent or service'. 12th cent.

FREELOVE: P OE *Frithulaf* 'peace-survivor'. 10th cent. An ancient and honoured name among the Anglo-Saxons.

FREEMAN: O OE *frēoman* 'free-born man'. 12th cent. [A First Fleet (convict) surname and also that of a clerk to the commissary].

FREEMANTLE, FREMANTLE: N OF *Fromentel* 'cold cloak', the name of a forest in France, and a nickname for one who was cold and ragged. 12th cent.

FREESTONE: P OE *Frēo-stān*, an Anglo-Saxon pers. name meaning 'free/noble stone'.

FRENCH: L OE *frencisc*, ME *frenche* 'a Frenchman'. 13th cent. There is also a form *ffrench*, so recorded in medieval manuscripts.

FREND see FRIEND. FRENSHAM see FRANSHAM. FRESHNEY see FRISKNEY.

FRESTON, FRISTON: L OE *Frisan* 'the *tūn* (village) of the Frisian people'. (Suffolk), *Fresetuna* DB.

FRETTER: O OF *frete* 'ornamental interlaced work with gold and jewels'. 'A gold fretter'. 14th cent.

FREW: N OE *frēo-frīge* 'free, noble'. FREWEN, FREWIN, FRUEN, FRUIN: N OE *Frēowine* 'noble friend'. DB.

FRIAR see FREAR.

FRIEND, FREND: N OE *frēond* 'friend'. 12th cent.

FRIGHT see FIRTH.

FRISBY: L OE + ON 'The *Frisians' býr* (homestead)'. (Leices), *Frisebi* DB.

FRISKNEY, FRESHNEY: L OE *Frescan ēa* 'fresh-water river'. (Lincs) 12th cent.

FRITH see FIRTH.

FROME, FROOME: L O Brit river-name R. *Frome*. (Dorset, Herefords, Som) OE Byname 11th cent.

FROST, FORST: N OE *forst* 'frost', frosty personality or frosty appearance (white hair and beard). DB.

FROUD(E), FROWDE, FROOD, FRUDE: N OE *frōd*, O Scand *frothi*, Norman *frodo*, all meaning 'old, wise and prudent'. 12th cent.

FRY(E): O OE *frēo* 'free', not a serf. 13th cent. [A First Fleet surname].

FRYER see FREAR.

FUCHE, FUDGE, FUGE, FUIDGE: P A pet-form of *Fulcher*. 12th cent.

FUGGLE(S) see FOWLE. FUGLER see FOWLER. FUKE see FOLK.

FULCHER, FULKER, FUTCHER, FOULCHER, FULLAGAR, VOLKER: P OG *Fulchar*, OF *Foucher* 'people (folk) army'. DB.

FULLER, VOLLER: O OF *fouleor* 'a fuller of cloth'. 13th cent. See also Tucker, Walker. [John Fuller, a convict, brought the name to Australia 1788].

FULLERTON: L OE 'The *tūn* (farm) of the *fuglere* (bird-catcher)'. (Hants).

FULLICK: L OE *fūl-wīc* 'foul (muddy) dairy farm'. 13th cent.

FULLWOOD, FULWOOD: L OE *fūl-wudu* 'foul (muddy) wood'. 14th cent.

FULTON: L OE *fūl-tūn* 'muddy farm'. FULWELL: L OE *'fūl-wielle* 'muddy spring'.

FUNK(E): N ME *funke* 'spark of fire'. 14th cent.

FUNNELL(E), FUNEL see FURNELL. FURBANK see FIRBANK.

FURBER: O OF *furbeor* 'a furbisher of armour'. 12th cent.

FURLONG, FORLONG(E), FURLONGER: L OE *furlang*, from *furh* 'furrow'. 13th cent. (The furlong was originally the length of a furrow in a common field of 10 acres.)

FURMAGE, FIRMAGE: O OF *fourmage*. Metonymic for a maker of cheese. 12th cent.

FURNEAUX: L OF from Fourneaux (Normandy). DB.

FURNELL, FOURNEL, FUNNEL(L), FUNNELLE, FUNEL: L OF From Fournal or Fournel (France). 12th cent.

FURNIVAL: L OF From Fournival (Oise, Orne) Normandy. 12th cent.

FURPHY, FURFY, FURFIE: P Ir *O Foirbhithe* 'descendant of perfect'.

FURSE, FURZE, FURZER: L OE *fyrs* 'furze-covered land'. 12th cent. [James Furzer, quartermaster on the *Sirius*, brought the name to Australia 1788].

FUSTER see FEWSTER.

FYFE, FIFE: L From Fife, Scotland, said to be named from *Fib*, son of *Cruithne*, king of the Picts.

FYNN see FINN. FYSH see FISH. FYSHWICK see FISHWICK.

G

GABB(E): N OF *gab* 'mockery, deceit', for *gabber* 'deceiver'. 13th cent.

GABLE: L ME *gavel* 'gable', 'mountain ridge like a gable'. (Cumb).

GABLER: O OF *gabelier* 'tax-collecter' or *gableor* 'usurer'. 12th cent.

GABRIEL(E), GABRIELLE: P Hebrew *Gabriel* 'Archangel'. 13th cent.

GADD: N OE *gad* 'goad', either a tormenting tongue or use of the goad, e.g., on cattle. GADSBY: L ON *Gaddr-bȳr* 'the farm of a Norseman called *Gaddr* (goad, sting)'. (Leices).

GADSEN: L OE 'The *denu* (dale) of an Anglo-Saxon nicknamed *Gǣte*, a derivative of *gat* 'goat'. (Herts).

GAFFNEY: P Ir *O Gamhna*, from *gamhain* 'calf'.

GAGE: O ONF *gauge* 'measure'. Metonymic for a measurer or tester. 14th cent.

GAGER: O OF *gauger* 'a gauger, exciseman'. Winton D. 1066.

GAILLARD see GALLIARD.

GAIN, GAINES, GAINS, GANE, INGHAM: N OF *engaigne* 'trickery, ingenuity'. DB. See also Ingham.

GAINFORD, GAINSFORD: L OE *gegn-ford* 'straight ford'. (Durham).

GAIR: Ir A rare Irish surname with an elusive etymology. Could it be *gáire* 'laughter' or *gáir* 'outcry'?

GAIT(E): O OF *gaite* 'watchman'. 13th cent.

GAITSKELL, GASKELL, GASKILL: L O Scand *geit-skali* 'goat-shelter'. (Cumb).

GALBALLY: Ir *de Gallbhaide* a rare Irish locality surname. 14th cent.

GALBRAITH: L SG *Gall-Bhreathnach* 'stranger, Briton', a name for Britons (Celts) who settled among the Gaels. 12th cent.

GALE: (i) P OF form of OG *Wale*. (ii) N OE *gāl* 'merry' or 'wanton'. 13th cent. (iii) O ME *gaylle* 'gaol'. Metonymic for a gaoler. 13th cent.

GALER, GAYLER, GAYLOR: O OF *jaioleur*, ME *jaoler* 'gaoler'. 13th cent.

GALES: L Central French form of OF *Wallis* 'Welsh'. 13th cent.

GALEY see GALLEY.

GALILEE: O OF *galilee* 'porch or chapel at church entrance', 'keeper of the galilee'. 14th cent.

GALL, GAUL: L Celtic (Ir, SG, Breton) *gall* 'foreigner', 'stranger', applied to Lowlanders in Scotland, Englishmen on the Welsh borders, and French immigrants in Brittany. 11th cent.

GALLACHER, GALLAGHER, GALLAHER: P Ir *O Gallchobhair* 'foreign help'. (Donegal).

GALLANT: (i) P OG *Waland*, OF *Galant*. DB. (ii) N OF & ME *galant* 'dashing, bold'.

GALLEN: P Ir *O Galláin*, from *gall* 'cock'. (Donegal)

GALLEY, GALLIE, GALEY: O OF *galie* 'a galley'. Metonymic for a galley-rower, often a slave or a criminal. 13th cent. (First use of galley in OE is *galea* in Asser's *Life of King Alfred*, 9th cent.)

GALLIARD, GAILLARD, GALLARD, GAYLARD, GAYLER: N OF *gaillard* 'gay, lively, brisk, spirited'. 13th cent.

GALLIFORD see GULLIVER.

GALLIOT(T): O OF *galiot* 'galley sailor, slave' or 'pirate'. 13th cent.

GALLON: (i) P OF *Galon*, from OG *Walo*. 13th cent. (ii) P Ir *O Galláin*, from *gallán* 'stone'.

GALLOP, WALLOP: N ONF *walop*, ME *wallop*, which became *gallop*, with the meaning 'rash, impetuous'.

GALLOWAY: L SG *gall-Gaidhel* 'foreigner Gael'. The name derives from an alliance between the Gaelic inhabitants of the area (then part of Northumbria) and the nearby Norsemen.

GALPIN: O OF *galopin* 'a messenger or page'. 12th cent. Later, 'turnspit, scullion in a monastery'.

GALSWORTHY: L OE *gagol-ōra* 'the bank where sweet myrtle grows'. (Devon) 16th cent. (OE *gagol* 'bog myrtle, sweet gale'.)

GALT, GAULT, GAUT(E): N ME *galte, gaute* 'boar, hog', an uncomplimentary nickname. 12th cent.

GALTON: L OE *gagol-tūn* 'the farm where sweet myrtle grows'. (Dorset).

GALVIN, GALVAN, GALLIVAN: P Ir *O Gealbhain* 'bright-white'.

GALWAY, GALWEY: P Ir *de Gallaidhe*. It is uncertain whether the name derives from Galway or from Galloway in SW Scotland. Probably the Ulster form is from Galloway and the Cork name from Galway.

GAMAGE, GAMMAGE, CAMIDGE, CAMMIDGE: L OF From Gamaches (Normandy). 12th cent.

GAMBELL, GAMBLE, GAMMEL, GEMMELL: N O Scand *Gamel* 'old'. DB. [A First Fleet (convict) surname].

GAMBLETON: L OE *gavel-tūn* 'the farm of the *gavelmen* (rent-paying peasants)'. (Som) (OE *gavel* 'rent'.)

GAME(S), GAMMAN(S), GAMMON(S): N ME *game* 'winner of the *gamen* (a medieval foot-race prize)'. 13th cent.

GAMLIN, GAMLEN, GAMBLIN(G): N O Scand A dim. of *Gammel*. DB.

GANDER: N OE *gan(d)ra* 'gander', from the same root as *gōs* 'goose', a bird-name common to the Indo-European languages, e.g., Lat *anser*, Sanskrit *hamsa*, Du and Ger *gans*, Sp *ganso*, Ir *gēis*. 13th cent.

GANDY: O 'Servant of *Game*'. 14th cent.

GANNON, MACGANNON: P Ir *Mag Thionnain* 'fair'. [A First Fleet (marine) surname].

GAPE(S): N OF *gape* 'feeble'. 13th cent.

GAPP(S): L ME *gappe* 'breach, chasm (in hills or wall)'. 12th cent.

GARBE, GARBER: O ONF *garbe* 'wheatsheaf', 'a binder of wheat into sheaves'. 13th cent.

GARBETT: GARBUTT: P OG *Gerbodo* 'spear-head'. DB.

GARD, GUARD: O OF *garde* 'guard, watchman'. 13th cent.

GARDEN, GARDYNE: O ONF *gardin*. Metonymic for a gardener. 12th cent.

GARDENER, GARDINER, GARDNER: O OF *jardinier* 'a gardener'. 12th cent. [A First Fleet (convict) surname].

GAREY, GEARY: (i) P ON *Geiri*, O Dan *Geri* 'spear'. DB. (ii) P Ir *O Gadhra*.

GARFIELD: L OE *gara-feld* 'triangular field'.

GARFORD, GARFORTH, GARFATH: L OE 'The ford of *Gāra*, an Anglo-Saxon'. (Berks, Yorks) 13th cent.

GARLAND: (i) L OE *gore-land* 'land at a point or cape'. 12th cent. (ii) O OF *garlande* 'a circlet of gold or silver, a coronet'. Metonymic for a maker of *garlandes*. 13th cent. [A First Fleet (convict) surname].

GARLIC, GARLICK: O OE *gārlēac* 'garlic'. Metonymic for a seller of garlic. 13th cent.

GARLING: L OE *gren-hlinc* 'green hill or

ridge', as at Garlinge (Kent), *Grenling* 10th cent.

GARMAN, GARMON, GARMENT: P OE *Gārmund* 'spear-protector'. 13th cent.

GARMONSWAY: L OE 'The *weg* (path) of *Gārmund*'. (Durham) 13th cent.

GARNER, GARNIER, GERNER: (i) P OF *Garnier*, a Norman pers. name. 12th cent, (ii) O OF *gernier* 'granary'. Metonymic for keeper of the granary. 14th cent.

GARNET(T): (i) P OF *Guarinot*, a dim. of *Guarin*. DB. (ii) O A variety of occupations: *garnetier* 'granary superintendent'; maker of *garnets*, either 16th cent. door-hinges or a form of hoisting tackle.

GARNON, GERNON, GRENNAN: N OF *gernon* 'with moustache'. Also *Algernon*. DB.

GARRAD, GARRED, GARRATT, GARRETT, GARROD: P A dim. of *Gerard*. 13th cent.

GARRAWAY, GARROWAY: P OE *Gārwīg* 'spear-war'. 12th cent.

GARRICK: L OE *gara-wīc* 'the dairy-farm at the gore (a triangular piece of land)'. (Lincs), *Gerewic* 1316.

GARSIDE: L ON *garthr* + OE *sīde* 'enclosure on a hill-slope'. (Lancs, Yorks).

GARSON: O OF *garcon* 'servant'. 12th cent.

GARTH(E): O ON *garthr*. Metonymic for keeper of the *garth* (paddock). 13th cent.

GARTON: L ON *garthr* + OE *tūn* 'farm with a paddock'. (Yorks) 12th cent.

GARVEY, GARVIE: P Ir & SG *Mac/O Gairbhith*, from *garbh* 'rough'. *Garvie* is the Scottish form.

GARVIN: P Ir *O Gairbhin*, from *garbh* 'rough'. (Co. Mayo).

GASCOIGN(E), GASCOINE, GASCOYNE, GASKIN: L OF *Gascuinz* 'a Gascon'. 12th cent.

GASH, GASON, GASS, GASSON see WACE. GASKELL see GAITSKELL.

GATE(S), GATER: L OE *geat* 'gate' (to forest, gap in the hills, etc.). 12th cent.

GATECLIFF, GATLIFF: L OE *gāta-clif* 'goats' cliff'. (Ches) 15th cent.

GATELY, GATLEY: L OE *gāta-lēah* 'goats' clearing'. (Norfolk) DB.

GATHERCOLE: N OE A nickname for a feeble person who 'gathered cold'. 14th cent.

GATT: O OE *gāt* 'goat'. Metonymic for 'goat-herd'.

GATTING: L OE 'The *ingas* (people) of an Anglo-Saxon nicknamed *Gāt* (wild goat)'.

GATWARD: O OE *geat-weard* 'gate-keeper'. 13th cent. See also Durward.

GAUKRODGER see GAWKRODGER.

GAUL see GALL.

GAULD: L SG 'Lowlander'. 16th cent.

GAULT, GAUT see GALT. GAUNSON see GAWENSON.

GAUNT, GANT: (i) L OF From Ghent (Flanders). DB. (ii) N ME *gant, gaunt* 'thin, haggard'. 13th cent. (iii) O Metonymic for Gaunter. 14th cent.

GAUNTER, GANTER: O OF *gantier* 'a maker/seller of gloves'. 12th cent.

GAVAN, GAVIN: P Ir *O Gábháin*, from *gábhadh* 'needy'. (Co. Mayo). See also Gavin.

GAVIN, GAVEN, GAUVIN, GAWNE: P AF *Gawain* 'white falcon', a name from the Arthurian legends. 13th cent. See also Gawne.

GAWKRODGER: N Yorks dial. *gawk* 'awkward Roger'. 16th cent.

GAWLER: O OE *gafol* 'debt', ME *gaveler* 'usurer, moneylender'. 12th cent.

GAWN(E): O Manx *Mac-an-Gabhain* 'son of the smith'. 15th cent. See also Gavin.

GAY: (i) L OF From Gaye (Normandy). 12th cent. (ii) N OF *gai* 'cheerful, lighthearted'. 13th cent.

GAYDON: L OE 'The *dūn* (hill) of *Gaega*'. (Warwicks).

GAYLARD, GAYLER see GALLIARD. GAYLER see GALER.

GAYMER: P OF *Gaimar*, from OG *Waimer*. 12th cent.

GAZE see WACE.

GEAKE: N ME *geke* 'simpleton'. 13th cent.

GEAR, GEER: N ME *gere* 'impulsive, wild'. 12th cent.

GEARING, GEERING: N ME *gering* 'glutton'. 12th cent.

GEARY, GERRY, GERRIE, GERREY: (i) P OF *Geri*, from OG *Geric*. 13th cent. (ii) N ME *gery* 'fickle, capricious'.

GEDDES: L SG From Geddes (Nairns) Scotland.

GEE see MACGEE. GEEVES see JEEVES.

GELDARD, GELDART: O OE *gelde-hierde* 'herdsman of the gelded cattle'. 13th cent.

GELDING, GILDING: ON *geldingr* 'gelded'. See Geldard.

GELL(E): P A pet-form of *Julian* or *Juliana*. 13th cent.

GEMMELL see GAMBLE. GENNER see JENNER.

GENTLE(S), GENTILE, GENTRY: N ME *gentil* 'well-born, courteous, noble'. 12th cent. Chaucer uses *gentil* for 'charming, compassionate, well-bred'.

GEOFFREY see JEFFREY.

GEOGHEGAN: P Ir *Mag Eachagáin*, a sept of the Ui Néill.

GEORGE: P Lat *Georgius* from Gk, OF *Georges*. Introduced into England by the Crusaders. 13th cent. In ancient Greece the name meant 'farmer, land-worker'. [The name was brought to Australia by Ann George (a convict) and Robert George (a sailor on the *Friendship*) 1788].

GERALD, GEROLD, JARROLD, JARROTT, JERROLD, FITZGERALD: P OG *Gerald* 'spear-ruler'. Introduced into England by the Normans. DB.

GERARD, GERRARD, GARARD, GARRARD: P OG *Gerard*, OF *Gerart* 'spear-brave'. DB.

GERRISH: N ME *gerysshe* 'wayward, wild'. 13th cent.

GERMAN(N), GERMAINE, JARMAN, JARMAIN, JERMAN, JERMYN: L Lat *Germanus*, OF *Germain* 'a German'. DB.

GERNER see GARNER. GERREY, GERRIE see GEARY.

GETHING(S), GETTENS, GETTINS, GITTINGS, GITTINS: N OW *Gethin* 'dusky'. 14th cent.

GIBB(S), GIBBES: P A pet-form of *Gilbert*. 12th cent.

GIBBEN(S), GIBBIN(S), GIBBON(S): P OF *Giboin* 'gift-friend'. 12th cent.

GIBLETT, GIBLIN(G): P A double dim. of *Gibb*. 12th cent.

GIBNEY: P Ir *O Gibne*, from *gibne* 'lock of hair'.

GIBSON, GIBBESON: P 'Son of *Gibb*'. 14th cent.

GIDDY: N OE *gydig* 'possessed, insane'. 12th cent. As with *Deeves* (deaf), the affliction probably ceased at the next generation, but the name became hereditary.

GIDLEY: L OE 'The *lēah* (clearing) of *Gydda*'. (Devon).

GIFFARD, GIFFORD: N OF *giffard* 'bloated, puffy'. DB.

GIGG(S): N ME *gigge* 'a flighty young woman'. 13th cent.

GILBERT, GUILBERT, FITZGILBERT: P OG *Gisilbert* 'hostage-bright'. DB. [The name was brought to Australia by Thomas Gilbert, master of the *Charlotte*, and Stephen Gilbert, a marine, 1788].

GILBEY, GILBOY: P Ir *O Giolla Bhuidhe*, from *buidhe* 'yellow'.

GILBOURNE: L ON *gil* + OE *burna* 'ravine with a stream'. [A First Fleet (convict) surname].

GILBY: L ON 'The *býr* (farm) of *Gilli*, a Norseman'. (Lincs).

GILBRIDE: P SG *Gille Brighde* 'St Bride's servant'. 12th cent.

GILCHRIST: P SG *Gillacrist* 'servant of Christ'; Ir *Mac Giolla Chriost* 'devotee of Christ'. 13th cent.

GILDEA, MACGILDEA, KILDEA: P Ir *Mac Giolla Dia* 'servant of God'.

GILDER, GUILDER: O OE *gyldan* 'a gilder'. 13th cent.

GILDERS: O OE *gield-heall* 'keeper of the guildhall'. 12th cent.

GILDERSLEEVE: N OE *gylden-slīefe* 'golden sleeve'. 13th cent.

GILDING see GELDING.

GILES, GYLES, JILES: P Lat *Aegidius*, from Gk. A miracle-working saint of the 7th cent. who identified himself with suffering humanity and hunted creatures. The name entered England as *Gilo*. DB.

GILFILLAN: P SG *Gille Fháolain* 'servant of St *Fillan*'. 13th cent.

GILFOYLE see GUILFOYLE.

GILKES: P OF 'Son of *Gillam*' (*Guillaume*).

GILKISON: P SG 'Son of *Gilchrist*'. 14th cent.

GILL: (i) L ON *gil*, ME *gille* 'ravine, deep glen'. 13th cent. (ii) P A pet-form of *Gillian*, producing surnames Gill, Gell, Jell.

GILL, MACGILL, MACKILL: O ON *Gilli*, Ir *Gilla*, Ir, SG & Manx *gille* 'servant'. DB.

GILLAM, GILLHAM, GILLIAM: P OF *Guillaume*, Fr form of *William*. 14th cent.

GILLARD: P OF *Guilard*, from Norman *Willard*.

GILLESPIE: O SG *Gilleasbuig* 'the bishop's servant'. 12th cent.

GILLET(T), GILLETTE, JILLETT: (i) P OF *Guilott*, a pet-form of *Guillaume*. 12th cent.

(ii) L ON *gil* + OE *hēafod* 'the head of the glen'. 14th cent.

GILLIES, GILLIS: P SG *Gille Iosa* 'servant of Jesus'. 12th cent.

GILLIGAN, GILLAN, GALLIGAN: (i) P Ir *Mac Giollagáin*, from *giolla* 'lad'. A Co. Derry surname preserved in Magilligan's Strand. (ii) N Ir *O Gealagáin* 'white, bright, silvery'.

GILLINGHAM: L OE 'The *hām* (homestead) of *Gylla*'. (Dorset, Kent, Norfolk).

GILLIVER: O OF *girofle*, ME *gilliver* 'clove', 'a grower/seller of cloves', a culinary spice. 13th cent.

GILLMAN, GILMAN: P OF *Guillemin*, a dim. of *Guillaume* (*William*). 13th cent.

GILMARTIN: P SG 'Son of the devotee of St *Martin*'.

GILMOUR, GILMORE, GILMER: P Ir & SG *Gille Moire* 'servant of the Virgin Mary'. 12th cent.

GILPIN: P A dim. of *Gilbert*. 13th cent. (Used by Cowper in 'John Gilpin'.)

GILROY, MACGILROY: P Ir & SG *Giolla Rua* 'servant of the red-haired lad'.

GINGER: O ME *gingivere* 'ginger'. Metonymic for a seller of ginger. 13th cent.

GINN, GYNN: O ME *ginne* 'a snare'. Metonymic for a trapper. 12th cent.

GIPP(S): P A pet-form of *Gilbert*. 12th cent. [Sir George Gipps, Governor of N.S.W., conferred with Capt Hobson of New Zealand, and proclaimed that land titles in New Zealand would not be recognised unless the land had been sold by the Crown, thwarting Sydney land sharks, 1840].

GIRDLER: O OE *gyrdel* 'belt or waist-cord', 'a maker of girdles'. 13th cent.

GIRTON, GURTON, GRETTON: L OE *greot-tūn* 'the farm on gravelly soil'. (Cambs, Glos) DB.

GISBORNE: L OE *gysel-burn* 'gushing stream'. (Yorks).

GITTING(S) see GETHIN.

GLADDEN, GLADDING, GLADING: P OE *glaeding*, a dim. of *glaed* 'glad'. 12th cent.

GLADMAN: P OE *glaed-mann* 'happy man'. DB.

GLADSTONE: L OE *glida-stān* 'the kites' stone'. Chiefly a Scottish surname.

GLADWIN: P OE *Glaedwine* 'glad friend'. DB.

GLANFIELD, GLENFIELD: L OE *claene-feld* 'clean (ploughed) field'. 12th cent.

GLANVILLE: L OF From Glanville (Normandy). DB.

GLASGOW: L OW *glas-cau* 'green hollow'. (Lanarks) 13th cent.

GLASS: O OE *glaes* 'glass'. Metonymic for a glazier.

GLASTONBURY: L Celtic *glasto*, OW *glaslys* 'woad'. (Som) (First recorded AD 601 as OW *Ineswytrin* 'woad island'. The Anglo-Saxons formed OE *Glaestingas* 'the people of *Glastonia*' + *īeg* 'island or burg', *Glaestingeberia* DB.

GLAYSHER, GLAZER, GLAZIER: O OE *glaes* 'a glass-maker'. 13th cent.

GLEAVE(S), GLAVE(S): O OF *gleive*, ME *gleyve* 'a lance'. Metonymic for a spearman (soldier). 12th cent.

GLEDHILL: L OE *glida-hyll* 'the hill where kites fly'. (Yorks) 13th cent.

GLEESON, GLISSAN: P Ir *O Glasain*, a Lower Ormond sept.

GLEN(N): (i) L Brit *glenno*, Welsh *glyn* 'valley'. (Leics) (ii) L From the lands of Glen in Traquair (Peebles) Scotland. 14th cent.

GLENDENING, GLENDINNING: L From Glendinning in Westerkirk (Dumfries) Scotland. 13th cent.

GLEW, GLUE: N OE *glēaw* 'wise, sagacious, prudent'. 12th cent.

GLIDE, GLEED, GLYDE: N OE *glida*, ME *glede* 'kite, vulture', 'a bird of prey'. 13th cent.

GLINTON: L OE *glind-tūn* 'farm with a hedge'. (Northants) [A First Fleet (convict) surname].

GLOSSOP: L OE 'The *hop* (small valley) of *Glott*, an Anglo-Saxon'. (Derbys).

GLOSTER, GLOUCESTER: L Brit *Glevum* 'bright, splendid place', changed by the Anglo-Saxons to *Glowe* + *ceaster* (Roman fort). DB. [A First Fleet surname].

GLOVER: O OE A deriv. of OE *glōf* 'glove'. 'A maker/seller of gloves'. 13th cent.

GLOZIER: O OF *gloser* 'to make glosses upon', 'an interpreter, commentator'. 13th cent.

GLYN(N), GLYNNE: L OW *glyn* 'valley'.

GODBEHERE, GODBEE, GODBER, GODBEER, GODBIER: N OE A phrase name 'God be here inne (this house)', for one who frequently uttered it. 13th cent.

GODBERT, GOBERT: P OG *Godebert* 'god-bright'. DB.

GODBOLD, GODBOLT: P OG *Godebald* 'god-bold'. DB.

GODDARD, GODARD: P OG *Godard* pagan 'god-hard'. 12th cent.

GODFREY: P OG *Godefrid*, OF *Godefroi* pagan 'god-peace'. DB. [A First Fleet (marine) surname].

GODLEY: L OE *gōd-lēah* (*gōd* 'good'). 'The good (fertile) clearing'. (Devon, Surrey, Sussex) 13th cent. [John Robert Godley, founder of the Canterbury Association, established the province of Canterbury, New Zealand, 1848].

GODMAN, GOODMAN: P OE *Godmann*. DB.

GODRICH, GOODRICH, GOODRIDGE, GOODRICK: P OE *Godrīc* pagan 'god-ruler'. DB.

GODSALL, GOODSELL: N OE *God sāwal* 'good soul', virtuous and true. 12th cent.

GODSMARK: N OE *God's mearc*, OF *marque*, ON *mörk* 'God's mark', a nickname for one doomed to die of the plague. One bearing the mark of the plague (buboes, Lat *bubo* 'groin', hence bubonic), regarded as a sign of Divine displeasure and therefore termed 'God's mark'. 13th cent.

GODSON, GOODSON: P OE pagan *god-sunu*, later, Christian *God-sunu* 'Godson', becoming a pers. name. DB.

GODWIN, GOODWIN: P OE *Godwine* 'God friend, protector'. DB. [Goodwin, a First Fleet (convict and marine) surname].

GOFF(E): O Ir & SG *gobha*, Cornish *gov*, Welsh & Breton *gof* 'smith, blacksmith'. 12th cent.

GOLD, GOOLD, GOULD: P OE *golde* 'gold', also OE for marigold (plant). DB. [Gould, a First Fleet (convict and crew) surname].

GOLDBOURNE, GOULBORN, GOULBOURNE: L OE *golde-burn* 'stream with marsh marigolds'. (Ches, Lancs) 14th cent.

GOLDBURG, GOLDBERG, GOLDBURGH: P OE *Goldburg* 'gold-fortress'. 12th cent.

GOLDEN, GOULDEN: N OE *gylden* 'golden (haired)'. 13th cent.

GOLDER, GOULDER: P OE *Goldhere* 'gold-army'. DB.

GOLDFINCH: N OE *goldfinc*, a nickname from the bird. 13th cent.

GOLDING, GOULDING: P OE *Golding*. DB.

GOLDRICK: P OE *Goldrīc* 'gold-ruler'. DB.

GOLDSMITH: O OE *goldsmith* 'a worker in gold'. 13th cent.

GOLDSTON(E), GOULDSTONE, GOULSTON, GOLSTON, GOLSON: (i) P OE *Goldstān* 'gold stone', a pers. name. DB. (ii) L OE 'The *tūn* (farm) of *Goldstān*'. (Kent, Salop) 14th cent.

GOLDWIN, GOLDWYN: P OE *Goldwine* 'gold friend'. DB.

GOLLAND, GOLLIN(S) see JOLIN. GOLLEY see GULLY.

GOMME, GOOM, GUM(M): N OE *gum*, three meanings: 'man, lord, hero'. 13th cent.

GOOCH, GOUDGE, GOUGE: N Welsh *coch* 'red', hair or complexion. 12th cent.

GOOD(E): N OE *gōd* 'good, good man'. DB.

GOODALL, GOODALE: N OE *gōd ealu*, nickname for a brewer of good ale. 12th cent. [William Goodall, a corporal, brought the name to Australia 1788].

GOODAY, GOODEY, GOODY: (i) L OE *gōd-haeg* 'good (fertile) meadow. 14th cent. (ii) N OE *gōd daeg* 'good day', a nickname for one who greeted all and sundry with this salutation, later to become thoroughly Australian. 14th cent.

GOODCHILD: N OE *gōd cild* 'good child', occasionally 'god child'. 13th cent.

GOODENOUGH: O OE *gōd cnafa* 'good knave, good servant'. 13th cent.

GOODERE, GOODA, GOUDA: P OE *Gōdhere* 'good army'. DB.

GOODERHAM, GOODRUM, GUTHRUM: P O Dan *Guthrum, Gudram* 'battle-dragon'. 12th cent. (*Gudram* was a Danish king of East Anglia.)

GOODES(S): P OE *Gōdhyse* 'good scion or warrior'. DB.

GOODEVE: P OE *godgifu* 'god-gift', a woman's name, also *Godiva*. DB.

GOODHEW: (i) P ON *Guthugi*. DB. (ii) N OE *gōd hewe* 'good servant'.

GOODIFF, GOODEY, GOODY: O OE *gōd-wīf* 'good wife', in ME 'mistress of the household'. (Hussey, Hussy is from *hūs-wīf* 'housewife' but has fallen from grace.) 14th cent.

GOODISON: P OE 'Son of *Godgȳth*, a woman's name meaning 'god battle'. 14th cent.

GOODLAKE, GOODLUCK, GULLICK: P OE *Gūthlāc* 'battle-play'. DB.

GOODMAN see GODMAN. GOODRICH, GOODRIDGE see GODRICH. GOODSELL see GOODSAL.

GOODSIR: N ME *gudsire* 'grandfather'. 14th cent.

GOODSON see GODSON. GOODWIN see GODWIN.

GOODYEAR, GOODYER, GOODGER, GOODIER: N ME *goodyere* 'good year', an oft repeated salutation. 13th cent.

GOOK: N ON *gaukr*, ME *gowke* 'cuckoo'. 13th cent. Most languages have a word for the cuckoo, Lat *cuculus*, OF *coucou*, OE *gēac*, Ger *kuckuck*. As a nickname it usually means 'fool'.

GOOSE: N OE *gōs* 'goose'. 12th cent. See also Gander.

GOOSEY, GOOZEE: (i) N OE *gōs-ēage* 'goose-eye'. 12th cent. (ii) L OE *gōs īeg* 'goose island'. 13th cent.

GORCH, GORDGE: O OF *gorge* 'throat', 'a maker of throat armour'. 12th cent.

GORDON: P SG *gor-din* 'great fort'. (Berwicks, Kincardines) Scotland. 12th cent.

GORE: L OE *gāra* 'cape, promontory, corner of land'. (Wilts) 12th cent.

GORHAM: L OE *gor-hām* 'dirty (muddy) homestead', or *gor-hamm* 'muddy meadow'.

GORMAN: P Ir *Mac* or *O Gormain*, from *gorm* 'blue'.

GORRELL: N OF *gorel* 'pig', 12th cent. or L OE *gor-hyll* 'muddy hill', 13th cent.

GORST: L OE *gorst* 'gorse'. 13th cent.

GORSTIDGE, GOSSAGE: L OE *Gos-ford-sīc* 'goose ford at the small stream'. 14th cent.

GORTON: L OE *gor-tūn* 'dirty (dungy) farm'. (Lancs) 13th cent.

GOSDEN: L OE *gōs-denu* 'goose valley'. 14th cent. GOSFORD: L OE *gōs-ford* 'goose ford'. (Devon, Oxon, Warwicks).

GOSLING: N ME *goslyng* 'little goose'. 13th cent.

GOSPER: N OE *godspel* 'gospel', 'glad tidings'. A phrase name.

GOSS(E), JOCE, JOSE, JOSS: P OG *Gozzo*, OF *Gosse, Josce*. 12th cent.

GOSSIP, GOSSOP: N OE *godsipp* 'godfather or godmother'. 13th cent.

GOTHAM: L OE *gāt-hām* 'homestead with goats'. (Notts) (Home of 'the wise men of Gotham', whose pretence of idiocy gained them respite from King John.)

GOTHARD: O OE *gāt-hierde* 'goat-herd'. 13th cent.

GOUDA see GOODER. GOUDGE see GOOCH.

GOUGH: N Welsh *coch* 'red' of hair or complexion. 13th cent. [Thomas Gough, a private, and his wife and son, brought the name to Australia 1788].

GOUL—For surnames beginning thus, e.g., Gould, see entries beginning 'Gol'.

GOW: O SG *gobha* 'smith'. 13th cent. See also Goff.

GOWEN see MacGOWAN.

GOWER(S): P OG *Godehar*, OF *Gohier* 'good army'. 12th cent.

GRACE, GRACEY, GRACIE: P Lat *Gracia*, from *gratia* 'grace'. 12th cent. [A First Fleet (convict) surname].

GRADY: P Ir *O Gradáigh*, from *gráda* 'illustrious'.

GRAF(F): O OF *grafe* 'pencil', *grafer* 'to write', 'a scribe or scrivener'.

GRAFHAM: L OE *graf-hām* 'homestead with a grove'. (Sussex, Hunts).

GRAFTON: L OE *grāf-tūn* 'farm by a grove'. 12th cent.

GRAHAM, GRAEME: L OE 'The *hām* (homestead) of an Anglo-Saxon called *Granta*'. Original place-name Grantham (Lincs), recorded in DB as both *Grantham* and *Graham*. William de *Graham*, a Norman, who owned the manor of Grantham, found the name too difficult to pronounce and called the place Graham. He later moved to Scotland, taking the Norman form of the name with him as his surname. Thus the name Graham was born. 12th cent.

GRANGE: O OF *grange* 'granary', 'worker at the granary for threshed grain'. 13th cent. GRANGER, GRAINGER: O OF *grangier* 'superintendent of the granary'. 11th cent. [Granger, a First Fleet (convict) surname].

GRANT, GRAND, LE GRAND: (i) P OE *Granta* (see Graham). (ii) N OF *grand*, *grant* 'great', usually 'big, tall'. 11th cent. [A First Fleet (marine) surname].

GRANTHAM see GRAHAM.

GRASSICK, GRACEY, GRASS: O SG *greusaich* 'decorator, embroiderer'. 16th cent.

GRAVATT, GRAVETT, GREVITT: L OE *grǣvet* 'little grove'. 12th cent.

GRAVE(S): (i) O ON *greifi*, O Sw *grefe* 'count, earl'. DB. (ii) O ME *greyve* 'steward of a landed property'. 12th cent. [A First Fleet (crew) surname].

GRAY, GREY, LE GREY: (i) L OF From Graye (Normandy). DB. (ii) N OE *graeg* 'grey (hair)'. 12th cent. [Both Gray and Grey are First Fleet (convict) surnames. Sir George Grey, British colonial administrator and statesman, when governor of New Zealand, bought large tracts of country for colonial settlement, leading to the Anglican settlement of Canterbury and the Presbyterian settlement of Otago].

GREALEY, GREALLY, GREALY, GREELEY, GRIDLEY: N OF *greslet* 'hailstone-marked' in the sense of 'pock-marked', a nickname for one who bears the marks of smallpox. DB. (ii) P Ir *Mag Raoghalloigh.*

GREASLEY, GRESLEY: L OE *grēosn-lēah* 'gravelly clearing'. (Notts) 13th cent.

GREATBATCH: L OE *grēat-baece* 'great beck', the big, broad stream.

GREATOREX, GREATORIX, GREATREX, GREATRIX: L OE *grēat* 'large, thick, big' (the sense of 'important, elevated' came later in ME) + OE *hraca*, dial. *rake* 'throat', used topographically for a gorge, defile, or pass. (The Rake, Sussex, is a pass on the Hants—Sussex border.) In northern England *rake* is dial. from OE *raca*, used of a pass, a rut, or a vein of ore. Guppy (see Bibliography) in 1890, found the surname concentrated in Derby, Staffs, Lancs, and derived it from Great Rocks, in Wormhill, Derbys, but a lost mining settlement (perhaps known anciently as *Grēatrakes*, which would have been the early form of the surname) is a more likely place of origin.

GREAVES, GREEVES, GREVE(S): L OE *graefe* 'grove'. (Lancs) 12th cent. See also Grave, Grieve.

GREED: A back-formation from Greedy and a nickname from avarice, cupidity. 12th cent. GREEDY: N OE *grǣdig* 'greedy, voracious, gluttonous'. 12th cent.

GREEF see GRIEVE.

GREEN(E), GRENE: L OE *grēne* 'green, the village green'. 12th cent. [Seven persons named Green arrived with the First Fleet 1788, one marine, five convicts, and the baby son of one of the female convicts].

GREENAWAY: L OE *grēne-weg* 'green way, path, road'.

GREENER: L OE *grēne-ora* 'green bank'. 13th cent. GREENFIELD: L OE *grēne-feld* 'green field or open plain'. 13th cent. GREENHALG: L OE *grēne-holh* 'green hollow'. 13th cent. GREENHAUGH: L OE *grēne-haga* 'green enclosure'.

GREENHEAD: L OE *grēne-hēafod* 'green hilltop', 13th cent. or *grēne-hod* 'green hood'. (Greenhood is the surname adopted by the actual person who was Robin Hood. A 13th cent. ballad to Robin Hood is mentioned in *Piers Plowman.*)

GREENHILL, GRINNELL: (i) L OE *grēne-hyll* 'green hill'. 12th cent. (ii) L OE *grīma-hyll* 'the haunted hill'. (Worcs), *Grimeshyll* in 816 AD. GREENHOUSE: L OE *hūs atte grēne* 'house on the village green'. 13th cent. GREENHOW(E), GREENHOUGH: L OE *grēne-hoh* 'green ridge or mound'. (Yorks, Norfolk) DB. GREENLEAF: L OE *grēne-clif* 'green cliff'. A place called Greencliff in Yorks is unrecorded after 1379, one of the 1,300 lost villages of England.

GREENLEY, GREENLY, GRINDLAY, GRINDLEY: L OE *grēne-lēah* 'green clearing'. (Staffs) 13th cent. GREENSLADE: L OE *grēne-slǣd* 'green glade'.

GREENSMITH: O OE *grēne-smith* 'copper-smith'. 16th cent. Regretfully, *Greensleeves* did not become a surname.

GREENWARD: O OE *grēne-weard* 'keeper of the village green'. 13th cent.

GREENWELL: L OE *grēne-wielle* 'grassy spring'. (Cumb, Durham) 13th cent.

GREENWICH: L OE *grēne-wīc* 'lush dairy farm'. (Kent) DB.

GREENWOOD: L OE *grēne-wudu* 'the greenwood'. 13th cent. [A First Fleet (female convict) surname. The Greenwood brothers secured one of the first leases on the Canterbury Plains].

GREER: P A dim. of *Grierson* (*Gregory*).

GREG, GREGG(S): P A short-form of *Gregory*. 13th cent.

GREGGOR, GREGOR: P The vernacular form of *Gregory*. 13th cent.

GREGORY, GREGORI: P Lat *Gregorius*, from Gk. 'to be watchful'. 12th cent. (Pope *Gregory* the Great sent St Augustine to Britain to convert the Anglo-Saxons to Christianity.)

GREIG, GRIEG: P Scots form of *Gregory*.

GRENVILLE, GRENFELL: L OF From Grainville-la-Teinturière (France). 12th cent. GRENFELL may also be L OE *grēne* + ON *fell* 'green fell or mountain'.

GRESHAM: L OE *gaers-ham* 'grazing farm'. 12th cent.

GRESTY: L OE *grǣg-stīg* 'badger-run'. (Ches) (ME *grey* 'badger'.)

GRETTON see GIRTON.

GREVILLE: L OF From Gréville (Normandy). 12th cent.

GREW(E): N OF *grue* 'crane (the bird)', 'long legs'. 13th cent.

GREWAL: O OF *gruel* 'fine flour', 'a miller or baker'. 14th cent.

GREY see GRAY.

GRIBBLE, GRIBBELL: L ME *gribbele* 'crabtree or blackthorn'. 14th cent.

GRIBBIN, GRIBBON see CRIBBEN.

GRICE: (i) N ON *griss*, ME *grice* 'pig'. (ii) N OF *gris* 'grey, grey-haired'. 12th cent.

GRIEVE(S), GREIF, GRIEF, GRIEFF, GREEF: O OE *gerēfa* 'a high official', e.g., governor of a province in Anglo-Saxon times. Later, 'overseer', 'farm bailiff'. Also, in areas of Scandinavian influence such as East Anglia, ON *greifi* 'steward'. 11th cent. See also Grave.

GRIFFIN, GRIFFEN: (i) P MW A pet-form of *Gruffud*, native to Wales and the border counties. Also introduced into the eastern counties of England by the Bretons who formed a significant part of the invading Norman army. DB. (ii) N OF *griffon* 'hook-nosed'.

GRIFFITH(S): P MW *Gruffyd*, from OW *Griph-iud* 'chief, lord'. 12th cent. [A First Fleet (marine and convict) surname].

GRILL(S): (i) N OE *grillan* 'to provoke, offend, gnash the teeth'. (ii) N ME *grill* 'fierce, cruel'. 14th cent.

GRIMBLE, GRUMBLE(S), GRIBBLE: P OG *Grimbald* 'helmet-bold'. DB.

GRIME(S), GRIMM, GRIMA, GRIMMER: (i) P ON *Grimr*, O Dan & O Sw *Grim*, pers. names of Viking invaders. DB. (ii) N OE *grim* 'fierce, grim', nickname for an Anglo-Saxon who was the equal of the Vikings. DB.

GRIMLEY: L OE *grima-lēah* 'the glade haunted by a spectre'. (Worcs).

GRIMMETT, GRUMITT, GRUMMET: (i) P ON *Grimhildr* 'helmet-battle'. (ii) P OG *Grimbald*, OF *Grimet* (see Grimble).

GRIMMOND: P SG A variant of *Mac Crimmon*. 16th cent.

GRIMSDALE: L ON 'The *dalr* (valley) of *Grimmr*, the masked one'. (Cumb) 14th cent.

GRIMSDITCH, GRIMDITCH: L ON *Grimr-dīc* (ancient earthworks). (Wilts) *Grimr*, a byname for the god *Odin*, related to OE *grima* 'a mask'. (*Odin* (*Woden*), the masked one, the self-concealing pagan god.)

GRIMSHAW: L OE 'The *scaga* (shaw, copse) of an Anglo-Saxon called *Grimm*'. (Lancs) 13th cent.

GRIMWARD, GRIMWADE, GRIMWOOD: L OG *Grimward* 'helmet-guard'. 12th cent.

GRINDER: (i) O OE *grindere* 'a grinder of corn, a miller'. (ii) 'a sharpener of iron tools (on a grindelstone)'. 13th cent.

GRINDLAY see GREENLEY.

GRINDROD: L OE *grēne-rod* 'green rod (small holding)'. One rod = a quarter-acre.

GRISDALE, GRISEDALE: L O Scand *gris* 'pig' + OE *dael*, 'valley with wild pigs'. (Cumb, Lancs) 14th cent.

GROGAN, GRUGAN: P Ir *O Gruagain*, 'descendant of *Gruag* (Hair). Grugan is an Ulster variant.

GRONOW: P OW *Guorgonui*. 14th cent.

GROOM(E): O OF *gromet* 'lad'; ME *grome* 'manservant'. Later, 'horse-groom', 'stable-groom'. 11th cent. (Bridegroom is from *brȳd-guma*, second el. 'man, lord, hero'.)

GROSS, GROSSE, GROS, GROSE: N Lat *grossus* 'thick', OF 'big, fat'. 11th cent.

GROSSET: P A dim. of *Gross*. 13th cent.

GROSVENOR: O OF *gros veneur* 'chief huntsman'. 12th cent.

GROVE(S), GROVER: L OE *grāf* 'grove, thicket'. [A First Fleet (convict) surname].

GRUBB(E): N ME *grubbe* 'short in stature'. 12th cent.

GRUMBLE see GRIMBLE. GRUMMITT see GRIMMET.

GRUNDY: P OF *Gundric* 'battle-power'. A Norman pers. name.

GUBB, GUBBIN(S): P OF *Giboin*. 12th cent.

GUEST: N ON *gestr* 'guest, stranger, traveller'. 11th cent. [A First Fleet (convict) surname].

GUILD: O OE *gield* 'member of a craft guild or worker at the guildhall'.

GUILFOYLE, GILFOYLE: P Ir *Mac Giolla Phóil* 'son of the devotee of St Paul'.

GUINESS see MAC GUINNESS.

GULLIVER, GULLIFORD, GALLIFORD: N OF *goulafre* 'glutton'. DB.

GULLY: N ME *golias*, from Hebrew *Goliath* 'a giant'. 12th cent.

GULSON see GOLDSTON. GUM(M) see GOMME.

GUMMER: P OE *Guthmaer* 'battle-famous'. 11th cent.

GUNN(S): P ON *Gunnr* 'battle'. 12th cent.

GUNNELL: P ON *Gunnhildr* 'battle-strife', a less than demure woman's name and that of the daughter of King *Cnut* (*Canute*). DB.

GUNNER: (i) O Dan *Gunnor*, ON *Gunvor*, a popular name among the Normans, who were descended from Viking stock. (ii) O ME *gonner* 'gunner'. (Gun was first recorded in the form *gonnes*, from *Gunnhildr*, in 1339).

GUNNING: P Ir *O Conaing*. See also Gunwin.

GUNNIS(S): L O Dan 'The *nes* (headland) of *Gunni*'. (Lincs) 12th cent.

GUNTER, GUNTHER: P OG *Gunter*, OF *Gontier* 'battle-army'. 11th cent. [A First Fleet (convict) surname].

GUNTHORP(E): L OE + O Dan 'The *thorp* (farm) of *Gunni*'. (Lincs, Norfolk, Rutland) 13th cent. [William Gunthorpe, bosun of the *Lady Penrhyn*, brought the name to Australia 1788].

GUNTON: L OE + O Dan '*Gunni's tūn* (farm)'. (Norfolk) 12th cent.

GUNWIN, GUNNING: P OG *Gundwine* 'battle-friend'. 12th cent.

GUPPY: L OE 'The *haeg* (enclosure) of *Guppa*, an Anglo-Saxon'. (Dorset) 14th cent.

GURLING see CODLING.

GURNARD: N ME *gurnard* 'a fish that grunts when caught', a nickname for a grumbler. 13th cent.

GURNEY: L OF From Gournai-en-Brai (Seine Inférieur) France. DB.

GURTON see GIRTON.

GUTHRIE: L SG from ON *gustr* 'windy', 'the windy place'. (Angus) Scotland.

GUTTERIDGE see CUTTERIDGE.

GUY(E), GYE, WHY(E): P OG *Wido*, OF *Guy*. DB. *Why* is the Norman form.

GUYER: O OF *guyour* 'guide'. 13th cent.

GUYMER: P OG *Wigmar* 'battle-famous'. 11th cent. See also Wymer.

GWILLIAM, GWILLIM: P Welsh variant of *William*. 14th cent.

GWINN, GWYN(N), GWYNNE, WYN(N), WYNNE: N OW *gwyn* 'fair, white'. 13th cent.

GWYTHER: P OW from Lat *victor* 'victor, conqueror'.

GYATT see WYATT. GYLES see GILES. GYNN see GINN.

H

HABERSHON: O OF & ME *haubergeon*. Metonymic for a maker of haubergeons, sleeveless coats of mail or scale armour. 13th cent.

HABGOOD see HAPGOOD.

HACK, HAKE(S): (i) N ON *Haki*, O Dan *Hake*, a Scandinavian nickname 'hook, crook'. (ii) N ME *hacchen* 'a meat-board for feeding falcons'. hence the medieval phrase *at hack and manger*, an envious nickname for one in clover. DB.

HACKER: O OE *haccian* 'to cut', 'a wood-cutter'. 13th cent.

HACKETT, HAGGET: N A dim. of ON *Haki* or O Dan *Hake*. DB.

HACKING: L OE 'The *ingas* (people) of *Hacca*, an Anglo-Saxon'. (Lancs) 13th cent. [The name was brought to Australia by Henry Hacking, quartermaster on the *Sirius* 1788. An explorer, Port Hacking, N.S.W., was named for him].

HACKLING, ACKLING: P ON A dim. of ON *Haki*. 12th cent.

HACKNEY: (i) L OE 'The *īeg* (island) of *Haca*, an Anglo-Saxon'. (Middx) 13th cent. (ii) O ME *hakenei* 'a hack-horse'. Metonymic for a keeper of hacks. 14th cent.

HADAWAY see HATHAWAY.

HADDEN: (i) L OE *heath-dūn* 'heather-hill'. (Devon, Derby, Dorset, Hants, Northants) 12th cent. (ii) L From the barony of Hadden (Roxburgh). 12th cent.

HADDOCK: N OF *hadoc*, nickname for a fish salter. 13th cent.

HADFIELD: L OE *haeth-feld* 'heather-covered field'. (Derbys) 12th cent.

HADLEY, HADLEE: L OE *haeth-lēah* 'heather-covered clearing'. (Essex, Middx, Suffolk, Sussex) 12th cent.

HAGAN, HAGEN, HAGON: P Ir *O Hagan, O hÁgáin*, from *óg* 'young'.

HAGGARD, HAGGART: N OF *hagard* 'wild, untamed'. 13th cent.

HAGGARTY see HEGARTY.

HAGLEY: L OE *hag-lēah* 'the *lēah* (clearing) in the hawthorn wood'. (Glos, Salop, Som, Staffs, Worces) [A First Fleet (convict) surname].

HAIG, HAIGH, HAGUE, HAGE: (i) L OF From La Hague (Manche) Normandy. 12th cent. (ii) L OE *haga* or ON *hagi* 'enclosure'. (Lancs) 13th cent.

HAILE(S), HAILS, HAYLES: (i) L Brit river-name *Haylebrok* (Glos). 13th cent. (ii) L OE From Hailes (Lothian) Scotland. 12th cent.

HAILEY, HALEY, HALLEY, HAYLEY: L OE *hīeg-lēah* 'hay clearing'. (Oxon) 13th cent.

HAILWOOD: L OE *halh-wudu* 'remote place in the wood'. (Lancs).

HAIM(S), HAYMES, HAMON: P OG *Hamo*, OF *Haim* 'home'. DB.

HAIN(S), HAINES, HAYNES, HEYNES, HANES: (i) P OG *Hagano* or O Scand *Hagne*. DB. (ii) L *haeg* 'hay meadow'. 13th cent. [Haines, Haynes, First Fleet (convict) surnames].

HALDANE, HALDEN, HALDIN: N Anglo-Scandinavian *Healfdene* 'half-Dane'. DB.

HALE(S): L OE *halh* 'remote valley'. 12th cent.

HALER, HAYLER, HAYLOR, HALLYER: O OF *haler* 'a carrier, porter'. 13th cent.

HALFACRE, HALFACREE: L OE *healf-aecer* 'half-acre homestead'. 13th cent.

HALFHEAD, HALFHIDE: L OE *healf-hīd* 'homestead on half a hide of land'. 13th cent. (One hide would support a free family; half a hide would have left them half hungry.)

HALFNIGHT(S): O OE *healf-cniht* 'a half-knight', holding land by paying his lord half the cost of an armed soldier for a set period. 12th cent.

HALFORD: (i) L OE *halh-ford* 'ford in a remote valley'. (Devon) (ii) L ME *hawkers' ford*. 12th cent.

HALFPENNY, HALPENNY: (i) N OE *healf-pennig*, a nickname for tenants at Halfpenny Field (Cambs) who were required to pay a half-penny an acre for the upkeep of nearby Needham Dyke. (ii) N A more general nickname of lost meaning. 13th cent. [A First Fleet (marine) surname].

HALFYARD: L OE *healf-yerd* 'a half-yard homestead'. 14th cent. (One *virgate* or *yerd* = 30 acres.)

HALIDAY, HALLIDAY, HOLIDAY, HOLYDAY, HOLLIDAY: N OE *hāligdaeg* 'holy-day', a name for one born on a holy day. 12th cent.

HALIFAX: L OE *hālig-fleax* 'holy flax field' (owned by the church). (Yorks).

HALL(S), HALLE: O OE *heall* 'a servant at the hall or manor house'. 12th cent. [Five persons named Hall (all convicts) arrived with the First Fleet 1788. In New Zealand, William Hall was one of Samuel Marsden's fellow missionaries].

HALLAM, HALLUM: L OE *halh* 'remote valley'. (Derbys, Yorks) [A First Fleet (Marine) surname].

HALLARD, HALLETT see ADLARD.

HALLAWAY see ALAWAY.

HALLER: O OE *atte heall* 'a worker at the hall'.

HALLEY: O OE A dim. of *Hall*.

HALLIWELL: L OE *hālig-wielle* 'the holy stream or spring'. 12th cent.

HALLORAN see O'HALLORAN.

HALIMAN, HALMAN: O OE *heall-mann* 'servant at the hall'. 13th cent.

HALLMARK see ALLMARK.

HALLOWES,, HALLAS: L OE *hagan-halh* 'enclosures in a remote valley'. (Worces) 13th cent.

HALLWARD, HALLARD: O OE *heall-weard* 'keeper of the hall'. 12th cent.

HALPIN: P Celtic A variant of *Alpin*.

HALSE: (i) N OE *heals* 'neck', a nickname from some peculiarity of the neck. 11th cent. (ii) L OE *heals* used topographically, 'a neck-spur or neck-like point of land'. (Som, Northants).

HALSTEAD, HALSTED, ALSTED: (i) L OE *heald-stede* 'cattle sheds'. (ii) O OE *heall-stede* 'worker at the hall buildings'. 12th cent.

HALTER: O OE *haelftre* 'a maker/seller of halters'. 13th cent.

HALTON: L OE 'The *tūn* in a *halh* (deep valley)'. 11th cent.

HAM(S), HAMME: L OE *hamm* 'meadow by a stream'. 13th cent.

HAMBLIN(G) see HAMLIN.

HAMBLEY: L OE 'The *lēah* (clearing) by the R. Hamble'. (Hants) [A First Fleet (crew) surname].

HAMER: L OE *hamor* or O Scand *hamarr* 'rock or cliff'. (Lancs).

HAMERSLEY: L OE *hamor-lēah* 'the clearing of the hammersmiths'.

HAMILTON: L OE *hamel-tūn* 'the *tūn* (homestead) by the scarred hill', (*hamel* 'maimed'). (Leices) The name was carried to Scotland by a man from Leices and took root in Lanarks. It was also carried to Russia where it was Russianised as *Gamentov*, but the bearer was nicknamed *Chomontov* 'horse-collar'.

HAMLIN, HAMLYN, HAMBLEN, HAMBLING: P OG *Haimo*. 12th cent. [James Hamlin and Alfred Brown, missionaries and explorers, spent five months travelling from Waikato to the Firth of Thames, New Zealand, 1834].

HAMMELL, HAMMILL: N OE *hamel* 'maimed'. 11th cent.

HAMMER: O OE *hamor* 'hammer'. Metonymic for a hammersmith. 13th cent.

HAMMERTON: L OE *hamor-tūn* 'the hammersmith's homestead'. (Yorks, Hunts).

HAMMOND, HAMMAN, HAMMON: P OG *Hamon*, OF *Hamond*. 12th cent.

HAMON see HAIM.

HAMPER: O OF *hanapier* 'a maker/seller of goblets'. 13th cent.

HAMPSHIRE, HAMSHERE: L OE 'The county of Hampshire, *Hamtunscir* in 755, named from *Hamtūn*, the early name of Southampton'. Surname 13th cent.

HAMPSON: P 'Son of *Hammond*'.

HAMPTON: (i) L OE *ham-tūn* 'home farm'. (ii) L OE 'The *tūn* in a *hamm* (water meadow)'. (iii) L OE *hēa-tūn* 'high farm'. Sometimes the farm was an important manor, e.g., Hampton Court, which became the palace of Cardinal Wolesey. 12th cent.

HANBURY: L OE *hea-burg* 'high fort'. (Staffs, Worces) 12th cent.

HANCOCK, HANDCOCK, HANCOX: P A dim. of *Hann*. 13th cent.

HAND(S): N OE *hand*, a nickname from some skill or deformity of the hand. 13th cent. [A First Fleet (marine) surname].

HANDFORD: L OE *hana* 'cock (wild bird) ford' or *hān* 'rocky ford'. 13th cent. [A First Fleet (convict) surname].

HANDLEY, HANLEY, HANLY: L OE *hēa-lēah* 'high clearing'. 12th cent. [A First Fleet (convict) surname].

HANGER: L OE *hangra* 'the wood on a steep slope, (Ches).

HANKIN(S), HANKING: N A dim. of *Hand*. 13th cent. HANKINSON: N 'Son of *Hankin*.

HANKS: (i) P ON A dim. of *Anki*, a Norse pers. name. 12th cent. (ii) P A Flemish pet-form of *John*.

HANLON see O'HANLON.

HANN: P (i) An abbreviation of *Johan*. (ii) a pet-form of *Henry*. 14th cent.

HANNAH, HANNA, HANNAY: (i) P Hebrew, a short-form of *Hanani* 'God has favoured me', a woman's name. (*Anna* is from the same source). (ii) L OE 'The *īeg* (island) of *Hana*, an Anglo-Saxon'. (iii) (Hannay) From a lost place in Scotland.

HANNEY: L OE *hanena-īeg* 'wild bird island'. (Berks), *Hannei* DB.

HANNIBAL see HUNNABLE.

HANNON: P Ir *O hAnnain*, a Munster surname derived ultimately from *Hannah*.

HANRAHAN: P Ir *O hAnradhain*, from *anradh* 'champion'.

HANRATTY: P Ir *O hAnrachain*, from *anrachtach* 'unlawful'.

HANSARD: O OF *hansard* 'a maker/seller of cutlasses, poniards'. 12th cent.

HANSELL see ANSELL.

HANSFORD see ANSFORD.

HANSON, HANSOM: P 'Son of *Hann*'. 14th cent.

HAPP(E), N ON *happ* 'lucky'. 12th cent.

HARBER, HARBOR, HARBOUR, ARBER: O OE *herebeorg* 'lodgings'. Metonymic for a lodging-house keeper, who would be called a *harberer*. 12th cent.

HARBISON see HERBERTSON. HARBUTT see HERBERT.

HARCOURT: (i) L OE *hearpere-cot* 'the harper's cottage'. (Salop) (ii) L OF From Harcourt (Eure) Normandy. (The name was first recorded in 1055, thus preceding the Norman Conquest.)

HARD(S), HARDES: L OE *heard* 'hard, firm ground'. 13th cent. (The name is from the fens where hard ground was rare.)

HARDACRE, HARDAKER: L OE *heard-aker* 'hard, stony, unproductive ground'.

HARDCASTLE: L OE + OF 'The hard (bleak) house'. (Yorks).

HARDEN: L OE *hara-denu* 'the hares' valley'. (Yorks).

HARDER(S): O OE *heardian* 'to harden', 'a hardener of metals'. 13th cent.

HARDIMAN: N OF *hardir* + OE *mann* 'bold man'. 14th cent.

HARDING, FITZHARDINGE: P OE *Hearding* 'harsh, severe' or 'hardy, bold'. 14th cent. See also Fitz.

HARDMAN: N OE *heardmann* 'a hard, severe man'. 12th cent.

HARDWICK: O OE *heordwīc* 'care at the sheep farm', 'a shepherd'. 13th cent.

HARDY, HARDEY, HARDIE: N ME from OF *hardi* 'courageous, daring'. 12th cent.

HARE: (i) N OE *hara* 'hare', a nickname for speed or timidity. (ii) N OE *hǣr* 'hairy'. 14th cent.

HARGREAVE(S), HARGRAVE, HARGROVE(S): L OE *hara-grāf* 'the grove frequented by hares'. (Ches, Northants, Suffolk) 12th cent.

HARKER: N OE *herkien, hearken* 'to listen', 'an eavesdropper'. 13th cent.

HARKEN(S): L A dim. of *Hard*. 12th cent.

HARKNESS: L OE 'The *naess* (headland) of an Anglo-Saxon called *Hereca*'. Mainly a Scottish surname.

HARLAND: L OE *hār-stān* 'hoary, greystone', used as a boundary mark. 13th cent.

HARLEY: L OE *hara-lēah* 'clearing frequented by hares'. (Salop, Yorks) 13th cent.

HARLOW(E): L OE *here-hlāw* 'the hundred meeting place, the mound of the people'. (Essex, Yorks, Northumb) 12th cent. For 'hundred' see Musto.

HARMAN, HARMON, HERMAN, HARIMAN: P OF *Hereman* 'warrior'. 11th cent.

HARMER, HERMER: P OG *Hermar* 'army-famous'. 12th cent.

HARMSWORTH: L OE '*Heremōd's worth* (homestead)'. (Middx) 14th cent. [A First Fleet (marine) surname].

HARNESS see ERNEST. HARNETT, HARNOT see ARNALD.

HAROLD, HARALD, HARROLD, HARRELL, HARRAD, HARROD: P OE *Hereweald*, O Dan & O Sw *Harald*, ON *Haraldr* 'army-power'. DB. In 1066 the name was held by both King Harold of England and *Harald Hardrada*, King of Norway. Following the Norman Conquest, the family of King Harold fled to Kiev, one of the great European cities of the Middle Ages, where they lived as émigrés, and Harold's daughter Gita married Prince Monomakh, grandson of Yaroslav, Grand Prince of Kiev Rus.

HARP: O OE *hearpe, sealthearpe* 'a salt sifter', from harp-shaped pan. Metonymic for a salt harvester. HARPER, HARPOUR: O OE *hearpere*, OF *harpeor*, AF *harpour* 'a harper or harp-maker'. 12th cent. [Both Harp and Harper are First Fleet (marine) surnames. Harper is also a convict surname. Bishop Harper was the first Bishop of Christchurch, 1864].

HARRADEN, HARRADINE: L OE *hearga-dūn* 'the hill with heathen temples'. (Beds, Northants) 14th cent.

HARRIMAN: O OE 'Servant of *Harry* (*Henry*)'. 14th cent.

HARRINGTON: L OE 'The *tūn* (settlement) of the people of *Haefer*'. 12th cent.

HARRISON, HARRISSON: P 'Son of *Henry*'. 14th cent. [A First Fleet (convict) surname].

HARROP: L OE *hara-hop* 'hares' valley'. (Northumb) 13th cent.

HARROWER: O ME *harwen* 'to harrow', 'a harrower'. 13th cent.

HARROWSMITH see ARROWSMITH.

HARRY, HARRIES, HARRIS, HARRISS, FITZHARRIS: P Often regarded simply as a pet-form of *Henry*, Harry is in fact the correct English form of *Henry*, and the name was so pronounced in the Middle Ages. The Lat form *Henricus* was used in documents. See also Fitz. 12th cent. [Harris, a First Fleet (crew and convict) surname].

HART(E): N OE *heort*, a nickname from the *hart* (male deer). 11th cent. [A First Fleet (crew and convict) surname].

HARTFORD see HEREFORD.

HARTIGAN: P Ir *O hArtagain*, from *art* 'stone'.

HARTLAND: L OE *heort-īeg* 'stag island'. (Devon) HARTLEY: L OE *heort-lēah* 'stag-clearing'. 12th cent. HARTMILL: L OE *heort-myln* 'the mill where harts roam'.

HARTRICK, HATTRICK see ARKWRIGHT.

HARTSHORNE: L OE *heort-horn* 'the headland with stags'. (Derbys) HARTWELL: *heorte-wielle* 'the stream where stags drink'. (Bucks, Northants, Staffs).

HARTY: P Ir *O hAthartaigh*, from *hartach* 'noisy'. (Cos. Tipperary, Cork).

HARVEY, HARVY, HARVIE, HERVEY: P OF *Herve*, O Bret *Haerviu* 'battle-worthy'. DB.

HARWIN: P OG *Hardwin*, OF *Harduin* 'firm friend'. DB.

HARWOOD, HAREWOOD: L OE *hār-wudu* 'the hoary (grey) wood'. 12th cent.

HASKELL see ASKELL. HASKEW see ASKEW. HASKIN see ASKIN.

HASLAM, HASLEM: L OE *haesel* 'the hazels'. (Lancs) 13th cent.

HASLEDAN, HASLEDEN see HAZELDEN.

HASLER, HASELER: L OE *haesel-ōfer* 'hazel slope'. (Staffs, Warwicks, Worces).

HASLOP, HASLIP, HEASLIP, HESLOP,

HISLOP, HYSLOP: L OE *haesel-hop* 'hazel-valley'. 15th cent.

HASLUCK: P O Dan & O Sw *Aslak*, ON *Aslakr*. DB.

HASSALL, HASSELL: L OE *haetse-halh* 'the witches corner'. (Ches).

HASSETT: P Ir *O hAiseadha*. A Thomond sept. (Co. Clare).

HASTIE, HASTY: N OF *hastif*, ME *hasty* 'quick, impatient'. Some may be from P *Asti*, a Norman form of ON *Asketill*. 12th cent.

HASTINGS: L OE From Hastings (Sussex), *Hastingas* in 790, named from the ancient *Haestingas* tribe, from OE *haest* 'violence, strife'. Surname DB.

HASWELL: L OE *haesel-wielle* 'the spring in the hazels'. (Durham) [A First Fleet (marine) surname].

HATCH: L OE *haecc* 'hatch, half-gate', e.g., gate to the forest. 12th cent.

HATCHARD see ACHARD.

HATCHER: L OE 'at the gate' (see Hatch). 13th cent. [A First Fleet surname].

HATFIELD: L OE *haethfeld* 'the field overgrown with heather'. 11th cent. [A First Fleet (convict) surname].

HATHAWAY, HATHWAY: (i) P OG *Hadewic* or *Heathuwīg* 'war-warrior'. DB. (ii) L *haeth-weg* 'the heath-way'. (Ann Hathaway became the wife of William Shakespeare.) [A First Fleet (convict) surname].

HATHERLEY: L OE *haegthorn-lēah* 'hawthorn-wood'. (Devon, Glos) [John Hatherley arrived as a carpenter on the *Sirius* 1788].

HATRY see DAWTREY.

HATT, HATTER: O OE *haett* 'a maker of hats'. 12th cent.

HATTERSLEY: L OE *hēahdeor-lēah* 'the deer wood'. (Ches).

HATTON: L OE *haeth-tūn* 'the farm on the heath'. [A First Fleet (convict) surname].

HAUGH: L OE *halh* 'nook, corner or remote valley'.

HAUGHEY: P Ir *O hEachaidh* (Donegal and Armagh).

HAUGHTON: (i) L OE *hōh-tūn* 'farm on a ridge'. (Notts) (ii) L OE *halh-tūn* farm in a remote valley'. (Ches, Durham, Lancs, Salop, Staffs).

HAVELOCK: L ON *hafleikr* 'sea-port'. 13th cent.

HAVERFIELD: L ON + OE *hafri-feld* 'oat-field'. 14th cent.

HAVERS: N OE *haefer* 'he-goat'. 12th cent.

HAVILL, HOVELL: L OF from Hauville (Eure) Normandy. DB.

HAWES: P OG *Hadewidis*, OF *Haueis* 'battle-wide'. 12th cent.

HAWK(E), HAWKES, HAWKS: (i) O OE *hafoc* 'hawk', 'a landholder by service of providing trained hawks for the lord owning the land'. Winton D. (In 1130, Ralph *Hauoc* owed the king's exchequer two gerfalcons or hawks in unpaid tax.) (ii) N OE *le Hauek*, a nickname for a cruel, savage individual. 13th cent. (iii) L ME *halke*, from OE *halh* 'nook, corner or secret valley'. [A First Fleet surname].

HAWKER: O OE *hafocere* 'hawker, falconer'. 13th cent. The surname may reflect *hawker* (now pedlar), an itinerant dealer in imported hawks who travelled between castles and manor houses trying to sell them.

HAWKIN, HAWKEN, HAWKING(S), HAVEKIN: O or N OE *havek-in*, a dim. of *Hafoc* (*Hawk*). 13th cent.

HAWKSEY, HAWKEY: N OE *hafoc-ēage* 'hawk's eye'. 12th cent.

HAWKSHAW: L OE *hafoc-sceaga* 'hawks' wood'. (Lancs) 13th cent.

HAWORTH: L OE *haga-worth* 'homestead by the enclosure'. (Yorks) 12th cent.

HAWTHORN(E): L OE *haguthorn* 'hawthorn'. (Durham).

HAWTRY see DAWTREY.

HAY(E), HAYES, HEY, HEYES: (i) P OE *Hēah*. 12th cent. (ii) L OE *(ge)haeg* 'the enclosure'. (Herefords, Westmorland) (iii) L ME *hay* 'forest enclosed for hunting'. [Hayes, a First Fleet (convict) surname; Hays, a FF (marine) surname].

HAYCOCK: P OE A dim. of *Hēah* (*Hay*). 13th cent. [Catherine Haycock, a female convict, brought the name to Australia 1788].

HAYDEN: P Ir *O hEideain*, a Co. Carlow sept, sometimes anglicised as Headon.

HAYDEN, HAYDON, HEYDON: L OE *heg-dūn* 'hay-down (hill)'. [A First Fleet (convict) surname].

HAYLAND, HIGHLAND, HYLAND: L OE *hēg-land* 'hay-land'. 13th cent.

HAYLES see HAILE. HAYLER see HALER. HAYLEY see HAILEY.

HAYMAN, HEYMAN, HYMAN: O OE *hēg-mann* 'a dealer in hay'. 14th cent.

HAYME see HAIM. HAYNE(S) see HAIN. HASELDEN see HAZELDEN.

HAYSOM: 'Son of *Hay*'. 13th cent.

HAYTER: L OE *Eofede-torr* 'the ivy rock'. (Devon) 13th cent.

HAYTON: L OE *hēg-tūn* 'hay-farm'. (Cumb, Notts, Salop, Yorks) 12th cent.

HAYWARD, HEYWARD: O OE *hege-weard* 'guardian of the enclosure'. 12th cent. [Elizabeth Hayward, a convict aged 13, brought the name to Australia 1788. In 1814 she owned a house valued at £8 in Sydney].

HAYWOOD, HEYWOOD: L OE *(ge)haeg-wudu* 'the enclosed wood'. 12th cent.

HAZARD, HAZZARD, HASSARD: N OF *hasard*, ME *hassard* 'a game of dice', nickname for a gambler. 12th cent.

HAZEL(L): L OE *haesel* or ON *hesli* 'hazel'. 12th cent. HAZELDEN(E), HAZELDEANE, HESELTINE: L OE *haeseldenn* 'hazel valley'. 13th cent. HAZELHURST: L OE *haesel-hyrst* 'hazel-wood'. 14th cent. HAZELTON, HESELTON: L OE *haesel-tūn* 'the farm with hazels'. (Essex, Glos, Herts, Yorks) 13th cent.

HAZLETT, HAZZLITT: L OE *haesel*, dial. *haeslett* 'hazel-thicket'. 14th cent.

HEAD(S): L OE *hēafod* 'head', used topographically as 'hill, head of valley, or place where stream rises' 12th cent.

HEADLEY, HEDLEY: L OE *hǣth-lēah* 'clearing overgrown with heather'. (Hants, Worces, Yorks) [Anthony Hedley, a sailor, arrived on the *Alexander* 1788].

HEAL(E), HEALES: L OE *heale* 'secluded place'. 12th cent.

HEALD: L OE *hielde* 'slope, declivity'. 12th cent.

HEALY, HELY: P Ir *O hEalaighthe* 'descendant of *Claimant*'. [A First Fleet (marine) surname].

HEAP: L OE *hēap* 'mound or heap'.

HEAPHY: P Ir *O hĒamhthaig*, a Co. Waterford surname recorded 1659. [Charles Heaphy, the New Zealand Company's draughtsman, arrived on the *Tory* 1839. In 1846, in company with William Fox, he discovered Lake Rotarua].

HEARD, HERD, HIRD, HORD, HURD: O OE *hierde* 'a herdsman'. 13th cent. [Capt Herd named Port Nicholson, later changed to Wellington, but the harbour still bears the original name].

HEARDER see HERDER. HEARL see EARL. HEARN see HERN.

HEASMAN: L OE *hǣs-mann* 'brushwood + man'. 13th cent.

HEATH, HEATHER: L OE *hǣth* 'heath'. 13th cent.

HEATHCOTE: L OE *hǣth-cot* 'cottage on the heath'. (Derbys, Warwicks) 12th cent.

HEATON: L OE *hēa-tūn* 'high homestead'. (Lancs, Northumb, Yorks).

HEAVEN(S): P OW An optimistic surname deriving from *Evans*. Heavens is 'Son of *Heaven*'.

HEBBLETHWAITE, HEBBLEWHITE, EBBELWHITE: L OE *hebble* + ON *thveit* 'the plank bridge at the *thwaite* (meadow or clearing)'. (Yorks) 14th cent.

HEBBURN, HEPBURN: L OE *hēa-byrg* 'high burial ground or tumulus'. (Durham, Northumb) 13th cent.

HEBDEN: L OE *heope-denu* 'the valley with rose hips'. (Yorks).

HECTOR: P Gk, name of the Trojan hero, son of *Priam*, usually translated as 'holding fast'. Used in Scotland to translate *Eachdonn*.

HEDGE(S): L OE *hecg* 'hedge enclosure'. 13th cent.

HEDLEY: L OE *haeth-lēah* 'the clearing overgrown with heather'. (Durham, Northumb).

HEGARTY, O'HEGARTY, HAGGERTY: P Ir *O hEigceartaigh* 'unjust'.

HEGINBOTHAM see HIGGINBOTHAM.

HEIGHT: L OE *hēah*, ME *heyt* 'hilltop'.

HELLER, HULLER, HELMAN: L OE *hyll*, ME *hull* 'hill'. 14th cent.

HELLIER, HELLYER, HILLIER, HILLYER: O OE *helian* 'to cover', 'a slater, tiler, roofer'. 13th cent. *Helian* is also 'to conceal' and may hide a nickname.

HELM(S): O OE *helm* 'a covering', used in dialects for cattle shelter and so for a herdsman. 12th cent.

HELY, HELEY see HEALY, ELY. HEMBRY see AMERY.

HEMMING(S): P O Dan *Hemming*, ON *Hemingr*. 11th cent.

HEMINGWAY, HEMMINGWAY: L O Scand + OE 'The path of *Hemming*'. (OE *weg* 'path'.)

HENDERSON: P 'Son of *Henry*'. 14th cent. [A First Fleet (crew and convict) name].

HENDRA: L Cornish *hen-dre* 'old homestead'. 14th cent.

HENDRIE: P Fr *Henri.* 16th cent.

HENDY: N ME *hendy* 'courteous, gentle, kind'. 12th cent.

HENLEY: L OE *hēa-lēah* 'high glade or clearing'. (Six counties, Surrey to Warwicks) 12th cent.

HENNESSEY, HENNESSY: P Ir *O hAoughusa* 'descendant of *Aoughus* (*Angus*)'.

HENRY, HENERY, FITZHENRY: P OG *Henric*, OF *Henri* 'home-rule'. DB. A popular Norman name. See also Fitz. [A First Fleet (female convict) surname].

HENSHAW: L OE 'The *haga* (enclosure) of an Anglo-Saxon called *Hethin*'. (Northumb), *Hetheneshalg* 1298.

HENSMAN, HINCKESMAN: O OE *hengest-mann* 'stallion-man', 'a groom'. Later, 'a squire or page of honour'. Still later, 'a sumpter-man, carrier'. 15th cent.

HENSTRIDGE: L OE *hengest-hrycg* 'stallions' ridge'. (Som) (Hengist and Horsa were the first Anglo-Saxons to lead an assault on Celtic Britain.)

HENWICK: L OE *hīwan-wīc* 'the dairy-farm of the household of the monks'.

HENWOOD: L OE *hīwan-wudu* 'the wood of the household of the nuns'.

HEPBURN see HEBBURN.

HEPWORTH: L OE *heop-worth* 'the homestead where rose-hips are plentiful'.

HERALD, HERAUD, HERROLD, HERROD: (i) P OE *Hereweald*, ON *Haraldr*, OG *Hairold*. DB. (ii) O OF *herault*, ME *herode* 'herald', medieval officer who uttered royal proclamations, officiated at tourneys, arranged state ceremonials.

HERBERT, FITZHERBERT: P OG *Hariberct*, OF *Herbert* 'army-bright'. Introduced into England at the Norman Conquest. DB. [A First Fleet (convict) surname].

HERDER, HEARDER, HORDER: O OE *hierde* 'a herdsman'. 14th cent.

HEREFORD, HERFORD, HARFORD, HERTFORD: L OE *heort-ford* 'the harts' ford'. (Herefords, Herts, Devon, Glos) DB. [A First Fleet (convict) surname].

HEREWARD, HARWARD: P OE *Hereweard* 'army-guard'. DB.

HERIOT, HERRIOT, HERRIOTT, HERRETT: (i) L ME *heriot*, an ancient legal term relating to the ownership of land. From Heriot (Midlothian) Scotland. (ii) L OE *hearg-geard* 'enclosure at the heathen temple'. (Hants) 12th cent.

HERITAGE, HERRITAGE: O OF *eritage*, ME *heritage* 'property, land by right of inheritance', 'an heir'. 13th cent. [A First Fleet (marine) surname].

HERMITAGE, ARMITAGE, ARMYTAGE: L OF & ME *ermitage, hermitage* 'hermitage'. 13th cent.

HERMITTE, ARMETT: O OF *ermite*, ME *hermite* 'a hermit, solitary religious ascetic'. 12th cent.

HERN(E), HEARN(E), HURN: L OE *hyrne* 'nook, bend or curving valley'. 13th cent. [William Hern arrived as steward on board the *Friendship* 1788].

HERON, HERRON: N AF *heron* 'heron'. A nickname from the bird for a tall thin man with long legs. 13th cent.

HERRICK: P O Dan & O Sw *Erik*, ON *Eirikr*. DB.

HERRING: O OE *haering* 'herring'. Metonymic for a seller of herrings. 12th cent.

HERST, HIRST, HURST, HORST: L OE *hyrst* 'wooded hill'. [Hurst, A First Fleet (marine) surname].

HESKETH: L O Scand *hestakeith* 'race course'. (Cumb) Horse-racing was a favourite sport among the Scandinavians in England. The racecourse in Cumb was *Hesteskeith* in 1155, more than 800 years ago. The place is now called Hesketh Grange.

HESLOP see HASLOP.

HETHERINGTON, ETHERINGTON: L OE *hǣth-tūn* 'the homestead on the heath or untilled land'. (Northumb) 13th cent.

HEW: O ME *hewe* 'a domestic servant'. 13th cent. See also Hugh.

HEWELL: P A dim. of *Hugh*. 13th cent.

HEWET(T), HEWAT, HEWIT(T), HOWAT(T), HOWETT, HOWITT, HUET(T): (i) P dim. of *Hugh*. 12th cent. (ii) L OE *hīewet* 'cutting (where trees have been felled)', 'the cleared place'. 13th cent.

HEWINS see EWAN. HEWISH see HUISH.

HEWLETT, HOWLETT, HULETT: P *Hugh-e-lot* double dim. of *Hugh*. 13th cent.

HEWLINS, HEWLINGS, HOWLING(S), HUELIN, HUGLIN, HULLIN(S): P OG *Huglin*, a dim. of *Hugo*, OF *Hugelin* or *Huelin*. Winton D.

HEWSON see HUGHSON. HEY, HEYES see HAY. HEYDON see HAYDEN. HEYMAN see HAYMAN. HEYNES see HAIN. HEYWARD see HAYWARD.

HEYWOOD: L OE *heah-wudu* 'high wood'. (Lancs).

HIBBARD, HIBBERT see ILBERT. HIBBIE see IBELL. HIBBS see IBBS.

HICK(S), HICKES, HIX: P A pet-form of *Ricard* (*Richard*). 13th cent.

HICKEY: P Ir *O hIcidhe*, from *iceadh* 'healer'.

HICKMAN, HIGMAN: O 'Servant of *Hick*'. 13th cent.

HICKSON: P 'Son of *Hick*'. 14th cent.

HIDE(S), HYDE(S): O OE *hīd* 'a hide of land', 'holder of a hide (120 acres)'. 12th cent. See also Halfhead.

HIGGENBOTHAM, HIGGENBOTTOM, HIGINBOTHAM, HIGGENBOTTOM: L OE *ǣcen-botm* 'oaken valley'. (Lancs) 13th cent.

HIGGINS, HIGGENS: P A dim. of *Higg*, a form of *Hick*, and all tracing back to *Richard*. 14th cent. HIGGS: P A variant of *Hick*. 13th cent.

HIGHAM, HYAM(S): L OE *hēah-ham* 'the high village'. 12th cent.

HILDEBRAND: P OG *Hildebrand* 'battle-sword'. DB.

HILDER: L OE *hylde* 'dweller on the slope'. 14th cent.

HILL(S), HILLE: L OE *hyll*, 'hill'. 12th cent. [Seven persons named Hill arrived with the First Fleet, five convicts and two crew members].

HILLARY, HILLERY, ELLERY: P Lat *hilaris*, OF *hilaire* 'cheerful, blithe'. 12th cent.

HILLIARD, HILLYARD: P OG *Hildigard* 'war-stronghold'. 12th cent.

HILLIER see HELLIER.

HILLING(S): L OE *hylling* 'hill-dweller'. 12th cent. HILLMAN: L OE *hyll-mann* 'dweller on the hills'. 14th cent. HILTON, HYLTON: L OE *hyll-tūn* 'hill-farm'. 12th cent.

HINCH: P OE *Hȳnca*, an Anglo-Saxon pers. name meaning 'wolf-cub'.

HINCHCLIFFE: L OE *henge-clif* 'overhanging cliff'. (Yorks) 14th cent.

HINCKESMAN see HENSMAN.

HINCKLEY: L OE 'The *lēah* (clearing) of an Anglo-Saxon called *Hȳnca* (wolf-cub)'. (Leics) 12th cent.

HIND(E), HINDS, HYND(S): N OE *hind* 'female deer'. 13th cent.

HINDMARSH: L OE *hind-mersc* 'the marsh of the hinds (deer)'.

HINE(S), HYNE(S): O ME *hīne* 'hind, peasant, servant'. 13th cent.

HINGSTON: L OE *hengest-tūn* 'stallion stud'. (Cambs).

HINTON: L OE *hīgna-tūn* 'the monks' or nuns' farm'. 13th cent.

HIPSLEY: L OE *hyppels-lēah* 'the stepping stones in the wood'. [A First Fleet (female convict) surname].

HIPWELL: L OE *hyppel-wiella* 'the stepping stones at the stream'. (Yorks).

HIRD see HEARD. HIRST see HERST. HISLOP see HASLOP.

HITCH, HITCHES: P A pet-form of *Richard*. 12th cent. HITCHCOCK, HITCHCOX, HISCOCK(S), HISCOX, HISCOTT: P A dim. of *Hitch*.

HITCHEN(S), HITCHIN(S), HITCHING(S), HICHENS: (i) P *Hich-un*, a dim. of *Hitch*. 13th cent. (ii) L OE 'The people of the *Hicce* tribe'. (Herts).

HITCHMOUGH: P ME *mough* 'relative by marriage', 'brother-in-law of *Hitch*'.

HOAD, HOATH: L OE *hǣth*, ME *hōth* 'heath'. (Kent) HOADLEY: L OE *hāth-lēah* 'heather-covered clearing'. (Sussex) 13th cent.

HOAR(E), HORE, ORE: (i) L OE *ōra* 'ridge'. (Sussex) (ii) N OE *hār* 'hoar', 'the hoary one, white-haired with age'. 12th cent. See also Orr.

HOBB, HOBBES, HOBBIS(S), HOBBS: P A pet-form of *Robert*. 12th cent. [Rev Hobbs, a Wesleyan missionary in New Zealand, 1835].

HOBDAY: O OE *daege* 'female servant', 'servant of *Hobb*'. 15th cent.

HOBSON, HOPSON: P 'Son of *Hobb*'. 14th cent. [Readthorn Hobson arrived Botany Bay 1788 as master of the storeship *Borrowdale*. In New Zealand, Capt William Hobson landed on 22 January 1840, with the authority of the British Government, hoisted the Union Jack and negotiated the Treaty of Waitangi with the Maori chiefs. He became the first governor of New Zealand].

HOCKADAY: N OE *Hōcor-daeg* 'Hockday', second Tuesday after Easter Sunday and half-yearly term day for payment of rents, a popular annual festival and an excuse for merry-making in rural England. A nickname for one born at Hocktide. 12th cent.

HOCKEY: (i) L OE *hocc-lēah* 'the clearing

overgrown with mallows'. (Essex), *Hocheleia* DB. (ii) L OE 'The *hlāw* (hill) of an Anglo-Saxon called *Hucca*'. (Warwicks).

HOCKHAM: L OE *hoc, holy-hoc*, 'hollyhock homestead'. 13th cent.

HOCKING: P O Fris A patronymic of *Hoc*, a Frisian pers. name (father of *Hildeburh* in *Beowulf*).

HODD(S), HODDES, HOOD: O OE *hōd* 'hood, head-covering'. Metonymic for a maker/seller of hoods.

HODDER: O OE A deriv. of *hōd*. 'A maker of hoods'. 13th cent.

HODGE(S): P A pet-form of *Roger*. 13th cent. HODGETT(S): P A dim. of *Hodge*. 14th cent. HODGKIN(S): P A dim. of *Hodge*. 14th cent. HODGSON: P 'Son of *Hodge*'. 14th cent.

HODKIN: P A pet-form of *Hugh*. 14th cent.

HODSON: P OG 'Son of *Odo*'. 14th cent. *Odo*, meaning 'riches', is the name of William the Conqueror's half-brother, the Bishop of Bayeux.

HOEY, HOY: P Ir *O hEochaidh*, an Ulster surname.

HOGAN: P Ir *O hOgáin*, from *óg* 'young'.

HOGBEN, HOGBIN: N OE *huck-bān* 'hip-bone', a nickname from some deformity of the hip. 15th cent.

HOGG(E): N OE *hogg* 'pig', an uncomplimentary nickname. 11th cent. Some may be from ON *högg* 'a ravine or cutting through trees'. The Cook's prologue in *The Canterbury Tales* suggests that *Hogge* was sometimes used for *Hodge*. Cook: 'I highte [am called] Hogg of Ware'. Host: 'Now tell on, gentil Roger, by thy name'. See also Hodge, a dim. of *Roger*. In Ireland Hogg is sometimes used as a synonym for *O'Hagan*. [A First Fleet (convict) surname].

HOGGARD, HOGARTH, HOGGETT: O OE *hogg-hierde* 'a hog-herd'. 13th cent.

HOILE(S) see HOYLE.

HOLBERT, HULBERT: P OE *Holdbeorht* 'gracious-bright'. 12th cent.

HOLBORN: L OE *holh-burna* 'the bourne (stream) in a deep ravine'. DB.

HOLBROOK: L OE *holh-broc* 'the brook in a hollow'. 12th cent. HOLCOMB(E): 'the deep valley'. 12th cent.

HOLD, HOULD: O ON *holdr* 'a nobleman ranking below a *jarl*, a Danish or Norwegian chief'. AD 905.

HOLDEN: L OE *hol-denu* 'a deep hollow or valley'. (Yorks) 13th cent.

HOLDER, HOULDER: O OE A deriv. of *healdan*. 'A possessor or tenant of land'. 13th cent.

HOLDING: O OE *healdan* 'to hold, inhabit', 'a landholder'.

HOLDSWORTH: L OE 'The *worth* (homestead) of *Halda*, an Anglo-Saxon'. 13th cent.

HOLE(S): L OE *holh* 'hollow' (small valley). 12th cent. HOLFORD: L OE *holh-ford* 'the ford in a hollow'. (Som) 12th cent. HOLGATE: L OE + ON *holh* + *gata* 'the hollow road'. (Yorks).

HOLLAND(S): L OE *hōh-land* 'land at the ridge'. (Essex, Lancs, Lincs) 13th cent. [A First Fleet (convict) surname].

HOLLIDAY see HALIDAY.

HOLLIER, HOLLYER: L OF A deriv. of *holegn* 'the hollies' (holly-trees). 14th cent.

HOLLIES, HOLLIS, HOLLING(S), HOLLINS, HOLLY: L OE *holegn*, ME *holie* 'holly-trees'. 13th cent. HOLLINGSWORTH: L OE *holegn-worth* 'homestead among the holly-trees'. (Ches, Lancs).

HOLLISTER: L OE The fem. form of *Hollier* 'dweller among the holly-trees'. 14th cent. (Tobias Hollister, a convict from Bristol, arrived on the *Alexander* 1788].

HOLLOWAY, HOLLWAY: L OE *holh-weg* 'the hollow (sunken) road'. 12th cent. [A First Fleet (convict) surname].

HOLM(E), HOLMES, HOLMS: L ON *holmr*, O Dan & ME *holm* 'island or dry land in a fen'. Some may be from OE *holen* 'holm-oak'. 12th cent. [A First Fleet surname].

HOLOHAN, HOOLAHAN, HOULIHAN: P Ir *O hUallachain*, from *uallach* 'proud'.

HOLROYD(E): L OE *'hoh-rōd* 'the clearing of one square rood in the hollow'.

HOLT, HOULT: L OE *holt* 'wood, forest'. 12th cent. [A First Fleet (crew) surname].

HOLYOAK(E): L OE *hālig-āc* 'the holy oak'. 12th cent. (On Rogation Days, three days before Ascension Day, the Gospel was read at the parish boundary oak. This became known as 'the holy oak'.)

HOME(S): (i) L OE *holm* 'island or dry land in a fen'. (ii) L ME *holm* 'holm-oak'. (iii) *Home, Hume* (Scottish) from the barony of Home (Berwicks).

HOMER: (i) O OF *heaumier* 'helmet-maker'. 13th cent. (ii) L OE *holm* 'holm-oak' or 'holly-bush'. (Devon) 13th cent.

HONE(S): L OE *hān* 'community stone or boundary stone'. 12th cent.

HONER: O OE A deriv. of *hān* 'stone', 'a tool sharpener, honer'. 13th cent.

HONEYMAN: (i) P OE *Hūnmann* DB. (ii) O OE *hunig-mann* 'honey dealer'.

HOOD see HOD.

HOOK(E), HUCK: L OE *hōc* 'hook, angle', 'bend or hill-spur'. 12th cent. Some may be N for a hook-nosed or crook-backed individual.

HOOKER: O OE *hōcere* 'a maker of hooks'. 12th cent.

HOOPER: O OE *hōp* 'hoop', 'a maker of hoops for casks, barrels'. 13th cent.

HOPE: L OE *hop* 'small enclosed valley'. 13th cent.

HOPKIN(S): P A dim. of *Hobb* (*Robert*). 13th cent. HOPKINSON: 'Son of *Hopkin*'.

HOPLEY: L OE *hop-lēah* 'a clearing in the valley'. [A First Fleet surname].

HOPPER: O A deriv. of OE *hoppian* 'to hop, leap, dance', 'a dancer'. 12th cent.

HOPWOOD: L OE *hop-wudu* 'the wooded valley'. (Lancs).

HORD see HEARD.

HORDER: O OE *hordere* 'treasurer, keeper of the hoard', also 'keeper of provisions in a large household'. OE Byname 1001. See also Herder.

HORDERN: L OE *hord-aern* 'the building in which the hoard is kept'. (Lancs).

HORE see HOAR.

HORLEY: L OE *horna-lēah* 'the clearing in a *horne* (a tongue of land)'.

HORN(E): (i) O OE *horn*. Metonymic for a horn-blower, or for a horner, maker of horn spoons, combs. DB. (ii) L OE *horna* 'tongue of land or bend in the stream'. (Rutland) 13th cent. [A First Fleet (convict) surname].

HORNBY: L O Sw 'The *býr* (farm) of a Swede called *Horni*' (Lancs), or ON 'The *býr* of a Norseman called *Hornbothi*' (Yorks). 12th cent.

HORNSBY: L ON 'The *býr* of a Norseman called *Orm*'. (Cumb).

HORROCKS, HORROX: L OE *hār-āc* 'the hoary (grey) oak'. (Lancs) 16th cent.

HORSBURGH: L OE *horsa-brōc* 'the horses' stream'. (Peebles) Scotland. 13th cent.

HORSEY: L OE *hors-īeg* 'horse-island'. (Norfolk, Som) HORSLEY: L OE *horsa-lēah* 'horse-pasture'.

HORSMAN, HORSEMAN: O OE *hors-mann* 'horse-keeper'.

HORSNAIL, HORSNELL: O OE *hors-naegl* 'a maker of horse-shoe nails'. 13th cent.

HORST see HERST.

HORTON: L OE *horh-tūn* 'the muddy farm'. OE Byname 1018.

HORWOOD: L OE *horh-wudu* 'the muddy wood' (Bucks), or *hār-wudu* 'the hoary (grey) wood' (Devon). 13th cent.

HOSBORN see HUSBORN.

HOSKER: P OE *Ōsgār* 'god-spear'. DB. Norman scribes at work with their -H- again.

HOSKIN, HOSKING(S), HOPKINS: P A dim. of O Scand names in *Ōsgood, Ōsbeorn*. Norman scribes prefixed such names with -H-, the better to suit their pronunciation. 13th cent.

HOST: O OF *oste* 'an inn-keeper'. 13th cent.

HOTCHKISS: A variant of *Hodgkin*.

HOUGH: (i) L OE *hōh* 'hill-spur'. (Ches) (ii) L OE *haga* 'enclosure'. (Lincs).

HOUGHTON: L OE 'The *tūn* (farm) in a *halh* (remote valley)'. 12th cent.

HOULIHAN see HOLOHAN.

HOUSTON: L *Hugh* + OE *tūn* (village). From the barony of Houston (Lanarks) Scotland. 13th cent.

HOVELL see HAVILL. HOW(E), HOWES, HOWS see HUGH.

HOWARD, HEWARD, HUARD, HUART: P OG *Hugihard*, OF *Huard* 'heart-brave'. DB. [A First Fleet (convict) surname].

HOWAT, HOWETT see HEWET.

HOWEL(L), HOWELS, HOWELLS: P OW *Houel*, O Bret *Howael, Huwel*, king of the West Welsh 926. In eastern England the name was introduced by the Breton contingent at the Norman Conquest. [Howell, a First Fleet (marine) surname].

HOWLETT see HEWLETT. HOWSON see HUGHSON. HOY see HOEY.

HOYLE(S), HOILE(S): L OE *holh* 'a hollow', Yorks dial. pronunciation.

HUBBOLD, HUBBLE: P OG *Hubald*, OF *Hubaut* 'mind-bold'. DB.

HUBERT, HUBBARD, HUBBERT, HOBART: P OG *Hubert* 'mind-bright'. DB.

HUCKER: O ME *hucke* 'to bargain', 'a street dealer'. 13th cent.

HUDD, HUTT(E): P A dim. of *Hugh*. 12th cent.

HUDDLESTON, HIDDLESTON: L OE 'The *tūn* (homestead) of *Hūdel*'. (Yorks) 12th cent.

HUDSON, HUTSON: P 'Son of *Hudd*'. 14th cent. [John Hudson, a nine-year-old convict and a former chimneysweep, brought the name to Australia 1788].

HUGGETT: P A variant of *Hewet* and a dim. of *Hugh*. 15th cent.

HUGGIN(S): P A dim. of *Hugh*. 13th cent.

HUGH, HUGHES, HUGO, HEWES, HOW(E), HOWES, HOWS, FITZHUGH: P OG *Hugo*, OF *Hue* 'heart, mind'. DB. A popular name in England after the Norman Conquest. Hugh, with its variants and dims., has produced some 90 different surnames. In Wales, Hugh assumes the form *Pugh*, from *ap Hugh* 'son of *Hugh*'. See also Fitz. [Six persons named Hughes arrived with the First Fleet, a marine and five convicts].

HUGHSON, HEWSON, HOWSON: P 'Son of *Hugh*'. 11th cent.

HUISH, HEWISH: L OE *hīwisc* 'household or family holding of land', a hide = 120 acres. 12th cent.

HUKIN(S), HEWKIN, HOOKINS, HOWKINS: P '*Hugh's* kin'. 14th cent.

HULBERT see HOLBERT.

HULL(S): (i) L OE *hulu*, ME *hule* 'hut or hovel'. (ii) L OE *hyll* 'hill'. (iii) P A pet-form of *Hugh*. 12th cent.

HULM(E), HUME: L O Dan *hulm* 'the holm (small island or land in a stream)'. (Ches, Lancs, Staffs) 12th cent. [A First Fleet (marine) surname].

HUMPHREY(S), HUMPHRIES, HUMPHRY(S), HUMPHERY: P OG *Humfrid* in Norman form. DB. [A First Fleet (convict) surname].

HUNGERFORD: L OE *hungor-ford* 'the ford where the people starved'. (Berks).

HUNT: O OE *hunta* 'huntsman'. 12th cent. HUNTER: O OE A deriv. of *huntian* 'to hunt', 'a huntsman'. 13th cent. [Hunt, a First Fleet (marine) surname. John Hunter arrived as second captain of the *Sirius*. He succeeded Phillip as governor of N.S.W.].

HUNTINGDON: L OE *hunta-dūn* 'huntsman's hill'. 11th cent. HUNTINGTON: L OE *huntena-dūn* or *huntena-tūn* 'the hill, or the village, of the huntsmen'. 13th cent.

HURFORD: L OE *hyrne-ford* 'the ford in a nook or corner'.

HURL(E) see EARL.

HURLEY: L OE *hyrne-lēah* 'the clearing in a corner of the wood'. 13th cent. [A First Fleet (convict) surname].

HURLSTONE: L OE *hyrdel-tūn* 'the farm surrounded by hurdles'. (Yorks) 15th cent.

HURREN: N OF *hurant* 'the shaggy-haired one'. DB. HURRELL: N 'shaggy, matted hair'. 12th cent.

HURST see HERST.

HUSBAND(S): O OE *hūsbonda* 'householder, farmer'. 12th cent.

HUSBORNE, HOSBORN: L OE *Hysseburnan*, an ancient river-name. (Beds).

HUSSEY: O ME *huswyf* 'housewife, wife of *hūsbonda*'. DB. [A First Fleet surname].

HUTCHIN(S), HUTCHINGS, HUTCHEN(S): P OF *Huchon*, from *Hue* (*Hugh*). 13th cent.

HUTHWAITE: L OE + ON *hōh-thveit* 'the clearing on a spur of land'. (Notts, Yorks).

HUTT see HUDD.

HUTTON: L OE *hoh-tūn* 'the homestead on a spur'. 12th cent.

HUXLEY: L OE *Hōc's leah* 'the clearing of *Hōc*, an Anglo-Saxon'. (Ches).

HUXTER: O ME *huckestere* 'a feminine pedlar'. 13th cent.

HUXTABLE: L OE *hōh-stapol* 'the staple (a post of some significance) on a spur of land'. (Devon).

HUYTON: L OE *hyth-tūn* 'the village by the landing place'. (Lancs).

HYAM(S) see HIGHAM. HYDE(S) see HIDE. HYLAND see HAYLAND. HYMAN see HAYMAN. HYND(S) see HIND. HYNE(S) see HINE. HYSLOP see HASLOP.

I

I'ANSON, IANSON: P for *Janson* (use of -I- due to 16th cent. similarity between I and J capital letters).

IBBERSON, IBBETSON, IBBITSON, IBBOTSON: P 'Son of *Ibbot*'. 14th cent.

IBBOTT, IBBETT: P A dim. of *Ibb* (*Isabel*) or of *Ilbert*. 13th cent.

IBBS, HIBBS: P A pet-form of *Isabel* or *Ilbert*. 14th cent.

IBELL, IBLE, HIBBLE: P A dim. of *Ibbs*. 14th cent.

ICK(E): P OE *Ica*, a pers. name preserved in Ickenham (Middx), Ickford (Bucks).

IDDON: O ON *Idunn*, from *unna* 'to love'. 12th cent.

IDE, IDA: P A Norman name from OG *Ida* (*id* 'to work, labour, get done'). 12th cent.

IDLE, IDEL(L): (i) P MW *Ithael* 'lord bountiful'. 12th cent. (ii) N OE *īdel* 'lazy'. (iii) L OE *īdel* 'uncultivated land'. (Yorks).

IFIELD: L OE *īw-feld* 'open land with yew-trees'. (Kent, Sussex).

IFOLD, IFOULD: L OE *īeg-falod* 'the sheep-fold in river-land'. (Sussex) 13th cent.

IGGLEDEN: L OE *igil-denn* 'the hedgehog pasture' (place where hedgehogs are plentiful). (Kent) 15th cent.

ILBERT, HIBBARD, HIBBERT: P OG *Hildeberht*, OF *Ilbert* 'battle-glorious'. 12th cent.

ILES, ILLES, ISLES, EYLES: L OF *isle* 'isle'. 13th cent.

ILIFF(E): P ON *Eilifr* 'ever-life'. 13th cent.

ILLINGWORTH: L OE 'The *worth* (settlement) of the people of *Illa*, an Anglo-Saxon'. (Lancs).

ILSLEY: L OE 'The *lēah* (clearing) of an Anglo-Saxon woman called *Hild*, whose name is a compound of 'war' and 'combat'. (Berks).

IMBER: (i) L OE 'The *worth* (homestead) of an Anglo-Saxon called *Imma*'. (Surrey), *Immewurth* 13th cent. (ii) L OE '*Imma's mere* (lake)'. (Wilts), *Imemerie* DB.

IMM: P A form of OG *Emma, Imma*. 13th cent. See also Emm.

IMPEY: L OE *imphaga* 'the enclosure made of saplings'. 14th cent.

IMRAY, IMRIE see AMERY.

INCE, INNES: L OW *ynys* 'the island or water-meadow'. (Ches, Lancs) 13th cent. See also Innes.

IND: L OE *ende* (of the village). 14th cent.

INGALL, INGOLD, INGLE(S): P ON *Ingialdr*, O Sw Inhaeld, Anglo-Scand *Ingald* '*Ing's* tribute'. DB. [Ingle, a First Fleet (convict) surname].

INGERSOLL, INGERSOLE, INKERSOLE: (i) L OE *hīgna-aecer* 'the field of the *hīwan* (monks)'. (Derbys) 13th cent. (ii) L OE *wyrhtena* 'the field of the *wrights* (workmen)'. (Notts) 14th cent.

INGHAM: L OE '*Inga's hām* (homestead)'. (Lincs, Norfolk, Suffolk) 11th cent. See also Gain.

INGLEBRIGHT, ENGELBERT: P OG *Engelbert*, OF *Engilbert* 'Angle-glorious'. DB.

INGLEBY: L O Scand *Englabȳr* 'the village of the English'. (Derbys, Lincs, Yorks), all *Englebi* in DB. These are Anglo-Saxon enclaves in the Danelaw.

INGLIS see ENGLISH.

INGRAM: P OG *Ingelramnis*, OF *Enguerran* 'Angle-raven'. 12th cent. [A First Fleet (convict) surname].

INGREY: P O Dan *Ingrith*, ON *Ingrithr*. DB.

INKPEN, INGPEN: L Brit *penn*, OE *ing*, both meaning 'hill'. (Berks) 13th cent.

INMAN: O OE *inn-mann* 'lodging-house keeper'. 14th cent.

INNES: L SG *inis* 'island'. From the barony of Innes in Urquhart (Moray) Scotland. 13th cent.

INSALL, INSOLE, INSULL: L OE From an abandoned village in Worces once known as Insoll, last seen on 17th cent. county map. Surname 14th cent.

INSKIP: L OW *ynys* 'island' + OE *cȳpe* 'osier basket (for catching fish)'. (Lancs) 13th cent.

INWOOD: L OE *inwudu* 'in-wood (home-wood)'. 14th cent.

IRBY, IREBY: L O Scand *Īrabȳr* 'the farm of the Irish'. (Derbys, Cumb) 13th cent.

IREDALE: L O Scand *Īra-dalr* 'the valley of the Irish'. (Cumb).

IRELAND: L OE *Īras* 'Irish', 'the man from Ireland'. 12th cent.

IREMONGER, IRONMONGER: O OE *īren-mangian* 'ironmonger'. 13th cent.

IRISH: L OF *Ireis* 'Irish', applied to both Irish and Scots Gaels in the Middle Ages. 12th cent.

IRONS see KENIRONS.

IRVIN(E), IRVING, ERVIN: L Brit (Celtic) river-name. From Irvine (Ayrs) or Irving (Dumfries) Scotland. 13th cent. [A First Fleet (convict) surname].

IRWIN(E), see ERWIN.

ISAAC(S), ISAACSON: P Hebrew 'God may smile favourably upon'. A popular name in medieval England and not exclusively Jewish. DB.

ISABEL, ISBEL(L), ISOBEL: P A form of *Elizabeth* developed in Provence and universal in France and Spain, as noted by William Camden in 1605. Surname 12th cent.

ISEMONGER: O OE *īsern-mangere* 'iron-merchant', 'ironmonger'. 12th cent.

ISBISTER: L ON 'The estuary or outermost settlement'. (Orkney).

ISHERWOOD: L OE The surname thrives in Australia, as well as in Britain, but the place from which it came, probably in Lancs, no longer exists, one of the 1,300 lost villages of England. 13th cent.

ISLIP: (i) L OE + OW 'The *slaep* (slippery place) on the R. Ise'. (Northants) (ii) L OE 'The *slaep* (slipway for porterage) on the R. Ight'. (Oxon).

ISMAY: P *Ismay, Ysemay*, a woman's name, from OG *Ismegi*. Celtic *Ismenia* may also have contributed to the surname. 13th cent.

ISSARD, ISSITT, ISSOTT, IZAT(T), IZZARD, IZZETT, EZARD: P OG *Ishild*, a compound of *is* and *vald* 'ice-rule' or *is* and *hild* 'ice-battle'. Latinised form *Isolda*, OF *Iseut*, Early English form *Isot, Izot*, Welsh *Essylt*. DB.

IVE(S): P OF *Ive, Yve, Yves*. A favourite name among the Normans and Bretons. Probably from OG *iv* 'yew'. DB.

IVOR, IVERS, IVERSON: P ON *Ivarr*, O Dan *Iwar*, O Sw *Ivar* 'yew-army'. DB. The yew was used for the bow, and 'yew-army' is 'army of archers'.

IVORY, IVERY: L OF From Ivry-la-Bataille (Eure) Normandy. DB.

J

JACK, JACKA, JACKE(S), JACKS, JAGG(S), JAKES, JEX: P ME The earliest and most popular pet-form of *John*, producing some 25 surnames. Langland used *Jagge the jogelour* in *Piers Plowman*. 12th cent.

JACKAMAN: P A dim. of *Jacqueme*, a Picard form of *James*. 14th cent.

JACKETT(S), JACOT: P A dim. of *Jack*. 13th cent.

JACKLIN(G): P A double dim. of *Jack*. 13th cent.

JACKMAN, JAKEMAN: O 'Servant of *Jack*'. 13th cent.

JACKSON, JACSON, JAGSON: P 'Son of *Jack*'. 14th cent. [A First Fleet surname].

JACOB(S), JACUBS: P Hebrew, Lat *Jacōbus*, used for both *Jacob* and *James*. In medieval England *Jacob* was not necessarily Jewish. 13th cent. [A First Fleet surname].

JACOBSON: P 'Son of *Jacob*'. 14th cent.

JACOBY: P Lat *Jacōbus*. 'Son of *Jacob* or *James*', 13th cent.

JACQUES, JAQUES, JAQUEST, JAQUET: P Most of these forms were introduced into England by Huguenots or other late entrants from France.

JAFFRAY, JAFFREY see JEFFRAY.

JAGGAR(S), JAGGER(S): O Yorks dial. *jagger* 'carrier, hawker, pedlar'. 14th cent.

JAGGARD: P A pet-form of *Jack* + OF Suffix *-ard*. 12th cent.

JAGO, JEGGO: P Cornish *Jago*, Welsh *Iago*, forms of *James*. 12th cent.

JAIN see JAN.

JAKINS, JAKENS: P A dim. of *Jak (James)*. 12th cent.

JAMES, FITZJAMES: P English *James* is from Lat *Jacōmus*, a late variant of *Jacōbus* (see Jacob). *James* was not recorded in England until 100 years after the Norman Conquest but gained in popularity with pilgrimages to the shrine of St *James* of Compostella beginning in 1148. Chaucer used *Seynt Jame* in 'The Shipman's Tale'. It became a frequent English name after the accession of James Stuart to the throne in 1603. Surname 12th cent. [A First Fleet surname].

JAMESON, JAMIESON, JAMISON: P 'Son of *James*', mainly Scottish. 14th cent.

JAN(S), JANE, JAIN, JAYNE(S), JEYNES: P Lat *Johannes, Johan* (*John*). 13th cent.

JANNINGS see JENNINGS.

JANSON: P 'Son of *Jan*'. 14th cent. See also I'Anson.

JARDIN, JARDINE: O OF *jardin* 'garden', 'a gardener'. 12th cent.

JARMAN, JARMAIN see GERMAN. JARRARD see GERARD.

JARRATT, JARRETT, JARROTT see GARRARD.

JARVIE: P A Scottish form of Jarvis.

JARVIS, JERVIS, JERVOIS(E): (i) P OG *Gervas*, OF *Gervaise*. 12th cent. (ii) L OF From Jervaulx (Yorks), pronounced *Jarvis*, a French name for an English place.

JASPER: P English form of OG *Kaspar*, popularised by the traditional belief that it was the name of one of the three Magi. 12th cent.

JAY(E), JAYS, JEYES: N OF *geai* 'jay (the bird)', nickname for a chatterer. 12th cent. [Jay, a First Fleet surname].

JEAN(S), JEANES, JEENS, JENNIS: P OF *Johan, Jehan, Jean.* 13th cent.

JEAVON see JEVON.

JEEVES, GEEVES: P OF A pet-form of *Geneviève*, patron saint of Paris. 12th cent. (P.G. Wodehouse used a woman's name to create a perfect gentleman's gentleman.)

JEFF(S): P A pet-form of *Geoffrey (Jeffrey)*. 14th cent.

JEFFCOAT(E), JEFFCOTT, JEFCOATE, JEFCOTT, JEPHCOTT: P A dim. of *Jeff.* 14th cent.

JEFFERSON: P 'Son of *Geoffrey (Jeffrey)*'. 14th cent.

JEFFREY(S), JEFFREE, JEFFRESS, JEFFERY(S), JEFFERIES, JEFFERIS, JEFFERY(S), GEOFFREY: P OG *Galfridus*, OF *Geuffroi, Jeufroi*, ME *Geffrey*. DB. [A First Fleet surname].

JEKYLL: P O Bret & Cornish *Iudicael*, introduced into England by the Breton contingent of Duke William's invading army. DB.

JENKIN(S), JENKING(S), JENKYN(S): P A dim. of *Jan (Johan)*. 13th cent. [A First Fleet surname].

JENNER, GENNER: O OF *enginior, engigeor* 'military engineer, maker of military machines, e.g., for assaulting castles'. 12th cent.

JENNET: P A dim. of *Jehan*, see Jean. 14th cent.

JENNIFER, JUNIPER: P Welsh *Gwenhwyvar*, from *gwen* 'fair, white' + *wyf* 'smooth, yielding'. 13th cent. *Guenevere*, the name of the wife of King Arthur, is from the same source.

JENNINGS, JENNENS, JANNINGS: P A dim. of *Jan (Johan)*. 13th cent.

JEPPESON, JEPSON: P 'Son of *Gepp*, a pet-form of *Geoffrey*'. 14th cent.

JEREMY: P Hebrew 'May Jehovah Exalt', Lat *Jeremias.* 12th cent.

JERMAN, JERMYN see GERMAN.

JEROME, JERROM, JERRAM: P Gk 'sacred name', OF *Jerome.* 12th cent.

JERROLD see GERALD. **JERVIS** see JARVIS.

JESSOP(P), JESSUP, JESSUP: P An ME version of *Joseph.* 13th cent.

JESSON, JETSON see JUDSON.

JEUDWINE: P AF A Norman form of OE *Goldwine.* 12th cent. See Goldwin.

JEW: (i) P A form of *Jull (Julian* or *Juliana)*. 13th cent. (ii) N A medieval nickname *le Jeu* 'the Jew'. 13th cent.

JEWELL: O OF *joel*, AF *juel.* Metonymic for a jeweller. 14th cent.

JEWKES see JUKES.

JEWRY, JURY, JUREY: L OF *jurie* 'the Jewry (Ghetto)'. 14th cent.

JEWSON: P 'Son of *Jull*'. 14th cent.

JEX see JACK. **JEYES** see JAY. **JEYNES** see JAN. **JILES** see GILES. **JILLETT** see GILLET.

JINKS: P A late variant of *Jenkin.* 16th cent.

JOAN, JOANES see JOHN.

JOB(E), JOBES, JUBB, JUPE, JUPP: (i) P Hebrew 'Hated, persecuted'. Sometimes non-Jewish from a part in a medieval play. 12th cent. (ii) N OF *jobe*, from Lat *joppus* 'a fool'. (iii) O ME *jobbe, jubbe* 'a vessel for holding liquor'. Metonymic for a maker of *jobbes.* 14th cent.

JOBBER: O ME Identical in meaning with *Job* (iii). 14th cent.

JOBERT, JOUBERT: P OG *Gautbert*, OF *Jobert.* 13th cent.

JOBLIN(G), JOPLING: OF *Job-el-in* a double dim. of *Job.*

JOCE, JOSE, JOSS see GOSS.

JOCELYN, JOSCELYN, JOSCELYN(E), JOSSELYN, JOSELIN, JOSLING: P OG *Gautselin*, OF *Goscelin, Joscelin.* DB.

JOEL(S), JEWELL, JOULE, JOELSON, JOLSON: P O Bret *Iudhael*, from *Iud* 'chief, lord' + *hael* 'generous'. DB.

JOHN(S), JOHNES, JOAN, JOANES, JONE, JONES, JOYNES, FITZJOHN: P Hebrew *Johanan*, Latinised as *Johannes*, OF *Johan, Jehan, Jean.* The fem. *Joan*, Latinised as *Johanna*, also contributed to the surname. The Welsh form is *Ieuan, Evan*, the Scottish *Ian*, Irish *Sean*, Spanish *Juan*, Italian *Giovanni*, German *Hans* (from *Johannes*), Russian *Ivan.* Many English surnames descend from *John* and its pet-forms. 12th cent. See also Fitz. [A First Fleet surname].

JOHNSON, JONSON, JOINSON, JOYNSON: P 'Son of *John*'. 13th cent. [A First Fleet surname].

JOHNSTON, JOHNSTONE: (i) P A variant of *Johnson.* (ii) L From Johnstone in Annandale (Dumfries) Scotland. 14th cent.

JOICE, JOISCE, JOICEY see JOYCE.

JOINER, JOYNER: O OF *joigneor* 'a joiner, worker with wood'. 12th cent.

JOLIN, JOLLAND, GOLLAND, GOLLIN(S): P *Joel-in*, a dim. of *Joel*. 13th cent.

JOLLIFF(E), JOLLEY, JOLLIE, JOLLY(E), JOLY: N OF *joliff* 'cheerful, lively, jovial'. 13th cent. [Edward Jollie, surveyor for the Anglican settlement of Canterbury, laid out the city of Christchurch. 1850].

JONATHAN, JONATHON: P Hebrew *Jonathan* 'Jehovah has given'. 13th cent.

JORDAN, JORDEN, JORDIN, JORDON, JOURDAIN, JOURDAN, JOURDON: P The River Jordan, the children of returning Crusaders baptised with water brought back from the river. *Jordan* is from Hebrew. 12th cent.

JORY: P Cornish form of *George*.

JOSEPH(S), JOSEY: P Hebrew 'May Jehovah add'. DB. [A First Fleet surname].

JOSHUA: P Hebrew 'Jehovah is generous'. The name became popular in England after the Reformation. The Hebrew form is *Jehoshea*.

JOUBERT see JOBERT. JOULE see JOEL.

JOWETT, JOWITT, JUETT: P A dim. of *Jull* (pet-form of *Julian* or *Juliana*). 12th cent.

JOY(E), JOYES: P OF *Joie* 'joy', a woman's name. 12th cent.

JOYCE, JOICE, JOISCE, JOSS(E), JOICEY, JOWSEY: (i) P O Bret *Iodoc*, a saint's name, son of *Iudicael*, a hermit of Ponthieu. Also a medieval woman's name. (ii) P Ir *Seoigh*, a family of Welsh origin which became one of the 'Tribes of Galway', and established their lands as 'Joyce's country'. 12th cent.

JOYNER see JOINER. JOYNES see JOHN. JUBB see JOB.

JUDD: P A variant of *Jordan*.

JUDE: P Hebrew *Judah*, Gk *Judas*.

JUDGE(S): O OF *juge* 'judge'. 14th cent.

JUDSON, JUTSON, JETSON: P 'Son of *Judd*'. 14th cent.

JUKES, JUCKES, JEWKES: P A short-form of O Bret *Iudicael*. 13th cent.

JULIAN(S), JULIEN, JULLIAN: P Lat *Julianus*, from *Julius*, name of a Roman *gens* (clan). *Julian* (masc.) and *Juliana* (fem.) both contributed to the surname. The name of 10 saints including St *Julian* the Hospitaller, patron saint of travellers. 12th cent.

JUNIPER see JENNIFER. JUPP see JOB.

JURD: P A pet-form of *Jordan*. 13th cent.

JURY see JEWRY.

JUST: P Lat *justus* 'just'. 13th cent.

JUSTER, JOESTER: O OF *justeur* 'a jouster in medieval tournaments'. 13th cent.

JUSTICE: O OF *justise* 'an officer of justice, judge'. 12th cent.

JUSTIN(S): P ON *Iosteinn*, Latinised as *Justinus*. The English surname is probably from the ON source. DB.

K

There is no letter K in the Old English alphabet. Some names beginning with K will be found under C.

KADWELL see CADWELL. KAIN(E) see CAIN. KAINES see CAINS. KALEY see CALEY. KANE see CANE, CAIN.

KANTER see CANTER. KAPLAN see CHAPLAIN. KARL(E) see CARL. KASER see CAYSER.

KATES see CATES. KATTE see CATT.

KAVANAGH, CAVANAGH: P Ir *Caomhanach*, a branch of the *Mac Murroughs*.

KAY(E), KAYES, KEAY(S), KEEYS, KEY(E), KEYES, KEYS: (i) P OW *Cai*, from Lat *Caius*. Also a Cornish and Breton name. 12th cent. Mallory's *Morte Darthur* (printed by Caxton in 1485) has Sir *Kay*, King Arthur's seneschal. (ii) L OF *cay*, ME *kay, key* 'quay'. (iii) N ON ka, ME *ME ka, kay* 'jackdaw', a nickname from the bird. In southern England this became *Coe*.

KEAN(E): P Ir *O Cathain*, from *cath* 'battle'. Occasionally a variant of Keen.

KEAR, KEER(S): O OE *caeg* 'key', a 'key-er, maker of keys'. 12th cent.

KEARNEY: P Ir *O Cearnaigh*, from *cearnach* 'victorious'.

KEARNS, KEARNES: P Ir *O Ciarain* (Co. Donegal).

KEARSEY see KERSEY. KEARSLEY see CARSLEY.

KEARTON: L O Sw + OE 'The *tūn* (homestead) of a Swede called *Kaerir*'. (Yorks).

KEARY: P Ir O *Ciardha* 'dark brown or black'.

KEAST: N OE *cēast* 'contentious, quarrelsome'.

KEAT(E), KEATES, KEATS, KEYTE,

KETT(S), KITE, KYTE: N OE *cȳta*, ME *kete* 'kite', a nickname from the bird, 'greedy, rapacious'. 12th cent.

KEATING: (i) P OW *Cethin* 'dark, fierce and ugly'. Originally a Welsh name but long settled in Ireland, where it became Ir *Céitinn*. (ii) P Ir *O Ceatfhadha* 'suave'. (iii) N OE *Cȳting*, a patronymic from *Cyta* 'Kite'. See Keat.

KEEBLE, KEABLE, KIBBLE: O OE *cycgel*, ME *kibble* 'cudgel', 'a maker/seller of cudgels'. 11th cent.

KEECH, KEATCH, KEITCH: N ME *keech* 'the fat of a slaughtered animal', used as a name for a butcher. Shakespeare uses the term in *Henry IV* and *Henry VIII*. 12th cent.

KEEGAN: P Ir *O Caogain*, a variant of *Aodhagain* (*Mac Egan*).

KEELEY, KEALEY: P Ir *O Caollaidh* 'graceful'.

KEELING: L OE *ceald-ing* 'the *ingas* (people) of an Anglo-Saxon nicknamed *Ceald* (Cold)'. [A First Fleet (convict) surname].

KEEN(E), KEENS: (i) P OE A short-form of names in *Cyne* or *Cīn*. 12th cent. (ii) N OE *cēne*, ME *kene* 'bold, brave' or 'learned, clever'. 13th cent.

KEEP: O OE *cēpan* 'keep, tower, stronghold (of a castle)', 'a guard or gaoler at the keep'. 14th cent.

KEEPENCE: N OE *cēpan* 'to sieze, hold on to' + ME *pens*, an abbreviation of pennies. A succinct description of a thrifty individual.

KEEVIL: L OE *cȳf-lēah* 'the wood where the tub-makers cut their timber'. (Wilts).

KEIGHLEY, KEIGHTLY: L OE 'The *lēah* (clearing) of *Cyhha*, an Anglo-Saxon'. (Yorks).

KEITH: L A Scottish locality name, e.g., from Keith Mains (Lothian). (*Mains* 'the home farm of a landed estate'.)

KELL(S): P ON *Kel*, short-form of *Ketill* (cauldron). 12th cent. Also in Ireland, *Kell* in Antrim, *Kells* in Cavan and Monaghan.

KELLAWAY, KELLEWAY see CALLAWAY.

KELLET(T): L ON *keld-hlith* 'the slope with a spring'. (Lancs, Westmorland) 12th cent.

KELLOGG: O ME *kellen-hogg* 'kill hog', 'a butcher or slaughterman'. 13th cent.

KELLOW: L OE *celf-hlaw* 'calf-hill'. (Durham). [Robert Kellow, a first lieutenant of Marines, brought the surname to Australia 1788].

KELLY, KELLEY, KELLIE: (i) P Ir *O Kelly*, *O Ceallaigh*, descendant of *Ceallach* 'war'. The form *Mac Kelly* is from Galway and the Isle of Man. (ii) L Cornish *celli* 'grove'. A place Kelly (Devon). 12th cent. [A First Fleet (convict and crew) surname. James Kelly was the first settler in the Invercargill district of New Zealand 1855. The district was named after William Cargill].

KELMAN: O ME *kelle*, from OF *cale*, 'a maker of cauls, coifs (head coverings for women)'. 13th cent. See also Call.

KELSEY: L OE 'The *ēg* (island or dry land in a fen) of *Cēli*, an Anglo-Saxon'. (Lincs).

KELTIE, KELTY: L From the lands of Keltie (Perths) Scotland. 17th cent. (Adam Keltie was servitor to the Chancellor of Scotland in 1628.) [James Keltie, first mate on the *Fishburn*, and later master of the *Sirius*, brought the surname to Australia 1788].

KELTON: L OE *celf-tūn* 'calf farm'. (Cumb).

KEMBER: O OE *cemban* 'to comb', 'a comber of wool or flax'. 14th cent.

KEMBLE, KEMBALL, KIMBALL, KEMBLE, KEMPLE: (i) P OW *Cyndel*, from *cyn* 'chief' and *bel* 'war'. 12th cent. (ii) P OE *Cynebeald* 'kin-bold'. 13th cent. (iii) L OE *cyne-belle* 'royal hill'. (Bucks) (Kipling uses Kimball O'Hara in his novel *Kim*.)

KEMP(E): O OE *cempa* 'warrior, athlete, wrestler'. OE Byname AD 902.

KEMPSTER: O OE *cemban* 'A female comber of wool or flax', comparable with *spinster*. 13th cent. See also Kember.

KENDAL(L), KENDELL, KENDLE: L Brit (Celtic) river-name + OE *dael*, 'the dale of the R. Kent'. (Westmorland) 14th cent. [Thomas Kendall was one of William Marsden's fellow missionaries in New Zealand, 1814].

KENIRONS: P Ir A Tipperary surname of uncertain origin, sometimes abbreviated to Irons, which appears to have become an independent surname.

KENNEALLY see KINNEALLY.

KENNEDY: P Ir and SG *O Cinneide* 'ugly head'. 12th cent. [A First Fleet (marine and convict) surname].

KENNERLY: L OE 'The *lēah* (clearing) of *Cyneweard*. (Devon) 13th cent.

KENNETT: L A Brit river-name, originally *Cunētiō*. (Wilts).

KENNINGTON: (i) L OE 'The *cyne-tūn* 'royal manor'. (Kent) (ii) L OE 'The *tūn* (farm) of *Cēna*, an Anglo-Saxon'. (Berks).

KENNY, KENNEY: P Ir (i) For O'Kenny *O Cionaoith*, an important Ui Maine sept. (Galway) (ii) P Ir For Mac Kenny, an Ulster variant of *Mac Kenna*.

KENRICK, KENDRICK: P OW *Cynwrig*, from *cyn* 'chief' and *gwr* 'hero'. 12th cent. See also Kerrich.

KENT: L O Brit (Celtic) *Kent* (the county), recorded as *Cantium* by Caesar in 51 BC and as *Cantia* by Bede in AD 730. Derived from Celtic *canto* 'borderland' or 'coast land'. Surname (the man from *Kent*) 12th cent. [Capt Kent took the first European vessel into Hokianga Harbour, Bay of Islands, New Zealand 1820].

KENTISH: L OF *Kenteis* 'Kentish (man)'. 12th cent.

KENTWELL, CANTWELL: L Brit + OE *Kennett* (river-name) to which *wella* (stream) has been added in Anglo-Saxon times. (Suffolk), *Kanewella* DB, *Kenetewell* 12th cent. The surname has also been established in Ireland since 12th cent., originally in the form *de Cantual* (of Kentwell).

KENWARD, KENNARD: P OE Either *Cenweard* 'bold guardian', or *Cyneweard* 'royal guardian'. 12th cent. (*Cyne* 'royal race', 'royal lineage'.)

KENWAY, KENNAWAY: P OE *Cēnwīg* 'bold war'. 12th cent.

KENWORTHY: L OE 'The *worthig* (enclosure) of an Anglo-Saxon called *Cyna* (royal)'. (Ches).

KENYON: L OW *cruc Enion* '*Enion's* mound', a bronze age barrow. (Lancs) 12th cent.

KEOGH: P Ir *Mac Eochaidh*, the name of three septs (Munster, Leinster, Roscommon). Ballymackeogh is named for one of the septs.

KEOWN see MAC OWEN. KER see CARR. KERBY see KIRBY. KERIN see KIERAN. KERLEY see KIRKLEY.

KERMODE: P A Manx contraction of *Mac Dermot* (*Mac Dhiarmada*). 15th cent.

KERR see CARR.

KERRELL, CROYLE: L OF From Criel-sur-Mer (Seine Inférieur) France. DB.

KERRICH, KERRIDGE, KENRICK, KENDRICK: P OE *Cynerīc* 'family ruler'. DB. [A First Fleet (marine) surname].

KERRIGAN: P Ir *O Ciaragáin*, from *ciar* 'black'. The sept gave its name to Ballykerrigan.

KERRY: P A variant of *Kendrick*. See Kenrick, Kerrich.

KERSEY: KEARSEY: L OE *caerse-īeg* 'watercress island'. (Suffolk) 13th cent.

KERSHAW: L ON *kirkja* + OE *scaga* or dial. *shaw* 'church wood'. (Lancs) 14th cent.

KERSLAKE: L OE *coerse-lacu* 'cress-stream'. 13th cent.

KERSLEY see CARSLEY. KESBY see KISBY. KESOR, KEYZER see CAYZER.

KESTEL(L), KESSEL(L): L Cornish 'The *kestel* (castle)'. 13th cent.

KETT(S) see KEAT.

KETTLE(S), KETELL, KITTEL(L), KITTLE: P OE *Cytel*, from ON *Ketill* '(sacrificial) caudron'. A Byname from 10th cent. [Charles Kettle and Alfred Wills, explorers, negotiated the Manawatu Gorge and travelled over the Rimutakas to the Hutt Valley 1842].

KETTLESTRING: L O Scand *strengr* 'a *string* (narrow vein of ore)', 'the *string* of a Scandinavian called *Ketil*'.

KEW: (i) L OF From Caieu, a lost place in the Pas-de-Calais, France. 12th cent. (ii) O OF *queu*, *keu* 'a keeper of an eating-house'. 12th cent.

KEWEN, KEWIN: P Manx From Ir *Mac Eoin* 'son of *John*'. 15th cent.

KEWISH: P Manx A contraction of Ir *Mac Uais* 'the noble's son'.

KEWLEY: L OF From Cully-le-Patry (Calvados) Normandy. DB.

KEY, KEYE, KEYES see KAY. KEYNES see CAINS. KEYTE see KEAT. KEYZER see CAYZER. KIBBLE see KEEBLE.

KIDD, KYD(D): N ON *kith*, O Dan & ME *kid* or *kide* 'a young goat'. 12th cent.

KIDDELL, KIDDLE: O OF *quidel* 'kiddle', a basket for catching fish at the weir. Metonymic for a fisherman at the kiddle. 13th cent.

KIDMAN: O ON *kith* 'kid, young goat', 'a kid-herd'. 13th cent.

KIDNEY: P Ir A synonym of *O Dubhain*, and a Co. Cork surname. [A First Fleet (convict) surname].

KIDSTON: L OE 'The *tūn* (homestead) of *Kide* (young goat)'. From Kidston in Peebles, Scotland. 12th cent.

KIERAN, KERIN: P Ir *O Ciarin*, from *ciar* 'dark brown or black'. A north Connacht sept.

KILBORN, KILBOURNE, KILBURN: L OE *cyclen-burna* 'the kiln by a stream'. (Derbys, Middx, Yorks).

KILBRIDE: L SG *cill*, from Lat *cella* 'cell, church' + St *Brigid*. From Kilbride (Ayrs, Lanarks) Scotland. 12th cent.

KILBY: L OE with O Scand influence *Cilda-tūn* 'the village of the young nobles'. (Leices) 12th cent. (OE *tūn* became ON *býr*.) [A First Fleet (convict) surname].

KILDEA see GILDEA.

KILLEN, MACKILLEN: P SG A patronymic of *Colin*, Ir *Mac Coilin*. A galloglas (mercenary Scottish soldier) surname.

KILLIP: P Manx A contraction of *Mac Philip*. 15th cent.

KILMINSTER: L OE 'The *mynster* (church) of an Anglo-Saxon called *Cydela*'. (Worces) 13th cent.

KILNER: O OE *cylene* 'kiln', 'a lime-burner'. 13th cent.

KILPATRICK: (i) P Ir *Mac Giolla Phadraig* 'devotee of St *Patrick*'. (ii) L SG From Kilpatrick (Dumbarton, Dumfries) Scotland. 13th cent.

KILROY: P Ir *Mac Giolla Rua*, from *rua* 'red'. See also Gilroy.

KIMBALL, KIMBLE see KEMBLE.

KIMBER: P OE *Cyne-burg* 'royal fortress', an Anglo-Saxon woman's name.

KIMBERLEY: L OE 'The *lēah* (clearing) of an Anglo-Saxon woman called *Cyneburg*'. (Norfolk, Warwicks) 12th cent. [A First Fleet (convict) surname].

KIMPTON: L OE 'The *tūn* (farm) of an Anglo-Saxon called *Cyma*'. (Hants), *Chementune* DB, (Herts), *Kamintone* DB.

KINCAID, KINKADE, KINKEAD: L SG From the lands of Kincaid in Campsie (Stirling) Scotland. 15th cent.

KING: N OE *cyng* 'king'. A nickname from playing the part in a medieval pageant or tournament. 12th cent. (Lieutenant Philip Gidley King, Governor of N.S.W. from 1800 to 1806, brought the surname to Australia 1788. Two marines and a convict named King also arrived with the First Fleet. John King was one of Samuel Marsden's fellow missionaries in New Zealand. 1814].

KINGHAM: L OE 'The *hām* (village) of the people of *Cǣga*, an Anglo-Saxon'. (Oxon), *Caningeham* DB.

KINGHORN(E), KINGHAN, KINGAN: L OE From the barony of Kinghorn (Fifes) Scotland. 12th cent.

KINGSBURY: (i) L OE 'The *burg* (fort) of an Anglo-Saxon called *Cyne*'. (Warwicks) (ii) L OE 'The king's burg'. (Middx, Som).

KINGSFORD: (i) L OE 'The ford of the people of *Cēna*, an Anglo-Saxon'. (Worces) where a place was called *Cenangaford* in 964. (ii) L OE 'The *Cyninges* (king's) ford'. (Warwicks) Surname 12th cent.

KINGSLEY: L OE *Cyninges lēah* 'the king's wood'. (Ches, Hants, Staffs) 13th cent.

KINGSMAN: O OE *cynemann* 'king's man', 'a man in the service of the king'. 12th cent.

KINGSON: P OE 'Son of *Cyne, Cyning*' (king, head of a kin, leader of a tribe). Winton D.

KINGSTON: L OE 'The *Cyninges tūn*', 'the king's farm or a royal manor'. The king had many manors and there are places of this name in 15 counties. Surname 12th cent.

KINGSWOOD: L OE *Cyninges wudu* 'The king's wood' (royal chase). 12th cent.

KINLAY, KINLEY: P Manx A contraction of Ir *Mac Cinnfaolaidh* 'wolf-head'.

KINNAIRD: L From the barony of Kinnaird (Perths) Scotland. 12th cent.

KINNEALLY, KENEALLY: P Ir *O Cinnfhaolaidh*, from *ceann* 'head' and *faol* 'wolf', 'wolf-head'. The barony of Connelloe was the original home of this name. (Munster).

KINRADE, KINRED: N OE *cynn-raeden* 'kin-condition' (kindred, family), a nickname from relationship.

KINSELLA: P Ir *Cinnsealach*, from an ancient clan name. A branch of the *Mac Murroughs*.

KINSEY: P OE *Cynesige* 'royal victory'. 13th cent.

KINSMAN: P OE *cynn-mann* 'a relative by blood or (less binding) by marriage'. 12th cent.

KIPLING: L OE *Cybbel-ingas* 'the *cots* (huts) of the *ingas* (people) of an Anglo-Saxon called *Cybbel*'. (Yorks).

KIPPAX: L OE + O Scand '*Cyppa's aesc* (ash-tree)'. (Yorks) Scand influence converted *aesc* to *ask* (ash), which became *ax*.

KIPPING, KIPPEN: N OE *cypping* 'fat'. DB. KIPPS: N 'Son of the fat man'. Winton D.

KIRK: L ON *kirkja* 'church', a frequent name in the Danelaw. 12th cent.

KIRKBY, KIRBY, KERBY: L ON *kirkbýr 'the village with a church'. 12th cent. [Kirby, a First Fleet (marine) surname].*

KIRKLAND: L O Scand *kirkja* 'church land' + ON *lundr* (wood). 12th cent.

KIRKMAN, KIRMAN: O ON *kirkja* + ME *man* 'custodian of a church'. 13th cent.

KIRKPATRICK: L SG 'The *kirk* (church)

dedicated to St *Patrick*'. A Scottish and Ulster surname.

KIRKWOOD: L ON *kirkja* + OE *wudu* 'church wood'.

KISBY, KESBY: L ON 'The *býr* (homestead) of a Norseman called *Kisi* (Cat)'. 12th cent.

KISS, CUSS: O OF Metonymic for *Kisser*. 14th cent. KISSER: O OF *cuisse* 'thigh', 'a maker of leather thigh-armour'. 13th cent.

KISSANE: P Ir *O Ciosáin*, from *cios* 'tribute'.

KITCHEN, KITCHIN: O OE *cycene* 'a kitchen worker'. 14th cent. KITCHENER: O OE A deriv. of *cycene* 'kitchen worker'. 14th cent.

KITE see KEAT.

KITT(S): P A pet-form of *Christopher*. 13th cent.

KITTLE see KETTLE.

KNAPE, KNAPMAN: O OE *cnapa* 'youth, servant'.

KNAPP: L OE *cnaepp* 'hill-top'. (Hants) 13th cent.

KNEAL(E): P Manx A contraction of *Mac Niall*. 15th cent.

KNEEBONE: L Cornish *carn-ebol* 'colt-enclosure'.

KNIGHT: O OE *cniht* 'youth, servant, retainer, feudal tenant bound to serve his lord as a mounted warrior, knight, soldier'. DB. Later, one of noble birth who had served as a squire or page, raised to honourable military rank. [A Marine sergeant, a marine sawyer, and a marine private, all following the tradition of military service, brought the name to Australia 1788].

KNIGHTON: L OE 'The *tūn* (village) of the knights'. (Nine places from Wight to Leices.) 12th cent.

KNIPE: L ON *gnipa* 'steep, overhanging rock'. (Westmorland) *Gnype* in 1314.

KNIVETT, KNEVITT: O OE *cniht* 'knight'. The surname derives from a Norman mispronunciation of 'knight'. For the curiosities of Norman pronunciation of Anglo-Saxon names see also Graham.

KNOCK: L Ir *cnoc* 'hillock'. (Westmorland).

KNOLL, KNOWLES: L OE *cnoll* 'hill-top'. (Devon, Dorset, Kent, Sussex) 12th cent.

KNOTT(S): (i) P O Dan *Knut*, ON *Knutr* (English pronunciation 'Canute'). DB. (ii) L OE *cnotta*, ME *knot* 'hill'.

KNOWLAN see NOLAN.

KNOX: L SG From Knock (Renfrews) Scotland. 13th cent. (Also Skye, Lewis, Mull.)

KRABBE see CRABB. KYD(D) see KID.

KYLE: L Brit From Kyle (Ayrs) Scotland, which bears the name of a British chieftain, *Coel*.

L

LACE: O OF *las*, ME *lace* 'cord'. Metonymic for a maker of cords or strings. 13th cent.

LACEY, LACY: L OF From Lassy (Calvados) Normandy. DB.

LACHLAN, LAUGHLAN, LAUGHLIN, LOUGHLIN, LAUGHLIN: L SG *lachlann* 'lake (fjord) land', i.e., Scandinavia. A name first applied to Vikings. 12th cent.

LACKEY see LECKY. LACOCK see LAYCOCK.

LADD(S): O ME *ladde* 'servant'. 12th cent.

LADE: L OE *lād* 'path, road, watercourse'. 13th cent.

LADYMAN: O OE *hlǣfdige-mann* 'the lady's servant'. 12th cent. (*Hlǣfdige* is from *hlaf* 'loaf' and an obsolete verb 'to knead', so the lady was originally a housewife rather than a superior female person.)

LAFFERTY see LAVERY.

LAIDLAW: L Supposedly a form of Ludlow (Salop) although mainly a Scottish surname. If so, OE *hlūde* (loud, referring to the nearby R. Teme) + *hlāw* 'low hill'. 'The hill by the rapid'.

LAIDLER: O OE *hlaedel* 'ladle', 'a maker/seller of ladles'. 13th cent.

LAIRD: Scottish variant of *Lord*, 'a land-owner'. 13th cent.

LAITHWAITE: L ON *hlatha-thveit* 'the clearing with a barn'. (Lancs).

LAKE, LACK: L OE *lacu* 'stream'. 12th cent.

LAKER, LAKEMAN: (i) L OE *lacu* 'by the stream'. 13th cent. (ii) O ME *leyker*, from ON *leikari* 'player, actor'. 13th cent.

LAKIN: P A dim. of *Lawrence* (*Laurence*).

LALOR, LAWLER: P Ir *O Leathlobhair*, from *leathlobar* 'half-sick', one of the 'seven septs of Leix', and the name of two Irish kings.

LAMB(E): (i) N OE *lamb* 'docile as a lamb' or an ironic nickname for a tough fighter. (ii) P An abbreviated form of *Lambert*. (iii) L A sign name; the Paschal Lamb was a common sign in medieval England. 12th cent.

LAMBARD, LAMBERT, LAMPERD, LAMPERT, LAMMERT, LIMBERT: P OG *Lambert*, OF *Lambert* 'land-bright'. DB.

LAMBERTON, LAMERTON: (i) L OE 'The *tūn* (farm) on Lumburn Water'. (Devon) 13th cent. (ii) L OE From the barony of Lamberton (Berwicks) Scotland. 12th cent. (The Devon place was *Lamburnan* c. 970.)

LAMBETH: L OE *lamb-hȳth* 'the *hȳth* (harbour) where lambs were shipped'. [A First Fleet (convict) surname].

LAMBIE, LAMBY: P ON *Lambi*, a Scottish surname, introduced by the Vikings. 12th cent.

LAMBKIN: P A dim. of *Lamb* (*Lambert*). 12th cent.

LAMBRIGG: L OE *lamb* + ON *hryggr* 'the ridge where lambs graze'. (Westmorland) 12th cent. LAMBOURNE(E), LAMBURN(E): L OE *lamb-burna* 'the stream where lambs are washed'. (Berks, Essex).

LAMEY see AMEY. LAMING see LOVEMAN.

LAMOND, LAMONT: O Ir *Lagmand*, from ON *Logmathr* 'lawman'. 13th cent.

LAMPORT: L OE *lang-port* 'the long market-place'. (Bucks, Herts, Kent, Northants, Som, Sussex).

LANCASHIRE, LANKSHEAR: L OE The county of Lancashire, *honor de Lancastre* in 1140. Surname 14th cent.

LANCASTER: L OE + Brit 'The Roman fort on the River Lune'. Surname 12th cent.

LANCE: P A Norman form of OG *Lanzo*. 12th cent.

LANCELOT(T): P A French double dim. of *Lance*. 13th cent.

LANCHESTER: L OE *lang-ceaster* 'the long Roman fort'. (Durham) 12th cent.

LAND, LAWN: L OF *lande*, ME *launde* 'glade, pasture'. (Leices) 12th cent.

LANDER(S) see LAVENDER.

LANDON: L OE *lang-dūn* 'long hill'. (Devon, Dorset, Kent, Warwicks).

LANDREY, LANDRY, LAUNDREY: (i) P OG *Landrie*, OF *Landri* 'land-ruler'. DB. (ii) O ME *Lavendrie*, from Lat *lavandarius*, OF *lavandier* 'worker in the wash-house'. 13th cent. (*Piers Plowman*: 'And laveth hem in the lavandry'.)

LANE(S), LOAN(E), LONE: L OE *lanu* 'lane'. 12th cent. [A First Fleet (convict) surname].

LANG, LANGE, LAING, LONG, LUNG: N OE *lang* 'long', i.e., 'tall'. Usually for a tall man, but *lange* means 'a long time' and may be for a tardy individual or an ancient one. OE Byname 10th cent. [Long, a First Fleet surname].

LANGDALE: L OE *lang-dael* 'long valley'. (Westmorland) 14th cent.

LANGDON: L OE *lang-dūn* 'long hill'. 11th cent. LANGFORD, LONGFORD: L OE 'long ford'. (Twelve counties, from Wilts to Derbys.) 12th cent. LANGHAM, LANHAM: L OE *lang-hām* 'the long village' or *lang-holm* 'long stretch of dry land in a fen'.

LANGLAND see LONGLAND.

LANGLEY, LONGLEY, LONGLY: L OE *lang-lēah* 'the long wood'. (Fifteen counties, from Bucks to Northumb.) 13th cent. [A First Fleet (female convict) surname].

LANGMORE, LONGMOOR, LONGMORE, LONGMUIR: L OE *lang-mōr* 'long moor or fen'.

LANGRIDGE, LONGRIDGE: L OE *lang-hrycg* 'the long ridge'. (Som).

LANGSHAW see LONGSHAW. LANGSTAFF see LONGSTAFF.

LANGSTON: L OE *lang-stān* 'long stone (megalith)'. (Devon) LANGTREE, LANGTRY, LANTRY: L OE *lang-treo* 'the tall tree'. (Devon) 12th cent.

LANGTON: L OE (i) *langa-tūn* 'the long village' or *lang-dūn* 'the long hill'. (Dorset, Lincs, Westmorland, Yorks), *Langetone* DB. (ii) 'The *tūn* (farm) of an Anglo-Saxon called *Tyrhtel*. (The Langton, Leices), *Terlintone* DB.

LANKEY: L Cornish *lan* 'church' + St *Cai*. (Devon) [A First Fleet surname].

LANSDOWN(E): L OE and dial. *langet-dūn* 'projecting ridge of hill'.

LANYON: L Cornish *lyn-yeyn* 'the cool lake'. (Cornwall).

LAPHAM: L OE 'The *hām* (homestead) of *Laeppa*, an Anglo-Saxon'.

LARCHER see ARCHER.

LARCOMBE: L OE 'The *cumb* (valley) frequented by *lāwerce* (larks)'.

LARDNER: O AF *lardiner* (i) 'Official in charge of the larder in a castle or manor-house'. (ii) 'Official supervising the pasturage of swine in the forest'. 12th cent.

LARGE: N OF *large* 'bountiful, generous'. 12th cent.

LARGENT see ARGENT.

LARK, LAVERACK, LAVERICK: N OE *lāwerce*, ME *larke*, a nickname from the bird. 13th cent.

LARKING see LORKING.

LARKIN(S): P A dim. of *Lawrence*.

LARMER, LARMOUR see ARMER.

LARNE: L Ir From Larne (N. Ireland), the stronghold of the legendary prince *Lahar*. [A First Fleet (convict) surname].

LARTER: N ME *lart* 'to trick, cheat, deceive'.

LARWOOD: L ME Probably *laverock-wudu* 'lark's wood'. (East Anglia).

LASCELLES: L OF From Lacelle (Orne) Normandy. 12th cent.

LAST: O ME *last*. Metonymic for a maker of lasts for shoe-makers. 14th cent.

LATCH, LETCH, LECHE, LEACH, LEECH: L OE *laecc*, ME *leche* 'the stream through boggy land'. (Ches) 12th cent. See also Leach.

LATHAM: L O Scand *hlatha* 'barn'. (Lancs, Yorks).

LATIMER, LATTIMER: O OF *latinier, latimier* 'a speaker, interpreter of Latin'. DB.

LATTA: Scottish form of *Lawtey*.

LATTER: O OE *laett* 'lath', timber used in house-building. 'A lath-maker'. 12th cent.

LAUDER, LAWDER, LAWTHER: L Brit, from Celtic *laour* 'ditch'. (Lauder, Berwicks), *Lawedir* 1250.

LAUGHLIN, see LACHLAN.

LAUGHTON: L OE *lēac-tūn* 'leek farm'. (Leices, Lincs, Sussex, Yorks) 12th cent.

LAUREL(S), LAWRELL: L OF *lorier*, from Lat *laurus* 'laurel (shrub)'. [Lawrell, a First Fleet (convict) surname].

LAURENCE: LAURANCE, LAURENS, LAWRANCE, LAWRENCE, LORENCE, LORENZ: P Lat *Laurentius* ('of Laurentum', an Italian city). A popular name in England in the Middle Ages, from St *Laurence*, martyred at Rome AD 258. Popular in Ireland also from St *Laurence* O'Toole (1130–80) Archbishop of Dublin. Surname 12th cent. [A First Fleet (convict and crew) surname].

LAURIE see LAWRY.

LAVENDER, LANDER(S): O OF *lavandier* 'washerman' or *lavandiere* 'washerwoman'. 13th cent. [George Lavender, bosun of the *Charlotte*, brought the name to Australia 1788].

LAVER: O OF *laver* 'to wash'. 'A washerman'.

LAVERACK see LARK.

LAVERT, LAFFERTY: P Ir *O Laithbheartaigh* 'valiant prince'.

LAVERY, LOWRY: P Ir *O Labhradha*, from *labhraidh* 'spokesman'.

LAW(S), LAWES: (i) P A pet-form of *Laurence*. 13th cent. (ii) L OE *hlāw* 'barrow, burial mound'. 13th cent.

LAWLER see LALOR.

LAWLESS: O ME *laweles* 'outside the law', 'an outlaw'. 14th cent.

LAWLEY: L OE 'The *lēah* (clearing) of *Lāfa*, an Anglo-Saxon'. (Salop).

LAWMAN: O ON *logmathr*, Anglo-Scand *lagman* 'a lawgiver', responsible for declaring the law. DB.

LAWN see LAND.

LAWREY, LAWRIE, LAWRY, LAURIE: P A dim. of *Laurence*. 12th cent.

LAWSON: P 'Son of *Law* (*Laurence*)'. 14th cent. [A First Fleet (crew) surname].

LAWTEY: N OF *leaute* 'loyalty'. 13th cent.

LAWTON: L OE *hlāw-tūn* 'the farm by a mound'. (Ches, Herefords) 12th cent.

LAX: N ON *lax*, OE *leax* 'salmon', a nickname for a salmon fisher/seller. 12th cent. (Teutonic *lax, leax* were replaced in ME by *samon*, from OF *salmo* 'salmon'.)

LAY see LEA. LAYLAND see LEYLAND.

LAYCOCK, LEACOCK, LACOCK: L OE *lacuc* 'streamlet'. (Wilts), *Lacoc* DB.

LAYMAN, LEYMAN: L OE *lēah* + *mann* 'dweller by the wood'. 14th cent.

LAYTON, LEIGHTON, LEYTON, LIGHTON: (i) L OE + Brit 'The *tūn* (farm) on the River Lea'. (Essex) (Lea is a Brit river-name, from Gaulish *Lugu* 'light', the name of a Celtic god.) (ii) L OE *lād-tūn* 'farm on a stream'. (Lancs) (iii) L OE *lēac-tūn* 'leek farm'. (Beds, Hunts, Lancs, Salop, Yorks) 12th cent.

LAZAR: N ME *lazare* 'the leper'. 13th cent.

LAZARUS: P Gk form of Hebrew *Eleazer* 'God helped', brother of Martha and Mary. Used as a Christian name in 17th cent. England.

LEA, LEE, LEGH, LEIGH, LEY(S), LAY(E), LYE(S): L OE *lēah*, ME *legh, leigh* 'wood, glade or clearing'. 12th cent. [Lee, a First Fleet (crew and convict) surname. In New Zealand, E. J. Lee opened up an overland route from Marlborough to Christchurch, 1851].

LEACH, LEECH, LECH(E), LEITCH, LISH: O OE *lǣce* 'physician'. 13th cent. See also Latch. LEACHMAN, LEECHMAN, LEISHMAN, LISHMAN: O OE *lǣce-mann* 'the physician's servant'. 13th cent.

LEACOCK see LACOCK.

LEADBEATER, LEADBETTER, LEADBITTER, LEABEATER, LIDBETTER: O OE *lēad-beatere* 'a worker in lead'. 13th cent.

LEADER, LEEDER, LEDDER: O OE *laeder* 'leader', of horse and cart, 'a carter'. 13th cent.

LEAF(E), LEEF: N OE *lēof* 'dear, beloved', a term of endearment and a nickname for a wife, husband, sweetheart. 12th cent.

LEAH, LEAR, LEER: L OE *lēah* 'glade, wood or clearing'. (Shakespeare's King Lear was legendary and British).

LEAHY: P Ir *O Laochdha* 'Descendant of *Heroic*'. A Munster surname.

LEAKE(E), LEEK(E): L OE *lece*, cogn. with *laecc* 'stream'. (Lincs, Notts, Yorks) 12th cent.

LEAL(E): N OF *leial*, ME *lele* 'loyal, faithful'. 13th cent.

LEAMAN see LOVEMAN.

LEAN(E): N OE *hlǣne* 'lean', 'the thin man'. 13th cent.

LEAPER, LEEPER: O OE *hlēapere* 'runner, courier, dancer'. 12th cent.

LEAPMAN: O OE *lēap-mann* 'a basket-maker' (*lēap* 'basket'). 13th cent.

LEARMOND, LEARMONT, LEARMONTH: L From Learmonth (Berwicks) Scotland. 15th cent.

LEARY see O'LEARY.

LEASE, LEESE: L OE *laes* 'pasture'. 13th cent. See also Leece.

LEATHERBARROW, LETHERBARROW: L ON *látr* 'lair' + OE *bearu* 'grove'. 'wild animal lair in the grove'. (Lancs).

LEAVER see LEVER.

LEAVEY, LEVEY, LEVI, LEVY, LEWY, LOVIE: P OE *lēofwīg* 'beloved warrior'. DB. Some variants may be more familiar as Jewish names, of entirely separate origin, Hebrew *Levi* or *Levy* 'pledged', third son of *Jacob* and *Leah*, son-in-law of *Zecharia*, Father of the priestly tribe.

LE BRASSEUR see BRASSEUR. LE BRETON see BRETON.

LECKIE, LECKEY, LECKY: L SG *leac* 'flat stones'. (Stirling) Scotland. Leckey is also an Irish surname.

LEDGER, LEGER: P OG *Leodedar*, OF *Legier* 'people-spear'. 12th cent.

LEDINGHAM: L OE 'The *hām* (homestead) where *leed* (reed meadow grass) grows'. (Lincs).

LEDWICH, LEDWIDGE: L OE 'The *wīc* (dairy-farm) of *Lēoda*, an Anglo-Saxon'. (Salop) 13th cent. (Irish-born opera singer William Ledwidge changed his name to Ludwig in the mistaken belief that this was the original form of the surname.)

LEECE, LEES(E): (i) P OF *Lece*, from Lat *laetitia* 'gladness'. 12th cent. See also Lettice. (ii) L OE *lēas*, plural of *lēah*, 'the clearings'. (Ches, Lancs) 13th cent.

LEEDER see LEADER. LEEF see LEAF. LEEK see LEAK. LEEMAN, LEMMON see LOVEMAN.

LEESON, LEASON: P 'Son of *Lece* (*Leece*)'. 14th cent.

LEETE see LEAT.

LE FANU(E): P OF A Huguenot surname formerly established in Normandy.

LEFEVRE see FEAVER.

LEGAT, LEGATE, LEGGET, LEGGATE: O or N OF & ME *legat* 'ambassador, diplomat', originally 'papal legate'. 11th cent. Usually a pageant name.

LEGG(E): N ON *leggr*, ME *legg* 'leg', a nickname from some peculiarity of the leg. 12th cent. (Shank was replaced by leg in ME but survives in surnames such as Cruikshank.) [Legg, a First Fleet (convict) surname].

LEGH see LEA. LE GRAND see GRANT. LE GREY see GRAY.

LEHANE: P Ir *O Liatháine*, from *liath* 'grey'.

LEICESTER, LESTER: L Brit river-name *Legra* or *Leire* 'the Roman fort on the River *Leire, Leire-ceaster*'. Surname 12th cent.

LEIGH see LEA. LEIGHTON see LAYTON. LEISHMAN see LEACHMAN. LEITCH see LEACH.

LEITHEAD, LEITHHEAD: L OE From the lands of Leithead (Lothian) Scotland.

LE MARE: O OF 'The Mayor'.

LENEHAN, LENIHAN: P Ir *O Leannacháin*. A Roscommon sept.

LENG(E): N OE *lang* 'tall'. 13th cent. See also Lang.

LENN see LYNN.

LENNON: P Ir *O Leannain*, from *leann* 'cloak'.

LENNOX: L SG From the district of Lennox (Dumbarton) Scotland. 14th cent.

LENTHAL(L), LENTELL: L OE 'The *halh* (corner) on the River Lent, a Celtic river-name'. (Herefords) 14th cent.

LENTON: (i) L OE 'The *tūn* (settlement) of an Anglo-Saxon called *Lēofa*'. (Lincs), *Lavingtone* DB. (ii) Brit + OE 'The *tūn* (farm) on the R. Leen (Brit river-name)'. (Notts), *Leutone* DB.

LEO, LEON: P OF *Leon*, from Gk 'lion'. *Leonie* is from the same source. 12th cent.

LEONARD, LENARD, LENNARD: P OG *Leonhard*, a compound of *levon* and *hard* 'lion-bold'. 13th cent. [A First Fleet (convict) surname].

LEOPARD, LEPPARD: N or L OF *léopard*, a nickname from leopards on a coat of arms or a sign name. 13th cent.

LEROY, LE ROY see RAY.

LESLEY, LESLIE, LESSLIE: (i) P OF A double dim. of *Lece* (*Leece*). 12th cent. (ii) L From Leslie (Fife) Scotland. 13th cent.

LESSELLS: Scottish form of *Lascelles*.

LESTER: L OF From Lestre (Manche) Normandy. 11th cent. See also Leicester.

LESTRANGE, L'ESTRANGE see STRANGE.

LE SUEUR: O OF 'The shoemaker'. A Channel Islands surname.

LETCH see LATCH.

LETCHER: (i) L OE *laecc, lecc* 'by the stream'. 13th cent. (ii) N OF *leceor*, ME *lechur* 'lecher'. 13th cent.

LETHBRIDGE: L OE 'The *brycg* (bridge) of an Anglo-Saxon whose name may have been *Lēofmǣr*'. From a lost place in Devon, one of the 1,300 lost villages of England. The place in Victoria is named from a railway construction worker.

LETT(S): P A pet-form of *Lettice*. 12th cent.

LETTICE: P Lat *Laetitia* 'joy, gladness'. 12th cent. See also Leece.

LEVER(S), LEAVER: (i) L OE *laefer* 'rush, iris'. (ii) N OF *levre* 'hare', nickname for a swift runner. 13th cent.

LEVERAGE, LEVERIDGE, LIVERY, LOVERIDGE: P OE *Lēofrīc* 'beloved ruler'. DB.

LEVERETT: (i) P OE *Lēofrǣd* 'dear-counsel'. Winton D. (ii) N AF *leveret* 'young hare', a nickname for alacrity or timidity. 13th cent.

LEVET(T), LEVITT, LIVETT: P OE *Lēofgēat* 'beloved *Gēat*', a woman's name. DB. (*Gēat* is the name of the tribe to which Beowulf belonged.)

LEVEY, LEVI, LEVY see LEAVEY.

LEVICK, LEFFECK: (i) P OE *Lēofeca*, a dim. of *Lēofa* 'dear, beloved'. 12th cent. (ii) O OF *eveske* 'bishop'. 12th cent.

LEVINGE, LEVINGS, LOVING, LOWING(S): P OE *Lēofing* 'dear friend'. DB.

LEW: (i) L OE *hlǣw* 'hill'. (Oxon, Devon) 12th cent. (ii) N AF *leu* 'wolf'. 12th cent.

LEWER see EWER.

LEWIN(S), LEWENS, LEVEN(E), LEVIEN, LEVIN, LEVINE, LOWEN: P OE *Lēofwine* 'dear friend'. DB.

LEWIS, LOUIS, LOWIS: P AF form of Frankish *Hlúdwig* 'loud battle'. 12th cent. *Hlúdwig* became Lat *Ludovicus* and *Chlodovisus*, Gallicised as *Clovis* and *Clouis*, from which French *Louis*. Introduced into England as *Lewis* soon after the Norman Conquest. Also used in Wales for *Llewelyn*. [Five persons named Lewis sailed with the First Fleet, two sailors, two marines, and a female convict].

LEWY see LEAVEY. LEY(S) see LEA. LEYDEN see LYDON.

LEYLAND, LAYLAND: L OE *laege-land* 'fallow land'. (Lancs) 12th cent.

LEYMAN see LAYMAN. LEYTON see LAYTON. LIDBETTER see LEADBEATER.

LIDDALL, LIDDEL(L), LIDDLE: L OE *Hlȳdan-dael* 'the valley of the River *Hlȳde*. (Cumb, Roxburgh) 12th cent.

LIDDANE see LYDON.

LIDDY: P Ir *O Lideadha*, a Dalcassian sept of Thomond.

LIGHT, LYTE: L OE *lēoht* 'light', 'the light place', e.g., a glade in the forest. 13th cent. (ii) N OE *lēoht* 'bright, active, carefree'. 13th cent.

LIGHTBAND, LIGHTBOND: N OE *lȳt-bonda* 'little peasant'. 12th cent.

LIGHTBODY: N OE *lēoht-bodig* 'bright, active person'. 14th cent.

LIGHTFOOT: N OE *lēoht-fōt* 'light foot', a nickname for a messenger, runner. 12th cent. [A First Fleet (convict) surname].

LIGHTON see LAYTON.

LILEY, LILLEY, LILLIE, LILLY: (i) P A pet-form of *Elizabeth*. 13th cent. (ii) L OE *lin-*

lēah 'the flax clearing'. (Berks, Herts) 14th cent.

LILLEYMAN, LILLYMAN, LITTMAN: N OE *lȳtelmann* 'little man'. Winton D.

LILLICO see LITHGOE.

LILLICRAP, LILLYCROP: N OE *lilie-cropp* 'head of herb', transferred to head of white-haired person. 14th cent.

LIMBERT see LAMBARD, LOMBARD.

LIMEBURNER: O OE *līm-beornan* 'a lime burner'. 13th cent. [A First Fleet (convict) surname, John Limeburner, who lived to 104].

LINACRE, LINAKER, LINEKER, LINEGAR: L OE *līn-aecer* 'flax field'. (Cambs, Lancs) DB.

LINCH, LINCK, LINK(S), LYNCH: L OE *hlinc* 'ridge, slope'. (Som, Sussex) 13th cent. See also Lynch. [Linch, a First Fleet (convict) surname].

LINCOLN: L A Celtic equivalent of Welsh *llyn* 'lake' (the River Witham widens here). DB.

LIND, LINE, LYNE(S): L OE *lind*, ME *line* 'lime-tree'. Sometimes from a pet-form of women's names in *Lina*, e.g., *Adelina, Emelina*. 12th cent.

LINDFIELD: L OE *linden-feld* 'lime trees in open country'. (Sussex).

LINDLEY, LINLEY: L OE *līn-lēah* 'flax clearing'. (Leices, Salop, Yorks).

LINDON: L OE An ancient form of Lincoln, see Lindsay.

LINDSAY, LINDSEY: L A Brit deriv. of *Lindon*, early name of *Lincoln*, + OE *ēg* (island). (Lincs), *Lindisae prouincia* c. 730.

LINEHAM, LYNAM, LYNHAM: L OE *līn-hām* or *līn-hamm* 'the homestead or water-meadow where flax is grown'. (Devon, Oxon, Wilts) 12th cent.

LINFORD, LINFORTH, LINFOOT: (i) L OE *hlyn-ford* 'maple-tree ford'. (Bucks) (ii) L OE *līn-ford* 'flax ford'. (Norfolk) 12th cent.

LINKLATER: L ON *lyng-kletrr* 'heather-covered rocks', an Orkneys surname. 15th cent.

LINN see LYNN.

LINNEY: P OE *Lindgifu* 'shield-gift'. 12th cent.

LINTON: (i) L OE *līn-tūn* 'flax farm'. (Derbys, Cambs, Herefords, Yorks) (ii) L OE 'The *tūn* (farm) of *Lilla*, an Anglo-Saxon'. (Kent) (iii) L Brit + OE 'The *tūn* on the River Lyne'. (Northumb).

LIPPIAT, LIPYEAT: L OE *hlīepgeat* 'leap-gate', a low gate or fence which deer can leap but sheep cannot. (Glos, Som).

LIPSCOMB(E): L OE *hlīep-cumb* 'the combe (valley) with a leap (chasm, water-jump, deep erosion)'.

LIPTON: L OE *hlīep-tūn* 'the farm by a leap (steep slope)'.

LISH see LEACH. LISHMAN see LEACHMAN.

LISK: L OE *Lisc*, an Anglo-Saxon stream-name meaning 'reeds'. [A First Fleet (convict) surname].

LISLE, LYLE, DE LISLE: L AF 'The isle', from Lille (Nord) France. DB.

LISSON: L OE 'The *tūn* (farm) of *Lill*, an Anglo-Saxon'. (Middx).

LIST: (i) P OG A pet-form of *Listhard* 'clever' or 'strong'. (ii) N OE *list* 'artful, cunning' or 'skilled, experienced'. (iii) O OF *liste* 'fringe, border', from which *lisse* 'lists or tiltyard' (palisades of the tournament field). A tournament official rather than a participant.

LISTER, LYSTER, LIDSTER, LESTER: O ME A deriv. of *lite* 'to dye', 'a dyer'. 13th cent.

LITCHFIELD: L OE *hlif-scylf* 'shelter by the hill or ledge'. (Hants), *Liveselle* DB.

LITHGOE, LITHGOW, LILICO, LYTHGOE: L SG From Linlithgow (Lothian) Scotland. 13th cent.

LITTLE, LYTTLE: N OE *lyīel* 'little'. OE Byname 10th cent.

LITTLEJOHN: N OE A popular nickname for a giant, e.g., Robin Hood's companion. 14th cent.

LITTLER: L OE *lȳtel-hrycg* 'the small ridge'. (Derbys) LITTLEWOOD: L OE *lȳtel-wudu* 'the small wood'. 13th cent.

LITTMAN see LILLEYMAN.

LIVERMORE: L OE *lifrig-mere* (*lifrig* 'clotted') 'the lake with thick water'. (Suffolk) 11th cent.

LIVERSAGE, LIVERSEDGE, LIVERSIDGE: L OE 'The *ecg* (ridge) of *Lēofhere*, an Anglo-Saxon'. (Yorks) 13th cent.

LIVESAY, LIVESEY: L OE *hlif-ēg* 'the shelter on the island'. (Lancs) 13th cent.

LIVETT see LEVET.

LIVINGSTONE, LIVINGSTON: L OE From Livingston (Lothian) Scotland. 12th cent. (The name is recorded as *Levingston* in charters of King David I to as late as 1688.) [John

Livingston, a marine carpenter on the *Sirius*, brought the surname to Australia 1788].

LLEWELLIN, LLEWELLYN, LLEWELYN: P Welsh *Hlywelin*, from *llyw* 'leader'. 12th cent. Also influenced by an early form of Fr *Louis*, see Lewis.

LLOYD(S), LOYD: N Welsh *llwyd* 'grey', 'hoary head'. 14th cent. [A First Fleet (convict) surname].

LOADER, LODER: O A deriv. of ME *lode* 'to load', 'a loader, carrier'. 13th cent.

LOAN see LANE.

LOBB: N OE *lobbe* 'spider', a nickname of lost meaning. 13th cent. Some may be from Lobb (Devon, Oxon) from an earlier meaning of *lobbe* 'an over-hanging rock'.

LOBSEY: L OE *lobbe-ēg* 'the island with an over-hanging rock'.

LOCH: L Scots form of OE *lacu* 'lake'. 13th cent.

LOCK(E): (i) N OE *locc* 'a lock of hair', 'curly head'. 12th cent. (ii) O OE *loc* 'keeper of the lock (river-barrier)'. 13th cent.

LOCKET(T) see LUCKETT.

LOCKHART: (i) P OG *Lochard* 'stronghold-hard'. 12th cent. (ii) O OE *loc-hierde* (*loc* 'stock enclosure'), 'a sheep or cattle herd'. 12th cent.

LOCKLEY: L OE *loc-lēah* 'the fenced clearing'. [A First Fleet (convict) surname].

LOCKWOOD: L OE *loc-wudu* 'the enclosed wood'. (Yorks) 13th cent.

LOCKYER: O OE A deriv. of *loc* 'a locksmith'. 13th cent.

LODDER: O OE *loddere* 'a beggar'. 13th cent.

LODGE: L OF *loge*, ME *logge* 'a temporary dwelling'.

LODWICK: L OE 'The *wīc* (dairy-farm) of *Lod*, an Anglo-Saxon'. [A First Fleet (crew) surname].

LOFT(S): O ME *lofte* 'upper chamber'. 'Servant of the upper chamber'. 13th cent.

LOFTHOUSE, LOFTUS: L ON *lopthús* 'the house with an upper floor'. (Yorks).

LOGAN: L SG 'the little hollow'. From Logan (Ayr) Scotland. 12th cent.

LOKER see LOOKER.

LOMAS, LOMAX: L dial. *lum* 'pool, a depression for the collection of water'. (Lancs).

LOMB, LOOMBE, LOOM, LOOMES, LOOMIS, LUMB: (i) N OE *lamb*, a nickname from the lamb. 12th cent. (ii) dial. *lum* 'pool'. (Lancs) 14th cent.

LOMBARD, LIMBERT: O Lat *Langobardus* 'long-beard', member of the German tribe which conquered and named Lombardy. In medieval England, Italian immigrants who became moneylenders and bankers, hence *Lombard* Street, London.

LONDON, LONNON, LUNDON, LUNNON: L Brit Pre-Roman city originally named by the Britons *Lyn-dyn*, and called by the Romans *Londinius*. The Brit name means 'the gravelly river-bed'. Early forms include: *AElfstan on Lundene* 10th cent., *Leofsi de Lundonia* 1066, *Bernardus Lundonie* 1086.

Names in LONG not recorded below may be found under LANG.

LONGBOTHAM, LONGBOTTOM: L OE *lang-botm* 'the long valley'. 14th cent.

LONGDEN: L OE *lang-dūn* 'the long hill'. (Salop), *Langedune* DB. [In New Zealand, J. Longden arrived on the *Barbara Gordon*, one of the early immigrant ships].

LONGFELLOW: N OE *lang-fēolaga* or ON *felage* 'tall fellow, partner, companion'. 15th cent.

LONGFIELD: L OE *lang-feld* 'long field'. (Kent) 14th cent. See also Longueville.

LONGHURST: L OE *lang-hyrst* 'long copse or wooded hill'. (Northumb).

LONGLAND, LANGLAND: L OE *lang-land* 'the long strip of land'. 13th cent. (Langland, author of *Piers Plowman*.)

LONGMAN, LANGMAN: N OE *lang-mann* 'tall man'. 13th cent.

LONGSHAW, LANGSHAW: L OE *lang-sceaga*, dial. *shaw* 'long wood'. (Derbys) 13th cent.

LONGSTAFF(E), LANGSTAFF: N OE *lang-staef* 'long staff', usually a badge of office and a nickname for a bailiff, constable, catchpoll, tipstaff. 13th cent. (Tipstaff 'tipped staff', truncheon with emblem of office.)

LONGSTREET: L OE *lang-straet* 'the long street', probably a Roman road.

LONGUEVILLE, LONGVILLE, LONGFIELD: L OF from Longueville-la-Gifart (Seine Inférieure) France. 12th cent.

LONGWORTH: (i) L OE *lang-worth* 'the long homestead'. (Berks) (ii) L OE *lang-ford* 'long ford'. (Herefords) *Langeford* 1242.

LONSDALE: L Brit + OE 'The valley of the *Lune*, Brit river-name'. 13th cent.

LOOK(E) see LUKE.

LOOKER, LOKER, LUKER: O OE *lōcian* 'to look, observe, take heed'. 'A Look-out guardian, a sentinel'. 13th cent.

LOOMES see LOMB.

LOONEY: P Ir *O Luanaigh* 'Descendant of *Warrior*'.

LOOS(E): L OE *hlōse* 'pigsty'. (Kent, Suffolk) 12th cent.

LORD: O OE *hlāford* 'loaf-ward, husband, master of the house'. 12th cent. (Lord of the manor, landowner, came later with the feudal system which was introduced by the Normans. The original meaning was Anglo-Saxon, i.e., before 1066, but the surname was not recorded before 12th cent.)

LORDING: O OE *hlāfording* 'son of the lord'. 12th cent.

LORENCE see LAURENCE.

LORIMER, LORRIMER: O OF *loremier* 'lorimer, spurrier', 'a spur-maker'. 12th cent.

LORING: L OF *le Lohereng* 'the man from Lorraine'. 12th cent.

LORKIN(G), LARKIN(S), LARKING(S): P Pet-forms of *Laurence*. 13th cent.

LORRAINE, LORAINE: L OF From Lorraine. 14th cent.

LOTHIAN: L OE In the 6th cent. the Angles colonised the country that became the Lothians as a part of Northumbria. Four hundred years later the English king Edgar granted the Lothians to Kenneth II, and they have remained the southeast central region of Scotland, embracing the counties of Edinburgh, Linlithgow, and Haddington. The name is therefore Anglian (Old English) rather than Scots Gaelic but the meaning has been lost.

LOTON: L OE 'The *tūn* (village) of the people of *Luca*, an Anglo-Saxon'.

LOTT: O OE *hlot* 'lot, portion', 'holder of an allotted share of land'. 13th cent.

LOUDEN, LOUDON, LOWDEN: L From Loudoun (Ayr) Scotland. 12th cent.

LOUGH: An Irish variant of SG *Loch*. An Ulster surname.

LOUGHLIN see LACHLAN.

LOUGHMAN, LOUGHNAN(E): P Ir *O Lachtnáin*, from *lachtna* 'grey'.

LOUIS see LEWIS. LOUND see LUND. LOURIE see LOWREY.

LOVAT: L Brit river-name identical with R. Lovat (Bucks) and R. Lavant (Sussex). From Lovat (Inverness) Scotland.

LOVE: P OE *lufu* 'love', a popular Anglo-Saxon woman's name. 11th cent. [A First Fleet (female convict) surname].

LOVEDAY, LOVEDEE: (i) P OE *Lēofdaeg* 'dear day', an Anglo-Saxon personal name. DB. (ii) N ME *love-day*, a day for the settlement of disputes and for pacifying families engaged in feuds. For one born on that day. 13th cent.

LOVEGROVE: L OE 'The *grāf* (grove) of an Anglo-Saxon called *Lufu* (Love)'.

LOVEJOY: N OE *lufu* + OF *joie* 'joy, delight'. 'Joyfully in love'.

LOVEL(L), LOWELL: N AF *lovel* 'wolf-cub', a dim. of AF *love*, from Lat *lupus* 'wolf'. 12th cent.

LOVELOCK: N OE *lufu-locc* 'love-lock (hair)', a wearer of artificial curls, 'a dandy'. 13th cent.

LOVEMAN, LOWMAN, LUFFMAN, LAMING, LEAMAN, LEAMON, LEEMAN, LEMMON, LEMAN, LEMON: (i) P OE *Lēofmann* 'beloved man'. DB. (ii) N ME *leofman, leman, lemman* 'lover, sweetheart'. 13th cent.

LOVERIDGE see LEVERAGE.

LOVERING: P OE *Lēofring* 'son of *Lēofhere*'. (*Lēofhere* 'beloved army'). DB.

LOVETT, LOVITT: N OF *louet*, a dim. of *lou* 'wolf'. 'Little wolf'. DB.

LOVIE see LEAVEY. LOVING see LEVINGE.

LOW(E), LOWES: P A pet-form of *Laurence*. 13th cent.

LOWDEN see LOUDEN. LOWEN see LEWIN. LOWER see EWER. LOWING see LEVINGE. LOWIS see LEWIS. LOWMAN see LOVEMAN. LOWNDES see LUND.

LOWRY, LOWREY, LOWRIE, LOUREY, LOURIE: P Scottish border forms of *Lawrey* and dims. of *Laurence*. 14th cent. See also Lavery.

LOWTHER, LOWDER: L A deriv. of ON *lauthr* 'froth', 'the foaming river'. (Westmorland).

LOXLEY: L OE 'The *lēah* (clearing) of an Anglo-Saxon called *Locc*'. (Staffs, Warwicks), *Locheslei* DB.

LOXTON: L Brit + OE 'The *tūn* (farm) on the River *Lox Yeo*'. (Som).

LUCAS: P Lat *Lucas*, from Gk, the learned form of *Luke*. 12th cent. [A First Fleet (marine and convict) surname].

LUCE, LUCIA: P Fem. form of Lat *Lucius*,

from *lux* 'light'. A popular name in medieval England from St *Lucia*, martyred at Syracuse. Surname 12th cent.

LUCKETT, LOCKET(T), LOCKITT: P A dim. of *Luke*. 13th cent.

LUCKEY, LUCKIE: P Scottish dims. of *Lucas*.

LUCKMAN: O 'Servant of *Lucas*'.

LUCY, LUCEY: L OF From Luce (Orne) Normandy. 12th cent.

LUDLOW: L OE *hlūd-hlāw* 'loud hill', 'the hill by the rapid' (beside the River Teme). (Salop).

LUFF: N OE *lēof* 'beloved'. 12th cent.

LUFFMAN see LOVEMAN.

LUKE, LUCK, LOOK(E): P Lat The popular form of Lat *Lucas*, from Gk *Lucania*. 13th cent.

LUKER see LOOKER. LUMB see LOMB.

LUMBY: L ON *lundr-býr* 'the homestead by a grove'. (Yorks).

LUMLEY: L dial. *lum* + OE *lēah* 'the clearing by a pool'. (Durham) 13th cent.

LUMSDEN: L OE From Lumsden (Berwicks) Scotland. 12th cent.

LUND, LUNT, LOUND, LOWNDS, LOWNDES: L ON *lundr* 'grove'. 12th cent.

LUNDIE: L ON From Lundie near Doune (Perths) Scotland, SG *lunnd* 'marsh'.

LUNDON, LUNNON see LONDON.

LUNDY: L ON *lundi* 'puffin' (the sea-bird). From Lundy Island (puffin island), *Insula de Lundeia* in 12th cent.

LUNG see LANG.

LUNN: OE *lund*, from ON *lundr* 'grove, copse'. (Lancs, Yorks).

LUNNEY: P Ir *O Luinig*. Co. Tyrone.

LUPTON: L OE '*Hluppa's tūn* (homestead)'. (Westmorland) 13th cent.

LUREY, LURIE: O ME *ewerye*, 'groom of the Ewery', supplying ewers of table water. 14th cent.

LUSCOMBE: L OE *hlōse-cumb* 'the valley with a pigsty'. (Devon).

LUSH: A short-form of *Lusher*. See Usher.

LUSHER see USHER.

LUSTY: P Ir *O Loiste*. Co. Donegal.

LUTHER: O OF *leuteor* 'a lute player'. 16th cent.

LUTTON: (i) L OE 'The *tūn* (village) of the people of *Luda*'. (Northants) (ii) L OE 'The *tūn* (farm) on the River *Hlūde* (loud river)'. (Yorks) (iii) L OE 'The *tūn* by a *luh* (pool)'. (Lincs).

LUTTRELL: N OF A dim. of *loutre* 'otter'. Metonymic for an otter-hunter. 12th cent.

LUTWYCHE: L OE *lōt-wīc* 'the outlying farm where the ditch has been cleared'. (Salop).

LUXFORD: L OE 'The ford of an Anglo-Saxon called *Lufu* (Love)'.

LUXTON: L OE '*Lugg's tūn* (farm)'. (Devon), *Luggeston* in 14th cent.

LYAL(L), LYEL(L): P A pet-form of *Lyon*. 14th cent.

LYDON, LIDDANE, LEYDEN: P Ir *O Loideain*, a Galway and Mayo surname.

LYLE see LISLE. LYNAM see LINEHAM.

LYNCH: P Ir *O Loingsigh*, from *loingeach* 'mariner', the name of several septs. See also Linch.

LYNDON: L OE *lind-dūn* 'lime-tree hill'. (Rutland).

LYNHAM see LINEHAM.

LYNN(E), LINN, LENN: L Brit *lindo* (Welsh *llyn*) 'lake' (see also *Lincoln*). 'The pool at the mouth of the River Ouse'. (Norfolk) 12th cent.

LYON(S): (i) P A development of *Leo*, of which it was the popular pronunciation. 12th cent. (ii) L OF From Lyon-la-Forêt (Eure) Normandy. 12th cent.

LYSAGHT see MAC LYSAGHT. LYSTER see LISTER. LYTE see LIGHT. LYTHGOE see LITHGOE. LYTTLE see LITTLE.

M

MABB, MAPP: P A pet-form of *Mabel*. 13th cent. [A First Fleet (marine) surname].

MABBOTT, MABBUTT: P A dim. of *Mabel*. 14th cent.

MABEE, MABEY: L Cornish From *Mabe* (believed to be formed from a saint's name). (Cornwall).

MABEL, MABLEY: P A popular form of *Amabel*. 12th cent. See Annable.

'Mac' means 'son of'. There is no difference in Scotland or Ireland between 'Mac' and 'Mc'; the latter is simply an abbreviation. For economy of space the abbreviation is used in this section.

MAC see MACK.

McADAM: P Ir & SG *MacAdaim* 'son of *Adam*'. 12th cent.

McADIE: P SG *MacAda*, from *Adie*. 16th cent.

McALASTER, McALLISTER: P SG *MacAlasdair* 'son of *Alexander*'. 15th cent.

McALEER: P Ir *Mac Giolla Uidhir* 'dun-coloured'. A Co. Tyrone sept.

McALEESE: P Ir *Mac Giolla Iosa* 'devotee of *Jesus*'.

McALLAN, McALLEN: P SG *MacAilin*, from *ail* 'rock'. 14th cent.

McALPIN(E): P Gallo Lat *Alpinus*, the name of several Pictish kings. 13th cent. (Kenneth *MacAlpin* killed the last of the Pictish kings, AD 840).

McANALLY see McNALLY.

McANDREW: P Scottish 'Son of *Andrew*'. 15th cent. St *Andrew*, patron saint of Scotland.

McARA: P Ir *Ara* 'charioteer'.

McARDLE, McARDELL: P Ir *Mac Ardghail* 'high valour'. A branch of the McMahons of Oriel.

McARTHUR, McCARTER: P SG *MacArtair* 'son of *Arthur*'. 16th cent.

McASKIE, CASKY: P SG *MacAscaidh*, a form of *Askell*. 14th cent.

McASKILL: P SG *MacAsgaill* 'son of *Askell*'. 14th cent. See Ashkettle.

McATEER: P Ir *Mac an tSaoir* 'craftsman'. An Ulster surname.

McAULEY, McCAUSLEY: P Ir & SG form of ON *Olafr* 'relic of the gods'.

McAULIFFE: P Ir *MacAmhlaoibh*. A Munster surname and a branch of the *McCarthys*.

McAUSLAN, McAUSLAND: P SG *Absalom*.

McAVOY see McEVOY.

McBEAN, McBAIN: P SG *MacBheathair*. 16th cent. A frequent surname in Ulster.

McBEATH, McBETH: P SG *MacBeatha* 'son of life'.

McBRAN, McBRAIN see BRAN.

McBRAYNE: O Ir *brehon*, SG *breithean* 'son of the judge'. 16th cent.

McBREARTY, McMURTY: P Ir *MacMuircheartaigh* 'son of *Murtagh*'.

McBRIDE: P Ir *Mac Giolla Bhrigde* 'devotee of St *Brigid*'. 14th cent. A Donegal surname. Also in Ulster of Scottish origin.

McBURNEY, McBURNIE: P Ir *Mac Biorna*, from ON *Bjarni* 'warrior'.

McCABE: N Ir *MacCaba*, from *caba* 'hood'. 14th cent.

McCAFFERTY: P Ir *MacEachmhacaigh* 'son of the steed rider'.

McCAFFRAY, McCAFFERY: P Ir *MacGafraidth* 'son of *Godfrey*'. 14th cent.

McCAHILL: P Ir *MacCathail* 'son of valour'. A Donegal surname.

McCAIG: P Ir *MacThaidhg*. A variant of *MacTeige*.

McCALL: P Ir & SG *MacCathail* (see McCahill). 14th cent.

McCALLION: P SG *MacCailin*, a galloglas (Scots mercenary soldier) surname.

McCALLUM: P Ir & SG *MacColuim*, from *colm* 'dove'.

McCALMAN, McCALMONT: P Ir *MacColmain* 'son of *Colman*'. In Scotland, a sept of the clan *Buchanan*.

McCAMBRIDGE: P SG *MacAmbrois* 'son of *Ambrose*'. Also an Ulster surname.

McCANN: P Ir *MacCana*, from *cano* 'wolf-cub'. [A First Fleet (marine) surname].

McCARLEY: P Ir A sept of the *MacFhearghaile*. A Connacht surname.

McCARROLL see CARROL.

McCARRON: P Ir *Mac Carrghamhna*, from *carr-gamhan* 'calf-face'.

McCARTHY: P Ir *MacCarthaigh*, from *Carthach* 'loving'. A leading sept in Ulster. [Charles McCarthy, bosun on the *Scarborough*, and John McCarthy, a marine, brought the name to Australia 1788].

McCHRISTAL see McCRYSTAL.

McCLEAN: P Ir *Mac Giolla Eáin* (or *Seán* 'John'), a galloglas (mercenary soldier) name of Scottish origin. See also Clean.

McCLEARY, McCLEERY: P Ir *Mac Giolla Arraith* (Ulster) or *Mac an Chleirigh* 'son of the *cleireach* (clerk)'. (Co. Cavan).

McCLELLAND see McLELLAN. McCLEMENT see McLAMON.

McCLINTOCK: P SG *Mac Giolla Fhionntain* 'devotee of St *Fintan*'.

McCLOSKEY, McCLUSKY: P Ir *MacBhloscaidh*, a branch of the *O'Cahans*, who used *Bhloscaidh* as a forename.

McCLOY: P SG *MacLughaidh* 'son of *Lewie*', a pet-form of *Lewis*. A branch of the clan *Stuart* of *Bute*.

McCLUNG: P SG *MacLuinge*, from *long* 'ship'.

McCLURE: P SG *Mac Gille Uidhir* 'devotee of St *Odhar* (sallow)'.

McCLYMONT see McLAMON. McCOLL see COLL.

McCOMB(E): P SG *MacThom* 'son of *Tom*'.

McCOMBIE: P SG *MacComaidh* 'son of *Tommy*', a sept of the clan *Mackintosh*.

McCONACHIE: P SG *MacDounchaidh* 'son of *Duncan*', a branch of the clan *Robertson*.

McCONNELL: P Ir *MacDhomhnaill* 'son of *Daniel*'. See also MacDonald.

McCONNOR see CONNOR. McCONVILLE see CONVILLE.

McCORKELL: P Ir *MacThorcaill*, from ON. A Donegal and Derry surname; in Scotland, a branch of the clan *Gunn*.

McCORMACK, McCORMICK: P Ir & SG *MacCormaic*, from *Cormac* 'chariot'. In Scotland, a branch of the clan *Buchanan-MacCormick* of *MacLaine*. 12th cent. [A First Fleet (female convict) surname].

McCORQUODALE: P SG *MacCorcadail* 'son of *Thorketill*'. 15th cent.

McCOUBREY: P SG *MacCuithbreith* 'son of *Cuthbert*'. 16th cent.

McCOURT: P Ir *Mac Cuairt*, an Oriel sept.

McCOY: P Ir *Mac Aodha* 'son of *Hugh*'.

McCREA, McCRAE: P SG *MacRaith*. Numerous in Ulster as McGrath. See also McRae. [McGrath, a First Fleet (convict) surname].

McCOSKER see McCUSKER.

McCRINDLE: P SG *MacRaonill* 'son of *Raonull* (*Ranald*)'. 15th cent.

McCROSSAN, McCROSSEN, McCROSSIN: P Ir *Mac an Chrosain*, an Ulster sept.

McCRUDDEN: P Ir A variant of *O'Rodain*. See O'Rodden.

McCRYSTAL, McCHRISTAL: P SG *Chrystal*, a dim. of *Christopher*.

McCUBBIN: P SG 'Son of *Cubbin* (*Gibbon*)', a dim. of *Gilbert*. 14th cent.

McCUE see CUE.

McCULLOCH, McCULLOUGH, McCULLAGH, McCOLLOUGH: P Ir & SG *Mac Cu Uladh* 'Hound of Ulster'.

McCULLY: P Ir A Co. Tyrone variant of *McCullagh*.

McCURDY: P Ir *MacMhuircheartaigh*, from O Scand *Myrkjartag* 'sea-ruler'.

McCUSKER, McCOSKER: P Ir *Mac Oscair*, from ON *Asgeirr* 'god-spear'.

McCUTCHEON, McHUTCHIN: (i) P Ir *MacUistin* 'son of *Hutcheon*'. (ii) P SG *MacUisdin*, a branch of the clan *MacDonald*.

McDAID, McDADE: P Ir *MacDaibheid* 'son of *David*'.

McDERMOT, McDERMAID, McDERMID: P Ir & SG A powerful Connacht sept, its chief styled 'Prince of Coolavin'. 15th cent.

McDEVITT: P Ir A variant of *MacDaid*.

McDONAGH: P SG *Mac Donnchaidh*, Ir *Mac Donnchadha* 'son of *Donagh*'.

McDONALD, McDONNELL, McCONNELL: P SG The first *MacDonald* was *Angus Mor*, son of *Donald* of Islay, grandson of *Somerled*, king of the Isles, who defeated the Norsemen in 1284 and submitted to the king of the Scots. The clan increased in power and its chief was styled 'Macdonald of Macdonald'. 13th cent. [A First Fleet (crew and marine) surname].

McDONOUGH: P SG 'Son of *Duncan*'. [A First Fleet (convict) surname].

McDOUGAL, McDOOL, McDOWALL, McDOWELL: Ir & SG *MacDhughaill* 'son of *Dhubgall* (*Dugald*)'. *Dugald* was one of the sons of *Somerled* (see McDonald). Of the same stock as the *Macdonalds*, the family chose the distinctive patronymic *MacDougal*. MacDowall, MacDowell are Ir variants of *MacDougal* (*MacDubhgaill* 'black foreigner'), the name of galloglasses (Scots mercenary soldiers) who entered Ireland from the Hebrides. 12th cent.

McDUFF: P SG *MacDhuibb* 'son of *Dubb* (black)'. 13th cent.

McDUNLEY see DONLEVY.

MACE: P A pet-form of *Matthew*.

McEACHAN, McEACHARN, McEACHEN, McEACHERN: P Ir *MacEachain* 'son of the horse-lord'. 15th cent.

McELLIGOTT: P Ir *MacUileagoid*, originally *Fitz Elias*, a Norman name.

McELROY, McILROY: P Ir *Mac Giolla Rua* 'son of the red-haired lad'. 14th cent.

McELWAIN see McILWAINE. McELWEE see McKELVY.

McENROE: P Ir *MacConruabha*, a Cavan and Leitrim name.

McENTYRE see McINTYRE.

McEVOY, McAVOY: P Ir *MacFiodhbhuide.* One of the 'seven septs of Leix'.

McEWAN, McEWEN: P SG *MacEoghainn* 'son of *Ewan, Ewen*'. 13th cent.

MACEY see MASSEY.

McFADDEN, McFADGEAN, McFADYEN, McFADZEAN: P Ir & SG *MacPháidin* 'son of *Páidin*', a dim. of *Pádraig* (*Patrick*). 13th cent.

McFAIL, McFALL, McPHAIL: P SG *MacPhail* 'son of *Paul*'. 15th cent.

McFARLAN(E), McFARLAND: P SG *MacPharlain* 'son of *Parlan* (*Bartholomew*)'. 14th cent. [Rev A. Macfarlane sailed as chaplain on the *Bengal Merchant*, the first immigrant ship from Glasgow bound for New Zealand, 1839].

McFARQUHAR: P SG *MacFearchair* 'son of *Farquhar* (man dear)'. 12th cent.

McFEE, McPHEE: P SG *MacDhuibhasithe* 'son of the black-haired man of peace'. 13th cent.

McGANN: P Ir A Connacht variant of *McCann.*

McGANNON see GANNON.

McGARRY: P Ir *Mag Fhearadhaigh*, from a pers. name *Feardhach* 'manly'.

McGEE, McGHEE, MAGEE, MAGGEE: P Ir *MacAoidh* 'son of *Aodh* (*Hugh*)'. 13th cent.

McGEORGE see McINDEOR.

McGERAGHTY, McGARRITY: P Ir *MagOireachtaigh* 'member of assembly'.

McGIBBON: (i) P Ir *MacFhibin*, a dim. of *Philip.* (ii) P SG 'Son of *Gibbon*'.

McGILCHRIST: P Ir & SG *Mac Giolla Chriost* 'son of the devotee of Christ', a Co. Longford and Connacht sept. In Ulster of Scottish origin.

McGILDEA see GILDEA.

McGILL, MAGILL: P Ir, SG & Manx *Mac an Ghoill* 'son of the lowlander or stranger'. 13th cent.

McGILLIGAN see GILLIGAN.

McGILLIVRAY, McGILVRAY: P SG *MacGillibhrath* 'son of the servant of judgement'. 16th cent.

McGINLEY: P Ir Mag *Fhionnghaile*, from *fionnghaile* 'fair valour'. (Co. Donegal).

McGINTY: P Ir *MagFhinneachta*, from *sneachta* 'snow'.

McGLASHAN: P Ir *MacGlasain*, from *glas* 'grey-green'. 'Son of the sallow lad'.

McGLOIN: P Ir *Mac Giolla Eoin* 'son of the devotee of St *John*'.

McGLYNN: P Ir *Mag Fhloinn*, from *flann* 'ruddy'.

McGOVERN: P Ir *MagShambrain*, from *samhra* 'summer'. A Breffny sept.

McGOWAN: P Ir & SG *Mac an Ghabhann* 'son of the smith'.

McGRATH see McCREA, McRAE.

McGREGOR, McGRIGOR: P SG 'Son of *Gregor* (*Gregory*).

McGUIGAN: P Ir *Mag Uiginn.* (Co. Tyrone).

McGUINESS, MAGUINESS, GUINESS: P Ir *MagAonghuis* 'son of *Angus*'.

McGUIRE, MAGUIRE: P Ir *MagUidhir*, from *uidhir* 'dun-coloured'. A Fermanagh sept.

McGUIRK, McGURK: (i) P Ir *Mag Oirc*, a Co. Tyrone sept. (ii) P SG *Mac Coirc*, from *Corc*, a pers. name meaning 'heart'.

MACHEN, MACHIN, MACHON see MASON.

McHENDRIE, McKENDRICK: P SG *MacEanring* 'son of *Henry*'. 14th cent.

McHUGH: Identical with McGee.

McHUTCHIN see McCUTCHEON.

McILRATH, McILWRAITH: P Ir & SG *Mac Giolla Riabhaigh*, from *riabhach* 'brindled'.

McILROY see McELROY.

McILVEEN: P Ir *Mac Giolla Mhin*, from *min* 'gentle'.

McILVRIDE: P Ir *Mac Giolla Brighde* 'son of the servant of St *Bride*'. 14th cent.

McILWAIN, McELWAIN: P Ir & SG *Mac Giolla Bhain*, from *ban* 'white'.

McINDEOR, McKINDEWAR, McGEORGE: P SG *Macindeoir* 'son of the stranger, pilgrim, sojourner'. See also Dewar.

McINERNY: O Ir *Mac an Airchinnigh* 'son of the *erenagh* (steward of church lands)'.

McINNES: P SG *MacAonghuis* 'son of *Angus*'. 16th cent.

McINTOSH: P SG *Mac an toisich* 'son of the chieftain'. 14th cent.

McINTYRE, McENTIRE: N Ir & SG *Mac an tSaoir* 'son of the wright or carpenter'. 13th cent. [A First Fleet (convict) surname].

McIVER, McIVOR: P SG *MacIomhair*, from ON *Ivaar* 'bow-army'. 13th cent. See also Ivor.

MACK, MAC: P O Ir *Maccus* A form of ON *Magnus.* 12th cent. Also Scottish.

McKAY, MACKAY, McKEE, MACKEY, MACKIE: P SG *MacAedha* 'son of *Aodh (Hugh)*'. The clan *Mackay* originated at Strathnaver. [A First Fleet (convict) surname].

McKECHNIE: P SG *MacEacharna* 'brown horse'. A branch of the clan *Macdonald.*

McKELL see KELL.

McKELLAR: P SG *MacEalair* 'son of *Ealair*, from Lat *Hilarius.* 15th cent.

McKELVY, McELWEE: P Ir *Mac Giolla Bhuide* 'son of the yellow-haired lad'.

McKENDRICK see McHENDRIE.

McKENNA: (i) P Ir *MacCionaoith*, a branch of the *Ui Neill* and lords of Truagh, (Co. Monaghan). (ii) P SG *Mac Cionaodha* 'son of *Cionaodh*'. 16th cent.

MACKENZIE: P SG 'Son of *Coinneach* (comely)'. 13th cent. [James McKenzie, long suspected of sheep duffing, drove 1,000 sheep from Cave, Canterbury, to south of Lake Tekapo, New Zealand, but nobody could prove that they weren't his own, 1855].

McKEON, McKEOWN: P Ir *MacEoghain* (Connacht), *MacEoin* (Ulster), both 'son of *John*'. See also McOwen. [A First Fleet (marine) surname].

McKERRAS: P SG *Mac Fhearghuis* 'son of *Fergus*'. (Duncan *M'Keras* was tenant of Kernach, Strogarty, 1483.)

McKIERNAN: P Ir *MacThighearnain*, from *tighearna* 'lord'.

McKILL see GILL.

McKILLOP: P Ir & SG *MacFhilib* 'son of *Philip*', a branch of the *MacDonald.*

McKINLEY, McKINLAY: P SG *MacFhionnlaoich* 'son of *Finlay* (fair hero)'.

McKINNEY: (i) P SG A branch of the clan *McKinnon.* See MacKinnon. (ii) P Ir *Mac Coinnigh* (Cos. Antrim and Tyrone).

McKINNON: P SG 'Son of the fair-born'. A clan originally of the Hebrides, whose chief was master of the household and marshall of the army of the Lord of the Isles. 14th cent.

McKNIGHT: P Ir *Mac an Ridire*, from *ridire* 'knight'.

McLACHLAN, McLAUCHLANE, McLAUGHLAN, McLOUGHLIN: P SG 'Son of *Lachlan*'. 13th cent. See also Lachlan.

MACLAE, MACLAY, MACLEAY: P SG *MacDhunnshleibhe* 'son of *Dounshleibhe*', a Ross and Argyle surname. 15th cent.

MACLAMON, MACLEMENT, McCLEMENTS, McCLYMONT: P SG *MacLaomuinn* 'son of *Lamont*'. 13th cent.

McLAREN, McLAUREN: P SG *MacLabhruinn* 'son of *Labhran* (*Laurence*)'. 16th cent.

McLEAN, MACLEAN, MACLAINE: P SG *Mac Gille Eoin* 'son of the servant of St *John*'. In Ireland, a galloglas (Scots mercenary soldier) surname. [Three convicts brought the surname to Australia 1788].

McLELLAN, McCLELLAND, McLELAND: P Ir & SG 'Son of *Lellan*'. In Ireland, an ancient sept of the *Mac Giolla Fhaolain* of Co. Sligo. [Charles McLellan, a convict, brought the surname to Australia 1788, and was one of the first settlers on Norfolk Island].

McLENAGHAN, McLENAHAN: P Ir *MacLeanachain*, from *leanach* 'possessing mantles (cloaks)'. An Ulster surname.

McLENNAN, McLENNON: P SG 'Son of the devotee of St *Finnan*'.

McLEOD: P SG *MacLeoid* 'Son of *Leod*'. 13th cent.

McLYSAGHT, LYSAGHT: P Ir *Mac Giolla Iasachta* 'a strange youth', supporting the tradition in Edward MacLysaght's (see Bibliography) family that a 14th cent. member of the *O'Briens* was transferred to another north Clare sept. Also the term *iasachta* contains an element meaning 'loaned'. An offshoot of the *O'Briens.*

McMAHON: P Ir *MacMathuna*, from *mathghamhan* 'bear'. The name of two septs (i) Thomond, descending from *Mahon O'Brien*, grandson of *Brien Boru*; (ii) Co. Monaghan, where the *MacMahons* are still numerous.

McMANUS: P Ir *MacMaghnuis*, from Lat *Magnus*, via ON. The principal *MacManus* sept is a branch of the *Maguires.* [A First Fleet (marine) surname].

McMARTIN: P Ir *Mac Máirtin.* In Co. Tyrone a branch of the *O'Neills. O Martáin*, a Westmeath surname. See also Martin.

McMASTER: P Ir & SG *Mac an Mhaighistir* 'son of the master'. (*Master* was a title conferred upon the eldest sons of Scottish barons.)

McMENAMIN: N Ir *MacMeanman*, from *meanma* 'high spirited'.

McMICHAEL see MICHAEL.

McMILLAN, McMULLAN, McMULLIN, McMULLEN: P SG *MacMhaolain* 'son of the tonsured one'. A Celtic cross at Kilmory Knap inscribed *Haec est crux Alexandri Macmulen* is evidence of the antiquity of the *MacMillan* clan.

McMINN: P SG *MacMinne* 'son of *Menzies*'.

McMURCHIE: P SG *McMhurchaidh* 'son of *Murchadh* (sea-warrior)'. 13th cent.

McMURRAY: P Ir *Mac Muireadhaig*, from the pers. name *Muireadhach*. See also Murdoch, Murray.

McMURROUGH: P Ir *MacMurchadha* also 'son of sea-warrior'.

McMURTY see McBREARTY.

McNAB(B): P SG *Mac an Abbadh* 'son of the abbot'. The *MacNabs* were known as 'the children of the abbot' but the chiefs of the clan were hereditary lay owners of the lordship of Glendochart.

McNACHTON, McNAUGHTON: P SG *MacNeachdainn* 'son of *Neachdain*', from Pictish *Nechtan* 'pure'. A charter granted to Gillechrist *Macnachdan* in 1267 identifies the clan with Loch Awe.

McNAIR: P SG A branch of the clan *MacNachton*. An Ulster surname.

McNALLY, McANALLY: P Ir *Mac an Fhailghigh*, from *failgheach* 'poor man'. A Mayo and Roscommon surname. The Ulster form is *Mac Con Ulaidh* 'son of the hound of *Ulidia*'.

McNAMARA, MACNAMARA: P Ir & SG *Mac-con-mara* 'son of the hound of the sea'. 14th cent. [A First Fleet (convict) surname].

McNEAL(L), McNEIL see NEAL.

McNEILLY: P Ir *Mac an Fhilidh*, from *fileadn* 'poet'. An ancient sept of Co. Antrim.

McNEVIN, McNIVEN: P Ir *MacCnaimhin*, from *cnamb* 'bone', a sept which has produced poets and physicians. Sometimes associated with a variant of *Niven*.

McNICHOLL, McNICKLE: P Ir *MacNiocaill* 'son of *Nicholas*', a Co. Tyrone surname.

McNULTY: P Ir *Mac an Ultaigh* 'son of the Ulsterman'.

McOMISH, MACCOMISH: P SG *MacThomais* 'son of *Thomas*'.

McOWEN, McCOWAN, MACKEOWN: P Ir & SG 'Son of *Ewen*'. See also McEwan, Owen.

McPHAIL see McFAIL. McPHEE see McFEE.

McPHERSON, MACPHERSON: O SG *Mac an Phearsain* 'son of the parson'. 15th cent.

McQUADE, McQUAID: P Ir *Mac Uaid* 'son of *Wat*'.

McQUARRIE, MACQUARIE: P SG *MacGuaire*, from *guaire* 'noble'.

McQUEEN, MACQUEEN: P SG *MacShuibhne*, from *suibhne* 'pleasant'. 13th cent.

McQUILLAN: P Ir *MacUighilin*, the name adopted by the Norman family of *Mandeville* which became an Irish sept.

McQUILLY: N Ir *Mac an Choilig*, from *coileach* 'cock'.

McRAE, McGRATH, MAGRATH: P Ir & SG *MacGraith, MagRaith* 'son of grace'. See also McCREA.

McRITCHIE see RITCHIE.

McSHANE: P Ir *Mac Seáin* 'son of *John*'.

McSWEENEY: P Ir *MacSuibhne* 'pleasant', of galloglas origin (armed retainer of a chief).

McTAGGART: O Ir & SG *Mac an tsagairt*, from *sagart* 'son of the priest'. 13th cent.

McTAGUE, McTEAGUE, McTEIGUE: O Ir *MacTaidh* 'son of the poet'.

McTAVISH: P SG *McTamhais* 'son of *Tammas* (*Thomas*)'. 14th cent.

McVEAGH, McVEIGH, McVEY: P Ir *Mac an Beatha*, from *beatha* 'life'. An Ulster surname.

McVICAR: O Ir *M'Bhiocair* 'son of the vicar'. 15th cent.

McWHINNIE: P SG Galloway form of *Mackenzie*.

McWHIRTER: O SG *MacCruiteir* 'son of the harper', a branch of the clan *Buchanan*.

McWILLIAM: P Ir *MacUilleim* 'son of *William*'.

MACY see MASSEY. MADDEN see O'MADDEN.

MADDISON, MADISON: P A variant of *Mathieson* (son of *Matthew*). 15th cent.

MADDOCK(S), MADDOX, MADDICK, MATTOCK(S), MATTICK: P OW *Matōc*, Welsh *Madog* 'good, goodly'. *Madoch* DB.

MADELEY: L OE 'The *lēah* (clearing) of an Anglo-Saxon nicknamed *Mada*, from *mād* (foolish)'. (Salop, Staffs).

MADGE, MAGGS: P A pet-form of *Madge* (*Margery*) or of *Margaret*. 13th cent.

MADGWICK: L OE '*Madge's wīc* (dairy-farm)'.

MADIGAN, MADDIGAN: P Ir *O Madagáin*. (Cos. Clare, Limerick).

MAGEE see McGEE. MAGER see

MAUGER. MAGILL see McGILL. MAGNALL see MANGOLD.

MAGNUS, MAGNUSSON: P ON *Magnus*, from Lat *magnus* 'great'. The choice of *Carolus Magnus* (*Charlemagne*) was followed by several Scandinavian kings. Surname 12th cent.

MAGRATH see McCREA, McRAE.

MAGSON: P 'Son of *Magg* (*Magaret*)'. 14th cent.

MAGUIRE see McGUIRE.

MAHAFFY: P SG A variant of McFEE.

MAHER see MEAGER. MAHONEY see O'MAHONEY. MAHOOD see MAUD.

MAHON: P Ir Although frequently used as a variant of McMahon, this is a distinct surname originating as *Mohan, O Móchãin.*

MAIDEN: N OE *maegden* 'maiden, virgin'. 12th cent.

MAIDENS: O OE 'A worker at the maidens' (nuns') house'. 13th cent.

MAIDMENT: O OE 'Servant of the maidens'. 13th cent.

MAIN(E) see MAYNE.

MAINPRICE, MAINPRIZE: N OF *mainpernor* 'nickname for a surety', one who pledges security for the appearance in a court of law of a bailed prisoner at the specified time. Langland uses the term in *Piers Plowman*.

MAINWARING, MANWARING, MANNERING: L OF *Mesnilwarin* 'the manor of *Warin*'. 12th cent. See also Waering.

MAIR: O SG *maor* 'officer', an official who executed legal writs, summonses. 13th cent. [Gilbert Mair, a merchant was one of the witnesses to the Declaration of the Independence of New Zealand by the Maori Chiefs, 28 October 1835].

MAITLAND: (i) N OF *maltalent* 'rude, discourteous'. 12th cent. (ii) L OF From Mautalant, France.

MAIZEY: L OF From Maizy (Aisne) Picardy. 12th cent.

MAJOR see MAUGER.

MAKEPEACE, MAKEPIECE: N OE *maccian* + OF *pais* 'make peace'. 13th cent.

MAKIN(S), MEAKIN(S), MEAKINGS, MEEKING(S): (i) P A dim. of *May*, a pet-form of *Mayhew*. 13th cent. (ii) N OE *maide-kin* 'little maid'. 14th cent.

MALCOLM: P SG *mael Coluimb* 'devotee of St *Columba*'. DB.

MALCOLMSON: P SG 'Son of *Malcolm*'. 13th cent.

MALE(S): N OF *masle* 'male, masculine, manly'. 12th cent.

MALIN(S), MALLIN: P A dim. of *Malle*, pet-form of *Mary*. 13th cent.

MALIS(S), MELLIS(H): P Ir & SG *maol Iosa* 'servant of Jesus'. 12th cent.

MALLAM: L ON *malghe* 'the sandy, gravelly place'. (Malham, Yorks), *Malgun* in DB.

MALLARD: N OF *malard* 'wild drake'. See also Maylard.

MALLET(T), MALET: (i) N OF *maillet*, a dim. of *mail* 'hammer', 'mace', a nickname for a knight proficient in the use of this weapon. DB. The mace became a symbol of authority in the parliament. (ii) P A dim. of *Mall* (*Mary*).

MALLEY see O'MALLEY.

MALLINSON, MALLISON: P 'Son of *Malin*'. 14th cent.

MALLORY, MALORY: N OF *maloret* 'the unlucky'. DB.

MALONE see O'MALONE. MALONEY see O'MOLONEY. MALLOY see O'MOLLOY.

MALPAS(S), MORPUSS: L OF *mal-pas* 'bad passage (path)'. 12th cent.

MALTBY: L O Dan 'The *býr* of a Dane called *Malti*'. (Lincs, Yorks) 12th cent.

MALTER: O A deriv. of OE *mealt* 'malt'. 'A maltster'. 13th cent.

MALVERN: L O Brit *moel-fryn* 'the bare hill'. (Worces).

MALYON: P A dim. of *Mary*, and a variant of *Marion*. 14th cent.

MAN(N): (i) P OE *Mann*, ON *Mannr*, a pers. name. DB. (ii) O OE The modern concept of *man* is totally different from that of medieval England. Then it usually meant 'bondman, vassal, servant' who, with his entire family, was the property of his master. (In 1279 Ralph de Ginges granted to Simon de Duntona, Peter Man son of Robert Man his nativus with all his family.)

MANCEL(L) see MANSEL.

MANCHESTER: L O Brit *mamucion* 'breast-hill' + OE *ceaster* 'fort'. (Lancs), *Mamesestre* in DB.

MANDER(S): L OF From Mandres (Eure) Normandy.

MANDEVILLE, MANVELL: L OF From Manneville (Seine Inférieure or Calvados), or Magneville (Manche) Normandy. DB.

MANGER, MONGER: O OE *mangere* 'monger', 'trader, dealer'. 13th cent.

MANGOLD, MAGNALL: O OF *mangonelle* 'a war machine for heaving rocks at the enemy'. 'A soldier operating the *mangonelle*'. 12th cent.

MANLEY, MANLY: L OE *mǣne-lēah* 'the wood held in common'. (Ches) 12th cent. (In 1788 Governor Phillip used a different meaning when he named Manly Cove after observing the proud bearing of a group of Aborigines.)

MANNERING see MAINWARING.

MANNERS: (i) L OF From Mesnieres (Seine Inférieure) France. DB. (ii) O OF 'a servant at the manor'. 12th cent.

MANNING: P OE *Mann* + suffix *-ing*, a pers. name. DB. [A First Fleet (marine) surname].

MANNIX: P Ir Anglicised form of *O Mainchin*, from *manach* 'monk'.

MANSEL(L), MANCEL(L): L OF From Maine or Le Mans (France). 12th cent.

MANSER: (i) P Hebrew *Manasseh* 'one who causes to forget'. 12th cent. Not exclusively a Jewish name. (ii) O A deriv. of OF *manche* 'handle, haft', 'a maker of hafts'. 13th cent.

MANSFIELD: L Brit + OE *Mam-feld* 'the open land beside the R. *Mam*'. (Notts) [A First Fleet (convict) surname].

MANSON: P 'Son of *Mann*'. 13th cent.

MANTEL(L), MANTLE: O OF *mantel* 'cloak'. Metonymic for a maker of mantles'. DB. (The early recording may be a nickname for one who habitually wore a mantle.)

MANTON: L OE 'The *mǣna-tūn* (farm held in common)' (Notts, Rutland, Wilts), or *malm-tūn* 'farm on sandy or chalky soil' (Lincs). 12th cent.

MANVELL see MANDEVILLE.

MAPLE(S): L OE *mapul* 'maple-trees'. 13th cent.

MAPP see MABB. **MARA** see O'MARA.

MARCH: L OE *mearc*, ME *marche* 'mark, boundary-mark'. (Cambs) 13th cent.

MARCHANT, MARCHAND, MARQUAND, MERCHANT: O OF *marchand* 'merchant/trader'. 12th cent.

MARCHBANK(S) see MARJORIBANKS.

MARCUS, MARKUS: P Lat *Marcus*, a Roman praenomen, derived from the god *Mars*.

MARCY: L OF from Marcy (Manche) Normandy. DB.

MARDEN: L OE (i) *mǣre-dūn* 'boundary hill'. (Sussex) (ii) *mier-denu* 'mares' pasture' (Kent) (iii) meare-denu 'boundary valley'. (Wilts).

MARES see MARRIS.

MARGETTS: P A form of *Margaret*, Lat *Margarita*, from Gk 'pearl'. 13th cent.

MARINER, MARRINER, MARNER: O OF *marinier*, AF *mariner* 'seaman, sailor'. 12th cent. [Marriner, a First Fleet (convict) surname].

MARION, MARRION: P A dim. of *Mary*, Hebrew 'wished-for child', and the same name as *Miriam*, producing Ir *Moire*, Fr *Marie*, Ger and Italian *Maria*, Russian *Marya* and *Masha*, English *Mary*, Scottish pet-forms *Maidie* and *Minnie*, and a popular U.S. form *Mamie*. Many English surnames derive from *Mary*. 13th cent.

MARJORIBANKS, MARCHBANK(S): L OE 'The banks or hillsides belonging to *Marjorie*'. Lands known as *Ratho-Marjoribankis* in the barony of Ratho (Lothian) Scotland were granted by King Robert Bruce as a marriage portion to his daughter *Marjorie* on her marriage in 1316 to *Walter*, High Steward of Scotland and ancestor of the royal house of *Stewart*. The lands eventually fell into the hands of a family named *Johnson* who assumed the surname *Marjoribanks*.

MARK(S): (i) P Lat *Marcus*. 13th cent. (ii) L OE *mearc* 'boundary'. (iii) L OF From Marck (Pas-de-Calais). DB.

MARKER: (i) P OG *Marchari* 'boundary-army'. 12th cent. (ii) O OE *mearcere* 'writer, notary'. 12th cent.

MARKHAM: L OE *mearc-hām* 'the boundary homestead'. (Notts) 12th cent.

MARLAND: L OE *mere-land* 'lake-land'. (Devon).

MARLBOROUGH: L OE *meargealla-beorg* 'gentian hill'. (Wilts), *Merleberge* in DB.

MARLER: O OF & ME *marle* 'marl (lime clay)', 'a quarrier of marl'. 13th cent.

MARLEY: L ME *martren* + OE *lēah* 'marten wood' (Yorks), or OE *myrge-lēah* 'merry wood' (Kent). 12th cent.

MARLOW: L OE *mere-lāfe* 'the drained lake'. (Bucks) DB.

MARMENT, MARMONT: L OF from Marmount, Lot-et-Garonne (Aquitaine) France.

MARNEY, MARNIE: L OF From Marigni (Manche) Normandy. 12th cent. [A First Fleet (convict) surname].

MARQUAND see MARCHANT.

MARR(S), MARRE: L O Sw *marr* 'marsh'. (Yorks, Aberdeens) 12th cent.

MARRIAGE: L OE *mǣre-haecc* 'boundary gate'. 13th cent.

MARRIOTT: P *Mari-ot*, a dim. of *Mary*. 12th cent.

MARIS(S), MARES: L OF From Marais (Calvados) Normandy. DB.

MARROW: N ME *marwe* 'companion, spouse, lover'. 13th cent.

MARSDEN: L OE *mercels-denu* 'valley of the mark (boundary)'. (Lancs, Yorks). [Samuel Marsden, a dedicated missionary who played a prominent part in New Zealand affairs long before the country became a British Colony, began his career there in 1814].

MARSH: L OE *mersc* 'marsh'. 12th cent.

MARSHALL, MASKELL, MASKILL: O OF *marescal* 'a shoeing smith, farrier, horse-doctor, a high official in a manor-house or castle, eventually the high office of Earl Marshall of England'. The original occupational name is in good company with *Smith, Faber, Feaver, Goff, Gove, Martel*, all 'smiths'. 11th cent. [Seven persons named Marshall brought the surname to Australia with the First Fleet, three crew members and four convicts, three of them women. Charles Marshall established a trading post at Waikato Heads, New Zealand, 1830].

MARSHMAN, MASHMAN: L OE *mersc-mann* 'the man on the marsh'. 12th cent.

MARSTON, MARSON, MERSON: L OE *mersc-tūn* 'the farm or homestead by the marsh'. (Nineteen counties from Yorks to Wight.) 12th cent.

MARTEL(L): O OF *martel* 'hammer'. Metonymic for a smith and for a maker of hammers including the iron-headed spiked club (mace) used in medieval warfare. DB.

MARTER, MARTYR: N OF *martre*, ME *marter* 'weasel'. 12th cent.

MARTIN(S), MARTEN(S), MARTYN: P Lat *Martinus*, a dim. of *Martius*, from *Mars*, god of war. Winton D. [Eight persons named Martin brought the surname to Australia with the First Fleet, one a marine, the others convicts. Sir William Martin, Chief Justice of New Zealand, accompanied Bishop Selwyn on some of his most hazardous journeys of exploration, 1842].

MARTON, MERTON: L OE *mere-tūn* 'the farm by a lake'. 12th cent.

MARVEL(L): (i) L OF From Merville (Nord, Somme) France. 13th cent. (ii) N OF *merveille* 'the marvel'. 13th cent.

MARVIN, MERVIN, MERVYN: P Welsh *Mervyn*, a popular name in medieval England. 13th cent.

MASLEN, MASLIN: (i) P OG *Mazelin*, a dim. of *Mazo*, OF *Masselin*. 12th cent. (ii) O OF & ME *maselin* 'mazer', a maple-wood bowl. Metonymic for a maker of wooden drinking-bowls. 13th cent.

MASON, MASSON, MACHEN, MACHIN, MACHON: O ONF *machun* 'mason, worker in stone'. 12th cent. [A First Fleet (marine and convict) surname].

MASSEY, MASSIE, MASSY, MACEY: P A pet-form of *Matthew*. DB. Also L OF From Macey or Marcy (Normandy) or Massy (Seine Inférieure) France. DB.

MASSINGHAM: L OE 'The *hām* (village) of the *ingas* (people) of an Anglo-Saxon called *Maessa*'. (Norfolk).

MASTER(S), MARSTERS: O OF *maistre*, ME *maister* 'master' of a farm, large house, orphanage, etc. 12th cent.

MASTERTON: L OE From the lands of Masterton (Dunfermline) Scotland. 13th cent.

MATHER(S), MATHUR: O OE *mǣthere* 'mower, reaper'. 13th cent. [A First Fleet (female convict) surname].

MATHIE, MATHIS, MATHYS: P A pet-form of *Matthew*. 12th cent. MATHIESON: P 'Son of *Mathie*'. 14th cent. MATSON: P 'Son of *Matt*'. [A First Fleet surname].

MATT(S), MATTES: P A dim. of *Matthew*. 13th cent.

MATTER(S), MATTAR: O OF *materas* 'mattress'. Metonymic for a maker of mattresses'. 14th cent.

MATTHEW(S), MATHEW(S): P Hebrew *Mattathiah* 'gift of Jehovah', Latinised as *Matthaeus*, OF *Mathieu*, introduced into England by the Normans. DB. [A First Fleet (marine) surname].

MATTINGLEY: L OE 'The *lēah* (clearing) of the *ingas* (people) of an Anglo-Saxon called *Matta*. (Hants) 12th cent.

MATTOCK(S), MATTICK see MADDOCK.

MAUCLARK, MOCKLER: N OF *mal, mau-clerc* 'bad cleric', maybe unfrocked. 12th cent.

MAUD(E), MAHOOD, MAWHOOD, MALD, MOULD(S), MOULT, MOWAT(T): P OG a compound of *mahti* 'strength' and *hildi* 'battle', producing the pers. name *Mahtildis*, from which *Matilda*, the name of

William the Conqueror's queen. *Matilda* is the Lat form; *Maud* was a popular form in medieval England. Many surnames derive from *Matilda* including those which have evolved from the pet-form *Till*. DB. [Mould is a First Fleet (convict) surname].

MAUDLING: P Hebrew *Magdalen* 'woman of Magdala'. 13th cent.

MAUDSLEY: MAWDSLEY: L OF + OE '*Maud's lēah* (clearing)'. (Lancs) 13th cent.

MAUDSON: P 'Son of *Maud*'. 14th cent.

MAUDUIT, MUDDITT: N OF *mal-duit* 'badly educated'. DB. (Few could read or write in 1066, so this man must indeed have been backward; perhaps he couldn't tell the bow from the string.)

MAUGER, MAGER, MAYGER, MAJOR: P OG *Madalgar*, OF *Maugier* 'council-spear'. DB.

MAUGHAM, MAUGHAN: L SG From Machan (now Dalserf in Lanarks) Scotland. 13th cent.

MAUND, MAUNDER: L OW *magen, maen* 'stone', used in original sense of 'plain'.

MAURICE, MORRICE, MORRIS(S), FITZMAURICE: P Lat *Mauritius* 'Moorish, i.e., dark, swarthy'. 12th cent. See also Fitz. [Morris, a First Fleet (crew and convict) surname].

MAW(E): L OE *māēdwe* 'meadow'. 13th cent. Also N OE *māge*, ME *maugh* 'female relative by marriage'.

MAWER, MOWER: O OE A deriv. of *māwan* 'to mow', 'a mower'. 13th cent. See also Mather.

MAWSON: P 'Son of *Maud* (*Matilda*) or of *Maw*. 14th cent.

MAXWELL: L Ir + O Scand + OE 'The *wiella* (stream) of *Maccus* (Irish-Scand form of *Magnus*)'. (Roxbys) Scotland. [A First Fleet (marine) surname].

MAY, LE MAY, MAYE(S), MAYS, MEY(S): N ME *may* 'virginal girl or youth'. 13th cent. No connection with the month, which is from OF *Mai*, from *Maia*, goddess of growth and increase, replacing OE *Thrimilce* 'month in which cows can be milked thrice in a day'. [May, a First Fleet (convict) surname].

MAYCOCK: P A dim. of *Mayhew* (*Matthew*) + the familiar *-cock*. 13th cent.

MAYER(S), MAYOR, MEIER, MEYER(S), MIERS, MYER(S): O OF *mire*, ME *meir, meyre* 'physician'. Occasionally from OF *maire* 'mayor'. The surname has been reinforced in 20th cent. by Ger *Meier* 'steward, bailiff, farmer'. 13th cent.

MAYHEW, MAYO: P OF *Mahieu*, a Norman pronunciation of *Matthew*. 12th cent.

MAYNARD: P OG *Maganhard*, OF *Mainard* 'strength-strong'. DB.

MAYNE(S), MAIN(S), MAINE: (i) P OG *Maino* 'strength'. 12th cent. (ii) L OF From the province of Maine (France). 12th cent. (iii) N OF *mayns* 'hands', from some dexterity or deformity, even severed as a medieval punishment, see Brisbane, Crakebone, Arless. 13th cent.

MEACHAM, MEACHEN, MEECHAM: O variants of *Machin* (*Mason*). 17th cent.

MEAD(S), MEADE: L OE *māēd* 'mead (meadow)'. 13th cent.

MEADER: O OE *medu* 'mead', *meduheall* 'mead-hall', 'a maker of mead (drink) or keeper of the *mead-heall* (drinking and banquetting-hall)'. 12th cent.

MEADOW(S), MEDEWE: L OE *māēdwe* 'by the meadow'. 13th cent.

MEADOWCROFT: L OE *maedwe-croft* 'the enclosed tillage or pasture by the meadow'. 13th cent.

MEADWAY, MEDWAY: L Brit river-name *Wey* + OE *medu* 'mead' (from colour of the river). 'The River Medway'. (Kent) 13th cent.

MEAGHER, MAHER: P Ir For *O'Meagher, O Meachair*, from *michair* 'kindly'.

MEAKIN(S) see MAKIN.

MEALE: O OE *melo*, a common Teutonic word from Aryan root, giving Du *meel*, Ger. *mehl*, ON *mjöl* 'meal (flour)'. Metonymic for a miller or seller of meal. 13th cent.

MEANEY, MEANY: P Ir *O Maonaigh*, from *maoineach* 'rich'. See also Mooney.

MEAR(S), MEARE(S), MEERS: L OE *mere* 'lake, pool'. (Som) 13th cent.

MEDLEY: L OE *midel-ēg* 'the middle island'. (Oxon) 15th cent.

MEDLICOTT: L OE *midel-cot* 'the middle cottage'. (Salop) 13th cent.

MEE: P Ir O *Miadhaigh*, from *miadhach* 'honourable'.

MEEK(S), MEEKE: N ON *mjúkr*, ME *meke* 'meek, humble, gentle'. 13th cent.

MEEKING(S) see MAKIN. MEIER see MAYER.

MEHAN: P Ir *O Miadhagáin*, from the pers. name *Miadhach*. Meaning as for *Mee*.

MEIKLEJOHN: N Scots from OE *micel* 'much, great', 'big John'. 15th cent.

MELBOURNE: (i) L OE *melde-burne* 'the stream where *milds* (a plant *Chenopodium*) grows'. (Cambs) (ii) L OE *mylu-burna* 'the mill stream'. (Derbys) (iii) L OE *midel-burna* 'the middle stream'. (Yorks).

MELDRUM: L SG *malg-druim* 'high-ridge', from Meldrum (Aberdeens) Scotland.

MELHUISH: L OE *moel-hīwisc* 'colourful *hide* (of land)'. (Devon) 13th cent.

MELLANBY: L Ir + ON 'The *byr* (farm) of *Maelmuire* (devotee of St *Mary*)'. (Cumb) 14th cent.

MELLER(S): O OE A deriv. of *mylen* 'mill', 'a miller'. 14th cent.

MELLOR: L Brit *moel-bre* 'the bare hill'. (Ches) 13th cent.

MELODY: P OF *melodie*, from Lat, 'song', a woman's name. 13th cent.

MELROSE: L Brit (Cumbric) *moelros* 'the bare moor', recorded by Bede as *Mailros*. (Roxburghs) Scotland.

MELSON see MILLSOM.

MELTON: (i) L OE *midel-tūn* (changed by Scandinavian influence to *methaltun*) 'the middle farm'. (Leices, Lincs, Norfolk, Yorks) (ii) L OE *māel-dūn* 'the hill with a cross'. (Suffolk).

MELVILLE: L OF From Emalleville (Normandy). 12th cent. Later examples are from Melville (Lothian) Scotland, named in 1161 by *Geoffrey de Mallaville*.

MEMBERY, MEMBREY: (i) L OW + OE *maen-burg* 'the stone fort'. (Devon) (ii) L OW + OE *min-burg* 'the border fort'. (Wilts).

MEMBRY see MOWBRAY.

MENZIES: L Scottish form of *Manners*, from Mesnieres (Normandy). The -z- represents a 'gh' sound and the surname is correctly pronounced 'mingies', but in Australia it will always be uncompromisingly *Menzies*. 15th cent.

MERCER, MERCIER: O OF *mercier* 'a merchant dealing in luxury fabrics, velvets, silks'. 12th cent.

MERCHANT see MARCHANT.

MEREDITH: P OW *Morgetiud*, Welsh *Meredydd*. 12th cent. [James Meredith, a captain-lieutenant of marines, arrived on the *Friendship* 1788].

MERRALL, MERRELL see MURIEL.

MERRETT, MERRIOTT, MERRIT(T): (i) P OE *Māerḡēat* 'Famous *Geat*'. DB. (ii) L OE *miere-geat* 'the mares' gate'. (Som) [A First Fleet (convict) surname].

MERRIMAN, MERRIMENT: N OE *myrge-mann* 'merry, happy man'. 14th cent.

MERRY: N OE *myrge* 'merry'. 13th cent.

MERRYWEATHER: N OE *myrge-weder* 'merry weather' for blithe temperament. 13th cent.

MERSON see MARSTON. MERTON see MARTON. MERVIN, MERVYN see MARVIN.

MESSENGER: O OF *messagier* 'a messenger'. 12th cent.

MESSER: O OF *messier* 'harvester, hayward'. 12th cent.

METCALF(E), MEDCALF(E): N OE *mete-cealf* 'a calf fattened for the table', a mocking nickname for a fat man. 13th cent.

METEYARD, MEATYARD: N OE *metan* 'to measure', *ymete* 'mete out', 'mark off', whence *metgeard* 'measuring stick'. Metonymic for a trader using the *metgeard* 'meteyard'. 'Ye shall do no unrighteousness in judgement, in meteyard, in weight, or in measure' (Lev, xix, 35). Shakespeare uses the term in *The Taming of the Shrew*—Grumio to the tailor: 'give me thy meteyard, and spare not me'.

METHUEN, METHVEN: L Brit '*maen* (mead) stone'. From Methven (Perths) Scotland. 13th cent.

METHWOLD: L OE *midel-wald*, with O Scand *methal* replacing *midel*, 'the middle wold (open forest-cleared upland)'. (Norfolk), *Methelwalde* in DB.

MEUX, MEWES, MEWS: L ON with Fr influence *mel-saer* 'the lake with sandy shores'. (Yorks) 12th cent.

MEW, MEWER, MUER(S), MURE: O OF *mue, mew* 'cage for moulting falcons'. 'The man in charge of the *mew*'. 12th cent. (The royal mews (falcon or hawk houses) at Charing Cross, London, were pulled down in 1534 and royal stables (no longer there) were erected on the site, hence the modern sense of *mews*.)

MEWETT: O OF A dim. of *Mew*. 13th cent.

MEY(S) see MAY. MEYER(S) see MAYER.

MEYNELL, MAYNALL, MENNELL: (i) P OG *Maginhild* 'battle-strength'. 13th cent. (ii) L OF From Mesnil (France). 12th cent.

MEYRICK: P OW *Meuric*, Welsh form of *Maurice*. 15th cent.

MIALL, MIELL, MYALL, MYHILL: P Variants of *Michael*. 16th cent.

MICHAEL(S), MAC MICHAEL: P Hebrew 'who is like the Lord?'. 12th cent.

MICHEL see MITCHELL.

MICHIE: P A Scottish dim. of *Mich* (*Michael*). 15th cent.

MIDDLECOMBE: L OE *midel-cumb* 'the middle valley'. [A First Fleet (convict) surname].

MIDDLEHURST: L OE *midel-hyrst* 'the middle copse (wood)'.

MIDDLEMAS(S), MIDDLEMISS: L OE *midel-mest* 'middlemost', a name applied to tenants of the middlemost part of Kelso, Scotland. 15th cent.

MIDDLETON: L OE *midel-tūn* 'the middle farm'. 12th cent. [A First Fleet surname].

MIDGLEY: L OE 'The clearing infested with midges'. (Yorks) [A First Fleet (convict) surname].

MIDHURST, MEDHURST: L OE *midel-hyrst*, meaning as for Middlehurst. (Sussex), *Middeherst* 1186.

MIER(S) see MAYER.

MIGNOT, MINET(T), MINNETT, MINNITT, MYNOTT: P OF A dim. of *Minna*, a woman's name. 12th cent. Also a Huguenot surname.

MILBOURNE, MILBURN, MILLBOURN(E): L OE *mylen-burna* 'mill-stream'. (Derbys, Northumb, Wilts, Westmorland). 12th cent. See also Melbourne.

MILES, MYLES: P OG *Milo*, OF *Miles*, from *milu* 'merciful'. DB. [A First Fleet (crew and convict) surname.]

MILFORD: L OE *mylen-ford* 'the ford by the mill'. (Derbys, Hants, Wilts, Yorks).

MILL: P A short-form of *Millicent*. 13th cent.

MILL(S), MILLES, MILLIS: (i) L OE *mylnum*. A locality name for one living by a mill. 14th cent. (ii) O OE *mylne* 'mill', 'a worker at the mill'. 12th cent. In a slow, laborious age entirely dependent upon human and draught animal power the invention of the water-mill was revolutionary. Some six thousand water-mills, all for grinding corn, are recorded in DB, and some of these are still working. [Mills, A First Fleet (convict) surname].

MILLER, MILLAR: O OE or ON A variant of *Milner*. 13th cent.

MILLETT: P A dim. of *Miles*. 13th cent.

MILLHOUSE: O OE *mylne-hūs* 'a miller'. 14th cent.

MILLICAN, MILLIKEN, MILLIKIN, MILLIGAN, MULLIGAN: N O Ir *Maelecan*, a double dim. of *mael* 'bald', used of a monk or disciple with shaven head. 13th cent.

MILLICENT: P OG *Amalasuintha*, a compound of *amal* and *swintha* 'work-strong'. In the form *Melisenda* it was the name of one of Charlemagne's daughters. Introduced into England in the form *Melisent*, it became a surname in 12th cent.

MILLIDGE, MILLEDGE: L OE *mylen-wīc* 'the mill with a dairy farm'. 12th cent.

MILLINGTON: L OE *mylen-tūn* 'the farm with a mill'. (Ches, Yorks) 12th cent.

MILLSOM, MILLSON, MILSOM, MELSOM, MELSON: P 'Son of *Miles*'. 14th cent.

MILLWARD, MILLWOOD, MILWARD, MILLARD, MULLARD: O OE *mylne-weard* 'keeper of a mill', 'a miller'. 13th cent.

MILN(E), MILNES, MYLNE: O OE *mylne* 'mill', 'a worker at the mill'. 13th cent.

MILNER, MILLNER: O OE *mylnere*, ME *melnere, mulnere*, or in areas of Scand influence *mylnari* 'a miller'. 13th cent.

MILROY: P A variant of Scots *MacIlroy* or Manx *MacGilroy*. See MacElroy.

MILTON: L OE *midel-tūn* 'middle farm' or *mylen-tūn* 'mill-farm', place-names in 18 English counties. OE Byname 972, Surname 13th cent. [A First Fleet (convict) surname].

MINCHIN: N OE *mynecen* 'female monk, nun', used as a nickname. 12th cent.

MINCHINTON: L OE *mynecen-tūn* 'the nuns' farm'. (Dorset, Glos).

MINER(S), MINOR(S): O OF *mineor, mineur* 'a miner' (in the early metal and coal workings). 12th cent.

MINET(T), MINNETT see MIGNOT.

MINGAY: P O Bret *Menguy*, a compound of *men* and *ki* 'stone dog'. 12th cent.

MINSHALL, MINSHULL: L OE *Monnes-scylf* 'the *scylf* (ledge, crag, shelf) of an Anglo-Saxon called *Monn*'. (Ches).

MINTER: O OE *myntere* 'moneyer, coiner'. 13th cent.

MINTO: L Brit & OW *mynydd* 'mountain'. From Minto (Roxburgs) Scotland.

MINTON: L OW *mynydd* + OE *tūn* 'the farm by the mountain'. (Salop).

MITCHAM, MITCHUM: L OE *micel-hām* 'the great homestead'. (Surrey) 12th cent.

MITCHEL(L), MICHELL: (i) P From *Michel*, popular pronunciation of *Michael* in the Middle Ages. 12th cent. (ii) N OE *micel* 'big, hefty'. See also Much. [The surname was brought to Australia with the First Fleet by William Mitchell, quartermaster of the *Sirius*, another William Mitchell, a corporal of marines, and Nathaniel, a convict, and Mary, a 17-year-old convict and her son Thomas].

MITCHELSON, MICHELSON: P 'Son of *Michel* (*Michael*)'. 14th cent.

MITFORD: L OE *mȳth-ford* 'the ford where the streams join'. (Northumb) 12th cent.

MOAT(E), MOTE: L ME *mote* 'mound, embankment, fortress surrounded by water'. 13th cent.

MOBBS: P A variant of *Mabb* and a pet-form of *Mabel*. 16th cent.

MOBERLEY, MOBBERLY: L OE *(ge)mōt-beorg-lēah* 'the glade in the woods with a mound for the assembly of the people'. (Ches) 12th cent.

MOCKLER see MAUCLERK. MOCKRIDGE see MOGGRIDGE.

MOFFAT(T), MOFFETT, MOFFITT, MUFFET(T): L ON *mȯr-thveit* 'the clearing on the moor'. From Moffatt in Annandale (Dumfries) Scotland. Also a Northumb and Cumb surname. 13th cent.

MOGG: P A pet-form of *Margaret*. 12th cent.

MOGGRIDGE, MOGRIDGE, MOCKRIDGE, MUGGERIDGE, MUGGRIDGE, MUGRIDGE: L OE 'The *hrycg* (ridge) of an Anglo-Saxon called *Mogga*'. (Devon) 16th cent.

MOIR: N SG *mor* 'big'. 14th cent.

MOISE see MOYSE.

MOLE: N OE *māl*, ME *mōl*. A nickname for an individual with a conspicuous mole.

MOLESWORTH: L OE 'The *worth* (homestead) of an Anglo-Saxon called *Mūl*'. (Hunts).

MOLIN(S): L OF From Molines (France). 13th cent.

MOLINEUX, MOLYNEUX: (i) O OF *molineur* 'miller'. See also Mulliner. (ii) L OF From Moulineaux (France). 13th cent.

MOLL(E): P A pet-form of *Mary*. 12th cent. MOLLET(T): P A dim. of *Moll*. 13th cent. MOLLISON: P 'Son of *Molly* (*Mary*)'. 16th cent.

MOLLOY see O'MOLLOY. MOLONEY see O'MOLONEY.

MOMPESSON, MUMBERSON: L OF From Montpinçon (Normandy). 14th cent.

MONAGHAN see O'MONAGHAN.

MONCRIEF, MONCRIEFF: L Brit + SG. From the lands of Moncrieff (Perths) Scotland. 13th cent.

MONDAY, MONDY: N OE *Mōnandaeg* 'Monday (moon day)'. (i) A nickname for one born on Monday. (ii) L A holder of *Mondayland*, land held by labour for the lord on Mondays. (Nothing to do with *Saint Monday*, holiday observed by workers exhausted by the week-end). [A First Fleet (marine) surname].

MONEY: (i) L OF From Monnai (Normandy). (ii) N OF *moigne* 'monk', a nickname for one who behaved like a monk.

MONEYPENNY, MONYPENNY: N This surname has been interpreted as 'many pennies', a nickname for a rich man or a miser, and OE *manig-penig* could be found to support this meaning. Unhappily, the original form of the name suggests a less felicitous meaning. Roger *Magnepeine* came out of the dauphinates of France in 1180, and by 1200 the name was recorded as *Monipenie*. In the hundred rolls of 1272 the name appears as *Manipeni*. From this *Moneypenny*.

MONGER see MANGER.

MONK(S), MONCK, MUNCK, MUNK: O or N OE *munuc* 'monk'. Probably for a servant of the monks or a name from playing the part in a medieval play. 11th cent.

MONKHOUSE: O OE *munuc-hūs* 'monk-house', 'a worker at the monastery'. 14th cent.

MONKS, MUNKS: O OE 'servant at the monks (monastery)'. 13th cent.

MONRO see MUNRO.

MONTACUTE, MONTAGU(E): L OF From Montaigu-le-bois or Montaigu (Manche) Normandy. 11th cent.

MONTEITH: L SG *mon* 'hill pasture'. From Monteith (Perths) Scotland. 13th cent.

MONTFORD, MONTFORT, MOUNTFORD: L OF From Montfort-sur-Risle (Normandy). DB. [Benjamin Mountford, who arrived in New Zealand on one of the First Four ships, was appointed Provincial Architect at Christchurch in 1864].

MONTGOMERIE, MONTGOMERY: L OF From Sainte-Foy-de-Montgomery and Saint-Germaine-de-Montgomery (Normandy). DB.

Robert de *Mundegumri* was the first of the Scottish line (1165). A descendant of the Irish branch of the family was Viscount Montgomery of Alamein.

MONTROSE: L SG 'The moor on the cape'. From Montrose (Angus) Scotland.

MOODEY, MOODIE, MOODY, MUDIE: N OE *mōdig* 'bold, brave'. 11th cent. [A First Fleet (convict) surname].

MOON(E), MUNN: (i) L OF From Moyon (Normandy). DB. (ii) O AF *moun, mun* 'monk'. 13th cent.

MOONEY: L Ir *O maonaigh*, from *maonach* 'wealthy'. [A First Fleet (crew) surname].

MOOR(E), MOORES, MOORS, MORE(S): (i) P OF *Maur*, from Lat *Maurus* 'the Moor'. 12th cent. (ii) L OE *mōr* 'moor, marsh'. DB. [A First Fleet (crew) surname].

MOORCROFT: L OE *mōr-croft* 'the small arable holding on the moor'. 14th cent.

MOORHEAD: L OE *mōr-heafod* 'the top of the moor' or 'the edge of the marsh'. (Northumb, Yorks) 13th cent. MOORHOUSE: L OE *mōr-hūs* 'the house on the moor'. 12th cent.

MORAN: P Ir *O Morain*. A Connacht sept. [A First Fleet (crew and convict) surname].

MORANT, MURRANT: N OF *demorant* (with loss of *-de*) 'a sojourner, stranger'. 12th cent.

MORCE, MORSE: P A variant of *Morris* (*Maurice*). 14th cent.

MOREL(L), MORRELL, MORRILL: N OF *more* 'brown, swarthy like a Moor'. 11th cent.

MORELAND, MORLAND: L OE *mōr-land* 'the land on the moor'. 13th cent.

MOREMAN, MORMAN, MOORMAN: L OE *mōrmann* 'moor or marsh dweller'. 13th cent.

MORGAN(S): P An ancient Celtic name of which the first el. is *mor* 'the sea', producing OW, O Bret and Cornish *Morcant*, Welsh *Morgan*, Ir *Muirgen*, Pictish *Morgunn*. 12th cent. [Three convicts named Morgan arrived with the First Fleet 1788].

MORIARTY: P Ir *O Muircheartaigh*, from *muircheartach* 'navigator'. See also Murtagh.

MORIN, MORREN, MORRIN: P OF *Morin*, a dim. of *More* (*Moor*). 11th cent.

MORLEY: L OE *mōr-lēah* 'the clearing on the moor'. 12th cent. [A First Fleet (crew) surname].

MORRIS(S) see MAURICE.

MORRISBY: L Lat + ON 'Morris's *bȳr* (farm)'. [A First Fleet (convict) surname].

MORRISEY, MORRISSEY: P Ir *O Muirgheasa*, from *muir-glas* 'sea-action'.

MORRISON, MORISON: P 'Son of *Maurice*'. 14th cent.

MORROW: L OE *mōr-rāw* 'the row (of cottages) on the moor'. (Cumb, Som).

MORT: N ME *murt* 'the stumpy one', short of stature.

MORTIMER: L OF From Mortemer (Seine Inférieure) France. DB. [John and Noah Mortimer, thought to be father and son, both convicts, brought the surname to Australia 1788. Noah married Mary Cottle and eventually settled in Hobart].

MORTLOCK: L OE 'The *lacu* (stream) of an Anglo-Saxon called *Morta*'. (Surrey).

MORTON: L OE *mōr-tūn* 'the farm on the moor'. 12th cent. [Micah Morton, master of the *Sirius*, brought the surname to Australia 1788].

MOSELEY, MOSELY, MOSLEY: L OE 'The *lēah* (clearing) of *Moll*, an Anglo-Saxon'. (Staffs) 12th cent. Alternatively, 'the clearing infested with *feld mȳs* (field mice)'. (Leices, Worces), *Muselei* DB, (OE *mūs* 'mouse'). [A First Fleet (convict) surname].

MOSES: P It is uncertain whether the name *Moses* is Hebrew or Egyptian. It was certainly a favourite Jewish name after the Dispersion (of the Jews among gentiles after the Captivity). In England, the pipe rolls of the 12th cent. record 38 persons with the name *Moses*. It sometimes was used by medieval Christians and the resulting surname is not necessarily Jewish. The DB form is *Moyses*. DB.

MOSS: P In ME *Moyes* or *Moyses* is used for *Moses*, and *Moss, Mosse* is an abbreviation of this form. *Moss* is also an L surname: OE *mōs* 'the moss, marsh or morass'. (Yorks) 13th cent.

MOSTYN: L OW *maes-amddiffynfa* 'the field of the fortifications'. (Flints) Wales.

MOTE see MOAT.

MOTHERS: P OE *mōdor*, ON *mothir*, O Dan & O Sw *modher* 'mother'. 11th cent.

MOTLEY, MOTTLEY, MOTLEE: L OE *mōt-lēah* 'the moot assembly clearing'.

MOTTRAM: L OE *mōt-aern* 'the moot (assembly or court) house'. 13th cent.

MOUAT(T), MOWAT(T): L OF From Montaut (France). 12th cent.

MOULD, MOULT see MAUD. MOULE(S) see MULE.

MOULTON: L OE 'The *tūn* (farm) of *Mūla*, an Anglo-Saxon'. 12th cent. [A First Fleet (crew) surname].

MOUNCEY, MOUNSEY, MUNSEY, MUNSIE: L OF From Monceaux (Normandy) or Monchaux (Seine Inférieure) France. DB.

MOUNT: L OE *munt* 'hill'. 13th cent.

MOUNTFORD see MONTFORD. MOWAT(T) see MAUD, MOUAT.

MOWBRAY, MULBERRY, MUMMERY, MEMORY, MEMBREY: L OF From Montbrai (Normany). 11th cent.

MOWER see MAWER.

MOXON, MOXOM: P 'Son of *Mogg* (*Margaret*)'. 14th cent.

MOYLAN see O'MOYLAN.

MOYLE: N SG *maol*, Cornish *moel* 'bald'. 13th cent.

MOYSE, MOYCE, MOYES, MOISE: P Variants of *Moses*.

MUCH, MUTCH: N ME *muche* 'big, hefty'. 13th cent. (*Much*, the miller's son in the Robin Hood legends.)

MUDDITT see MAUDUIT. MUDIE see MOODEY. MUER(S), MURE see MEW. MUFFETT see MOFFAT. MUGGERIDGE see MOGGRIDGE.

MUDGE: P A variant of *Madge*/*Magg*.

MUIR, MURE: L Scottish form of OE *mōr* 'the moor'. 13th cent. MUIRHEAD: L A Scottish name from OE *mōr-heafod* 'the head of the moor'. 14th cent.

MULCASTER, MUNCASTER: L OE 'The *ceaster* (Roman fort) occupied by *Mūla*, an Anglo-Saxon'. (Cumb) 13th cent.

MULDOON: P Ir *O Maolduin*, from *dun* 'fort', the name of three septs, in Ulster, Co. Clare and Co. Galway.

MULCAHY: P Ir *O Maolchathaigh*, from St *Cathach*.

MULE, MOULE(S): N OE *mūl*, OF *mule*, ME *moul* 'the obstinate one'. 12th cent.

MULHALL: P Ir *O Maolchathail* 'devotee of St *Cathal*', *maol* 'bald, tonsured'.

MULHOLLAND: P Ir *O Maolchalann* 'devotee of St *Calann*', the name of several septs.

MULLARD see MILLWARD.

MULLET(T): N OF *mulet* 'mussel', 'a seller of mussels'. 13th cent.

MULLIGAN see MILLICAN.

MULLIN(S), MULLEN(S), MULLINGS, MULLAN(E): (i) L OF From Moulin, several places in France. 12th cent. (ii) P Ir *O Maolain*, from *maol* 'tonsured'. [Mullen, Mullins, First Fleet (convict) surnames].

MULLINER, MULLINGER: O OF *molinier* 'miller'. 13th cent.

MULVEY: P Ir *O Maoilmhiadhaigh*, from *miadhach* 'honourable'.

MULVIHILL: P Ir *O Maoilmhichil* 'devotee of St *Michael*'.

MUMBERSON see MOMPESSON.

MUMFORD, MUNFORD: L OE 'The ford of *Munda*, an Anglo-Saxon'. (Norfolk).

MUMMERY see MOWBRAY. MUNCK, MUNK see MONK. MUNCASTER see MULCASTER. MUNCEY see MOUNCEY.

MUNDAY, MUNDIE, MUNDY: P ON *Mundi* 'protector'. 13th cent.

MUNDEN: L OE 'The *denu* (valley) of *Munda*, an Anglo-Saxon'. (Herts).

MUNDON, MUNTON: L OE 'Munda's *dūn* (hill)'. (Essex).

MUNN see MOON.

MUNNINGS: P OE *Munding* 'son of *Munda*', an Anglo-Saxon pers. name meaning 'protector'. DB.

MUNRO(E), MONRO(E): L In Ireland, where the name probably originated, Ir *Mac an Rothaich* 'from the foot of the R. Roe (Co. Derry)'. In Scotland, the *Munro* clan traces back six centuries to Robert *Munro* of Foulis (Ross). [A First Fleet (female convict) surname].

MUNSEY see MOUNCEY.

MURCH: N ME *murche* 'dwarf'. 14th cent.

MURCHIE see McMURCHIE. MURCHISON see McMURCHIE.

MURDOCH: O SG *Murdoch* 'mariner', from O Ir *Muireadhac* or OW *Mordoc*. DB.

MURE see MUIR.

MURGATROYD: L OE 'The *rod* (dial. *royd*, clearing) of *Margaret*', a lost place in Yorks. 14th cent.

MURIEL, MURRELL(S), MURRILL, MERRALL, MERRELL, MERRIL(L): P A Celtic name, OW *Meriel*, *Meryl*, Ir *Muirgheal* or *Muirgel* 'sea-bright'. Also introduced into eastern England by the Bretons at the Norman Conquest. 11th cent.

MURPHY: P Ir *O Murchadha* 'sea-warrior'. The most numerous surname in Ireland. The chief of the *O Murphys* uses the form *O Morchoe*. *MacMurphy* is the Ulster form, but the 'O' and 'Mac' prefixes are seldom used with this surname. [A First Fleet (convict) surname].

MURRANT see MORANT.

MURRAY, MURREY, MURRIE: L SG From Moray. One of the oldest names in Scotland, and the family name of the dukes of Atholl. 12th cent.

MURTAGH: P Ir *O Muircheartaigh*, from *Muircheartach* 'navigator'. See also Moriarty.

MURTON: L OE *mōr-tūn* 'the farm on the moor'. (Durham, Northumb, Westmorland, Yorks) 13th cent.

MUSCOTT: L OE *mūs-cot* 'the cottages overrun with mice'. (Yorks).

MUSGRAVE: MUSGROVE: L OE *mūs-grāf* 'the grove infested with mice'. 13th cent.

MUSSARD, MUSSARED: N OF *musard* 'absent-minded'. DB.

MUSTERS: L OF From Moutiers-Hubert (Normandy). DB.

MUSTO(E), MUSTOW: L OE *mōt-stōw* 'moot-stow', the hundred meeting place. 14th cent. (A *hundred* 'division of a county in England, intended to contain one hundred families'. The total population of England towards the end of the 14th cent. was not more than 2.5 million.)

MUSTON: (i) L OE *mūs-tūn* 'the farm infested with mice'. (Leics) (ii) L ON + OE 'The *tūn* of a Norseman called *Músi*. (Yorks).

MUTER: O OE *mōtere* 'mooter, public speaker, speaker at the moot'. 12th cent.

MUTTON: O OF *mouton* 'sheep'. Metonymic for OF *moutonier* 'shepherd'. 12th cent.

MYALL see MIALL. MYER(S) see MAYER.

MYERSCOUGH: L ON *myrr-skogr* 'the marshy wood'. (Lancs).

MYLECHREEST, MYLCHREEST: P Manx *Mac Giolla Chreest* 'son of the servant of Christ'. 16th cent.

MYLES see MILES. MYNOTT see MIGNOT.

MYTTON: L OE *mȳth-tūn* 'the farm where the streams meet'. (Salop, Warwicks, Yorks) 13th cent.

N

NAGLE, NAGEL, NANGLE: L Ir *de Nogla*, originally Norman *de Angulos*.

NAIRN: L Celtic From Nairn, Scotland, named from the R. *Nairn*, which flows into the Moray Firth at Invernairn, *Invernaren* in 12th cent.

NAISH see ASH.

NAISMITH, NASMYTH, NAYSMITH: O OE *cnif-smith* 'knife smith', 'a cutler'. 13th cent.

NALDER see ALDER.

NANCARROW: L Cornish *nans-carrow* 'the valley of the stags'.

NANCE: L Cornish *nans* 'valley'.

NANGLE see ANGLE, NAGLE.

NANKERVIS: L Cornish *nans-kervys* 'the valley of the stags'.

NANKIVELL: L Cornish *nans-Cyfel 'Cyfel's* valley'.

NAPIER, NAPPER: O OF *napier*, from *nappe* 'napery, table-linen'. 'Naperer, in charge of the linen in a manor-house or castle'. 12th cent.

NASH see ASH.

NATHAN: P Hebrew biblical name of a prophet in the time of *David*.

NATION: P An English variant of Hebrew *Nathan*. [A First Fleet (marine) surname].

NAUGHTON see McNACHTON.

NAVE: O OE *cnafa* 'knave, youth, servant'. 13th cent.

NAY see NYE.

NAYLER, NAYLOR: O OE A deriv. of *naegle* 'nail', 'a maker of nails (wooden pegs)'. 13th cent.

NEAL(E), NEIL(L), NIGEL, NILES, NIHILL, McNEAL, McNEIL: P O Ir *Niall*, SG *Niall* 'champion'. DB. Brought to England by the Normans, and from Ireland by Norwegian invaders of Yorkshire. Latinised as *Nigellus* through mistaken association with *niger* 'black', producing *Nigel*. [Neal, a First Fleet (convict) surname].

NEAT(E): O OE *nēat* 'ox, cow'. Metonymic for a cowherd. *Nēat* is also 'a tenant, vassal working for a lord', indicating his lowly status. 13th cent.

NEAVE(S), NEEVE(S), NEVE: N OE *nefa*, ME *neve* 'nephew'. 13th cent.

NEEDHAM: L OE *nīed* 'poverty' + *hām* 'homestead', 'the poor, needy homestead'. (Derbys, Norfolk, Suffolk) 13th cent. [A First Fleet (convict) surname].

NEGUS: A surname of uncertain origin. Possibly from Welsh *neges* 'message' and metonymic for a messenger.

NEIGHBOUR: L OE *nēahgebūr* 'neighbour', literally 'nigh-boor' (peasant, husbandman). 13th cent.

NEILSON, NILSON: P SG 'Son of *Neil*', derived from *Njall*, Norse form of Ir *Niall*.

NELL: P O Ir *Nel, Niall*, see Neal. 13th cent.

NELMS see ELM.

NELSON: P 'Son of *Nell*'. 14th cent. [A First Fleet (crew) surname].

NESBIT(T), NISBET(T): L OE *byht*, 'from *būgan* 'to bow, bend', preceded by ME *nese* 'nose'. 'The nose-like bend'. (Berwicks, Northumb, Durham) 12th cent.

NESS: L OE *ness*, ON *nes* 'the headland or cape'. (Ches, Glos, Salop, Yorks) 12th cent.

NETHERBY: L OE *nither-ēg* 'the lower island'.

NETTLETON: L OE *netele-tūn* 'the farm overgrown with nettles'. (Lincs) 13th cent.

NEVE see NEAVE. , NEVIN see NIVEN.

NEVILL(E), NEVILE: L OF From Néville (Seine Inférieure), Neuville (Normandy) or other places of similar name in France. DB.

NEW: N OE *nīwe*, ME *newe* 'a newcomer'. 13th cent.

NEWALL: L OE *nīwe-heall* 'the new hall or manor-house'. 12th cent.

NEWBOLD, NEWBOULD, NEWBOULT: L OE *nīwe-byldan* 'the new building'. 12th cent.

NEWBON, NEWBOND: O OE *nīwe-bonda* 'the new serf, peasant, churl'. 13th cent. See also Bond.

NEWBURY, NEWBERRY: L OE *nīwe-burg* 'the new fort'. (Berks).

NEWBY: L ON *nýr-býr* 'the new farm'. (Cumb, Westmorland, Yorks).

NEWCOMB(E): N OE *nīwe-cumen* 'the newly-arrived stranger'. 12th cent.

NEWELL see NOEL.

NEWEY: L OE *nēowe-haga* 'the new enclosure'. 14th cent. NEWHAM: L OE *nēowe-hām* 'the new homestead'. (Northumb, Yorks) NEWLAND(S): L OE *nēowe-land* 'the newly cleared land'. (Glos, Lancs, Worces, Yorks) 12th cent.

NEWLYN: L 'The church of St *Newelina*' (Cornwall), *Sancte Neuline* in 1264. Also Newlyn near Penzance, earlier *Luelyn*.

NEWMAN, NYMAN: N OE *nēowe, nīwe* + *mann* 'the new man, newcomer'. 12th cent.

NEWPORT: L OE *nēowe-port* 'the new town' (esp. one with a harbour or market). (Devon, Essex, Monmouth, Salop, Wight). NEWSTEAD: L OE *nīwe-stede* 'the new place, settlement, village'. (Lincs, Notts, Northumb, Yorks). NEWTON: L OE *nēowa-tūn* 'the new settlement or village'. *Newton* is found in most counties and is the most frequent place-name in England. DB.

NEWSOME, NEWSOM, NEWSON, NEWSHAM: L OE *nēowan-hūsum* 'new houses'.

NEY see NYE.

NIBLETT: P A double dim. of *Isobel*.

NICHOLAS, NICHOL(L), NICHOLLS, NICOL(L), NICOLAS: P Lat *Nicolaus*, from Gk 'victory people'. A popular name in medieval England with many pet-forms and dims., resulting in some 30 variant forms. St *Nicholas*, Bishop of Myra c. 300, patron saint of children, sailors, pawnbrokers and wolves, a strange and incongruous collection. See also McNichol. [A First Fleet (marine and convict) surname. In New Zealand, John Nicholas was one of Samuel Marsden's fellow missionaries, 1814].

NICHOLSON, NICOLSON: P 'Son of *Nichol* or *Nicholas*'. 15th cent.

NICKLEN, NICKLIN: P A dim. of *Nick* (*Nicholas*). 14th cent.

NICKSON, NIXON: P 'Son of *Nick*'. 14th cent.

NIGEL, NILES, NIHILL see NEAL.

NIGHTINGALE: N OE *nihtegale* 'night singer', the nightingale. A nickname for a sweet voiced singer. 12th cent.

NIMMO: A Scottish surname of lost origin.

NISBET see NESBIT.

NIVEN, NEVEN, NEVIN: P Ir & SG *Naomhin* 'little saint', Latinised as *Nevinus*. 13th cent.

NOAD, NOADES, NODES: L OE *ād*, ME *ode* 'the pyre, ash-heap'. The name derives from *atten ode*. 13th cent.

NOAK(S), NOAKE(S) see OAK.

NOAR: L OE *ōra* 'steep slope or bank', ME *atten ore*. 13th cent.

NOBBS: P A pet-form of *Robert*. 13th cent.

NOBLE(S): N OF *noble* 'noble, high-born,

distinguished' or ironically the reverse. 12th cent.

NOCK see OAK. NOE see NOY.

NOEL, NEWELL, NOWELL, NOWILL: P OF *Noël*, from birth or baptism at Christmas. 12th cent.

NOICE see NOY. NOKE(S) see OAK.

NOLAN, KNOWLAN(D), NOWLAN(D): P Ir *O Nualláin*, from *nuall* 'shout'. The chief of the *Nolan* sept held hereditary office under the kings of Leinster. [A First Fleet (convict) surname].

NOONAN, NUNAN: P Ir *O Nuanain*, from *ionmhain* 'beloved'. A Munster surname.

NORBURY: L OE *north-burg* 'the northern fort'. (Ches, Derbys, Salop, Surrey).

NORFOLK: L OE *Northfolc* 'the northern people', as distinct from those of the southern part of East Anglia (Suffolk). *Nordfolc* in DB.

NORGATE: L OE *north-geat* 'the north gate' (of a castle or walled town). 12th cent.

NORMAN(D): (i) L OE *Northmann* 'a Scandinavian, Norseman'. DB. (ii) L OF *Normand* 'a Norman'.

NORRIS(S), NORREYS, NORRISH: (i) O OF *norrice* 'nurse'. 13th cent. (ii) L AF *norreis* 'northerner', applied to an immigrant from the north of England to the south. 12th cent. [A First Fleet (marine and convict) surname].

NORTH: L OE *north*, ON *northr* 'the man from the north'. 13th cent.

NORTHAM: L OE *north-hām* (homestead) or *hamm* (water-meadow). (Devon, Hants) 13th cent. NORTHCOTE, NORTHCOTT, NORCOTT: L OE 'The northern cottage'. 12th cent.

NORTHEY: L OE *north-ēg* 'north island' or *north-ēa* 'north river'. 12th cent.

NORTHORPE, NORTHROP: L OE *north-thorp*, 'the northern village'. (Lincs, Yorks) NORTHOVER: L OE 'The northern bank of the R. Yeo'. (Som).

NORTON: L OE *north-tūn* 'the northern settlement or village'. A frequent place-name. [Michael Norton, a cook's boy in a marine company, brought the name to Australia 1788. In 1863, when he was 103 years of age, he was living in Sydney].

NOTLEY: L OE *hnutu-lēah* 'the nut-wood'. (Berks).

NOTT: N OE *hnott* 'close-cropped or bald'. 12th cent.

NOTTAGE: N ME *notehach* 'a nut-cracking bird', for one who cracked nuts with his teeth. 13th cent.

NOTTINGHAM: L OE 'The *hām* (homestead) of an Anglo-Saxon called *Snot*'. *Snotinge-ham* DB.

NOURSE see NURSE. NOWELL see NOEL. NOWLAN see NOLAN.

NOY, NOYCE, NOYES, NOE, NOICE: (i) P Hebrew *Noah* 'long lived'. 12th cent. (ii) N From the same source, a nickname from playing the part in a medieval play.

NUGENT: L OF From Nogent, one of several places in France. 12th cent.

NUNAN see NOONAN.

NUNN, NUNNS: O OE *nunne* 'nun', originally a pagan priestess; in Christian times a woman devoted to the religious life who has taken vows and lives in a convent. 12th cent. Nunns is 'servant at the nunnery or convent'. There was also a nickname for a man thought to be meek and demure as a nun, and the surname is probably from this source. [Nunn, a First Fleet (convict) surname].

NURSE, NOURSE: O OF *nurice* 'nurse'. 14th cent. See also Norris. [A 14-year-old convict brought the surname to Australia 1788].

NUTT: N OE *hnutu* 'nut', an unexplained nickname from the 12th cent.

NUTTALL: L OE *hnutu-haugh* 'the little valley with nut-trees'. (Notts) 12th cent.

NUTTER: (i) O OE *nōtere* 'scribe, writer'. (ii) O OF *note* 'note'. Metonymic for a note-taker, secretary. 13th cent.

NYE, NAY, NEY: L OE *ēg*, prefixed by ME *atten* 'at the island'. 13th cent.

NYMAN see NEWMAN.

O

OADE, OATES, OATS, OTT(E), OTTEN, OTTON(E): P OG *Odo, Otto*, OF *Odes, Otes* 'riches'. DB. (Odo, Bishop of Bayeux, was half-brother to William the Conqueror.)

OAK(E), OAKS, OKE, NOAK(S), NOAKE(S), NOCK, NOKE(S): L OE *āc*, ME *oke* 'oak', 'the oak-tree'. 13th cent.

OAKDEN, OGDEN: L OE *āc-denu* 'oak valley'. (Lancs) 13th cent. (Ogden, a First Fleet (convict) surname].

OAKEY see OKEY.

OAKLEY, OKELY: L OE *āc-lēah* 'oak clearing'. 12th cent.

OAKMAN: N OE *āc mann* 'oak-man', a nickname 'strong as an oak'. 13th cent.

OATLEY: (i) L OE *āte-lēah* 'the clearing used for growing oats'. (Oteley, Salop), *Otley* 1280. (ii) 'The *lēah* of an Anglo-Saxon called *Otta*'. (Otley, Suffolk), *Otelega* DB, (Otley, Yorks), *Otelai* DB.

OBORN(E): L OE *wōh-burna* 'winding stream'. (Dorset) 14th cent.

O'BOYLE see BOYLE. O'BRAY see BRAY.

O'BRIAN, O'BRIEN, O'BRYAN, O'BRYEN: P Ir *O Briain* 'descendant of *Brian*'. [A First Fleet (marine) surname].

O'BYRNE see BYRNE. O'CALLAGHAN see CALLAGHAN. O'CARROLL see CARROL.

OCKENDEN: L OE 'The *dūn* (hill) of an Anglo-Saxon called *Wocca*'. (Essex).

OCKHAM: L OE 'The *hām* (homestead) of *Occa*, an Anglo-Saxon'. (Rutland, Surrey).

O'CONNELL: P Ir *O Conaill*, a Co. Kerry sept.

O'CONNOR: P Ir *O Conchobhair* 'descendant of *Conchobhar* 'high-will'. See also Connor. One of the O'Connor septs provided the kings of Connacht.

O'DARGAN see DARGAN.

O'DEA: P Ir *O Deaghaidh*, a Co. Clare sept.

ODELL: L OE *wād-hyll* 'woad hill'. (Beds) 12th cent. This surname is also found in Ireland as O'Dell from settlement of an English family.

ODGER(S), OGIER: P OG *Odger* 'wealth-spear'. DB. [Edward Odgirs, a marine, brought his unrecorded variant of the surname to Australia 1788].

ODLIN: P OG *Odelin*, a double dim. of *Odo*. DB. See also Oade.

O'DOHERTY see DOUGHARTY. O'DONAHUE, O'DONAGHUE see DONOGHUE.

O'DONNELL: P Ir O *Domhnaill* 'descendant of *Domhnall* of Kilmacrenan barony in Co Donegal'. The name of several septs.

O'DONOVAN see DONOVAN. O'DOWD see DOWD. O'DRISCOLL see DRISCOLL.

O'DWYER: P Ir *O Duibhir* 'dun-coloured', a Tipperaray sept.

O'FARRELL see FARRELL.

OFFER: O OF *orfrer*, from *orfreis* 'a maker of *orphrey* (gold embroidery)'. 13th cent. OFFICER: O OF A corruption of *orfroisier* 'a maker of *orphrey*'. 13th cent.

OFFORD: L OE *uppe-ford* 'the upper ford'. (Hunts) 13th cent.

O'FLAHERTY see FLAHERTY. O'FLYNN see FLYNN.

OGBORNE, OGBOURNE, OGBURN: L OE 'The *burna* (stream) of an Anglo-Saxon called *Occa*'. (Wilts).

OGDEN see OAKDEN.

OGG(E): N SG *ogg* 'young'. See also Hogan.

OGILVIE: L SG From the barony of Ogilvie in Glamis (Angus) Scotland. 12th cent.

OGLE(S): L OE 'The *hyll* (hill) of *Ocga*, an Anglo-Saxon'. (Northumb) 12th cent.

O'GORMAN see GORMAN. O'GRADY see GRADY. O'HAGAN see HAGAN.

O'HALLORAN: P Ir *O hAllmhuráin*, from *allmhurach* 'pirate', the name of two septs, Co. Galway and Co. Clare.

O'HANLON: P Ir *O hAnluain* 'champion', originally an Ulster sept.

O'HARA: P Ir *O hEaghra*, a predominantly Co. Sligo sept of the barony of Leyny.

O'HARE: P Ir *O hEir*, an Oriel sept, mainly of Co. Armagh and Co. Louth.

O'HEALEY see HEALEY. O'HEARNE see AHEARNE.

O'HEHIR: P Ir *O hAichir*, from *aichear* 'bitter'

O'KANE: P Ir *O Catháin*, an Ulster sept. See also Cain.

OKE see OAK.

O'KEEFFE: P Ir *O Caoimh*, from *caomh* 'gentle'. A Co. Cork surname. The sept provided early kings of Munster.

O'KELLY see KELLY. OKELY see OAKLEY.

OKEY, OAKEY: P O Dan *Aki*, O Sw *Ake*. DB. Also OE *āc-haeg* 'oak copse'. [A First Fleet (convict) surname].

OLD(E), OULD: N OE *eald* 'old', sometimes used for the older rather than the younger in a family. A 10th cent. Byname.

OLDEN see ALDEN. OLDER see ALDER.

OLDERSHAW: L OE *alor-sceaga* 'alder-wood'. 14th cent.

OLDFIELD: L OE *eald-feld* 'the old field'. 13th cent. [A First Fleet (convict) surname].

OLDHAM: L OE *eald-hamm* 'the old water-meadow' or ME *ald-holm* 'old fenland'. (Lancs) 13th cent.

OLDROYD: L OE *eald* + Yorks dial. *royd*

(OE *rod* 'rood'), 'old clearing'. 14th cent.

O'LEARY: P Ir *O Laoghaire* 'calf-keeper'. One of the most ancient of Irish surnames and a sept of the *Corca Laoidhe*. Co. Cork and Muskerry.

OLIPHANT: ME A surname of uncertain origin. In *Boethius* (Book III, Prose VIII) Chaucer uses ME *olifaunt* (from OF *olifant*) for elephant. OF *olif* 'olive-branch' has also been suggested. Either L for the hostelry sign of elephant, or N for a peace-maker.

OLIVE: P Lat *oliva* 'olive'. A saint's name. 12th cent.

OLIVER, OLIVIER: P Charlemagne's peer *Oliver* (of the heroic legend *Roland and Oliver*) was 8th cent., and the name must originally have been Germanic, but it is usually attributed to OF *olif* or *olivier* 'olive-branch', symbol of peace. DB.

OLLERENSHAW: L OE *aelren-sceaga* 'alder shaw (wood)'. (Derbys) 14th cent.

OLLEY, OLLIE see DOYLEY. OLLIER see OYLER.

OLLIFF(E), OLIFF(E): P ON *Oleifr* 'ancestral-relic', the name of a Norwegian king. 13th cent.

O'LOAN: P Ir *O Luain*, from *luan* 'hound (warrior)'.

O'LOUGHLIN: P Ir *O Lochlainn*, a Co. Clare sept.

O'MADDEN: P Ir *O Madain*, from *mada* 'dog'.

O'MAHONEY: P Ir *O Mathghamhana*, from *mathghamhan* 'bear'. A Munster sept.

O'MALLEY: P Ir *O Maille*, a Co. Mayo sept renowned for their exploits on the Atlantic coast.

O'MALONE: P Ir *O Maoileoin* 'devotee of St *John*'.

OMAN, OMOND: P ON *Hamundr* 'high protector'. A surname of the Orkney and Shetland islands. 11th cent.

O'MARA, O'MEARA: P Ir *O Meadhra*, from *meadhar* 'merry'.

O'MOLLOY: P Ir *O Maolmhuaidh* 'noble'. Originally a Co. Offally sept.

O'MOLONEY: P Ir *O Maoldhomhaigh* 'servant of the church'.

O'MONAGHAN: P Ir *O Manachain*, from *manach* 'monk'.

O'MOYLAN: P Ir *O Maoileain*, a Munster surname. Generally used without the prefix.

O'MULLAN(E): P Ir *O Maolain*, the name of three septs, Co. Galway, Co. Derry, Co. Cork.

O'NEAL, O'NEIL see NEAL.

ONIAN(S), ONION(S): O OF *oignon* 'onion', 'an onion seller'. 13th cent. See also Ennion.

ONLEY: L OE *āna-lēah* 'the lonely wood'. (Northants).

ONSLOW: L OE 'The *hlāw* (barrow, burial mound) of *Andhere*, an Anglo-Saxon'. (Salop) *Andreslave* in DB.

OPENSHAW: L OE *open-sceaga* 'open shaw (unenclosed wood)'. (Lancs).

OPIE: P A dim. of names in *Osbert*, originating in Cornwall as *Oby*.

ORANGE: P OF *Orenge*, a woman's name in medieval England, derivation perhaps from OF *orenge*, ME *orenge*, the fruit, ultimately from Arab. *naranj*, Pers. *narang*.

ORBELL: P Lat *Orabilis* 'apt to be entreated', a woman's name. 13th cent.

ORCHARD: (i) O OE *ortgeard, orceard* 'orchard'. Metonymic for an orchardist. (ii) L From the same derivation, 'Orchard'. (Devon), *Orceard* in 9th cent. (iii) L Welsh *argoed* 'the wood (as shelter)'. (Dorset).

ORD(E): (i) L OE *ord* 'point, sword', used topographically for 'ridge'. (Northumb) 13th cent. (ii) L SG From Ord (Peebles, Banff) Scotland.

O'REGAN see REGAN. O'REILLY see REILLY.

ORFORD: (i) L OE *uferra-ford* 'upper ford'. (Lancs) (ii) L OE *ōra-ford* 'ford at the sea-shore'. (Suffolk) (iii) L *Ira-ford* 'the Irish ford'. (Lincs).

ORGAN: O OE *organe*, ME *organ*. Metonymic for a maker or player of musical instruments. 13th cent.

ORGEL, ORGILL: N OF *orgueil* 'pride', 'the proud one'. 12th cent.

ORME(S), ORAM: P O Scand *orm* 'serpent'. DB.

ORMEROD: L ON + OE '*Ormr's rod* (clearing)'. (Lancs).

ORMISTON: L ON + OE '*Ormr's tūn* (farm)'. (Lothian, Roxburgh) Scotland.

ORMSBY: L ON '*Ormr's býr* (farm)'. (Lincs, Norfolk, Yorks) [A First Fleet (crew) surname].

O'RODDEN: P Ir *O Rodáin*, from *rod* 'strong'.

O'ROURKE: P Ir *O Ruairc*, from a Norse pers. name. A Breffny sept.

ORR, ORE: (i) L OE *ōra* 'shore, slope, ridge'. (Berks, Som, Suffolk, Sussex) 13th cent. (ii) N SG *odhar* 'dun, sallow'. 16th cent. See also Hoar.

ORRELL: L OE *ōra-hyll* 'hill with a ridge'. (Lancs).

ORRIS: P Lat *Horatius*, name of a Roman gēns (clan). 12th cent.

ORTON: L OE Either *ōfer-tūn* 'border or river-bank farm' or *ufera-tun* 'the upper farm'. (Hunts, Leices, Northants, Warwicks, Westmorland). OE Byname 11th cent.

ORWELL: L OE *ord-wella* 'the spring at the hill-ridge'. (Cambs) DB.

ORWIN: P OE *Eoforwine* 'boar-friend'. DB.

O'RYAN: P Ir *O Maoilriain*. (Co. Tipperary) [A First Fleet (convict) surname].

OSBORN(E), OSBOURNE, OSBURN: P O Dan *Asbion* 'god-bear'. DB. [A First Fleet (convict) surname].

OSGOOD: P O Dan *Asgautr*, also with ON and O Sw forms. DB.

O'SHAUGHNESSY: P Ir *O Seachnasaigh*, a sept which claims descent from *Daithi*, the last pagan king of Ireland.

O'SHEA: P Ir *O Seagdha* 'descendant of stately'.

OSMOND, OSMUND, OSMAN, OSMENT: P OE *Ōsmund* 'god-protector'. Norman form *Osmund* from ON *Asmundr*. DB.

OSTLER: O OF *ostelier*, ME *ostiler* 'an innkeeper or keeper of lodgings, originally in a monastery'. Later 'a stableman'. 12th cent.

O'SULLIVAN: P Ir *O Súileabháin*, from *súil* 'eye'. Second el. obscure. A Munster surname.

OSWALD: P OE *Ōsweald* 'god-ruler' or ON *Ásvaldr*. DB. St *Oswald*, King of Northumberland. 7th cent.

OSWIN: P OE *Ōswine* 'god-friend'. 13th cent.

O'TOOLE: P Ir O *Tuathail*, from *tuathal* 'people-mighty', a powerful Leinster sept.

OTT(E), OTTEN, OTTON see OADE.

OTTER: (i) P OE *Ohthere*, from ON *Óttar* 'terrible army'. DB. (ii) O ME *oter* 'otter'. Metonymic for an otter-hunter. Some may be from places on the Otter River (Som).

OUGHTRED, OUTRED, OUTHRED: P OE *Ūhtrǣd* 'dawn-counsel'. DB.

OULD see OLD.

OUTLAW: N ON *útlagi*, ME *outlawe* 'an outlaw', outlawed, banished. 13th cent.

OVENS: O OE *ofen* 'oven or furnace', 'worker at the iron or charcoal-furnace'. 13th cent.

OVER: L OE *ōfer* 'seashore' or *ofer* 'slope, ridge'. 13th cent.

OVERALL, OVERELL: L OE *ufera*, ME *overe-heall* 'the upper hall'. 13th cent.

OVEREND: L ME *overe* + OE *ende* 'the upper end (of settlement, village)'. 13th cent.

OVERTON: L OE *ufera-tūn*, ME *overe* replaced *ufera*, 'the upper farm'. 12th cent. [A First Fleet (marine) surname].

OWEN(S): P OW *Ouen*. DB. See also Ewan. [Joseph Owen, a 64-year-old convict, brought the name to Australia 1788. On arrival he lived in a cabin that he made under a rock at Millers Point].

OWLES: N OE *ūle* 'owl', an unexplained nickname. 12th cent. [A First Fleet (convict) surname].

OXBOROUGH: L OE *oxan-burg* 'the fort used as an enclosure for oxen'. (Norfolk) 13th cent.

OXENBOULD: L OE *oxan-bold* 'the dwelling-place with oxen'. (Salop), *Oxibola* DB.

OXFORD, OXENFORD: L OE *oxan-ford* 'the ford used by oxen'. DB.

OXLADE: L OE *āc-slaed* 'oak-valley'. 13th cent.

OXLEY: L OE *oxa-lēah* 'the ox-pasture'. 13th cent.

OYLER, OLLIER: O OF *olier* 'a seller of oil'. 13th cent.

OZANNE: P *Osanna*, a woman's name from a Hebrew word meaning 'save pray', Latinised as *Hosanna*. 12th cent.

P

PACE, PAICE, PEACE: P OF *pais* (Lat *pax*), ME *pese* 'peace, concord'. 13th cent.

PACEY, PACY: L OF From Pacy-sur-Eure (Normandy). 12th cent.

PACK(E), PAIK, PAKES: P OF *Paque* 'Easter', a pers. name for one born during the Easter festival. 13th cent.

PACKARD: P OF *Paque* + suffix *-hard* (brave, strong). 13th cent.

PACKER: O A deriv. of ME *packe* 'to pack', 'a wool-packer'. 13th cent.

PACKHAM: L OE 'The *hām* (homestead) of *Pacca*, an Anglo-Saxon'. PACKWOOD: L OE '*Pacca's wudu* (wood)'. (Warwicks), *Paggewod* 11th cent.

PADDOCK: (i) N ME *padduc* 'toad', a nickname. 13th cent. (ii) L OE *pearroc* 'paddock, enclosure'.

PADDON: L OE '*Padda's dūn* (hill)'.

PADLEY: L OE 'The *lēah* (clearing) of *Padda*, an Anglo-Saxon'. (Derbys) 13th cent.

PAGE: O OF *page* 'page', a boy in a knight's service and in training for knighthood. 13th cent. [A First Fleet (convict) surname].

PAGET(T), PADGET(T): O OF A dim. of *Page*. 14th cent. [A First Fleet surname].

PAIN(E), PAYEN, PAYN(E), PAGAN, FITZPAYNE: P Lat *Paganus*, OF *Paien*, ME *Pain(e)*. Originally 'a villager, country-dweller', later 'a heathen' (for a reluctant worshipper). DB. See also Fitz. [A First Fleet (convict) surname].

PAINTER, PAYNTER: O OF *peintour* 'a painter'. 13th cent. [A First Fleet (crew) surname].

PAISH see PASH.

PAISLEY: L From Paisley (Strathclyde) Scotland, *Paisleth* in 12th cent.

PALFREY, PALFREYMAN: O OF 'The groom in charge of the palfreys (saddle-horses)'. 12th cent.

PALLANT: L OF *palatin* or OE *palendse* (Lat *palatinus*) 'palace'. From the Pallant, a quarter of Chichester in which the Archbishop of Canterbury has palatine rights. 13th cent.

PALLIS: L OF *palis* 'palisade, fence'. 14th cent.

PALLISER, PALLISTER, PALSER: O A deriv. of OF *palis*, 'a maker of palings or fences'. 14th cent.

PALMER: N OF *palmer* 'palmer, pilgrim to the Holy Land', from the custom of returning pilgrims carrying a palm-branch. 12th cent. [A First Fleet (crew and convict) surname].

PANKHURST: Either L from a minor Sussex place (*hyrst* 'wood') or P a variant of *Pentecost*.

PANNELL see PAYNELL.

PANTER, PANTHER: O OF *panetier* 'an official in a large household in charge of the pantry and supplies of bread'. In a monastery also distributing loaves to the poor. 12th cent.

PANTON: L OE 'The *tūn* (farm) by the ridge'. (Lincs).

PAPE: N OF *pape* 'pope', a pageant name. 11th cent.

PAPIGAY, POBJOY: N OF *papegai* 'parrot', a nickname for the winner of a contest of 'shoot the *papegai* (wooden parrot)' set high on a steeple, an archery contest. 14th cent.

PAPWORTH: L OE 'The *worth* (homestead) of an Anglo-Saxon called *Papa*'. (Cambs).

PARAMORE, PARRAMORE: N OF & ME *par amour* 'with love', nickname for a lover. 13th cent.

PARDEW, PARDEY, PARDY, PARDO(E): N An oath name *par Dieu* 'by God', a nickname for one who frequently used this oath. 13th cent.

PARDNER, PARDON, PARTNER: O OF 'The pardoner', a licensed seller of indulgences, remissions of punishment due for sins. 14th cent.

PARFAIT, PARFETT, PARFIT(T), PERFECT: N OF *parfeit*, ME *parfit, perfit* 'perfect', 'well educated, accomplished'. 12th cent. [A First Fleet (marine) surname].

PARGETER: O OF *parjeter* 'a decorative plaster craftsman' 12th cent. (Ipswich, Suffolk, has fine examples of this medieval craft.)

PARHAM, PERHAM, PERRAM: L OE *pere-hām* 'the *hām* (homestead) with pear-trees'. (Suffolk, Sussex) DB.

PARIS, PARRIS, PARISH, PARRISH: (i) L The Gaulish tribe the *Parisii* gave its name to the French capital. 'From Paris'. 12th cent. (ii) P OF popular form of (St) *Patrick* (Lat *Patricius* 'patrician'). [Parish, a First Fleet (convict) surname].

PARK(E), PARKS: L OF *parc* 'lists, enclosure, park'. 13th cent. [Robert Park served as assistant surveyor for the New Zealand Company, 1839].

PARKER(S): O OF *parquier* 'parker, park-keeper'. DB. (An early sense of *parc* was an enclosed space held by royal grant for keeping game.) [A First Fleet (convict and marine) surname].

PARKIN(S), PARKYN(S), PERKIN(S): P A dim. of *Peres* (OF *Piers*), popular medieval form of *Peter*. 14th cent. [Parkin, a First Fleet (convict) surname].

PARKINSON: P 'Son of *Parkin/Perkin*'. 14th cent. [Jane Parkinson, a convict, and her three-year-old son Edward, embarked on the *Friendship*. Jane died at sea. Edward survived to bring the surname to Australia 1788].

PARMENTER, PARMETER, PARMITER: O OF *parmentier* 'a tailor'. 12th cent.

PARNELL, PARNWELL, PURNELL: P Derived from a woman's name *Petrōnilla*, fem. dim. of Lat *Petrōnius*, a saint's name and that of a Roman family. 13th cent.

PARR, PARRACK: L OF *pearr, pearroc* 'enclosure, paddock'. (Notts, Lincs, Lancs) 13th cent. [Parr, a First Fleet (convict) surname].

PARROTT, PARRATT, PARRETT, PEROT, PERRETT, PERROT(T), PORRETT, PORRITT: (i) P Dims. of *Perre* (*Peter*) + suffix *-et, -ot.* DB. (ii) N A nickname from the parrot, although the bird itself was nicknamed from *Perrot.*

PARRY: P Welsh *ap Harry* 'son of *Harry*'. 15th cent.

PARSEY see PERCY.

PARSLOE, PARSLOW, PARSLEY, PASLEY, PASHLEY: N OF A phrase-name *Passelewe* 'cross the water', applied to a pilgrim, crusader, merchant, who travelled overseas. [Ann Parsley, a convict, brought the surname to Australia 1788].

PARSON: O OF *persone*, ME *persoun* 'priest, parson'. 12th cent.

PARSONAGE: L OF *personage* 'benefice'. 'Dweller at the parson's house', presumably the parson.

PARSONS: O 'The parson's servant'. 14th cent. [A First Fleet (marine) surname].

PARTINGTON: L OE 'The *tūn* (settlement) of the people of *Pearta*, an Anglo-Saxon'. (Ches) 13th cent.

PARTON: L OE *pere-tūn* 'pear orchard'.

PARTRIDGE: N OF *perdrix*, ME *pertriche* 'partridge', a nickname from the bird. 12th cent. [A First Fleet (convict) surname].

PASCAL(L): P Fr *Pascal*, Lat *paschalis* 'pertaining to Easter'. 13th cent.

PASCOE: P A pet-form of *Pask*, from ME *paske* 'Easter'. 14th cent.

PASH, PASK(E), PAISH: P ME *pasche*, from OF *pasque*, from Hebrew *pesakh* 'passing-over'. A pers. name for one born at Easter. 13th cent.

PASKIN(S): P MW *Pascen*, from Lat *Pascentius.* Paskins is 'son of *Paskin*'.

PASLEY see PARSLOE.

PASS: P ME *pasche.* Meaning identical with *Pash.* 13th cent.

PASSANT: O OF *passe avant* 'a front-runner', perhaps also for a herald or a messenger. 12th cent. (OF *passe avant* 'go on in front'.)

PASSMORE: L OF *passe mer* 'cross the water (lake)'. (Devon, Hants) 12th cent.

PASTERFIELD see BASKERVILLE.

PASTOR: O AF *pastour* 'herdsman, shepherd'. 12th cent.

PATCH: P ME Meaning identical with *Pash.* PATCHET: P A dim. of *Patch.*

PATE(S), PATEMAN, PATMAN: P pet-forms of *Patrick.* 12th cent.

PATERNOSTER: O Lat *paternoster* 'Our Father', the opening words of the Lord's prayer. Metonymic for a maker of rosaries, chaplets. (Paternoster Row by St *Paul's* Cathedral was once a centre of this industry.) 12th cent.

PATIENCE: N ME *patience*, from Lat *patiens* 'to endure', a morality play name.

PATMORE, PATTEMORE: L OE 'The *mere* (lake) of an Anglo-Saxon called *Patta*'. (Herts) 13th cent.

PATON, PATTON, PATTEN: (i) P A dim. of *Patrick.* 13th cent. (ii) L OE 'The *tūn* (village) of *Peatta's* people'. (Salop) 13th cent.

PATTEN, PATTIN: O OF *patin*, ME *paten* 'a clog worn by monks'. Metonymic for a patten maker. 12th cent.

PATRICK, PATTRICK, FITZPATRICK: P O Ir *Patraicc*, from Lat *Patricius* 'patrician'. See also Fitz. 12th cent. [A First Fleet (convict) surname].

PATTERSON, PATERSON: P 'Son of *Patrick*'. 15th cent.

PATTINSON, PATTISON: P 'Son of *Paton* (*Patrick*)'. 13th cent.

PAUL(E), PAWLE, POLE(S), POOLE, POWELL: P Lat *Paulus* 'small'. 12th cent. See also Powell.

PAULEY, PAULLEY, PAULY, PAWLEY: P A pet-form of *Paul.* 13th cent.

PAULIN(G): P A dim. of *Paul.* 13th cent.

PAVER, PAVIER, PAVIOUR: O OF *paveur* 'paviour, paver', 'a pavement layer', a highly skilled craft including laying of stone, marble, tiled floors in English cathedrals. 13th cent.

PAVETT, PAVITT: P A dim. of *Pavey.* 16th cent.

PAVEY, PAVY: (i) P *Pavia*, a woman's name, probably OF from *pavie* 'peach'. 12th cent. (ii) L It. From Pavia (Lombardy).

PAW(E), POE, POWE: N OE *pāwa*, ON *pá*, ME *pō* 'peacock'. 11th cent.

PAWLETT, PAULET(T): (i) P A dim. of *Paul*. (ii) L OE *pāl-flēot* 'the *fleet* (stream) with poles or stakes' (probably for mooring).

PAXTON: L OE 'The *tūn* (farm) of an Anglo-Saxon called *Paecc*'. (Hunts) 12th cent.

PAYN(E) see PAIN.

PAYNELL, PANNELL, PENNELL: P OF *Payenel*, dim. of *Payen*. See Pain. DB.

PAYNTER see PAINTER.

PAYTON, PAYTEN, PEYTON: L OE '*Pǣga's tūn* (farm or enclosure)'. (Suffolk). 13th cent. [Payton, a First Fleet (convict) surname].

PEACE see PACE. PEACH, PEACHEY see PETCH.

PEACOCK(E), POCOCK: N OE *pēacocc*, ME *pecok, pocok* 'peacock', a bird of gorgeous plumage. DB. In the 14th cent. allegorical poem *Piers Plowman* the sin of pride is introduced in the proud-hearted person of Petronella Peacock. *See also Sheldrake*.

PEAK(E), PEEK: L OE *pēac* 'hill, peak'. (Peak District, Derbys). 12th cent.

PEAR, PEEAR, PEER, PERE: N OF *peer*, ME *pere* 'a peer, paragon' or 'companion'. 13th cent.

PEARCE, PEARS see PIERCE.

PEARCEY, PEARCY, PIERCEY, PIERCY: L OF *perce-haie* 'pierce-hedge', a nickname for one adept at wriggling through hedges or fortifications, 'a skirmisher or a poacher'. DB.

PEARL, PEARLMAN, PERLMAN: O OF *perle* 'pearl'. Metonymic for a trader in pearls. 13th cent.

PEARMAN: O OE *peru-mann* 'a grower/seller of pears'. 13th cent.

PEARSON, PEIRSON, PIERSON: P 'Son of *Piers* (*Peter*)'. 14th cent.

PEART: N OF & ME *apert* 'forward, bold, malapert' or 'open, unconcealed'.

PEASCOD, PESCOD, PESCUD, PESCOTT, PESKETT: O OE *peose-codd* 'pea-bag', 'peapod'. 'A grower/seller of peas'. 13th cent.

PEASE: O OE *peose* 'pea'. Metonymic for a seller of peas. 13th cent.

PEASEY see PIZEY.

PEAT(E), PEATTIE, PEET: P dims. of *Peter*.

PEBERDY see PEPPERDAY. PECHEY see PETCH.

PECK: (i) O ME *pekke* 'a measure', e.g., for corn. Metonymic for a measurer or a maker of *pekkes*. 12th cent. (ii) L A variant of *Peak*. 13th cent. [A First Fleet (convict) surname].

PECKHAM: L OE *pēac-hām* 'homestead by the hill'. (Kent).

PEDDAR, PEDDER, PEDLER, PIDLER: O ME *pedde* 'pannier'. 'A carrier of goods for sale, a pedlar, hawker'. 12th cent.

PEEBLES: L Brit *pebyll* 'tents, pavilions'. From the county town (Peebles) of Peeblesshire, Scotland, *Pebles* 1126.

PEEL(E), PEILE, PIEL(E): (i) L OF *pel, piel* 'pole, stake', 'palisade'. 13th cent. (ii) N OF *pel* 'pole', a nickname for a tall, thin person. 13th cent. [Charles Peal, bearing an unrecorded version of the surname, arrived with the First Fleet 1788].

PEGG: (i) O ME *pegge*. Metonymic for a maker of wooden pegs, e.g., for building. 12th cent. (ii) P A dim. of *Margaret*, an altered form of *Meg*.

PEGGRAM, PEGRAM, PEGRUM see PILGRIM.

PEGLER: O W. Midlands dial. *pegler* 'patcher, unskilled workman'.

PELL(S): P A pet-form of *Peter*. 13th cent. PELLATT, PELLETT: P A dim. of *Pell*. 13th cent.

PELLEW, PELLOW: N OF *pel de lou* 'wolf-skin'. 12th cent.

PELLY: N OF *pele* 'bald'. 13th cent.

PEMBERTON: L Brit *penn* + OE *bere-tūn* 'the barley farm by the hill'. (Lancs) 13th cent.

PENDEGAST see PRENDERGAST. PENDER see PINDAR.

PENDLEBURY: L Brit *penn* 'hill' + OE *hyll* (also) 'hill' + *burg* 'fort or manor'.

PENDLETON: L The first two elements of Pendlebury + OE *tūn* 'farm or enclosure'.

PENFOLD see PINFOLD.

PENGELLEY, PENGELLY, PENGILLY: L Cornish *pen-kelly* 'the head (end) of the copse'. 13th cent.

PENMAN: O OF & ME *penne*, from Lat *penna* 'feather (quill)' + OE *mann*. 'A scribe'. (*Penknife* is from sharpening quills.)

PENN: (i) L Brit *penn* 'hill'. (Bucks, Staffs) 12th cent. (ii) L OE *penn* '(sheep) pen, fold'.

PENNELL see PAYNELL.

PENNEY, PENNIE, PENNY, PENNING(S): N OE *pening, penig*, a nickname from the coin. 13th cent. The English coinage was based on the silver penny from the reign of *Offa* (797) to that of Edward III who introduced a gold florin in 1344. Silver pence, which had become much debased in value, ceased to be used for general circulation in the reign of George II, but are still struck as part of the royal alms on Maundy Thursday. The copper penny was not introduced until 1797. The nickname, first recorded in the 13th cent., must have been for a man of means who actually possessed a silver penny (22½ gr. of silver at that time) or even had one of the gold pennies, worth 20 silver pence, which were struck experimentally by Henry III in 1257. In *Henry IV* Shakespeare has Falstaff speak of 'gilt twopences'. [John Penny, a convict, brought the surname to Australia 1788].

PENNINGTON: L OE *pening-tūn* 'penny rent farm'. (Lancs).

PENNYCUICK: L Brit *pen-cog* 'cuckoo hill'. (Lothian) 14th cent.

PENNYFATHER, PENNEFATHER: N OE *pening-faeder* 'a niggard, miser'. Winton D.

PENROSE: L Cornish *pen-ros* 'top of the heath or moor'. (Cornwall, Devon) 12th cent.

PENSON: P 'Son of *Penn*'. 13th cent.

PENTECOST: P OF *Pentecost* (Whitsun), for one born during the festival of Pentecost. 12th cent.

PENTLAND: L 'The land of the Picts'. In Old Norse the Picts are referred to as *Péttar* or *Péttir*, and Pentland as *Péttland*. (Midlothian) Scotland.

PEPALL, PEOPLES: P OF A pet-form of *Pepin*. 13th cent.

PEPEREL, PEPPERELL see PEVERALL.

PEPIN, PEPPIN, PEPYS, PIPPIN: P OG *Pipin, Pepin*, OF *Pepin*, from the root *bib-* 'to tremble'. A popular name in France from the Carolingian monarchy. Introduced into England at the Norman Conquest. DB.

PEPPER: O OE *pipor* 'pepper'. Metonymic for a 'pepperer, spicer'. 12th cent.

PEPPERDAY, PEBERDY: N OF *pape-Dieu* 'Pope-God', an oath name 'by the Pope-God'. 12th cent.

PERCEVAL, PERCIVAL: P OF From Perceval (Calvados) Normandy. 12th cent. Popularised by the 12th cent. poet Crestien de Troyes, who used *Perceval* as the name of his hero in the epic poem. [Percival, a First Fleet (convict) surname. Augustus Perceval arrived in New Zealand on the *Barbara Gordon*, one of the early migrant ships. Ten ships chartered by the New Zealand Company sailed from London, Glasgow and Plymouth in 1839, carrying a total of 1,123 settlers and officials].

PERCY, PARSEY, PURSEY: L OF From one of several places called Percy in Normandy, from a Gallo-Roman pers. name. DB.

PERE see PEAR. PERES, PERRIS see PIERCE. PERFECT see PARFAIT. PERHAM, PERRAM see PARHAM. PERKIN(S) see PARKIN. PERLMAN see PEARL. PEROT, PERRETT see PARROTT.

PEROWNE: P OF From the same source as *Perrin*. A Huguenot surname.

PERRIMAN, PERRYMAN: L OE *pere* + *mann* 'the pear-tree man', from his abode by a pear-tree. 13th cent.

PERRIN(S), PERRING, PERREN: P A dim. of *Perre* (*Peter*). 12th cent.

PERRY, PERRIE, PIRIE, PIRRIE: L OE *pirige, pirie* 'pear-tree'. 12th cent. [Perry, a First Fleet (marine and convict) surname].

PESCOD, PESCOTT, PESKETT see PEASCOD.

PESTEL(L), PISTOL: O OF *pestel* (for use with mortar). Metonymic for a spicer or a druggist. 13th cent.

PETCH, PECHEY, PEACH, PEACHEY: N OF *peche, pechie*, from Lat *peccatum* 'sin'. DB. However sinful, *Peche* was the name of the Bishop of Coventry in 1123.

PETER(S), PETRE: P Lat *Petrus*, from Gk 'rock'. *Peter* is the learned form; *Peres* (Fr *Piers*) was popular in medieval England. *Peters* has become a frequent Welsh surname. DB. PETERSON: P 'Son of *Peter*'. 14th cent.

PETHARD: N OF *peter* 'to break wind' + suffix *-hard*. An indecent nickname. 13th cent. See also Petter.

PETHER(S), PITHER(S): P A form of *Peter* used in Ireland and Cornwall. 13th cent.

PETHERBRIDGE, PETHYBRIDGE: L OE 'The *brycg* (bridge) of an Anglo-Saxon called *Pidda*'. (Devon).

PETO: L OF From Poitou (France). 13th cent.

PETRIE, PETRY: P A Scottish dim. of *Peter*, and sometimes of *Patrick*. 15th cent. [Henry Petrie, a marine sergeant, and John Petery, a convict with an unrecorded variant, brought the surname to Australia 1788].

PETT(S) see PITT. PETTENGELL see PORTUGAL.

PETTER: N OF *peter* 'to break wind'. 13th cent. However indecent it may be considered now, Rolland le *Pettour* held land in Suffolk by serjeantry of presenting himself before the king (Henry III) at Christmas to do 'a jump, a whistle and a fart'. In later times farting at court fell into disfavour. By the time of Elizabeth I it was considered a solecism. It is recorded that a courtier, on making a deep bow before the Queen, had the misfortune to break wind. Covered in confusion, he withdrew and went into voluntary exile in France. Years later he was presented to the Queen on one of her Progresses. 'Sir, we greet you,' said Queen Elizabeth I, 'We hath forgot the fart.' In France, the surnames *Pétard, Pétour, Pétot* and *Pétain* all descend from OF *peter.*

PETTIFER, PETTAFOR, PETTIFORD: N OF *pedefer* 'iron foot', a nickname for a tireless marcher; sometimes for an old soldier who had lost a foot. OE Byname. 11th cent.

PETTIGREW: N OF *petit cru* 'small growth', a nickname for one of stunted growth. 13th cent.

PETTINGELL see PORTUGAL.

PETTIT(T), PETTET, PETIT: N OF *petit* 'little', 'the small one'. DB. [John Pettit (a boy convict) brought the surname to Australia 1788].

PETTMAN see PITMAN.

PETTY: N OF *petit* 'little'. 12th cent.

PEVERALL, PEVERELL, PEVERILL, PEPEREL, PEPPERALL, PEPPERELL: N OF *peurel, pevre* 'pepper', nickname for a hot-tempered individual. 12th cent.

PEW see PUGH. PEYTON see PAYTON. PHAIR see FAIR. PHARAOH see FARRAR. PHEAR see FEAR.

PHELAN, WHELAN, WHALEN: P Ir *O Faolain*, from *faol* 'wolf'.

PHEMISTER see FEMISTER. PHILBY, PHILBEY see FILBY.

PHILCOX: P A pet-form of *Philip.* 13th cent.

PHILIP(S), PHILIPP(S), PHILLIP(S), PHILP(S), PHELP(S): P Lat *Philippus*, from Gk 'horse-lover'. Also a woman's name *Philippa.* 12th cent. [Admiral Arthur Phillip, Commander of the First Fleet and first Governor of N.S.W., together with Mary Phillips, convict, Richard Phillips, convict, Thomas Phillips, a marine mason, and William Phillips, a sailor on the *Sirius*, brought the surname to Australia 1788].

PHILIPSON, PHILLIPSON: P 'Son of *Philip*'. 14th cent.

PHILLIMORE: P OF *Filimor* 'most famous'. [A First Fleet (convict) surname].

PHILPOT, PHILPOTT(S), PHILLPOT: P A dim. of *Philip.* 14th cent. [A First Fleet (marine) surname].

PHIN see FINN.

PHIPPS: P A pet-form of *Philip.* 13th cent.

PHIZACLEA see FAZACKERLEY. PICK see PIKE.

PICKARD: L OF From Picardy. William the Conqueror's invading army contained followers from Picardy but the earliest recording of the name is 12th cent.

PICKER(S): O OE A deriv. of OE *pīc* 'pike', 'a maker of pikes'. 12th cent.

PICKERING: L OE *Pīcōringas* (*pīc-ōra*), a tribal name, 'people of the ridge'. (Yorks) 12th cent.

PICKETT, PICOT, PIKETT, PIGGOT(T), PIGOT(T): P OF A dim. of *Pick, Pike* + suffix *-et, -ot.* DB. See also Pike. [Pigott, a First Fleet (convict) surname].

PICKFORD: L ME *pigge-ford* 'pig-ford'. 13th cent.

PICKLES: L ME *pighel* 'small enclosure'. (Lancs, Yorks).

PICKMAN: O OE The meaning is identical with that of *Picker.* 13th cent.

PICKUP: L OE *pīc-copp* 'the hill with a peak'. (Lancs).

PICKWELL: L OE *pīc-wielle* 'the spring at the peak of the hill'. (Leices).

PICKWORTH: L OE 'The *worth* (homestead) of an Anglo-Saxon called *Pīca*'. (Lincs).

PICTON: L OE '*Pīca's tūn* (farm)'. (Ches, Yorks) 12th cent.

PIDGEON, PIGEON: N OF *pipjon* 'pigeon'. Two meanings are conventionally offered for this nickname, 'one easily plucked' and a manipulation of *petite.* Neither fits the facts. William Caxton, a prolific writer and translator as well as Britain's first printer, in his *The Myrrour of the World*, described the pigeon as a young dove: 'The douve is a symple byrde, and of her nature nourisheth well the pigeons of another dove'. The Anglo-Saxons described both the pigeon and the dove in a single word, OE *culfre*, which also gave rise to a nickname, *Culver.* The surname was first recorded in 1200 but the use of the term 'pigeon' as the gullible victim of a swindler did not gain currency until the 16th cent. *Pigeon* may be a metonym for a breeder of pigeons, or a nickname for one of soft and gentle demeanour.

PIDLER see PEDDAR.

PIE, PYE: (i) O OF & ME *pie, pye* 'a pieman, maker/seller of pies'. 14th cent. (ii) N A nickname from the magpie, originally the *pie*, which was later prefixed with the name *Mag*. 12th cent.

PIEL see PEEL.

PIERCE, PIERS, PEARCE, PEARS, PEIRCE, PERES, PERRIS, PERSE: P OF *Piers* (*Peter*). 12th cent. See also Peter.

PIERCEY see PEARCEY.

PIERPOINT, PIERPONT: L OF *pierre-pont* 'stone bridge', from Pierrepont (Seine Inferieure) or one of several places of similar name in Normandy. DB.

PIERSON see PEARSON.

PIGG(E): N OE *picg*, ME *pigge* 'pig'. DB. PIGGINS: N A dim. of *Pigg*, 'little pig'.

PIGGOT(T) see PICKETT. PIGRAM see PILGRIM.

PIKE, PYKE, PICK: These surnames derive from OE *pīc* 'point', used variously for O 'a pikeman (foot soldier armed with a pike)'; L 'a sharp pointed hill'; N nickname from pike (the fish) so named from its sharp pointed jaw, and usually for a seller of pike, and from pick for a tall, thin person. DB.

PILCHER: O OE *pylece*, ME *pilche* 'a garment made of fur', 'a maker of *pilches*'. 13th cent.

PILE, PYLE: L OE *pīl* 'a post or stake', probably a boundary post. 13th cent. [A First Fleet (female convict) surname].

PILGRIM, PEGRAM, PEGRUM, PIGRUM: N OF *pelegrin*, ME *pilegrim* 'one from foreign parts', 'a pilgrim', usually applied to one who had made the pilgrimage to the Holy Land or to Rome. 12th cent.

PILKINGTON: L OE 'The *tūn* (settlement) of the people of *Pīleca*, an Anglo-Saxon'. (Lancs) 12th cent.

PILL, PELL: L OE *pyll* 'stream, creek'. 12th cent.

PILLEY: L OE *pīl-lēah* 'the wood where piles (stakes) were cut'. (Hants, Yorks).

PILLING: L OE *pylling* 'streamlet'. 13th cent.

PILLINGER see BULLINGER.

PIMM, PYM(M): P *Pymme*, a medieval woman's name, from Gk *Euphemia*. 12th cent. See also Effemy.

PIMLOTT: P A dim. of *Pimm*. 16th cent.

PINCHBECK, PINCHBACK: L A Lincs surname and name of a village. This is fen country and the second el. is OE *baece* 'stream', as in several other Lincs and Cambs places such as Wisbech, Holbeach. The first el. is uncertain. It may be either OE *pinca* 'finch' or an unrecorded OE *pinc*, thought to be 'minnow'. Lincs was within the Danelaw, its names subject to Scand influence. 'Minnow stream' would be an agreeable meaning. *Pincebec* DB. Surname 12th cent.

PINCHEN, PINCHIN, PINSON, PINSENT: N OF *pinçon*, Norman *pinchon* 'finch'. A nickname from a lively, cheerful little bird. 12th cent. See also Finch.

PINDAR, PINDER, PENDER: O OE A deriv. of *pyndan* 'to impound, shut up'. An officer of a manor responsible for impounding stray animals. 13th cent. [A First Fleet (female convict) surname].

PINE, PYNE: (i) N OE *pīn*, OF *pin* 'pine (tree)', a nickname for a tall, thin man. 11th cent. (ii) L OF From Le Pin (Normandy) or some other French place with a similar name. 12th cent.

PINFOLD, PENFOLD: O OE *pundfald*, cogn. with the verb *pyndan* (see Pindar), dial. *pinfold, penfold*, 'the keeper of the *pinfold* (pound)'. 13th cent.

PINK, PINCH: N OE *pinca* 'chaffinch', a nickname from the little song-bird. 11th cent. See also Pinchen.

PINKERTON: L OE *pinca-tūn* 'the enclosure enlivened with finches'. A Scottish surname from Lothian.

PINKNEY: L OF From Picquigny (Somme) France. DB.

PINN: O OE *pinn* 'pin'. Metonymic for a pin-maker. 13th cent.

PINNELL, PINEL: N OF *pinel* 'a diminutive pine tree', a curious nickname. DB.

PINNOCK: N ME *pynnuc* 'hedge-sparrow'. 12th cent.

PIPE: (i) P A variant of *Pepin*. DB. (ii) O OE *pīpe* 'pipe', metonymic for a piper.

PIPER, PYPER: O OE *pīpere* 'a player on the pipe'. 12th cent.

PIPKIN: P A dim. of *Pipe*. [A First Fleet (female convict) surname].

PIPPIN see PEPIN. PIRIE see PERRY. PISTOL see PESTELL. PITHER see PETHER.

PITMAN, PITTMAN, PETTMAN, PUTMAN: L OE *pytt-mann* 'the pit or hollow-man'. 12th cent.

PITNEY: L OE 'The *ēg* (island) of an Anglo-Saxon called *Pytta*'. (Som).

PITT(S), PETT(S), PUTT: L OE *pytt* 'pit or hollow'. (Kent, Hants) 12th cent.

PITTAWAY: L OE 'The *weg* (way, path) of an Anglo-Saxon called *Pytta*'.

PIZEY, PIZZEY, PEASEY, PUSEY: L OE *pisu-ēg* 'pea island'. (Pusey, Berks) 13th cent.

PLACE: (i) L OF & ME *place* 'the market place'. (ii) L OF *pleix* 'an enclosure with a quickest hedge as fence'. 13th cent.

PLAMPIN see BLAMPHIN.

PLANK: L ME *planke* 'narrow foot-bridge'. 13th cent.

PLANT(E): O OE & OF *plante*, ME *plant*. Metonymic for a gardener. 13th cent.

PLATER, PLATTER: (i) O A deriv. of ME *plate* 'a maker of plate-armour'. 13th cent. (ii) O A deriv. of OF *plaitier* 'to plead', 'a pleader, advocate'. 13th cent.

PLATT(S): L (i) OE *plaet* 'a small patch of land'. (ii) Lancs dial. *plat* 'foot-bridge'. 13th cent.

PLAYER: O OE *plegere* 'player, athlete'. 13th cent.

PLAYFAIR: N OE *plegian-feolaga* 'brisk, active partner', not necessarily at play, and nothing to do with fair play. 13th cent.

PLAYFORD: L OE *pleg-ford* 'the ford where sports are held'. 12th cent.

PLEASANCE: (i) P A woman's name *Plaisance*, from OF *plaisance* 'pleasure, pleasing'. 13th cent. (ii) L From Piacenza (earlier *Placentia*) Italy. 13th cent.

PLENTY: N OF *plente*, an envious nickname for one who had everything in abundance. 13th cent.

PLEW(S), PLEWE(S): L OE *plōh* 'plough (land)'.

PLIMMER see PLUMMER.

PLOWMAN, PLEWMAN: O OE *plōh-mann* 'ploughman'. 13th cent. [A First Fleet (marine) surname].

PLOWRIGHT: O OE *plōh-wyrhta* 'a ploughwright, maker of ploughs'. 13th cent.

PLUCKNETT, PLUNKETT: L OF From Plouquenet (Ille-et-Vilaine) Brittany. 12th cent.

PLUM, PLUMB(E): O OF *plomb* 'lead'. Metonymic for a plumber. 13th cent.

PLUME, PLUMER, PLOMER: (i) L OE *plūme* 'plum (tree)'. (ii) O OF *plume* 'feather', 'a dealer in feathers'. 13th cent.

PLUMMER, PLIMMER: (i) O OF *plummier* 'plumber'. (ii) As in Plume (i). 12th cent.

PLUMLEY: L OE *plūme-lēah* 'the clearing with plum-trees'. (Ches, Hants).

POAD, POAT(E), PODD: N ME *pode* 'toad', a nickname. (Pode of Pode Hall.) 13th cent.

POBJOY see PAPIGAY.

POCKLEY: L OE 'The *lēah* (clearing) of an Anglo-Saxon who appears to have been called *Pohha*', but he may have borne the unrecorded name *Poca*. (Yorks) *Pochelac* in DB.

POCOCK see PEACOCK. POE, POWE see PAW. POEL see POWELL.

PODMORE: L ME *pode* + OE *mōr* 'frog-marsh'. (Staffs), *Podemore* DB, Podimore (Som).

POE see PAW.

POGG(S): P A variant of *Mogg* and a pet-form of *Margaret*. 13th cent. POGSON: P 'Son of *Pogg*'. 13th cent.

POIDEVIN, PORTWIN(E): L OF From Poitou, France. DB.

POINTER, POYNTER: (i) O OF *pointe* 'a maker of points for fastening doublet and hose'. 13th cent. (ii) Late ME 'A pointer of brickwork, roofing tiles'.

POINTON, POYNTON: L OE 'The *tūn* (settlement) of *Pohha's* people'. (Lincs) 12th cent. [Thomas Poynton, an Irish catholic and ex-convict, settled on the Hokiangu, New Zealand, and started business as a timber merchant, 1829].

POLE(S) see PAUL, POOL.

POLGLASE: L Cornish *pol-glās* 'green/blue pool'. 13th cent.

POLKINHORNE: L Cornish *pol-Kynhorn* 'the pool of the iron-chief'.

POLLARD: (i) P A dim. of *Paul*. 13th cent. (ii) N ME *poll* + suffix *-ard*, a nickname for cropped head or bulging head. [R. Pollard arrived in New Zealand on the *Barbara Gordon*, one of the early immigrant ships].

POLLITT: P Gk *Hippolytus*, famous for his virtue and his misfortunes. 12th cent. The surname evolved through *Yppolitus, Ippollitis, Polytes*.

POLLOCK, POLLACK: L A dim. of SG *poll* 'pool'. (Renfrews) Scotland.

POLMEAR: L Cornish *pol-mur* 'the big pool'.

POLSON, POULSON: P 'Son of *Paul*'. 14th cent.

POMEROY, POMERY, POMROY: L OF From La Pommeraye (Calvados) or places of similar name in Normandy. DB.

POMFRET, PONTEFRACT: L Norman French *punt-freit* 'the broken bridge'. (Yorks) 12th cent.

POND: L ME *pond*, from OE *pund* 'enclosure'. 'An artificially banked pool'. The surname is for one who lived by the pond.

PONSONBY: L OF nickname *Puncheon* + ON *býr* '*Puncheon's farm*'. (Cumb) 14th cent.

PONT, PUNT, DUPONT: L OF *pont* 'bridge'. 13th cent.

PONTER, PUNTER: O A deriv. of ME *pont, punt* 'keeper of the bridge'. 13th cent.

POOK(E), POUCK: N OE *pūca* 'elf, goblin', 12th cent. (Kipling, *Puck of Pook's Hill.*)

POOL(E), POLE(S), POLL(E): (i) L OE *pōl* 'pool'. (ii) P Variants of *Paul.* 12th cent. [Pool, a First Fleet (female convict) surname].

POOLEY: L OE *pōl-ēg* 'low-lying land near the pool' or *pōl-haeg* 'the enclosure by the pool'. [Elizabeth Pooley, a convict, brought the name to Australia 1788].

POOR(E), POWER(S): (i) L OF *Pohier* 'a Picard'. The original name appears to have been *Le Poer*. 12th cent. (ii) N OF *povre, poure* 'poor', the opposite of *Plenty*. 13th cent. [Poor and Powers, First Fleet (convict) surnames].

POPE: N OE *pāpa*, ME *pope*, from playing the part of pope in a medieval pageant. 13th cent. [David Pope, a convict, brought the surname to Australia 1788].

POPPETT, POPPITT: N OF *poupette* 'a little baby', an intriguing nickname. *Poppett* was the original form of puppet but the doll worked by strings did not appear until the 16th cent.

POPPLE: L OF *poplier*, from Lat *pōpulus*, producing dial. *popple* 'poplar (tree)'.

POPPLETON: L OE *popel-tūn* 'pebbly farm'. (Yorks).

POPPLEWELL: L OE *popel-welle* 'the pebbly stream'. (Yorks).

PORRETT, PORRITT see PARROTT.

PORT, PORTE: (i) L OF From Port-en-Bessin (Calvados) Normandy. DB. (ii) L OE *port*, OF *porte* 'the castle/town gate'. 12th cent. (iii) L OE *port* (a word of several meanings) 'harbour, market town'. 13th cent.

PORTER(S): (i) O OF *portier* 'door/gate-keeper'. DB. (ii) O OF *porteour* 'burden carrier, porter'. 13th cent. [James Porter, ship's boy on the *Prince of Wales*, brought the name to Australia 1788].

PORTMAN: O OE *portmann* 'townsman', cf. Alderman. 13th cent. (A citizen chosen to administer the affairs of a borough.)

PORTUGAL, PETTENGELL, PETTINGALE, PETTINGELL: L ME *Portingale* 'Portugal', 'a Portugese'. 12th cent.

PORTWIN(E) see POIDEVIN. POSER see POYSER.

POSTLE(S), POSTILL: N OE *apostol* 'apostle', a pageant-name. 12th cent.

POSTLETHWAITE: L ME *apostel-thwaite* (from ON *thveit*) 'the clearing of a man nicknamed *Postle*'. (Cumb) 15th cent.

POTHECARY: O OF *apotecaire*, from Lat *apothēcārius* 'storekeeper'. ME *apotecarie* 'spice/store-keeper'. Later, 'compounder of drugs, apothecary'. 13th cent.

POTT(S): (i) P A dim. of *Philpot* (*Philip*). (ii) O OE *pott*. Metonymic for a maker of pots. (iii) L OE *pott*, used topographically, 'hole or pit'. 13th cent.

POTTER: O OE *pottere* or OF *potier* 'a maker of pots', usually earthenware. 12th cent.

POTTINGER: O OF *potagier* 'a soup/broth maker'. 13th cent.

POULDEN: L OE *pōl-denu* 'the valley with a pool'. (Som) [A First Fleet (marine) surname].

POULSON see POLSON.

POULTER: O OF *pouletier* 'a poultry dealer'. 13th cent.

POULTON: L OE *pōl-tūn* 'the enclosure by a pool'. (Lancs, Ches).

POUND(S), PUND: O OE *pund* 'enclosure', 'keeper of the pound for stray animals'. 13th cent. See also Pindar, Pinfold.

POUNDER: O OE *pounder* 'a maker of weights' or 'an impounder of stray animals'. 12th cent.

POUNTNEY, POULTNEY: L OE 'The *ēg* (island) of an Anglo-Saxon called *Pulta*'. (Leices) 14th cent.

POURIE, POWRIE: L SG From Powrie in Errol, parish of Murroes, Scotland. Henry of *Pourie* was a juror on an inquest at Roxburgh in 1361.

POVEY: N A dial. name for the barn-owl and a nickname for one of puffed-up appearance.

POWDERLEY, POWDERLY: L OE *lēah* + an unrecorded OE word cogn. with Du *polder*. 'The clearing on the reclaimed land'.

POWELL: P Welsh *ap* 'Son of *Howel*'. 13th cent. See also Paul. [A First Fleet (female convict) surname].

POWER see POOR.

POWIS, POWYS: L OW From Powis (North Wales).

POYNTER see POINTER. POYNTON see POINTON. PRATER see PREATER.

PRATT, PRITT: N OE *praett* 'a trick, a stratagem', nickname for a cunning or astute individual. OE Byname 11th cent. [General Thomas Pratt served in the Maori Wars].

PRATTEN: N A dim. of *Pratt.*

PREATER, PRATOR: O Lat *praetor* 'leader, chief', used in the sense of 'reeve' (bailiff, steward, magistrate). 12th cent. [A First Fleet (marine) surname].

PREECE, PREES: P Welsh *ap* 'Son of *Rhys*'. 13th cent. Prees may also be L Welsh *pres, prys* 'brushwood or covert'.

PRENDERGAST, PENDEGAST: A surname of uncertain origin with connections in Pembrokeshire and Berwicks (Scotland). Perhaps of Norman origin. The name has long been established in Ireland as *de Priondragas.* 13th cent.

PRENTICE, PRENTIS: O OF *aprentis* 'apprentice', originally applied to a pupil at a medieval craft, later used as a nickname. 13th cent.

PRESCOT(T), PRISCOTT: O OE *prēost-cot* 'servant at the priest's cottage', sometimes house or manor. 12th cent.

PRESLAND see PRIESTLAND. PRESS see PRIEST.

PRESSICK: L OE *prēost-wīc* 'the priests' dairy farm'. (Ayrs, Bucks, Northumb, Surrey).

PRESSLEY see PRIESTLEY. PREST see PRIEST.

PRESTER: O OF *prestre* 'priest'. 13th cent.

PRESTON: L OE *prēost-tūn* 'the priests' farm'. 12th cent.

PRESTWICH, PRESTAGE, PRESTIDGE: L OE *prēost-wic* 'the priests' outlying farm'. (Lancs) 13th cent.

PRETTY: N OE *praetigg* 'artful, clever, wily', 14th cent., or ME *prety* 'handsome'.

PREW, PROW, PRUE: N OF *prou*, ME *prew, prue* 'valiant'. 13th cent. PREWETT: N A dim. of *Prew* and with the same meaning. 13th cent.

PRICE, PRYCE, PRYSE: (i) P Welsh *ap* 'Son of *Rhys*'. 14th cent. See also Preece. (ii) O OF & ME *pris* 'price'. Metonymic for a setter of market prices. 13th cent. [Price, a First Fleet (convict) surname].

PRICKETT, PRITCHETT, PRITCHATT: N ME *priket* 'pricket', a male fallow-deer in its second year. 13th cent. See also Brocket.

PRIDE, PRYDE: (i) N OW *prid* 'precious, dear' or 'costly'. (ii) N ME *pride* 'pride', a morality-play name in which the virtues were extolled and the vices condemned. The morality plays belong mainly to the 15th cent. and the name was first recorded two centuries earlier. Also a pageant-name. 13th cent.

PRIDEAUX, PRIDAY: L Cornish *prȳ-tyas* 'clay-covered'. *Pridias* in 12th cent. (cf. Welsh *pridd* 'earth, soil'.)

PRIDHAM see PRUDHOMME.

PRIEST, PREIST, PRESS: (i) O *prēost* 'priest'. OE Byname 10th cent. (ii) N A nickname for one of priestly appearance or ironically for one who would never have been admitted to the priesthood.

PRIESTLAND, PRESSLAND: L OE *'prēost-land* 'the priests' land'. (Devon, Surrey) 13th cent.

PRIESTLEY, PRIESTLY, PRESSLEY: L OE *prēost-leah* 'the priests' wood or clearing'. (Beds, Herts, Notts, Wilts, Yorks) 12th cent.

PRIGG(E): N A nickname of uncertain origin. It has been used to denote (i) a tinker or thief, (ii) a haggler (Scottish), (iii) a coxcomb or fop, (iv) a person of excessively precise morals, manners or speech. But it could be a form of ME *prikke*, see Pryke. 12th cent.

PRIME: (i) N OE *prim* 'first', originally the first hour of the ecclesiastical day. (ii) OF *prim, prime* 'fine. delicate'. 13th cent.

PRIMROSE: L Brit *pren-rhos* 'tree of the moor', a Scottish surname from places in Berwicks, Midlothian and Fifes. Not recorded until 15th cent., *Primrose* was a surname in 13th cent., perhaps from the woodland flower, ME & OF *primerole*, from Lat *primula.*

PRINCE, PRINS: N Lat *princeps* 'chief, leader', OF *prince* 'prince', a pageant-name. 12th cent.

PRINGLE: L ON 'The *gil* (ravine) of a Norseman called *Pin*'. (Selkirks) Scotland.

PRIOR, PRIER, PRYER, PRYOR: O OE *prior*, OF *priur* 'prior' (officer of religious house next to abbot). Originally a surname of office. As with priest, later a nickname. 12th cent. [A First Fleet (convict) surname].

PRISCOTT see PRESCOTT.

PRITCHARD, PRICHARD: P Welsh *ap* 'Son of *Richard*'. 16th cent. [A First Fleet (convict) surname].

PRITT see PRATT.

PROBERT, PROPERT: P Welsh *ap* 'Son of *Robert*'. 16th cent.

PROBIN, PROBYN: P Welsh *ap/ab* 'Son of *Robin*'. 16th cent. Also Brobyn.

PROCTER, PROCTOR, PROCKTER: O Lat *procurator*, ME *proketour* 'an attorney in a spiritual court'. 13th cent. [James Proctor, a seaman on the *Sirius*, brought the surname to Australia 1788].

PROPHET, PROFFITT: N OF *prophete* 'prophet, soothsayer', a nickname for one who had played the part in a medieval mystery play. 13th cent.

PROSSER: P Welsh *ap* 'Son of *Rosser* (*Rodger*)'.

PROTHERO(E), PRYDDERCH: P Welsh *ap* 'Son of *Rhydderch*'. 16th cent.

PROUD(E): N OE *prūt, prūd* 'proud, arrogant'. OE Byname 11th cent.

PROUDFOOT: N OE *prūd-fōt* 'proud foot', a nickname for one who walked with a haughty step. 12th cent.

PROUDLOCK: L OE *prūd-loca* 'the stronghold of an Anglo-Saxon called *Prūd* (Proud)'.

PROUDMAN: O 'Servant of *Proud*'. 14th cent.

PROUST: O ME *prevost* 'provost'. 13th cent.

PROVOST, PROVEST, PROVIS: O OE *prafost* 'provost (head of a religious chapter)'. 12th cent.

PROWSE, PROUSE: N OF & ME *prouse* 'strong, valiant'. 13th cent.

PRUDENCE: P Lat *prudentia* 'prudence', a woman's name. 13th cent.

PRUDHOMME, PRIDHAM: N OF *prudhomme* 'an honest, upright man', 'a good man and true'. Used of a knight or freeholder summoned to serve on the jury or on the king's council. 12th cent.

PRUE see PREW.

PRUNTY, PRONTY, BRÖNTE: P Ir *O Proinutigh* 'bestower, generous person'. An Ulster surname. The variant *Brönte*, assumed by the father of the famous authoress, is better known than the original surname.

PRYCE see PRICE. PRYDE see PRIDE. PRYER, PRYOR see PRIOR.

PRYKE: O ME *prike, prikke* 'a point'. Metonymic for a maker of pointed instruments or weapons, e.g., lances, spears. 13th cent.

PRYOR see PRIOR.

PUCKLE, PUCKELL' N OE *pūcel* 'little elf, goblin' or L 'the goblin hollow'. 13th cent.

PUCKERIDGE: L OE *pūca-ric* 'the goblin's stream'. (Herts).

PUDSEY: L OE 'The *īeg* (island or river-land) of an Anglo-Saxon nicknamed *Pudoc* (wen, wart)'. (Yorks).

PUGH(E), PEW: P Welsh *ap* 'Son of *Hugh*'. 16th cent. [Edward Pugh, a convict, brought the surname to Australia 1788].

PUGSLEY: L OE 'The *lēah* (clearing) of an Anglo-Saxon called *Pocg*'. (Devon).

PULFORD: L OE *pōl-ford* 'the ford by a pool'. (Ches) PULHAM: L OE *pōl-ham* 'the homestead by a pool'. (Dorset).

PULLAN, PULLEN, PULLIN: N OF *pullian* 'colt', 'lively, untamed'. 12th cent.

PULLAR, PULLER: (i) N OE *pullian-hara* 'pull-hare', a nickname for a hare-catcher. 12th cent. (ii) L OE *pull-ōra* 'pool or creek bank'. 14th cent.

PULLINGER see BULLINGER.

PULMAN, PULLMAN: L OE *pull-mann* 'pool' + 'man'. 16th cent.

PUMFREY, PUMPHREY: P Welsh *ap* 'Son of *Humphrey*'. 16th cent.

PUNCH: P OF *ponz, ponce*, ONF *ponch*, from Lat *Pontius* 'the man from Pontus in Asia Minor'. The reference is to a saint *Pontius* whose cult gathered many adherents in the Middle Ages and popularised the name. The name is also for a dandy much concerned with his points and as such a nickname (see Pointer). 12th cent.

PUNCHARD: P ONF *Ponchard*, a dim. of OF *Ponce*. 13th cent.

PUNCHEON: N OF *poinçon* 'awl, punch', a nickname of obscure meaning. 12th cent.

PUND see POUND.

PUNSHON: P A dim. of OF *Ponce*. 12th cent. See also Punch.

PUNT see PONT. PUNTER see PONTER.

PURCELL: N OF *pourcel* 'piglet'. 12th cent.

PURCHAS(E), PURCHES(E), PURKISS: O OF *purchas* 'pursuit, hunting, chase, pillage'. Curiously, this became an occupational name for a messenger/courier. 12th cent.

PURDAY, PURDEY, PURDIE, PURDY(E), PURDU(E): N OF *pour Dieu* 'for God's sake', an oath-name for one who was constantly uttering it. 13th cent.

PURNELL see PARNELL.

PURSE, PURSER: O OE *purs* 'a purse, pouch-maker'. 12th cent.

PURSEY see PERCY.

PURVIS, PURVES: O AF *purveier* 'to

provide'. 'a purveyor to a large household'. 13th cent.

PUSEY see PIZEY. PUTMAN see PITMAN.

PUTNAM: L OE 'The *hām* (homestead) of an Anglo-Saxon called *Putta*'. (Herts) 13th cent.

PUTT see PITT.

PUTTOCK, PUTTICK: N OE *puttoc* 'kite (the bird)', 'greedy'. OE Byname 11th cent. Also DB.

PYATT, PYETT: N A dim. of OF *pye* 'magpie'. 13th cent.

PYE see PIE. PYKE see PIKE. PYLE see PILE. PYM(M) see PIMM.

PYMONT: L OF From Pimont (Manche) Normandy and Seine Inférieure.

PYNE see PINE. PYPER see PIPER.

Q

QUADLING see CODLIN.

QUAIF(E): O OF *coif*. Metonymic for a *coifier*, maker of *coifs* (close-fitting cap covering skull and back and sides of head). 12th cent.

QUAINTON: L OE *Cwēne-tūn* 'the Queen's manor'. (Berks), *Chentone* DB.

QUALTER, QUALTROUGH: P Manx form of *Mc Walter*. 15th cent.

QUANT: N OF *quoint*, ME *quante* 'clever, smart, crafty'. 13th cent.

QUANTICK, QUANTOCK: L Brit *Cantuc*, name of a range of hills. (Som).

QUANTRILL, QUINTRELL: N OF *cointerel* 'a fop, beau, dandy'. 12th cent.

QUARMBY, WHARMBY: L ON *kvern-býr*, (ON *kvern* corresponds with OE *cweorn quern*, hand-mill). 'The farm with a quern'. (Yorks), *Cornebi* DB.

QUARRELL: O OF *quarrel* 'a square-headed bolt (arrow) for cross-bolt or arbalest'. Metonymic for a maker of bolts or for an arbalester. 12th cent.

QUARRIE, QUARRY: (i) P A Manx form of *Macquarrie*. 14th cent. (ii) O OF *quarrere* 'quarry'. Metonymic for a quarrier. 13th cent.

QUARTERMAIN(E): N AF *quatremayns* 'four-hands', a nickname for a mail-fisted warrior. 12th cent.

QUAYLE, QUAIL: (i) P Manx form of *Mc Fail*. 16th cent. (ii) N OF *quaille* 'quail', 'amorous but timid', from supposed characteristics of the bird. 14th cent.

QUEEN: N OE *cwēn* 'queen', a pageant-name.

QUENNELL, QUINNELL: P OE *Cwēnhild* 'woman-war'. DB.

QUICK(E): (i) L OE *cwic* (*bēam* or *trēo*) 'aspen or poplar (tree)'. 11th cent. (ii) P OE *cwic* 'alive, brisk, nimble'. 13th cent.

QUICKLEY: N OE *cwiclīc*, ME *quiklich* 'nimbly, quickly, in a lively fashion'. 13th cent. Mistress *Quickly* was hostess of a tavern in Eastcheap, London, in Shakespeare's *King Henry IV, Part II*.

QUIGG: P Ir *O Cuaig*, a Co. Derry sept.

QUIGLEY: N Ir *O Coigligh* 'descendant of Unkempt'.

QUILL: P Ir *O Cuill*, from *cuill* 'hazel'.

QUILLIAM: P Manx form of *Mc William*.

QUILTER: O A deriv. of OF *cuilte*, 'a maker of quilts', a name also long established in Co. Kerry, Ireland. 12th cent.

QUILTY: P Ir *O Caoilte*, from *caoile* 'slender'. Co. Limerick.

QUIN(N): P Ir *Mc Quinn, O Quinn*, from *conn* 'counsel'. Also Manx. 11th cent.

QUINCY, QUINCEY, QUINSEY: L OF From Cuinchy (Pas-de-Calais) or other places of similar name in France. 12th cent.

QUINLAN: P Ir *O Caoinleain*. The Munster sept of this name claims to descend from *Laoghaire*, King of Ireland.

QUINNEY: P Manx 'Son of *Connaidh* the crafty' 15th cent.

QUINTON: (i) P Lat *Quintinus* 'fifth born', a popular name in France, introduced into England by the Normans. DB. (ii) L OE *Cwēn-tūn* 'the Queen's manor' (Glos, Northants, Worces) 12th cent. See also Quainton. (iii) L OF From St Quentin (Manche) Normandy, enshrining the name of St *Quentin* of Amiens. DB.

QUINTRELL see QUANTRELL.

QUIRK(E): P Manx form of *Mc Cuirc* 'son of *Corc* (heart)'.

QUIXLEY: L OE 'The *lēah* (clearing) of an Anglo-Saxon called *Cwīc*'. (Yorks).

QUODLING see CODLIN.

R

RABBATT(S), RABBITT(S): (i) P OG *Rabbodo* 'counsel-messenger'. DB. (ii) P A dim. of *Robert.* 13th cent.

RABONE see RAWBONE.

RABY: L O Scand *rā-bý* 'the homestead by the boundary mark'. (Ches, Durham).

RACKHAM: L OE *hreac-ham* '(hay) rick homestead', 'the homestead near a hayrick'.

RACKSTRAW, RAXSTRAW: N OE *raca* 'rake' + *strēaw* 'rake-straw', 'heap up every trifle', nickname for a miser.

RADBONE see RATHBONE.

RADBURN, RADBONE: L OE *hrēod-burna* 'the stream where reeds grow'. 12th cent.

RADCLIFF(E), RATCLIFF(E): L OE *rēade-clif* 'the red cliff'. (Bucks, Devon, Leices, Lancs, Warwicks) 12th cent.

RADFORD, REDFORD, RETFORD: L OE *hrēod-ford* 'the reedy ford'. 13th cent. [A First Fleet (marine) surname].

RADLEY: L OE *rēade-lēah* 'the red clearing'. (Berks, Devon) 12th cent.

RADNAGE, RADNEDGE, RADNIDGE: L OE *rēadan-āc* 'the red oak'. (Bucks).

RADSTONE: L OE *rōd-stān* 'the rood stone (a cross)'. (Northants).

RADWELL, REDDALL, REDDELL: L OE *rēade-wielle* 'the red spring or stream'. (Herts) 12th cent.

RAE: N A Scottish form of *Roe.* 13th cent.

RAFE, RAFF see RALF.

RAFFERTY: P Ir *O Raithbheartaigh* 'prosperity-wielder'.

RAFFLES: N A dim. of *Raff* (*Ralph*). In medieval England a game of chance played with three dice (OF *rafle*) may have contributed a nickname for a gambler.

RAFTER: P Ir *O Reachtabhair*, from *reacht* 'decree'. A Kilkenny sept.

RAFTERY: P Ir *O Reachtaire*, with the same meaning as *Rafter.* A Connacht sept.

RAGG see WRAGG.

RAIN(E), RAINES, RAYNE: (i) P OF *Reine*, from Lat *Regina*, a pers. name. 12th cent. (ii) L SG From Rayne (Aberdeens) Scotland. (iii) N OF *raine*, a nickname from the frog. [Thomas Raine, in partnership with David Ramsay and Gordon Brown, set up a flax and timber trading depot at Horeke on Hokianga Harbour, 1827].

RAINBIRD: P OG *Raginbert*, OF *Rainbert* 'mighty-guardian'. DB.

RAINBOW, RAYBOULD, RIMBAULT: P OG *Raginbald*, OF *Rainbaut* 'might-bold'. DB.

RAINER see RAYNER.

RAINEY, RAINNIE, RENNIE, RENNY: P Scottish pet-forms of *Reynold.* 15th cent. In Ireland *McRaighne, O Raighney.* See also Reaney.

RAINFORD: L OE *'Regna's ford'*. (Lancs) (*Regna*, an OE pers. name.)

RAINGER see RINGER.

RAKE: L OE *hrace* 'throat', used in the sense of 'pass'. (Sussex) 13th cent.

RALEIGH, RALLEY, RAWLEY: L OE *rēada-lēah* 'the red clearing'. (Devon, Essex) 12th cent.

RALF(E), RALPH(S), RALLS, RAFE, RAFF, RAW(E), RAWLE(S): P OG *Radulf*, Norman *Raulf.* DB.

RALLING, RALLIS see RAWLIN.

RAM, RAMM: N OE *ramm*, a nickname from the ram. 12th cent.

RAMAGE: N OF *ramage*, a hawking term 'living in the branches'. As a nickname, 'wild'. 13th cent.

RAMSAY, RAMSEY: L OE *hramsa-ēg* 'wild garlic island'. (Essex, Hunts) OE Byname 11th cent. In the 12th cent. Simund *de Ramesie* left the Hunts place and went to live in Scotland, hence the Scottish Ramsays. [A First Fleet (convict) surname. David Ramsay and his partners Gordon Brown and Thomas Raine established a flax and timber trading business at Horeke on Hokianga Harbour, New Zealand, 1827].

RAMSBOTTOM: L OE *hramsa-botm* 'wild garlic valley'. (Lancs) 12th cent.

RAMSDEN: L OE *hramsa-denu* 'wild garlic valley'. (Essex) 12th cent.

RAMSHAW see RAVENSHAW.

RAND(S), RANCE: L OE *rand* 'brink, edge'., river-bank or edge of a dyke or embankment. (Lincs, Yorks) 12th cent. Also P A pet-form of *Randolph.*

RANDALL, RANDELL, RANDLE(S): P A dim. of *Rand* (*Randolph*). 12th cent. [The surname was brought to Australia by John Randall, a negro convict, who arrived with the First Fleet 1788].

RANDOLPH: P ON *Rannulfr* 'shield-wolf', introduced into England by the Normans. 11th cent. Perhaps also from OG *Rannulf* 'raven-wolf'. 12th cent.

RANGER: O OF & ME *ranger* 'gamekeeper'.

RANK: N OF & ME *ranc* 'strong, proud'. 14th cent.

RANKIN, RANKEN: P A dim. of names in *Rand*, e.g., *Randulf*.

RANSLEY see RAWNSLEY.

RANSON, RANSOM(E): P 'Son of *Rand* (*Randolph*)'. 14th cent. [A First Fleet (crew) surname].

RAPER see ROPER. RASH, RASCH see ASH.

RASHLEIGH: L OE *aesc-lēah* 'ash glade' (Devon) 13th cent.

RATCLIFF see RADCLIFF.

RATH: L Ir One of the rare Irish locality names, from a place in Louth.

RATHBONE, RADBONE: L Celtic *rath* 'circular fort', *rath-ban* 'the white fort'.

RATTENBURY: L OE *rēada-burg* 'the red fort'.

RATTIGAN: P Ir *O Reachtagáin*, from *reacht* with the same meaning as *Rafter*.

RATTRAY: L Celtic (Brit or SG) from *rath* 'a circular fort' (Perths) Scotland.

RAVEN(S): P OE *Hraefn* or ON *Hrafn* a pers. name from the bird, popularly regarded as rapacious. DB.

RAVENSCROFT: L OE 'The *croft* (small holding of land) of an Anglo-Saxon called *Hraefn*'. (Ches).

RAVENSHAW, RAMSHAW, RANSHAW, RONSHAW, RENSHAW: L OE *hraefn-sceaga* (dial. *shaw*) 'the raven-wood'. (Derbys, Warwicks) 14th cent.

RAWBONE, RABONE: N ON *rá-bein* 'roe-bone', nickname for a fast runner, 'swift as a roe'. 13th cent.

RAWCLIFF(E), ROCKCLIFFE, ROWCLIFF: L O Scand *rauthr* + OE *clif* 'red cliff'. (Cumb, Devon, Lancs, Yorks) 12th cent.

RAWLE(S), RAW(E) see RALF. RAWLEY see RALEIGH.

RAWLIN(S), RAWLING(S), RALLING, RALLIS: P A dim. of *Ralf* (*Ralph*). 13th cent.

RAWNSLEY, RANSLEY: L OE 'The *lēah* (clearing) of an Anglo-Saxon called *Hraefn* (*Raven*)'. (A lost place in Yorks.) 14th cent.

RAWSON: P 'Son of *Ralf* (*Ralph*)'. 14th cent. [Isabella Rawson, a convict and a former school mistress, brought the surname to Australia 1788].

RAWSTHORN(E), RAWSTRON, ROSTEN, ROSSON, ROSTRON: L ON 'The thorn-bush of a Norseman called *Rauth* (*Red*)'. (Ches) 13th cent.

RAY(E), REY, LE ROY: N OF *rei* 'king', from acting the part in a medieval play or pageant or a mocking nickname for an excessively proud individual. 13th cent. See also Rea.

RAYBOULD see RAINBOW.

RAYMOND, RAYMONT, RAYMENT: P OG *Raginmund*, OF *Raimund* 'counsel, might-protection'. 12th cent. [Raymond, a First Fleet (convict) surname].

RAYNE see RAIN.

RAYNER, RAYNOR, RAINER, REINER, REYNA, RENNER: P OG *Raginhari*, OF *Rainer, Renier* 'counsel, might-army'. DB.

REA, REE, RAY(E), REY, REAY, RYE: L OE *ēa* 'water/stream' or *ēg, īeg* 'island or dry land in a fen'. The initial R appears in ME *at ther ie, atte rie*. 13th cent. See also Rey, Rye.

REACE see RHYS.

READ(E), REED, RED(D), REID: (i) N OE *rēad* 'red' of hair or complexion. OE Byname 11th cent. Reid is the Scottish form. (ii) L OE *rēod, rīed, rȳd* 'a clearing' or *hrēod* 'reed (bed)'. 13th cent. (An ancient runic inscription on the Rök stone at Östergötland, Sweden, records *Reid* as a tribal name. Translation: 'This I tell who nine generations ago . . . with the Reidgoths . . . Theodric the bold, king of the sea-warriors, ruled over Reid sea shores'. This suggests the possibility that *Reid* was introduced into Scotland by the Vikings, a form unrelated to the OE name.) [Reed, a First Fleet (convict) surname, and Reid (a crew) surname. Gabriel Read was the first to find a rich seam of gold at Otago, New Zealand, 1861].

READER, REDER, REEDER: O ME A deriv. of *redyn* 'to thatch with reed', 'a thatcher'. 13th cent. See also Thatcher.

READETT, RIDDETT: L OE *hrēodet* 'reed bed'. 13th cent.

READING, REDDING, REDDIN, RIDDING, RIDING, RYDING: L OE 'The *ingas* (people) of an Anglo-Saxon called *Rēada* (Red)'. (County town of Berks.) 13th cent.

READMAN, REEDMAN, REDMAN: O OE *hrēod-mann* 'a cutter of reeds'. 13th cent. [John Redman, a marine, his wife Elizabeth, and a son James, brought the surname to Australia 1788].

READWIN, REDWIN: P OE *Raedwine* 'counsel-friend'. 12th cent.

READY, READDIE, READDY, REDDIE,

REDDY, REEDY, REIDY: (i) N OE *raede* 'ready, prompt'. 13th cent. (ii) P Ir *O Riada*, from *riad* 'spirited'.

REAGAN, REGAN, O'REGAN: P Ir *O Riagain*, the name of three septs, Leix (one of the 'Tribes of Tara'), Thomond (akin to *Brian Boru*), the third akin to the *McCarthys*.

REANEY, RAINEY, RENNIE: P Ir *MacRaighne*, from *Reginald*. (West Meath) P.H. Reaney (see Bibliography) identifies his own surname with a minor place in Sheffield, Yorks.

REARDON, RIORDAN: P Ir *O Rioghbhardain* 'descendant of royal bard'.

REAVELL see REVEL. RED see READ. REDDALL see RADWELL.

REDFERN: L OE *rēad-fearn* 'red fern'. A Lancs surname.

REDFORD see RADFORD.

REDGRAVE: L OE *hrēod-graef* 'the reedy ditch'. (Suffolk).

REDHEAD, READHEAD: N OE *rēad-hēafod* 'red head (hair)'. 13th cent.

REDMOND: (i) P Ir *Reamonn*, a Hiberno-Norman surname. (ii) P Ir *McReamoinn*, a Connacht branch of the *Burkes*. [A First Fleet (marine) surname].

REE see REA. REECE, REES see RHYS. REED see READ. REEDER see READER.

REESON: O 'Son of the reeve'. 13th cent.

REEVE: O OE *rēfa* 'reeve' (steward, bailiff). 13th cent.

REEVES: O OE 'The reeve's servant'. 13th cent.

REID see READ.

REILLY, O'REILLY: P Ir *O Raghailligh*, an east Breffny sept, its ancient ancestral lands in Co. Cavan. [A First Fleet (marine) surname].

REINER see RAYNER.

REITH: N A Scottish surname from Brit or OW *rheitheg* 'rhetoric', 'an orator, preacher'.

RELF(E), RELPH: P OG *Ricwulf*, OF *Riulf* 'power-wolf', introduced into England by the Normans but not recorded until 12th cent.

REMINGTON: L OE *Rima* or *Riming*, a river-name. 'The *tūn* (farm) on the R. *Riming*'. (Rimington, Yorks), *Renitone* DB.

REMFREY, REMFRY, RENFREE: P OG *Rainfrid* 'might-peace'. DB.

RENAUD see REYNOLD.

RENDELL: P A pet-form of names in *Rand-*, preserved in Rendlesham, Suffolk. See also Randall.

RENGGER see RINGER. RENNARD see REYNARD. RENNELL see REYNOLD.

RENNER: O ME A deriv. of *rennen* 'to run', 'a messenger, courier'. 12th cent. See also Rayner.

RENNIE see RAINEY, REANEY. RENSHAW see RAVENSHAW.

RENTON: L OE 'The *tūn* (farm) of *Regna's* people'. (Berwicks), *Regninton* c.1100.

RENWICK: L OE 'The *wīc* (outlying farm) of an Anglo-Saxon called *Hraefn* (Raven)'. (Cumb).

RETFORD see RADFORD.

RETTER: (i) O OE *ret* 'to soak', *rettery* 'place where flax is retted', 'a retter of flax'. (ii) O OF *retier* 'a maker of fishing-nets'. 13th cent.

REVEL(L), REVILL(E), REAVELL: N OF *revel* 'revelry, rebellion', *reveler* 'to rebel', also 'to make tumult'. Nickname for a boisterous merrymaker. 12th cent.

REW, RUE: L OE *raew*, ME *rew* 'row (of houses, cottages)'. 13th cent.

REX: N Lat *Rex*, the reigning king, a pageant name.

REY see RAY, REA.

REYNARD, RENNARD: P OG *Raginhard*, OF *Reinart* 'counsel-brave'. DB. Introduced into England by the Normans.

REYNOLD(S), REYNELL, RENAUD, RENNELL: P OG *Raginald*, OF *Reinald* 'counsel-might'. DB. Both the OG and OF forms were introduced into England by the Normans. [A First Fleet (marine) surname].

RHODES, RHOADES, ROAD(S), ROYDS: L OE *rod* 'clearing'. 13th cent. The Gk island and its knights influenced the surname, hence the intrusive -H-. [William Barnard Rhodes transported forty head of cattle from Sydney to stock the first cattle station on New Zealand's South Island at Akaroa, 1839].

RHYS, REACE, REECE, REES(E), RICE: P OW *rīs*, Welsh *rhys* 'fiery', the name of a Welsh king. DB. [Rice, a First Fleet (convict and marine) surname].

RICH, RICHES, RITCH: (i) N OF & ME *riche* 'rich'; also OE *rīce* 'powerful, noble, mighty, rich'. (ii) P A dim. of *Richard*. (iii) L OE *ric* 'stream', sometimes becoming 'reach' in place-names. Surname 12th cent.

RICHARD(S), RITCHARD, RICARD, RICKARD(S), RICKART, RICKET,

RICKETT(S): P OG *Ric(h)ard*, Anglo-Norman *Ricard* 'powerful-brave'. DB. One of the most popular names introduced into England by the Normans. RICHARDSON: P 'Son of *Richard*'. 14th cent. [Eight persons named Richards, and three named Richardson, arrived with the First Fleet 1788. Of these three were marines and eight were convicts].

RICHER, RICKER(S): P OG *Richer*, OF *Richier, Ricier* 'power-army'. DB. A surname largely absorbed by *Richard*.

RICHEY, RICHIE see RITCHIE.

RICHMOND: L OF From Richemont ('splendid hill'), various places in France, or from Richmond (Yorks), named from one of the French places. Richmond, Surrey is too late to have influenced the surname. 12th cent.

RICK(S), RIX: (i) P A pet-form of *Ricard* (*Richard*). 13th cent. (ii) L West Saxon *rixe*, a metathesised form of OE *risc* 'rush', also *risc* in west country dial. 'Dweller by the rushes'. 13th cent.

RICKSTON: L OE *ric-tun* 'the farm with a stream or ditch'. [A First Fleet (convict) surname].

RICKWARD, RICKWOOD: P OG *Ricwald* 'powerful-guardian'. 12th cent.

RIDAL, RIDDELL: L OE *ryge-dael* 'the valley where rye is grown'. (Westmorland, Yorks). 12th cent. Riddell may also have an ecclesiastical meaning from OF *ridel* ME *riddel* 'altar-curtain'. [John Riddel, a seaman on the *Charlotte*, arrived 1788].

RIDDETT see READETT. RIDDING see READING.

RIDE, RYDE: L OE *rīed, rȳd* 'the clearing'. 12th cent. See also Read (ii).

RIDER, RYDER: O OE *rīdere* 'rider', 'a mounted soldier, messenger, courier'. Also a mounted forest officer, one of whose duties was to lead the king in hunting. 12th cent.

RIDGE: L OE *hrycg* 'the ridge'. 12th cent. RIDGEWAY, RIDGWAY: L OE *hrycg-weg* 'the ridge way (road or path)'. 12th cent.

RIDGEWELL, RIDGWELL: L OE *hrēod-wielle* 'the reedy stream'. (Essex) 13th cent.

RIDLEY: L OE *rydde-lēah* 'the clearing, cleared land', or *hrēod-lēah* 'the reedy clearing'. (Ches, Essex, Kent, Northumb) 13th cent.

RIGBY: L ON *hryggr-býr* 'the farm on the ridge'. 12th cent. Rigbey is a variant form.

RIGDEN: With all the appearance of a L name, this is in fact P a double dim. of *Ricard* (*Richard*), originally *Ricdun*. 14th cent.

RIGG(S), RIGGE: L ON *hryggr* 'ridge'. 12th cent.

RIGNEY: P Ir *O Raigne*, a variant of *O Raighne* (*Rainey*).

RILEY, RYLEY: L OE *ryge-lēah* 'the rye clearing'. (Lancs) 13th cent. In Ireland sometimes used as a variant of *Reilly*.

RIMBAULT see RAINBOW.

RIMER, RIMMER, RYMER: O AF *rimour, rymour* and a deriv. of ME *rimen* 'to *rime* (rhyme)', 'a *rimer*, poet'. 13th cent. See also Doggrell. [Joseph Rimmer, a seaman on the *Charlotte*, brought the surname to Australia 1788].

RING(E): O OE *hring*. Metonymic for a maker of rings, either jewellery or for chain mail. 12th cent.

RINGER: O OE A deriv. of *hringan* 'to ring', 'a bell-ringer'. 13th cent.

RINGER, RENGGER, RAINGER: P OG *Reginger*, OF *Rainger* 'counsel-spear'. 12th cent. (Richard *Renger*, alderman, was mayor of London 1221.)

RINGROSE: N OE *hring-rōse*, a 13th cent. nickname of lost meaning.

RIORDAN see REARDON.

RIPLEY: L OE *ripel-lēah* 'the strip clearing' (Derbys, Hants, Surrey, Yorks) 12th cent.

RIPON, RIPPON: L OE 'The Anglian *Hrype* tribe'. (Yorks).

RIPPINGALE: L OE 'The *halh* (remote valley) of the *ingas* (people) of an Anglo-Saxon called *Hrep*'. (Lincs).

RISBY: L O Scand *hris-býr* 'the farm in the brushwood'. (Lincs, Suffolk, Yorks). [Edward Risby, a convict, brought the surname to Australia 1788].

RITCHIE, RICHEY, RICHIE(S): P Scottish dim. of *Rich* (Richard). 16th cent.

RIVERS: L OF From La Rivière (France). DB.

RIVETT: O OF & ME *rivet* 'a small bolt'. Metonymic for a rivetter or metal-worker. 14th cent.

RIXON: P 'Son of *Rick*', a dim. of *Richard*. 15th cent.

ROACH, ROCH, ROCHE: L OF From Les Roches (Seine Maritime) France. DB. Some may be from Roche (Cornwall), from OF *roche* 'rock', *la Roche* in 1233. In Ireland, a Hibernicised Norman name *de Róiste*, originally established in Munster and

Wexford. [Roach, a First Fleet (crew and convict) surname].

ROAD(S) see RHODES.

ROADNIGHT: O OE *rādcniht* 'road knight', 'a mounted servant or retainer'. 13th cent.

ROAKE see ROKE.

ROAN, RONE: L OF From Rouen (Normandy). 12th cent.

ROBB(S), ROBE: P A dim. of *Robert*. 12th cent.

ROBBERDS see ROBERT.

ROBBIE: P A Scottish dim. of *Robb*, a dim. of *Robert*. 16th cent.

ROBBINS, ROBENS see ROBINS.

ROBERT(S), ROBART(S), ROBBERDS: P OG *Rodbert*, OF *Robert* 'fame-bright'. DB. Introduced into England by the Normans during the reign of Edward the Confessor. [Five persons named Roberts arrived with the First Fleet, three convicts and two marines].

ROBERTSON, ROBERSON: P 'Son of *Robert*'. 14th cent. [A First Fleet (convict) surname].

ROBEY: (i) P A variant of *Robbie*. (ii) L O Scand *rā-by* 'the farm at the boundary mark'. (Durham), *Raby* in 14th cent.

ROBIN(S), ROBYNS, ROBBINS, ROBENS: P Dims. of *Rob*, a pet-form of *Robert*. 12th cent.

ROBINSON, ROBISON: P 'Son of *Robin*'. 14th cent. [Six persons named Robinson arrived with the First Fleet, four convicts and two crew members].

ROBOTHAM see ROWBOTHAM.

ROBSON: P 'Son of *Rob* (*Robert*)'. 14th cent.

ROBY: L OE Identical in meaning with Robey (ii). (Lancs).

ROCHE see ROACH.

ROCHELLE, ROCKALL, ROCKELL: L OF From La Rochelle (France). 12th cent.

ROCHER: L OF *roche* 'by the rock'.

ROCHESTER: L Recorded by Bede c. 730 as *Hrofaescaestre* 'the Roman fort *Hrofi*', a clipped form of the Brit name *Durobrivis* 'the bridges of the stronghold'. The DB form is *Rouecestra*, (Kent). Rochester (Northumb) may also have contributed to the surname.

ROCHFORD: L OE *raecces-ford* 'the ford of the hunting dog'. (Essex, Worces) 12th cent.

ROCK(S) see ROKE. ROCKCLIFF(E) see RAWCLIFF.

RODD: L OE *rod*, dial. *royd* 'a clearing in the forest'. (Herefords).

RODDEN, RODEN: P Ir *O Rodáin*, from *rod* 'strong'. A Donegal surname. In England, OE *rā-denu* 'the roe-bucks' valley'. (Som).

RODERICK: P OG *Hrōdrīc* 'fame-powerful'. Introduced into England by the Normans.

RODNEY: L OE 'The *ēg* (island or dry land in a fen) of an Anglo-Saxon called *Hroda*'. (Som) 13th cent.

ROE: N OE *rā*, ME *rō* 'roe-deer', a nickname for a swift runner. 11th cent. See also Rae, Rea.

ROEBUCK: N OE *rā-bucc* 'roe-buck', with the same meaning as *Roe*. 13th cent.

ROFFEY: L OE *rāhhege* 'deer-fence, enclosure for roe-deer'. (Sussex) 13th cent.

ROGAN: P Ir *O Ruadhagain*, from *ruadh* 'red' An Oriel sept.

ROGER(S), RODGER(S): P OG *Rodger*, OF *Roger*, *Rogier* 'fame-spear'. DB. Introduced into England by the Normans. Rodgers is the Scottish form. ROGERSON: P 'Son of *Roger*' 14th cent. [Rogers, a First Fleet (convict and marine) surname].

ROHAN: L OF From Rohan (Morbihan) Brittany. 12th cent.

ROKE, ROAKE, ROCK(E), ROCKS, ROOK(E): L These surnames all derive from OE *āc* 'oak', the short vowel in ME sometimes producing the 'Rock' form. ME *atter oke*, *atte roke* 'at the oak'. 12th cent.

ROLAND, ROLANCE see ROWLAND.

ROLF(E), ROLPH, ROLES, ROLLO, ROLL(E), ROLLES, ROFF(E), ROFE, ROLLS, ROW(E), ROWES, ROWLES, RUFF, RULE: P An O Scand name O Dan, O Sw *Rolf*, ON *Hrólfr*, frequent in the Danelaw. Also introduced into England by the Normans in the Lat form *Rollo*, which developed a number of variants. DB. Some of these surnames occur from other sources, e.g., Row.

ROLLAND, ROLLANS see ROWLAND.

ROLLER: O OF & ME *rolle* 'a roll or piece of parchment', 'a maker/seller of parchment/vellum'. (Parchment from sheep or goat skin, vellum from calf skin.)

ROLLESTON, ROLLSTON, ROLSTON, ROULSTON, ROWLSTON(E): L ON 'The *tūn* (farm) of a Norseman called *Hrolfr*'. (Leices, Notts, Staffs, Wilts, Yorks) 12th cent.

ROLLIN, ROLLING(S), ROLLINS, ROLIN, ROLING: P Dims. of *Roll* (*Rolf*). 12th cent.

ROLLINSON, ROLLASON, ROLLISON, ROLINSON: P 'Son of *Roland*'. 16th cent.

ROLT: P ON *Hroaldr*. DB. (A First Fleet (female convict) surname].

ROMAIN, ROMAN(S): L OF *Romeyn* 'a Roman'. 13th cent. [A First Fleet (convict) surname].

ROME, ROOM(E): L ME 'A pilgrim from Rome', as in Romer. 13th cent. Still pronounced 'Room' in Shakespeare's time.

ROMER, ROOMER, RUMMER: L ME *romere* 'a returned pilgrim from Rome'. Perhaps also L OF from Roumare (Seine Inférieure) France. 12th cent.

ROMNEY: L OE *rūm-ēa* 'spacious river'. (Kent) DB.

RONALD(S): P A Scottish form of *Reynold*. 15th cent.

RONSON see ROWNSON. ROOBOTTOM see ROWBOTTOM.

ROOK(E), ROOKES, ROOKS, RUCK: N OE *hrōc* 'rook', a nickname from the bird, perhaps for one of gregarious nature, or with a raucous voice. Other meanings have occurred at various periods including 'sharper' and 'simpleton'. 12th cent. See also Roke.

ROONEY: P Ir *O Ruanaidh*, a Co. Down surname. Sometimes an abbreviation of Mulrooney.

ROOT, ROOTES, ROOTS: (i) N OE *rōt* 'glad, cheerful, bright'. OE Byname 10th cent. (ii) O ME *rōte* 'psaltery', 'a player on the rote or psaltery'. See also Rutter.

ROPE, ROOPE, RUPP: O OE Metonymic for *Roper*. 14th cent. [A First Fleet (convict) surname]. ROPER, RAPER, RAPIER: O OE A deriv. of *rāp* 'rope', 'a roper', maker of rope. 13th cent. [George Raper, a midshipman on the *Sirius*, brought the surname to Australia 1788. He recorded the flora and fauna of Norfolk Island in watercolours and drew several species of birds that are now extinct].

ROSE, ROYCE, ROYSE: (i) P OF *Rothaid* 'fame-kind'. The Norman form *Rohese*, *Royse* became *Rose* in ME. (ii) L A sign-name 'at the sign of the rose'. (*Rothais* in DB.) *Rose* is also a Jewish ornamental surname. ROSENBERG: L 'rose-hill'.

ROSEMAN, ROSAMOND: P OG *hros-mund* 'horse-protection'. 12th cent.

ROSEVEAR(E): L Cornish *ros-mur* 'the big moor or heath'.

ROSKEN see RUSKIN.

ROSS: (i) P OG *Rozzo*, a pet-form of names in *Hrod-*. DB. (ii) L OF From Rots (Calvados) Normandy. DB. (iii) L Welsh *rhōs* 'promontory'. (Herefords, Lancs, Northumb) [A First Fleet (marine) surname including Major Robert Ross, lieutenant-governor of the colony, and John Ross, promoted to second lieutenant of marines although only nine years old].

ROSSER: P Welsh form of *Roger*. See also Prosser. [A First Fleet (marine) surname].

ROSSON, ROSTEN, ROSTRON see RAWSTHORN.

ROTH: L OE *roth* 'clearing'. 14th cent.

ROTHERHAM: L Brit + OE 'The *hām* (homestead) by the R. Rother'. (Yorks) 13th cent.

ROTHMAN: L OE *roth* + *mann*. Identical in meaning with *Roth*. 14th cent.

ROTHWELL, ROWELL: L OE *roth-wielle* 'the clearing with a spring'. (Lincs, Northants, Yorks) 12th cent.

ROUGH, RUFF: (i) N OE *rūh* 'rough', a nickname. 13th cent. (ii) L OE *rūh*, used topographically, 'the rough, uncultivated ground'. 14th cent. [A First Fleet (convict) surname].

ROUGHLEY: L OE *rūh-lēah* 'the rough clearing'. 14th cent.

ROULSTON see ROLLESTON.

ROUND(S), ROUNCE: N OF *roond* 'rotund, corpulent'. 12th cent.

ROUNTREE see ROWNTREE. ROURKE see O'ROURKE.

ROUS(E), ROWSE, RUSE, RUSS: N AF & ME *rous* 'red', of hair or complexion. 13th cent. [Rouse, a First Fleet (convict) surname].

ROUSEL, ROUSSEL see RUSSEL.

ROUT: L OE *rūht* 'the rough, untilled ground'. 13th cent.

ROUTLEDGE, RUTLEDGE: L OE From a lost place on the Scottish-English border. 15th cent.

ROW(E): L OE *rāw* 'the row or street (of houses, cottages)'. 12th cent. See also Rolf. [A First Fleet (convict) surname].

ROWAN: L O Dan *rön* 'rowan (mountain-ashtree)'. Dan *rön* 'red' from berries.

ROWBOTHAM, ROWBOTTOM, ROBOTHAM, ROOBOTTOM: L OE *rūh-botm* 'the rough, untilled valley'. 16th cent.

ROWDEN, ROWDON: L OE *rūh-dūn* 'the rough (broken) hill'. (Devon, Herefords, Wilts) [A First Fleet (marine) surname].

ROWELL: L OE *rūh-wielle* 'the rough hill with a spring'. (Devon) 14th cent. See also Rothwell.

ROWER, ROYER: O OF *rouer* 'wheelwright', 12th cent.

ROWLAND, ROLLAND, ROLLANS, ROLAND, ROLANCE: P OG *Hrodland*, OF *Rollant, Rolant* 'famous land'. *Roland*, the most famous of the peers of *Charlemagne*. The name was introduced into England by the Normans. DB. Some may be L O Scand *rā-lundr* 'the wood of the roe deer'. (Derbys), *Ralunt* in DB.

ROWLATT: P A pet-form of *Rowland*. 14th cent.

ROWLES see ROLF. ROWLSTON(E) see ROLLESTON.

ROWLEY: L OE *rūh-lēah* 'the rough, probably neglected clearing'. 13th cent.

ROWLING(S), ROWLINS: P A pet-form of *Rowland*. 12th cent.

ROWLINSON, ROWLISON: P 'Son of *Rowland*'.

ROWNEY: L OE *rūh-haeg* 'the rough (overgrown) enclosure'. (Beds, Essex, Herts, Worces) 13th cent.

ROWNSON, RONSON: P A Lancs form of *Rowlandson*. 16th cent.

ROWNTREE, ROUNTREE: L ME *rown* from O Dan *rön*, + OE *trēo* 'the rowan (mountain ash) tree'. 13th cent.

ROWSELL: N A dim. of *Rowse* (*Rous*). See also Russell.

ROXBURGH: L OE *Hrōc-burh* 'the fort of an Anglo-Saxon called *Hrōc* (Rook)'. Roxburgh, Scotland.

ROY: N OF *roi* 'king'. A pageant-name. 13th cent. See also Ray.

ROYAN: P Ir A variant of *O'Ruane*, centred on Gortyroyan, near Ballinasloe.

ROYCE see ROSE. ROYDS see RHODES. ROYER see ROWER.

ROYLE: L OE *ryge-hyll* 'rye-hill'. 13th cent.

ROYSTON: L OE *Roese* + OF *croiz* + OE *stān*. Lady *Roese* (Lady Righteous) set up a cross and a priory was established. Later came a village, recorded as *Croyroys* 1262. The earliest name was *Crux Roaisie* 1184. The name translates as '*Roese's* stone'. (Herts).

RUCK see ROOK.

RUDD: N OE *rud, rudig* 'ruddy' of complexion. 12th cent.

RUDDER: (i) P OE *Rudda*, an Anglo-Saxon pers. name. (ii) O A variant of *Rutter*.

RUDDICK, RUDDOCK, RUDDUCK: N OE *rudduc* a nickname from the robin. 12th cent.

RUDGE: (i) N OF *ruge* 'red (hair/beard)'. 12th cent. (ii) L OE *hrycg* 'ridge'. (Glos, Salop).

RUDHAM: L OE 'The *hām* of an Anglo-Saxon called *Rudda*'. (Norfolk), *Rudeham* in DB. (*Hām* 'homestead').

RUDKIN: N A dim. of *Rudd*.

RUDYARD: L OE *rūde-geard* 'the yard where rue (herb) grows'. (Staffs), *Rudierd* DB. Shakespeare: 'I'll set a bank of rue, sour herb of grace' (*Richard II*).

RUE see REW. RUFF, RULE see ROLF, ROUGH.

RUFFLER: From *ruffle*, of unknown origin. N 'One of a class of vagabonds', 'a proud, swaggering, arrogant fellow'. [A First Fleet (convict) surname].

RUGELEY, RUDGLEY: L OE *hrycg-lēah* 'the clearing on a ridge'. (Staffs).

RUMBALL, RUMBELL, RUMBOLD, RUMBLE(S): P OG *Rumbald* 'famous-bold'. DB.

RUMMER see ROMER.

RUMP: N ME *rumpe* 'buttocks', a nickname for one with an ungainly posterior. 11th cent.

RUMSEY: L OE 'The *ēg* (island) of an Anglo-Saxon called *Rūm*'. (Hants).

RUNCIE: O ME *runcy* 'nag'. Metonymic for *Runcieman*. 13th cent.

RUNCIEMAN: O 'The man in charge of the *runcies* (small riding horses)'.

RUNDALL, RUNDELL, RUNDLE: (i) N OF *Rondel*, a dim. of *Round*. 12th cent. (ii) L OE *rūm-dael* 'wide valley'. (Kent) 13th cent.

RUPP SEE ROPE. RUSE, RUSS see ROUS.

RUSH: L OE *rysc* 'rush' (among the rushes). 14th cent. RUSHER, RISHER: O OE 'a cutter/seller of rushes'. 13th cent. RUSHBROOK: L OE *rysc-brōc* 'the rushy brook'. (Suffolk) RUSHFORTH: L OE 'the rushy ford'. (Lancs, Norfolk, Suffolk).

RUSHMER, RUSHMORE: L OE *rysc-mere* 'the rushy lake or pond'. (Suffolk).

RUSHTON: L OE *rysc, risc-tūn* 'the farm or village among the rushes'. (Ches, Northants, Staffs), *Rusitone, Risetone* DB.

RUSHWORTH: L OE *rysc, risc-worth* 'the homestead among the rushes'. (Yorks).

RUSKIN, ROSKIN: P A dim. of forms in *Ross*. 13th cent.

RUSSEL(L), RUSSILL, ROUSEL(L), ROUSSEL(L): N OF *rous-el*, a dim. of *rous* 'red', of hair, beard or complexion. 11th cent. [A First Fleet (marine and convict) surname].

RUST: N OE *rūst* 'rust', 'rust-coloured of hair/beard'. OE Byname 1016.

RUSTON, RUSTOM: L OE *hris-tūn* 'the farm in the brushwood', (Norfolk) or OE *hrōst-tūn* 'the farm(-house) with a strange roof', (Yorks) or ON + OE 'the *tūn* of a Norseman called *Hrór*', (Yorks). Surname 12th cent.

RUTH: N ME *reuthe* 'pity', either taking pity or deserving of pity. Not to be confused with the woman's pers. name, which is from Hebrew. [A First Fleet (convict) surname].

RUTHERFORD: L OE *hryther-ford* 'the oxen-ford'. (Roxburghs, Yorks) 12th cent.

RUTHVEN: L SG *ruadh* 'red'. Second el. obscure, probably 'place'. 'The place with red earth or rocks'. (Perth) Scotland.

RUTLEDGE see ROUTLEDGE.

RUTTER: O OF *roteor* 'a player on the rote (a stringed instrument)'. 13th cent. See also Root. Some may be from OF *routier* 'highwayman'.

RYAL(L): (i) L OE *ryge-hyll* 'the hill where rye grows'. (Northumb) (ii) P Ir A variant of *Ryle*.

RYAN see O'RYAN. RYDE see RIDE. RYDER see RIDER. RYDING see READING.

RYE: (i) O OE *ryge* 'rye'. Metonymic for a grower of rye. (ii) L OE *ēa* 'stream' or *ēg* 'island', see Rea.

RYLAND(S), RYLANCE: L OE *ryge-land* 'the land where rye grows'. 13th cent.

RYLE(S): P Ir *O Raghail*. Ryall and Riall are variants of this surname which may be related to *O Raghailligh* (O'Reilly).

RYLEY see RILEY.

RYMAN: L OE *ēg* (island) or *ēa* (stream) + *mann* 'man', 'the island or stream man'. See also Rea.

RYMER see RIMER.

S

SABAN, SABIN(E): P Lat *Sabinus*, ancient Italian people of the Apennines. The surname is from St *Sabinus* or St *Sabina* (fem.) popular saints' names in England. 12th cent. SABLIN: P A double dim. of *Sabina*. 12th cent.

SABER see SEABER.

SACH: O OF *sachier*. Metonymic for Sacker. 13th cent.

SACKER, SECKER, SAKER: O A deriv. of OE *sace* or ON *sekkr* 'sack'. 'A maker of sacks, sackcloth'. 13th cent.

SACKVILLE, SACKWILD: L OF From Sauqueville (Seine Inférieure) France. DB.

SADD: N OE *saed*, originally 'satiated', becoming *sadde* 'serious, firm' in ME. DB. The DB tenant, Roger *Sad* 1086, must have been satiated.

SADDINGTON: L OE 'The *tūn* (farm) of the *ingas* (people) of an Anglo-Saxon called *Sǣgēat*'. (Leics).

SADDLER, SADLEIR, SADLER, SADLIER: O A deriv. of OE *sadol* 'saddle', 'a maker of saddles'. 13th cent.

SAGAR, SAGER, SAGGERS, SEAGER(S), SEEGER, SEGAR, SEGER: P OE *sǣgār* 'sea-spear'. DB.

SAGE: N OF *sage* 'wise'. 12th cent. Petronilla *la Sage* was a wise woman in 1206. Her predecessors were wise men.

SAILER, SEILLER: O OF *sailleor, saillur* 'dancer'. 12th cent.

SAINES, SAINS: P OE *Sǣwine* 'sea-friend'. DB.

SAINSBURY, SAINSBERRY: L OE 'The *burh* (fort) of an Anglo-Saxon called *Sǣwine*'. (Glos) 12th cent.

SAINT, SANT: N OF *sant*, AF & ME *seint* 'saint', a nickname, probably ironical. 13th cent.

ST CLAIR see SINCLAIR. SAINTER see SENTER.

ST JOHN: P OF From St Jean, various places in France. 12th cent. See also John.

ST LEGER, ST LEDGER: L OF From St Léger (France). 12th cent. See also Ledger.

SAIT: P OE *Sǣgēat* 'sea-Geat'. DB.

SAKER see SACKER.

SALAMAN, SALAMON, SALOMAN, SALMON(D), SALMONS, SAMMAN,

SAMMON(S), SOLOMON: P OF *Salomon*, from Hebrew *shalom* 'peace'. Forms other than *Solomon* are not exclusively Jewish. DB.

SALE(S): (i) L OE *salh* 'sallow', a low-growing willow. (ii) O OE *sael* 'hall', 'a servant at the hall'. 13th cent.

SALINGER, SELINGER: L OF From St Léger (Manche) Normandy. 12th cent.

SALISBURY, SALESBURY, SALSBURY: L OE Originally Old Sarum (Wilts). The Anglo-Saxons found a Brit name which they changed to *Searu-burg* 'armour-fort'. The Normans, unable properly to pronounce *Searu*, substituted -l- for -r-, hence Sealusburg (Salisbury). Salesbury (Lancs) has also contributed to the surname.

SALKELD: L OE *salh-hylte* 'sallow (willow) wood'. (Cumb).

SALKIN, SAWKINS: P A dim. of *Saul* or *Salamon*. 14th cent.

SALLAWAY see SALWAY.

SALLITT: N OE *saelida* 'seafarer, pirate'. DB.

SALLOWS, SALLIS(S): L OE *salh, sealh* 'the sallows (willows)'. 13th cent.

SALT, SAULT: L OE *selte* 'salt-pit'. (Staffs) 12th cent.

SALTER: (i) O OE *sealtere* 'a maker/seller of salt'. 13th cent. (ii) O OF *sautere* 'psaltery', 'a player on the psaltery (a stringed, harp-like instrument)'. 13th cent.

SALTMARSH: L OE *sealt-mersc* 'the salt (brackish) marsh'. (Glos, Herefords, Yorks) 12th cent. [A First Fleet (convict) surname].

SALTON: L OE *salh-tūn* 'the farm among the sallows'. (Yorks) 13th cent.

SALVAGE see SAVAGE. SALVIN see SAUVAIN.

SALWAY, SALWEY, SALLAWAY, SELWAY: P OE *Sǣlwīg* 'prosperity-war'. 12th cent.

SAM(S), SAMME, SAMS: P A pet-form of *Sampson*. 13th cent.

SAMBELL, SAMBER see SEMPLE.

SAMBROOK(E): L OE *sand-brōc* 'the sandy brook'. (Salop) 13th cent.

SAMMAN, SAMMON see SALAMAN. SAMPLE see SEMPLE.

SAMSON, SAMPSON, SANSOM(E), SANSON: (i) P Hebrew *Shimshon*, from *shemesh* 'sun'. The great strength of the biblical character popularised the name among Christians in England. (ii) P Welsh & Breton *Samson*, a Welsh bishop, established the abbey of Dol in Brittany. He died there and was venerated as a saint by the Bretons. In 1066 the Breton contingent of Duke William's army introduced the name into England. DB. (iii) L OF A third source of the surname is from places called Saint Samson in Seine Inférieure and in Eure and Calvados, Normandy. DB. [A First Fleet (convict) surname].

SAMUEL(S): P Hebrew *Shemuel* 'Name of God'. A 12th cent. surname in England. Not exclusively Jewish, and a favourite given name after the Reformation.

SANCTUARY, SANTRY: L OF *saintuarie*, ME *seintuarie* 'a shrine', for one who has taken sanctuary in a church or monastery.

SANDS, SANDES, SANDYS: L OE *sand* 'sandy soil or the sands'. 13th cent.

SANDARS, SANDER(S), SAUNDER(S): P A pet-form of *Alexander*. 13th cent.

SANDELL(S), SANDEL: L OE *sand-hyll* 'the sandy hill'. 13th cent. [A First Fleet (crew) surname].

SANDEMAN: O 'Servant of *Sander* or *Saunder*'. 14th cent.

SANDERSON, SAUNDERSON: P 'Son of *Sander* or *Saunder*'. 14th cent. [Saunderson, a First Fleet (convict) surname].

SANDEY, SANDY, SANDAY: (i) L OE *sand* 'the sandy place'. (Beds) (ii) P ON *Sandi*, a pers. name. 13th cent.

SANDFORD, SANDIFORD, SANFORD: L OE *sand-ford* 'sandy ford'. (Berks, Devon, Dorset, Westmorland, Yorks) 12th cent. SANDHURST: L OE *sand-hyrst* 'sandy hillock'. (Berks, Glos, Kent) SANDLING, SANDLIN: L OE *sand-hlinc* 'sand bank'. [Sandlin, a First Fleet (convict) surname].

SANGER, SANGSTER: O OE *sangere*, fem. *sangestere* 'chorister'. 13th cent.

SANKEY, SANKI: L A Brit river-name, *Sanki* in 1202. (Lancs).

SANTER, SAUNTER: L OF *sanz-terre* 'landless'. 13th cent. See also Senter. (The name equates with *Lackland*, King John's nickname.)

SANTLER, SANDLER: L OF From Saint-Lô (Manche) Normandy or Saint-Laud (Maine-et-Loire) or other places of similar name in France. 12th cent.

SAPER see SOPER.

SARGANT, SARGEANT, SARGENT, SEARGEANT, SERGEANT: (i) O OF *sergent* 'a tenant by military service under the rank of knight'. 12th cent. (ii) O 'An official charged with summoning offenders before the court and with enforcing judgements'.

SARSON: N OF *Sarrazin* 'Saracen', a nickname for a swarthy person. 12th cent.

SASSON, SASSOON: P Hebrew *Sason* 'joy'.

SATCHEL(L): O OF *sachel* 'small bag'. Metonymic for a maker of small sacks, bags. 13th cent. See also Sacker.

SATCHWELL see SETCHFIELD.

SAUL, SAWL(E): P Hebrew *Saul* 'asked for', the name of the first king of Israel. As an English surname 12th cent.

SAUVAIN, SAVIN, SALVIN, SELWIN, SELWYN(E): P Lat *Silvanus*, from *silva* 'wood' the name of a forest deity, and of a Roman martyr. 12th cent. [Bishop George Augustus Selwyn, churchman and explorer, brought succour to the wounded of both sides in the Maori wars, 1842].

SAVAGE, SAVIDGE, SAUVAGE, SALVAGE: N OF *sauvage* 'savage, wild'. DB.

SAVIGNY: L OF From Savenay (Calvados) Normandy. DB.

SAVIL(L), SAVILLE, SAVEAL(L), SAVELL, SAYWELL, SEVILLE: L From Sauville (Vosges) or Sainville (Eure-et-Loire) France. 13th cent.

SAWELL see SEWALL. SAWKINS see SALKIN.

SAWYER(S): O A deriv. of ME *saghe, sawe* 'to saw', 'a sawer of timber'. 13th cent. [A First Fleet (crew) surname].

SAXBY: (i) L O Scand 'The *býr* (farm) of a Scandinavian settler called *Saxi*'. (Leices, Lincs) 12th cent. (ii) N OF *sacqépée* 'draw sword', a nickname for a fencing master, becoming *Sakespey* in 13th cent.

SAXON, SAXTON, SEXTON: L OE *Seax-tūn* 'the farm of the Saxons'. (Cambs, Yorks) 13th cent.

SAYBURN see SEABORN.

SAYCE, SEYS: L O Welsh *sais* 'Englishman, i.e., Saxon'. 13th cent.

SAYER(S), SAYRE, SARE, SEAR(S), SEARES, SEEARS, SEERS: (i) P A Norman name, early examples, *Saher, Seir, Saerus*, probably Germanic in origin. 12th cent. (ii) O A form of *Sawyer*. 13th cent. (iii) O ME *assayer* 'a food-taster' or 'an assayer of metals'. (iv) O A deriv. of OE *secgan* 'to say', 'a tribal sayer, reciter'.

SAYNOR see SENIOR.

SCAIFE: N ON *skeifr*, northern dial. *scafe* 'awkward, crooked, wild'. 13th cent.

SCALES, SCHOLES, SCOLES: L ON *skáli* 'huts/sheds'. (Cumb, Lancs, Yorks) 13th cent.

SCAMMELL: N OE *scamol* 'table, bench for sale of meat' and by extension, 'butchery, meat-market' (which became *shambles*).

SCANLAN, SCANLON: P Ir *Mac/O' Scannlain*, from *scannal* 'contention'.

SCARBOROUGH, SCARBORO, SCARBROW: L ON 'The fort of a Norseman nicknamed *Skarthi* (hare-lip)'. (Yorks).

SCARF(E), SCARFF: N ON *skarfr* 'cormorant', a nickname from the voracious seabird. 13th cent.

SCARGILL: L An O Scand hybrid name. O Sw *skrake* (a fish-eating diving bird) + ON *gil* 'ravine, narrow valley'. 'The valley of the mergansers'.

SCARLETT: O & N OF *escarlate* 'a rich fabric', not necessarily red. 'A maker or habitual wearer of scarlet'. 12th cent.

SCATTERGOOD: N ME *skater-gode* 'squander goods, wealth', a nickname for a spendthrift rather than a philanthropist. Charity, however benevolent, is seldom scattered. 13th cent.

SCHADE see SHADE.

SCHOFIELD, SCHOLFIELD, SCOFFIELD, SCOFIELD: L ON + OE *skáli-feld* 'the field with a hut'. 14th cent.

SCHOLAR, SCHOLER, SCOLLARD, SCOULAR, SCOULER, SCOULLER: L ON *skáli-erg* 'the shieling (grazing ground) with a shepherd's hut'. 14th cent.

SCOBIE, SCOBBIE: L SG From a lost place in Perths, Scotland. [A First Fleet (female convict) surname].

SCOTLAND: L Gaelic *Scoti* + OE *land*. DB.

SCOTNEY: L OF From Etocquigney (Seine Inférieure) France. 12th cent.

SCOTT: L Gaelic *Scoti* and OE *Scott*, originally an Irishman, later a Gael from Scotland. Also a border name and in eastern England from settlement there in the 12th cent. [A First Fleet (marine, crew and convict) surname. In New Zealand Giles Gilbert Scott designed Christchurch Cathedral, 1860].

SCOTTON: L OE 'The *tūn* (settlement) of the Scots'. (Lincs, Yorks) 12th cent.

SCRIMGEOUR, SCRYMGEOUR, SCRIMSHAW: O OF *escremisseor* 'fencing-master', an illegal occupation in medieval London, where fencing-masters were classed with rogues and vagabonds, stage-players, bearwards, gipsies and other undesirable characters. 12th cent.

SCRIVEN(S), SCRIVENER, SCRIVENOR: O OF *escrivein* 'writer, clerk, copier of manuscripts'. 13th cent. [Philip Scriven, foremastman of the *Lady Penrhyn*, brought the surname to Australia 1788].

SCRUBY: P ON *Skroppa*, a Norse pers. name preserved in Scrooby (Notts), *Scrobi* DB, *Scruby* 1242.

SCRUTTON, SCRUTON: L ON + OE 'The *tūn* (farm) of a Norse *jarl* (earl) called *Scurfy*'. (Yorks) 14th cent.

SCUDAMORE see SKIDMORE.

SCULLIN: P Ir *O Scollain*, a Derry sept.

SCULLION: (i) P Ir A dim. of Scully. (ii) O OF 'a menial kitchen servant'.

SCULLY: P Ir *O Scolaidhe* 'student'. (Leinster) [A First Fleet (marine) surname].

SCULTHORP(E): L ON 'The *thorp* (farm) of a Norseman called *Skuli*'. (Norfolk).

SCUTT(S): (i) P A variant of *Scott*. (ii) ME *scut* 'the tail of a hare, displayed when the hare is fleeing', a nickname for one who regards discretion as the better part of valour. 12th cent.

SEABERG, SEABURY, SABER, SIBERRY, SIBERY, SIBREE: (i) P OE *Sǣburh* 'sea-fortress'. 12th cent. (ii) L OE *seofon-beorgas* 'the seven hills' (Seaborough, Dorset). 13th cent.

SEABORN, SIBBONS, SAYBURN: P OE *Sǣbeorn* 'sea-warrior'. 12th cent.

SEABROOK: L OE *sǣge-brōc* 'the trickling, slow-moving brook'. (Bucks).

SEACH see SYKES.

SEACOMBE, SECOMB(E): L OE *sǣ-cumb* 'the combe (valley) by the sea'. (Ches).

SEAGER see SAGAR.

SEAGRAVE, SEAGROVE, SEGRAVE: L OE *sēath-grāf* 'the grove by the pool'. (Leices) 12th cent.

SEAL(E), SEEL, ZEAL: L OE *sealh* (willow)' or OE *sele* 'hall'. (Kent, Surrey, Sussex) 12th cent.

SEAMAN, SEAMONS, SEEMAN, SEMAN, SEMMANS: O OE *sǣmann* 'seaman, sailor, pirate'. DB. Also P a pers. OE name from the same source, which may account for the DB entry.

SEAMER, SEAMOUR: (i) P OE *Sǣmǣr* 'sea-famous'. DB. (ii) O OE *sēamere* 'tailor' 12th cent. [John Seamour, a convict who was sentenced to transportation for cutting down trees in a nursery garden, arrived on the *Scarborough* 1788].

SEAR, SEARES see SAYER.

SEARL(E), SEARLES, SERLE, SERRELL: P ON *Sorli*, cogn. with OE *searu* 'armour'. A Norman pers. name. DB.

SEATON, SETON: L OE *seten* 'cultivated land', (Kent) or *sǣ-tūn* 'the farm or settlement by the sea or lake', (Cumb, Devon, Durham, Northumb, Rutland, Yorks). 13th cent.

SEAVER(S), SEVER(S): P OE *Sǣfaru* 'sea-passage', an Anglo-Saxon woman's name. 12th cent. [William Sever, master of the *Lady Penrhyn*, brought the surname to Australia 1788, having previously been named Otoo (king) by the people of Tahiti].

SEAWARD see SEWARD.

SEBASTIAN: L Lat *Sebastānus* 'man from Sebastian (city in Pontus)'.

SEDDON: L ON *set* + OE *dūn* 'the flat-topped hill'. (Lancs) 14th cent.

SEDGER: O OE A deriv. of *secg* 'sedge', 'a worker with sedge, thatcher with reeds'. 12th cent.

SEDWAY: A surname of uncertain origin. Perhaps L OE *secg-weg* 'the sedgy (reedy) way, path'. [A First Fleet (convict) surname].

SEDWICK, SEDGEWICK, SIDGWICK: (i) L OE *secg-wīc* 'the dairy farm among the sedge (reeds)'. (Sussex) (ii) L O Scand + OE *Siggi's wīc*. (Westmorland) 14th cent.

SEE: L OE *sǣ* 'sea, lake, pool'. 13th cent.

SEEAR, SEERS see SAYER.

SEED(S): (i) P OE A short-form of names in *Sidu*, e.g., Seduuinus, from OE *sidu* 'manner, purity, morality'. DB. (ii) O OE Metonymic for Seedman.

SEEDHOUSE: O OE *sǣd-hūs* 'gardener in charge of the seed-house'. [A First Fleet (marine) surname].

SEEDMAN, SEEDSMAN, SEDMAN: O OE *sǣdmann* 'seedsman, a dealer in seeds'. 13th cent.

SEEGER see SAGAR. SEEL see SEAL.

SEELEY, SEALEY, SEALY, CEELEY, CEILEY, ZELLEY: N OE *saelig* 'happy, prosperous, blessed', a nickname for one so blessed and also a woman's name in the Middle Ages. A pity that the word later came to mean 'silly'. 12th cent.

SEEMAN see SEAMAN.

SEFTON: L ON *sef* + OE *tūn* 'the enclosure

overgrown with rushes'. (Lancs).

SEGAR, SEGER see SAGAR. SEGRAVE see SEAGRAVE. SEIGNIOR see SENIOR.

SELBY, SELBIE: L OE *seletūn*, with O Scand influence, 'the farm among the sallows (willows)'. (Yorks) 12th cent.

SELDEN, SELDON: L OE *sealh-denu* 'willow valley'. (Devon, Sussex) 12th cent.

SELF(E): P OE *Sǣwulf* 'sea-wolf'. DB.

SELINGER see SALINGER.

SELLAR(S), SELLER(S), SELLORS, CELLIER, ZELLER: O (i) OF *celier* 'cellar', AF & ME *celerer* 'official of a large house or monastery in charge of the cellar and provisions'. 12th cent. Later used of a taverner. (ii) OF & ME *seller* 'sadler'. 11th cent. (iii) OE *sellan*, ME *sellen* 'a seller, dealer in the market'. 12th cent. Winton D.

SELLEY, SELLY: L OE *scylf-lēah* 'the wood on a slope or ledge'. (Worces) See also Sealey, Shelley.

SELLICK, SELLECK: L OE *saege-strēamlic* 'sluggish water (stream, creek)'.

SELLMAN, SELMAN, SILMAN: N OE *saelig-mann* 'happy man'. 12th cent.

SELSHAW: L OE *sell-sceaga* (dial. *shaw*) 'the herdsman's hut by the spinney (small wood)'. [A First Fleet (convict) surname].

SELVESTER see SILVESTER. SELWAY see SALWAY. SELWIN, SELWYN see SAUVAIN.

SELWOOD: L OE *sealh-wudu* 'the sallow (willow) wood'. (Som).

SEMAN see SEAMAN. SEMKEN see SIMKIN. SEMMENS see SIMMONDS.

SEMPLE, SAMBELL, SAMPLE: L OF From Saint-Pol (Pas-de-Calais, Nord) or one of several places in France called Saint-Paul. 12th cent.

SENDALL: O OF 'A dealer in *sendal* (silken cloth)'. 13th cent.

SENIOR, SEIGNIOR, SENYARD, SAYNOR: N OF *seignour* 'lord', a nickname for a churl who aped the lord of the manor. Sometimes used to distinguish the senior member of a family from a junior of the same name. 12th cent.

SENNETT see SINNETT.

SENTER, SAINTER, SANTER, CENTRE: O OF *saintier* 'a bell-founder'. 12th cent. See also Center.

SERGEANT see SARGANT. SERLE see SEARL.

SERMIN, SERMON, SURMON, SURMAN: O OF *sermounier* 'speaker, preacher'. 13th cent.

SERVICE, SERVIS, SERVAIS: O OF *cervoise* 'ale', a name for a taverner. 12th cent.

SESSIONS: L OF From Soissons (Aisne) France. 12th cent.

SETCHFIELD, SATCHWELL: L OF From Secquevilles, Normandy. 12th cent.

SETON see SEATON.

SETTER: (i) O OF *saietier* 'a silk-weaver'. (ii) O ME *setten* 'to set' (ornaments on garments e.g., church vestments), 'an embroiderer'. (iii) O OE *settan* 'to set' (stones worked by the mason), 'a stone-mason's setter'. The surname is 13th cent.

SEVER(S) see SEAVERS.

SEVIER, SIVIER, SIVYER: O OE A deriv. of OE *sife* 'sieve', 'a sieve-maker'. 13th cent.

SEVILLE see SAVIL.

SEWALL, SAYWELL: P OE *Sǣweald* 'sea-power'. DB.

SEWARD, SEWART, SEAWARD, SUART: (i) P OE *Sǣweard* 'sea-lord'. DB. (ii) P OE *Sigeweard* 'victory-lord'. DB. (iii) P O Dan *Siward* with the same meaning as (ii). (iii) O OE *sū-hierde* 'sow-herd'. 14th cent.

SEWELL: (i) P OE *Sigeweald* 'victory-rule'. DB. (ii) L OE *seofon-welle* 'seven springs'. (Beds, Devon, Northants, Oxon) 12th cent.

SEWTER see SOUTAR.

SEXTON: O OF *secrestein*, AF *segerstaine* 'sacristan'. 12th cent. See also Saxon.

SEYMOUR(E): L OF From Saint-Maur-des Fossés (Seine) France. 12th cent. Seamer (Yorks) has also contributed to the surname.

SHACKEL(L), SHACKLE, SHAKLE: (i) P Anglo-Saxon *Skakel*, from O Sw *Skakli* or ON *Skokull*. (ii) O ME *schackel* 'shackle (fetter)', 'a maker of shackles'.

SHACKERLEY: L OE *scēacere-lēah* 'the wood of the robbers'. (Lancs).

SHACKLADY see SHAKELADY.

SHACKLETON: L OE *scacol-tūn* 'the farm on a tongue of land'. (Yorks).

SHADDICK, SHADDOCK, SHADWICK see CHADWICK.

SHADBOLT: O OE *scēotan-bolt* 'shoot bolt (arrow with a heavy head)'. 'An archer'.

SHADE, SCHADE: (i) L OE *scēad* 'boundary'. (ii) N ME *schade* 'shade, shadow', a nickname for a thin man. 13th cent.

SHADWELL: L OE *scēad-wielle* 'boundary stream'. (Middx, Norfolk, Yorks) 13th cent.

SHAKELADY, SHACKLADY: N OE *sceacan*, ME *schaken-ladie*, a nickname of uncertain meaning. Perhaps a 14th cent. domestic tyrant, or a libertine.

SHAKESBY: O Identical in meaning with *Saxby* (ii). 13th cent.

SHAKESHAFT: N OE *sceacan*, ME *schaken*, + OE *sceaft* 'shaft, spear', a nickname for a spearman, foot-soldier. 14th cent.

SHAKESPEAR(E): N ME *spere* 'spear'. Identical in meaning with *Shakeshaft*. 13th cent. (OE *sceacan* 'to shake, brandish'.)

SHALLCROSS see SHAWCROSS.

SHANAHAN: P Ir *O Seanachain*, from *sean* 'old'.

SHANK(S): N OE *sceanca* 'shank, shin', a nickname from some deformity of the leg or from a peculiar gait. OE Byname 11th cent.

SHANLEY: P Ir *Mac Seanlaoich*, from *sean-laoch* 'old hero'. A Connacht sept.

SHANNON: P Ir *O Seannachain*, a contracted form of *Shanahan*, in which the basic element is *sean* 'old'.

SHARD, SHEARD: L OE *sceard* 'cleft, gap (in the hills)'. 13th cent.

SHARDLOW: L OE sceard-*hlāw* 'the cleft (indented) mound'. (Derbys).

SHARKEY: P Ir *O Searcaigh*, from *searcach* 'loving', a Co. Tyrone name.

SHARMAN, SHEARMAN, SHEERMAN, SHERMAN: O OE *scēarra-mann* 'shears-man', 'a shearer of woollen cloth'. 13th cent. [Sheerman, a First Fleet (convict) surname].

SHARP(E): N OE *scearp* 'sharp, keen, smart, quick'. OE Byname 11th cent.

SHARPLES(S): L OE *scearp-lāes* 'steep meadow'. (Lancs) 13th cent.

SHARROCK see SHORROCK.

SHAW(E), SHAVE, SHAY, SHEA: L OE *scaga*, dial. *shaw* 'copse, thicket, grove, small wood'. (Berks, Dorset, Lancs, Som, Wilts) 12th cent. [Shea, a First Fleet (marine) surname].

SHAWCROSS, SHALLCROSS: L OE *scacul-crūc* 'shackle-cross (a cross equipped with a shackle or fetter for the detention of malefactors)'. 14th cent.

SHEA: P Ir *O Seagdha* 'descendant of *Stately*'. See also Shaw.

SHEARER, SHERAR, SHERER, SHERA: O OE A deriv. of OE *sceran* 'to cut': (i) 'a sheep-shearer', (ii) 'a cutter who shears the nap from cloth'. 13th cent.

SHEATHER: O OE A deriv. of OE *scēath* 'sheath', 'a maker of sword-sheaths'. 13th cent.

SHEDDON, SHEDDEN: L OE *scead-dūn* 'the hill with a shelter'. (Essex).

SHEEHAN, SHEAHAN, SHEAN: P Ir *O Siodhachain*, from *siodhach* 'peaceful'.

SHEEN: L OE *Scēon*, from *scēo* 'huts, sheds'. (Staffs, Surrey) Richmond, Surrey, was originally Sheen, changed to Richmond after the accession to the throne of the earl of Richmond, Henry VII, in 1485.

SHEER, SHEERS, SHEAR: N OE *scaere* 'bright', a nickname for a bright, fair person. 12th cent.

SHEERMAN see SHARMAN.

SHEFFIELD: L OE (i) 'The *feld* (field) on the River *Sheaf*. (Yorks) (ii) *scēap-feld* 'the sheep-field'. (Sussex) (iii) *scēo-feld* 'the field with a shelter'. (Berks).

SHEIL, SHIEL: (i) P Ir *O Siadhail*, an Ulster sept. (ii) P SG *Seile*, river at Loch Shiel and river at Invershiel (Ross and Cromarty). The names of both rivers derive from the pre-Celtic root *sal-* 'stream, flowing water, current'.

SHELDON: L OE *scylf-denu* 'the steep-sided valley' (Devon); L OE *scylf-dūn* 'the hill with a shelf' (Warwicks); L OE *schēle* 'shed, hut' + the nearby place. Haddon (Derbys). 12th cent.

SHELDRAKE, SHELDRICK: N dial. *sheld* 'dappled, pied'. A nickname from the sheldrake, a bird of the duck family, with bright, parti-coloured plumage. 12th cent. Peacock is a comparable nickname.

SHELL: L OE *scylf* 'bank, shelf'. (Worces).

SHELLEY, SHELLY: L OE *scylf-lēah* 'the clearing on a steep slope or ledge'. (Essex, Suffolk, Northumb, Yorks) 12th cent.

SHELTON: L OE *scylf-tūn* 'the enclosure on a bank or ledge'. (Beds, Norfolk, Notts, Salop, Staffs) 12th cent.

SHEPARD, SHEPEARD, SHEPERD, SHEPHARD, SHEPHEARD, SHEPHERD, SHEPPARD, SHEPPERD, SHEPPHARD, SHEPPEARD: O OE *scēap-weard* 'sheep-ward' or *scēaphyrde* 'shepherd'. Some may be OE *scip-weard* 'ship-master'. 13th cent. [Shepherd and Shepphard are First Fleet (convict) surnames].

SHEPHERDSON: O OE 'Son of the shepherd'. 14th cent.

SHER(R) see SHEER. SHERA, SHERAR see SHEARER.

SHERATON: L Identical in meaning with *Scruton* (see Scrutton).

SHERGOLD: N OE *scīr-gold* 'bright gold', 'for one with golden hair'.

SHERIDAN: P Ir *O Sirideain* (Co. Longford), a literary family.

SHERIFF, SHERRIFF, SHIRRIFF, SHREEVE: O OE *scīrgerēfa* 'sheriff'. OE Byname 11th cent.

SHERLOCK: N OE *scīr-loc* 'golden hair'. OE Byname 11th cent.

SHERMAN see SHARMAN.

SHERRARD, SHERRATT: P OE *scīr* + OF suffix *-ard* 'bright-hardy'. 13th cent.

SHERRY: P Ir *Mac Searraigh*, from *searrach* 'foal'. An Ulster sept.

SHERWIN, SHERWEN: N OE *sceran-wind* 'cut-wind'. A nickname for a swift runner. 12th cent.

SHERWOOD: L OE *scīr-wudu* 'the shire wood' (belonging to the shire). (Notts), *Shirewuda* 1164.

SHIELD(S): (i) O OE *scild* 'shield'. Metonymic for a maker of shields. 12th cent. (ii) L ME *schēle* 'a shepherd's summer shed'. (Durham, Northumb) 14th cent.

SHILLING: N OE *scilling* 'shilling', a nickname from the silver coin, perhaps for rent or other land charge. 12th cent. See also Halfpenny. *Scilling*, from the Anglo-Saxon tribal name *Scillingas*, may also have contributed to the surname.

SHILLINGTON: L OE 'The *tūn* (settlement) of the people of *Scyttel*, an Anglo-Saxon'. (Beds)

SHIMMIN: P Manx *McSimeen* 'son of *Simon*'. 14th cent.

SHINE: P Ir *O Seighin*, from O Ir *seigene* 'small hawk'.

SHIP(P): O OE *scip* 'ship'. Metonymic for a seaman, sailor. Occasionally L from the sign of the ship. 13th cent.

SHIPLEY, SHIPLEE: L OE *scēap-lēah* 'the sheep pasture'. 13th cent.

SHIPMAN: O OE *scip-mann* 'shipman, seaman'. 12th cent.

SHIPPERBOTTOM see SHUFFLEBOTHAM.

SHIPTON: L OE *scēap-tūn* 'sheep farm'. (Dorset, Glos, Hants, Oxon, Salop).

SHIPWAY: L OE *scēap-weg* 'the sheep way, track'.

SHIRLEY: L OE *scīr-leah* 'the clearing where the shire *moot* (assembly) was held'. (Derbys, Hants, Surrey, Warwicks) 13th cent.

SHIRT: L OE *scyrte* 'skirt-land', 'the detached piece of land'. 12th cent.

SHOBROOK(E): L OE *sceocca-brōc* 'the goblin brook'. (Devon).

SHOESMITH, SHOOSMITH: O OE *scōh-smith* 'shoeing-smith, horseshoe-maker'. 13th cent.

SHOOTER, SHOTTER, SHUTER: O OE A deriv. of *scotian* 'to shoot', 'a shooter, archer'. 12th cent.

SHORE(S): L ME *schore* 'shore'. 14th cent. [A First Fleet (convict) surname].

SHORROCK(S), SHARROCK(S): L OE *scorian* 'steep, rocky', or *scora-āc* 'the steep, oak-grown slope'. (Lancs) 14th cent.

SHORT(T), SHORTER: N OE *sceort* 'short', 'the short one'. 12th cent.

SHORTHOSE, SHORTHOUSE, SHORTIS, SHORTUS: N A translation of OF *curt-heuse*, 'short-hose', for various leg-coverings. 13th cent.

SHORTLAND: L OE *scyrte-land* 'skirt-land', i.e., 'cut-off land, a detached block of land'. 12th cent.

SHOWERS: N A deriv. of OE *scūfan* 'to thrust, push' and a nickname for a determined, thrusting individual. 13th cent.

SHRAPNEL: N OF *charbonnel* 'small and dark' (*charbon* 'coal, charcoal'), corrupted to *Shrapnel* via *Sharpnel*. 13th cent.

SHREEVE see SHERIFF.

SHRIMPTON: L OE *scrimman* 'to shrink', 'the shrunken or contracted village', probably destined to become one of the 1,300 lost villages of England.

SHUFFLEBOTHAM, SHIPPERBOTTOM: L *scēap-wella-bothm* 'the sheep-wash valley'. (Shipperbottom, Lancs) 13th cent.

SHUTE: L OE *scēat* 'parkland'. (Devon), *Schete* in 1228.

SHUTER see SHOOTER.

SHUTT: O OE *scytta* 'shooter, archer'. OE Byname 11th cent.

SHUTTLEWORTH: L OE *scytel-worth* 'the enclosure with a bolted gate'. (Derbys, Lancs, Yorks) 13th cent.

SIBLEY, SIBLY: P Gk *Sibyl*, Lat *Sibilla*, name of the priestess who uttered the oracles. A popular woman's name in England after the Norman Conquest. Surname 13th cent. (The lady who married *Robert*, son of the Conqueror, was named *Sibylla*.)

SIBREE see SEABER.

SIBSON: P 'Son of *Sibb*', a pet-form of *Sibyl*. 14th cent.

SIBTHORPE: L OE 'The *thorp* (farm) of an Anglo-Saxon called *Sibba*'. (Notts), *Sibetorp* DB.

SIDDALL, SIDELL, SIDDLE: L OE *sīd-halh* 'the spacious nook'. (Lancs, Yorks).

SIDE, SYDE(S): L OE *sīde*, ME *side* 'long hill slope'. 13th cent.

SIDEBOTHAM, SIDEBOTTOM: L OE *sīd-bothm* 'the wide valley'. (Ches) 13th cent. Polite pronunciation in sensitive circles *Siddibottarm*.

SIDGWICK see SEDGWICK.

SIDNEY, SYDNEY: L OE *sīd-īeg* 'the wide, well-watered land'. (Surrey, Lincs) 14th cent. Sydney, capital of New South Wales, was named for Viscount Sydney, Secretary of State. The name could not be more appropriate; Sydney is as wide and well-watered as anywhere in the world.

SIER see SIRE. **SIKES** see SYKES.

SILCOCK(S), SILCOX: P A short-form of *Silvester*. 13th cent.

SILK: O OE *seolc* 'silk'. Metonymic for a silk-weaver or a dealer in silk. 12th cent.

SILLS: P A dim. of *Silvester*. 14th cent.

SILLIBOURNE, SILABON, SILBURN: N OE *saelig-bearn* 'happy, blessed child'. 13th cent.

SILMAN see SELLMAN.

SILVER: (i) O OE *silfor* 'silver'. Metonymic for a silversmith. 13th cent. (ii) L OE *seolfre*, *sylfre* 'the silvery stream'. 14th cent.

SILVERSTONE: L OE 'The *tūn* (farm) of an Anglo-Saxon called *Saewulf* (sea-wolf)'.

SILVERTHORN(E): L OE *seolfre-thorn* 'the silver thorn-bush'. [A First Fleet (convict) surname].

SILVESTER, SYLVESTER: L Lat *Silvester* 'forest-dweller', a deriv. of *silva* 'wood'. The name of three popes. 13th cent.

SIM(M), SIMMS, SIMS, SYMS, SIME(S), SYME(S): P A pet-form of *Simmond* or *Simon*. 14th cent. [Simms, a First Fleet (crew) surname].

SIMCOCK(S), SIMCOX, SINCOCK: P *Sim* + *cock*, a dim. of *Simon*. 13th cent.

SIMEON, SIMION: P Hebrew *Shimeon* 'hearkening'. Surname 13th cent.

SIMINGTON, SYMINGTON: L Hebrew *Symon* + OE *tūn* '*Symon's* farm'. (Ayrs, Lanarks, Midlothian) Scotland.

SIMKIN(S), SIMPKIN, SEMKEN: P *Sim-kin*, a dim. of *Sim* or *Simon*. 12th cent.

SIMMONDS, SIMMONS, SIMMEN(S), SEMMENS, SIMOND(S), SYMMONS, SYMONDS, SYMONS, FITZSIMMONS: A surname of several origins which are now indistinguishable: (i) Hebrew *Simon*, (ii) ON *Sigmundr*, (iii) O Dan *Sigmund*, (iv) OG *Sigmund*. All are patronymics, the last three meaning 'victory-power'. DB.

SIMON(S), SYMON(S): P Hebrew *Shimeon*. 12th cent. See also Simeon, Simmonds.

SIMPSON, SIMSON: P 'Son of *Simm* (*Simon*)'. 14th cent.

SINCLAIR, ST CLAIR: L OF From either of two places called Saint-Clair in Normandy. DB. The frequency of the surname is partly due to the adoption by tenants of the name of their overlord, esp. in Caithness and the Orkneys. [Duncan Sinclair, master of the *Alexander*, brought the surname to Australia 1788].

SINGER(S): O OE A deriv. of OE *singan* 'to sing', 'a singer'. 13th cent.

SINGLE: L OE *sengel* 'the burnt clearing'. 13th cent.

SINGLETON: L OE *sengel-tūn* 'the farm at the burnt clearing'. (Lancs, Sussex) 12th cent.

SINNETT, SINNOTT, SENNETT, SENNITT, SYNNOT(T), SYNOTT: P OE *Sigenōth* 'victory-bold'. 12th cent.

SIRE, SIER, SIRR, SURR, SYER: N OF *sire*, ME *sire*, *sier* 'master', a nickname rather than occupational. 12th cent.

SIRED, SIRETT, SYRAD, SYRED, SYRETT: P OE *Sigerǣd* 'victory-counsel'. DB.

SISMORE, SIZMUR: N OF *sis mars* 'six marks', a nickname from the coin. 15th cent. (A mark varied in value, originally half pound of silver.)

SISSON(S), SISSEN(S): P 'Son of *Ciss* (*Cecily*)'. 13th cent. [Mr Sisson, cook on the *Lady Penrhyn*, brought the surname to Australia 1788].

SIVIER, SIVYER see SEVIER.

SIXSMITH: O OE *sicol-smith* 'a sickle/scythe smith'.

SKEAT(S), SKEATES, SKETT, SKEET: N ON *skjotr* 'swift, fleet of foot'. DB.

SKEGG: N ON *skegg* 'beard', for a wearer of one. 14th cent.

SKELTON: L An O Scand form of OE *scelftūn* 'the farm on a steep bank or ledge'. (Cumb, Yorks) 12th cent.

SKENE: L SG *sceathin* 'bush, shrub'. (Aberdeens) Scotland.

SKERRATT, SKERRETT, SKERRITT: O OF *escheruis* 'water parsnip'. Metonymic for a grower/seller of parsnips. 13th cent.

SKEWES, SKUSE: L Cornish *skewys* 'shelter'.

SKIDMORE, SCUDAMORE: L OE *scīte-mōr* 'the muddy, dungy moor'. 12th cent.

SKILBECK: L O Scand *skill* 'to separate' + ON *bekkr* or OE *bece* 'stream', 'the boundary stream'.

SKILLMAN: N ON *skilamathr* 'trustworthy man'. 13th cent.

SKINNER: O ON *skinn* 'skin', 'a skinner, stripper of hides'. 13th cent.

SKIPPER: (i) N A deriv. of ME *skip*, 'a leaper, jumper'. 13th cent. (ii) O ME from Du *skypper* 'master of a ship'.

SKIPWORTH: L OE *scēap-worth* 'the sheep enclosure'.

SLACK: (i) L ON *slakki* 'the shallow valley'. 13th cent. (ii) N OE *slēac* 'languid, inactive, negligent'. 12th cent.

SLADE: L OE *slaed* 'glade'. 13th cent.

SLATER, SCLATER, SLATTER: O A deriv. of OF *esclate*, ME *sclate* 'slate', 'a slater, roofer with slates'. 13th cent. [A First Fleet (convict) surname].

SLATTERY: P Ir *O Slatara*, from *slatra* 'strong'. A Co. Clare surname.

SLAUGHTER: (i) L OE *slōhtre* 'a slough, muddy place'. (Glos) 12th cent. (ii) O A deriv. of ME *slahter* 'slaughter', 'a slayer of animals'. 13th cent.

SLAVEN: N OF *esclavine*, ME *slaveyn* 'a pilgrim's mantle', and a nickname for a wearer of one. 12th cent.

SLAY, SLEIGH, SLEITH, SLEATH, SLY: N ME *slez*, from ON *slaegr* 'clever, cunning, expert, skilful'. 13th cent.

SLAYTER, SLAYTOR: O A deriv. of OE *slyht* 'slaughter', 'a slaughterer, butcher'. 14th cent.

SLEE: L OE *slēa* 'the grassy slope'. 13th cent.

SLEEMAN, SLEIMAN, SLIMAN, SLYMAN: N ME *slez-man* 'clever, sagacious man'. 13th cent.

SLIM: L OE *slīm* 'slime', 'the slimy (muddy) place'.

SLINGSBY: L ON 'The *býr* (homestead) of a Norseman called *Slengr*'. (Yorks).

SLOAN(E), SLOYAN: P Ir O *Sluaghain*, from *sluagh* 'army, host'.

SLOCOMBE, SLOCUM: L OE *slāh-cumb* 'sloe (blackthorn fruit) valley'. (Wight).

SLOMAN, SLOWMAN, SLUMAN: L OE *slōh* + *mann* 'the man at the slough (swamp or miry place)'. 14th cent.

SLOPER: O ME *slope* 'a maker/seller of slops (loose outer garments such as smocks)'. 13th cent.

SLOUGH, SLOW: L OE *slōh* 'slough, mire'. 12th cent. See also Sloman.

SLY see SLAY.

SMAIL(S), SMAILES, SMILES: (i) L OE From the lost village of *Smeghel* (Sussex), one of the 1,300 lost villages of England, from *smēagel* 'burrow' or 'badger-hole'. 13th cent. (ii) N A Scottish variant of *Small*, as at Smailholm (Roxburgh).

SMALE(S), SMALL(S), SMEAL(L), SMEALLIE: (i) N OE *smael* 'small, slender, thin'. 13th cent. (ii) L OE *smael*, used topographically, 'the narrow water (burn)'. (Northumb), *Smale* in 1279.

SMALLEY: L OE *smael-lēah* 'the narrow clearing/wood'. (Derbys) 14th cent.

SMALLMAN: O OE 'A land-tenant of inferior status to a *thane* or *dreng*', OE *smaelmann*. See Glossary for thane and dreng.

SMART: N OE *smeart* 'brisk, prompt, active'. 12th cent.

SMEATON, SMEETON: (i) L OE *smithatūn* 'the smiths' enclosure'. (Leices, Yorks) 12th cent. (ii) From Smytheton (Midlothian), with the same meaning as (i), originally *Smithetun* 1124.

SMEDLEY: L OE *smēthe-lēah* 'the smooth level clearing'.

SMEE: N OE *smēthe* 'smooth, suave'.

SMEETH: (i) N OE identical in meaning with *Smee* (ii) O A variant of *Smith*.

SMETHURST: L OE *smēthe-hyrst* 'the smooth. symmetrical wooded hill'.

SMILEY see SMYLIE.

SMITH, SMYTH(E), SMYE: O OE *smith*, the form of the name unchanged in over a thousand years. An occupational surname meaning 'worker in metals, smith, farrier blacksmith'. First recorded as an OE Byname c. 975 and therefore pre-Conquest. Early examples in England include the Lat form *Faber* DB. Most European languages have an equivalent surname, Celtic *Goff, Goffe, Gove*, Cornish *Angove*, OF *Mareschal*, which contributed the English surname *Marshall*, German *Schmidt*, Italian *Farrari*, Russian *Kuznecov*, Polish *Kowalski*, Spanish *Herrera*, Czech *Kovar*. The smith was an important man in medieval times, making and repairing swords, lances, armour, defensive iron-works for castles and many other articles such as agricultural tools. He was both the technologist and the technician, the engineer and the mechanic of his day. Because of this, and also perhaps because he was not quite so close to the heat of battle, there are many more Smiths today than Archers, Knights, Bowmans, and other bearers of the surnames descending from the Middle Ages. See also Feaver, Ferrar, Gow, McGowan, Marshall, Martell. [Twenty-one persons named Smith arrived with the First Fleet 1788. Of these 6 were female convicts, 10 were male convicts, 2 were marines, and 2 were crew members. Also, somewhat surprisingly, a James Smith arrived on the *Lady Penrhyn*, having apparently paid his own passage. Capt R.A. Smith was surveyor-general to the New Zealand Company, 1839].

SMITHER(S): O OE A deriv. of *Smith*, 'smith, hammerman'. 14th cent. (An itinernant or journeyman smith.)

SMITHERMAN, SMITHYMAN, SMYTHYMAN: O OE *smithy-mann* 'a worker at the smithy'. 14th cent. SMITHIES: 'Worker at the smithy'. 14th cent. SMITHSON: 'Son of the smith'. 13th cent.

SMOLLETT: N OE *smael-hēafod* 'small head'. 14th cent.

SMYLEY, SMYLIE, SMILEY: L OF A Scottish surname, originally from Semilly, France. Also numerous in the northern counties of Ireland from Scottish settlement in Co. Tyrone.

SNAILHORN: L OE *snaegl-horn* 'the snail-infested corner of land'. [A First Fleet (convict) surname].

SNAITH: L ON *sneith* 'the detached piece of land'.

SNAPE: L OE *snaep*, from ON *snap* 'winter grazing, i.e., poor pasture'. (Suffolk) 13th cent.

SNEDDEN: L OE *snǣd-denu* 'the piece of woodland in the valley'.

SNELL(E): N OE *snel* 'active, brisk, bold'. 12th cent. SNELLING: A variant of Snell and with the same meaning.

SNELSON: L OE '*Snell's tūn* (farm)'. (Ches), *Snelestune* DB.

SNIDER, SNYDER(S): O OE A deriv. of *snithan* 'to cut', 'a cutter, tailor'. 14th cent.

SNODGRASS: L OE *snod-graes* 'the smooth, level grass'.

SNOOK(E), SNOOKS, SNOOKES: (i) L OE *snōc* 'a projecting point of land'. (ii) N OE *snōc* used as a nickname for one with a long, pointed nose. DB.

SNOW: N OE *snāw* 'snow', a nickname for one with snow-white hair. 13th cent.

SNOWBALL: N OE *snāw* + ME *bal* 'snowball', for a white patch of hair. 13th cent.

SNOWDEN, SNOWDON: L OE *snāw-dūn* 'the snowy hill' (where the snow lingers). 13th cent.

SNUGG(S): N ME *snug*, probably from Dan *snyg* 'tidy'. Snug entered the English language in the 16th cent., originally as a nautical term. As a nickname it means 'well-sheltered, trim, comfortable'. It was known to Shakespeare (*Snug*, a joiner, in *A Midsummer Night's Dream*).

SOAMES, SOMES: L OE *sǣ-hām* 'the homestead by the lake'. (Cambs) 11th cent.

SOAN(E), SOANES see SON. SODEN see SOWDEN.

SODWICK: L OE *suth-wīc* 'the south(ern) dairy farm'. [A First Fleet (crew) surname].

SOLLAS, SOLLARS, SOLIS: N OF *solaz*, ME *solas*. An agreeable nickname and a word of many meanings. Chaucer used it to express amusement, pleasure, playfulness, solace, comfort, consolation, relief, diversion, joy and ease. 13th cent.

SOLLY: (i) P A double dim. of *Solomon*. (ii) L OE An English surname of uncertain etymology, first recorded in the form *Sawlew* 1398, and perhaps originating at the manor of Soles in the parish of Nonington, Kent. (iii) P Ir *Mac Soilligh*, from *soilbh* 'agreeable', but recorded as *O'Soilligh* in 17th cent. money rolls for Co. Monaghan.

SOLOMON see SALAMAN. SOLTAN see SOWDEN. SOMER(S) see SUMMER.

SOMERSET: L OE *Sumorsaete* 'the people of Somerset', later becoming the name of the county. 12th cent.

SOMERVELL, SOMMERVILLE, SOMERVAILLE, SOMMERVILLE, SUMMERVILLE: L OF From Someville

(Somme) or Graveron-Sémmerville (Nord) France. 12th cent.

SOMNER see SUMMER.

SON, SONE(S), SOAN(E), SOANS: N OE *sunu*, ME *sone* 'son', 'descendant'. *Son* is one of the oldest words in the English language and is found in recognisable form in most of the languages which go back to the parent Indo-European including Ger. *sohn*, Du. *zoon*, ON *sunr*, Gothic *sunus*, Sanskrit *sūnu*. As a nickname it may have been used of the younger or junior male in the family. 12th cent as a surname.

SOOTHILL, SUTTLE: L OE *sōt* 'soot' + *hyll*, 'the charcoal-burner's hill'. (Yorks) 12th cent.

SOPER, SOAPER, SAPER: O A deriv. of OE *sāpe* 'soap', 'a maker/seller of soap'. 12th cent.

SORBIE, SORBY, SOWERBY, SURBEY, SURBY: L ON *saurr-býr* 'the muddy, boggy farm'. (Cumb, Lancs, Yorks, Westmorland) 12th cent.

SORREL(L): N OF *sorel* 'reddish-brown', of hair or beard. 12th cent.

SOTHEBY: L ON *suthr-i-býr* 'south in the village'. 12th cent.

SOTHERAN, SOTHERON, SOTHERN, SOUTHAN, SOUTHERN: L OE *sūtherne* or ON *suthraenn* 'from the south'. 13th cent.

SOUTAR, SOUTER, SOUTTER, SOWTER, SUTER, SUTTER: O OE *sūtere* 'shoe-maker'. 13th cent.

SOUTH: L OE *sūth* 'south', 'from the south'. 13th cent. SOUTHALL: L OE *sūth-heall* 'the south hall'. 13th cent. SOUTHAM: L OE *sūth-hām* 'the southern homestead'. (Glos, Warwicks) 12th cent.

SOUTHERLAND see SUTHERLAND.

SOUTHEY: L OE *sūther-ēg* 'the southern island'. 13th cent.

SOUTHGATE: L OE *sūth-geat* 'the south gate (of castle or town)'. 12th cent.

SOUTHWELL: L OE *sūth-wielle* 'the south stream'. SOUTHWICK: L OE *sūth-wīc* 'the outlying farm or dairy farm to the south'. OE Byname 10th cent.

SOWDEN, SODEN, SOLTAN, SOLDEN, SULTAN: N OF *soudan* 'sultan' (the Soldan of the Saracens). A pageant-name. 12th cent.

SPACKMAN see SPEAKMAN.

SPAIN: (i) L OF From Epaignes (Eure) Normandy. 12th cent. (ii) L OF *Espaignart* From Spain.

SPALDING, SPAULDING: L OE A 7th cent. tribal name *Spaldingas*, the *ingas* (people) of the *Spaldas* tribe, who inhabited the fens of Lincs, Hunts and Northants. Surname 12th cent.

SPARE: N OE *spaer* 'frugal, sparing'. 12th cent.

SPARK(E), SPARKES, SPARKS: N ON *sparkr* 'sprightly'. 12th cent. [Sparkes, a First Fleet (convict) surname].

SPARLING, SPERLING, SPURLING: P OE *Spyrling*, an Anglo-Saxon pers. name. 12th cent. An early form of the name is *Esperling* (1173); *esperlinge* is OF for smelt, a fish of the salmon family, suggesting a nickname for a dealer in smelts.

SPARROW: N OE *spearwa* 'sparrow', used of a 'flutterer', a confused, agitated person. 12th cent.

SPARROWHAWK: P/N OE *spearhafoc* 'sparrow-hawk', an Anglo-Saxon pers. name as well as a nickname. DB. In the 14th cent. a bearer of this name was posted as an outlaw.

SPEAK, SPEAKS, SPECK: (i) N OF *espeche* 'woodpecker', a nickname for a gaily dressed bird or perhaps a stutterer. DB. (ii) L OE *spǣc* 'brushwood'. (Speke, Lancs), *Spec* in DB.

SPEAKMAN, SPACKMAN: O ME *spekeman* 'spokesman, advocate'. 12th cent.

SPEAR(E), SPEARS, SPEER(S): O OE *spere* 'spear'. Metonymic for spearman, soldier. 12th cent. SPEARMAN: O OE 'spearman'. 14th cent.

SPEED: N OE *spēd* 'speed, success, wealth, power'. 12th cent.

SPEIGHT, SPEAIGHT: N OE *speoht* 'woodpecker'. 13th cent. See Speak for meaning.

SPELLMAN, SPELMAN: O OE *spell*, from *spellian* 'to speak, discourse', 'a speaker, preacher, professional story-teller, deliverer of homilies'. 13th cent.

SPENCE: O OF *despense*, ME *spence* 'larder', 'man in charge of the buttery'. [A First Fleet (convict) surname].

SPENCER: SPENSER: O OF *despensier* 'dispenser of provisions, butler, steward'. 12th cent. [A First Fleet (convict and marine) surname].

SPENDER: O OF *despendour* 'a steward'. 13th cent.

SPENDLOVE, SPENLOW: N OE *spendan* 'to spend, squander' + *lufu* 'love', 'a gallant'. 13th cent.

SPERLING see SPARLING. SPERRING see SPURREN.

SPICE, SPICER: O OF *espicier* 'a dealer in spices', also 'an apothecary'. 12th cent.

SPIER(S), SPEIR(S), SPYER(S): O OF *espier* 'to spy', 'a watchman, spy'. 13th cent.

SPILLANE: P Ir *O'/Mac Spealain*, from *speal* 'scythe'.

SPILLER: N OE *spillan* 'to squander', 'a waster' or *spillere* 'a parasite', also 'a jester'.

SPILLMAN: O *spilemann* 'a jester, juggler'. 11th cent.

SPILSBURY: L OE *spēol-burg* 'the look-out fort'. (Oxon). 12th cent.

SPINDLER: O OE *spinel* 'spindle', 'a maker of spindles'. 13th cent.

SPINK(S): N ME *spink* 'a finch, chaffinch', an unexplained nickname. See also Finch. 12th cent. (The chaffinch is a little songbird, said to delight in chaff.)

SPINNER: O A deriv. of OE *spinnan* 'to spin', 'a spinner of wool or yarn'. 13th cent.

SPITTLE(S), SPITTAL: O OF *(h)ospital*, ME *spitel* 'hospital (hostel for travellers)', 'a servant at the hospital'. 13th cent.

SPOONER: O OE *spōn* 'spoon'. Metonymic for a maker of spoons. 14th cent.

SPOOR(S) see SPURR.

SPRAGG(E), SPARKE: N ON *spraek* 'lively cheerful, active'. 14th cent.

SPRING: N ME *spring* 'spring, a young shoot', a nickname for an eager young person. 13th cent.

SPRINGALL: O AF *springalde* 'a medieval war engine, a massive catapult'. Metonymic for the soldier operating the *springalde*. 12th cent.

SPRINGER: N A deriv. of OE *springan* 'to jump'. A nickname 'nimble, lively'. 12th cent. SPRINGETT: N A dim. of *Spring*, 'an eager young person'. 12th cent.

SPRINGFIELD: L OE *Springinga-feld* 'the field with a spring'. (Essex).

SPRINGHAM: L OE *spryng-hām* 'the homestead by a spring'. [A First Fleet (convict) surname].

SPRINGMORE: L OE *spryng-mōr* 'the moor or fen with a spring'. [Charlotte Springmore, a female convict, brought the surname to Australia 1788].

SPROAT, SPROT(T), SPROTTE, SPROD: N OE *sprot*, ME *sprote* 'sprout, twig', used of a son, youngster. DB.

SPRY: N Doubtless a nickname for an agile, active, nimble person, but the origin declines to be uncovered. The word first came into use in the 18th cent.

SPURLING see SPARLING.

SPURR, SPOOR(S): O OE *spura, spora* 'spur'. Metonymic for a spurrier, a maker of spurs. 13th cent.

SPURREN, SPERRING, SPURRIER: O OF *esperun* 'a maker of spurs'. 12th cent.

SPYER see SPIER.

SQUIRE(S), SQUIER: O OF *escuyer*, ME *squyer* 'shield-bearer, esquire'. 12th cent. [The surname was brought to Australia in 1788 by Mr Squires, second mate of the *Lady Penrhyn*, and James Squires, highway robber and convict, who was eminently successful in the colony, a farmer, brewer, district constable, banker and taverner].

STACE: P A short-form of *Eustace*. 12th cent.

STACEY, STACY: P A dim. of *Stace*. 13th cent.

STACK: O ON *stakkr*, ME *stack* 'hay-stack'. Metonymic for a stacker (builder of stacks). 12th. Also STACKER.

STACKPOOLE, STACKPOLE: P A Norman name of OF origin, originally *de Stacpul*. 12th cent.

STAFF: N OE *staef* 'staff, stick', a nickname for a thin, lean person, so used by Chaucer. 12th cent.

STAFFORD: (i) L OE *stān-ford* 'stony ford'. (Dorset) (ii) L OE *staeth-ford* 'the ford by the landing-place'. (Staffs) Surname DB.

STAGG: N OE *stagga* 'stag', a virile male, robustly masculine. 12th cent.

STAINER, STEINER: O A deriv. of ME *steyne* 'to stain', 'a stainer, painter'. 14th cent.

STAINES: L OE *stāne* 'stone', a milestone on the nearby Roman road. 13th cent.

STAINTON see STANTON.

STALKER: N OE *stealcian*, ME *stalke* 'to stalk, move stealthily', a nickname for a hunter. 12th cent.

STAMER: N OE *stamera* 'stammerer'. OE Byname 11th cent., suggesting that this was a fairly common affliction.

STAMFORD: L OE *stān-ford* 'the stony ford'. (Lincs, Northumb, Yorks).

STAMMER(S), STANMORE: P OE *Stān-māēr* 'stone-fame'. DB. Also *stān-mere* (lake).

STAMP: L OF From Etampes (Seine-et-Oise) France. 12th cent.

STANBOROUGH, STANBURY: P/L OE *Stānburh*, an Anglo-Saxon woman's name. DB. There are also places of this name with the same meaning (stone-fort) in Devon, Lancs and Yorks.

STANBRIDGE: L OE *stān-brycg* 'the stone bridge'. (Beds, Hants).

STANDEN: L OE *stān-denu* 'the stony valley'. STANDON: L OE *stān-dūn* 'the stone hill'. (Berks, Herts, Wight).

STANDING: L OE A variant of *Standen*. 16th cent.

STANDISH: L OE *stān-edisc* 'the stony pasture'. (Glos, Lancs) 13th cent.

STANFIELD, STANDFIELD: L OE *stān-feld* 'the stony field'. (Norfolk, Staffs) [Daniel Standfield, a marine, brought the surname to Australia 1788].

STANFORD: L OE *stān-ford* 'the stony ford'. See also Stamford.

STANGER: (i) L OE *stān-gāra* 'the stony gore (triangular piece of land)'. 14th cent. (ii) L ON *stongr* 'pole', probably a boundary mark. 14th cent.

STANHOPE: L OE *stān-hop* 'the stony valley'. (Durham) 13th cent.

STANIFORD, STANIFORTH: L OE *stān-ford* 'the stony ford'. (Yorks) 13th cent.

STANILAND: L OE 'stony-land'. 13th cent.

STANISTREET: L OE *stān-strǣet* 'stony-street', probably a Roman road.

STANLEY: L OE *stān-lēah* 'the stony clearing'. (Derbys, Durham, Glos, Staffs, Wilts, Yorks) 12th cent. [A First Fleet (convict) surname. Capt Stanley, commander of the naval vessel *Britomart*, forestalled an attempt by the French to claim the Banks Peninsula of New Zealand and proclaimed British sovereignty, 1840].

STANMORE see STAMMER.

STANNARD, STANNETT: P OE *Stānheard* 'stone-hard'. DB.

STANNAS, STANNERS, STANNUS: L OE *stān-hūs* 'the stone house'. 13th cent.

STANTON, STAINTON, STAUNTON, STENTON: L OE *stān-tūn* 'the farm on stony ground'. OE Byname 11th cent. Stanton (Som) is '*tūn* by the stone circle'.

STANWAY: L OE *stān-weg* 'the stone (paved) way' probably a Roman road.

STANWELL: L OE *stān-wielle* 'the stony stream'. (Middx).

STANYER see STONEHEWER.

STAP(P): L OE *staepe* 'step', probably stepping stones. 13th cent.

STAPLE(S): L OE *stapol* 'pillar, post'. (Kent, Som) 13th cent. This may equally well be OE *stēpel* 'steeple, tower'; steeple-chase had originally a steeple as goal, long before church steeples were built, and this may have been a permanent feature from which a place-name and surname were formed. STAPLETON, STAPYLTON: L OE The *tūn* (farm) by the *stapol* or *stēpel*. 12th cent.

STARK(E), STARKS: N OE *stearc* 'rigid, unyielding, stiff'. 13th cent.

STARKEY, STARKIE, STARKY: N A dim. of *Stark*. 13th cent.

STARLING, STERLING: N OE *staerling* 'starling', a nickname from the bird. DB.

STARR: (i) P OE A pers. name from OE *steorra* 'star'. DB. (ii) L ME *sterre* 'star', a sign-name. (iii) N OE *steorra*, a word that has hardly changed since the parent Indo-European, e.g., Sanskrit *star*. Used as a nickname for an exceptional person (revived in 20th cent. theatre), or for one with rare knowledge of the stars and their courses.

START(E), STURT: L OE *steort* 'promontory'. 12th cent.

STARTIFANT, STURTEVANT: N A combination of ME *sterten* and AF *avaunt* 'start forward', a nickname for a pursuivant, a state messenger ranking below a herald. 12th cent.

STATHAM: L OE *staethe-hām* 'the homestead by the landing-place or embankment'. 15th cent.

STAUNTON see STANTON.

STAVELEY: L OE *staef-lēah* 'the clearing where staves may be cut'. (Derbys, Lancs, Westmorland, Yorks).

STAWELL: L OE *stān-wielle* 'the stony stream or spring'. (Som).

STEAD, STEDE, STEED(E): (i) N OE *stēda* 'stallion, stud-horse', a nickname for a person of high spirits and stamina. 12th cent. (ii) L OE *stede* 'a landed estate' and O in a transferred sense for the steward of such an estate. 13th cent.

STEADMAN, STEDMAN: O OE *stede-mann* (i) 'a mounted warrior', (ii) 'a groom charged with the care of war-horses', (iii) 'a stud farmer'. 13th cent.

STEARMAN: (i) O OE *stēor-mann* 'steer-man, herdsman'. (ii) *stēora-mann* 'steersman, pilot'. 12th cent.

STEBBING(S), STEBBINS: L OE *stubbing* 'cleared land'. See also Stubbings.

STEEL(E), STEELL: N OE *stēle, stȳle* 'steel', a nickname for one true as steel. 13th cent.

STEEPER: O A deriv. of ME *stepe*, from OE *stīepan*, 'to steep'. 'A steeper of flax'. 14th cent.

STEER(E), STEERS, STEAR(S): O OE *steor*, a 'steer-herd'. 13th cent.

STEFFAN, STEFFEN see STEPHEN. STEGELS, STEGGAL(S) see STILE.

STEIN, STEYNE(E), STAIN, STAINES, STAINS: P O Dan *Sten*, ON *Steinn*. DB. Later introductions are from OHG *Stein* 'stone'. See also Staines.

STEINER see STAINER.

STELLING: L OE *stiellan* 'the cattle-fold'.

STENNING, STEYNING: L OE 'The *ingas* (people) of an Anglo-Saxon called *Stāen* (Stone)'. (Sussex), *Staninges* DB.

STENTON see STANTON.

STEPHEN(S), STEFFAN, STEFFEN(S), STEVEN(S), STIVEN(S): P Gk *Stephanos* 'Crown'. Introduced into England by the Normans, and a popular medieval name. DB. [A First Fleet (marine) surname].

STEPHENSON, STEVENSON, STEPHINSON: P 'Son of *Stephen*'. 14th cent.

STERLING see STARLING, STIRLING.

STERN(E), STEARN(S): N OE *styrne* 'strict, severe, austere'. 13th cent.

STERNBECK: L OE *stāener* + ON *bekkr* 'the *beck* (brook) on stony ground'.

STEWARD, STEWART, STEUART, STUART: O OE *stīweard, stigweard* 'steward': (i) 'steward (seneschal) of a manor or castle'; (ii) 'controller of a large household'; (iii) 'manager of a landed estate'. The royal house of *Stuart* dates from the accession of Robert the Steward as Robert II of Scotland. Surname 12th cent. [A First Fleet (convict and marine) surname].

STEWARDSON, STEWARTSON: O 'Son of the steward'. 12th cent.

STEYN(E) see STEIN. STEYNING see STENNING.

STIBBARD: L OE *stig-byrde* 'path by the river or road bank'. (Norfolk).

STICKELLS see STILES.

STIFF(E): N OE *stīf* 'stiff, unbending, obstinate'.

STIG: L OE *stig* 'stye, pen' or *stīg* 'narrow path, track'.

STILE(S), STYLE(S), STEGGALL, STEGGEL, STICKELLS, STEGALL, STEGGLE(S): L OE *stigol, stigel* 'stile', from *stīgan* 'to ascend'. (The countryside abounded in footpaths and stiles, hence the large number of variant surnames.) 13th cent.

STILEMAN, STILLMAN: L OE *stigel* + *mann* 'by the stile'. 13th cent.

STILGOE: L OE *stigol* 'stile' (by metathesis).

STIMPSON, STIMSON, STINSON: P 'Son of *Stephen*'. 16th cent.

STIRLING, STERLING: L From Stirling, city in Scotland. See also Starling. A Brit name, *Strivelin* in 1147.

STIVEN see STEPHEN.

STOCK(S): L OE *stocc* 'stump of a tree'. 13th cent. OE *stocc* also came to mean 'pillory'.

STOCKBRIDGE: L OE *stocc-brycg* 'the foot-bridge made of tree-stumps or a tree-trunk'. (Hants).

STOCKDALE: L OE *stocc-dael* 'the valley of tree-stumps'. (Cumb, Yorks) 14th cent. [A First Fleet (convict) surname].

STOCKELL, STOCKILL: L OE *stocc-helde* 'the slope with tree-stumps'. (Yorks) 13th cent. [James Stockell, a sailor, arrived with the First Fleet 1788].

STOCKER: O OE A deriv. of *stocc* 'a grubber of tree-stocks'. 13th cent.

STOCKHAM: L OE *stoccum*, plural of *stocc* 'tree-stumps'. (Ches).

STOCKING: L OE *stoccing* 'the ground cleared of tree-stumps'. 13th cent.

STOCKLEIGH, STOCKLEY, STOCKLE: L OE *stocc-lēah* 'the wood where tree-stumps were extracted'. (Devon, Durham, Staffs) 13th cent.

STOCKMAN: L OE Identical in meaning with *Stocker*. 13th cent.

STOCKTON: L OE *stocc-tūn* 'the log-built homestead'. (Ches, Durham, Norfolk, Salop, Wilts, Warwicks, Worces, Yorks).

STOCKWELL: L OE *stocc-wielle* 'the stream with a tree-trunk foot-bridge'. (Surrey).

STODART, STODDARD, STODDART, STUDDARD, STUDDEARD, STUDDERT: O OE *stōd* 'stud (of horses)', 'a horse-keeper, breeder'. 12th cent.

STOKER: O OE identical in meaning with *Stocker*. 13th cent. [A First Fleet (convict) surname].

STOKES, STOOKE(S), STOAKS: L OE *stoc* original meaning the rather vague 'place'. Later given a special meaning 'monastery, cell', hence 'holy place', but other meanings have been noted, e.g., cattle-farm, dairy-farm, usually an outlying farm. The name was often in the plural *stocu*. A frequent place-name and surname. 11th cent. [In New Zealand, Robert Stokes opened up an alternative route to Wairarapa by climbing the Rimutakas, 1841].

STOKOE: L OE *stocc* + O Scand *haugr* 'the mound/ hillock with tree-stumps'.

STONE(S): L OE *stān*, plural *stānas* 'stone' or 'stones', usually a stone of some significance such as a boundary stone or hundred (shire subdivision) stone. (Berks, Hants, Kent, Som, Staffs, Worces) 13th cent. [A First Fleet (convict) surname].

STONEHAM, STONHAM: L OE *stān-hām* 'the stony homestead'. 16th cent.

STONEHEWER, STONIER, STANYER: O OE *stān* + a deriv. of *hēawen* 'to hew', 'a stone-cutter, quarrier of stone'. 13th cent.

STONEHOUSE: L OE *stān-hūs* 'the stone house' (most were timber, wattle and daub). (Devon, Glos) 13th cent.

STONESTREET: L OE *stān-straet* 'a Roman road'. 13th cent.

STONEY: L OE *stān-ēg* 'the stony island or gravelly low-lying land'. 14th cent.

STONOR, STONER: L OE *stān-ora* 'the stony ridge'. (Oxon).

STONROCK see STURROCK.

STOODLEY, STUDLEY: L OE *stōd-lēah* 'the horse-pasture'. (Devon).

STORER, STORAH, STORRAR: O A deriv. of ME *storen* 'to store': (i) 'keeper of provisions for a large household', (ii) 'a wool-storer'. 14th cent.

STOREY, STORIE, STORY, STORRIE, STORRY: P ON *Stóri*, a pers. name. DB. [John Storey, a sailor on the *Charlotte*, brought the surname to Australia 1788].

STORK: N OE *storc* 'stork', 'long-legs'. 12th cent.

STORM(S): N OE *storm* 'storm, tempest', 'tumult, disturbance', a nickname for one of stormy temperament. 12th cent.

STORR: N ON *storr* 'big', for a large, heavy man. 12th cent.

STOT(T): N OE *stot* 'a nag, a jade'. 12th cent.

STOTHARD, STOTHART, STUTTARD: O ME *stott-hierde* 'a keeper of horses or bullocks, steers, heifers'. 13th cent. In *Piers Plowman*, Passus xix, *stot* 'a young oxen'.

STOUT: (i) N OE *stūt* 'gnat', 'an irritating little person'. (ii) N OF *estolt*, ME *stout* 'stout' in the sense of bold, stout-hearted. 12th cent.

STOW(E): L OE *stōw* 'holy place', e.g., monastery or church. 12th cent.

STOYLE: OF *estoile*, ME *stoyle* 'star', with the same meaning as *Starr*. 12th cent.

STRACHAN, STRAHAN, STRAUGHAN: L SG From Strachan (Kincardines) Scotland, from SG *srath* 'valley'. 12th cent.

STRADBROKE: L OE *straēt-brōc* 'the brook by the Roman road'. (Staffs).

STRAKER see STRIKER. STRANG see STRONG.

STRANGE, LESTRANGE: L OF *estrange* 'stranger, foreigner'. 12th cent.

STRATFORD: L OE *straēt-ford* 'the ford where a Roman road crossed the river'. (Beds, Bucks, Essex, Middx, Suffolk, Warwicks, Wilts) DB.

STRATTON: L OE *straēt-tūn* 'the homestead, farm or settlement by a Roman road'. A frequent place-name. 12th cent. (Stratton (Cornwall) has its own meaning: Old Cornish *stret* 'stream + *ystrad* 'valley', 'the valley of River Strat'.)

STREET(E), STREAT: L OE *straēt* 'street, Roman (paved) road'. 12th cent.

STREETER, STREATER: L OE 'One who lived on the street (Roman road)'. 13th cent.

STRETCH: N OE *strec* 'strong, violent'. 12th cent. [A First Fleet (convict) surname].

STRETTON: L OE identical in meaning with *Stratton*. 13th cent.

STRICKLAND: L OE *steorc-land* 'pasture for bullocks/heifers'. (Westmorland). 12th cent.

STRIKE, STRIKER, STRAKER: O *strike*, a word formed from OE *strīcan* 'to stroke', and a flat stick used in the measurement of a bushel of wheat. Metonymic for an official responsible for the accuracy of the measure. 13th cent.

STRINGER: O OE A deriv. of *streng* 'string, cord'. 'A maker of string for bows, a stringer of bows'. 12th cent.

STRINGFELLOW: N OE *strenge, strang-fēolaga* 'strong fellow, partner', a reliable comrade. 13th cent.

STRODE see STROUD.

STRONG(E), STRANG: N OE *strang*, ME *strong* 'strong', a strong man. 12th cent.

STROUD, STRODE, STROOD: L OE *strōd* 'marshy land overgrown with brushwood'. (Kent, Glos, Middx) 12th cent.

STRUDWICK: L OE *strōd-wīc* 'the dairy farm in marshland'.

STRUTHERS: L OE *strother*, from *strōd* 'marshy, boggy land'. (Fifes) Scotland.

STUART see STEWARD.

STUBB(E), STUBBS: (i) L OE *stobb* 'the tree-stumps'. (Yorks) 12th cent. (ii) N OE *stybb* 'stub', 'short and stumpy'. OE Byname c. 1000.

STUBBING(S), STUBBIN(S): (i) N OE *stybbing* 'the stumpy one'. 12th cent. (ii) L ME *stubbing* 'the cleared land'. 13th cent.

STUDDARD see STODART.

STUDHOLME: L OE *stōd-holm* 'horse-island'. [Michael and John Studholme were pioneers in the settlement of Waimate District, Canterbury, New Zealand, 1853].

STUMBLES: L OE *stumbel* 'tree-stumps'. 13th cent.

STURDEE, STURDY: N OF *estordet* 'fierce, reckless'. In ME this came to mean 'fierce in combat, impetuously brave'. 11th cent.

STURGE(S), STURGESS, STURGISS: P O Scand *Thorgisl*, *Thorgils* '*Thor's* hostage'. The name appears in Old Norse, Old Swedish and Old Danish. DB.

STURGEON: N OF *esturgeon* 'sturgeon', a nickname from the fish, probably for a seller of sturgeons, a fish-monger. 13th cent.

STURMAN: O O Dan *styreman* 'steersman', perhaps also master of a ship. DB.

STURROCK, STONROCK: L OE *stānrocc* 'the high rock'. 13th cent.

STURT see START. STURTEVANT see STARTIFANT. STUTTARD see STOTHARD. STYLE see STILE. SUART see SEWARD.

SUCH, SUTCH, CHUCK: L OF *souche* 'tree-stump'. 12th cent.

SUFFOLK: L OE *sūth-folc* 'the southern folk'. As a surname 'the man from Suffolk'. 13th cent.

SUGDEN: L OE *sugga-denu* 'the valley frequented by titlarks'. (Yorks) 14th cent.

SUGGATE, SUGGETT, SUGGITT: L Variants of *Southgate*.

SULLIVAN see O'SULLIVAN. SULTAN see SOWDEN.

SUMMER(S), SOMMER(S), SOMER(S): O OF *somier* 'sumpter'. Metonymic for a sumpter-man (pack-horse driver). 13th cent. [Summers, a First Fleet (convict) surname].

SUMMERSCALE, SUMMERSGILL, SUMMERSKILL: L ON *sumer-skáli* 'herdsman at the summer-huts'. 14th cent.

SUMMERVILLE see SOMERVELL.

SUMNER, SOMNER: O OF *somoneor*, AF *sumenour*, 'a summoner', 'a minor official who cites and warns offenders to appear in court', also 'one who summons sinners before an ecclesiastical court'. 12th cent.

SUMPTER: O OF *sometier* 'driver of a pack-horse'. 12th cent. See also Summer.

SUMSION, SUMPTON: N Lat *assūmptum* From birth or baptism on the Feast of the Assumption, fifteenth day of August.

SUNDERLAND: L OE *sundorland* 'separate land'. (Cumb, Lancs, Durham).

SUPPLE: N OF *souple* The meaning has varied over the centuries: 'submissive', 'bending the knees', 'pliant, adaptable, fawning', 'lithe, nimble'.

SURBEY see SORBIE.

SURGEON: O AF *surgien* 'surgeon'. 13th cent. (The surgeon was often also the barber, who extracted teeth and amputated limbs.)

SURMAN, SURMON see SERMIN.

SURPLICE, SURPLIS: O OF *sourpelis*, AF *surplis* (from Lat *pellicia* 'fur garment'). Originally worn over fur garments in unheated medieval churches, now only by clerics and choristers in comparative comfort. Metonymic for a maker of surplices.

SURR see SIRE.

SURTEES: L AF *sur* + Brit *Tees* 'by the River Tees'. (Durham) 12th cent.

SUSAN: P Hebrew *Shushannah* 'lily'. A medieval surname. 12th cent.

SUTCLIFF(E): L OE *sūth-clif* 'the south cliff'. (Yorks) 13th cent.

SUTER, SUTTER see SOUTAR.

SUTHERLAND: L ON *suthroen* + OE *land* 'the southern land', i.e., south of Norse colonies in the Orkneys and Shetlands. From Sutherland, Scotland. 14th cent.

SUTTLE: N AF *sotil* 'subtle, clever, crafty'. 13th cent. See also Soothill.

SUTTON: L OE A widespread place-name, appearing in most counties. OE *sūth-tūn* 'the southern farm or settlement'. DB.

SWADDLING, SWADLING: P OE *Sweartling*, an Anglo-Saxon pers. name, preserved in Swadlincote (Derbys).

SWAIN, SWANE, SWAYN(E): O ON *Sveinn* or O Dan, O Sw *Sven* 'boy, servant', also 'peasant, swineherd'. DB. SWAINSON: 'Son of *Sveinn*'. 14th cent.

SWAINSTON: L ON '*Sveinn's tūn* (farm)'. *Tūn* is OE.

SWALLOW: (i) N OE *swealwe* 'swallow', a nickname of elusive meaning. In addition to the bird, a broad arrow and the pennant of a lance were called a swallow. Perhaps the clue lies in the fact that the swallow is a migratory bird. (ii) L OE *swelg* 'whirlpool' as at Swallow (Lincs). 12th cent.

SWAN(N): (i) O OE *swān* 'herdsman, swineherd, peasant'. 12th cent. (ii) L 'The Swan', a sign-name. (iii) N A nickname from the swan, perhaps for purity or a swan-like neck.

SWANNELL: P ON *Svanhildr*, a woman's name. 12th cent.

SWANNICK, SWANWICK: L OE *swān-wīc* 'the outlying farm of the swineherds'. (Derbys, Hants) OE Byname 11th cent.

SWANSON: O/L/N 'Son of *Swan*'.

SWANTON: L OE *swāna-tūn* 'the farm of the swineherds'. (Kent, Norfolk) 12th cent.

SWARD: (i) P A development of OE *Sweord*, an Anglo-Saxon pers. name preserved in Swardeston (Norfolk). (ii) L OE *sweard* 'skin, rind', in ME a sward of earth, 'the turf or grassy land'.

SWART: N OE *sweart* or ON *svartr* 'swarthy'. DB.

SWAYNE see SWAIN.

SWEATMAN, SWEETMAN: N OE *Swētmann* 'sweet man', 'dear, beloved man'. DB.

SWEENEY see MAC SWEENEY.

SWEET, SWETE: N OE *swēte* 'pleasant, agreeable', also 'fragrant'. DB.

SWEETAPPLE: N OE *swēte-appel*. A term of endearment and a nickname. 13th cent.

SWEETING: P/N OE *Swēting* 'darling, sweetheart'. A nickname which early became a pers. name. 12th cent.

SWEETINGHAM, SWETENHAM, SWEETNAM, SWETTENHAM: L OE 'The *hām* (homestead) of an Anglo-Saxon called *Swēta (Sweet)*'. (Ches) 13th cent.

SWEETSER, SWITZER: N OE *swēte* + ME *sire* 'sweet sir', 'dear master'. 14th cent.

SWIFT: P/N OE *swift* 'swift, fleet'. A pers. name as well as a nickname from the bird. 12th cent.

SWINBURN(E), SWINBOURN(E): L OE *swīn-burna* 'the (wild) pig brook'. (Northumb) 13th cent. SWINDELL(S): L OE *swīn-dael* 'pig-valley'. (Lancs) SWINDEN: L OE *swīn-denu* 'pig-valley'. SWINFIELD: L OE *swīn-feld* 'pig field'. SWINTON: L OE *swīn-tūn* 'pig-farm'. (Lancs, Yorks).

SWINYARD: O OE *swīn-geard* 'worker at the pig-enclosure'. 14th cent.

SWORD(S): O OE *sweord* 'sword'. Metonymic for a sword-maker. 12th cent.

SWYNNERTON, SWINNERTON: L OE *swīnford-tūn* 'the farm by the pig ford'. (Swynnerton, Staffs) 12th cent.

SYDENHAM: L OE *sīd-hamm* 'the wide water-meadow'. (Devon, Oxon, Som) 12th cent.

SYDE see SIDE. SYDNEY see SIDNEY. SYER see SIRE.

SYKES: L OE *sīc* 'gully, dip, hollow', also 'a small stream'. 12th cent.

SYLVESTER see SILVESTER. SYME see SIM. SYMINGTON see SIMINGTON. SYMMONS, SYMONS see SIMMONDS, SIMON. SYMS, SYMMS see SIM. SYNNOTT see SINNETT. SYRED see SIRED.

T

TABARD, (i) O OF *tabart*, ME *tabard* 'a sleeveless coat still worn by heralds on ceremonial occasions'. Metonymic for a maker of *tabards*. 13th cent. (ii) L A sign-name. Chaucer's pilgrims assembled at the *Tabard*, an inn at Southwark, London.

TABER, TABOR, TABERER: O OF *tabour* 'a tabor (drum)', 'player on the tabor', 'a drummer'. OF *tabour* from Pers. *tabīra* 'drum'. 12th cent.

TADD: N OE *tādige, tāde* A nickname from the toad.

TAFT see TOFT.

TAGART, TAGGART: O Ir The complete form of this Ulster surname is Mc Entaggart, *Mac an tSagairt* 'son of the *Sagart* (priest)'.

TAGUE see TEAGUE.

TAILFORD: L OE *taegl-ford* 'the ford at the narrow, projecting land'.

TAIT: N ON *teitr* 'cheerful, jolly'. 12th cent.

TALBOT(T): P OG *Dalabod*, OF *Talebot*, a pers. name. 12th cent.

TALL: N OE *tael* 'swift, prompt, valiant'. This is the original meaning. The sense of tall, lofty is 16th cent.

TALLBOY: O OF *taille-bosc* 'cut-wood', 'a wood cutter'. DB.

TALLENTIRE: L Brit, O Bret, O Cornish, OW *tal-en-tir* 'the end of the land'. (Cumb), *Talentir* 1200.

TALLON: P OG *Talo*, OF *Talon*, a pers. name which appears to be related to OF *talon* 'claw'. 12th cent.

TALMADGE, TALMAGE, TOLLEMACHE: N OF *talemache* 'knapsack'. 12th cent.

TAME: L A Brit river-name (Staffs, Warwick) meaning 'dark river'. Also R. Tame (Lancs, Yorks) with the same meaning. The R. Thames is from the same root, cogn. with Sanskrit *Tamasā*, a tributory of the Ganges (*tamasā* 'dark'). Thame (Oxon) is recorded as *Tame* in DB and this is probably the source of the surname.

TAMLIN, TAMLYN, TAMBLING, TAMPLIN: P A double dim. of *Tam* (*Tom*). See also Tomlin.

TANCRED: P OG *Tancrad* 'thought-counsel'. 13th cent. [H.J. Tancred arrived in New Zealand on the *Barbara Gordon*, one of the early ships].

TANDY: P A dim. of *Andrew*.

TANGUY, TINGAY, TINGEY: P O Bret *Tanguy, Tengi, Tingi*, the name of a Breton saint, O Bret *tan-ci* 'fire-dog'. Also a Cornish name.

TANKARD: (i) P OG *Tancard* 'thought-hard'. 12th cent. (ii) O OF *tanquart* Metonymic for a maker of tankards. 13th cent.

TANNER: O OE *tannere* or OF *taneor* 'a tanner of leather'. 12th cent.

TANSEY: L OE *tān-īeg* 'the island at the branch of the river'. (No connection with the herb tansy, used in the Middle Ages to repel fleas, ward off the plague, and relieve cramps in the leg.)

TANSLEY: L OE *tān-lēah* 'the valley branching from the main dale'. (Derbys).

TAPER: O OE *tapur* 'taper'. Metonymic for a maker of tapers (candles). 14th cent.

TAPLIN: P A dim. of *Tapp*.

TAPNER: O OF 'A maker of *chalons* and *burel* (coverlets and blankets of coarse woollen cloth)'. 13th cent.

TAPP(E), TEAPE: P OE *Taeppa*, a pers. name preserved in several place-names such as Taplow (Bucks). 12th cent.

TAPPER: O OE *taepere* 'tapper of casks, a beer-seller'. 11th cent.

TAPPIN(G): P 'Son of *Tapp*'. 13th cent.

TAPSELL: L OE '*Tapp's (ge)sell* (animal shelter)'. [Philip Tapsell and Henry Williams were the first Europeans to venture into Rotarua, 1831].

TARBERT, TARBUTT see TURBARD.

TARBOCK, TARBUCK: L OE *thorn-brōc* 'thorn-brook', with a change in the initial letters to meet the needs of Norman pronunciation. (Lancs).

TARGETT: O OF *targa* 'shield', 'a maker of small round shields'. The sense of archery target is 18th cent.

TARLETON, TARLTON: L OE 'The *tūn* (farm) near the thorn-bushes'. (Lancs, Glos) 12th cent. Originally *Thornton*, changed by Norman pronunciation.

TARR: O OE *teoru* 'tar', 'a worker with tar', probably on ships. [A First Fleet (marine) surname].

TARRANT: L A variant of *Trent*, a Brit river-name. (Dorset) 12th cent.

TARRAS see TERRAS. TARRY see TERREY.

TARTE: O OF *tarte* 'a kind of loaf'. Metonymic for a maker of *tartes*. 13th cent.

TARVES: O OF *talevas* 'a massive target, set in the ground on a pike'. A maker/seller of *talevas*, or one changed with responsibility for it. 12th cent.

TARVIN: L OW *terfyn* 'boundary'.

TASH see ASH.

TASKER: O ME *taske* 'assessment, reckoning'. A deriv. of *taske*, applied to a thresher of corn, a 'task-worker, piece-worker' as distinct from a day labourer. 13th cent.

TATAM, TATUM, TATHAM: L OE *Tāta's hām* 'Tate's homestead'. (Lancs) 13th cent.

TATE: P OE *Tāta*, an Anglo-Saxon pers. name. 11th cent.

TATTERSHALL, TATTERSHAL: L OE 'The *halh* (corner or angle of land) of an Anglo-Saxon called *Tathere*'. (Lincs), *Tateshale* DB. Surname 12th cent.

TAUNTON: L Brit + OE 'The *tūn* (farm) on the River *Tone*'. (Som).

TAVERNER, TAVERNOR, TAVENER, TAVENDER: O OF *tavernier*, AF *taverner* 'a tavern-keeper'. 12th cent.

TAYLOR, TAYLER: O OF *tailleur*, AF *taillour* 'a tailor'. 12th cent. [A First Fleet (convict) surname].

TAZELAAR, TESLER, TESSLER: O A deriv. of OE *taesel*, 'a teaser of woollen cloth (with a teasel)'. 13th cent.

TEAGUE: (i) P Ir *MacTaidhg*, a surname with several variants, *Teige, Tigue, Tighe*, usually with *Mac* prefix. (ii) N Cornish *tek* 'fair, beautiful'. [Cornelius Teague, a convict, brought the surname to Australia 1788].

TEAL(E), TEALL: N ME *tele* 'teal', an unexplained nickname from the water-fowl. 12th cent.

TEAPE see TAPP. TEARALL see TIRRELL.

TEASDALE, TEESDALE, TEASDELL: L Brit + OE 'The *dael* (valley) of the River *Tees*'. 13th cent.

TEASEL: O OE *taesel*. Metonymic for a teaser of woollen cloth. See also Tazelaar.

TEBB: P A pet-form of *Tebbold* (*Theobald*). 12th cent.

TEBBET, TEBBATT, TEBBIT, TEBBUTT: P Variants of *Theobald*.

TEE: L OE *ēa* 'water, stream'. In ME *atte ēa*. 14th cent.

TEELING: P Anglo-Irish *Taoilinn*, a Co. Meath surname.

TEGART, TEGGART: O OE *tegga* 'a young sheep', 'a shepherd'. 14th cent.

TEGG, TIGG: O Metonymic for *Tegart*, 'a shepherd'. 13th cent.

TELFER, TELFORD: N OF *taille fer* 'cut iron', a nickname for one with the skill and strength to cleave through the armour of his adversary. 11th cent.

TEMBY: L Brit + ON 'The *býr* (farm) on the River Teme'.

TEMPANY: O OF *tympan, tympany* 'a drum, timbrel or tambourine', 'a drummer, player on the timbrel or tambourine'. 13th cent. See also Preface.

TEMPEST: N OF *tempeste*, ME *tempest* 'storm, agitation, perturbation'. A nickname for one exhibiting these uncomfortable characteristics. 12th cent.

TEMPLAR, TEMPLER: O OF A member of the Knights Templars, a military and religious organisation founded early in the 12th cent., its members consisting of knights, chaplains and men-at-arms.

TEMPLE: O OF The founder of the Knights Templars was called Hugo of the Temple, and there is no doubt that the surnames *Temple* and *Templar* originated with Hugo and his knights, but not all of those bearing these surnames can claim descent from the Knights Templars. In the 18th cent. more than one hundred foundlings were baptised with these names at the Temple in London.

TEMPLEMAN: O 'A servant or tenant of the Knights Templars', who owned lands in Cambridgeshire, where the name *Temple* survives in farms which have descended from the manors.

TEMPLETON: L OF + OE 'The *Templar's tūn* (farm)'.

TENCH: N OF *tenche* 'a fat, sleek fish'. 12th cent. [Captain Watkin Tench, who later wrote two books on the early settlement in N.S.W., arrived with the First Fleet 1788].

TENNANT, TENNENT: O OF *tenant* 'a holder of a tenement (land by any tenure)', 'a holder or possessor of land'. 14th cent. [A First Fleet (convict) surname].

TENNYSON, TENNISON: P & L A variant of *Denison*, with substitution of T for D, a not infrequent occurrence, e.g., *Dandy/Tandy*. 14th cent.

TERRAS, TERRIS, TERRACE, TARRAS: (i) L OF *terras*, from Lat *terra* 'earth'; OF *terrasse* 'earthen mound, raised bank, terrace cultivation, e.g., vineyard'. The form *Terras* is from the Dauphiné. (ii) L From Tarras in the parish of Rafford (Moray) Scotland. Adam *de Tarays*, monk, 1375; Jacobus *Terras*, Succentor (Preceptor's deputy in a cathedral) 1569 (Black).

TERREY, TERRY, TERRIS, TARRY, TORREY, TORRY: P OG *Theudoric* 'people-rule', OF *Thierry, Tierry, Terri*. DB.

TESLER, TESSLER see TAZELAAR.

TESTAR, TESTER: N OF *testard*, a disparaging deriv. of *teste* 'head', 'big-head'. 12th cent.

TETLEY: L OE 'The *lēah* (glade or clearing) of an Anglo-Saxon called *Tāta* (Tate)'.

THACKER: O OE A deriv. of *thacian* 'to thatch', 'a thatcher'. 14th cent.

THACKERAY, THACKRAH, THACKRAY, THACKERY: L ON *thak-rá* 'the nook providing reeds for thatching'. 14th cent. [A First Fleet (female convict) surname].

THAIN, THANE, THAYNE: O OE *thegn* 'a servant, follower, nobleman, courtier', the name meant all of these at different periods. Surname 12th cent.

THATCHER: O OE a deriv. of OE (Anglian form) *thaeccan* 'to cover, thatch', 'a thatcher'. 13th cent. See also Thacker, Theaker. [John Thatcher, a marine, brought the surname to Australia 1788].

THAXTER: O OE The feminine form of *Thacker*, a peculiarly Norfolk surname, where it has largely absorbed *Thatcher*. 13th cent.

THEAKER: O ON *thekja* 'to cover', 'a roofer (thatcher or tiler)', recorded in the City of York. 12th cent.

THEAKSTON(E): L OE 'The *tūn* (farm) of an Anglo-Saxon called *Thēodec*'. (Yorks),

Eston DB. [A First Fleet (crew) surname, John Theakston, who had a son by Ann Yeates, a convict. Ann later had two children by Judge Advocate David Collins, and so helped to establish these surnames in Australia].

THELWALL, THELWELL: L OE *thel-wǣl* 'the deep pool by a plank bridge'. (Ches).

THEOBALD, TEBBET(T), TEBBIT(T), TEBBUT(T), TIBAL, TIBBLES, TIBBELS, TIDBALL: P OG *Theudobald* 'people-bold', OF *Theobald*. DB. The vernacular pronunciation in earlier centuries was *Tibbald*.

THEODORE: P Gk *Theodorus* 'God-gift'. The name of an Archbishop of Canterbury in the 7th cent.

THEW, THEWES, THOW: O OE *thēow* 'bondman, slave'. 12th cent.

THICK: N ME *thikke* 'thick-set, stocky'. 13th cent.

THICKETT, THICKITT: L OE *thicce-hēafod* 'the thick headland', either a blunt headland or one thick with vegetation. (Yorks).

THIN, THYNNE: N OE *thynne* 'lean, slender'. 13th cent.

THINGWALL: L ON *thingvollr* 'the assembly field'. (Ches), *Tinguelle* DB.

THIRGOOD see THURGOOD. THIRKELL. THIRKILL see THURKELL. THIRKETTLE see THURKETTLE.

THIRLEY: L OE *thyrel* 'the deep hollow'.

THIRLWALL, THIRLWELL: L OE *thyrel-weall* 'the holed wall', a gap in the Roman wall. (Northumb).

THIRSK: L O Sw *thraesk* 'lake, fen'. (Yorks), *Tresc* DB.

THIRTLE see THURKELL.

THISTLETHWAITE, THISTLETHWAYTE: L OE *thistel* + ON *thveit* 'the meadow overgrown with thistles'. (A lost place in Cumb.) THISTLETON: L OE *thistel-tūn* 'the farm with thistles'. (Lancs, Yorks) 13th cent.

THOM(S): P A pet-form of *Thomas*, mainly Scots. 14th cent.

THOMAS, TOMAS: P An Aramaic word meaning 'twin', and the name of one of the twelve apostles. A rare name in England before the Norman Conquest and borne only by a priest, but popular thereafter, especially after the murder of *Thomas* Becket (St *Thomas* of Canterbury). Surname DB. [Seven persons named Thomas arrived with the First Fleet, four of them convicts, two marines, and the wife of one of the marines].

THOMASON, THOMASSON: P 'Son of *Thomas*'. 14th cent.

THOMLEY see TOMLEY. THOMLINSON see TOMLINSON. THOMMEN see TUMMAN.

THOMPSETT, THOMSETT, TOMPSETT, TOMSETT: P *Thomas-et*, a dim. of *Thomas*.

THOMPSON, THOMSON, TOMPSON, TOMSON: P 'Son of *Tom* (*Thomas*)'. 14th cent. [Five persons named Thompson arrived with the First Fleet, a marine, a seaman and three convicts].

THORBURN, THOBURN, THURBON, TURBIN: P ON *Thorbiorn*, O Dan & O Sw *Thorbiorn* 'Thor-bear', anglicised as *Thurbeorn* 'Thor-warrior'. DB.

THORLEY: L OE *thorn-lēah* 'the thorny clearing'. (Herts, Wight).

THORMAN see THURMAN.

THORN(E): L OE *thorn* 'thorn-bushes'. (Som, Yorks) 12th cent.

THORNBOROUGH, THORNBURY, THORNBERRY, THORNBER: L OE *thorn-beorge* 'thorn-hill'. (Bucks, Yorks) 12th cent. Those from Devon, Herefords, Northumb are 'the *burg* (fort) protected by a thorn hedge'.

THORNCROFT, THORNCRAFT: L OE *thorn-croft* 'small holding overgrown with thorn-bushes'. THORNDIKE, THORNDYKE: L OE *thorn-dīc* 'the thorny ditch'. 17th cent.

THORNEYCROFT: L OE meaning identical with *Thorncroft*. THORNHILL: L OE *thorn-hyll* 'the hill covered with thorn bushes'. (Derbys, Dorset, Wilts, Yorks) 13th cent. THORNLEY: L OE *thorn-lēah* 'thorny wood or clearing'. (Durham, Lancs). THORNTHWAITE: L OE + ON *thorn-thveit* 'the thorny enclosure or meadow'. (Cumb, Westmorland, Yorks) THORNTON: L OE *thorn-tūn* 'the farm with thorn bushes'. 12th cent. [A First Fleet (convict) surname].

THOROGOOD, THORGOOD, THOROWGOOD see THURGOOD.

THORP(E): L OE & O Dan *thorp* 'farm, hamlet or village', a frequent place-name and especially common in the Danelaw. 12th cent.

THORSBY: L O Scand 'The *by* (farm) of a Scandinavian settler called *Thori*'. (Cumb).

THORY, TORY: L O Dan *Thorir*, a Danish pers. name. Norman difficulties with pronunciation produced *Tory*. (See also *Graham, Grantham*). DB.

THOW see THEW.

THRALE, THRALL: O OE *thrǣl*, ON *threal*

'a villein, serf, bondman'. An ancient name of lowly status but first recorded as a surname 14th cent. See also Bond.

THRASHER, THRESHER: O OE A deriv. of *therscan* 'to thresh', 'a thresher'. 13th cent.

THREADER: O OE *thrǣd* 'thread', 'a threader of shuttles in a weaving mill'. 14th cent.

THREADGOLD, TREADGOLD: N OE *thrǣd-gold* 'thread gold', 'an embroiderer'. 12th cent.

THRELFALL: L OE *thrǣl-fall* 'the thrall's clearing', place where trees had been felled. (Lancs) 13th cent.

THRELKELD: L OE *thrǣl* + O Scand *kelda* 'spring', 'the spring of the serfs'. (Cumb).

THRIFT: N ME *thrift*, from ON *thrīfa* 'thrive'. The original meaning and therefore the meaning of the surname was 'success, prosperity'. 14th cent. See also Firth.

THRING: L OE *trēo-hangra* 'the tree-grown slope'. (Herts), *Treunge* DB, *Trehanger* 13th cent. Eventually the place-name became Tring and the surname *Thring*.

THRIPP: L A variant of *Thorp*, found in some place-names, e.g., Westrip (Glos).

THROCKMORTON, THROGMORTON: L OE *throc-mere-tūn* 'the farm by the lake with the trestle-supported bridge or pier'. (Worces), *Trochemerton* 12th cent.

THROSBY: L ON A variant of *Thorsby*.

THROSSELL, THRUSSELL: N OE *throsle* 'throstle', a nickname from the bird. 13th cent.

THROWER, TROWER: O OE A deriv. of *thrāwan* 'to throw', 'a thrower of raw silk into silk thread'. 13th cent.

THRUSH: N OE *thrysce* 'thrush (the bird)', a melodious nickname. 12th cent.

THURGAR: P O Scand *Thorger* 'Thor-spear'. DB. Also a Norman name.

THURGOOD, THORGOOD, THOROGOOD, THOROUGHGOOD, THORROWGOOD, THIRGATE: P ON *Thorgautr*, O Dan & O Sw *Thorgot* 'Thor-Geat'. 12th cent.

THURKELL, THURTELL, THIRKELL, THIRKILL, THIRTLE, TURKEL, TURTLE, TUTTLE, TOGHILL: P ON *Thorkell*, O Dan *Thorkil*, contracted forms of ON *Thorketill*. DB.

THURKETTLE, THIRKITTLE, THIRKETTLE: P ON *Thorketill* 'Thor's (sacrificial) cauldron'. DB.

THURLEY: THURLEIGH: L OE *thǣre-lēage* '(at) the glade'. (Beds).

THURLOW, THURLOE, TRILLO: L OE *thrȳp-hlāw* 'the hill for the assembly of the host (army)'. Surname 13th cent.

THURMAN, THORMAN: P O Scand *Thormund* 'Thor's protection' or *Thormoth* 'Thor's wrath'. DB.

THURSTON, THURSTING, TUSTIAN, TUSTIN(G), TUTON, DUSTING: P ON *Thorsteinn*, O Dan *Thorsten* 'Thor's stone', anglicised as *Thorstān*. The Norman form *Turstinus* became *Tustin(g), Tutin* in England. DB.

THWAIT(E), THWAYTES, TWAITE, TWAITS, TWITE: L ON *thveit* 'a meadow, enclosure, or forest clearing'. 12th cent.

THYNNE see THIN. **TIBALD** see THEOBALD.

TIBB(S): P A pet-form of both *Isabel* and *Tibald*. 13th cent.

TIBBETS, TIBBETT(S), TIBBITS, TIBBITT(S), TIBBATTS, TIBBOTT(S): P Dims. of *Tibb* (*Isabel*) or *Tibald* (*Theobald*). 14th cent.

TIBBLES see THEOBALD.

TICE: (i) P OE *Tica*, a pers. name. (ii) N OE *ticcen* 'kid', a nickname for one of skittish disposition.

TICEHURST, TYCEHURST: L OE *ticcen-hyrst* 'the kids' wood'. (Sussex).

TICKLE, TICKEL: L OE 'The *hyll* (hill) of an Anglo-Saxon called *Tica*'. (Yorks) 12th cent.

TICHNER, TICKNER see TWITCHEN.

TIDBURY: L OE 'The *burg* (fort) of *Tuda*, an Anglo-Saxon'. (Hants).

TIDDEMAN, TIDMAN, TIDYMAN, TYDEMAN, TITMAN, TITTMAN: O OE *tethingmann* 'the chief man of a tithing (ten householders)'. 12th cent.

TIDDSWELL, TIDESWELL, TIDSWELL: L OE 'The *wielle* (stream or spring) of an Anglo-Saxon called *Tidi*'. (Derbys) 12th cent.

TIDDY: L Cornish & OW A river-name deriving from *tud* 'good'.

TIDMARSH: L OE 'The *mersc* (marsh) of an Anglo-Saxon called *Tydda*'. (Berks).

TIDY, TIDEY: N OE *tīd* 'time', 'timely'. Also dial. 'plump, shapely, comely'.

TIERNAN: P Ir *MacTighearnan*, from *tighearna* 'lord'.

TIERNEY: P Ir *O Tighearnaig*, from *tighearna* 'lord'. Not surprisingly, there is much confusion with Tiernan.

TIFFANY, TIFFEN, TIFFIN: P OF *Tifaine*, from Gk *Theophania* 'the manifestation of God'. A popular name for girls born on the Feast of the Epiphany. 12th cent.

TIGG see TEGG. TIGHE see TEAGUE.

TIGHT: N OE *thight* 'solid, staunch, tight, trustworthy'.

TILBROOK: L OE 'The *brōc* (brook) of an Anglo-Saxon called *Tila*'. (Hunts).

TILBURY: L OE '*Tila's burg* (fort)'. (Essex).

TILDEN: L OE '*Tila's denu* (valley)'.

TILDESLEY, TILDSLEY, TILSLEY, TYLDESLEY: L OE 'The *lēah* (glade) of *Tiwald*, an Anglo-Saxon'. (Lancs) 13th cent.

TILER, TILLIER, TYLER: O OF *tieuleor* 'tiler, tile-maker'. 12th cent.

TILLER, TILLIER, TILLYER: O OE *tilian* 'to till', 'a farmer, husbandman, farm labourer'. 13th cent.

TILLETT, TILLOTT: P A dim. of *Matilda*. 13th cent.

TILLEY, TILLIE, TILLY, TYLEE, TYLEY: (i) P Identical with Tillett. (ii) O Identical with Tiller. DB. [Tilley, a First Fleet (convict) surname].

TILLING: P OE A development of the pers. name *Tila*, see Tilbrook, etc. 13th cent.

TILLMAN: O OE *tilmann*. Identical in meaning with *Tiller*. 12th cent.

TILSED: L OE 'The *hide* of an Anglo-Saxon called *Tidwulf*'. (A hide of land, sufficient to support one free family.) (Wilts).

TIMBERLAKE: L OE *timber-lacu* 'the wood beside the stream where timber may be extracted'. (A lost place in Worces.) 13th cent.

TIMBRELL: O OF *timbre* 'a player on the timbrel/tambourine, a drummer'.

TIMINS: P A dim. of *Timm*. [A First Fleet (marine) surname].

TIMM(S), TIMME, TIMS, TIMBS, TYM, TYMM(S): (i) P OE *Tima*. (ii) P OG *Timmo*. Both pers. names. 13th cent.

TIMMERMAN, TIMBERMAN: O OE *timber-mann* 'a dealer or worker in timber'. 14th cent.

TIMPERON: L OE *timperon*, from *timber-aern* 'timber building'. 14th cent.

TINDAL(L), TINDALE, TINDELL, TYNDALE, TYNDALL: L OE 'The *dael* (valley) of the River Tyne', formerly a Brit river-name *Tina*. (Cumb) 12th cent.

TINGAY, TINGEY see TANGUY.

TINGLE: O OE *tyngyl* 'a small nail'. Metonymic for a maker of *tyngyls*. 13th cent.

TINKER, TINKLER: L OE *tinker* 'an itinerant mender of pots, kettles, etc.'. Tinkler is the northern and Scottish form. In Ireland also a gipsy. 13th cent.

TINSLEY, TINSLAY: L OE 'The *hlāw* (mound or barrow) of an Anglo-Saxon called *Tynne*'. (Yorks).

TIPLADY, TOPLADY, TOPLASS: N ME *tope, tup* (the lady), a term in general use; Shakespeare uses it in *Othello*, Act I, Scene I. A nickname for a libertine. But as Oscar Wilde observed, 'Every saint has a past, every sinner has a future', and in 1775 Rev. Augustus Toplady wrote the hymn 'Rock of Ages'. Surname 13th cent.

TIPLER, TIPPLER: O ME *tipeler* 'a tapster, seller of ale'. 13th cent.

TIPPER: O OE A deriv. of *typpe* 'to tip, e.g., with metal'. 'A maker of metal arrow tips'. 12th cent.

TIPPETT: P A double dim. of *Theobald*. 13th cent.

TIPPING: P A dim. of *Tibb*. 13th cent.

TIPPINS: P 'Son of *Tipping*'. 14th cent.

TIRRELL, TERRELL, TERRILL, TEARALL, TYRELL, TYRRELL: (i) P ON 'Son of *Turold*'. DB. (ii) N OF A Nickname from *tirer* 'to draw, pull on the reins', for one of stubborn character. DB. [Tyrell, a First Fleet (convict) surname].

TISBURY: L OE 'The *burg* (fort) of an Anglo-Saxon called *Tissi*'. (Wilts).

TISDALE, TISDALL, TISDELL: L OE 'the *dael* (valley) of *Tissi*'.

TITE, TYTE: N ON *titt* 'prompt, swift, eager'.

TITLEY: L OE 'The *lēah* (clearing) of *Titta*, an Anglo-Saxon'. (Herefords).

TITMARSH: L ON *tittr-mersc* 'the marsh where tits fly'.

TITMAS, TITMUS(S): N ON *tittr*, ME *titmose* 'titmouse' (second el. from OE *māse*, a bird-name). A nickname for a small person.

TITTERTON: L OE 'The *tūn* (enclosure) of *Titta*, an Anglo-Saxon'.

TOBEY, TOBY, TOBIAS: P Hebrew *Tobia*. *Toby* is the vernacular form. 12th cent. Hebrew meaning: 'Jehovah is good'.

TOBIN: (i) P Ir A Hibernicised Anglo-Norman name, originally *St Aubyn*. (ii) P A dim. of Hebrew *Tobias*.

TOD(D): N ME *tod, todde* 'fox', 'crafty'. 12th cent.

TODHUNTER: O ME *tod* + OE *hunta* 'fox-hunter'. 14th cent.

TODMAN: O ME *tod-man* 'fox-hunter'. 13th cent.

TOFT(S), TAFT: L O Scand *toft* 'homestead'. (Cambs, Lincs, Norfolk, Warwicks) 12th cent.

TOGHILL see THURKELL. TOKE see TOOK.

TOLE: P OE *Tola* or ON *Toli*, pers. names. 12th cent.

TOLHURST: L Southern dial. of OE *toll* 'a clump of trees' + OE *hyrst* 'wooded hill'. 'Hilly woodland'.

TOLL, TOLLES, TOWLE: (i) P OE *Toll*, a pers. name. 13th cent. (ii) L southern counties dial. *toll* 'a clump of trees'. 14th cent.

TOLLAND, TOLAND, TOLAN: L OE *Tān-land* 'land on the River Tone'. (Som) [A First Fleet (marine) surname].

TOLLEMACHE see TALMADGE.

TOLLER, TOLER, TOWLER: (i) O OE *tollere* 'a tax gatherer'. 12th cent. (ii) L OW *toll-thur* 'the stream in the hollows'. (Dorset) 12th cent.

TOLSON see TOWNSON.

TOM(S), TOMES: P A pet-form of *Thomas*. 13th cent.

TOMAN see TUMMAN.

TOMBS, TOOMBES, TOOMBS: P Variants of *Toms*. 14th cent.

TOMKIN(S), TOMKYN(S), TOMPKIN: P A dim. of *Tom*. 14th cent.

TOMKINSON: P 'Son of *Tomkin*'. 14th cent.

TOMLEY, THOMLEY: L OE *thuma-lēah* 'thumb-wood', thumb meaning dwarves or fairies (as in Tom Thumb). (Oxon), *Tumbeleia* DB. Surname 13th cent.

TOMLIN(S), TOMALIN, TOMBLIN: P A double dim. of *Tom*. 14th cent.

TOMLINSON, THOMLINSON: P 'Son of *Tomlin*'. 14th cent. [A First Fleet (marine) surname].

TOMPSETT see THOMPSETT. TOMPSON see THOMPSON.

TONBRIDGE, TUNBRIDGE: L OE 'The *brycg* (bridge) of an Anglo-Saxon called *Tunna*'. (Kent) DB.

TONE see TOWN.

TONER: (i) L OE *tūn* 'farm, village or town'. 13th cent. See also Town. (ii) P Ir *Ó Tomhrair*, from a Norse pers. name. An Ulster surname.

TONG(E), TONGS, TONGUE: (i) L OE *tunge* 'tongue of land'. (Leices) (ii) L OE *tang* 'tongs', i.e., 'fork of the river'. (Kent, Lancs, Salop, Yorks) 12th cent. (iii) N OE *tunge*, nickname for a fault-finder, scold, chatter-box.

TONKIN: P A Cornish form of *Tomkin*.

TONKS: P A dim. of *Thomas*.

TOOGOOD, TOWGOOD, TUGWOOD: N ME An ironical nickname 'too good'. 12th cent.

TOOHEY, TOOHY see TUOHY.

TOOK(E), TOKE, TUKE: P ON *Toki*, O Scand *Toke*, a pers. name. DB.

TOOKEY, TUCKEY: P ON *Toki*, O Dan *Toke*, O Sw *Tuke*. DB.

TOOLE see O'TOOLE.

TOOLEY, TOLEY: P ON *Toli*, a pers. name. DB.

TOOMBS see TOMBS. TOOMEY see TWOMEY. TOON see TOWN.

TOOP(E): P O Dan *Topi*. DB.

TOOTH: N OE *tōth* 'tooth', a nickname for one with a prominent, outstanding tooth. 13th cent.

TOOTHILL, TOOTALL, TOOTELL, TOOTILL, TUTHILL, TUTILL: L OE *tōt-hyll* 'the look-out hill'. (Essex, Lincs, Middx, Lancs, Warwicks) 12th cent.

TOOVEY see TOVEE.

TOPHAM: L OE 'The *hamm* (river-land) of an Anglo-Saxon called *Topp*'

TOPLADY see TIPLADY.

TOPP: P OE *Topp* or ON *Toppr*. 12th cent.

TOPPER: O ME A deriv. of *toppe* 'a tuft of fibre, e.g., flax on a distaff'. 13th cent.

TORBETT see TURBARD.

TORR, TORRA, TORRE: (i) L OE *torr* 'rocky hill/peak'. 12th cent. (ii) N OF *tor* 'bull'. 13th cent.

TORRANCE, TORRENS: L SG *torran* 'hillock'. (Stirlingshire, Lanarks, Kilbride) Scotland. 16th cent.

TORREY see TERREY. TORY see THORY.

TOSHACH, TOSHACK: O Ir & SG *toiseach* 'chief, leader'. (*Taoiseach* is the title of the prime minister of the Irish Republic.)

TOUGH, TOW(E): N OE *tōh*, ME *togh, tow* 'tough, steadfast, tenacious'. 13th cent.

TOULSON see TOWNSON.

TOURS, TOWERS: L OF From Tours (Indreet-Loire) France. 12th cent. See also Tower.

TOUSSAINT: N OF *tous-saints* 'all saints', for one born on All Saints Day.

TOUT: N ME *toute* 'buttocks, rump', a word familiar to Chaucer who uses it in 'The Miller's Tale'. ME *rumpe*, from O Dan *rumpe*, was also in use and persisted; Pepys wrote in the Diary (1660) 'Boys now do cry "kiss my parliament" '. Surname 13th cent.

TOVEE, TOVEY, TOOVEY: P ON *Tofi*, O Dan *Tovi*, introduced into England by a follower of Canute. DB. TOVELL: P *Tofa Hildr* 'daughter of *Tofi*'. DB.

TOWER: (i) L OE *tūr* or OF *tour* 'tower' (dweller thereby or therein). 12th cent. (ii) O OE A deriv. of *tāwian* 'to taw', 'a tawer, dresser of white leather'. 13th cent.

TOWGOOD see TOOGOOD. TOWLE see TOLL. TOWLER see TOLLER.

TOWN(E), TOWNS, TONE, TOON, TUNE: L OE *tūn*, originally 'a fence', later expanded to 'farm or homestead', then to 'village', and eventually to 'town'.

TOWNEND, TOWNSEND, TOWNSHEND: L OE *tūn-ende* 'at the end of the town or village'. 13th cent.

TOWNER: O OE *tolnere* 'a tax-gatherer' or OE *tūn* + *-er* 'farm worker'. 13th cent.

TOWNLEY: L OE *tūn-lēah* 'the farm clearing'. (Lancs) 13th cent.

TOWNSON, TOLSON, TOULSON: P A colloquial pronunciation of *Tomlinson*. 16th cent.

TORREY, TORRY see TERREY. TORY see THORY.

TOY(E): N OE (*sulh*) *ge teog* 'an agricultural implement', cogn. with Du *tuig* of the same meaning. Probably a nickname associated with a farm implement. The name occurs in Winchester in 1066. Winton D. The sense of dalliance, plaything does not occur until c. 1530. Also an Irish surname, *O Toghdha* 'descendant of chosen'.

TOYNTON: L OE 'The *tūn* (farm) of *Teoda's* people'. (Lincs).

TOZER: O OE A deriv. of *tāsian* 'to tease', 'a teaser with teasels', 'a comber or carder of wool'. 13th cent.

TRACEY, TRACY: (i) L OF From Tracy-Bocage or Tracy-sur-Mer (Calvados) Normandy. 12th cent. (ii) P Ir *O Treasaigh*, from *treasach* 'war-like'.

TRAFFORD: (i) L OE *trog-ford* 'valley ford'. (Ches) (ii) L OE A Normanised form of *Strēt-ford* (*Strǣt-ford*) 'ford on the Roman road'. (Lancs) (iii) L OE *traeppe-ford* 'ford by the (otter) trap'. (Northants).

TRAIN: N OF *traine* 'guile', a nickname for a trapper, hunter. 12th cent.

TRAINER, TRAINOR, TREANOR, TRAYNOR: O ME *trayne* 'to lay a train, snare', 'a trapper'. 13th cent.

TRANTER, TRENTER: O Lat *travetarius* 'a carrier, waggoner'. 12th cent.

TRAVERS, TRAVES, TRAVIS(S): O ME *travers, traves, travis*, terms used at river crossings, bridges, town gates, where travellers were obliged to pay a toll. From this a name for the collector of tolls. 12th cent.

TRAYNOR, TREANOR: P Ir *Mac Threinfhir* 'Son of the strong man'. See also Trainer.

TREADGOLD see THREADGOLD.

TREADWELL, TREDWELL: N OE *tredan-wel* 'tread well', a nickname for one with a fancy gait. 13th cent.

TREASURE: O OF *tresor*, ME *treysour* 'wealth'. Metonymic for a treasurer. 12th cent.

TREBILCOCK: L Cornish Either *tre-pyl-cok* 'homestead by the cuckoo-haunted hill' or *tre-pilicock* 'favourite homestead'.

TREBLE: O OF from Lat *triplus*. 'A treble singer, or player on a musical instrument with high notes, e.g., a treble recorder or fipple flute'.

TREDGETT, TRUDGETT: O ME *treget* 'jugglery, trickery'. Metonymic for a juggler. 12th cent.

TREDINNICK: L Cornish *tre-redenek* 'homestead in a fern-brake' or *tre-dynek* 'homestead by the little fort'.

TREE(S), TREEN, TREWIN: L OE *trēow* 'tree', plural *treen*. 14th cent. *Treen* is also a Cornish surname, *tre-ryn* 'homestead on the hillside'.

TREFFREY, TREFFRY: L Cornish *tre-vre* 'homestead on the hill'.

TREGEAR: L Cornish *tre-ke* 'homestead surrounded by a hedge' or *tre-ger* 'homestead by a fort'.

TREGELLAS, TREGELLES, TREGELLIS: L Cornish *tre-gellys* 'the hidden homestead'.

TREGONING, TREGONNING: L Cornish *tre-ke-onnen* 'homestead with a belt of ash-trees'.

TREHARN, TREHEARN: P OW *Trahaearn*, a pers. name and that of a 9th cent. Welsh prince.

TRELAWNEY, TRELAWNY: L Cornish *tre-lonow* 'homestead in the grove'.

TRELEAVEN, TRELEVEN: L Cornish *tre-leven* 'the level homestead'.

TRELOAR: L Cornish *tre-lowarth* 'homestead with a garden'.

TREMAINE, TREMAYNE: L Cornish *tre-meyn* 'the stone homestead'.

TREMBATH: L Cornish *tre-an-bagh* 'homestead in a nook or corner'.

TREMELLING: L Cornish *tre-melyn* 'the mill homestead'.

TREMENHEERE: L Cornish *tre-men-hyr* 'the homestead by the menhir (long-stone)'.

TREMLETT: L OF From Les Trois Minettes (Calvados) Normandy. 12th cent.

TRENCH: L OF *trenche* 'the ditch or cutting'. 14th cent.

TRENCHARD: O OF *trenchier* 'to cut', 'a swordsman'. DB.

TRENGOVE: L Cornish *tre-an-gof* 'the homestead of the smith'.

TRENDALL, TRENDELL, TRINDALL, TRINDLE: L OE *trendel* 'circle', e.g., circular hill, earthworks or stone circle. 14th cent.

TRENOWATH, TRENOWETH: L Cornish *tre-noweth* 'new homestead'.

TRENT: L A Brit river-name, originally *Tristanton*.

TRENTER see TRANTER.

TRESEDER, TRESIDDER: L Cornish *tre-Seder* 'the homestead of a family called *Seder*'.

TRETHEWEY, TRETHEWY: L Cornish *tre-thewi* 'the homestead of a family called *Dewi*'. 13th cent.

TRETHOWAN: L Cornish *tre-thewin* 'the homestead of a family called *Dewin*'. 13th cent.

TRETT: N ME *tret*, of the features, 'neat, handsome, shapely'. 12th cent.

TREVELLICK: L Cornish *tre-velynyk* 'homestead by the little mill' or 'the walled homestead'. 13th cent.

TREVELYAN, TREVILLIAN: L Cornish *tre-melin* 'the mill homestead'.

TREVOR: (i) L Welsh *tre-mawr* 'the large village'. (Anglesey, Caernarvon, Denbys) Wales. (ii) L Cornish *tre-Mvor 'Mor's* homestead'. In Ireland the name takes the form *O Treabhair*.

TREW see TRUE.

TREWARTHA: L Cornish *tre-wartha* 'the upper homestead'.

TREWEEK(E): L Cornish *tre-gwyk* 'the homestead in the wood'.

TREWHELLA: L Cornish *tre-ughella* 'the high homestead'.

TREWIN: L Cornish *tre-gwyn* 'the fair or white homestead'. See also Tree.

TREWMAN see TRUEMAN.

TRIBE: P Lat *tribus*, OF *tribu* 'tribe', originally applied to the three divisions of the Romans.

TRICKER: N OF *trique*, ME *trik* 'trickery', a nickname for a cheat, trickster. 13th cent.

TRICKETT: N OF *trichet*, Norman-Picard *tricard* 'cheat, deceiver'. 12th cent.

TRIGG(S), TRIGGER: N ON *tryggr* 'true, faithful, trustworthy'. 12th cent. Also a Cornish surname, from an ancient hundred recorded c. 880 as *Triconscir*.

TRILLO see THURLOW. TRIMBLE see TRUMBLE.

TRIMBY: L ON *thyrnir-býr* 'the homestead at the thorn-bush'. (Westmorland) [A First Fleet (convict) surname].

TRIMMER: O OE *trymman* 'to arrange, strength, fortify'. The original sense survives in nautical language, e.g., *trim the ship, in fighting trim*.

TRINDALL, TRINDLE see TRENDALL.

TRINDER: O OE *trendan* 'to turn round, roll', ME *trend* 'to twist, plait' + *tryndelle* 'a spindle'. 'A spinner or braider'. 13th cent.

TRIPE, TRIPP: O OF & ME *tripe*. Metonymic for a tripe-seller. 12th cent. [C.G. Tripp opened up new grazing country in Canterbury, New Zealand 1855].

TRIPPETT: O OF *tripot*, ME *tripet* 'an evil scheme, a malicious trick'. 12th cent. [Susannah Trippett, a female convict, arrived with the First Fleet 1788].

TRIST: O OF & ME *triste* 'an appointed rendezvous in hunting'. Probably a name for the huntsman responsible for the arrangements. 13th cent.

TRISTRAM, TRUSTRAM: P Celtic *Drystan*, from *drest, drust* 'tumult, din'. 12th cent.

TRITTON: L OE *trēo-tūn* 'the *tūn* (farm) by the tree(s)'. (Yorks), *Tretone* DB and now Treeton, and as Lower observed in 1860, so curtly pronounced as *Tritton*.

TRIVETT: N OF *trefet* 'trivet'. A curious nickname; nobody has three feet. But nothing stands more firmly than a trivet and this must be the meaning of the nickname, 'stand-firm'.

TROLLOP(E): L ON *troll* + OE *hop* 'Trolhop', 'the valley of the trolls (goblins)'. (Northumb) 15th cent.

TROLOVE see TRUELOVE. TROMAN see TRUEMAN. TRONSON see TRUNCHION.

TROTH: N ME *trothe* 'loyal, faithful'. 14th cent.

TROTT: N AF *trote* 'old woman, hag'. 12th cent.

TROTTER: O OF *trotier* 'a trotter, messenger'. 12th cent.

TROUNCE, TROUNCER: O OF *tronche* 'club, cudgel', 'a maker/seller of cudgels'. 12th cent.

TROUT: N OE *trūht* 'trout', a nickname for a trout look-alike. 12th cent.

TROWBRIDGE: L OE *trēo-brycg* 'wooden bridge (consisting of a tree-trunk)'. (Wilts) 12th cent.

TROWEL(L): L OE *trēo-wielle* 'the stream with a tree-trunk bridge'. (Notts) 12th cent.

TROWER see THROWER.

TROY: (i) L OF From Troyes (Aube) France. 12th cent. (ii) P Ir *O Troiththig* 'descendant of Footsoldier'.

TRUANT: N OF *truand* 'vagabond, rogue'.

TRUDGETT see TREDGETT.

TRUE, TREW, TROW: N OF *trēowe*, ME *trow* 'faithful, loyal, trustworthy'. 12th cent.

TRUELOVE, TROLOVE: N OE *trēowe-lufu* 'faithful love'. 13th cent.

TRUEMAN, TRUMAN, TREWMAN, TROMAN: N OE *trēowe-mann* 'true, faithful man'. 13th cent.

TRUMBLE, TRUMBULL, TRIMBLE: P OE *Trumbeald* 'strong-bold'. 13th cent.

TRUMPER: O OF *trompeor* 'trumpeter'. 13th cent.

TRUNCHION, TRONSON, TROUNSON: N OF & ME *tronchon* 'stump', a nickname for a short, stout man. 13th cent. Later a nickname for a minor official armed with a club or cudgel responsible for keeping the peace.

TRUNDLE: O OE *trendel* 'ring, circle', applied in 16th cent. to a wheel or castor, especially in 'trundle-bed', a small bed for use of a servant, which could be rolled under the high bed. Pepys, 9 October 1667: 'So all to bed. My wife and I on the high bed in our chamber, and the maid in the trundle-bed.' The surname is metonymic for a maker of trundles.

TRUSCOTT: L OE *trēzl-cot* 'the cottages on the Trysull stream, *Trēzl* in Anglo-Saxon times and now called Smestow Brook'. *Trēzl* is probably a Brit (Celtic) name. Surname 13th cent.

TRUSLOVE, TRUSLER, TRUSSLER: N OF *trusser* 'to truss, bind' + AF *love* 'wolf', 'bind wolf', a nickname for a wolf-hunter. 13th cent.

TRUSSEL(L): O OF + ME *troussel* 'packet', also the mould used in the stamping of coins. 'A maker/user of *troussels*'. 12th cent.

TRUSTRAM see TRISTRAM.

TRY(E): N ME *trie* 'good, choice, excellent'. 13th cent.

TUBB(S), TUBBY: L O Scand *Tubbi, Tubbe*. DB.

TUBMAN: O ME *tubbe*. 'A cooper, maker of tubs'. 15th cent.

TUCK: P O Dan *Tuk*, O Scand *Tukka*, a pet-form of *Thorketill*. A familiar name from the Robin Hood legends. 12th cent.

TUCKER, TUCKWELL: O OE A deriv. of *tūcian* 'to tuck, to full', 'a tucker, fuller in the textile industry'. 13th cent. See also Fuller, Walker.

TUCKERMAN: O OE Identical in meaning with *Tucker*. 17th cent.

TUCKEY see TOOKEY.

TUDOR: P The Welsh form of *Theodore*. The surname of the royal house which ruled England from 1485 to 1603. 13th cent.

TUGWOOD see TOOGOOD. TUKE see TOOK.

TULIP: N OF *tulipe*, from Turkish pronunciation of Persian *tulbend* 'turban'. A nickname for a wearer of a turban. Also for a showy person. The flower is so named from similarity in shape to a turban. 16th cent.

TULL: (i) L OF From Tulle (Corréze) France. (ii) O OF *tulle* 'a seller of *tulle* (silken fabric)' (iii) N OF *tulle*, used by Chaucer in the sense 'to allure, entice'.

TULLOCH, TULLOCK: L SG *tulach*, a hill-name. (Aberdeens, Ayrs, Perths, Ross) Scotland.

TULLY: P Ir *Mac Tuile*, from *tuile* 'flood'. The name has sometimes been anglicised as *Flood*.

TUMMAN, TUMMON, THOMMEN, TOMAN: L OE *tūnmann* 'villager'. 13th cent.

TUNBRIDGE see TONBRIDGE. TUNE see TOWN.

TUNNEY: P O Dan *Tunni*, O Sw *Tunne*. DB.

TUNNICLIFF(E), DUNNICLIFF(E): L OE

tūn-wiella-clif 'the enclosure on a slope with a stream'. (Lancs) 13th cent.

TUNSTALL: L OE *tūn-steall* 'the site of a farmstead'. 12th cent.

TUOHY, TOOHEY: P Ir *O Tuathaigh*, from *tuathach* 'ruler'.

TURBARD, TURBET, TURBOTT, TORBETT, TARBERT, TARBUTT: P A hybrid name, O Scand *Thor* + Ger. *-bert*, producing Norman *Turbert*, and introduced into England by the Normans. DB.

TURBIN see THORBURN.

TURK: (i) P O Scand An abbreviated form of *Thorkell*. DB. (ii) N OF *Turc*, a nickname for an uncouth or aggressive individual introduced into England by returning crusaders.

TURKEL see THURKELL.

TURLEY: P Ir *Mac Toirdealbhaig*, from *Turlough*, a pers. name and a form of *Terence*. (Cos. Armagh and Down.)

TURNBULL: N OE *turnian-bula* 'turn bull', a nickname for a brave, strong man. 14th cent.

TURNER: (i) O OF *tornie* 'tourney', 'an official at a tournament', or *tornoieor* 'a jouster in tournaments'. 12th cent. (ii) O OF *tornour* 'a turner, worker at the lathe'. [Six persons named Turner arrived with the First Fleet, four convicts, a marine and his wife].

TURNEY: L OF From Tournai (Normandy). DB.

TURNPENNY: N ME phrase 'turn a penny', 'one intent on turning a profit', 'a keen dealer, haggler'. 13th cent.

TURPIN: P ON *Thor*, the god, and the ethnic *Finnr* combine in *Thor-Finn*, which the Normans converted to *Turpin* to suit their pronunciation. DB.

TURREFF, TURRIFF: P Anglo-Scand hybrid *Thor-gifu* 'Thor-gift'. 12th cent.

TURRILL, TURRELL: P O Dan *Thorild*, a woman's name. DB.

TURTLE: N OE *turtle*, a nickname from the turtle-dove, 'a constant lover'. See also Thurkell.

TURTON: L ON + OE 'The *tūn* (enclosure) of a Norseman called *Thori*'. (Lancs).

TURVEY: L OE *turf-ēg* 'turf island (the island with good grass)'. (Beds).

TURVILL(E): L OF From Turville-la-Campagne (Eure) Normandy. 12th cent. (There is a place *Turville* in Bucks, but this was *Turfeld* until 19th cent. The surname is from the Normandy place.)

TUSTIAN, TUSTIN see THURSTAN. TUTHILL, TUTILL see TOOTHILL. TUTON see THURSTAN. TUTCHENER see TWITCHEN.

TUTT: P OE *Tutta*, an Anglo-Saxon pers. name. preserved in Tuttingham (Norfolk), 'the *tūn* (settlement) of the *ingas* (people) of *Tutta*'.

TUTTLE see THURKELL.

TUTTLEBEE, TUTTLEBY: L ON '*Thurkell's býr* (farm)'. (Yorks) 13th cent.

TWAIT see THWAITE.

TWEEDALE, TWEDDELL, TWEDDLE, TWEEDLE, TWADDELL: L Brit + OE 'The *dael* (valley) of the River Tweed (on the English-Scottish border)'. The river-name is ancient, *Tuidi* c. 730, *Tweode* c. 890, belonging to the root *tevā* 'swelling, powerful' and is related to Sanskrit *tavās* 'powerful'. Surname 13th cent.

TWEEDIE, TWEEDY: L Scots. From a place in Stonehouse, Scotland, of unknown origin. The name does not derive from the R. Tweed.

TWELL(S): L OE *wielle* 'spring or stream'. 16th cent. See also Attwell; *Twell* was originally *Attwell*, the initial A having been lost.

TWEMLOW: L OE (be) *twǣm hlāwum* '(by) two hills'. (Ches).

TWESBOURNE: L OE *twisla-burna* 'the forked stream'. [A First Fleet (marine) surname].

TWIFIELD: L OE *twifeld* 'the double field'. [A First Fleet (convict) surname].

TWIGG(E): N OE *twigge* 'a slender shoot', a nickname for a slender, willowy person. 13th cent.

TWINDLEY: L OE *betwēon-lēah* 'between the wooded glades'.

TWINE, TWINER: O OE *twīn* 'thread, string', ME *twīnen* 'to twine', 'a twiner or twister of thread'. 14th cent.

TWINING, TWYNING: L OE *betwēon-ēam* 'between the streams', to which *ing* (*ingas* 'people') was added later. (The people were those of *Bituinaeum*, an Anglo-Saxon of the 9th cent.)

TWISS: L OE *twisla* 'confluence, junction, fork of a river'. (Lancs) [A First Fleet (crew) surname].

TWIST: L OE The name is associated with Twiston (Lancs), OE *twisla-tūn* 'farm in the fork of the river'. (Lancs).

TWITCHEN, TWITCHING(S), TUTCH-ENER, TWITCHIN: L OE *twi-cen* 'road junction, cross-roads'. (Devon) 13th cent.

TWITE see THWAITE.

TWIZEL(L): L OE *twisla* 'the fork of the Rivers Till and Tweed'. (Northumb) 12th cent.

TWOMEY, TOOMEY: P Ir *O Tuama*. A Munster surname.

TWYFORD: L OE *twi-ford* 'the double ford', probably over a river with two arms.

TYCEHURST see TICEHURST. TYDEMAN see TIDDEMAN.

TYE: L OE *tēag* 'enclosure (of land)'. (Essex, Kent, Suffolk) 13th cent.

TYLDESLEY see TILDESLEY. TYLEE, TYLEY see TILLEY. TYLER see TILER. TYM see TIMM.

TYNAN: P Ir *O Teimhneain*. A Connacht sept. [Thomas Tynan, a marine private, brought the surname to Australia 1788].

TYNDALE: TYNDALL see TINDAL. TYRRELL see TIRRELL.

TYSOE: L OE *tiges-hōh* 'the spur of land dedicated to the god *Tig* (*Tīw*, the war-god)'. (Warwicks).

TYSON: N OF *tison* 'a fomenter of strife'. DB.

TYTE see TITE.

TYTHERLEIGH: L OE *tīedre* 'fragile' + *lēah* 'the sapling wood'. (Devon, Hants).

U

UDALL, UDELL: L OE *ēow-dell* 'the valley of the yews'. (Lancs).

UDEN: L OE *ēow-denu* 'yew-dale'.

UFFORD: L OE 'The *worth* (homestead) of an Anglo-Saxon called *Uffa*'. (Northants, Suffolk) 12th cent.

ULLETT see WOOLVETT.

ULLMAN(N), ULMAN(N): O OF *uille*, ME *oyle* + ME *man* 'a maker/seller of oil'. 13th cent.

ULLRICH, ULRICK see WOOLRICH. ULMER see WOOLMER.

ULPH: P O Dan & O Sw *Ulf*, ON *Ulfr* 'wolf'. DB.

ULYATE see WOOLVETT.

UMFREVILLE: L OF From Umfreville (Manche) Normandy. 12th cent.

UMPELBY, UMPLEBY: L ON 'The *byr* (farm) of a Norseman called *Anlaf*. (Anlaby, Yorks), *Umlouebi* DB. Surname 13th cent.

UNCLE(S), UNGLES: P ON *Ulfketel, Ulfkell* 'wolf-cauldron'. DB.

UNDERCLIFFE: L OE *under-clif* 'at the foot of the cliff'. UNDERDOWN: L OE *under-dūn* 'below the hill'. 12th cent. UNDERHILL: L OE Identical with *Underdown*. 13th cent. UNDERWATER: L OE *under-wielle* 'below the stream'. 13th cent. UNDERWOOD: L OE *under-wudu* 'below the trees', i.e., within the forest. 12th cent. [James Underwood, shipwright and convict, brought the surname to Australia 1788. He made a successful career in the colony as a shipwright and merchant].

UNSWORTH: L OE 'The *worth* (homestead or enclosure) of *Hund*, an Anglo-Saxon'. (Lancs).

UNTHANK: L OE *unthances* 'without leave', a squatter's farm. 13th cent.

UNWIN: (i) P OE *Hūnwine* 'young bear-friend'. DB. (ii) N OE *unwine* 'unfriend, enemy'.

UPFOLD: L OE *uppe-falod* 'the upper (sheep) fold'. UPHAM: L OE *up-hām* 'the upper manor or village'. UPHILL: L OE *uppan-pylle* 'above the creek'. (Som) 12th cent. *Opopille* DB.

UPJOHN: P Welsh *ap* 'Son of *John*'. 17th cent.

UPSALL: L O Scand *upp-salir* 'the upper hall'. (Yorks), *Upsale* DB.

UPSTON(E), UPSON: L ON + O Dan 'The *tūn* (farm) of a Scandinavian settler called *Ubbi*'. (Suffolk), *Upbestuna* DB. Surname 13th cent.

UPTON: L OE *upp-tūn* 'the upper farm or village'. OE Byname 10th cent. A frequent place-name.

URBAN: P Lat *Urban* (*urbānus*) 'of the city'. The name of seven popes and of a 3rd cent. saint. Surname 12th cent.

URE: L O Brit *Isurā*, a river-name identical with Gaulish *Isura*, a tributary of the Danube. In OE *Isūra* became *Īor*, and in ME *Yōr*. *Ure* occurs c. 1540.

UREN: P O Brit, OW, O Bret *Urien, Urbgen*, an essentially Celtic name, found mainly in Cornwall, to which it may have been introduced from Brittany.

URQUHART: L In 1652, Sir Thomas *Urquhart* published a fanciful pedigree in which he traced the family to a Prince Achaia in ancient Greece in 2139 BC. However this may be, the name is Brit *ar cardden* 'by the wood', and there are places of this name in

Inverness, Moray, Ross and Cromarty, from which the surname derives. 14th cent.

URSELL: P *Ursel*, a dim. of Lat *ursus* 'bear'. 12th cent.

URWIN see ERWIN.

USHER: USSHER, LUSHER: O OF (le) *ussier*, AF *usser*, ME *usher* 'door-keeper, usher'. 13th cent. [A First Fleet (convict) surname].

USSELL, UZZELL: N OF *oisel* 'bird', a nickname. 12th cent.

UTTERIDGE: P OE *Ūhtrīc* 'dawn-powerful'. 14th cent.

UTTING: P OE A patronymic from the Anglo-Saxon pers. name *Utta*. 12th cent.

V

VACHER, VATCHER: O OF *vachier* 'cowherd'. 13th cent.

VAGG see FAGG. VAILLANT see VALIANT. VAINE see FANE.

VAISEY, VAZEY, VEASEY, VESEY, VOISEY, VOYSEY, FACEY: N OF *envoisié*, AF *enveisé* 'playful'. DB.

VALANCE see VALLANCE. VALDER see FALDER.

VALE, VAIL(E): L OF *val*, ME *vale* 'valley'. 12th cent.

VALENTINE, VALINTINE, VALLINTINE: P Lat *Valentinus*, from *valens* 'strong'. The name of a 3rd cent. saint. 12th cent.

VALET(T), VARLET: O ME *valet* from OF *vaslet* (a dim. of *vassal* 'serf'). 'A manservant'.

VALIANT, VAILLANT: N OF *vaillant* 'courageous, sturdy'. 12th cent.

VALLANCE, VALANCE: L OF From Valence (Drôme) France. 12th cent. [A First Fleet (crew) surname].

VALLIN(S): L OF From Valognes (Manche) Normandy. DB.

VALLIS: L OF From Valois, Ile-de-France. 13th cent.

VAN, VANN(E) see FANN. VANE(S) see FANE. VANNER see FANNER. VARNAL see FARNALL.

VARLEY: L OE *fearn-lēah* 'the ferny clearing'. (Varley, Devon), earlier *Fernlegh*. Some may be OF from Verley, France.

VARROW, VAREY, VARY: O A late variant of *Farrow* (*Farrar*), with the original meaning 'smith, farrier'. 17th cent.

VASS, VASSALL: O OF *vasse, vassal* 'vassal, servant'. 13th cent.

VASSIE: L OF from Vassy (Calvados) Normandy. 12th cent.

VAUGHAN: N Welsh *fychan*, from *bychan* 'small'. 13th cent.

VAUSE, VAUX, VOCE: L OF From one of the many places called Vaux in France. DB.

VAVASOUR, VAVASSEUR: O OF *vavasour* 'a feudal tenant ranking immediately below a baron'. 12th cent.

VAYNE see FANE.

VEAL(E), VEALL, VEEL: N OF *viel*, a nickname from the calf. 13th cent.

VEARE see VERE.

VECK, VICK: O OF *le evesk* 'the bishop'. 13th cent. See also Levick (ii).

VEIL, VAIL: O OF *de la veille* 'of the watch', 'a watchman'. 12th cent.

VEITCH: O OF *vache* 'cow'. Metonymic for a cowherd. Mainly a Scottish surname; also settled in Fermanagh and Cavan, Ireland.

VENABLES: L OF From Venables (Eure) Normandy. 12th cent.

VENDER: O OF *vendeor*, AF *vendour* 'seller, dealer'. 12th cent.

VENES(S), VENIS(S), VENNS: L OF From Venoix (Calvados) Normandy. 12th cent.

VENN see FENN.

VENNALL, VENNEL: L OF *venelle* 'lane, alley'. 13th cent.

VENNER: O OF *veneur* 'huntsman'. 12th cent. See also Fenner.

VENNICKER: L OE *fenn-wīc* 'the dairy farm in the marsh'.

VENTER(S), VENTRESS, VENTRISS, VENTRICE: N ME *aventurous* 'venturous'. 17th cent.

VENTON: L OE *fenn-tūn* 'the farm in the fens'. (Devon) 13th cent.

VENTRE, VENTUR(E): N ME *aventure* 'chance, hazard'. 13th cent.

VENTURA: N OF A deriv. of ME *aventure* 'the adventurer'. 13th cent.

VENUS: L A variant of *Venes*.

VERDEN, VERDON, VERDUIN: L OF From Verdun (Manche, Eure) Normandy. DB.

VERE, VEAR, VEARE, DE VERE, DEVERE: L OF From Ver (Manche, Calvados) Normandy. DB.

VERGIN, VERGO see VIRGIN.

VERITY: N OF *vérité* 'the truthful one'. 13th cent.

VERNALL see FARNALL.

VERNAY, VERNEY, VARNEY: L OF From Saint-Paul-de-Vernay (Calvados) Normandy. 13th cent.

VERN(E) see FERN.

VERNON: L OF From Vernon (Eure) Normandy. DB.

VERRAN: L Cornish *Saint Veryan, Elerchi* DB.

VERRIER, VERRIOUR: O OF *verrier*, AF *verrer* 'a glazier, worker in glass'. 12th cent.

VESEY see VAISEY.

VESSEY: L OF From Vessey (Manche) Normandy. DB.

VIAL(S), VIALL, VIEL, VIDAL(E), VITAL: P Lat *vitalis* 'living, vital'. DB. ME *vital* 'full of vitality' may have produced a nickname in 14th cent.

VIAN: L OF From Vienne (Calvados) Normandy. 12th cent.

VICAR, VICKER: O AF *vicaire* 'vicar', acting as parish priest in absence of the parson. 13th cent.

VICARAGE, VICKRIDGE, VICKRESS: O OF 'Servant of the *Vicary*'. 14th cent.

VICARS, VICCARS, VICKARS, VICKERS: O OF 'Servant at the *vicar's*'. 14th cent.

VICARY, VICARI, VICCARY, VICKARY, VICKERY: O Lat *vicārius* 'vicar'. 13th cent.

VICK see VECK.

VICKERMAN: O AF 'The vicar's servant'. 14th cent.

VICTOR: P Lat *victor* 'conqueror'. 12th cent.

VIDEAN see VIVIAN. VIDLER see FIDLER.

VIGAR, VIGGOR, VIGOR, VIGOUR(S), VIGURS: N OF *vigoros*, AF *vigrus* 'strong, hardy' or *vigor* 'vigorous, lively'. 13th cent.

VILLAIN, VILLIN: O AF *villein* 'a serf, bondman, servile tenant bound to a manor'. 12th cent.

VILLAR, VILLIERS, VILLIS: L Lat *villāre* 'outlying farm', probably from one of the many places called Villiers in France. 12th cent.

VILLY: L OF From Villy (Calvados) Normandy. 12th cent.

VINCE: P A short-form of *Vincent*. 17th cent.

VINCENT, VINCETT, VINSEN, VINSON: P Lat *Vincentius*, from *vincens* 'conquering'. Introduced into England 12th cent.

VINCK see FINCH.

VINE(S), VIGNE(S): O OF *vigne* 'vine', 'worker in the vineyard'. 13th cent. (Vine-growing, introduced into England by the Romans, flourished in the Middle Ages. There are still places called Vineyards in southern England.)

VINEN: O OF *vignon* 'vine-dresser'. 14th cent.

VINER, VYNER: O OF *vigneour*, AF *viner* 'vine-grower'. 12th cent.

VINTER, VINTOR, VINTINER: O AF *vineter* 'vintner, wine-merchant'. 12th cent.

VIPAN, VIPOND, VIPONT, VIPPOND: L OF From Vieuxpont (Calvados) Normandy. 12th cent.

VIRGIN, VERGIN, VIRGO, VERGO: N A miracle play-name, for one who had played the part of the Virgin Mary. 13th cent.

VIRTUE: N OF *vertu*, a nickname for a virtuous person or ironically for a vicious one.

VISE, VIZE, VYSE: L OF *devise* 'boundary', which also contributed the place-name Devizes (Wilts). Surname 14th cent.

VITAL see VIAL.

VIVASH: N OF *vivace* 'lively, vivacious'.

VIVIAN, VIVIEN, VYVYAN, VIDEAN, VIDGEN, FIDDIAN: P OF *Vivian, Vivien*, from Lat *Vivianus* (*vivus* 'living'). 12th cent.

VIZARD see WISHART. VOAK see FOLK. VOCE see VAUS.

VOLANT(E): N OF *voler* 'to fly', 'agile, nimble'. 13th cent.

VOLK(E), VOLKES see FOLK. VOLKER see FULCHER. VOLLER see FULLER. VOULES, VOWELL see FOWLE. VOYSEY see VAISEY. VYNER see VINER.

W

WACE, WASE, WASH, WASON, WASS, WASSON, GASH, GASON, GASS, GASSON, GAZE: P OG *Wazo*, O Fris *Watso*, OF *Gace*. DB.

WADDELL: L OE From Wedale (Edinburgh) Scotland.

WADDIE, WADDY see WALTHEW.

WADDINGTON: L OE 'The *tūn* (settlement)

of the *ingas* (people) of *Wada*, an Anglo-Saxon'. (Yorks) 12th cent.

WADDS: P Anglo-Scand A short-form of *Waltheof*. 14th cent. See Walthew.

WADE, WAIDE: (i) P OE *Wada*, a pers. Anglo-Saxon name which gained popularity along the North Sea coast from the sea-giant legend. DB. (ii) L OE *waed* 'ford'. 12th cent.

WADEMAN, WADMAN, WODEMAN: (i) O OE *wād-mann* 'woad-man', a supplier of woad, a widely used blue dye obtained from the plant. 13th cent. (ii) O ME *wōdman* 'woodman'. 13th cent.

WADEY see WALTHEW.

WADHAM: L OE '*Wada's hām* (village)'.

WADLEY: L OE *wāden-lēah* 'the glade where *wād* (woad) grows'.

WADSWORTH, WORDSWORTH: L OE '*Wada's worth* (homestead)'. (Yorks) 13th cent.

WAGER: O ME *wacher* 'watchman'. [Benjamin Wager, a convict, brought the surname to Australia 1788].

WAGG: N ME *waggen* 'to shake' (with laughter), 'a droll fellow, a wit'.

WAGHORN(E): N OE *wagian-horn*, a nickname for a horn-blower (trumpeter). 14th cent.

WAGSTAFF(E): O OE *wagian-staef*, a nickname for a beadle. 13th cent.

WAILES see WALES.

WAIN(E), WAYNE: O OE *waegn* 'wain'. Metonymic for a maker/driver of wains, waggons, carts. 14th cent.

WAINMAN, WENMAN, WHENMAN: O OE *waegn-mann* 'waggoner'. 13th cent.

WAINWRIGHT: O OE *waegn-wyrhta* 'wainwright', 'wain, wagon-builder'. 13th cent. [A First Fleet (female convict) surname].

WAIT(E), WAITES, WAITS, WATES, WAYT, WAIGHT(E), WEIGHT, WHAIT(E), WHAITES: O OF *gaite*, ONF *waite* 'town watchman'. 12th cent. (The town waits were also the town's band of musicians, the origin of Christmas minstrels.)

WAKE: N ON *vakr* 'watchful, alert'. 12th cent. (Hereward was an early bearer of this nickname.)

WAKEFIELD: L OE *wacian-feld* 'the field for the annual wake (vigil followed by merry-making), and the venue for wake-plays, such as the Towneley Plays'. (Yorks), *Wachefeld* DB. [Edward Gibbon Wakefield founded the New Zealand Company, bringing capital and labour together to promote orderly and progressive settlement, 1837. The Company's first expeditionary ship, the barque *Tory*, sailed from Plymouth 1839].

WAKEHAM: L OE 'The *hamm* (river-meadow) of *Wake*, an Anglo-Saxon'. 13th cent.

WAKELEY, WAKLEY, WAKERLEY: L OE '*wācor-lēah* 'the willow glade'. 14th cent.

WAKELIN(G), WAKELAM, WALKLIN(G): P Norman French *Walchelin*, a double dim. of OG *Walho*. DB.

WAKEMAN, WAKERMAN: O ME *wake-man*, 'watch, vigil-man'. 12th cent. *Wakeman* was also the former title of the mayor of Ripon (Yorks), where the town hall bears the motto: 'Except ye Lord keep ye cittie, ye Wakeman waketh in vain'.

WALBANCK, WALBANK. WALLBANK: L OE *wella* + ME *banke* 'the bank of the stream'. 14th cent.

WALBOURNE, WALBURN: L OE *walh-burna* 'the brook of the Welsh'. 12th cent. [Walbourne, a First Fleet (convict) surname].

WALBROOK: L OE *walh-brōc* 'the brook of the Welsh (Britons)'. 12th cent. (Walbrook is one of London's four lost rivers. The others are the Fleet, the Tyburn, and the Westbourne. All have gone underground before they reach the Thames. Only Walbrook and Fleet have given rise to surnames.)

WALBY, WAUDBY: OE + ON *weall-by* 'the farm at the (Roman) wall'. (Cumb).

WALCH see WALSH.

WALCOT(T): L OE *wealh-cot* 'the cottage of the serfs'. 12th cent.

WALD(E), WAUD, WOLD: L OE *wald*, *weald* 'the wold (cleared forest)'. 12th cent.

WALDEN: L OE *wealh-denu* 'the valley of the Britons'. (Essex, Herts, Yorks).

WALDER: L OE A deriv. of *wald* 'open forest dweller'. 13th cent.

WALDIE, WALDY see WALTHEW.

WALDRAM, WALDREN, WALDRON: P OG *Waleran*, OF *Galeran* 'stranger-raven'. DB.

WALE(S), WAILES: (i) P OG *Walo*, OF *Galon*. 12th cent. (ii) N ME *wale* 'goodly, meritorious'. 13th cent. (iii) L OE *walh* 'foreign, i.e., Welshman, Briton'. (iv) L OE *walu* 'ridge, bank'. 13th cent. Some may be from Wales (Yorks), OE *Walas* 'the Welsh'.

WALFORD: (i) L OE *wealt-ford* 'the shaky, unsteady ford, i.e., difficult to cross'. (Dorset) (ii) L OE *Wealh-ford* 'the ford of the Welsh'. (Herefords) 13th cent.

WALKDEN: L OE *Walce-denu* 'the valley of the Walce stream'. (Lancs).

WALKER: O OE *wealcere* 'fuller' (in the cloth trade). 13th cent. See also Fuller, Tucker. [A First Fleet (crew and convict) surname].

WALKLATE, WALKLETT: P *Walk-el-et* a double dim. of OG *Walho*. 14th cent.

WALKLEY: L OE 'The *lēah* (clearing) of an Anglo-Saxon called *Walaca*'. (Yorks).

WALL(S): L OE *wall, weall* usually a Roman wall, as at London, Colchester, Oxford, Northumb, or a Roman station as at Staffs (*Letocetum*), or the wall of a town elsewhere. 12th cent. [A First Fleet (marine and convict) surname].

WALLER(S): (i) O A deriv. of ME *walle* 'a builder of walls'. 13th cent. (ii) N OF *gallier* 'a coxcomb, a fop'. 13th cent.

WALLINGTON: (i) L OE 'The *tūn* (farm) of the people by the wall or embankment'. (Norfolk) (ii) L OE *Weala-tūn* 'the farm of the Welsh (Britons)' (Berks, Hants, Surrey) (iii) L OE 'The *tun* of *Waendel's* people' (Herts).

WALLIS, WALLACE: L Anglo-French *Walleis* 'Welshman, Celt': (i) Britons of Strathclyde. (ii) Welshmen of the border counties—Warwicks, Worcs, Staffs. (iii) Bretons of East Anglia. Wallace is the Scottish form. 12th cent.

WALLMAN: O 'Servant of *Wale*'. 12th cent.

WALLOP see GALLOP.

WALLWORK: L OE *Weala-worth* 'The *worth* (enclosure) of the Welsh (Britons)'.

WALLWORTH: L OE Identical in meaning with *Wallwork*.

WALMSLEY: L OE *wald-(ge)mǣre-lēah* 'the *lēah* (clearing) near the *wald* 'wood' *(ge)mǣre* (boundary mark)' (Walmersley, Lancs).

WALPOLE: (i) L OE 'The *pōl* (pool) by the wall (Roman bank)'. (Norfolk) (ii) L OE 'The *pōl* of the *wealh* (Welsh, Britons, serfs)' (Suffolk) 12th cent.

WALSH(E), WALCH: L OE *wǣlisc*, ME *walsche* 'foreign, Welsh'. 13th cent. See also Welsh. [A First Fleet (convict) surname].

WALSINGHAM: L OE 'The *hām* (village) of the *ingas* (people) of an Anglo-Saxon called *Wǣl*'. (Norfolk), *Walsingeham* DB.

WALTER(S), FITZWALTER, FITZWATER: P OG *Walter* 'mighty-army', introduced into England during the reign of Edward the Confessor. DB. See also Fitz.

WALTHAM: L OE *weald-hām* 'the *hām* (homestead) in the wood or on the *wold* (cleared forest)'. A frequent place-name. 12th cent.

WALTHEW, WALTHO, WADDIE, WALDIE, WALDY, WADDY: P Anglo-Scand *Waltheof* 'battle-thief' (snatching victory in battle). DB.

WALTON: L OE The many places called *Walton* have various meanings from which surnames have derived, e.g., 'the *tūn* (homestead, village, town) on a *wold* (cleared forest)', 'the *tūn* of the serfs', 'the *tūn* by a stream', 'the *tūn* with a wall or bank'. Most of these places are in DB. The surname is 12th cent. [A First Fleet (crew) surname].

WANLESS: N ME *wanles* 'luckless'. 15th cent.

WANN: N OE *wann*, now 'wan, pale', but the original sense was dark. Chaucer uses *wan* in 'The Knight's Tale': 'the sea was wan'. 13th cent.

WANNA: N OE *wana* 'lacking, wanting, in poverty'.

WANNER: L An ancient stream-name, preserved in *Wannerton*, (Worces).

WANSEY: L OF From Wanchey (Seine Inférieure) France. DB.

WANT, WHANT: (i) L ME *want*, a dial. form of *went*, OE *wendan* 'to turn', hence 'cross-roads'. (ii) N ME *want*, from Ger 'mole, *molewarp*', a nickname from the mole. 14th cent.

WARBOYS, WORBOYS: (i) L O Scand *varthi-buskr* 'the beacon in the bushes'. (Hunts) 13th cent. (ii) N OF *garder-bois* 'guard wood', a nickname for a forester. 13th cent.

WARBURTON: L OE 'The *tūn* (farm) of an Anglo-Saxon called *Wǣrburg*'. 13th cent. [Ann Wharburton, a convict, brought her unrecorded variant of the surname to Australia 1788].

WARBY: L ON *varthi-býr* 'the village with a beacon'.

WARD(E), WARDS: O OE *weard* 'watchman, guard'. 12th cent. [A First Fleet (convict) surname].

WARDEN: (i) O AF *wardein* 'warden, porter, gate-keeper, sentinel'. DB. (ii) L OE *weard-dūn* 'watch hill'. (Beds, Durham, Kent, Northumb, Northants) 13th cent.

WARDILL, WARDLE, WARDALE, WARDALL, WARDEL(L): L OE *weard-hyll* 'watch hill'. (Ches, Lancs) 13th cent.

WARDLAW, WARLOW: L OE *weard-hlāw* 'watch hill'. (Derbys, Staffs).

WARDLEY: L OE *wer-lēah* 'the clearing by a weir'. (Rutland).

WARDMAN: L ME *werde* 'marsh' 'marshman'. 14th cent.

WARDROBE, WARDROP, WARDROPER, WARDROPPER: O OF *garderobier*, ONF *warderobier* 'an official in a large household in charge of the robes'. 13th cent.

WARE(S): (i) N OE *waer* 'astute, prudent'. 13th cent. (ii) L OE *wer* 'weir' (as at Ware, Herts, which is on the R. Lea). DB. [Charlotte Ware or Weir, a convict, brought the surname to Australia 1788].

WAREHAM: L OE *wer-hām* 'the homestead by a weir'. (Dorset).

WAREING, WARING, WARRING, WEARING, FITZWARIN: P OG *Warin*, OF *Guarin*, a popular Norman pers. name. DB. (Fulke *FitzWarine*, a young knight, was assigned by William the Conqueror to the defence of the Welsh Marches.)

WARFIELD: L OE *waernanwella-feld* 'the field or open country by the wrens' stream'. (Berks).

WARHAM: L OE *wer-hām* 'the homestead by a weir'. (Herefords).

WARK: L OE *weorc* 'fort'. (Northumb).

WARLOCK, WORLOCK, WARLOW: N OE *waerloga* originally 'fiend, traitor'. Later, 'sorcerer, wizard'. 13th cent.

WARMAN: (i) P OE *Waermund* 'faith-protector'. 12th cent. (ii) O OE *waru-mann* 'merchant, chapman'. 13th cent.

WARN(E), WARNES, WEARN(E), WORN(E): L OE *wagen-fenn* 'the quaking fen'. (Devon) 13th cent.

WARNER, WORNER: P OG *Warinhar*, ONF *Warnier*, a frequent Norman pers. name. 12th cent.

WARR(E), DELAWARE: N OF *de la guerre*, *de la werre* 'of the war', a nickname for a warrior. 12th cent.

WARREN, WARRAN: L OF From La Varenne (Seine Inférieure) France. DB.

WARRENER, WARRINER, WARRENDER: O OF *warrennier* 'a game warden'. 12th cent.

WARRINGTON: L OE (i) 'The *tūn* (settlement) of the *ingas* (people) of an Anglo-Saxon called *Wāer*'. (Lancs) (ii) 'The *tūn* of *Wāerheard's* people'. (Bucks).

WARRY see WERRY.

WARTER: L OE *weargtrēo* 'gallows, gibbet', 'the gallows tree'. (Yorks) 13th cent.

WARTERS: A variant of *Waters*. 17th cent.

WARTON: L OE *weard-tūn* 'the look-out place'. (Lancs, Northumb, Warwicks) 12th cent.

WARWICK, WARRICK: L OE *waering-wīc* 'the dairy farm by the weir'. (Warwicks) DB.

WASE, WASH see WACE.

WASHINGTON: L OE 'The *tūn* (settlement or colony) of the *ingas* (people) of an Anglo-Saxon called *Wassa*'. (Durham, Sussex) 14th cent.

WASS: L OE *waesse* 'swamp'. (Yorks) Also a variant of *Wace*.

WASSALL, WASSELL, WASTALL, WASTELL: O OF *wastel* 'a fine bread or cake'. Metonymic for a baker of *wastels*. 12th cent.

WATCHORN: L OE *waecce-aern* 'watch-house, guard-house'.

WATER(S), WATTERS: P A variant of *Walter*, persisting from the normal medieval pronunciation. 12th cent. [A First Fleet (crew) surname].

WATERER: O A der. of OE *waeterian* 'to water', 'a water-seller or farm worker leading cattle to water'. 15th cent.

WATERFIELD: L OF From Vatierville (Seine Inférieure) France. 12th cent.

WATERHOUSE: L OE *waeter-hūs* 'the house by the water' or 'the house with a moat'. 14th cent. [A First Fleet (crew and convict) surname].

WATERMAN: (i) O 'Servant of *Walter*'. 13th cent. (ii) O OE *waeter-mann* 'water-carrier'. 12th cent.

WATERSON, WATTERSON: P 'Son of *Walter*'. 14th cent.

WATERWORTH: L OE *waeter-worth* 'the homestead by the water'.

WATES see WAITE.

WATKIN(S), WATKIS(S): P A dim. of *Walter*. 13th cent. [A First Fleet (female convict) surname. Rev James Watkin entered New Zealand as a Wesleyan missionary, 1835].

WATKINSON: P 'Son of *Watkin*'. 15th cent.

WATLING: P OE *Hwaetling*, son of *Hwaetel*, a deriv. of OE *hwaet* 'bold, brave, active'. This Anglo-Saxon name is preserved in Whatlington, Sussex.

WATMORE see WHATMOOR.

WATMOUGH, WHATMOUGH, WHATMUFF: P *Wat*, a pet-form of *Walter* + OE *māga* or ME *maugh* 'relative'. '*Wat's* brother-in-law'. 14th cent.

WATSON: P 'Son of *Wat*'. 14th cent. [Thomas Watson and John Watson, convicts, and Robert Watson, quartermaster and sail-maker on the *Sirius*, brought the surname to Australia 1788. Robert Watson was reputed, among others, to have been the first to set foot on the eastern coast of Australia].

WATT(S): P A pet-form of *Walter*. 13th cent. [A First Fleet (crew and marine) surname].

WATTON: L OE *wād-tūn* 'the *tūn* (farm) where woad grows' (Herts), or 'the *tūn* of an Anglo-Saxon called *Wada* (Norfolk), *Wadetuna* DB, or OE *weta-dūn* 'the wet hill' (Yorks).

WAUD see WALD.

WAUDBY: L OE + ON 'The *býr* (homestead) on the wold (cleared forest)'. (Yorks) See also Walby.

WAUGH: L The name used by the Angles for the Britons of Strathclyde, *Walh* 'foreigner'. 13th cent. [The surname was brought to Australia 1788 by William Waugh, a sailor on the *Alexander*].

WAVELL: L OF From Vauville (Manche) Normandy. DB.

WAX, WAXMAN: O OE *weax* 'a seller of wax', probably beeswax. 12th cent.

WAY(E), WEY: L OE *weg* 'way, road, path'. 12th cent.

WAYGOOD: L OE *weg-gōd* 'the good road', probably a Roman road.

WAYLAND: L OE *weald-land* 'woodland'.

WAYLETT: L OE *weg-ge-lǣte* 'cross-roads'. 13th cent.

WAYMAN see WYMAN. WAYNE see WAIN. WAYT see WAIT. WAYMARK see WYMARK.

WEAR, WEIR, WERE: O OE *wer* 'fish-trap', 'fisherman at the weir'. 13th cent.

WEARING see WAREING. WEARN see WARN. WEATE see WHEAT. WEATHERALL see WETHERALL. WEATHERBY see WETHERBEE. WEATHERHEAD see WETHERHEAD.

WEATHERLEY: L OE *wether-lēah* 'the sheep pasture'.

WEAVER: O OE A deriv. of *wefan* 'to weave', 'a weaver'. 13th cent. Some surnames may be from R. Weaver (Ches), a Brit river-name.

WEBB: O OE *webba* (or fem. *webbe*), 'a weaver'. 12th cent. [A First Fleet (crew) surname].

WEBBER: O OE A deriv. of OE *web*, 'a weaver'. 13th cent.

WEBLEY: L OE 'The *lēah* (clearing) of *Wibba*, an Anglo-Saxon'. (Herefords).

WEBSTER: O OE *webbestre* 'a female weaver', frequently used also of men. 13th cent.

WEDDERBURN: L OE *wether-burna* 'the sheep-wash stream'.

WEDGE: O OE *wecg* 'wedge-cake, simnel cake'. Metonymic for a baker of *wedges*. (This was a rich, ornamental boiled cake for which there was a demand at the Easter and Christmas festivals.)

WEDGEWOOD, WEDGWOOD: L OE *wecg-wudu* 'the wedge-shaped wood'. (Staffs).

WEDLAKE, WEDLOCK: L OE *wīd-lacu* 'the wide stream'. (Devon).

WEEDON: L OE *weoh-dūn* 'the hill with a heathen temple'. (Bucks, Northants).

WEEKES, WEEK(S) see WICH.

WEEKLEY: L OE *wice-lēah* 'the wych-elm wood'. (Northants).

WEIGHT(E) see WAIT, WIGHT. WEIGHTMAN see WIGHTMAN. WEIR see WEAR.

WELBOURN, WELBORN, WELBURN, WELLBOURN(E), WELLBORN(E), WELLBURN: L OE *welle-burna* 'the brook flowing from a spring'. (Lincs, Norfolk, Yorks) 12th cent.

WELBY: L OE + ON *wella-býr* 'the farm by a spring'. (Leices, Lincs) 12th cent.

WELCH see WELSH.

WELCOME: (i) L OE *wella-cumb* 'the valley with a stream'. (Devon) 13th cent. (ii) N OE *wilcume* 'welcome'. 'a welcome guest'. 13th cent. (iii) N OE *wel-cemban* 'well groomed'. 13th cent.

WELDON, WELLDON: L OE *wielle-dūn* 'the hill with a spring'. (Northants) 12th cent.

WELFARE: WELLFARE: N OE *wel-faru* 'full, abundant, life', a nickname for one who was doing very well. 13th cent.

WELFIT(T): N OE *wel-fēdan* 'well fed', a nickname for a fat man. 12th cent.

WELHAM: L OE *wella-hām* 'the homestead by the stream/spring'. (Leices) 14th cent.

WELK, WILK: (i) O OE *weolc* 'whelk' (earlier *welc, wilc*). Metonymic for a gatherer/dealer in whelks, either as food or for their purple dye. (ii) N OE *hwylca* 'pustule, boil', a nickname for a persistent sufferer from boils or carbuncles. (iii) N ME *welk, welken*, 'withered, shrivelled'.

WELLAND: L Celtic + OE *Wen-land* 'land beside the *Wen* stream'. (Worces), *Wenelande* 12th cent. The Welland River (Northants, Leices, Rutland, Lincs) did not produce a surname.

WELLER, WHELLER: O A deriv. of OE *wellan* 'to boil', 'a salt-boiler'. 13th cent.

WELLESLEY: L OE *welle-leah* 'the glade with a stream', Wellesley in Wells (Som). 13th cent. The surname of the dukes of Wellington.

WELLING(S): L OE *Wellingas* 'people by the stream', preserved in Wellingham (Lincs, Norfolk, Sussex).

WELLINGTON: L OE 'The *ingas* (people) of *wēo-lēah* (temple in the woods) + *tūn* (farm)'. (Herefords, Salop, Som), early forms *Weolintun, Weolingtun* 1038 and 904.

WELLMAN, WELMAN: L OE *wella-mann* 'by a spring or stream'. 14th cent.

WELL(S): L OE *wellum* 'springs, streams'. (Norfolk, Som) 12th cent. See also Attwell, Atterwell.

WELSH, WELCH: L OE *wēalisc* 'foreign', the Anglo-Saxon name for Celtic, Welsh, British people. 13th cent. See also Walsh. [A First Fleet (convict) surname].

WELTON: L OE *welle-tūn* 'the village by a stream'. (Cumb, Lincs, Northants) 12th cent.

WEMYSS: L SG *uaim* + ME suffix -s-, 'caves'. (Fife) Scotland. 13th cent.

WENDEN: L OE *wende-denu* 'the winding (stream)valley'. (Essex), *Wendena* DB.

WENMAN see WAINMAN.

WENN, WEN: L OE *wenn* 'wen, wart', used topographically of a mound or barrow. 14th cent.

WENSLEY: L OE 'The *lēah* (glade) sacred to the pagan god *Wōden*'. (Derbys, Yorks) 12th cent.

WENT: (i) L Brit river-name. (Yorks). (ii) L ME *went* 'cross-roads'. 13th cent.

WENTWORTH: L OE 'The *worth* (enclosure) of an Anglo-Saxon who bore the nickname *Wintra* (*Winter*)'. (Cambs, Yorks) 13th cent.

WERE see WEAR.

WERRY, WARRY: P OG *Werric*, OF *Guerri*. DB.

WERTH see WORTH. WESKER see WISHART.

WESLEY, WESTLEY: L OE *westan-lēah* 'the western clearing'. (Cambs, Devon, Lancs, Suffolk) 11th cent.

WEST: L OE *west* 'the man from the west'. 12th cent. [A First Fleet (marine and convict) surname].

WESTALL: L OE *west-heall* 'the western hall'. (Suffolk).

WESTBROOK: L OE *west-brōc* 'the western brook'. (Berks, Kent, Wight) 13th cent. [A First Fleet (marine) surname].

WESTBURY: L OE *west-burg* 'the western fort'. (Bucks, Glos, Hants, Salop, Som).

WESTCOTT, WESTACOTT, WESCOT(T): L OE *west-cot* 'the west cottage'. 12th cent.

WESTERMAN: L OE 'The newcomer from the west'. WESTERN, WESTREN: L OE *westerne* 'the man from the west'. 12th cent. WESTGATE: L OE *west-geat* 'the west gate' (of castle or walled town). WESTHORP(E), WESTROP(E), WESTROPP, WESTRUP: L OE *west-thorp* 'the west outlying farm'. (Suffolk) 12th cent.

WESTLAKE: L OE *west-lacu* 'west of the stream'. 13th cent. [A First Fleet (convict) surname; Edward Westlake, transported for stealing a leg of mutton, became a sheep grazier in Tasmania].

WESTMAN: L ON *vestmathr* 'the man from the west', probably Ireland. 12th cent.

WESTMORE: L OE *west-mere* 'the west lake'. 14th cent.

WESTON: L OE *west-tūn* 'the west farm' or 'west of the village'. DB.

WESTWOOD: L OE *west-wudu* 'west of the wood' (Kent) or 'the west wood' (Warwicks, Worces, Wilts). 13th cent. [A First Fleet (convict) surname].

WETHERALL, WETHERILL, WEATHERALL, WEATHERILL, WETHERELL: L OE *wether-halh* 'the corner of land where wethers are grazed'. (Cumb) 14th cent.

WETHERBEE, WETHERBY, WITHERBY: L ON *wether-býr* 'wether farm'. (Yorks) 13th cent.

WETHERHEAD, WETHERED,

WEATHERHEAD: O OE *wether-hierde* 'wether-herd', 'shepherd'. 12th cent.

WETTON: L OE *waet-dūn* 'the wet hill'. (Staffs).

WEY see WAY. WEYMAN see WYMAN. WEYMARK see WYMARK.

WEYMOUTH: L Brit + OE *Wey-mūth* 'the mouth of the River Wey'. (Dorset).

WHAIT(E), WHAITES see WAIT. WHALAN see PHELAN.

WHALE, WHALL: N OE *hwael*, ME *whal* 'whale', a nickname for a large, bulky man with a huge appetite. 13th cent. There was also a nickname WHALEBELLY OE *hwael-bylig*, but it has probably been absorbed by *Whale*.

WHALEBONE: O OE *hwael-bān*. A metonym for a dealer in whalebones, from which various articles were made, originally the tooth of the walrus.

WHALEY: L OE *weg-lēah* 'the clearing by a road'. (Ches).

WHALLEY: L OE *hwealf-lēah* 'the clearing by the rounded hill'. (Lancs) 12th cent.

WHANT see WANT.

WHARF(E): (i) O OE *hwerf* 'wharf', 'a worker at the wharf'. 14th cent. (ii) L *Wharfe*, a Brit river-name, *Weorf* (winding river) in 963. (iii) L ON *hvarf* 'bend, corner'. (Yorks), *Qwarf* in 1297.

WHARTON: L OE (i) *hwearf-tūn* 'the farm by the shore or embankment'. (Westmorland). (ii) *waefre-tūn* 'the farm by the winding stream'. (Ches, Herefords) (iii) *weard-tūn* 'the watch, look-out place'. (Lincs) Surname 14th cent.

WHATLEY see WHEATLEY.

WHATMAN, WHEATMAN: P OE *Hwaetmann* 'bold, brave man'. DB.

WHATMORE, WATMORE: L OE *waet-mōr* 'the wet (boggy) marsh'. (Salop).

WHEADON: L OE *hwǣte-dūn* 'wheat hill'.

WHEAT(E), WEATE: N OE *hwaet* 'sharp, brisk, active'. 12th cent.

WHEATLEY, WHATLEY: L OE *hwǣt-lēah* 'The wheat clearing'. (Essex, Lancs, Notts, Oxon, Yorks) 11th cent.

WHEATON: L OE *hwǣte-tūn* 'the wheat farm'. (Leices, Notts).

WHEELDON, WHEELDEN, WHEILDON, WHELDON: L OE *hwēol-denu* 'the curving valley'. 13th cent.

WHEELER: O OE A deriv. of *hwēol* 'wheel', 'a wheel-maker, wheelwright'. 13th cent. [A First Fleet (convict) surname].

WHEELWRIGHT: O OE *hwēol-wyrhta* 'wheelwright', 'a maker of wheels and wheeled carts'. 11th cent.

WHELAN see PHELAN. WHELLER see WELLER. WHENMAN see WAINMAN.

WHETTER: O OE A deriv. of *hwettan* 'to whet, sharpen', 'a tool-sharpener'. 14th cent.

WHICKER see WICKER. WHIGHT see WIGHT. WHILESMITH see WILDSMITH. WHILEY see WILEY.

WHINFIELD, WINFIELD: L ME *whin* + OE *feld* 'the field overgrown with gorse'.

WHINNEY: L ME *whin* + OE *ēg* 'the gorse-covered island'. 14th cent.

WHIPP: P OE *Wippa*, an Anglo-Saxon pers. name, preserved in Whippingham, (Wight).

WHISKER see WISHART.

WHISSON, WISSON: L OF From Wissaut (Pas-de-Calais) France. DB.

WHISTLER: O OE *hwistlere* 'a player on the pipe, flute'. 13th cent.

WHITAKER, WHITTAKER: L OE *hwīt-aecer* 'white acre, white field'. (Lancs) 12th cent. [A First Fleet (convict) surname].

WHITBREAD, WHITEBREAD: O OE *hwīt-brēad* 'white bread' or *hwǣte-brēad* 'wheat bread', 'a baker of best bread'. 13th cent.

WHITBY: L OE + O Scand *hwīt-by* 'the white village'. (Ches, Yorks), *Witebi* DB.

WHITCHER, WITCHER: O OE *hwicce* 'chest', a maker of chests'. 12th cent.

WHITCOMBE: L OE *withig-cumb* 'willow valley' or *wīd-cumb* 'wide valley'. (Dorset, Wight, Wilts) 12th cent.

WHITE, WHYTE, WITT(E), WITTS: (i) P OE *Hwīta*, an Anglo-Saxon pers. name. DB. (ii) N OE *hwīt* 'white', for fair hair or complexion. (iii) L OE *wiht* 'a bend or curve in river or road'. 13th cent. [John White, chief surgeon of the First Fleet, Peter White, sailmaker on the *Sirius*, John White, ship's boy on the *Alexander*, James White, a marine, and James White, a convict, brought the surname to Australia 1788].

WHITEFIELD: L OE *wiht-feld* 'the field at a bend'. (Derbys, Kent, Northants, Northumb) 12th cent.

WHITEFORD, WHITFORD: L OE *hwīt-ford* 'the white ford'. The first is mainly a Scottish form. The second is from Whitford (Devon), *Witefort* DB.

WHITEHALL: L OE *hwīt-heall* 'the white hall'.

WHITEHEAD: N OE *hwīt-hēafod* 'white-head', for fair or white hair or *hwīt-hōd* 'white hood'. 13th cent.

WHITEHORN(E), WHITHORN: L OE *hwīt-hūs* 'the white house'. (Whithorn, Wigtown), Scotland. In AD 730, *Bede* recorded that this white house (*Hwitan AErne*) was so called because it was built of stone, in contrast to the wattle and daub huts in which the people lived.

WHITEHOUSE, WHITTERS: (i) L OE *hwīt-hūs* 'whitewashed or stone house'. 14th cent. (ii) N OE *hwīt-halse* 'white neck'.

WHITELAM, WHITLAM, WHITLUM: N OE *hwīt-lamb* 'white lamb', a nickname for an innocent, an incorruptible, or one steeped in piety. 14th cent.

WHITELAW: L OE *hwīt-hlāw* 'the white hill', places in Scotland. 13th cent.

WHITELEY, WHITELY, WHITLEY: L OE *hwīt-lēah* 'white clearing'. 12th cent.

WHITELOCK, WHITLOCK: N OE *hwīt-locc* 'white lock' (of hair). DB.

WHITEMAN, WHITMAN, WITTMAN: P OE *Hwītmann*, an Anglo-Saxon pers. name, meaning 'fair (complexioned) man'. 12th cent.

WHITEMORE, WHITMORE: L OE *hwīt-mōr* 'white moor or swamp'. (Staffs, Devon) 12th cent.

WHITEOAK see WHITTOCK.

WHITER, WHITTER: O OE A deriv. of OE *hwītian* 'to make white', 'a white-washer'. A busy trade. Important buildings were kept in sparkling condition outside with whitewash, among them Corfe Castle (Dorset) and the White Tower (the Keep of the Tower of London). 12th cent.

WHITESIDE: L OE *hwīt-sīde* 'the white slope' (of hill). 13th cent.

WHITESMITH: O OE *hwīt-smith* 'a tin-smith'. 13th cent.

WHITEWAY: L OE *hwīt-weg* 'the white way', probably a chalk road. 13th cent.

WHITHAM see WITHAM.

WHITING, WHITTING, WITTING: P OE *Hwīting*, a patronymic from *Hwīta* (White), 'son of *Hwīta*'. 11th cent. Some are from a nickname 'fair of hair or complexion'. [A First Fleet (convict) surname].

WHITMARSH: L OE *hwīt-mersc* 'the white marsh'. 13th cent.

WHITNEY: L OE *hwīt-ēg* 'the white island'. 13th cent.

WHITSON: P OE 'Son of *White*'. 14th cent.

WHITTAKER see WHITAKER.

WHITTAL(L): L OE *hwīt-halh* 'the white corner of land' (probably chalky).

WHITTARD: P OE *Wihtheard* 'elf-brave'. 12th cent.

WHITTERS see WHITEHOUSE.

WHITTINGHAM: L OE 'The *hām* (village) of the *ingas* (people) of an Anglo-Saxon called *Hwīta* (White)'. (Lancs, Northumb, Lothian) 12th cent.

WHITTINGTON: L OE 'The *tūn* (farm) of *Hwīta's* people'. (Derbys, Glos, Lancs, Northumb, Salop, Staffs, Warwicks, Worces) 12th cent.

WHITTLE, WHITTELL: L OE *hwit-hyll* 'the white hill'. (Oxon, Lancs, Northumb) 13th cent.

WHITTOCK, WHITEOAK: P OE *Hwīttuc*, a dim. of *Hwīt*. 14th cent.

WHITTON: L OE 'The *tūn* (farm) of an Anglo-Saxon called *Hwīta*'. (Durham, Middx, Northumb, Salop) Those from Lincs are L OE *Hwītan-ēg* '*Hwīta's* island', probably dry land in a fen.

WHITTY: N OE *hwīt-ēage* 'white-eye', for one with light-coloured eyes.

WHITWORTH: L OE 'The *worth* (enclosure) of *Hwīta*. (Durham, Lancs) 12th cent.

WHY(E) see GUY. WHYMAN see WYMAN. WHYTE see WHITE. WIBER see WYBER.

WIBLIN: P A Norman double dim. of *Wibbe*, which may be from the OE name *Wibba*. 12th cent.

WIBROW see WYBER.

WICH(E), WICK(E), WICKES, WICKS, WIX, WYKE(S), WEEKES, WEEKS: L OE (i) *wīc* 'dairy farm'. (ii) *wice* 'wych (elm)'. 11th cent.

WICKEN, WICKIN(S): L OE *wīcum* 'dairy farms'. 13th cent.

WICKENDEN: L OE *wīcum-denu* 'the dairy-farm in the valley'. 12th cent.

WICKER, WHICKER: O OE A deriv. of *wīc* 'a worker at the dairy-farm'. 13th cent.

WICKET(T) see WIGGETT.

WICKHAM, WHICKHAM: L OE *wīc-hām* 'the village with a dairy-farm'. 13th cent. [A First Fleet (female convict) surname].

WICKING: (i) O ON *Vikingr*, O Dan & O Sw *Viking*. (ii) O OE *wīcing* 'pirate'. DB.

WICKMAN: O OE *wīc-mann* 'dairy-farm man'. 12th cent.

WIDDECOMBE, WIDDICOMBE, WITHYCOMBE: L OE *wīthig-cumb* 'willow valley'. 12th cent.

WIDDOWS, WIDDAS, WIDDER(S): N OE *widewe* 'widow'. 13th cent. WIDDOWSON: N 'Son of the widow'. 14th cent.

WIDGER: P OE *Wihtgār* 'elf-spear'. DB.

WIDMER: L OE *wīthig-mere* 'the pool in the willows'.

WIGAN, WIGGAN, WIGGIN: (i) P O Bret *Uicon*. The OF form of the name, *Wighen* was introduced into England at the Norman Conquest. DB. (ii) L *Tref Wigan* '*Wigan's* homestead'. (Lancs).

WIGG: N OE *wicga* 'beetle', a nickname. 12th cent.

WIGGETT, WICKET(T): P O Dan *Vigot*. DB.

WIGHT, WEIGHT, WHIGHT: N ME *wiht* 'valliant, strong, agile'. 12th cent.

WIGHTMAN, WEIGHTMAN: (i) P OE *Wihtmann* 'elf-man'. (ii) N ME *wiht* 'brave, strong man'. 13th cent.

WIGLEY: L OE *wicga-lēah* 'the clearing infested with beetles or earwigs'. (Derbys).

WIGMORE: L Welsh *gwig mawr* 'the big wood'. (Herefords).

WIGNALL, WIGNELL: L OE 'The *haga* (haugh, enclosure) of an Anglo-Saxon called *Wicga* (Beetle)'. (Norfolk).

WIGNEY: L OE *wicga-ēg* 'the island infested with insects'.

WILBERFORCE: L OE 'The *foss* (ditch) of an Anglo-Saxon woman called *Wilburg* (Will-Fortress)'. (Yorks).

WILBY: L OE *wīthig-by* 'the farm among the willows' (Norfolk), or L OE *wilig-bēag* 'circle of willows' (Suffolk) 12th cent.

WILCHER see WILTSHIRE.

WILCOCK, WILCOX: P *Wilcoc*, a pet-form of *William*. 13th cent. [Samuel Wilcock and Richard Wilcox, both convicts, brought the surname to Australia 1788].

WILCOCKSON, WILCOXON: P 'Son of *Wilcock*'. 14th cent.

WILD(E), WYLD(E): (i) N OE *wilde* 'wild, violent'. DB. (ii) L OE *wilde* (noun) 'waste, wilderness'. 12th cent.

WILDBLOOD: N OE *wilde-blōd* 'wild blood', a nickname for a rake. 14th cent.

WILDER: N OE *wildēor* 'wild deer'. 14th cent.

WILDGOOSE, WILLGOSS, WILLGOOSE: N OE *wilde-gōs* 'wild goose'. 12th cent.

WILDING, WILLDING: N OE A deriv. of *wilde*, 'the wild one'. 13th cent.

WILDISH: WILDASH: L OE *wealdisc* 'of the Weald'. (Kent) 13th cent.

WILDMAN: N OE *wilde-mann* 'the wild man of the woods'. 14th cent.

WILDSMITH, WILESMITH: O OE *hwēol-smith* 'wheelsmith, maker of iron parts for wheels'. 14th cent. See also Wheelwright.

WILES, WYLES: O OE *wīl* 'trick, trap'. Metonymic for a trapper or fisherman at the fish-traps'. 12th cent.

WILEY, WHILEY, WYLIE, WYLLIE: L OE *wilig-lēah* 'willow wood'. 12th cent.

WILFORD: L OE *wilig-ford* 'the ford among the willows'. (Notts, Suffolk) 12th cent.

WILFRED: P OE *Wilfrith* 'will-peace'. 11th cent.

WILK(E), WILKES, WILKS, WILCK(E): P OE A short form of *Willock*. 13th cent.

WILK see WELK.

WILKIE: P A Scottish double dim. of *William*. 15th cent.

WILKIN(S), WILKEN(S), WILKING(S): P A dim. of *Will* (*William*). 12th cent. [A First Fleet (convict) surname].

WILKINSON: P 'Son of *Wilkin*'. 14th cent.

WILKSHER see WILTSHIRE.

WILL(E), WILLES, WILLS: P A short form of *William*. 13th cent. [Alfred Wills and Charles Kettle, explorers, negotiated the Manawatu Gorge and travelled over the Rimutakas to the Hutt Valley, 1842].

WILLARD: P OG *Widelard* or OE *Wilheard* 'will-brave'. DB.

WILLET(T), WILLATS, WILLETTS, WILLOTT, WILLITS: P dim. of *Will* (*William*). 13th cent.

WILLIAM(S), WILLEMS: P OG *Willihelm* 'will-helmet', Norman form of Fr *Guillaume*. Introduced into England at the time of the Conquest. DB. [Twelve persons named Williams arrived with the First Fleet, of whom nine were convicts. Henry Williams and Philip Tapsell were the first Europeans to visit Rotorua, 1831. In 1840, Henry Williams, a missionary who spoke the Maori language, advised the Maori chiefs on the Treaty of Waitangi].

WILLIAMSON: P 'Son of *William*'. 14th cent.

WILLING: P A dim. of *Will* (*William*).

WILLIS: P A form of *Will*. 14th cent.

WILLMAN, WILMAN: O 'Servant of *Will*'. 13th cent.

WILLMOT(T), WILMOT(T): P A dim. of *William*, with OF suffix *-ot*. 13th cent.

WILLOCK(S), WILLOX: P OE Forms of *Willoc*. 13th cent.

WILLOUGHBY: L OE + ON *wilig-býr* 'the farm among the willows'. (Leices, Lincs, Notts, Warwicks) 12th cent.

WILLSHEAR see WILTSHIRE.

WILMER: P OE *Wilmǣer* 'will-famous'. 13th cent.

WILMORE, WILLMORE: L OE *wilde-mōr* 'the waste, uncultivated moor or fen'. 13th cent.

WILSON: (i) P 'Son of *Will* (*William*)'. 14th cent. (ii) L OE A few bearers of this surname may be from *Wilson* (Leices), *Wifeles thorp* (farm) c. 972. [Seven persons named Wilson arrived with the First Fleet, four convicts and three crew members].

WILTON: L OE (i) 'The *tūn* (village) on the R. Wylye' (Brit river-name, short form *Wil*). (Wilts) (ii) *wilg-tūn* 'the farm among the willows'. (Cumb, Herefords, Norfolk, Yorks) (iii) *wiell-tūn* 'the farm with a spring'. (Som, Wilts, near Burbage) Surname DB.

WILTSHIRE, WILCHER, WILSHAW, WILSHIRE, WILKSHER, WILLSHAW, WILLSHER, WILLSHIRE: L OE *Wiltunscir* 870 'the shire dependent on *Wilton*'. In c. 800 the Wilts people are described as *Wilsaetan* 'dwellers on the Wylye'. Surname 12th cent.

WIMBLE: N Northern dial. form of O Dan *vimmel* 'quick, active, nimble'.

WIMMER: P OE *Winemǣer* 'friend-famous', an Anglo-Saxon pers. name. 12th cent.

WIMPLE: O OE *wimpel* 'veil'. Metonymic for a weaver/maker of wimples. 12th cent.

WINBOLT: P OE *Winebeald* 'friend-bold'. 12th cent.

WINCH, WYNCH: L/O OE *wince* 'winch'. 'Dweller or worker at the winch' (for hauling boats, etc). 13th cent.

WINCHCOMBE: L OE *wincel-cumb* 'remote valley'. 13th cent.

WINCHESTER: L Brit + OW *Gwent* + Lat *castra*, Brit town, Roman city, and the Anglo-Saxon capital of England until the time of Edward the Confessor. DB.

WINDEL, WINDLE: L OE *windbǣre-hyll* 'the windy hill'. (Yorks, Lancs) 12th cent.

WINDER: (i) O OE A deriv. of *windan* 'to wind', 'a wool winder'. 13th cent. (ii) L OE *wind* + ON *erg* 'the shelter against the wind'. (Cumb).

WINDHAM, WYNDHAM: L OE 'The *hām* (homestead) of an Anglo-Saxon called *Wigmund*'. (Wymondham, Leices, Norfolk). 13th cent.

WINDLEY: L OE *winn-lēah* 'the glade with good pasture'. (Derbys).

WINDOW: L ME *wind-oge*, from ON *vind-auga* 'eye-hole' (replacing OE *ēagduru* 'eye-door') 'the watch, look-out hole'.

WINDRIDGE: P OE *Wynrīc* 'joyful-ruler'. DB. Some may be from Windridge (Herts), L OE *winn-hrycg* 'the pasture ridge'.

WINDRUM: L OE + ON *wind-ergum* 'the wind shelters'.

WINDSOR: L OE *windan-ōra*, from *windan* 'to wind' and *ōra* 'bank'. The meaning has never been established beyond doubt. Both 'winding shore' and 'landing place with a windlass' have been suggested. Probably the Anglo-Saxons who named the place thought of it simply as 'a landing place on the winding bank of the river'. Windsor has an illustrious history. The Saxon king Edward the Confessor had a royal residence here, and William the Conqueror laid the foundation of the first Windsor Castle in 1070. (i) The surname of the British royal family. (ii) A surname from the place-name. DB.

WINDUS, WINDERS: O OE *windan-hūs* 'a worker at the winding-house', 'a weaver or maker of threads, yarn'. 14th cent.

WINE(S), WYNE(S), WYNESS: N OE *wine* 'friend'. 12th cent. (The OE word for wine (drink) is *wīn*.)

WINFIELD, WINGFIELD: L OE *winn-feld* 'meadow pasture'. 13th cent. See also Whinfield.

WINGATE, WINGATT, WINDEATT, WINNIATT: L OE *wind-geat* 'wind-gate', a windy gap, pass in the hills. (Devon, Durham, Northumb) 12th cent.

WINGRAVE, WINGROVE: L OE 'The *grāf* (grove) of an Anglo-Saxon called *Wing*'.

WINKWORTH: L OE 'The worth (homestead) of *Wineca*, an Anglo-Saxon'.

WINN, WYNN(E), WYNNES: N OE *wine* 'friend'. 12th cent. See also Wine.

WINNEY, WINNY: P OE *Wyngeofu* 'joy-battle'. 12th cent.

WINSBURY: L OE 'The *burg* (fortified manor) of an Anglo-Saxon moneyer called *Winuc*'. (Som).

WINSLADE: L OE 'The *flōde* (channel or stream) of an Anglo-Saxon called *Wine* (friend)'. (Hants).

WINSLOW: L OE 'The *hlāw* (burial mound) of *Wine*'. (Bucks) 14th cent.

WINSOR, WINCER, WINSER, WINZER: L OE These surnames are from Winsor (Devon, Hants) the meaning of which appears to be identical with that of Windsor (Berks).

WINSPEAR, WINSPER, WINSPUR: L OE *spura* 'spur'. 'The hill-spur of *Wine*, an Anglo-Saxon'.

WINSTANLEY: L OE 'The *lēah* (clearing) of an Anglo-Saxon called *Wynn-stān* (joy-stone)'. (Lancs) 13th cent.

WINSTON: L OE (i) '*Wine's tūn* (farm)'. (Durham) (ii) '*Wynsige's tūn*'. (Wight) (*Wynsige*, an Anglo-Saxon name meaning 'Joy'.) Surname DB.

WINTER(S), WINTOUR, WYNTER(S): (i) P OE *Winter, Wintra*, pers. Anglo-Saxon names. (ii) N OE *winter*, a nickname for one with a sad and miserable face. 12th cent. [A First Fleet (crew) surname].

WINTERBORNE, WINTERBOURNE, WINTERBURN: L OE *winter-burna* 'the winter stream', one that flows only in winter. (Berks, Dorset, Yorks, Wilts) 12th cent.

WINTERBOTHAM, WINTERBOTTOM: L OE *winter-bothm* 'the valley used only in winter'.

WINTERFLOOD: L OE *winter-flōd* 'the land flooded in winter'.

WINTERTON: L OE (i) 'The *tūn* (farm) of an Anglo-Saxon called *Wintra*. (Lincs) (ii) 'The *tūn* used only in winter'. (Norfolk) Nearby is Somerton, to which the people and farm animals moved in summer. Surname DB.

WINTON, WYNTON: L OE (i) *wīthig-tūn* 'the farm among the willows'. (Lancs) (ii) 'The *tūn* of an Anglo-Saxon called *Wina*'. (Yorks) (iii) 'The *winn-tūn* (pasture (grazing) farm)'. (Westmorland) Surname 12th cent.

WINYARD, WYNYARD: O OE *wīngeard*. Metonymic for a worker at the vineyard. 13th cent.

WIRRALL: L OE 'The *halh* (river-meadow) where *wīr* (bog myrtle) grows'. (Ches).

WIRTH see WORTH.

WISDOM: N OE *wīsdōm* 'wisdom, sagacity, knowledge'. 12th cent.

WISE, WYSE: N OE *wīs* 'wise'. OE Byname 11th cent. [A First Fleet (marine) surname].

WISEMAN: N OE *wīs-mann* 'a wise, sagacious, discreet man' or ironically 'a fool'. Occasionally 'a wizard, magician'. 12th cent.

WISHART, WISKAR, WISKER, WHISKER, VIZARD: P ONF *Wiscard*, from ON *viskr* 'wise' + French suffix *-ard*. 12th cent.

WITCHER see WHITCHER. WITHYCOMBE see WIDDECOMBE.

WITHAM: (i) L OE 'The *hām* (homestead) of *Witta*, an Anglo-Saxon'. (Som) (ii) L OE 'The *hām* of the *wita* (counsellor)'. (Essex, Lincs) 13th cent.

WITHER(S): P ON *Vitharr*, O Dan *Withar*. DB.

WITHERBY see WETHERBEE.

WITHERIDGE: L OE *wīthig-hrycg* 'the willow ridge'. (Devon) 13th cent.

WITHEY, WITHY: L OE *wīthig* 'willow (tree)'. 13th cent.

WITHINGTON: L OE *wīthig-tūn* 'the farm in the willows' (Ches, Herefords, Lancs, Salop), or '*Widia's dūn* (hill)' (Glos).

WITHNALL, WITHNELL: L OE *wīthig-hyll* 'willow hill'. (Lancs).

WITNEY: L OE 'The *īeg* (island) of an Anglo-Saxon called *Witta*'. (Oxon).

WITT see WHITE. WITTING see WHITING. WITTMAN see WHITEMAN.

WITTON, WITTEN: L OE (i) *wīc-tūn* 'the dairy farm'. (Warwicks, Worces) (ii) *widu (wudu)-tūn* 'the farm by a wood'. (Norfolk, Northumb, Yorks) (iii) 'The *tūn* (farm) of *Witta*, an Anglo-Saxon'. (Lancs) [A First Fleet (convict) surname].

WITTY, WITTEY: N OE *wittig* 'wise, sagacious, reasonable'. The current meaning of witty (amusing, droll) is from ME *witty* and may have contributed to the surname. 13th cent.

WIVELL: P OE *Wifel* 'Beetle'. The pers. name survives in Wivelsfield (Sussex) and Wiveliscombe (Som).

WIX see WICH. WODEHOUSE see WOODHOUSE.

WOGAN: P English form of Welsh *Gwgan*, a dim. of *gwg* 'a scowl, a frown'. 13th cent.

WOLD see WALD.

WOLF(E), WOLFS, WOOLF(E), WULF(F), WOOF(F): N OE *wulf* 'wolf'. 12th cent.

WOLFENDEN, WOOLFENDEN, WOFF-

ENDEN, WOFFINDIN, WOLFENDALE: L OE *wulf-denu* 'the valley of wolves'. (Lancs).

WOLFORD see WOOLARD.

WOLFRAM: P OE *Wulfrūn*, a pers. Anglo-Saxon name. 12th cent.

WOLL see WOOLL. WOLLMAN see WOOLMAN. WOLRICH, WOLRIGE see WOOLRICH.

WOLSELEY, WOLSEY, WOLSLEY, WOOLSLEY: L OE *Wulfsige* 'wolf-victory'. DB. A frequent pers. name in Suffolk, producing the surname of Cardinal *Wolsey*.

WOLSTENHOLM: L OE 'The *holm* (island in a creek) of an Anglo-Saxon called *Wulfstan*'.

WOMBWELL, WOMBELL, WOMBLE: L 'The *wielle* (spring) of an Anglo-Saxon called *Wamba*, from *wamb* (belly, stomach)'.

WOOD(E), WOODS, WOD: (i) L OE *widu, wudu* 'forest, wood, grove, timber'. (ii) N OE *wōd*, ME *wod, wode* 'inspired', e.g., by the god *Woden*, also 'frenzied, wild, distracted'. Shakespeare (*Midsummer Night's Dream*): 'And heere am I, and wood within this wood'. Surname 13th cent. [Three convicts named Wood, and a marine named Woods brought the surname to Australia 1788].

WOODALL see WOODHALL.

WOODBINE: L OE *wudu-binde* 'wood-fetter', 'woodbine', OE name for honeysuckle.

WOODBRIDGE: L OE *wudu-brycg* 'wooden bridge'. WOODBURN: L OE *wudu-burna* 'the stream in the wood'. WOODBURY: L OE *wudu-burg* 'the wooden fort or fort in a wood'.

WOODCOCK: N OE *wuducocc*. The woodcock was popularly supposed to be stupid, hence a nickname for a simpleton. 12th cent. [A First Fleet (convict) surname].

WOODCRAFT, WOODCROFT: L OE *wudu-croft* 'the enclosure by the wood'. 12th cent.

WOODEN: L OE *wulf-denu* 'wolves' valley'. (Northumb).

WOODERS see WOODHOUSE.

WOODFORD: L OE *wudu-ford* 'the ford by the wood'. (Ches, Cornwall, Essex, Northants, Wilts).

WOODGATE, WOODYATT: L OE *wudu-geat* 'the gate into the wood'. (Dorset) 12th cent.

WOODHALL, WOODALL: L OE *wudu-heall* 'the hall in the wood', sometimes 'the hall for a forest court'. (Herts, Lincs, Yorks) 12th cent.

WOODHAM(S): L OE *wudu-hām* 'homestead in the wood'. 12th cent. [A First Fleet (convict) surname].

WOODHEAD: L OE *wudu-hēafod* 'wood-head', 'the top of the wood'. (Ches, Derbys, Devon, Yorks) 13th cent.

WOODHOUSE, WODEHOUSE, WOODER(S): L OE *wudu-hūs* 'the house in the wood'. (Leices, Yorks) 12th cent. [A First Fleet (marine) surname].

WOODIER, WOODGER: O OE *wudu-hēawere* 'wood-hewer, wood-cutter'. 13th cent.

WOODING, WOODIN: L OE *wudung* 'the wood-cutting place'. 13th cent.

WOODLAND(S): L OE *wudu-land* 'woodland'. (Devon, Dorset, Kent, Som) 12th cent.

WOODLEY, WOODLEIGH: L OE *wudu-lēah* 'the glade in the wood'. (Berks, Ches, Devon) 12th cent.

WOODMAN: P & O OE *Wudumann*, both a pers. Anglo-Saxon name and an occupational name for a worker in the woods. DB. [Jonathon Woodman, a marine, brought the surname to Australia 1788 and settled on Norfolk Island].

WOODMANSEY: L OE *wudu-mann-sae* 'the woodman's pool'. (Yorks).

WOODRIFF(E): O OE *wudu-rēfa* 'wood reeve, bailiff of the woodland'. 13th cent.

WOODROFF(E), WOODROOF(E), WOODRUFF(E), WOODRIFF(E): N OE *wudurofe* 'woodruff', a sweet-scented herb, a nickname for one who used it as a perfume. 12th cent.

WOODROW: L OE *wudu-rāw* 'the row of cottages in the wood'. (Wilts, Worces) 13th cent.

WOODSTOCK: L OE *wudu-stoc* 'place, probably holy place, in the wood'. (Oxon).

WOODWARD: O OE *wudu-weard* 'wood guard, keeper', 'a forester'. 12th cent.

WOODWELL: L OE *wudu-wiella* 'the spring in the woods'.

WOODYATT see WOODGATE. WOOF see WOLF.

WOOKEY: L OE *wōcig* 'noose, snare', 'animal trap'. (Som).

WOOLBANK: L OE *wielle* + ME *banke* 'the bank of the stream'.

WOOLCOCK, WOOLCOTT: L OE Late variants of *Walcot*. [Woolcott, a First Fleet (convict) surname].

WOOLF(E) see WOLF. WOOLFENDEN see WOLFENDEN.

WOOLFREY: P OE *Wulfrith* 'wolf-peace'. DB.

WOOLGAR, WOOLGER: P OE *Wulfgār* 'wolf-spear'. DB.

WOOLHOUSE, WOOLASS: O OE *wull-hūs* 'a worker at the wool-house (warehouse)'. 13th cent.

WOOLL, WOLL: L OE *wielle, wella* (southern dial. *woll, wooll*) 'spring, stream'. 13th cent.

WOOLLAN(D), WOOLLON, WOOLAM, WOOLAND: L OE *winn-land* 'meadow-land'.

WOOLLARD, WOLFORD, WOOLFORD: (i) P OE *Wulfweard* 'wolf-ward', an Anglo-Saxon pers. name. DB. (ii) L OE *wulf-geard* 'enclosure to protect flocks from wolves'. (Warwicks) 12th cent.

WOOLLER: O OE A deriv. of *wull* 'wool', 'a dresser/seller of wool'. 14th cent.

WOOLLETT see WOOLVETT.

WOOLLEY, WOOLEY: L OE (i) *wulf-lēah* 'the wolves' wood'. (Berks, Devon, Hunts, Sussex, Wilts, Yorks) (ii) *wulf-hyll* 'the wolves' hill'. (Northumb) (iii) *wilege* 'the clearing by a stream'. (Som) Surname 13th cent.

WOOLMER, ULMER: P OE *Wulfmǣr* 'wolf-famous'. DB.

WOOLNER, WOOLNOUGH: P OE *Wulfnōth* 'wolf-boldness'. DB.

WOOLRICH, WOOLRYCH, WOOLDRIDGE, WOOLRIDGE, WOLRICH, WOLRIGE, WOLVERIDGE, ULRICH, ULRICK: P OE *Wulfric* 'wolf-powerful'. DB.

WOOLSLEY see WOLSELEY.

WOOLSTON(E): P OE *Wulfstān* 'wolf-stone'. DB.

WOOLVEN: P OE *Wulfwine* 'wolf-friend'. DB.

WOOLVETT, WOOLLATT, WOOLLETT, WOLLETT, ULLETT, ULYATE: P OE *Wulfgēat* '*wolf-Geat*'. DB. *Geat* (*Geata*) is the name of *Beowulf's* tribe.

WOOLWICH: L OE *wull-wīc* 'wool-farm'. (Kent).

WOOSTER see WORCESTER.

WOOTON, WOOTTON, WOOTTEN, WOTTON: L OE *wudu-tūn* 'the farm near the wood'. OE Byname 11th cent. A frequent place-name.

WORBOYS see WARBOYS.

WORCESTER, WOOSTER: L Brit + OE *Wigoran-ceastre* 'the Roman fort of the *Wigoran* tribe'. Surname 12th cent.

WORDSWORTH see WADSWORTH.

WORGAN: P Welsh *Gwrgan*, a pers. name. [Lieut George Worgan, a Naval surgeon, brought the surname to Australia 1788].

WORK, WORKMAN: O OE *weorc* and *weorcmann*. *Weorc* is also used of buildings, e.g., fortifications, churches, cathedrals, so no doubt both Work and Workman are occupational names for men engaged in the building industry. The term applied to the foreman, *weorcgerēfa*, did not produce a surname. 13th cent.

WORLE, WORLEY: L OE *wōr-lēah* 'the wood-grouse wood'. (Som, now Avon).

WORLEDGE, WORLIDGE, WORLLEDGE: N OE *weorthlīc* 'noble, distinguished'. 15th cent.

WORLOCK see WARLOCK.

WORMALD: L OE 'The *wella* 'spring' of an Anglo-Saxon woman called *Wulfrūn*' (Yorks), or '*Wyrma's hyll* (hill)' (Derbys). 14th cent.

WORMLEIGHTON, WORMLEATON: L OE *wielm-lēac-tūn* 'the leek farm beside a welling stream'. (Warwicks).

WORMLEY: L OE *wyrm-lēah* 'the clearing swarming with snakes'. (Herts, Lincs, Suffolk, Surrey).

WORN see WARN. WORNER see WARNER.

WORRAL(L), WORRELL: L OE *wir-haga* 'the enclosure where bog myrtle grows'. (Ches, Yorks) 13th cent.

WORSDALE: L Brit + OE *Wyre-dael* 'the valley of the Wyre', Brit river-name. (Lancs) 14th cent. [A First Fleet (convict) surname].

WORSLEY: L OE *weorf-lēah* 'the pasture for draught cattle'. (Worces) 13th cent.

WORSTHORNE: L OE 'The *thorn* (thorn-bush) of an Anglo-Saxon called *Wurth* (*Worthy*)'.

WORSWICK, WORSICK: L OE *ūr-wīc* 'the wild cattle farm'. (Urswick, Lancs).

WORTH, WERTH, WIRTH: O OE *worth* 'enclosure'. Metonymic for a worker at an outlying farm. 12th cent.

WORTHING: L OE 'The *ingas* (folk) of an Anglo-Saxon called *Wurth* (*Worthy*)'. (Sussex) 12th cent.

WORTHINGTON: L OE '*Wurth's tūn* (farm)'. (Lancs, Leices) 12th cent.

WORTHY: L OE *worthig* 'enclosure, homestead'. (Hants) Winton D.

WORTMAN: O OE *wyrt-mann* 'a grower/seller of herbs and vegetables'. 13th cent.

WOTHERSPOON: L OE *wudu-spōn* descriptive of a physical feature, such as 'a small wooded valley', cf. Wothersome (Yorks) *wudu-husum* 'houses in the wood' and Wotherton (Salop), *wudufordtūn* 'farm by a ford at the wood'.

WOTTON see WOOTON.

WRAGGE, RAGG: P O Dan *Wraghi*, a pers. name. 12th cent.

WRAIGHT see WRIGHT.

WRAY, WROE: L ON *vra* 'the remote, isolated place'. 12th cent.

WREN(N), WRAN: N OE *wrenna* 'wren', a nickname. The wren bears a royal name in some other languages, e.g., Lat *rēgulas* 'petty king, prince', French *roitelet*, Ger. *zaunkönig*, apparently in allusion to its golden crest. The wren is tiny but is the king of birds, shrewd, towny, and a singer, its call-note ending with an impatient 'tick, tick, tick'. 13th cent.

WRENCH, WRINCH: N OE *wrenc*, ME *wrench* 'wile, trick, artifice'. 12th cent.

WREY: N ME *wrye* 'bent, twisted, crooked'. 14th cent.

WRIGHT, WRAIGHT: O OE *wryhta* 'carpenter, joiner'. 13th cent. [Nine persons named Wright arrived with the First Fleet, of whom five were convicts, two were marines, and two were marines' wives].

WRIGHTSON: O 'Son of the wright'. 14th cent.

WRIGLEY: L OE *wrigels-leah* 'the glade overhung with tall trees'. (Lancs) 14th cent.

WRITER: O OE *wrītere* 'writer, copier of manuscripts'. 13th cent.

WROTH: N OE *wrath* 'angry, fierce'. 13th cent.

WULF(F) see WOLF.

WYARD, WYARTT: P OE *Wīgheard* 'war-brave', a pers. name. 12th cent.

WYATT, GYATT: P A dim. of OF *Guy* or OG *Wido*. 12th cent.

WYBER, WYBREW, WYBROW, WHYBRO, WIBER(G), WIBROW: P OE *Wīgburh* 'war-fortress', an Anglo-Saxon woman's name. 12th cent.

WYBERD, WYBURD: P OE *Wīgbeorht* 'war-bright'. DB.

WYBORN, WYBURN, WYBRON: P OE *Wigbeorn* 'war-hero', an Anglo-Saxon pers. name. 13th cent.

WYE: L OE *wēoh* 'holy place, heathen temple'. (Kent) 13th cent. Some may be a variant of *Guy*.

WYKE see WICH. WYLD(E) see WILD. WYLES see WILES. WYLIE see WILEY.

WYMAN, WEYMAN, WAYMAN, WHYMAN: P OE *Wīgmund* 'war-protection' or ON *Vigmundr*, O Dan & O Sw *Vimund*. DB. The Scandinavian names derive from Danelaw areas such as Leices, Lincs and Norfolk.

WYMARK, WAYMARK, WEYMARK: P O Bret *Wiuhomarch* 'worthy to have a horse'. DB.

WYMER: P OE *Wīgmǣr* 'battle-famous' DB.

WYN, WYNNE see GWINN. WYNDHAM see WINDHAM. WYNE, WYNESS see WINE. WYNN(E) see WINN. WYNNIATT see WINGATE. WYNTER see WINTER. WYNTON see WINTON. WYNYARD see WINYARD. WYSE see WISE.

Y

YABSLEY: L OE '*Eabbe's lēah* (clearing), *Eabbe*, an Anglo-Saxon.

YALE: L Welsh *ial* 'the fertile upland'.

YALLAND, YELLAND, YOLLAND: L OE *eald-land* 'the old (cultivated) land'. 13th cent.

YAPP: N OE *gēap* 'bent, crooked', in the sense of 'cunning, deceitful', but the word also means 'intelligent, shrewd'. 12th cent.

YARBOROUGH, YERBURY: L OE *eorthburh* 'earth fortification'. (Lincs), *Gereburg* DB.

YARD(E): O OE *gerd* 'a holder of a *gerd* (yard) of land (a virgate = 30 acres)'. 13th cent.

YARDLEY, YEARDLEY: L OE 'The *lēah* (wood) where yards (spars, etc.) were cut'. (Essex, Northants, Worces, Som) 12th cent.

YARKER, YORKER: O ME A deriv. of *yerk* 'to stitch', 'a shoemaker'. 14th cent.

YARNTON: L OE *earding-tūn* 'dwelling-place, manor'. (Oxon).

YARROW: L SG from Ir *garbh* 'rough stream'. (Selkirks) Scotland.

YARWOOD: L OE *earn-wudu* 'eagle-wood'.

YATE(S), YEATES, YEATS: (i) L OE *geat*

'gate', e.g., of town, castle, enclosure. (ii) O OE *geat*. Metonymic for a gate-keeper. Surname 12th cent. [Yeates, a First Fleet (female convict) surname. Rev William Yate entered New Zealand as a missionary, 1831].

YATMAN, YEATMAN: L OE *geat-mann* 'gate-man'. 16th cent.

YAXLEY, YASLEY: L OE *gēac-lēah* 'cuckoo wood'. (Hunts, Suffolk) [A First Fleet (convict) surname].

YEADON: L OE *hēa-dūn* 'high hill'. (Yorks).

YEALLAND, YELLAND: L OE *hēa-land* 'high land'. (Lancs).

YEANDLE, YANDELL, YANDALL: L OE *gēandele* 'steep', probably a steep-sided valley.

YEARBY: L O Scand *Efri-býr* 'the upper village'. (Yorks).

YEARD: P OE *Eorēd*, a pers. Anglo-Saxon name, preserved in Yeardsley (Ches).

YEARSLEY: L OE *eofor-lēah* 'the wild boar's wood'. (Yorks).

YEATES see YATES. YEATMAN see YATMAN.

YEEND: L OE *(aet) gē ende* '(at) ye/the end' (of the road/village).

YELDHAM: L OE *gield-hām* 'yield village', the village on which a special tax was levied. (Essex).

YELL: A locality surname from Yell, Shetland.

YELLAND see YALLAND, YEALAND.

YEO, YEA: L OE *ēa* or *ēow* 'river' or 'yew'. The River Yeo in Devon is 'the river on whose banks yews grow'. 13th cent.

YEOMAN, YEAMAN: O ME *yoman* 'a country landowner qualified by possessing free land to serve on juries and vote for the knight of the shire'. In medieval England fighting men ranked in order: knight, squire, yeoman, knave. Earlier, a servant or attendant in a noble house, ranking between a sergeant and groom, or between a squire and a page. Surname 13th cent.

YEOWARD, YEOWART see EWART. YEOWELL see YOULE. YERBURY see YARBOROUGH.

YEWDALE, YEWDALL, YEWDELL: L OE *ēow-dael* 'yew-tree valley'. (Lancs).

YEWEN see EWAN. YOELL, YOEWELL see YOULE. YONG(E) see YOUNG.

YONWIN: P OE *Geongwine* 'young friend', a pers. Anglo-Saxon name. 11th cent.

YORK(E): L Brit The original name of York was *Ebórakon* c. 150, derived from a Brit pers. name *Eburos*. By 644 this had been changed by popular etymology to *Eoforwicceaster* 'the boar farm at the fort'. This led the Scandinavians to describe the place as *Iorvic*, which later contracted to *Iork*. And so to *York*, as far from the original name as could be imagined. Surname 12th cent.

YOUARD, YOUD: O OE *ēow-hierde* 'ewe-herd, shepherd'.

YOUATT see EWART. YOUENS see EWAN.

YOULDON, YOULDEN: L OE *eald-dūn* 'old hill'. (Devon).

YOULE, YOUELL, YOUL(L), YEOWELL, YUILE, YUILL, YULE: N OE *geōl*, ON *jól* 'Yule'. A nickname for one born or baptised during the Christmas festival. Surname 12th cent.

YOUNG(S), YONG(E): N OE *geong* 'young', a nickname, 'youthful, vigorous', sometimes used to distinguish the junior from the senior in a family. 12th cent. [Seven persons named Young arrived with the First Fleet 1788. One of these was Richard Young, steward on the *Lady Penrhyn*, who had sailed round the world with Captain Cook. The others were a marine sergeant and his wife and two sons, and two convicts].

YOUNGER: N A distinguishing name, 'the younger', from OE *geong*, and in this sense a variant of *Young*. 12th cent.

YOUNGHUSBAND: O OE *geong-hūsbonda* 'young farmer'. 13th cent.

YOUNGMAN, YOUNKMAN: O OE *geong-mann* 'young servant'.

YOUNGSON: N OE *geong-sunu* 'young son'. 13th cent. [A First Fleet (convict) surname].

YOUNSON: P 'Son of *Ewan*'. 13th cent.

YOXALL: L OE *geoc-halh* 'a yoke of oxen as a measure of land in a remote valley', (*geoc* 'yoke', *halh* 'a remote valley'.) (Staffs).

YUILE see YOULE. YVE see IVE.

Z

ZEAL see SEAL.

ZELLER see SELLAR.

ZELLEY see SEELEY.

Bibliography

Attwater, Donald, *The Penguin Dictionary of Saints*, Harmondsworth, 1965.
Bardsley, C.W., *Dictionary of English and Welsh Surnames*, London, 1901.
Benson, Morton, *Dictionary of Russian Personal Names*, Philadelphia, 1964.
Black, George F., *The Surnames of Scotland*, New York, 1946.
Bronsted, Johannes, *The Vikings*, Harmondsworth, 1960.
Bryant, Arthur, *The Age of Chivalry*, London, 1963.
Camden, William, *Remaines Concerning Britaine*, London, 1605. Reprinted Toronto, 1984.
Chadwick, Nora, *The Celts*, Harmondsworth, 1970.
Chapman, Don, *1788: The People of the First Fleet*, Sydney, 1986.
Clark, Sir George, *English History*, Oxford, 1971.
Cottle, Basil, *The Penguin Dictionary of Surnames*, Harmondsworth, 1967.
Coulton, G.G., *Medieval Panorama*, Cambridge, 1947.
Dauzat, Albert, *Dictionnaire étymologique des noms de famille et prénoms de France*, Paris, 1951.
de Breffny, Brian, *Irish Family Names*, New York, 1982.
Ekwall, Eilert, *The Concise Oxford Dictionary of English Place-Names*, Oxford, 1936.
Fidlon, Paul G., and Ryan, R.J., *The First Fleeters*, Sydney, 1981.
Fox-Davies, A.C., *Complete Guide to Heraldry*, London, 1909.
Galbraith, V.H., *Domesday Book*, Oxford, 1974.
Graham-Campbell, J., *The Viking World*, New York, 1980.
Grekov, B., *Kiev Rus*, Moscow, 1959.
Guppy, H.B., *Homes of Family Names in Great-Britain*, London, 1890.
Hinde, Thomas (Ed.), *The Domesday Book—A Survey*, London, 1985.
Hook, J.H., *Family Names*, New York, 1982.
Johnson, Stephen, *Later Roman Britain*, London, 1982.
Kaganoff, Benzion, C., *A Dictionary of Jewish Names*, New York, 1977.
Kochan, Lionel, and Abraham, Richard, *The Making of Modern Russia*, Harmondsworth, 1963.
Laing, L. and J., *Anglo-Saxon England*, London, 1982.
Lower, A.M., *A Dictionary of the Family Names of the United Kingdom*, London, 1860.
McEvedy, C., *Penguin Atlas of Ancient History*, Harmondsworth, 1967.
McEvedy, C., *Penguin Atlas of Medieval History*, Harmondsworth, 1961.
Mackie, J.D., *A History of Scotland*, Harmondsworth, 1964.
MacLysaght, Edward, *The Surnames of Ireland*, Dublin, 1969.
Morgan, T.J. and P., *Welsh Surnames*, Cardiff, 1985.
Munro, R.W., *Kinsmen and Clansmen*, Edinburgh, 1971.
Nicolaisen, W.F.H., *Scottish Place-Names*, London, 1976.
Poole, A.L., *From Domesday to Magna Carta*, Oxford. 1951.
Public Record Office (London), *Domesday 1086*.
Public Record Office (Hampshire), *Winton Domesday 1086–1125*.

Reaney, P.H., *A Dictionary of British Surnames*, London, 1958.
Reaney, P.H.,. *The Origin of Place-Names*, London, 1960.
Reed, A.H., *The Story of New Zealand*, Wellington, 1945.
Salway, Peter, *Roman Britain*, Oxford, 1981.
Savage, Ann (Translator), *The Anglo-Saxon Chronicles*, London, 1982.
Sherley-Price, L. (Translator), *Bede—A History of the English Church and People (AD 731)*, New York, 1985.
Smiles, Samuel, *The Huguenots*, London, 1876.
Smith, E.C., *New Dictionary of American Family Names*, New York, 1956, Reprinted 1973.
Stenton, Sir Frank, *Anglo-Saxon England*, Oxford, 1943.
Topp, E.J., *Early New Zealand*, Melbourne, 1958.
Thorpe, Lewis, *The Bayeux Tapestry*, London, 1973.
Trevelyan, G.M., *English Social History* (Vol. 1.), London, 1949.
Unbegaun, B.O., *Russian Surnames*, Oxford, 1972.
Vaughan-Thomas, W., *Wales: A History*, London, 1985.
Wagner, A.R., *English Genealogy*, Oxford, 1960.
Ward, J., *Information Relative to New Zealand*, Christchurch, 1839, reprinted 1975.
Withycombe, E.G., *The Oxford Dictionary of Christian Names*, Oxford, 1945.
Wood, Charles T., *The Age of Chivalry*, London, 1970.
Woulfe, Patrick, *Irish Names and Surnames*, Dublin, 1923.
Zenovsky, S.A., *Medieval Russia's Epics, Chronciles and Tales*, New York. 1963.